# Knowledge Management
# in Practice

# Knowledge Management in Practice

## Connections and Context

Edited by
T. Kanti Srikantaiah, Ph.D.
Director, Center for Knowledge Management, and Professor
Dominican University

and

Michael E. D. Koenig, Ph.D.
Professor and Former & Founding Dean
College of Information and Computer Science
Long Island University

ASIST Monograph Series

Published on behalf of
American Society for Information Science and Technology by

Information Today, Inc.
Medford, New Jersey

*First printing, 2008*

*Knowledge Management in Practice: Connections and Context*

Printed and bound in the United States of America.

**Library of Congress Cataloging-in-Publication Data**

Knowledge management in practice : connections and context / edited by T. Kanti Srikantaiah and Michael E.D. Koenig.
    p. cm.
    "Published on behalf of the American Society for Information Science and Technology."
    Includes bibliographical references and index.
    ISBN 978-1-57387-312-3
    1. Knowledge management. I. Srikantaiah, Taverekere. II. Koenig, Michael E. D. III. American Society for Information Science and Technology.
  HD30.2.K63726 2008
  658.4'038--dc22

2007050338

President and CEO: Thomas H. Hogan, Sr.
Editor-in-Chief and Publisher: John B. Bryans
Managing Editor: Amy M. Reeve
ASIST Monograph Series Editor: Samantha Hastings
VP Graphics and Production: M. Heide Dengler
Cover Designer: Jacqueline Walter Crawford and Bonnie Weisbrod
Copyeditor: Dorothy Pike
Proofreader: Penelope Mathiesen
Indexer: Beth Palmer

# Contents

Introduction ........................................................... ix

Acknowledgments ....................................................... xi

Roadmap ............................................................... xiii

Companies and Organizations Mentioned ................................. xxi

## Introductory Chapters: The Three-Dimensional Expansion of KM

Foreword .............................................................. 3

Chapter 1: KM Is Here to Stay ......................................... 5
   *Michael E. D. Koenig, Long Island University*

Chapter 2: KM Moving into Stage IV? The Extra-Organizational Stage ..... 9
   *Michael E. D. Koenig, Long Island University*

Chapter 3: Knowledge Management Expansion: Content Management,
  Project Management, Competitive Intelligence, Environmental
  Scanning, and Knowledge Audit ................................. 17
   *T. Kanti Srikantaiah, Dominican University*

Chapter 4: KM: The New Business Potpourri or Seeing the Forest Rather
  than Just the Trees ........................................... 43
   *Michael E. D. Koenig, Long Island University*

## Part I: Identifying the Knowledge

Foreword .............................................................. 49

Chapter 5: Representing and Managing Context: Toward Knowledge
  Resource Planning ............................................. 51
   *Kavi Mahesh, PES Institute of Technology*
   *J. K. Suresh, Infosys Technologies Ltd.*

Chapter 6: Knowledge Audits: Establishing a Context for
  Leveraging Knowledge ......................................... 79
   *Lynda W. Moulton, LWM Technology Services*

Chapter 7: PKM: A Bottom-Up Approach to Knowledge Management ........... 95
   *Dave Pollard, Meeting of Minds, Consulting Services*

# Part II: Knowledge Management Strategy

*See also the Roadmap*

Foreword . . . . . . . . . . . . . . . . . . . . . . . . . . . . . . . . . . . . . . . . . . . . . . . . . . . . . 113

Chapter 8: Knowledge Strategy: The Linkage Between Business Strategy
        and Knowledge Management . . . . . . . . . . . . . . . . . . . . . . . . . . . . . . . . 115
        *Joseph Kasten, Dowling College*

Chapter 9: You Want Systems But You Need Strategy . . . . . . . . . . . . . . . . . . . . . . . 125
        *Bob Boiko, Metatorial Services Inc.*

Chapter 10: Knowledge Management in Strategic Context . . . . . . . . . . . . . . . . . . . . . 155
        *Robert N. McGrath, University of Maryland University College*

Chapter 11: Knowledge Services: The "Why" of Knowledge Management . . . . . . . . . . . . 169
        *Albert J. Simard, Natural Resources Canada*

# Part III: Knowledge Management Techniques and Technology

Foreword . . . . . . . . . . . . . . . . . . . . . . . . . . . . . . . . . . . . . . . . . . . . . . . . . . . . . 201

Chapter 12: How to Build a Smart Search System Using Taxonomies
        and Ontologies . . . . . . . . . . . . . . . . . . . . . . . . . . . . . . . . . . . . . . . . . . 203
        *Denise A. D. Bedford, World Bank*

Chapter 13: Video Management and the Transfer of Knowledge
        through Audiovisual Material . . . . . . . . . . . . . . . . . . . . . . . . . . . . . . . . . 223
        *Suliman Hawamdeh and Hazem Refai,*
        *University of Oklahoma*

Chapter 14: Knowledge Discovery, Metadata, and Semantic Interoperability . . . . . . . . . . 239
        *Denise A. D. Bedford, World Bank*

Chapter 15: Knowledge Management: Best Practices in the InfoTech Sector . . . . . . . . . . . 257
        *Madanmohan Rao, Asian Media Information and*
        *Communication Centre*

# Part IV: Knowledge Sharing

*See also the Roadmap for Communities of Practice on Collaboration and Collaborated Tools*

Foreword . . . . . . . . . . . . . . . . . . . . . . . . . . . . . . . . . . . . . . . . . . . . . . . . . . . . . 275

Chapter 16: Sharing Knowledge: Problems, Root Causes, and Solutions . . . . . . . . . . . . . . 277
> Laurence P. Chait, Chait and Associates, Inc.

Chapter 17: Digital Libraries and Librarians in the Learning Organization . . . . . . . . . . . . 289
> Kate Marek, Dominican University

Chapter 18: Corporate Blogs and Communities of Practice . . . . . . . . . . . . . . . . . . . . . . . . . 303
> Qiping Zhang, Long Island University
> Shanshan Ma, Drexel University

# Part V: Knowledge Management Measurement and Assessment

*See also the Roadmap*

Foreword . . . . . . . . . . . . . . . . . . . . . . . . . . . . . . . . . . . . . . . . . . . . . . . . . . . . . . . . . . . . . . 323

Chapter 19: Measuring Knowledge in Organizations: The Organizational
> Knowledge Assessment Tool . . . . . . . . . . . . . . . . . . . . . . . . . . . . . . . . . . . . . . . 325
> > Ana Flavia Fonseca, University of Joao Pessoa
> > Arnoldo Fonseca, Consultant

Chapter 20: Knowledge Management Measurement: An Agenda for
> Organizations and Economies . . . . . . . . . . . . . . . . . . . . . . . . . . . . . . . . . . . . . . . 341
> > Alton Y. K. Chua and Abdus Sattar Chaudhry,
> > Nanyang Technological University

# Part VI: Knowledge Management and Project Management

Foreword . . . . . . . . . . . . . . . . . . . . . . . . . . . . . . . . . . . . . . . . . . . . . . . . . . . . . . . . . . . . . . 355

Chapter 21: Knowledge Management in Software Projects . . . . . . . . . . . . . . . . . . . . . . . . 357
> C. S. Shobha, Perot Systems

Chapter 22: Running Successful Collaboration Software Pilots . . . . . . . . . . . . . . . . . . . . . 375
> Joe Hutchinson and Patti Anklam, Hutchinson Associates,
> Consulting Services

# Part VII: Knowledge Preservation

*See also the Roadmap*

Foreword . . . . . . . . . . . . . . . . . . . . . . . . . . . . . . . . . . . . . . . . . . . . . . . . . . . . . . . . . . . . . . 401

Chapter 23: Transfer of Long-Term Knowledge and Expertise: A Case
            Study in the Nuclear Sector . . . . . . . . . . . . . . . . . . . . . . . . . . . . . . . . . . . . . . . 403
                *Françoise Rossion, Ernst & Young Consultancy*

Chapter 24: An Alternative Knowledge System at the World Bank: A Case
            Study of the World Bank's Indigenous Knowledge for
            Development Program . . . . . . . . . . . . . . . . . . . . . . . . . . . . . . . . . . . . . . . . . . . 415
                *Deepa Srikantaiah, University of Maryland*
                *Claudia Rueger, World Bank*

## Part VIII: Knowledge Management in Government

*See also the Roadmap*

Foreword . . . . . . . . . . . . . . . . . . . . . . . . . . . . . . . . . . . . . . . . . . . . . . . . . . . . . . . . 443

Chapter 25: Knowledge Networking in a Public Service Agency:
            Contextual Challenges and Infrastructural Issues . . . . . . . . . . . . . . . . . . . . . . 445
                *Elisabeth Davenport, International Teledemocracy Centre*
                *Louise Rasmussen, Napier University*

Chapter 26: Knowledge Management in the Federal Sector: A Review
            and Critique   . . . . . . . . . . . . . . . . . . . . . . . . . . . . . . . . . . . . . . . . . . . . . . . . . 463
                *Roland G. Droitsch, KM21 Associates*


About the Contributors . . . . . . . . . . . . . . . . . . . . . . . . . . . . . . . . . . . . . . . . . . . . . . 483

Index  . . . . . . . . . . . . . . . . . . . . . . . . . . . . . . . . . . . . . . . . . . . . . . . . . . . . . . . . . . . . 497

# Introduction

The most important point to be made in this introduction is that **the reader should use the Roadmap**. The Roadmap is a guide to the themes interwoven throughout this book. As is typical of any book of this type, our book is clustered into sections based on the major themes of the chapters. Thus, the table of contents, with its section names and chapter titles, is a good introduction to the book and its major themes, but it is still only a partial guide. Themes and chapters enjoy a many-to-many relationship. Almost inevitably, a chapter will touch on, sometimes in considerable depth, themes other than its major theme. Almost equally inevitably, more than one chapter will touch on a theme. The problem of course is that the theme will often be discussed in a chapter whose name does not make that obvious.

The Roadmap is a list of the major themes in this book, with a brief discussion of where that theme appears, and in what context, and often with what conclusions are drawn. Note: There are more than twice as many important themes as there are subject sections in the table of contents. The co-editors would be delighted if all readers read the entire book, but they are realistic enough to know that most readers will delve into a book of this sort (multi-chapters, multi-authors) with particular interests in mind. The Roadmap is designed precisely to facilitate that sort of delving, to provide a rich supplement to the table of contents, and to guide the reader to where a theme is discussed, particularly to where that would not be obvious solely from the table of contents.

The reader should also note that at the beginning of each section there is a Foreword, which combines something of a mini-abstract of the chapters in that section, with a brief discussion of how the chapters interrelate.

Why another book on knowledge management (KM)? The most obvious reason is that KM, and interest in KM, continues to grow. In fact, the continuing growth of KM is so dramatically different from the patterns of other recent business hot topics that we have devoted a small introductory chapter following this introduction, entitled "KM Is Here to Stay," precisely to illustrate and document this point.

That is not the only reason for this book, however. Another reason is the continued expansion of KM into new areas and in many cases the recognition that old areas, for example competitive intelligence, are quite logically part of KM. In the first major section of the book, the Introductory Chapters, this expansion is described as having three parts:

1. Expansion I: The Fourth Stage of KM = Context and Extra Organizational Knowledge
2. Expansion II: The Overlap and Convergence with Content Management, Project Management, Competitive Intelligence, Environmental Scanning, and Knowledge Audit
3. Expansion III: KM is the New Business Potpourri. Rather than be repetitive, the reader is directed to the foreword in the Introductory Chapters Section for a quick summary of the three themes, and to the chapters themselves for a more complete discussion.

Another way of making the point: As KM is expanding our notion of itself, KM is changing and expanding, and that change and expansion warrants new attention.

Another reason for this book is that KM is a very operational discipline without as yet much of an academic foundation. The result is that many of the best presentations on KM appear not in a well-structured, retrievable disciplinary literature, but rather at trade shows and conferences where they are presented to small audiences of KM professionals, or often people moving into KM positions, and afterwards in many cases they functionally disappear. Such presentations are in fact a major source for chapters in this book. The co-editors made a practice of attending such conferences, particularly those of the Conference Board (now sadly in abeyance) and KMWorld, cherry picking from those conferences and asking the presenters to turn their topic into a book chapter. This is now the third book on KM that the co-editors have put together primarily in this fashion. In some ways these volumes serve for the field of KM as something of a "key recent papers on …" or an "annual review of …" but one that appears every three or four years. Perhaps the time has come for an annual review of KM.

# Acknowledgments

The editors would like to acknowledge the contributions of the chapter authors. In this rapidly growing field of KM, this book would not have been possible without their full cooperation. We would like to thank them not only for their specific chapters but also for the insights, suggestions, and guidance they have provided for the editors. We also would like to thank Selenay Aytac, David Master, Luciana Marulli-Koenig, Jayashree Srikantaiah, Laurie Murphy, and Kristen Snyder in assisting the completion of the manuscript on time.

We would also like to thank the editorial staff at Information Today, Inc., who, having worked with us before, were still willing to undertake it again, especially John B. Bryans, Editor-in-Chief, who provided valuable and timely guidance and support in the completion of the manuscript, Dr. Samantha Hastings for undertaking the editorial responsibilities, and Amy M. Reeve, Managing Editor.

<table>
<tr><td>Michael E. D. Koenig</td><td>T. Kanti Srikantaiah</td></tr>
<tr><td>Long Island University</td><td>Dominican University</td></tr>
</table>

# Roadmap

## INTRODUCTION

The Roadmap is a pointer to the themes covered in this book, and where they are covered. It leads the reader to themes and chapters that are not obvious from what a reader most often does with a book of this type: simply peruse the table of contents. The reader interested in a particular knowledge management (KM) theme or topic should peruse both the Table of Contents and the Roadmap. In addition to the nine sections of the book:

- The Three-Dimensional Expansion of KM
- Identifying the Knowledge
- KM Strategy
- KM Techniques and Technology
- Knowledge Sharing
- KM Measurement and Assessment
- KM and Project Management
- Knowledge Preservation
- KM in Government

which of course are major themes in this book, there are 18 topics/themes expanded upon in the Roadmap:

- Case Studies
- Collaboration and Collaboration Tools
- Communities of Practice (CoPs)
- Education and Training
- KM Audits
- KM in Government*
- KM Measurement and Assessment*
- Knowledge Preservation*
- Organizational Structure and KM
- Pain Points
- Personal Knowledge Management (PKM)

- Selling KM
- Social Network Analysis
- Stages of KM Development
- Storytelling (see also Selling KM)
- Strategy for KM*
- Taxonomies, Ontologies, and Metadata
- Trust

(* indicates Roadmap themes that overlap with a section name and that lead to additional material on that theme)

# THEMES

## 1. Case Studies

There are a number of descriptions of KM implementations of sufficient detail that they function in the nature of case studies:

- Davenport & Rasmussen (Chapter 25) describe semi-aborted KM implementation in a major U.K. public agency.
- Rossion (Chapter 23) describes KM implementation at ONDRAF-NIRAS, a Belgian nuclear materials regulatory agency.
- Chait (Chapter 16) describes KM implementation at Arthur D. Little, Inc.
- Rao's chapter (Chapter 15) contains mini abstracts of KM systems at 16 info-tech sector companies.

## 2. Collaboration and Collaboration Tools

- Chait (Chapter 16) examines roadblocks to sharing and techniques, particularly "The Seven Methods of Influencing Behavior," to remove or detour around those roadblocks.
- Hutchinson & Anklam (Chapter 22) discuss collaboration software pilot programs and their management (see also the theme: Communities of Practice).
- Zhang & Ma (Chapter 18) specifically discuss the role of corporate blogs in enhancing collaboration.
- Pollard (Chapter 7) focuses on Personal Knowledge Management (PKM), and the user perspective on developing collaboration and using collaboration tools.

- Marek (Chapter 17) discusses the role of Digital Libraries in the Learning Organization.

## 3. Communities of Practice

- Zhang & Ma (Chapter 18) specifically discuss the role of corporate blogs in enabling and encouraging communities of practice.
- Rao (Chapter 15) discusses the extent of CoPs in a number of companies in the info-tech sector.
- Moulton (Chapter 6) describes the use of the Knowledge Audit to discover actual and potential CoPs and to facilitate their development.
- Davenport & Rasmussen (Chapter 25) describe the attempt to build CoPs in a major U.K. public agency (see also Theme 2, Collaboration and Collaboration Tools).

## 4. Education and Training

- Droitsch (Chapter 26) describes the development of SCORM (Shareable Content Object Reference Model) for the delivery of digital educational content.
- Marek (Chapter 17) touches on the role of the digital library for education and training.

## 5. KM Audits

- Shobha (Chapter 21) briefly mentions the utility of the KM audit as a tool for project management.
- Moulton (Chapter 6) concentrates on the Knowledge Audit process.
- T. K. Srikantaiah (Chapter 3) discusses the role of the Knowledge Audit in KM in some depth.
- Rao (Chapter 15) describes the "8 Cs" audit technique for evaluating KM systems.
- Chait's (Chapter 16) "why" technique is a KM audit technique.
- Marek (Chapter 17) discusses the Knowledge Audit in the context of designing digital libraries to support KM.

## 6. KM in Government

- Droitsch (Chapter 26) discusses KM in U.S. government departments and agencies.
- Davenport & Rasmussen (Chapter 25) discuss the KM implementation in a major KM public agency.

- Chua & Chaudhry (Chapter 20) discuss KM metrics, including those used by several governments and quasi-governmental organizations.
- D. Srikantaiah & Rueger (Chapter 24) discuss a KM system for indigenous knowledge being developed by the World Bank.

## 7. KM Measurement and Assessment

*See the Foreword to Part V, KM Measurement and Assessment*

- Chua & Chaudhry (Chapter 20, full chapter) describe the metrics used in various organizations, and classify them.
- Fonseca & Fonseca (Chapter 19, full chapter) describe the Organizational Knowledge Assessment (OKA) tool being developed by the World Bank Institute.
- Hutchinson & Anklam (Chapter 22) describe metrics used for the evaluation of pilot KM collaboration systems.

## 8. Knowledge Preservation

*See Part VII, Knowledge Preservation*

- Shobha (Chapter 21) discusses Project Management and KM and points out the utility of not treating projects as silos, rather the need for retention of knowledge and the transfer of lessons learned from one project to subsequent projects.
- Rossion (Chapter 23) describes the development of a KM system in a nuclear technology environment, one with a very long half-life, where preservation of knowledge is a key issue.
- D. Srikantaiah & Rueger (Chapter 24) describe the development of a KM system specifically for indigenous knowledge at the World Bank with issues of preservation very much in mind.
- Davenport & Rasmussen (Chapter 25) discuss "memory practices" in the context of, in this case, unsuccessful implementation of a KM system.
- Hawamdeh & Refai (Chapter 13) discuss the use of video for Project Exodus in the U.S. Department of Defense for processing the knowledge of retiring employees.
- Marek (Chapter 17) addresses some issues of sustainability in the creation of digital library support for KM.

- Mahesh & Suresh (Chapter 5) in their prescriptive of Knowledge Resource Planning describe a fourth stage of KM that is long term and preservation oriented.

## 9. Organizational Structure and KM

- Droitsch (Chapter 26), in describing development in KM in U.S. government departments and agencies, describes the maladaptive consequences upon KM of organizational structures mandated by the Clinger-Cohen (Information Technology Management Reform) Act of 1996.
- Davenport & Rasmussen (Chapter 25) analyze a major and largely unsuccessful KM initiative at a major U.K. public agency, a failure due in no small degree to "shifting regimes of power." They analyze these developments through the lenses of signification, domination, and legitimation.
- McGrath (Chapter 10) reviews the classic literature on industry evolution, life cycle parameters, organizational theory, etc., much of it relating to organizational structure, and relates it to KM, particularly the knowledge conversion mechanism, appropriate to different states.

## 10. Pain Points

- Boiko (Chapter 9) demonstrates how to use the "Strategy Statement" technique to find the pain points.

An interesting aside is how often the theme of finding the pain points—where an organization feels pain—surfaced in the editors' previous book, *Knowledge Managment Lessons Learned*, whose theme was "lessons learned," a theme taken implicitly from the organizational viewpoint, and how comparatively seldom in this volume, whose theme is "context."

## 11. Personal Knowledge Management (PKM)

- Pollard (Chapter 7, full chapter) writes about PKM as the basis for good KM strategy and design.
- Hutchinson & Anklam (Chapter 22) discuss running collaboration software pilots and emphasize the PKM aspect.

## 12. Selling KM

- Fonseca & Fonseca (Chapter 19) describe the useful effect of the Organizational Knowledge Assessment (OKA) tool as a mechanism for creating KM awareness and for selling KM.
- Moulton (Chapter 6) discusses the utility of the Knowledge Audit as a tool for selling KM.
- Chait (Chapter 16) discusses selling KM and using "The Seven Methods of Influencing Behavior" tool to modify behavior and effect the sale.
- Rossion (Chapter 23) describes the use of the Knowledge Management House metaphor to sell the idea of KM.

## 13. Social Network Analysis

- Pollard (Chapter 7) discusses SNA in the context of people (expertise) finding and canvassing.

## 14. Stages of KM Development

- Koenig (Chapter 2, full chapter) reviews the stages of KM to date, and argues that KM is moving into stage IV.
- T. K. Srikantaiah (Chapter 3) also briefly reviews those stages of development.
- Mahesh & Suresh (Chapter 5) suggest in their conclusion that the Knowledge Resource Planning model they propose is what the fourth stage of KM is evolving toward.

## 15. Storytelling

*See Theme 12, Selling KM*

- Hawamdeh & Refai (Chapter 13) discuss the use of video storytelling in preserving the knowledge of retirees, particularly Project Exodus of the U.S. Department of Defense.

## 16. Strategy for KM

There are four chapters in the section on Knowledge Management Strategy:

- Boiko (Chapter 9) discusses the use and development of "Strategy Statements" to develop KM strategy.
- Kasten (Chapter 8) develops a typology of knowledge strategies based on an in-depth study of a number of organizations.

- McGrath (Chapter 10) reviews the classic organizational and business literature, particularly in terms of knowledge conversion mechanisms appropriate to particular organizational states and consequent KM strategy.
- Simard (Chapter 11) looks at modern networked organizations and derives organizational frameworks and knowledge value chains. (These chapters are discussed in somewhat more detail in the foreword to Part II, Knowledge Management Strategy.)

Also discussing KM Strategy:

- Moulton (Chapter 6) discusses the Knowledge Audit as a tool to discover and develop contextual relevancy and drive strategy.
- Rao (Chapter 15) introduces the "8 Cs" Audit Tool as a technique to develop KM strategy.
- Pollard (Chapter 7) develops bottom-up driven Personal Knowledge Management (PKM) as a tool to drive KM strategy development.
- Davenport & Rasmussen (Chapter 25) use the lenses (viewpoints) of signification, domination, and legitimation as tools with which to examine KM strategy.

## 17. Taxonomies, Ontologies, and Metadata

*See Part I, Identifying the Knowledge*

- Bedford (Chapter 12, full chapter) writes "How to Build a Smart Search System Using Taxonomies and Ontologies."
- Bedford (Chapter 14, full chapter) writes "Knowledge Discovery, Metadata, and Semantic Interoperability."
- Mahesh & Suresh (Chapter 5) stress the importance of metadata in representing context, which they describe as the core problem in KM.
- Marek (Chapter 17) stresses the importance of metadata in building digital libraries to support KM.

## 18. Trust

- Moulton (Chapter 6) introduces trust as one of the things to focus on and chart in an Information Audit.

# Companies and Organizations Mentioned

APEC (Asia-Pacific Economic Cooperation) – Chua & Chaudhry (Chapter 20), short description of metrics used re KBE (Knowledge Based Economy)

Arthur Andersen – Chua & Chaudhry (Chapter 20), short description of metrics used

Arthur D. Little – Chait (Chapter 16), description of KM operations

Australian Bureau of Statistics – Chua & Chaudhry (Chapter 20), short description of metrics used for KM

Bristol Myers Squibb – Moulton (Chapter 6), describes KM organization

Companhia Hidroelétrica do Saõ Francisco – Fonseca & Fonseca (Chapter 19), role in development of the Organizational Knowledge Assessment Tool

DARPA – Droitsch (Chapter 26), "handle" system for large digital databases

Department of Defense, ADL (Advanced Distributed Learning) Initiative – Droitsch (Chapter 26), development of SCORM (Sharable Content Object Reference Model)

Department of Education – Droitsch (Chapter 26), lack of uptake of SCORM

Department of Labor – Droitsch (Chapter 26), KM systems

EDS – Rao (Chapter 15), thumbnail description of KM operations

EMC – Rao (Chapter 15), thumbnail description of KM operations

Ernst & Young – Pollard (Chapter 7), personal productivity improvement

Fuji Xerox – Chua & Chaudhry (Chapter 20), short description of "Eureka" system

Fujitsu Consulting – Rao (Chapter 15), thumbnail description of KM operations

Hill & Knowlton – Pollard (Chapter 7), automatic content harvesting

Hughes Software Systems – Rao (Chapter 15), thumbnail description of KM operations

i2 – Rao (Chapter 15), thumbnail description of KM operations

IBM – Rao (Chapter 15), thumbnail description of KM operations

i-flex – Rao (Chapter 15), thumbnail description of KM operations

Infosys Technologies – Chua & Chaudhry (Chapter 20), short description of metric used in KM; Rao (Chapter 15), thumbnail description of KM operations

KPMG – Pollard (Chapter 7), personal productivity improvement

Lend Lease Corporation – Pollard (Chapter 7), people finding, just in time conversing

Microsoft – Chua & Chaudhry (Chapter 20), short description of metrics used

MITRE – Rao (Chapter 15), thumbnail description of KM operations

Novell – Rao (Chapter 15), thumbnail description of KM operations

OECD (Organisation for Economic Co-operation and Development) – Chua & Chaudhry (Chapter 20), short description of metrics used in KBE (Knowledge Based Economy)

Open Text – Rao (Chapter 15), thumbnail description of KM operations

Oracle – Rao (Chapter 15), thumbnail description of KM operations

PuSA (unnamed public sector agency in the U.K.) – Davenport & Rasmussen (Chapter 25), maladaptive implementation of KM

SAS – Rao (Chapter 15), thumbnail description of KM operations

Serviçio Federal de Processsamento de Dados – Fonseca & Fonseca (Chapter 19), role in development of the Organizational Knowledge Assessment Tool

Sun Microsystem Philippines – Rao (Chapter 15), thumbnail description of KM operations

Unisys – Rao (Chapter 15), thumbnail description of KM operations

University of Maryland University College – Fonseca & Fonseca (Chapter 19), role in development of Organizational Knowledge Assessment tool

University of Oklahoma – Hawamdeh & Refai (Chapter 13), role of DoD's (Department of Defense) Project Exodus

World Bank Institute – Fonseca & Fonseca (Chapter 19), development of the Organizational Knowledge Assessment Tool

Xerox – Rao (Chapter 15), thumbnail description of KM operations

# Introductory Chapters

---

# The Three-Dimensional Expansion of KM

# The Three-Dimensional Expansion of KM

## FOREWORD

This section presents the extraordinary expansion in the understanding of what knowledge management (KM) is and what it represents. Chapter 1, KM Is Here to Stay, briefly traces the origin of KM and several clear stages of development, and argues that what can be described as a fourth stage is emerging, an emphasis upon and a clearer understanding of the importance of external (to the organization) information-business and political developments, technology, connecting to customers, suppliers, vendors, dealers, alumni, etc. This is in contrast to KM's "traditional" emphasis upon the "Firm's Knowledge." Partly driven by this change is an accompanying emphasis upon context and the understanding of context for the implementation of KM. This awareness of context has of course been driven to a great extent by the expansion and the application of KM principles in new areas and new directions, which are of course different contexts. New contexts have forced more attention upon context. This increased emphasis upon context and upon the inclusion and importance of information external to the organization is the subject of Chapter 2, KM Moving into Stage IV? The Extra-Organizational Stage.

Chapter 3, Knowledge Management Expansion: Content Management, Project Management, Competitive Intelligence, Environmental Scanning, and Knowledge Audit, delineates KM's increasingly recognized overlaps with and increasing convergence with already existing information and knowledge-based management processes and procedures—content management, project management, competitive intelligence, environmental scanning, and knowledge audit. Content management is arguably a child of KM, and we might also point a finger in the direction of Sarbanes-Oxley legislation when discussing the parenthood, but the others can all be described as pre-KM through Knowledge Audit, developed as information auditing by Forest W. (Woody) Horton in the 1970s, which almost disappeared from sight and trendiness until it reappeared under KM. What has happened is that these have all now begun to be perceived as existing as compo-nents of and under the umbrella of KM.

Chapter 4, KM: The New Business Potpourri or Seeing the Forest Rather than Just the Trees, ponders an interesting question. After two decades of business hot topics, each one succeeding another, the procession ceased just about the same time as the dot-com bust (which some perceive as a cause-and-effect relationship). This chapter notes, however, that a very high number (more than 20) and a very high proportion of those hot topics were, in some important sense, about the man-agement of information or knowledge. The chapter then speculates that what is happening is a recognition of the "forest for the trees." Instead of enthusiasm for the latest hot topic, the latest tree, KM is being recognized as the forest of those information and knowledge-related trees. When a new tree emerges or is discov-ered, it is no longer viewed in splendid isolation as the new big thing, with sub-sequent let-down and disappointment, but rather it is seen as exciting and new to be sure, but as only one of many trees in the KM forest. This, it can be argued, is a stage of maturity both for KM and for managerial and business perspectives.

In short, the scope and meaning of KM is expanding in several directions. The danger is that the term KM is becoming a portmanteau of so much generality that it loses much of its utility.

# CHAPTER 1

# KM Is Here to Stay

Michael E. D. Koenig
Long Island University

The late 20th century was unusually full of business enthusiasms, hot topics, and recipes for success. (See Chapter 4, KM: The New Business Potpourri or Seeing the Forest Rather than Just the Trees, for further discussion of that phenomenon.) We can be blunt and admit that many of them were fads, but KM is quite unlike any of the rest, both the substantive hot topics and those merely temporarily trendy. It is quite literally in a class by itself.

One could begin to recognize that difference a few years ago. In 2002, Ponzi and Koenig, building on previous work by Abrahamson, who had looked at previous business "fads," demonstrated that KM was behaving quite unlike those other management topics, and that KM was at the very least an unusual and long lasting management fad. Previous management fads (as measured by the number of articles in the business literature on the topic) showed a consistent pattern of boom and bust over a roughly 10-year cycle, with four or five years of explosive logarithmic growth followed by an only slightly longer period of almost equally dramatic decline. Figures 1.1a–c show the graphs for "Quality Circles," "Total Quality Management," and "Business Process Reengineering." Notice how similar the pattern is.

The profile of KM however is dramatically and fundamentally different. See the chart in Figure 1.2.

With four more years of data since the Ponzi and Koenig article, it is clear that KM is now in a pattern all its own, an initial four- or five-year burst of explosive growth, but since then a pattern of stable mature growth—not a pattern of boom and bust, but a pattern of boom and continuity.

That, of course, is one of the reasons for this book: KM continues to flourish and we continue to examine and refine the concepts of what KM consists of and what constitutes necessary and sufficient conditions for its success.

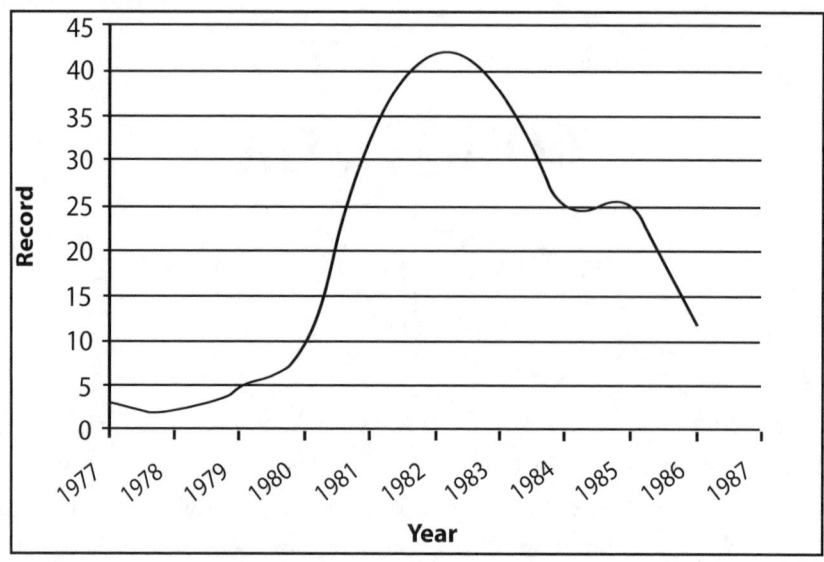

**Figure 1.1a   Typical business enthusiasm life cycles: The Lifecycle of Quality Circles, 1977–1986 (Source: Abrahamson, 1996)**

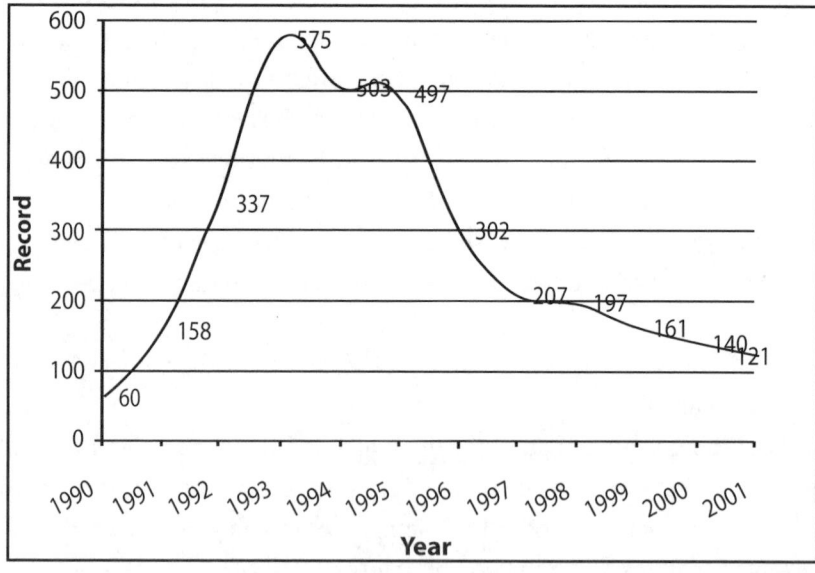

**Figure 1.1b   Total Quality Management, 1990–2001 (Source: Abrahamson, 1996)**

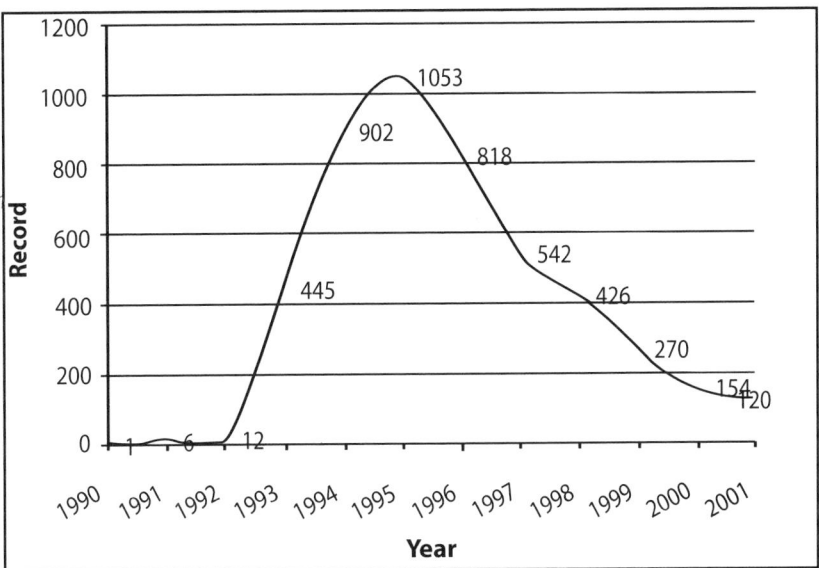

**Figure 1.1c  Business Process Reengineering, 1990–2001 (Source: Abrahamson, 1996)**

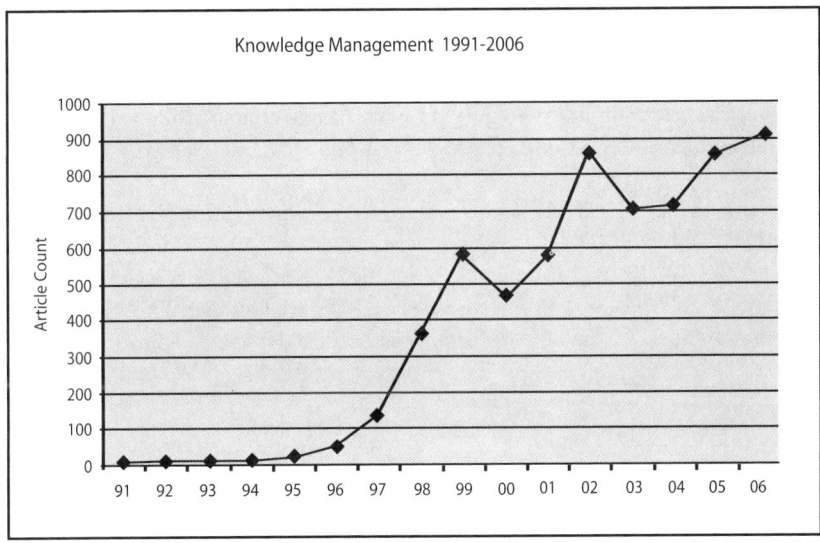

**Figure 1.2  KM growth**

In any case, though, it's just, **"Nice to know that KM is here to stay."**

**Note:** The graphs in Figures 1.1a–c and 1.2 derive from the simple technique of counting the year's articles in the business literature with the phrase "knowledge management" in the title of the article. It can be anticipated that as KM becomes more routine, this technique will need to become more sophisticated. For example a title with the phrase "communities of practice" is clearly a KM article, but would not be counted. There is of course an obvious advantage, from illustrating a time series point of view, to continue to count the same thing.

This technique, which assumes that almost all KM articles will have that phrase in the title, was perhaps quite valid in the initial years after the emergence of KM as a concept, but it clearly becomes less credible and less complete as KM grows and spawns offspring such as "communities of practice" or "enterprise content management," and those offspring begin to have conferences devoted to them and become broad subjects in their own right. The implication of that spawning is that our simple technique is in danger of underestimating KM the more the field grows. Given that likely underestimation, the contour of the KM growth curve is doubly dramatic.

# REFERENCES

Abrahamson, Eric. (1996). Managerial fashion. *Academy of Management Review*, *21*(1): 254–285.

Abrahamson, Eric, & Fairchild, Gregory. (1999). Management fashion: Lifecycles, triggers, and collective learning processes. *Administrative Science Quarterly*, *44*: 708–740.

Koenig, Michael E. D. (2005). KM moves beyond the organization. *Information Services and Use*, *25*(2): 87–93.

Ponzi, Leonard J., & Koenig, Michael E. D. (2002). Knowledge management: Another management fad? *Information Research*, *8*(1), 8 pages, October 2002, with Leonard J. Ponzi (first author). Available at informationr.net/ir/8-1/paper145.html

# CHAPTER 2

# KM Moving into Stage IV? The Extra-Organizational Stage

Michael E. D. Koenig

Long Island University

Is knowledge management (KM) entering a new growth stage, a fourth stage, or is it merely maturing? To date, there have been three clearly observable stages of KM development. It is useful to review them briefly. Note that new stages don't replace earlier stages, they merely add emphasis to aspects of KM that, although there all along, were inadequately recognized previously. (If you are familiar with the literature on KM stages, skip this bit, and go to "Now, Stage Four.")

## The Three Stages of KM

Stage One – "By the Internet out of Intellectual Capital"

Information Technology

Intellectual Capital

The Internet (including intranets, extranets, etc.)

Key Phrases: *best practices*, later replaced by the more politic *lessons learned*

Stage Two – Human and Cultural Dimensions, the HR, Human Relations Stage

Communities of Practice

Organizational Culture

The Learning Organization (Senge)

Tacit Knowledge (Nonaka) incorporated into KM

Key Phrase: *communities of practice*

Stage Three – Content and Retrievability
Structuring Content and Assigning Descriptors (index terms)
Key Phrases: *content management* and *taxonomies*

## Stage One

The initial stage of KM was driven primarily by IT, information technology. That first stage has been described in an equestrian metaphor as "by the Internet out of intellectual capital." Organizations, particularly the large international consulting organizations, realized that their stock in trade was information and knowledge, that often the left hand, as it were, had no idea what the right hand knew, and if they could share that knowledge, then they could avoid reinventing the wheel, underbid their competitors, and make more profit. When the Internet emerged, they realized that the intranet flavor of the Internet was a god-given tool to accomplish that knowledge coordination and sharing. The first stage of KM was about how to deploy that new technology to accomplish those goals.

Those large international consulting organizations then realized quickly that many of their customers shared exactly the same problems, and that the expertise they were building for themselves could also be a product, an expertise, that they could purvey to those customers. A new product needs a name and a theme or rationale. The name for their new product was Knowledge Management and the theme/rationale justifying it was *intellectual capital*, a theme that coincidentally had emerged as a hot topic in the business literature only a couple of years earlier, and that provided a wonderful rationale for the importance of KM. The first stage might be described as the "If only Texas Instruments knew what Texas Instruments knew" stage, to revisit a much quoted aphorism. The hallmark phrase of Stage 1 was first *best practices* to be replaced by the more politic *lessons learned*.

## Stage Two

The second stage of KM can be described simply as adding the recognition of the importance of the human and cultural dimensions. The second stage might be described as the "If you build it they will come is a fallacy" stage—the recognition that "If you build it they will come" is a recipe that can easily lead to quick and embarrassing failure if human factors are not sufficiently taken into account. As this recognition unfolded, two major themes from the business literature were brought into the KM fold. The first was Senge's (1990) work on the learning organization. The second was Nonaka's (1995) work on tacit knowledge and how to discover and cultivate it. Both were not only about the human factors of KM implementation and use, they were also about knowledge creation as well as knowledge sharing and communication. The hallmark phrase of Stage 2 was *communities of practice*.

## Stage Three

The third stage was the awareness of the importance of content, and in particular an awareness of the importance of the retrievability and therefore of the importance of the arrangement, description, and structure of that content. Since a good alternate description for the second stage of KM is the "it's no good if they don't use it" stage, then in that vein, perhaps the best description for the new third stage is the "it's no good if they can't find it" stage, or perhaps "it's no good if they try to use it but can't find it." Another bellwether is that TFPL's (2001) report of its October 2001 Chief Knowledge Officer (CKO) Summit stated that for the first time taxonomies emerged as a topic, and it emerged full blown as a major topic. In TFPL's summarization of the results of that summit, the largest boldest word was **taxonomy**. The hallmark phrases emerging for the third stage are *content management* (or enterprise content management) and *taxonomies*.

### The Missed Opportunity

The unfortunate aspect of Stage Three is that, to a very large degree, it represented a substantial amount of wheel spinning and wheel reinvention. The KM community has been trying to reinvent the domain of taxonomy, precisely what librarians have long known, studied, and developed as classification. Despite some work pointing out the obvious contribution of librarianship (Koenig & Srikantaiah, 2002), the community of KM practitioners unfortunately remained largely unaware of that pool of expertise. Taxonomies are often perceived by the KM community as emanating from natural scientists, not from librarians and information scientists. To be sure, meaning #2 in Webster's for taxonomy is "classification, especially the orderly classification of plants and animals," but **meaning #1** in Webster's is "**the study of the general principles of classification,**" that is, librarianship and information science. The KM community, it appears, didn't read the dictionary. If business professionals and KM staff could visualize what they have in mind when they talk about taxonomies, and only a few could adequately do that, what would constitute that picture is something very similar to MESH: the carefully structured compendium of Medical Subject

Headings compiled by the National Library of Medicine. There is still too little awareness that taxonomies and classificatory structures like MESH are the natural and long established domain of librarians/information scientists.

## Now, Stage Four

Now, however, a fourth stage of KM can be seen to be emerging. This stage is the awareness of the importance of information and knowledge external to the organization. The inclusion of information and knowledge external to the organization is not new to KM. One need only think of the World Bank and the high visibility of their KM program and their very deliberate development of communities of practice (COPs) specifically designed to encompass experts external to the bank, to make that point. That being said, however, the overwhelming emphasis of KM to date has been to mobilize and make accessible the organization's information and knowledge. Perhaps the most basic mantra of KM has been the "If only Texas Instruments knew what Texas Instruments knew" refrain, the classic metaphoric example of what KM is all about, making *an organization's* knowledge more usable and more productive.

KM's traditional emphasis upon just an organization's internal knowledge can be best illustrated by quoting two of the most frequently quoted and used definitions of KM:

> Knowledge management is a newly emerging interdisciplinary business model dealing with all aspects of knowledge *within the context of the firm*, including knowledge creation, codification, sharing, learning, and innovation. Some aspects of this process are facilitated with information technologies, but knowledge management is, to a greater degree, about organizational culture and practices. (Ruggles, 1998)

> A discipline that promotes an integrated approach to identifying, capturing, evaluating, retrieving, and sharing all of *an enterprise's information assets*. These assets may include databases, documents, policies, procedures, and previously uncaptured expertise and experience in individual workers. (Wildermen, the Gartner Group, 1999)

The mainstream KM mindset up until now of focusing only on the firm's or the organization's or the enterprise's information and knowledge assets could hardly be clearer. Note that while Ruggles is an individual author and may be expressing a more particular view, the Gartner Group is a major high profile consulting firm and its definition is in effect a description of the product, KM consulting, that they are offering, and in this their product description they are limiting KM to "an enterprise's information assets."

This narrow emphasis of KM is now broadening. The phenomenon is particularly observable in the papers and topics discussed in the arena of the annual KM World Conference.

Several threads have converged to drive this new emphasis:

- **The extension of intranet-based KM systems to extranet-based systems:** The first and most obvious application of Internet technology was to make an "intranet" of it, to use the Internet as an access-controlled network for the company. A next logical step was to use the same access control mechanisms to build an "extranet" so that persons outside the organization, vendors, suppliers, dealers, major customers, and so on could be included. This has proceeded much more slowly, however, as security, particularly for for-profit corporations, is a major concern. How do you know that your competitor is not posing as a vendor of your products, or has not acquired a vendor of your products precisely so as to have access to some of your information? It was precisely this lack of a need to be concerned about competitive information that allowed the World Bank to so quickly move into extranet-based communities of practice. However as security techniques have improved, the willingness of corporations to extend communities of practice onto extranets so as to incorporate the knowledge of "outsiders" has correspondingly increased. A good example is Caterpillar Inc., who brought in dealers and independent repair facilities to their communities of practice. They agonized for months over what sort of nondisclosure form to use to allow access from outside the organization, produced what they jokingly called the mother of all nondisclosure forms, and then discovered that those outside the firm barely glanced at it before signing.
- **Concern about the knowledge about to be lost as post-war baby boomers are beginning to hit retirement age:** Corporations are beginning to realize that KM, in the form of communities of practice, is a wonderful tool to address this issue. If retirees are encouraged to remain as active members of one or more communities of practice, then their

knowledge is not lost, and the retiree may well be able to contribute valuable knowledge: "Back when we introduced the model 812, we had similar teething problems, and the solution turned out to be that ..." The organization has also gained, at minimal cost, important good will among their retirees and among the local communities where those retirees live.

Increasingly the realization is dawning that the notion of successfully debriefing and capturing the employees' knowledge before they leave the organization, keeping it in-house as it were, is for the most part a pipe dream. Why?

1. The chance that the teething problems of the model 812 will come up in that "data dump" interview, even an extended one, before the employee retires is somewhat minimal.

2. The chance that someone in the organization will actually try to look for relevant information in those "data dumps" at or near the critical time is even more minimal.

3. Even if someone does search, the chance of finding the right information and making the connection is also small. One might find the problems with the model 812 by searching under, let us say "lubrication problems," but the chances that the old timer will have used some other phraseology to describe the situation is probably equally high. If one attempts to develop a taxonomy and index the data dumps, the cost is very high and the improvement in performance likely to be meager.

4. The response is very likely not as simple as "back when we introduced the model 812, we had similar teething problems, and the solution turned out to be that ..." It is more likely to be something like "back when we introduced the model 812, we had similar teething problems, and the situation here puts me in mind that what's causing the problem could be ... and a possible field fix might be ..." In short, the great utility of the old timers knowledge is likely to be not just the knowledge per se, but the ability to apply that knowledge to a new situation, and it is probably the old timer who has that ability, not the person who looks it up in the data dump.

The solution isn't the data dump and thereby attempting to keep the knowledge in-house; the solution is opening up the organization's communities of practice to the alums and to selected members of the world outside the organization. Caterpillar Inc. again is an organization that has been particularly pro-active in this use of KM for their "alums," and it was success in this venture that led them to go still further afield as described previously.

- **A repeat of the same broadening phenomenon that occurred with Management Information Systems (MIS)**: After MIS were introduced in the 1970s, there came a rebound of disillusionment with the field of MIS. Much of that disillusionment was a function of the fact that what the MIS system contained was typically only the organization's raw and partially aggregated transaction information, purchases, production data, sales, etc., useful data and information to be sure, but not the information constituting the bulk of what an executive typically needed for those decisions near the top of the managerial decision-making pyramid. For those decisions, what was typically needed was external contextual data, not the transactional data in the typical MIS system. This realization drove an awareness of the importance of external information, and it also drove a partial rebranding of MIS, relaunched as DSS (Decision Support Systems), a terminology designed to avoid overselling those transactional data based systems and to avoid implying that they had all the data or information that an executive needed. That same awareness is gradually developing in the KM world, the awareness that much of the key information needed for critical decisions lies outside the corporation or organization, and that the ideal KM system should provide appropriate links to the world outside the organization.

The result is a greatly increased emphasis upon external information. It should also be noted that another emphasis emerging simultaneously is that of the importance of situating information and knowledge in context. This is in fact another facet of the same evolution, the awareness that the importance, the usability, and the value of information is a function of how it relates to other information. New knowledge derives from the combination of information, either the juxtaposition of existing information, or the addition of new information to existing information. If I have seen further than others, it is because I have stood on the shoulders of giants …

Is this really a new stage four? Or just a maturation of KM? Probably the best answer is the latter. The distinction is hardly as clear as those between the previous stages and the continuity is greater with context emphasis long apparent in many cases. Yet, it is a very heightened emphasis, and that emphasis is the theme of this book.

# REFERENCES

Abrahamson, Eric. (1996). Managerial fashion. *Academy of Management Review, 21*(1): 254–285.

Abrahamson, Eric, & Fairchild, Gregory. (1999). Management fashion: Lifecycles, triggers, and collective learning processes. *Administrative Science Quarterly, 44*: 708–740.

Davenport, Thomas, & Prusak, Larry. (2003). *What's the big idea?* Boston: Harvard Business School Press.

Koenig, Michael E. D., & Srikantaiah, T. Kanti. (2002). The business world discovers the assets of librarianship. *Information Outlook, 6*(4): 14–18.

Nonaka, Ikujiro, & Takeuchi, Hirotaka. (1995). *The knowledge-creating company: How Japanese companies create the dynamics of innovation.* New York: Oxford University Press.

Ponzi, Leonard, & Koenig, Michael E. D. (2002). Knowledge management: Another management fad? *Information Research, 8*(1). Available at informationr.net/ir/8-1/paper145.html

Ruggles, Rudy L., III. (1997). *Knowledge management tools.* New York: Butterworth-Heinemann.

Senge, Peter M. (1990). *The fifth discipline: The art and practice of the learning organization.* New York: Doubleday/Currency.

TFPL. (2001). *Knowledge strategies–corporate strategies.* [TFPL's 4th International CKO Summit]. London: TFPL. Available at www.tfpl.org

Wildermen, Jack. (1999). *Knowledge management: Moving from academic concepts to fundamental business practice.* Stamford, CT: InfoEdge for the Gartner Group.

# CHAPTER 3

# Knowledge Management Expansion: Content Management, Project Management, Competitive Intelligence, Environmental Scanning, and Knowledge Audit

T. Kanti Srikantaiah

Dominican University

Knowledge management (KM) has evolved from the techno-centric applications to intellectual capital-centric applications. When KM started, the focus was purely internal to the organization and the application of technology within the organization to resolve issues. Gradually, over the years, KM has broadened its scope to include learning organizations and the information profession to cover knowledge beyond and outside the organization. Today, KM, true to its interdisciplinary nature, is more matured and advanced, embracing, among others, Content Management, Competitive Intelligence, Project Management, Environmental Scanning, and Knowledge Audit, where KM tools are applied regularly to manage knowledge. This chapter summarizes the expanded role of KM describing those areas.

## STAGES OF KNOWLEDGE MANAGEMENT

Koenig and Srikantaiah (2004) recognize three stages in KM in terms of its evolution. The first stage of KM "by the Internet out of intellectual capital" is driven by IT. Organizations, particularly large international organizations, realized their stock is information and knowledge; that often the left hand, as it were, had no idea what the right hand knew; and if they could share that knowledge, they would avoid reinventing the wheel and increase profits. This resulted in applying IT to the full extent and concentrating on intellectual capital and the

Internet (including intranets, extranets, and so on). The key phrase here is "best practices," later replaced by "lessons learned."

The second stage of KM, described simply, added recognition of the human and cultural dimensions. This stage could be described as the "if you build it they will come is a fallacy" stage; that is, the recognition "if you build it they will come" as a recipe that can easily lead to quick and embarrassing failure if human factors are not sufficiently taken into account. With this recognition, two major themes from the business literature were brought into the KM fold. The first work was by Senge (1990) on learning organization. The second was the work by Nonaka and Takeuchi (1995) on tacit knowledge and how to discover and cultivate it. They were also concerned with knowledge creation and sharing and communication. The hallmark of this stage is "communities of practice."

The third stage is the awareness of the importance of content, and focuses on the importance of retrievability and therefore the importance of arrangement, description, and structure of content. A good alternate description is the "it's no good if they can't find it" stage. The hallmarks of this stage are "content management" and "taxonomy."

As KM is in the domain of stable mature growth, which entails expanding and changing, a fourth stage of KM seems to be emerging, which expands the KM application in the areas of Content Management, Competitive Intelligence, Project Management, Environmental Scanning, and Knowledge Audit.

## KNOWLEDGE MANAGEMENT

### Historical Background

At the individual level, all wise men are attributed to have managed knowledge since the beginning of our human civilization. Great thinkers of the world had accumulated a tremendous amount of knowledge in their heads and when they shared their knowledge, civilizations evolved. In the western society, philosophers like Aristotle and Plato have laid strong foundations for knowledge. In science and literature, individuals have contributed heavily toward knowledge to benefit the public and the society. However, this writing does not deal with those thinkers and their knowledge; it instead focuses on organizational knowledge in both for-profit and nonprofit sectors.

Today, KM focuses on the intellectual capital contributing to economic and social development and emphasizes sustainability in organizations.

## Current Background

Currently, at the organizational level, KM is attributed to organizational assets. KM is a product of the 1990s and is a hot topic in organizations with many practitioners drawn from different disciplines, such as business, engineering, education, epistemology, communication, and information management, among others. KM embraces those disciplines and treats knowledge as an entity dynamically embedded in networks, processes, repositories, and people. Over the last few years, KM has emerged explosively through an interdisciplinary approach dealing with all aspects of knowledge in organizations, including knowledge creation, codification, organization, sharing, and application. Therefore, we can define KM as the systematic process of identifying, capturing, organizing, and disseminating/sharing explicit and tacit knowledge assets that add value within an organization. These assets may include databases, documents, policies, and procedures, as well as previously uncaptured expertise in individual workers.

Organizations have realized that knowledge is power—but only if it is readily accessible, organized, analyzed, and displayed to solve the needs of users. KM addresses the problem of poor quality and poorly organized information and knowledge in both the for-profit and nonprofit sectors. KM focuses on the proper access and delivery methods for explicit knowledge on the desktop and also concentrates on tacit knowledge, unknown and unavailable to most people. In the U.S. alone, more than 15 billion dollars are spent in the area of KM. The KM perspective looks at assets in a new way at the organizational level, which includes: people, customers, databases, documents, products, processes, and services.

## KNOWLEDGE MANAGEMENT CONTINUUM

Knowledge is part of our culture. We have been able to track down knowledge ever since human beings began communicating with each other.

On a continuum, as Davenport (1997) expressed, KM starts with *data*, which is based on raw facts, figures, or statistics. When these raw facts are contextualized, categorized, calculated, corrected, and condensed, it leads to codification and becomes explicit, in other words, *information*. When this information is applied by users through comparisons, conversations, connections, and consequences, it becomes *knowledge*. In other words, knowledge focuses on experience, values, and the context in which information is applied to a message and thus embraces both explicit and tacit knowledge. The last segment of the KM continuum is *wisdom*, which reflects on sound and effective decisions made, based on knowledge. Wisdom is a collective application of knowledge in action by wise men and women.

## Why Knowledge Management Now?

Why KM now? There are several reasons.

First, there is the advancement of technology. We had never experienced the advantages of technology tools before, say, 15–20 years ago. The Internet, laptop, cell phone, BlackBerry, and Pilot are just a few examples of the technological tools that have altered our working lifestyle as well as our social lifestyle. The benefits of harnessing this technology to manage knowledge have given an advantage to organizations in managing their assets. In today's work environment our work life revolves around these technologies.

Second, there is the exploding nature of online information. Gone are the days when we had all information packages in the hard copy format (on paper). With thousands of Web sites, search engines, e-mails, and so forth, digital information is taking over hard copy format in most areas. Digital information is growing each day and has become part of our culture; it is here to stay. As the ratio of electronic information vs. hard copy information is leaning toward the digital area, KM has become a functional necessity.

Third, organizations have to compete for their survival. These days, organizations are acquired, merged, and claim bankruptcy if they do not compete with others to sustain viability in the industry. Also, many organizations are operating in the global context, which poses more strategic challenges. In order to stay competitive and survive, organizations are establishing their own KM systems.

Fourth, with the regulatory reforms at the national levels and fast growing global environment, organizations have realized that the culture of the organization should change from hoarding to sharing knowledge. The KM systems that are set up in organizations promote an organization-wide knowledge sharing culture. Collaboration among various units of the organization in a synergic way will increase the trust and work morale of staff resulting in increased productivity. Also, it will cut costs and fulfill the goals and objectives of the organization effectively. KM plays a key role in accomplishing this aspect.

Fifth, organizations are influenced by external economic conditions and internal political conditions (management styles). The current environment dictates increased productivity with fewer resources. In order to achieve this, knowledge in the organization needs to be managed properly. KM experts are setting up systems to accomplish this objective to increase productivity levels while resources are cut.

Last (but not the least), the skills of information professionals are absolutely necessary to make KM work. At the present stage, KM has absorbed content management, project management, competitive intelligence, environmental scanning, and knowledge audit as KM is applied in those areas.

## Types of Knowledge

KM deals with both explicit and tacit knowledge. *Explicit knowledge* deals with codified knowledge that is documented and is in the domain of structural capital. In contrast, *tacit knowledge* is the know-how and know-what, the knowledge people hold in their possession, which is the domain of human and customer capital. Knowledge resides with individuals, their conversations, internal records, external publications, data warehouses, internal and external databases, best practices, intranet, and Internet. Nonaka and Takeuchi (1995) described four basic patterns of explicit and tacit knowledge, addressing it as SECI: socialization, externalization, creation, and internalization.

- **From Tacit to Tacit:** When an individual shares tacit knowledge with another face-to-face or through other modes (socialization)
- **From Explicit to Explicit:** When an individual combines discrete pieces of explicit knowledge and creates a new product (creation)
- **From Tacit to Explicit:** When the organization deals with a knowledge base by codifying experience, insight, and opinion into a form that can be reused by others (externalization)
- **From Explicit to Tacit:** When staff members internalize new or shared explicit knowledge and then use it to broaden, extend, and rethink their own tacit knowledge (internalization)

The last two may provide a challenge in KM: from tacit to explicit and explicit to tacit. Although it is easy to identify these two areas, it depends on the organizational culture and structure.

Srikantaiah and Koenig (2001) describe the various categories of explicit and tacit knowledge. Explicit knowledge exists in organizations in a wide variety of forms. Here is a sample list:

- Commercial print publications (books, periodicals, and reports)

- Internal records (business records, archives)
- Sound recordings, video recordings, graphic material, etc.
- Data warehouses
- Internal databases (text, numerical)
- External databases (text, numerical)
- E-mail
- Intranet
- Internet
- Best Practices
- Self-study material
- Newsletters
- Others

Tacit knowledge is vital to KM. KM practices aim to draw out the tacit knowledge people have, what they carry around with them, and what they observe and learn from experience, rather than what is usually explicitly stated. Davenport and Prusak (1998) state studies have shown that managers get two-thirds of their information and knowledge from face to face meetings or phone conversations. These days, many organizations are establishing physical areas that are dedicated and designed to facilitate tacit knowledge transfer.

In the area of tacit knowledge there also is a wide variety of categories. Here is a sample list:

- Face-to-face conversation
  - Formal
  - Informal
- Telephone conversations
  - Formal
  - Informal
- Video conferences and presentations
- Individual knowledge and expertise
- Top management support
- Outside experts
- Mentoring
- Coaching
- Study tours
- Client knowledge
- E-mail
- Other

Today's organizations benefit from organizing explicit knowledge (both external and internal) and by capturing tacit knowledge (people skills, ideas, values, motivation, and so on), which is the core of KM.

# Content Management

## Background

Content is knowledge—if accessible, organized, managed, analyzed, and delivered to meet the user's needs. Too often, the right content is not found or found too late. Over the last few years, content management has emerged explosively with an interdisciplinary approach dealing with all aspects of content management, which includes creation, codification, organization, sharing, and application. Managing content requires many skills from a variety of fields—technology, management, and information science, among others.

## Definition

In simple terms, content management can be described as the art of locating, selecting, acquiring, processing, managing, and disseminating content. It is certainly more than a Web development in organizations. McQueen (2001) defines content management as the strategic application of technology, content, and people resources to leverage business processes and create competitive advantage. He elaborates that content management strategy should assist in three areas: people as Content Contributors (creators, acquiring content); as Content Consumers (consuming content); and as Content Managers (managing the content and CM technologies). Therefore, content management deals with managing content in organizations and making available the right knowledge relevant to users at the right time. This knowledge must be current, relevant, and useful in application. Content management cuts through many areas and assimilating concepts: KM, document management, competitive intelligence, Web development, library and information services, and e-commerce, among others.

## Principles

Irrespective of the perspective, servicing from content involves five basic principles: understanding user needs, acquiring the essential content, selecting the appropriate content, storing and managing the content, and disseminating the content. User needs assessment is an important activity in content management. The needs of users depends on the individuals and the culture of the organization. These needs may be met through internal resources or by reaching out to external sources. These needs are to be properly assessed and evaluated before designing and developing a content management system in the organization. Boiko (2002) poses several questions: What does content mean to users? How can content be acquired, processed, and stored? Where are content resources located in the organization? Who has the responsibility to manage the content? What are the information flows within the organization? How does the organization relate to the outside world? How do people share content? How should IT provide the necessary infrastructure to the users of content? What are the costs and benefits? How does it fulfill the organizational objectives?

Content is managed in organizations to increase productivity, improve efficiency, provide economic growth, enhance social capital, provide sustainability, and enhance customer satisfaction. Content management involves capturing relevant content, performing market analyses, and maintaining databases, documents, best practices, policies, procedures, products, and services, as well as previously uncaptured expertise in individual workers.

## Explicit and Tacit Content

The information in a content management system is generally of three types: unrecorded knowledge that people carry in their heads, recorded knowledge generated internally, and knowledge acquired from external sources. The first type is generally known as tacit knowledge and is the most difficult to deal with in accessing and sharing content. Examples are already provided in the previous section.

On the other hand, explicit knowledge deals with codified knowledge. It covers both internally generated knowledge and externally available knowledge. Examples are already provided in the previous section.

## Content Management System

The effectiveness of a content management system (CMS) is similar to any other information system. It revolves around response time, accuracy (validity), throughput, relevancy, economy, reliability, efficiency, security, legal framework, quality, etc.

The creation of content maps may facilitate an understanding of the content of organizations. This map may include people, processes, databases, products, documents, repositories, services, customers, and relationships. The volume of content, internally generated and available externally, in organizations can be overwhelming. If one looks at the total possible content including media and telephone conversations, the volume can be very high. Brown (2000, p. 15) estimated that the World Wide Web alone encompasses about six terabytes of text data—and that estimate is now very much out of date. Content is the nucleus of tacit/explicit knowledge, and an appropriate infrastructure is required to manage content. Two major components of that infrastructure are technology and the training of staff who service and support the CMS. Content management systems strategy (CMSS) must be developed in accordance with the philosophy and the direction of an enterprise's use of content.

Managing content could be centralized or distributed depending on the policy of the organization. In a centralized service unit, it may be difficult to keep content close to staff and to their needs. In a decentralized function, there may be a number of information purveyors involved in content management and distribution, such as database administrators, librarians, record managers, help desks, HR, finance, and administration, among others. In a decentralized environment, communities of practice can be established giving staff with common interests a chance to voluntarily participate and share content/knowledge. Content can be organized around topical areas that are valuable to the community.

## Systems Study

Understanding the problem completely and with clarity is absolutely essential. In order to achieve this, a systems study is recommended. Assessing user requirements and determining costs and benefits is part of a systems study and is extremely helpful in designing a content management system (CMS). First, an overview of the content management in the organization need to be examined. Second, mapping of explicit knowledge and tacit knowledge needs to be conducted. Third, user community needs must be identified in order to clearly understand the communities of practice. Fourth, knowledge sharing activities in the organization need to be examined and evaluated. Once the systems study provides a solid analysis of these aspects, then a content management system can be designed and implemented. Content management systems need to be implemented by carefully reviewing policies and procedures of the organizations, evaluation of the content, and with appropriate software applications. An evaluation of vendor driven systems vs. one built in-house should be done to make a proper decision.

Warren (2001) says that the process of content management begins when an organization realizes that it needs a system to manage content. Content is no longer solely the product published on paper. Other formats are dominating the field, including electronic and CD formats.

## Issues

There are numerous major issues connected with content management:

- **Online/electronic:** Often print material needs to be converted into electronic format for easier access.
- **Legal framework:** Copyright, proprietary rights, and similar issues need to be sorted out and legally protected.
- **Organizational culture:** Is the organization ready to implement CMS? What kind of change management is required?
- **User profiles/needs analysis:** What are the real needs of users? Are need profiles available to disseminate content?
- **Cost:** Design cost, implementation and installation, and general ongoing maintenance costs are accounted for.
- **Training:** For the success of a CMS, the staff who provide services need to be well trained.
- **Software:** Appropriate software needs to be selected for effectiveness.

## Software Applications

Content has become the important domain of technologists. In today's environment, content cannot be managed through manual processes.

One needs an electronic platform, meaning the application of appropriate software, to manage content. Apart from the ones that are developed in-house, there are a large number of software packages available on the market to handle many aspects of content management. As already stated, CM software depends on the sector to be dealt with and the type of application intended. There are more than 100 vendors currently claiming to offer content management (CM) products and expertise. The latest KM World Buyers' Guide lists more than 30 software packages available on the market. Among others, they include: Bauter, BCI Knowledge Group, Cannon U.S.A., Citrix Systems Inc., Eclipsys Corporation, Entopia, Filenet Corporation, FORMTEK, Hummingbird Ltd., Hyperware, IBM Corporation, Identitech, iManage, IMR Alchemy, Insystems, IT Factory Inc., Neotix, Participate Systems Inc., Ptech Inc., Quiver Inc., SER Solutions Inc.,

Softfront Software, Softheon Inc., Symtrax, Tower Software, Universal Document Management Systems (UDMS), and Websoft systems. The descriptions of these packages are provided in the guide. The scope and functionality of these packages depends upon what the organizations are trying to do with their content such as structured vs. unstructured data, document management, and process integration, among others. Priscilla Emery (2001) evaluates eight software applications of content management in her article and presents informal guidelines about what to look for in software vendors. She discusses the following packages: BroadVision, ePrise, FileNET, Intranet Solutions, Interwoven, Vignette, Cytura, and FatWire, and provides a critical evaluation of them. The software market landscape is ever changing, and it can be difficult for an organization to make the right decision about which product to select for its KM efforts. Selection of software depends on the sector and the type of application. Software vendors claim that their product can manage content through creating, locating, acquiring, processing, storing, and disseminating to users. The supplier side, however, is very much in flux with significant mergers and acquisitions, with new vendors emerging frequently, and with many vendors scaling back their operation's size to be more in line with the reality of the market. Realistically, many of these vendors are likely not to survive (Emery, 2001).

## Future

The content management industry is several billion dollars strong with investments growing rapidly into the area. A greater number of organizations will implement CMS in the future, and the industry will grow exponentially, including software and services.

## Competitive Intelligence

This field is adapted from tools and technologies used by intelligence agencies. Larry Kahaner (1996) defines Competitive Intelligence (CI) as a systematic program for gathering and analyzing information about your competitors' activities and general business trends to further your own organization's goals. The Society for Competitive Intelligence Professionals (SCIP) echoes that definition (www.scip.org/ci). SCIP, established in 1986, has more than 7,000 members and is recognized as an authority in the competitive intelligence field.

The application of KM is essential as the aim of CI is to understand business processes, industry trends, market forces, and strategic impact factors. Also, CI involves differentiating between the unique challenges of various competitors in order to assess their readiness, as expressed by their capability, capacity, and willingness to act. CI uses KM to understand the marketplace and competitors, as well as lessons learned from the success and failure of other organizations. CI as part of KM has intrinsic value as a modern business decision-making tool. CI goes beyond traditional market research to deliver details that executives rely upon in formulating corporate strategy. In managing knowledge, CI's functions revolve around collecting data and turning it into information providing the context, analyzing information and converting it into knowledge, and from knowledge deriving intelligence, which is made available to decision makers to apply to yield results.

According to SCIP, 80 to 90 percent of all information is public knowledge and centered around: new competitors, actions of competitors, new markets, changes in marketplace, new legislation, new technology, and so on. These areas can be explored by using primary sources as well as secondary sources.

The sources of information for CI may include:

- Government documents (public domain information) at the federal, state, and local levels
- Annual reports
- Speeches
- Financial reports
- Commercial books and popular and technical periodicals
- News media, television, radio, and the like;
- Online databases (Dialog, LexisNexis, Dow Jones, etc.)
- The Internet
- Tacit knowledge of individuals
- Others

Stephen H. Miller, in his article "Competitive Intelligence—An Overview" (Source: SCIP Web site), quotes Herring (1998) that CI life cycle activities include: planning and direction (working with decision makers to discover and hone their intelligence needs), collection activities (conducted legally and ethically), analysis (interpreting data and compiling recommended actions), dissemination (presenting findings to decision makers), and feedback (taking into account the response of decision makers and their needs for continued intelligence). CI focuses on external information and knowledge, and, as KM started its expansion to the external environment, CI utilizes many KM tools. CI reports allow management to position themselves strategically to sustain competition. Today, CI is practiced all over the world and has a global significance. KM's aim is to add value to the organization making use of information and knowledge collected through CI.

# Project Management

PMBOK Guide (Project Management Institute, 2004) defines a project as "a temporary endeavor undertaken to create a unique product or service." According to the PMBOK Guide, every project will have the following components: Integration, Scope, Time, Cost, Quality, Human Resources, Communications, Risk, and Procurement. The interrelationships that exist among these components dealing with management of such knowledge make the project a success or failure. The Project Management Institute (PMI) is a leading authority in project management with more than 210,000 members. In every project, there is communication, performance reporting, information and knowledge distribution, documentation, and stakeholder management activities. In order to perform these functions effectively, knowledge needs to be managed and the tools and techniques of KM are absolutely necessary to produce results. Therefore, KM is an important function in project management. Important benefits also include "lessons learned" in managing projects and best practices. There are many driving factors for KM in the project area.

First, the advancement of technology requires that projects manage knowledge in professional, industrial, regulatory, market, and customer areas. Second, the explosive nature of outside information has made KM a basic requirement in projects. Third, projects need to be completed on time for survival; KM helps to leverage knowledge in such competition. Fourth, regulatory reforms and a fast growing global environment encourage the transition from hoarding knowledge to sharing knowledge. Fifth, projects are influenced by economic conditions and internal political conditions and the slogan: "to do more with less resources" fits all projects. In order to accomplish this, KM is absolutely essential.

Some of the questions raised in the discussion group in "KM for PM" (www.knowledgeboard.com/cgi-bin/item.cgi?id=428) are dealt with here: Projects are temporary with start date and completion date. Capitalizing on lessons learned from the previous projects through KM is a fundamental necessity for any success in the ongoing project. How can the experiences of previous projects be captured and in what format? How do we establish policies and procedures in disseminating codified knowledge? How can one tap the knowledge for ongoing projects? What needs to be saved? What is the role of project management structures in facilitating knowledge sharing? Since many carry tacit knowledge on projects, how can they be captured? In many cases, multiple projects are managed with interrelated resources and KM will have immense value. However, often project team members are not afforded the luxury of time to record their experiences and even if it were possible it would be ignored or receive a low priority. As information accumulates with projects and as it progresses, knowledge should be made available for the success of the project. Some questions for KM in projects could be: How can we efficiently and effectively share knowledge between projects? What information is useful and value adding? What information does not require saving?

KM in projects has the following benefits:

- **Strategic advantage:** With available knowledge widely dispersed and fragmented, projects teams often waste valuable time and resources in "reinventing the wheel" or failing to access the highest quality knowledge and expertise that is available.

- **Retention:** Without effective mechanisms in place to capture knowledge of experienced employees, project teams may be making costly mistakes or have to pay again for knowledge they once had on hand.

- **Sharing of best practices:** Projects could cut costs by taking the knowledge from their best performers and applying it in similar situations elsewhere.

- **Global environment:** Using knowledge from one project/assignment to other projects/assignments and applying it in another culture.

- **Successful innovation:** Other companies applying KM methods have found that through knowledge networking they can create new products and services faster and better.

Therefore, because of these many benefits, managing knowledge is the most important task for the success of any project.

# ENVIRONMENTAL SCANNING

Choo (2001) states that *environmental scanning* is the acquisition and use of information about events, trends, and relationships in an organization's external environment, the knowledge of which would assist management in planning the organization's future course of action. This is where KM is helpful in tracking down the three categories of information sources, which are human resources, textual resources, and online resources. KM emphasizes an understanding of the organization and its environments, information culture in the organization, and information needs of the organization and users, and also helps the organization in learning and unlearning. One of the KM tools used in environmental scanning is the application of SWOT analysis. SWOT analysis is an excellent tool for organizational planning, especially in the strategic planning area, and provides important information to information professionals, project managers, and managers. SWOT provides analysis of strengths, weaknesses, opportunities, and threats.

The term environmental scanning was coined by Francis Aguilar in the 1960s (1967) who defined it as "the activity of acquiring information … about events and relationships in the outside environment, the knowledge of which would assist top management in its task of charting the company's future course of action." It also includes the analysis of social, political, economic, scientific, and technical trends. It cautions decision makers on the trends and changing external environment. Porter (1985) outlined five forces that organizations have to watch out for: bargaining power of customers, bargaining power of suppliers, threat of new entrants, threat of substitute products, and intensity of competitive rivalry. In terms of KM, in addition to tuning in to those external conditions, it also focuses on the internal environment of information politics and culture. Through KM, organizations scan the environment in order to understand the external forces of change so that they may develop effective responses, which secure or improve their position in the future and also the internal environment to determine resources, staff morale and motivation, management, and productivity. Through environmental scanning one can avoid surprises, identify strengths and weaknesses, identify threats and opportunities, gain competitive advantage, and plan strategically. Scanning helps knowledge managers understand the information seeking behaviors focusing on information needs, information seeking, and information use.

The professional literature points to case studies where successful companies benefited from environmental scanning and KM. From the KM perspective,

Subramanian's study (Subramanian, Fernandes, & Harper, 1993) of Fortune 500 companies indicated that there is a strong correlation between organizational performance, profitability, and growth with scanning.

Environmental scanning concentrates on tracking down both tacit knowledge (personal knowledge and experience) and explicit knowledge (rule based and codified) to help the organization. Through environmental scanning, organizations can track down the continuously created new knowledge by capturing tacit knowledge to develop creative insight and the shared, explicit knowledge by which the organization develops new products and innovations (Nonaka & Takeuchi, 1995, p. 60).

KM reflects on Coates's (1985, p. 26) objectives on environmental scanning:

- Detecting scientific, technical, economic, social, and political trends and events important by those trends and events
- Defining the potential threats, opportunities, or changes for the institution implied by those trends and events
- Promoting a future orientation in the thinking of management and staff
- Alerting management and staff to trends that are converging, diverging, speeding up, slowing down, or interacting

Organizations have to decide which level of scanning is suitable for them to manage knowledge. Organizations can have regular and continuous scanning done to keep the proper health of the organization in order to prosper economically, socially, and through growth. Organizations may decide on a periodic/regular scan to assess their standing on knowledge and how it is used; organizations may opt for irregular or ad hoc scanning only when they notice a problem in KM.

Wikipedia (wikipedia.org) provides a long list of indicators at the macro environment for the environmental scanning and to manage knowledge. Briefly, they include: the economy (GNP or GDP, etc.), government (political climate, taxes, etc.), legal (environmental protection, copyright and intellectual property rights, etc.), technology (efficiency of infrastructure, etc.), ecology (production processes and customer buying habits, etc.), socio-cultural (demographic factors such as population size, age, education, income, etc.), potential suppliers (labor supply, quality, etc.), material suppliers (quality, quantity, price, etc.), and service providers. All these macro areas thrive on knowledge and proper management of knowledge as a fundamental necessity.

# KNOWLEDGE AUDIT

A knowledge audit is different from an information audit—a technique that has been in practice for many years—although a knowledge audit includes an information audit as well. A knowledge audit dwells upon the politics and culture of the information and knowledge environment and also evaluates the external environment in the areas of social, economic, political, and technological aspects. Henczel (2001a), an authority on information audits, recognizes seven stages in the audit process. They are: planning, data collection, data analysis, data evaluation, communicating recommendations, implementing recommendations, and a look at the information audit as a continuum. These seven stages are applied while conducting a knowledge audit.

As a starting point, the objectives for the audit should be clear to succeed in knowledge audit. The purpose of a knowledge audit should be documented and methodology should be spelled out in order to achieve that purpose. The role of knowledge in the organization and the organizational culture needs to be understood including: mission and goals, operations, human resources, finance, processes, and technology. There is a need to scan the stakeholders both inside and outside the organization to get a clear idea in terms of knowledge acquisition, KM, and knowledge use. Carrying out a knowledge audit is the first critical step in understanding KM in the organization. A knowledge audit will also expose existing infrastructure and align KM with business strategy. The steps in a knowledge audit may include:

- Establishing a steering committee
- Identifying important business strategies
- Identifying the nature of knowledge resources
- Identifying the knowledge that staff need to do their work
- Developing a profile of knowledge workers
- Identifying the people who carry critical knowledge in fulfilling the organizational objectives
- Examining processes for key issues and critical content
- Setting goals and benchmarks

A knowledge audit is qualitative in nature in contrast to a financial audit, which tends to be quantitative. A typical knowledge audit will look at the organization's knowledge assets and point out through knowledge mapping the inventory, gaps, duplication, etc. in knowledge. It can also determine the knowledge flows in the organization and issues surrounding those flows, and evaluate the existing tech-nology infrastructure supporting KM.

Some examples of situations in which a knowledge audit can be beneficial include (source: www.nelh.nhs.uk/knowledge_management/kmz/audit_toolkit.asp):

- You are about to embark on creating a KM strategy and need to establish exactly "where you are now."
- People are having difficulty in finding the information and knowledge they need to make key decisions.
- Useful sources of information and knowledge are frequently stumbled across by accident.
- There is duplication of information and knowledge gathering activities across different departments or teams, and hence duplication of costs.
- Questions are being raised about the value of KM systems, initiatives, or investments.
- When findings from research and development are not making their way into practice quickly enough.

The Web site also reiterates the steps in a knowledge audit, which were already discussed, including: identifying knowledge needs; assessing the knowledge needs of stakeholders—both internal and external; creating a knowledge map that reveals knowledge assets in the organization and provides an inventory of both explicit and tacit knowledge and where gaps exist; and understanding knowledge flows—how it moves around in the organization under established policies and practices. An analysis of knowledge flows will allow you to further identify gaps in your organization's knowledge and areas of duplication; it will also highlight examples of good practice that can be built on, as well as blockages and barriers to knowledge flows and effective use. It will show where you need to focus atten-tion in your KM initiatives in order to get knowledge moving from where it is to where it is needed. A greater percentage of knowledge exits in tacit format, and a knowledge audit should not focus only on explicit knowledge that is the key fac-tor in an information audit.

Ann Hylton (www.crm2day.com) says that a knowledge audit should always be the first major stage of a KM initiative. A KM program or system should never be implemented without a knowledge audit having been conducted. Most impor-tantly the precursor to big spending on KM technology is a proper knowledge audit to determine exactly what tools and solutions are most appropriate to enable better KM by the knowledge people in the organization.

Knowledge is the most important asset any organization can own—through its employees, partners, suppliers, customers, and competitors. A knowledge audit will strengthen these assets.

# FINAL NOTE

There is a definite correlation between KM and economic growth, as evidenced by a significant contrast in the social and economic indicators between the developed and developing countries. The World Bank has provided some startling statistics on the differences between the advanced and less developed countries. It lists, based on GNP, 200+ countries as: low income economies, lower-middle-income economies, upper-middle-income economies, and high-income economies. An analysis of these developed and developing countries through KM, competitive intelligence, project management, environmental scanning, and the knowledge audit reveals a significant difference in the KM factors that have contributed to the considerable disparities not only in wealth, but also in education, population, GNP per capita, adult literacy rate, infant mortality, health services, and other indicators of poverty and prosperity. To improve the situation, knowledge should be managed for better results.

Professional literature reveals, in the U.S. private sector, organizations involved in sectors such as energy, automobile, research and development (R&D), manufacturing, insurance, finance, education, agriculture, telecommunications, and transportation have invested heavily in KM and have benefited by the results. The investment pattern is catching on in many parts of the world, and recent additions to the KM area are the two most populated countries in the world, China and India. In most situations, the technology side of KM has high visibility in market terms of supply and demand, and policies relating to them become embedded in the various official documents. In order to sustain the growth, countries should adapt KM on a balanced scale (score card) emphasizing budget allocation and information policies. Applying KM on this sound platform will contribute to low inflation and concomitant monetary policies around the globe.

In the knowledge economy, the countries need to do a lot of work defining strategies and creating conditions to acquire and manage knowledge as quickly as possible. A conducive knowledge environment in those countries should encompass regulations protecting investment, intellectual property, and individual privacy, with regulated communication networks and sound education policies, creating conditions for knowledge to grow—both through the acquisition of external information and stimulating the creation of indigenous information.

In the 21st century, it is perhaps not over the top to say that KM will become the core of all human activities (considering the field started only 15–20 years ago). KM has made a real impact in organizations around the world by demonstrating how to grow and sustain growth.

From the KM perspective, all the discussed areas are essential in managing knowledge in an enterprise. As information and communication technologies continue to grow rapidly and dominate in the 21st century, KM applications will become critical in the knowledge life cycle, from the knowledge creation stage to the knowledge dissemination stage. The expanded application of KM through content management, competitive intelligence, project management, environmental scanning, and the knowledge audit have resulted in economic benefits and healthy competition in every sector and all aspects of human life.

# REFERENCES

Abell, Angela. (2000). Skills for knowledge environments. *Information Management Journal, 34*(3): 33–41.

Adams, Katherine C. (2001). The Web as a database: New extraction technologies and content management. *Online, 25*: 27–32.

Aguilar, Francis J. (1967). *Scanning the business environment.* New York: Macmillan.

Alavi, Maryam, & Tiwana, A. (2002). Knowledge integration in virtual teams: The potential role of KMS. *Journal of the American Society for Information Science and Technology, 53*(12): 1029–1037.

Alper, Joseph. (1998). Assembling the world's biggest library on your desktop. *Science, 281*(5384): 1784–1786.

Anantatmula, Vittal S. (2005). Outcomes of knowledge management initiatives. *International Journal of Knowledge Management, 1*(2): 50–67.

Blair, David C. (2002). Knowledge management: Hype, hope or help? *Journal of the American Society for Information Science and Technology, 53*(12): 1019–1028.

Boiko, Bob. (2001). Understanding content management. *Bulletin of the American Society for Information Science & Technology, 28*: 8–13.

Boiko, Bob. (2002). *Content management bible.* New York: Hungry Minds.

Bontis, Nick. (2001). Assessing knowledge assets: A review of the models used to measure intellectual capital. *International Journal of Management Reviews, 3*(1): 41–60.

Booth, A., &. Haines, M. (1994). Information audit: Whose line is it anyway? *Health Libraries Review, 10*(4): 224–232.

Bouthillier, France, & Shearer, Kathleen. (2002). Understanding knowledge management and information management: The need for an empirical perspective. *Information Research*, 8(1).

Breeding, Bret. (2000). CI and KM convergence: A case study at Shell Services International. *Competitive Intelligence Review*, 11(4): 12–24.

Broadbent, Marianne. (1998). The phenomenon of knowledge management: What does it mean to the information profession? *Information Outlook*, 2(5): 23–36.

Brown, Ian D. (2000). *What can technology offer? Notes on technical developments for the non-technical*. Available at www.alpsp.uk/journal.htm

Brown, John Seeley. (1998). Organizing knowledge. *California Management Review*, 40(3): 90–112.

Brown, John Seeley, & Duguid, Paul. (2000). Balancing act: How to capture knowledge without killing it. *Harvard Business Review*, 78(3): 73–80.

Browne, Mairead. (1997a). The field of information policy: 1. Fundamental concepts. *Journal of Information Science*, 23(4): 261–275.

Browne, Mairead. (1997b). The field of information policy: 2. Redefining the boundaries and methodologies. *Journal of Information Science*, 23(5): 339–351.

Burnett, Simon, Illingworth, Lorraine, & Webster, Linda. (2004). Knowledge auditing and mapping: A pragmatic approach. *Knowledge and Process Management*, 11(1): 25–37.

Burwell, Helen P. (2004). *Online competitive intelligence: Increasing your profits using cyber-intelligence*. 2nd ed. Tempe, AZ: Facts on Demand Press.

Choo, Chun Wei. (2000). Working with knowledge: How information professionals help organizations manage what they know. *Library Management*, 21(8): 395.

Choo, Chun Wei. (2001). *Information management for the intelligent organization: The art of scanning the environment*. 3rd ed. Medford, NJ: Information Today, Inc.

Choudhury, Vivek, & Sampler, Jeffrey L. (1997). Information specificity and environmental scanning: An economic perspective. *MIS Quarterly*, 21(1): 25–53.

Chourides, Pieris, Longbottom, David, & Murphy, William. (2003). Excellence in knowledge management: An empirical study to identify critical factors and performance measures. *Measuring Business Excellence*, 7(2): 20–45.

Coates, J. F. Inc. (1985). *Issues identification and management: The state of the art of methods and techniques* (Research Project 2345-28). Palo Alto, CA: Electric Power Research Institute.

Cross, Rob, & Prusak, Laurence. (2002). The people who make organizations go–or stop. *Harvard Business Review*, 80(6): 105–112.

Davenport, Thomas H. (1997). *Information ecology: Mastering the information and knowledge environment*. New York: Oxford University Press.

Davenport, Thomas H., De Long, Thomas H., & Beers, David W. (1998). Successful knowledge management projects. *Sloan Management Review*, 39(2): 43–57.

Davenport, Thomas H., Eccles, Robert G., & Prusak, Laurence. (1992). Information politics. *Sloan Management Review*, 34(1): 347–368.

Davenport, Thomas H., & Prusak, Laurence. (1998). *Working knowledge: How organizations manage what they know*. Boston: Harvard Business School Press.

Dhansukhlal, Jasna, & Chaudhry, Abdus Sattar. (2002). Performance measures for knowledge management. *Journal of Information and Knowledge Management*, 1(1): 27–39.

Drucker, P. (1993). *The post-capitalist society*. New York: Harper Business/HarperCollins.

Emery, Priscilla. (2001). The content management market: What you really need to know. *Bulletin of the American Society for Information Science, 28*: 22–26.

Evans, Phillip, & Worster, Thomas. (1997). Strategy and the new economics of information. *Harvard Business Review, 75*(9): 71–82.

Fahey, L. (1998). The eleven deadliest sins of knowledge management. *California Management Review, 40*(3): 265–277.

Frishhammar, Johan. (2002). Characteristics in information processing approaches. *International Journal of Information Management, 22*(2): 143–156.

Gillman, P. (1997). What information audits tell you about user needs. *State Librarian, 42*(3): 43–55.

Handzic, Meliha. (2003). An integrated framework of knowledge management. *Journal of Information and Knowledge Management, 2*(3): 245–252.

Hansen, Morten, Nohria, Nitin, & Tierney, Thomas. (1999). What's your strategy for managing knowledge? *Harvard Business Review, 77*(2): 107–114.

Hasanali, F., & Leavitt, P. (2003). *Content management: A guide for your journey to knowledge management best practices*. Houston: American Productivity and Quality Center.

Hedlund, Gunnar. (Summer, 1994). A model of knowledge management and the n-form corporation. *Strategic Management Journal, 15*: 73–90.

Henczel, Susan. (2001a). *The information audit: A practical guide*. Munich: Saur.

Henczel, Susan. (2001b). The information audit as a first step towards effective knowledge management. *Information Outlook, 5*(6): 48–57.

Herring, Jan P. (1998). What is intelligence analysis? *Competitive Intelligence Magazine, 2*(1): 13–16.

Holsapple, Clyde W., & Joshi, K. D. (2004). A formal knowledge management ontology: Conduct, activities, resources, and influence. *Journal of the American Society for Information Science and Technology, 55*(7): 593–612.

Hylton, Ann. (2002). *The importance of the knowledge audit for leveraging customer knowledge*. Available at www.crm2day.com

Kahaner, Larry. (1996). *Competitive intelligence: How to gather, analyze, and use information to move your business to the top*. New York: Simon & Schuster.

Koenig, Michael, & Srikantaiah, Taverekere K. (2004). *Knowledge management lessons learned: What works and what doesn't*. Medford, NJ: Information Today, Inc.

Leonard, Dorothy. (1998). The role of tacit knowledge in group innovation. *California Management Review, 40*(3): 112–143.

Leonard, Dorothy, & Straus, Susan. (1997). Putting your company's whole brain to work. *Harvard Business Review, 75*(4): 111–121.

Levett, Gavin P., & Guenov, Marin D. (2000). A methodology for knowledge management implementation. *Journal of Knowledge Management, 4*(3): 258–270.

Liebowitz, Jay. (2000). Developing knowledge management metrics for measuring intellectual capital. *Journal of Intellectual Capital, 1*(1): 54–67.

Liebowitz, Jay, et al. (2000). The knowledge audit. *Knowledge and Process Management, 7*(1): 3–10.

McInerney, Claire, & Day, Ronald. (2002). Knowledge management and the dynamic nature of knowledge. *Journal of the American Society for Information Science and Technology*, *53*(12): 1009–1018.

McQueen, Howard. (2001). Taste, snack, & meal: Content management in three courses. *EContent*, *24*: 26–31.

Metaxiotis, Kostas, & Psarras, John. (2003). Applying knowledge management in higher education: The creation of a learning organization. *Journal of Information and Knowledge Management*, *2*(4): 353–359.

Miller, Jerry P. (1994). The relationship between organizational culture and environmental scanning: A case study. *Library Trends*, *43*(2): 170–205.

Nevis, Edwin C., DiBella, Anthony J., & Gould, Janet M. (1995). Understanding organizations as learning systems. *Sloan Management Review*, *40*(2): 73–85.

Nonaka, Ikujiro. (1991). The knowledge-creating company. *Harvard Business Review*, *69*(12): 96–104.

Nonaka, Ikujiro. (1994). A dynamic theory of organizational knowledge creation. *Organizational Science*, *5*(1): 14–37.

Nonaka, Ikujiro. (1998). The concept of "ba": Building a foundation for knowledge creation. *California Management Review*, *40*(3): 40–55.

Nonaka, Ikujiro, & Takeuchi, Hirotaka. (1995). *The knowledge-creating company: How Japanese companies create the dynamics of innovation*. New York: Oxford University Press.

O'Dell, Carla. (1998). If only we knew what we know: Identification and transfer of internal best practices. *California Management Review*, *40*(3): 154–175.

Orna, Elizabeth. (2000). The human face of information auditing. *Management Information*, *7*(4): 40–42.

Pervan, Graham, & Ellison, Ruth. (2003). Knowledge management practices and attitudes of IT departments: Do they practice what they preach? *Journal of Information & Knowledge Management*, *2*(1): 15–31.

Phillips, Fred, Delcambre, Lois, & Weaver, Mathew. (2005). Knowledge management: A re-assessment and case. *Knowledge, Technology & Policy*, *17*(3–4): 65–82.

Polyani, M. (1967). *The tacit dimension*. New York: Doubleday.

Porter, Michael E. (1979). How competitive forces shape strategy. *Harvard Business Review*, *57*(2): 137–145.

Porter, Michael E. (1985). *Competitive advantage*. New York: The Free Press.

Project Management Institute. (2004). *A guide to the project management body of knowledge. PMBOK guide*. 2004 edition. Atlanta: Project Management Institute.

Robertson, G. (1994). The information audit: A broader perspective. *Managing Information*, *1*(4): 34–36.

Robertson, G. (1997). Information auditing: The information professional as information accountant. *Managing Information*, *4*(4): 31–35.

Senge, Peter. (1990). *The fifth discipline: The art and practice of the learning organization*. New York: Currency Doubleday.

Shelfer, Katherine. (2001). A roadmap for the successful implementation of competitive intelligence systems. *Information Outlook*, *5*(7): 34–44.

Srikantaiah, Taverekere K., & Koenig, Michael. (2001). *Knowledge management for the information professional*. Medford, NJ: Information Today, Inc.

Stewart, Thomas, A. (2001). *The wealth of knowledge: Intellectual capital and the twenty-first century organization*. New York: Currency Doubleday.

Subramanian, Ram, Fernandes, Nirmala, & Harper, Earl. (1993). Environmental scanning in US companies: Their nature and their relationship to performance. *Management International Review*, *33*(3): 271–286.

Subramanian, Ram, Kumar, Kamalesh, & Yauger, Charles. (1994). The scanning of task environments in hospitals: An empirical study. *Journal of Applied Business Research*, *10*(4): 104–115.

Townley, Charles T. (2001). Knowledge management and academic libraries. *College & Research Libraries*, *62*(1): 44–55.

Ulrich, Dave. (1998). Intellectual capital equals competence x commitment. *Sloan Management Review*, *39*(2): 126–144.

Vail, Edmond F., III. (1999). Mapping organizational knowledge: Bridging the business-IT communication gap. *Knowledge Management Review*, *39*(2): 10–15.

Valentin, E. K. (2001). SWOT analysis from a resource-based view. *Journal of Marketing Theory and Practice*, *9*(2): 54–69.

Warren, Rita. (2001). Information architects and their central role in content management. *Bulletin of the American Society for Information Science and Technology*, *28*: 14–17.

Wenger, Etienne C., McDermott, Richard, & Synder, William. (2002). *Cultivating communities of practice: A guide to managing knowledge*. Boston: Harvard Business School Press.

Wenger, Etienne C., & Snyder, William M. (2000). Communities of practice: The organizational frontier. *Harvard Business Review*, *78*(1): 139–145.

Xu, Xianzhong M., et al. (2003). Some U.K. and U.S.A. comparisons of executive information systems in practice and theory. *Journal of End User Computing*, *15*(1): 1–19.

# RECOMMENDED WEB SITES

APQC, www.apqc.org

BRINT, www.brint.com

CIO.com, www.cio.com

Google, www.google.com

IBM, www.ibm.com

The Kaieteur Institute for Knowledge Management, www.kikm.org

K & M Protection, www.kmpro.com

KM Resources: KM Case Studies, www.icasit.org/km/resources/kmcases.htm

KMCI, www.kmci.org

Knowledge Connections, www.skyrme.com

The Knowledge Management Resource Center, www.kmresource.com

KnowMap: The Knowledge Management, Auditing and Mapping Magazine, www.knowmap.com

Society of Competitive Intelligence Professionals (SCIP), www.scip.org

Special Libraries Association (SLA), www.sla.org
Sveiby Knowledge Management, www.sveiby.com
TFPL, www.tfpl.com
University of Technology Sweden, www.uts.edu.au
Wikipedia, wikipedia.org
World Bank, www.worldbank.org

# KM: The New Business Potpourri or Seeing the Forest Rather than Just the Trees

Michael E. D. Koenig

Long Island University

As pointed out in the introduction, the late 20th century was full of business enthusiasms, hot topics, and fads, but knowledge management (KM) has become quite unlike any of the rest in terms of its sustained growth and staying power. The introduction illustrates graphically and quantitatively that it is quite literally unique among those topics and enthusiasms.

The argument that we make here is that it is not just quantitatively different, but that it is also quite qualitatively different, and different in a fundamentally important way.

What is that fundamentally important difference? Think of all the management fads and enthusiasms of the late 20th century, 1975–2000. What is striking is how many of those management fads, enthusiasms, and topics have to some considerable degree to do with the management of information (knowledge) or the management of information technology (IT), or the management of information functions.

Following is a list of the management fads, enthusiasms, and topics that meet those criteria. There have been quite a few indeed. There are very few management hot topics left over that don't meet those criteria.

**Information/Knowledge Related Business Enthusiasms and Hot Topics of Last Quarter Century** (listed in rough chronological order with the most recent first):

- Enterprise Content Management (ECM)
- Supply Chain Management
- Customer Relationship Management (CRM)
- E-business

- Enterprise Resource Planning
- Knowledge Management (KM)
- Intellectual Capital
- Data Warehousing/Data Mining
- Core Competencies
- Business Process Re-engineering
- The Shift from Hierarchies to Markets, both Economic and Political
- Competitive Intelligence (CI)
- Total Quality Management (TQM) and Benchmarking
- Information Technology (IT) and Organizational Structure
- Information Resource Management (IRM)
- Enterprise-Wide Information Analysis (IBM Inc.)
- Management Information Systems (MIS) to Decision Support Systems (DSS) and the Importance of External Information
- IT as Competitive Advantage
- Managing the Archipelago (of Information Services)
- Information Systems Stage Hypotheses (Gibson & Jackson, 1987; Koenig, 1986; Marchand, 1983; McFarlan, McKenney, and Pyburn, 1983; Nolan, 1978; Rockart & Scott Morton, 1984; and Zachman, 1987)
- Decision Analysis
- Data Driven Systems Design (the fundamental basis of Structured Programming)
- IT and Productivity
- Minimization of Unallocated Cost

The conclusion that jumps out is that these topics are the trees in a forest, a forest of information and knowledge (small 'k') management, whose scope and importance we are still coming to recognize.

Furthermore, it is beginning to appear that KM is graduating from being just one of many names on that list to becoming the name for that forest of all the trees of information and knowledge (small 'k') management.

What is also striking is that after a quarter of a century of business fads, there have been no new significant business fads in the last few years. The conventional explanation offered for that paucity of new fads is that the dot-com bust created a period of skepticism and a climate unreceptive to new enthusiasms and new topics. The more likely explanation is the one of the forest and the trees: Fads come and go and we have begun to realize that the important phenomenon to recognize is the forest. As new trees are observed, for example, enterprise content management, they can be recognized as part of the forest, and they will be far less likely to be touted as the newest greatest thing that will solve all problems.

The forest is certainly not going away, nor is it static; new trees will emerge, but KM is morphing and expanding in scope to be the name of that forest. We have always had trouble defining KM, and now we have another definition, or more exactly a new metaphor, *KM is the name for that newly recognized forest of all the trees of information and knowledge (small 'k') management.*

# References and Further Reading

## Hot Topics and Fads

Abrahamson, Eric. (1996). Managerial fashion. *Academy of Management Review*, *21*(1): 254–285.

Abrahamson, Eric, & Fairchild, Gregory. (1999). Management fashion: Lifecycles, triggers, and collective learning processes. *Administrative Science Quarterly*, *44*: 708–740.

Koenig, Michael E. D. (2005). KM moves beyond the organization. *Information Services and Use*, *25*(2): 87–93.

Ponzi, Leonard J., & Koenig, Michael E. D. (2002). Knowledge management: Another management fad? *Information Research*, *8*(1). Available at informationr.net/ir/8-1/paper145.html

## Forest

Koenig, Michael E. D. (2000). Information driven management, the new but little perceived, business zeitgeist. *Libri*, *50*(3): 174–190.

## Stages

Gibson, Cyrus, F., & Jackson, Barbara Bund. (1987). *The information imperative: Managing the impact of information technology on business and people.* Lexington, MA: D.C. Heath.

Koenig, Michael E. D. (1986). The convergence of computers and telecommunications: Information management implications. *Information Management Review*, *1*(3): 23–33.

Marchand, Donald A. (1983). Strategies and tools in transition? *Business and Economic Review*, *29*(5): 4–8.

McFarlan, F. Warren, McKenney, James L., & Pyburn, Phillip. (1983). The information archipelago: Plotting a course. *Harvard Business Review*, *16*(1): 145–156.

Nolan, Richard L. (1978). Managing the crises in data processing. *Harvard Business Review*, *57*(2): 115–126.

Rockart, John F., & Scott Morton, Michael. (1984). Implications of changes in information technology for corporate strategy. *Interfaces*, *14*(1): 84–95.

Zachman, John A. (1987). A framework for information systems architecture. *IBM Systems Journal*, *26*(3): 276–292.

# Part I

---

# Identifying the Knowledge

# Identifying the Knowledge
## Foreword

The three chapters in this section all focus on finding and identifying the appropriate and useful knowledge: Who has it and where is it? Moulton (Chapter 6) carefully instructs one on how to conduct a knowledge audit in the context of knowledge management (KM). The phrase "in the context of KM" is used because the concept of the Knowledge Audit, then called an information audit, originated in the 1970s with Woody (Forest W.) Horton before KM was even used as a phrase. After a period of inattention, the knowledge audit has re-emerged with a vengeance as a basic tool of KM, and it has re-emerged in large measure precisely as a consequence of the awareness of the importance of understanding context. Moulton's chapter goes beyond the obvious to emphasize information and knowledge flows, and the auditor's need to understand, appreciate, and chart aspects such as truth, respect, and following.

Pollard, in his chapter (Chapter 7) on Personal Knowledge Management (PKM), advocates, from a different viewpoint, much the same process. His emphasis is upon a bottom-up approach to KM, which is in effect how to define PKM, a technique in which the emphasis is upon identifying how the person interacts with others and with knowledge, and building tools to make that individual more effective. The chapter contains a very useful and suggestive table contrasting traditional KM with PKM. Although written and approached very differently, the congruence between Chapters 6 and 7 is marked. One should not read one without the other.

Mahesh and Suresh (Chapter 5) identify the attribution of context to knowledge as the core KM problem. They propose a new model for KM, Knowledge Resource Planning (KRP), in which the tagging of knowledge entities with the attributes that reflect their context, at least some of which must be done by subject experts, is a very central component of any large organization's operation. They argue that in a true knowledge organization, Enterprise Resource Planning (ERP) will be transformed into KRP with the emphasis put not on Supply Chain

Management (SCM), but on Knowledge Supply Management (KSM). They illustrate the type of context attribution needed with the example of a person-with-the-knowledge expertise location system. They argue that such a KRP approach will allow the extension of KM into areas now relatively unaffected by KM, such as recruitment, performance analysis, and outsourcing. They include a fairly detailed example for the case of performance analysis. In short, the chapter is a very ambitious sketch of a future scenario for KM, but with sufficient detail to be very thought provoking.

# CHAPTER 5

# Representing and Managing Context: Toward Knowledge Resource Planning

Kavi Mahesh

PES Institute of Technology

J. K. Suresh

Infosys Technologies Ltd.

This chapter addresses the questions of how context can be represented and managed in knowledge management (KM) and how this can lead to a much broader scope for applying KM to make knowledge-based decisions in a variety of functions in an organization. Borrowing the work on knowledge representation from Artificial Intelligence and cognitive sciences, the authors hypothesize that context must be represented using knowledge-level attributes that make the capture, classification, retrieval, and re-application of knowledge effective and efficient. Extending this beyond the traditional scope of KM in an organization to include functions such as recruitment, performance assessment, compensation and benefits, and outsourcing, the authors predict that the field of KM in its fourth stage and beyond will develop into Knowledge Resource Planning as a way of managing most functions in the organization by making knowledge-based quantitative decisions. The link between core KM and the newly inducted knowledge-based functions will be through the representation of context using knowledge attributes, not merely a shared corporate taxonomy.

## INTRODUCTION

### Context and Knowledge Transfer

What do we manage in KM? It is important to understand what we manage in order to manage it well. Much has been written about how either KM is the same as information management or that it is different from it only in levels of abstraction (Grey, 1998; Skyrme, 1997; Zack, 1999). In this chapter, we begin by trying to understand the core problem of KM based on studies of what is knowledge and how it is transferred from one person to another in an organization (Firestone, 2001; Fuller, 2002; Ruggles, 1997). We model KM as a problem of matching contexts using *knowledge attributes* and highlight the role of context in making knowledge transfer and re-use effective.

KM is essentially about *knowledge* and about the *transfer of knowledge*. In general, members of an organization possess different kinds of knowledge. The purpose of KM is to facilitate effective transfer of the knowledge to others who have a need for the knowledge in the context of carrying out their responsibilities in the organization. Other activities such as capturing, storing, and retrieving knowledge and its metadata are merely instrumental to the core objective of transferring knowledge to needy members of the organization. For the purposes of the present discussion, we assume that the person who receives the knowledge is a rational agent with sufficient capabilities to apply the knowledge effectively in his or her context for the benefit of the organization.

A knowledge need may arise in a variety of contexts as a part of any organizational process. For example, a knowledge need may arise in understanding the market, answering a customer's queries, designing a solution to a problem, or planning an event. In a small organization, the way to obtain the necessary knowledge to satisfy the need is usually apparent to the person responsible for the process. For example, the person may know whom to ask in the organization to obtain the right knowledge. In large organizations, it is unlikely that the person will know everybody else or every "place" in the organization (physical, such as libraries and file cabinets with records, or virtual, such as intranet Web sites, databases, and digital repositories) so as to determine the right person or place from whom to seek the knowledge.

In an ideal organization, anyone who needs some knowledge is always in close proximity (not just physically but also in terms of organizational roles and relationships) to a person who possesses that knowledge. In reality, this is true to a large extent only in small organizations. In large organizations, several other orthogonal or conflicting considerations prevent an organization from being structured exactly in the way prescribed here. For example, knowledge use may have to be geographically removed from the source due to conflicting needs of proximity such as to customers. In such organizations, there is a greater need for KM with its constituent technologies and systems to bridge the resulting gaps in locations, time zones, languages, and cultures.

The context of a knowledge need is usually not identical to the context of the knowledge source, that is, the context in which the knowledge was earlier acquired or applied. A key problem in KM is the matching of present and prior contexts so that any differences between the two can be recognized and bridged over by applying suitable transformations to the concerned piece of knowledge.

The conventional scope of KM is limited to the transfer and re-use of knowledge in organizational functions where the need for knowledge is already recognized (e.g., research, product development, consulting, and customer support). It is possible to extend the scope of KM to functions where current practice does not involve making knowledge-based quantitative decisions (e.g., recruitment, inventory, and supply chain management). We explore briefly the potential broader scope of KM later in the chapter.

## Modes of Knowledge Transfer

Before we discuss the matching of contexts in KM, let us consider for a moment how knowledge is transferred from its source to its point of use. The original and time-tested means for transferring knowledge is *directly* from one member to another in a synchronous communication between the two. Direct transfer of knowledge in an organization can be one-way—through teaching, training, and consulting. It can also be mutual—through collaboration where both (or all) collaborating parties provide as well as obtain some knowledge from others.

For all direct transfers, the scope and role of KM, in addition to providing the necessary communication infrastructure, is to manage the meta-knowledge or knowledge representation (Brachman & Levesque, 1985; Davis, Shrobe, & Szolovits, 1993; Minsky, 1975) of who knows what in the form of an expertise directory that classifies what people know in a systematic way. KM can also facilitate direct transfer by setting up organizational groups (or communities) for ownership, nurturing, and accumulation of knowledge in various areas of interest. A secondary role may be to capture some of the knowledge being transferred during collaboration so that it can be shared in indirect ways at a later time.

Direct transfer is very effective since it sets up a shared context between the source and the point of assimilation or use. This is often facilitated by mechanisms of human conversation such as negotiation, dialogue for clarification, pedagogy, and other nonverbal elements of human interaction (Grice, 1975; van Dijk

& Kintsch, 1983). However, for the purposes of KM in a large organization, direct transfer is not scalable due to time constraints; difficulties in synchronizing knowledge exchange; member attrition; and wide geographical, cultural, linguistic, and time-zone spreads.

Indirect knowledge transfer was first enabled by early inventions of writing, paper, and printing, leading to the widespread use of written communication in the form of books, papers, reports, and letters. It has been further enriched in the recent past by the introduction of computers, computer networks, and their applications such as the Internet, e-mail, messaging, and other online storage and communication technology.

In an indirect transfer, the communication can be asynchronous. The two parties may not know each other and may never meet each other. As such, the knowledge must be embodied in suitable content (documents, images, and other hypermedia and multimedia elements). In addition, in the absence of the establishment of a shared context between the source and the user of knowledge, the embodiment must necessarily be accompanied by sufficient metadata to capture the original context associated with the knowledge. Typically metadata that represents context includes ontological classifications (Rosch, 1978; Sowa, 1999; Web Ontology Language—OWL), background axioms, and other organizational descriptors of context such as the roles and projects involved.

Indirect transfer requires an agent to store and manage the knowledge embodiment and metadata to make it available to needy members. Agents can be publishers, libraries, or information stores such as Web sites, KM systems, online discussion forums, and so on. Indirect transfer also requires a mechanism for matching contexts. To be effective in large organizations with many sources of knowledge and large amounts of embodied content and metadata, this mechanism needs to have a sufficiently rich representation of context. *Representing context to make its matching effective, in essence, is the core problem of KM.*

## The KM Problem: Representing Context

In both direct knowledge transfer through collaborative KM solutions and indirect transfer through repositories in content-based KM solutions, recognizing present and prior contexts and identifying the differences between them play a central role in determining the effectiveness of the KM solution, without which the KM solution will essentially be a keyword-based search engine. There is a need for KM technology and systems to bridge the gap between present and prior contexts of knowledge creation, sharing, or application. The richness with which context is captured and represented is a critical factor in determining the effectiveness of finding relevant knowledge. In particular, attributes of the context at the *knowledge level* (Mahesh & Suresh, 2004; Newell, 1982) are crucial in improving the precision and recall (Baeza-Yates & Ribeiro-Neto, 1999; Salton, 1983) of context matching.

Context can be represented as a signature, the attributes of which capture essential elements of the context that can be matched effectively against (the signatures of) other contexts. The process of assigning a signature to the context of (the embodiment and metadata of) each piece of knowledge is called *classification*. It may be noted here that typical classification systems, such as the Dewey Decimal System for subject classification, tend to be inadequate for the purpose of KM due to many reasons, including the variety of knowledge types involved in a KM solution and the dynamic nature of the ontology of subject areas that are of interest to a typical organization.

An attempt to represent context using only data or information attributes is usually grossly inadequate. As an example, consider having only a data-level representation of context. A member of the organization has a knowledge need and is trying to locate a document that might satisfy the need. This would amount to trying to find relevant knowledge by matching contexts at the data-level, such as by asking "Find previous contexts where we had used a large MS Word file to answer questions." Data attributes such as the byte size or word count of the document or its format are unlikely to be known in the context of the knowledge need.

Similarly at the information level, if we try to match contexts we may be trying to answer questions of the kind "Find previous contexts where we had used a whitepaper that had the keyword 'Java.'" Such attempts suffer from problems of precision akin to those well known in the world of information retrieval and Web search engines (Baeza-Yates & Ribeiro-Neto, 1999). Although information attributes such as the title or author of the document, like data attributes, might provide a good match to existing content, they are unlikely to be known in the present context of knowledge need. KM must provide a much more effective solution to the problem of matching contexts using rich representations of context with knowledge attributes. Such a solution is not as infeasible in KM as it is in Web search, primarily because the context is better understood, more predictable, and can be captured effectively in doing KM within a particular organization than while serving an unknown customer searching for content from a very vast collection for an unknown purpose.

## The Core KM Problem

Finding the right piece of knowledge or the right expert in the context of a given knowledge need is a nontrivial problem in a large organization where there are a number of potential matching prior contexts (or appropriate generalizations and abstractions of such contexts) in which the organization obtained or used knowledge. Thus, the core problem for KM in a large organization is one of matching the context of a knowledge need to a number of prior contexts so as to identify ones that are most relevant and applicable to the present need. The prior context may be one of acquiring the knowledge and embodying it in various forms of content (e.g., a document published within or outside the organization), of capturing the metadata about the expertise possessed by a member of the organization, or of having applied knowledge to satisfy a previous need. However, the KM problem often becomes easier because of shared organizational cultures and processes that complement the role of technology in well-managed organizations.

A critical sub-problem of matching context effectively is the extraction of a subset of the attributes—called *knowledge attributes*—of present and prior contexts so as to be able to efficiently find relevant matches between the two in the presence of large numbers of such prior contexts. In Figure 5.1, we illustrate how knowledge attributes, unlike *data* and *information attributes,* provide the necessary richness to the representation of context to enable effective matches of contexts.

## The K in KM: Knowledge Representation

What is the K in KM? Is it knowledge itself or a representation of knowledge that we manage? It is useful to think that the K in KM stands for *knowledge representation*, and, in particular, for a *set* of *knowledge attributes* that truly represents the context of knowledge creation, capture, or re-use as well as the quality, value, goal, and applicability of the knowledge. A KM solution solves the core KM problem by enabling sharing of readily updateable knowledge by effective matching of present and prior contexts using knowledge-level attributes.

Intuitively, it seems appropriate to think that KM needs to manage much more than just data or information (Davenport, 1998; Davenport & Prusak, 1998; Sveiby, 1994). Data, for the present purposes, is any collection of bits and bytes with a known structure. For example, a sequence of bytes or characters or a table

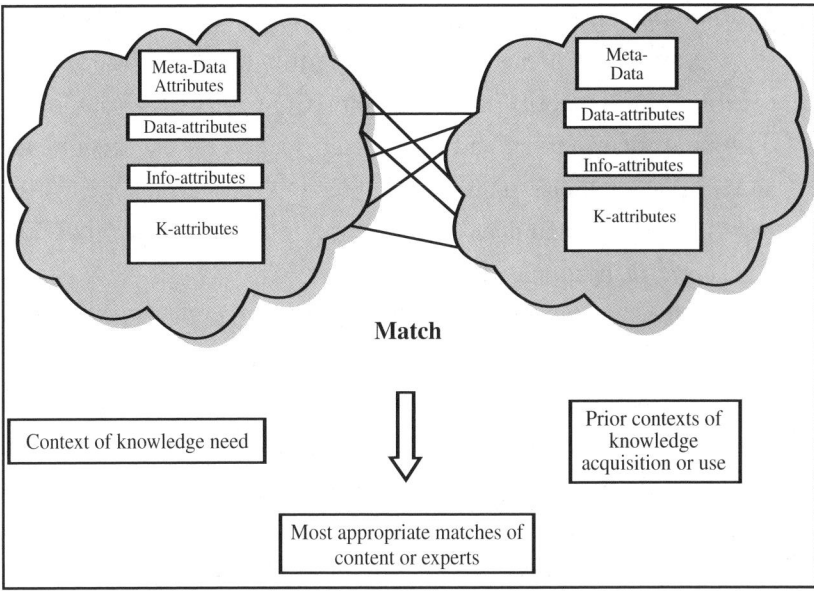

**Figure 5.1  Matching contexts: The core**

with rows and columns of numbers is data. Information is data endowed with sufficient context and semantics to be useful to the reader. For example, a database manages data such as a table of telephone numbers and e-mail addresses; application software supplies context and semantics to the numbers and strings stored in the table to be able to serve useful information to the user, such as the contact information for a particular person in the organization. It may be noted here that the term *content management* merely refers to information management where the information is in text, video, and other unstructured or semi-structured forms (as opposed to structured data that is typically in databases and spreadsheets).

## What Is in a Context: Knowledge Attributes

A context is represented by a set of attributes at the following three levels, together called *metadata*:

1. *Data Attributes:* These are attributes of the context that a machine can assess. Metadata attributes at this level include attributes such as record structure, syntax, size, encoding, file type, image resolution, whether compressed, whether encrypted or password protected, which software program to use for editing, whether printable, and so on.

2. *Information Attributes:* These are attributes that a human with no deep knowledge of the domain can assess. Attributes at the information level constitute the majority of the Dublin Core attributes (dublincore.org/documents/dcmi-terms) and include language, dialect, version, template and format, author's name, date, previous usage statistics, ISBN, an expert's telephone number and addresses, document type, confidentiality and access restrictions, and so on.

3. *Knowledge Attributes:* These are attributes that only an expert in the domain can assess. At this level, the attributes describe the content, quality, value, applicability, and purpose of knowledge itself. They include aboutness (Bruza, Song, & Wong, 1999), gist (Wical, 1999), ontological mappings, intended target audience, background assumed, quality and value ratings and reviews, author's knowledge profile, conditions or constraints to be considered in applying the knowledge, and so on.

An important distinction between knowledge and information attributes is that while data and information attributes are about the *container* or embodiment of the knowledge (i.e., a knowledge asset such as a document or a person), knowledge attributes are about the knowledge *contained* in the container. Also, k-attributes, unlike the constructs of knowledge representation languages in artificial intelligence (Brachman & Levesque, 1985; Davis, et al., 1993), are not meant to encode the knowledge itself. Rather, like data and information attributes, they serve to represent metadata about the knowledge.

K-attributes enable better matching of contexts and more effective application of the knowledge by:

1. Normalizing against differences in language and usage, culture and views of the world, terminologies used, and domains of interest. This is likely to improve the *precision* and *recall* of context matching.

2. Enabling the measurement of the quality of knowledge, thereby improving the *ranking* of matching contexts.

3. Providing grounding for a piece of knowledge in a space of all knowledge present in the organization by linking it implicitly with other assets in related areas or through other similarities in knowledge attributes (e.g., in terms of applicability). This is likely to improve the *recall* of context matching.

4. Taking the KM solution beyond the embodiment of knowledge by representing attributes of applicability of knowledge to specific contexts of re-use. This is likely to improve the *effectiveness* of knowledge re-use.

5. Enabling the KM solution to build tools for facilitating the exchange of knowledge through interactive dialogues in content-based solutions and conversational assistants in collaborative solutions.

In addition, k-attributes also enable other KM functions such as:

1. Identifying gaps or lack of currency in organizational knowledge to help the organization to plan for filling the gaps through recruitment, training, or outsourcing.

2. Measuring and tracking of the knowledge dynamics of the organization, i.e., the various pathways and volumes of knowledge flow across or within communities in the organization and the demographic patterns of these flows. Measurement of internal and external benefits of KM such as brand value and intellectual capital value is also enabled partially by knowledge attributes. The contribution of an individual or a team can also be measured in terms of knowledge attributes.

3. Expanding the scope of KM to cover other organizational functions as illustrated later in this chapter.

4. Aggregating knowledge by synthesizing composite assets from multiple pieces of knowledge.

5. Integrating KM and business systems and processes at a semantic/knowledge level.

6. Building automatic question answering, FAQ generation, and message or query routing tools.

7. Providing subscription, personalization, and customization services to users.

8. Helping authors construct knowledge embodiments.

9. Automatically classifying knowledge embodiments or profiles of experts.

10. Judging the motivations and goals of knowledge workers and designing schemes for promoting KM.

## Types of K-Attributes

Data attributes are of different types such as format, size, encoding, and security attributes. Information attributes are also of several types such as those pertaining to authorship/ownership, source, title, version and history, language, and so on. On similar lines, there are five primary types of knowledge attributes that essentially answer these questions: What is it? How much is in it? How good is it? What is it meant for? How do we use it?:

- **K-content attributes (What is it?):** K-attributes that describe the content of knowledge and help determine its relevance for a context, thereby improving precision
- **K-value attributes (How much is in it?):** K-attributes that quantify the amount, utility, potential, and contribution of knowledge to enable KM functions such as benefit measurement, intellectual capital assessment, and identification of knowledge gaps in the organization
- **K-quality attributes (How good is it?):** K-attributes that help us measure knowledge quality, thereby improving efficiency and effectiveness of its re-use as also the measurement of value
- **K-goal attributes (What is it meant for?):** K-attributes that represent the goals and purposes of people, processes, and systems, thereby enabling better integration of KM with business systems and processes as well as enabling KM to assist knowledge sharing and collaboration
- **K-applicability attributes (How do we use it?):** K-attributes of context and its assumptions that make re-use more effective

Table 5.1 summarizes this classification of data, information, and knowledge attributes into the five types depending on what questions they answer.

It may be noted here that the Dublin Core attributes (DCMI terms, dublincore. org/documents/dcmi-terms) are a mix of mostly information-level and a few knowledge-level attributes.

A suitable language is needed to represent k-attributes along with other data and information attributes to capture and manage metadata for KM. Recent standards and recommendations from the work on the Semantic Web are ideally suited for this purpose. A combination of XML, XML Schema, RDF, RDFS, and OWL can be used to define schemas and store all the metadata for KM purposes (Mahesh & Suresh, 2005). These representations need to be engineered suitably to be effective in KM implementations in large organizations (Mahesh & Suresh, 2006).

In such a knowledge representation language for KM, data attributes are represented primarily in the XML Schema language. Information attributes are rendered using resource descriptions in RDF on the foundation of a suitable RDFS schema. OWL serves as the language (both syntax and semantics) for

## Table 5.1  Types and examples of data, information, and knowledge attributes

| | | Data (What a machine can assess) | Information (What a person with no domain knowledge can assess, e.g., a librarian) | Knowledge (What an expert can assess) |
|---|---|---|---|---|
| 1 | **Content: What is it?** | File type, data type | Content type (e.g., whitepaper, not just MS word file), language, title | Subject area, topic, ontology concept, theme, aboutness[1], gist[2], summary, keyword |
| 2 | **Quantity/Value: How much is in it?** | Byte size, # of records, # of files | Completeness (w.r.t template), number of diagrams and examples, domain and range of information | Current value to organization, potential value, contribution to prior projects, authority and ownership of subject area |
| 3 | **Quality: How good is it?** | Checksum, well-formedness, format, font, resolution | Matches template, grammatical correctness, clarity, contrast | Quality rating, reviews, comments, popularity, frequency of use |
| 4 | **Goal or Purpose: What is it meant for?** (Why is it there?) | For viewing on handheld, for printing | To calculate taxes, for ID card, for a graduate course | Intended purpose, target audience, people and team goals |
| 5 | **Applicability: How do we use it?** | Mapping to application, whether zipped, encrypted, password protected | For review, not for critical applications, not for export, need-to-know basis, reference only | Constraints on application, assumptions made, ease of generalization or specialization, self-containedness, extra-functional requirements |

1. Aboutness (Bruza et al, 1999) is a generalization of the idea of subject or topics. Instead of merely placing the piece of knowledge in one or more bins of classification system, aboutness enables one to answer the question "is this about x where x may be a complex description of a context (e.g., a logical combination of several subjects with various further restrictions, conditional relaxations of constraints, etc.)."

2. A gist (Wical, 1999), as opposed to an abstract or a summary, need not be a condensed piece of text. Rather, it can be a complex representation of the essential contents of a piece of knowledge that can enable the user to visualize the contents from any chosen point of view.

representing the classification system and therefore the k-content attributes. Other types of k-attributes are also rendered as RDF statements.

## ILLUSTRATION: EXPERTISE DIRECTORY USING K-ATTRIBUTES

Let us consider the example of building an expertise directory in an organization for its members to find the right person to contact in order to meet a particular knowledge need. This example illustrates how the use of knowledge attributes improves the effectiveness of a KM function—expertise locator—that is within the conventional scope of KM.

Information-level attributes enable us to build directory systems for looking up an employee or member of an organization. In a typical person look-up tool, one can find contact information about one or more persons if other information attributes of the persons are known. For example, if you know their names, you can find their e-mail addresses or telephone numbers. If you know what department or project they work for, you can find similar contact information about them. Typically you can also search or browse to identify the right person even if only partial information, such as their first name only or their role in the organization, is known.

Unfortunately, KM requires a better directory system. As illustrated earlier in the case of finding a document to meet a knowledge need, one can rarely identify information attributes such as a person's name or e-mail address from the context of the need. What is more likely to be extracted from the present context is the subject area and type of knowledge being sought. How can we build a member directory that can tell us who, among all the people that are expected to have the desired knowledge, is most likely to cooperate and enable you to meet the knowledge need most effectively in the present context?

Such a knowledge-level expertise directory can only be built by making use of appropriate k-attributes. The system must not only know what areas of knowledge each person possesses, it must also have assessments of the quality, value, and applicability of the knowledge in addition to knowing the goals and motivations of the persons. The proposed expertise directory will therefore use the data, information, and knowledge attributes shown in Table 5.2. Using the knowledge attributes, the expertise locator, given a context of a knowledge need, can attempt to find a few persons in the organization who not only have the most relevant knowledge of the highest quality and value but are also most likely to share that knowledge effectively in the present context.

Figure 5.2 shows a snapshot of data, information, and knowledge attributes in the expertise locator for one person. While the data in the figure is artificial, it serves to illustrate the number and variety of k-attributes needed for the expertise directory to function much more effectively than a telephone directory for the purposes of finding the right expert in the organization to satisfy a knowledge need.

Without the knowledge attributes, the expertise locator operating at only the data and information levels can at best match keywords in the present context to keywords present in all the information kept about employees.

On similar lines, in the case of an online search system for a library, building the capability to answer questions of the kind "Which textbooks do we have on database management systems?" is rather straightforward given the maturity of

## Table 5.2  Data, information, and knowledge attributes for context matching in an expertise locator

| Type of Attribute | Sample Attribute | Justification |
|---|---|---|
| **Data Attributes** | Employee number | Created for data management/security purposes |
| | ID card/badge number | |
| | Password for log-in | |
| | Photograph | Not processed at information level in current technology, e.g., cannot search or query using these attributes |
| | Digitized signature | |
| | Voicemail greeting message | |
| **Information Attributes** | Name | Inherent attributes that are likely to be queried (unlike password, photograph, or voicemail greeting), e.g., "Find all Smiths" or "Find all female employees from Virginia" or "Find all Ph.D.s in the training department" |
| | Gender | |
| | Date of birth | |
| | Addresses | |
| | Telephone/fax numbers | |
| | E-mail addresses | |
| | Web site URLs | |
| | Department | |
| | Project, location | |
| | Reports to | |
| | Qualifications | |
| **Knowledge Attributes** | Areas of knowledge, experience (contexts of knowledge acquisition), skills | K-content attribute: establishes relevance in present context |
| | Expertise or depth in each area | K-value attribute: improves precision of context matching (who has the most relevant knowledge for the present context) |
| | Rating by peers in each area | K-quality attribute: improves ranking of matching persons (how good is the knowledge) |
| | Approachability, availability, willingness to help, feedback from previous collaborations (with contexts), style, and communication and interpersonal skills | K-applicability attributes: improve ranking of matching persons (how likely is the person to share the knowledge for the present context) |
| | Career goals, personal business commitment, and personal preferences | K-goal attributes: help make knowledge exchange more effective (how to motivate the person to share) |

technologies such as information retrieval and databases. On the other hand, if the query is "Which books cover database tuning?" the system may have to manage information attributes well to find out which book's table of contents has chapters on database tuning. At the next level, if the query is "Which is the best book for explaining database tuning?" a carefully designed set of k-attributes has to be acquired and managed well to answer the query effectively (i.e., with good precision, recall, and ranking of matching contexts).

# KNOWLEDGE RESOURCE PLANNING: THE FUTURE OF KM?

The current state of practice of KM in organizations seems to be characterized by an almost exclusive focus on the use of knowledge as a productive internal resource, with a primary thrust on its sharing and re-use in those segments of functions (such as sales, marketing, and production) where the results and returns

| K-Value: KGPA = 3.78 / 10.0 | | |
|---|---|---|
| **Area** | **Experience** | **Value (0–10)** |
| Web services | 6 months | 2.5 |
| .Net | 8 months | 4.0 |
| RFID | 2 months | 1.0 |
| Java prog. | 2 years | 6.5 |
| GUI develop | 3 projects | 3.3 |
| Architecture | 2 projects | 8.5 |
| SOA design | 1 project | 0.5 |
| Web develop | 1 project | 4.5 |
| Insurance | 4 months | 1.5 |
| Mutual funds | 16 months | 5.0 |

**Figure 5.2  Snapshot showing k-attributes of a person in the expertise directory**

are relatively more visible, speedier to achieve, and easier to measure. However, a number of other areas deal with knowledge indirectly in developing and sustaining organizational capabilities and competencies, the effects of which are likely to be less immediate, while being critical to its long-term performance. Planning for personnel recruitment, training, and allocation of personnel to projects, for example, are all functions that supply, or improve the quality of, competent human resources whose knowledge is needed to execute various steps in business processes.

In its evolution, therefore, the knowledge organization must view all functions from the vantage point of knowledge and make all decisions by its relevant application. Even if many functions currently operate without applying knowledge and its attributes, a good KM solution should take them into account; otherwise, when a future need arises for their transformation into knowledge-based decision making processes, a redesign of the KM solution will prove expensive and may even stall or reverse the ascent of the organization toward greater maturity in KM. In attempting to thus broaden the focus of KM, this section briefly considers how decisions in these functions can be based on knowledge attributes, using a *knowledge model* of an organization that maps the flow of knowledge through its people, their groupings, processes, and systems acting on behalf of people. The model is an abstract representation of an organization wherein people are considered as knowledge sources and the roles they play are seen essentially as assignments made to satisfy particular knowledge needs.

## A Knowledge Model of the Organization

The knowledge model of a modern organization includes typical knowledge-related functions such as education, training, research, and KM as well as functions such as human resources (including recruitment, compensation, and assessment), enterprise resource planning, supply chain management, and sales and marketing (including customer relationship management). Placing knowledge at the very center through an inversion of the common command and control view of an organization enables a systematic study of the effects of knowledge and its management on a larger number of functions. In Figure 5.3, knowledge is represented in the

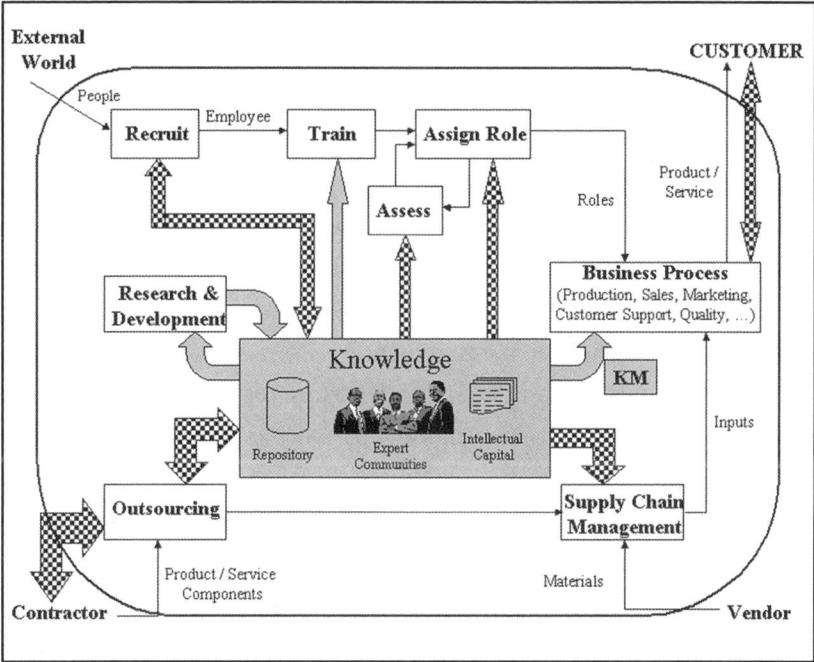

Figure 5.3  Knowledge model of an organization showing current scope of KM (shaded) and potential knowledge flows to be managed in the expanded scope (checkered arrows)

form of multiple content repositories and expert communities distributed throughout the organization as well as formal intellectual capital assets such as patents, copyrights, and registered designs, and current KM practice and future scope are demarcated clearly.

## Resource Planning

As indicated before, several key functions in the organizations including recruitment, personnel assignment (staffing), performance assessment, supply chain management (SCM), outsourcing, and other parts of enterprise resource planning (ERP) involve important decision making steps where KM principles are typically not applied rigorously. For example, recruitment and training are often planned using ad hoc procedures, rules of thumb, and historical data that have been developed over time without consciously applying quantified data about knowledge needs, levels, and quality.

Personnel allocation to projects and departments is done based mainly on skills, but often other considerations such as availability, proximity, convenience, or persistent departmental loyalty or ownership take prominence. This results in inefficiencies that go undetected since, traditionally, project performance is measured predominantly through simple metrics of quality, productivity, and finance. For example, a person allocated to a project may meet or exceed performance expectations, albeit unenthusiastically, in spite of being disinterested in the work assigned. His knowledge and interests could have been put to better use in a different project that is more closely related to his interests, thereby delivering better long-term value for the organization, the loss of which goes undetected in the current system of performance measurement.

It therefore becomes necessary to consider measures and metrics derived from KM as critical supplements to conventional parameters in making such key decisions in the organization. Ideally, personnel allocation to projects may be based solely on best matches of knowledge needs to the expertise and experience of personnel. Recruitment, driven principally by knowledge needs, may be viewed as a process by which the organization essentially acquires knowledge that is brought in by the new members. Such a knowledge view of the organization entails, for example, an application of the principles and methods of supply chain management to treat processes such as recruitment, training, and project allocation as nodes in the supply chain of knowledge in the organization.

Using this concept, customers can be treated as both useful sources and recipients of knowledge that the organization possesses or generates during the course of an engagement. Customer relationship management (CRM) can change its focus to *customer knowledge management* (CKM), which includes both managing the knowledge relationships between the customer and the organization and the more mundane (yet valuable and effort intensive) management of knowledge about customers. Similarly, outsourcing, a key element of any modern global organization, can be treated as both a way of importing knowledge into the organization and a way of supplying knowledge to enable the vendor to deliver a product or service.

Finally, barring very compelling counter arguments, organizational structure ought to reflect the areas of knowledge in which the organization operates. It is common today to have geographical, linguistic, or other non-knowledge-centric divisions in the organization, resulting in unwarranted fragmentation of knowledge by creating departmental or geographical barriers and distances between knowledge sources and points of knowledge need. Some of the need for conventional KM can be eliminated if the organization is structured so that knowledge needed by any member in any business process is available locally in the same group. It may be noted that locality here refers more to the ability to communicate and connect together than to geographic proximity and can be ensured through communication and networking infrastructure.

ERP is transformed in a true knowledge organization into *knowledge resource planning* (KRP): how to plan for and acquire knowledge sources, be they members or training courses or outsourcing contractors. Managing the supply chain of knowledge shifts the focus from the SCM of materials, components, and their inventory to a process of *knowledge supply management* (KSM), thus enabling an organization to not only rationalize all decision making processes using knowledge, but also to employ knowledge as a critical yardstick to measure realized value.

The evolution of KM into KRP and the consequent broadening of the role of KM in managing an organization is only possible through effective managing of information about the context of knowledge using a rich set of knowledge attributes as outlined earlier in this chapter. Context and its representation using k-attributes will serve as the foundation for integrating all business applications across the organization at the knowledge level. Without them, the only link between KM and other business systems is a shared classification system that is clearly insufficient by itself to enable knowledge-based quantitative decision making.

An important consequence of formally dealing with value realization as a product of material and knowledge transformations is that the traditional quality and productivity parameters tend to become smaller components of a broader range of metrics that include additional knowledge-centric parameters such as the leverage of existing knowledge for effective delivery of output and contribution to organizational knowledge needs. In order to appreciate how knowledge metrics assume significance in this, and to explore how they might be constructed and used, it is critical to revisit and investigate the complex problem of value transformation through knowledge that intensely affects the business performance of the new-age organization.

## Value Transformation and Organizational Performance

In recent decades, rapid globalization of markets, development of large production bases and supply chains across geographies, growing sophistication of end-user needs, and an intense search for a competitive edge in an environment of constant technological flux have resulted in an increased complexity and variability of products and services: in themselves, or through their influence on their operational environment. Largely as a consequence, the roles of people, processes, and especially knowledge have come to be recognized as central to value creation. This, in turn, has prompted a search, by no means completely successful presently, for a reliable means to manage the various dimensions of value associated with these roles and thereby ensure predictability and repeatability in the production process (Suresh & Mahesh, 2006).

A corollary to these developments is the pervasion of knowledge infusion and knowledge based decision making at many more steps in the production process than ever before. The resulting amplification of the share of knowledge in the creation of goods and services has led to a few nettlesome problems, an important one among which is related to the estimation of the effort and costs involved in creating the output. The often quoted trends of time and cost overruns in the development of information technology (IT) systems (Standish Report, 2001) seem to indicate a widespread prevalence of this problem, although some recent studies (Standish Report, 2006) seem to question the gravity and extent of the problem, or differ with the degree of pessimism projected by the report (Jørgensen & Moløkken, 2006). Nevertheless, it is undeniable that the translation of the mental processes of a large number of collaborating people (including customers) into a sensible product is a complex task that is arguably affected by challenges related to often conflicting individual and collective interpretations, decision making, and integration of a networked set of logical and physical components that make up a software system. While the recent widespread practice of utilizing historical data and sophisticated process frameworks such as the Capability Maturity Model (CMM, www.sei.cmu.edu/cmm) have helped put software engineering as a discipline on a firmer footing, the core problem of estimation of effort and cost does not appear to be fully conquered at present.

A second, and more difficult, problem arises in assessing value additions and transformations across business processes. Where knowledge flows and knowledge-based decision making dominate the processes, assignment of value perforce has to base itself largely on measures of their effects and inter-relationships. While a critical component of the effort involved in producing a service or a good is in making reasoned decisions that serve as the basis for action (that involves further reasoning, such as in encoding knowledge or in integrating it into a good or service), the quantum of effort itself is a variant influenced by the quality and type of these decisions, whose effects are usually apparent only at a later point in time, either from the standpoint of post-fact analysis or from that of applying corrective measures. Moreover, in the absence of calipers, gauges, scales, or meters that can measure with precision the attributes of the inputs or of the output, it is difficult to quantify or qualify precisely the knowledge that is applied at various stages in its creation. In an effort to create a more sound basis for assessing value contribution, current approaches seem to augment the traditional by introducing a mix of knowledge-centric, although somewhat subjective, considerations such as of function (e.g., sales, production and after-sales service), of the relative stage and complexity of the project life-cycle (e.g., requirement gathering, testing, deployment, or implementation with new technologies), and of the need for fulfillment of strategic or operational objectives (e.g., deal size and types, client and industry types, and geography of deployment). In practice, the percolation in recent years to the departmental or individual level of measures related to not only the financial aspects but also the customer, business process and learning dimensions of organizational strategy and implementation, utilizing methodologies such as the balance card (Kaplan & Norton, 1996), seems to indicate a growing awareness of the need to deem knowledge generation and use as an essential part of the assessment of value addition. Nonetheless, value ascription continues to largely rely upon (the currently not very well understood) estimates of knowledge stocks and flows, the valuation by markets for the product or service, and the supply and demand characteristics of skills and competencies.

It may be noted that distributed knowledge infusion and a broader diffusion of decision making across the business processes are by no means the preserves of new economy organizations driven by information and communication technologies (ICT). Such effects of complexity may be induced in larger segments of the production process by various factors including competition, efforts to enhance customer satisfaction, operations across multiple locations, need for cost control, variability of product or service ranges, and internationalization and localization requirements. Besides, continued flux in technologies and difficulties in streamlining and deskilling significant portions of the production process pose further difficulties in dealing with complexity.

In summary, these problems may be considered to be manifestations of an increased coupling between the traditional means of production (the machines of the industrial era) and the new means of production (that predominantly exist within the head of the worker) in the organizations and markets of the new economy. A noteworthy consequence of this development is that value analysis has become more challenging due to the large number of factors that affect its infusion, many of which arise from the knowledge-centric nature of productive work in today's organizations. Of late, the continuing interest in developing standards, measures, and analytical bases to better understand and manage business performance appears to be an important part of the evolution of value analysis.

## PERFORMANCE ASSESSMENT

A key sub-problem of the value chain analysis arises in the assessment of the performance of individuals in an organization. In recent years, given that a large fraction of employees in contemporary organizations use knowledge as an important means of production in their work, performance measures have begun to gradually shift, from a strong focus on financial outcomes, toward including nonfinancial and behavioral factors that influence the organizational environment, of which balance sheet results are considered but one of the consequences.

In the performance management process, goals are set for an employee to achieve over a defined period of time and are typically expressed through parameters related to customer relationships, partnership with collaborating groups in the organization, learning and development, and the like, in addition to the customary parameters of budget and finance. Over time, process and management reviews and explicit feedback obtained from internal partners and customers would constitute the necessary information to both drive performance and derive indices related to the targets set for the employee. The assessment of an individual's performance can then be made through an interview process, usually with the above data supplemented by context establishment, elaboration, clarification, and discussion.

While the process outlined here appears robust, a closer examination would reveal an opportunity for developing a knowledge-based approach to assessment that can help improve the effectiveness of performance management. Such an approach would focus on the knowledge dimension of an individual's work, not only as obtained from the formal systems (e.g., project work-flow systems) that provide indices of performance, but also from non-formal systems (e.g., KM systems) across the enterprise that can index the contributions of an individual that benefit others in the organization. It would be based on a model of the employee as an active agent in multiple knowledge eco-systems, playing various roles such as of a consumer or provider of knowledge at different times (Figure 5.4). In this model, an individual interacts with the project, engagement, and organizational knowledge ecosystems through systems, processes, role definitions, and people networks.

In actual practice, formal and informal knowledge exchange between various eco-systems supplement project team interactions in the process of conversion of plans and schedules, derived from customer requirements, into deliverables facilitated through goal setting. In a scenario where the engagement is large and has many participating roles, project health and progress are dynamic functions of both upstream factors (e.g., implicit and explicit customer needs that often lead to evolving requirements) and downstream factors (e.g., budget utilization, status and quality of outputs at various milestones) in the business process. Individual effort in the process is directed toward actions that serve to achieve overall goals such as functionality, quality, and customer satisfaction, while simultaneously optimizing on risks, margins, and schedules. While processes and systems facilitate individual effort and results, reviews and feedback provide additional tools to collectively manage the plans and schedules. In this setting, project performance essentially depends on the competencies, and the efficient channeling of knowledge into action, of individuals interacting with each other within the project

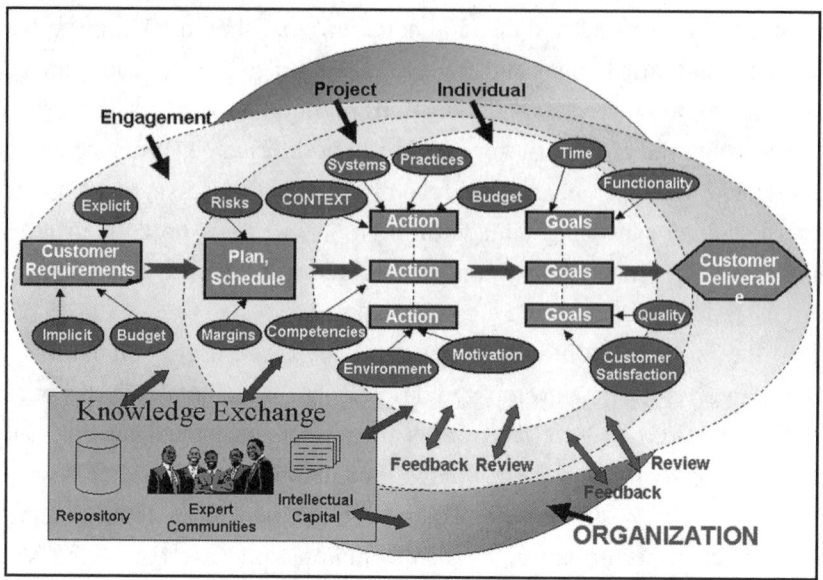

**Figure 5.4  A conceptual view of interactive knowledge ecosystems in the service industry at the individual, project, and engagement levels**

ecosystem. The ability to leverage knowledge effectively is dependent on both the systemic capability of KM and individual competencies and actions that aid the invocation, additionally, of the engagement and organizational eco-systems in the process of knowledge exchange.

The various dimensions of individual competencies such as expertise, knowledge sharing, and learning abilities impact not only project performance, but also the organizational environment comprising similar dimensions of peer and customer groups, through formal and informal interactions with people and systems (Figure 5.5). Consequently, the collective efforts of a project team not only lead to project performance, but also to actual and potential changes in the knowledge levels of individuals and systems within and beyond the project.

In this background, individual performance can be assessed based on inputs of several kinds from formal systems associated with the project as well as the KM and other informal systems that form the internal environment of the organization as a whole as shown in Figure 5.5. A sample set of parameters that can form the basis for the evaluation are shown in Table 5.3, and it may be noted that they are

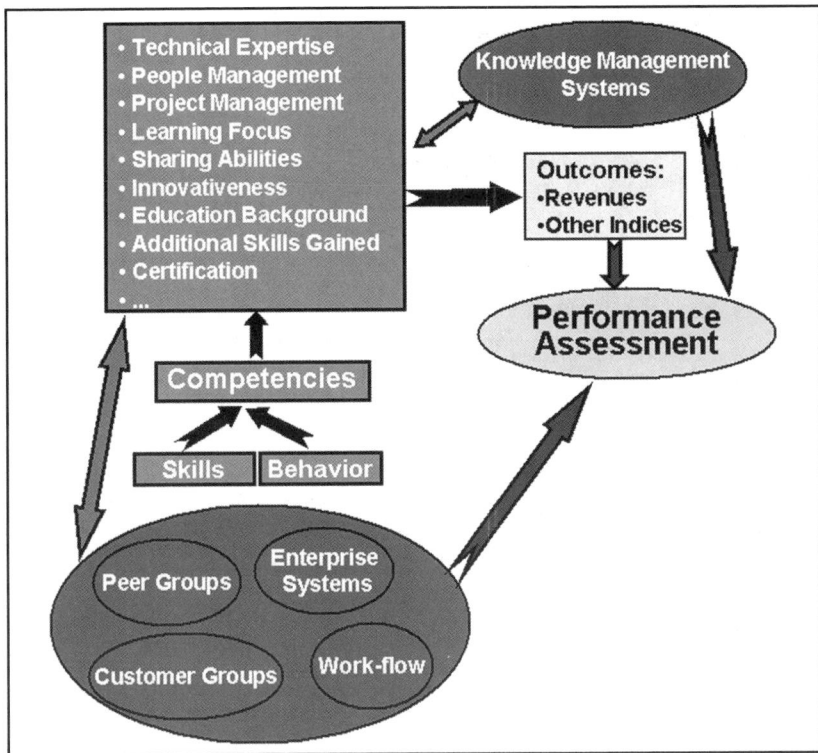

**Figure 5.5 Performance assessment: What to measure**

essentially related to the knowledge of the individual, the project, the organization, and the customer as it pertains to individual and collective actions and their results. These parameters are evaluated in terms of qualitative and quantitative measures through enterprise and workflow systems that capture project progress indicators and data, as well as periodic feedback from peers, subordinates, and customers (both internal and external). To make the assessment parameters more effective, the measures can be normalized against a role average or maximum, or ranked into bands to aid the relative placement of individual performance across the organization.

Additional evaluation of the parameters is provided by KM and informal systems that aid an estimation of the knowledge of the individual in terms of its relevance, value, quality, applicability, and realized benefits to different contexts of knowledge needs across the organization. As just described, normalization of the measures would be helpful in easier relative evaluation. A further use of these

## Table 5.3  Parameters for evaluation of individual performance

| Parameter | Attributes Derivable from Enterprise and Workflow Systems | Attributes Derivable from Non-Formal Systems |
|---|---|---|
| Technical Expertise | Quality and quantity of output, problem solving ability | Numbers and types of knowledge contributions to organizational systems, ratings of their quality, value, applicability, and reported benefits to other projects from users |
| People Management | Approachability, availability, attrition and retention rates and quality of manpower in team | Numbers and types of interactions with different role players across organization and ratings from users on approachability and quality of interactions |
| Project Management | Plan and schedule implementation, quality and productivity, handling uncertainty, learning from failures | Numbers and types of interactions with similar projects across the organization |
| Learning Focus | Ability to learn, ability to understand project needs | Non-formal courses completed, new areas of knowledge contribution and their ratings by users |
| Sharing Abilities | Willingness to help others, owning responsibility to share | Ratings by users of willingness to share knowledge and quality, value, and applicability of the interactions |
| Innovativeness | Approach to problem solving, working toward patents and copyrights | Instances of problems solved in a different domain, user ratings of innovativeness of knowledge interactions |
| Additional Skills Gained | New skills in specific areas that may affect business | Updates to skill profile by the individual and the ratings of the new skills by users |

systems is in its ability to substantiate evaluations derived from formal systems, for example, in eliciting specific instances of innovative work and their ratings by beneficiaries across the organization to reinforce a conclusion from formal systems (using, say, output measures, feedback from customers and peers) that a particular individual ranks high in creativity and innovation.

The measures shown in Table 5.3 for both types of systems would need to be further specialized to suit the needs of evaluation of different roles. For example, a data analyst role in the organization may have fewer measures in the people management dimension than a recruiter role in the human resources department, for which additional measures such as the number of high performers recruited, new sources of recruitment developed, and ratios of job offers made to actual joins may have to be considered. In addition, the parameters and the measures need to be weighted to reflect their relative effect on the overall character and expectations of the role. For example, a Java trainer or a junior programmer in a software development team may be assigned less weight for project management than a project manager, while a domain expert in actuarial analysis may be given less weight for technical expertise in comparison with a software architect. It may be noted that KM and informal systems can be useful in gauging an individual's relationship with the organizational environment, by providing indicators of an individual's preferences, knowledge, vision, sharing abilities, and the like as additional measures in the assessment process. In addition, it helps provide discriminatory inputs, as for example, through an estimation of technical expertise to differentiate the contributions of two individuals playing the same role and having similar scores from enterprise and workflow systems, but differing in their contributions to the organizational knowledge exchange. A further use of these systems is in incorporating the time value of knowledge in the assessment scheme, for example, in giving weight to the ratings of successful re-use by the individual, in present times, of past knowledge contributions of others, as well as of the past contributions of the individual being re-used by others across the organization.

However, it may be noted that the scope of such evaluation in actual practice varies significantly across organizations, and can be justifiably pursued only for roles where knowledge plays an important part in the course of their fulfillment. Thus, for example, a knowledge-based approach to performance assessment may be readily applicable to a majority of the employees in a consulting or a high-technology organization, while it may be applicable to a small number of employees in a highly automated production system with little variability of process or product.

## CONCLUDING REMARKS

In its fourth stage of evolution, KM needs to build a strong conceptual foundation not only to improve the effectiveness of its implementation but also to aid the pervasion of its practice across more organizational functions than at present. In attempting either, however, an important challenge lies in its ability to clearly distinguish itself from both information and data management, which in turn could help the creation and deployment of systems to enable efficient knowledge exchange practices that go beyond keyword searches, taxonomies, and simple ontologies. As illustrated in this chapter, at the heart of this potential transformation lies the idea of context representation in KM, which can be developed through knowledge-level attributes that describe the different dimensions of knowledge such as its content, value, quality, and applicability. Furthermore, knowledge attributes can constitute a refined means to develop quantitative and qualitative measures for assessing the maturity of KM implementation, identifying gaps in organizational knowledge, and integrating KM with business systems and processes at a semantic or knowledge level.

A successful movement toward KM that is structured primarily through context representation using knowledge attributes can also prospectively provide greater credibility to a knowledge centric view of the organization that would enable it to rationalize all its decision making processes across functions using knowledge as the principal yardstick, an idea that we termed Knowledge Resource Planning.

# References

Baeza-Yates, Ricardo, & Ribeiro-Neto, Berthier. (1999). *Modern information retrieval.* New York: ACM Press and Addison Wesley.

Brachman, Ronald J., & Levesque, Hector J. (Eds.). (1985). *Readings in knowledge representation.* Los Altos, CA: Morgan Kaufmann.

Bruza, Peter, Song, Dawei, & Wong, Kam-Fai. (1999). Fundamental properties of aboutness. *Proceedings of the 22nd annual international ACM SIGIR conference on R&D in information retrieval* (pp. 277–278). New York: ACM Press.

Davenport, Thomas H. (May 1998). From Data to Knowledge. *Oracle Magazine, 6*(3): 12–16. Available at www.oracle.com/oramag/ oracle/98-May/ind2.html

Davenport, Thomas H., & Prusak, Laurence. (1998). *Working knowledge: How organizations manage what they know.* Boston: Harvard Business School Press.

Davis, Randall, Shrobe, Howard, & Szolovits, Peter. (1993). What is a knowledge representation? *AI Magazine, 14*(1): 17–33.

Firestone, J. M. (2001). Key issues in knowledge management. *Knowledge and Innovation, Journal of the KMCI, 1*(3).

Fuller, Steve. (2002). *Knowledge management foundations.* Boston: KMCI Press and Butterworth-Heinemann.

Grey, Denham. (August 1998). *Knowledge management and information management: The differences.* Available at www.smithweaversmith.com/km-im.htm

Grice, H. Paul. (1975). Logic and conversation. In Peter Cole & Jerry L. Morgan (Eds.), *Syntax and semantics: Vol. 3. Speech acts* (pp. 41–58). New York: Academic Press.

Jørgensen, Magne, & Moløkken, Kjetil. (2006). How large are software cost overruns? *A Review of the 1994 CHAOS Report, Simula Research Laboratory.* Available at www.simula.no/research/engineering/publications/Jorgensen.2006.4/downloadPdfFile

Kaplan, Robert S., & Norton, David P. (1996). *The balanced scorecard: Translating strategy into action.* Boston: Harvard Business School Press.

Mahesh, Kavi, & Suresh, J. K. (2004). What is the K in KM technology? *The Electronic Journal of Knowledge Management, 2*(2): 11–22. Available at www.ejkm.com

Mahesh, Kavi, & Suresh, J. K. (2005). Tutorial notes from "XML Schema Languages for Knowledge Representation and Management" at IICAI-2005: The Second Indian International Conference on Artificial Intelligence, Pune, India, December 2005.

Mahesh, Kavi, & Suresh, J. K. (2006). Engineering a semantic intraWeb for Knowledge Management. Presented at KMAP-2006: The 3rd Asia Pacific International Conference on Knowledge Management, Hong Kong, December 2006.

Miller, F. J. (October 2002). I = 0 (Information has no intrinsic meaning). *Information Research*, *8*(1).

Minsky, Marvin. (1975). A framework for representing knowledge. In Patrick Henry Winston (Ed.), *The Psychology of Computer Vision* (Chapter 6). New York: McGraw-Hill, 1975. (Reproduced in Allan Collins & Edward E. Smith (Eds.) (1988). *Readings in Cognitive Science*. Los Altos, CA: Morgan Kaufmann.)

Newell, Allen. (1982). The knowledge level. *Artificial Intelligence*, *18*: 87–127.

Newman, Brian, & Conrad, Kurt W. A framework for characterizing knowledge management methods, practices, and technologies. The Knowledge Management Forum. Available at www.km-forum.org

Rosch, E. (1978). Principles of categorization. In Eleanor Rosch & Barbara B. Lloyd (Eds.), *Cognition and Categorization*, Hillsdale, NJ: Erlbaum. (Reproduced in Allan Collins & Edward E. Smith (Eds.) (1988). *Readings in Cognitive Science*. Los Altos, CA: Morgan Kaufmann.)

Ruggles, Rudy L., III. (Ed.). (1997). *Knowledge management tools.* Boston: Butterworth Heinemann.

Russell, Bertrand. (1926). Theory of knowledge. *The Encyclopaedia Britannica*. Chicago: Encyclopædia Britannica, Inc.

Salton, Gerald. (1983). *Introduction to modern information retrieval.* New York: McGraw-Hill.

Skyrme, David. (1997). From information management to knowledge management: Are you prepared? *Proceedings OnLine '97* (December 9–11, 1997).

Sowa, John F. (1999). *Knowledge representation: Logical, philosophical, and computational foundations.* Pacific Grove, CA: Brooks Cole.

The Standish Report. (2001). Extreme chaos. The Standish Group International.

The Standish Report: Does it really describe a software crisis? (2006). *Communications of the ACM*, *49*(8), 15–16.

Suresh J. K., & Mahesh, Kavi. (2006). *Ten steps to maturity in knowledge management: Lessons in economy.* Oxford, UK: Chandos Publishing.

Sveiby, Karl-Erik. (October 1994). What is information? Available at www.sveiby.com. au/Information.htm

van Dijk, Teun A., & Kintsch, Walter. (1983). *Strategies of discourse comprehension.* New York: Academic Press.

Wical, Kelly. (1999). *Point of view gists and generic gists in a generic document browsing system.* US Patent, US5918236.

Wilson, T. D. (2002). The nonsense of "knowledge management." *Information Research*, *8*(1).

Zack, Michael H. (1999). Managing codified knowledge. *Sloan Management Review*, *40*(4): 45–58.

# CHAPTER 6

# Knowledge Audits: Establishing a Context for Leveraging Knowledge

Lynda W. Moulton

LWM Technology Services

Knowledge audits play a critical role in establishing contextual relevancy for any activity that has play in the knowledge management/knowledge leveraging arena of an organization. It is the author's experience that several overlapping audits are useful to fully understand and build the context around people, their work activities, and the products of their applied knowledge. As patterns of practice relating to knowledge flow and transfer are uncovered, auditors often find it useful to revisit subjects from earlier evidence gathering to "clear up" misconceptions and to create a more comprehensive view of current operations. Review and re-runs give auditors opportunities to unearth more support needs and "wishes" from the participants, and to validate the probable usefulness of contemplated knowledge leveraging programs.

What follows is an attempt at a practical framework for a series of audit activities with a goal of illuminating bottlenecks in the flow of knowledge, poor capturing, organizing, and leveraging practices. What we are seeking are both fundamental flaws in how an organization identifies, values, and leverages the knowledge assets it has, and the special activities that are beneficial and might be candidates for scaling to a wider audience or other beneficiaries.

Who should conduct an audit, in terms of professional position and training, is highly variable. Rarely do people come into any organization with specific training for this role. A key ingredient is that the project has a strong leader with the ability and skills to map a coherent plan for doing the audit, and who champions the reasons for doing one in the first place. It is not a role that should be assigned to a skeptic or reluctant participant. Another factor to seek in the leader is having a broad and solid understanding of the work of the organization and how all groups and departments fit together to "get work done." Often, professionals from organization development, human resources, or library and information services have that perspective and enough experience with all groups to meet the challenge. Information professionals also have the service orientation. If they have been proactive in their work, they will have established contacts throughout the organization to begin the project with an aggressive roadmap to individuals who can participate and contribute information.

Finally, this essay examines four concepts that are increasingly entering the discussion in the KM realm: complexity, synchronicity, asymmetricity, and orthogonity. Each has relevant play in the field; together they contribute to what appear to be insoluble problems of harnessing knowledge. The results of multi-faceted audits must take these into account to ultimately create an interlocking model of how components work in harmony for healthy knowledge flow.

## Organization Structures—Phase I (Discovery)

Knowledge management (KM) is first about people, their knowledge and expertise and their connections to others. Larry Prusak has noted that individual stars are not the most critical success factors in organizations; well connected teams of people that contribute collaboratively are. It is for that reason that we begin our knowledge inventory with people, for they will lead us to these important communities and the products of their knowledge.

Organization charts are only one view of an organization, and their static nature usually belies informal relationships that exist to truly get work done. Organizations often tackle reorganizations or restructuring to correct business problems in the mistaken belief that if the structure is logical, problems will go away. The author has shifted thinking over several decades as she moved from some highly structured and even rigid organizations to observe those in a constant state of reorganization. The key rests in leadership, which can exist in both formal and informal structures. Learning and understanding both types of structures is crucial to getting the "big picture" right. Because organization structures can also have great influence on employees' awareness of themselves and how they related to others, they can be strong factors in knowledge sharing and behavioral conditioning.

*Formal organization structures* may reflect management's view of how divisions, departments, and groups should be organized to achieve corporate goals. In younger organizations, it is just as likely to reflect how individuals in an early stage divided up responsibilities for different areas of the business because of their own professional strengths or biases learned from previous organizations. The knowledge auditor should not only explore what the formal structure is, but also try to understand why it is and how well it is being supported by the current and active leadership. If there are inherent weaknesses and if managerial roles are not being well integrated with needs and goals, the knowledge audit analysis should reflect a possibility that change is afoot or likely soon.

Formal structure is important as a guide for identifying the people the auditor needs to contact and learn about. People in organizations often behave in accordance with a self-referencing model of how they relate to the whole. In a hierarchical structure, those in the lower rungs may view the formal structure as a framework that distances them from responsibility, key decisions, and decision makers. Conversely, if the organization structure, hierarchical or not, makes sense in the context of the business goals, individuals will find security and connections in knowing that the framework supports their work and lends trust that the leaders know what they are doing. Auditors using formal charts to find leaders to interview should then explore how those leaders understand the structure and apply it to their own business behaviors. The resulting responses can inform an auditor about the usefulness or potential weakness of that structure on knowledge flows. At the same time, it will help the auditor to know where else to look for knowledge leveraging frameworks of a less formal nature.

*Informal structures* evolve to meet organizational needs and to move agendas forward whenever and wherever formal structures and processes can't meet demands. They occur and are necessary in all organizations, regardless of the health of formal structures. In KM parlance these are often referred to as *communities of practice* or *CoPs*. They often begin in an ad hoc manner but become formalized as teams, steering committees, or special interest groups, and may last for a few months or several years. They frequently form the basis of new formal groups within organizations. Their existence and potential importance cannot be ignored in a knowledge audit because these groups harbor some of the best collective expertise and collaborative work of organizations. While formal organization structures rarely keep up with pressing business demands, CoPs can form and morph rapidly establishing alternative frameworks for getting work done.

A case in point is documented in presentations by Dr. Harvey Wiener at Bristol Myers Squibb from his Connecticut offices. While working as a scientist at BMS he began to leverage peer relationships and networks to foster collaboration by sharing learning and content resources. Over time the group experimented with building mini-portals to share information among themselves; this informal group developed a model that became known as the Knowledge Desktop, an internal brand. It was exported through a group led by Dr. Wiener in his new role heading the Knowledge Integrated Resources (KIR) group. They then functioned as a formal entity within corporate Knowledge and Information Management providing consultancy and service, content management training and support, and team business practices, and at the time of this writing, they have helped both formal groups and CoPs launch over 500 Knowledge Desktops. When we caught up with Harvey a couple of years later, KIR had been unbundled from and moved to the Pharmaceutical Research Institute, Informatics Division. This is a good example of how *user needs for sharing knowledge in a mutually fulfilling context* dictated a practice that was formalized and then morphed to serve other needs. Their needs were not satisfied through normal channels in an organization, so a CoP initiated a solution. Once formalized, this group would have appeared in an audit of the formal structure. Most organizations are filled with efforts of this type that need to be discovered in an audit to ensure the survey will result in a complete picture of where knowledge is being concentrated and leveraged in the organization.

Management can use the results of an audit to temper impulses to restructure an organization by viewing informal groups as beneficial, self-organizing ways of creating stability. Putting off a frenzy of reorganizing can avoid turmoil, allowing organizations to find their equilibrium more naturally. Nurturing and encouraging CoPs is not only helpful to the organization but affirms also the importance of people who lead these efforts and empowers individuals who participate. Allowing them to operate and acknowledging them encourages employees to be a part of collaboration efforts.

## Your Role as Auditor—Using Organization Structures

Audits need to be structured and efficient. There is no expectation that every person or even every group will be surveyed. You may be tasked to perform an audit by a department or leader who is seeking information to explore the need for a knowledge initiative or you may be the primary mover. Regardless, moving purposefully to a conclusion with solid results that will support the initiative requires a process whose outcome is defensible.

Your ultimate conclusions and recommendations will be tested and/or debated. You want to avoid the risk that they are seen as biased, incomplete, or unfocused. Success is more likely if you demonstrate fairness and an understanding of organizational realities. Therefore, informing yourself about the formal organization is a good starting point for finding connections that may be meaningful for a larger audit. Couple that with personal inquiries and discussions with people in the organization who have the respect of peers, subordinates, and superiors. Ask them who they believe are good candidates to be interviewed about the information needs of a department, group, team, or project. It will help to have an organization diagram to direct the conversation to specific groups that you believe may have knowledge intensive needs or outputs and to identify who in those groups would be willing contributors.

Seek an introduction to recommended individuals by the recommender, if you don't know them, or introduce yourself by stating the reason for wanting a discussion:

- Tell them who suggested a discussion and why they are considered an important candidate.
- Schedule a time to talk.
- Let them know how much time you would like, in the range of 30 to 45 minutes, but try to schedule a time when you know that you both will be available for longer if the conversation is flowing productively.
- Prepare a questionnaire with a minimal number of questions and tell your subject how many; three to six is a reasonable number. If they know that the list is very long, they are likely to abbreviate their responses in the attempt to keep the session short. Letting them know that you have only a few questions is apt to encourage them to be expansive and really open up about things that are meaningful and useful, early in the discussion.
- Be clear during all phases about what you can attribute by source and what is being shared with you in confidence to be used only in the aggregate.

So, what are the types of things you might ask and what do you really want to learn? These questions are the key to getting at the facts that will guide the next phases of the audit and fuel the final audit analysis. Beginning with an open-ended question like, *"Tell me about your position here and your job function; expand, if you would, on some of your most critical information needs."* Some individuals will be off and running with an opening like that but you may need to tease information out of others. Follow up questions might include:

- Who are some of your best sources for information about?
- What are some of the best resources here in X Corporation for information about?
- Are there any outside services or experts you tap to learn more about?
- Do you find any roadblocks to certain types of information? What are they?
- In the best of all possible worlds, how do you think X Corporation should be helping employees find the information sources they need to do their work?
- What would help and encourage employees to share the products of their own work and research with others?

Take as many notes as you can or, with permission, tape the conversations.

Let's assume that you have more time, and the person you are interviewing has not been very talkative or responsive to your initial, open-ended question and follow-up. If you go in with three prepared questions, the second might be, *"What is the principal role of your group? How do members of the group collaborate with each other?"* Follow-up to this track would include questions to discover clarity of missions, how people work with each other, and, most important, barriers to successful collaboration or successful models for sharing and enhancing each other's work results.

Finally, don't conclude any interview without asking for names of other people who might have insights into information finding, using, and sharing behaviors in the organization. A final question might be, *"Who else would you recommend that I speak with who seems to have a good handle on how to find and use information efficiently and produces good results? Or, do you know anyone who has expressed ideas about how we could manage information more effectively in the company?"*

Very soon after each interview, transcribe your notes or audio recording and follow up quickly by phone or e-mail to get clarification.

## Reporting and Communication

The net output that you are seeking in the first series and all subsequent interviews and queries is a map of:

- Who is connected to whom, formally and informally?
- What are their formal roles and job descriptions while also learning about informal relationships and roles?
- Where do expertise, methods, differing views of the organization reside?
- What are the successful knowledge sharing engagements and practices?
- What are the barriers to information and knowledge transfer?
- What are the cultural behaviors that are dictating successes or failures to share and leverage knowledge?

The map needs to be comprehensive, reflecting as many points of view as you can assemble in a reasonable amount of time. Good analytical work is time consuming. You need to be able to spot trends and repeating evidence quickly to decide when you have enough information to make generalizations and draw useful conclusions. You can't drag out the interviewing process for too long a period because, having had these discussions with subjects, they will soon begin wondering where you are going with the results and whether they can expect improvements and changes.

Reporting needs to be made to the appropriate stakeholders, but you may want to also seek permission to share at least a summary of results with interview subjects. Visualization of results in the form of pictures and charts of trends and relationships to business goals will interest your subjects. In any event, be quick to follow up with a thank you for their time and comments about the next steps in your process, even if you cannot share the full analysis and report. Remember that one reason for a knowledge audit is people-to-people collaboration and improving their access to critical resources. You need their interest, buy-in, and enthusiasm as you move through stages of a process. They are your constituents in this effort but also your partners in establishing a successful outcome, so you want to share what you learn, where you are heading, and what they can expect.

## PROGRAMS, PROJECTS, AND PRODUCTS—PHASE II (WHERE KNOWLEDGE IS CREATED AND APPLIED)

Much of what has been revealed about formal and informal structures can also be investigated about specific programs, projects, and products. Using the information gathered in Phase I, try to create a visual structure of the human network of relationships that make up both formal and informal working connections.

You may have ended up with a formal structure that looks similar to the chart shown in Figure 6.1.

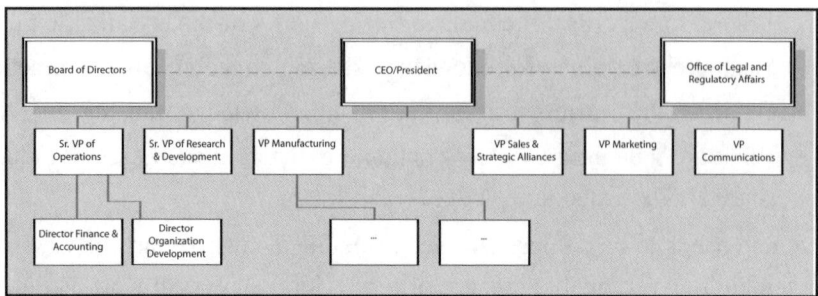

**Figure 6.1   Typical organization chart (partial)**

A schematic of the human networking interconnections for exploring potential product development in an engineering firm might look more like Figure 6.2.

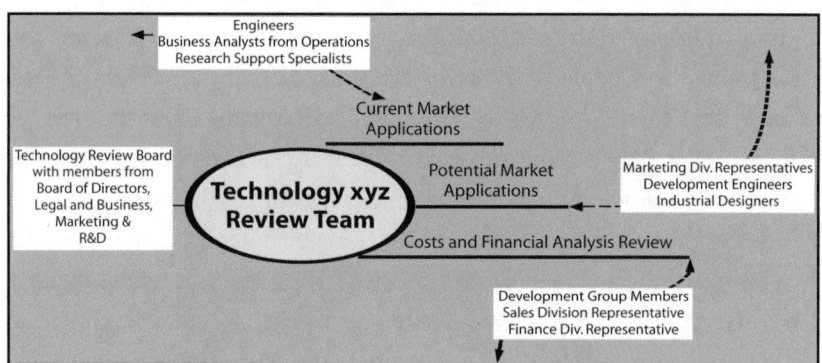

**Figure 6.2   Typical communities of practice assembled from
diverse groups for a project**

Each node containing members from different formal groups is a CoP, a potential source of not only information about their own activities, but also a resource on where else to find expertise. Their methods for gathering information and sharing it within the group are noteworthy commentary about beneficial practices that work for them. You can also ask about technologies they employ and difficulties they have keeping track of and retrieving content.

Typical CoPs might also be found working on issues like:

- Process improvements
- Business and legal issues
- Technology infrastructure planning
- Project planning
- Project management facilitation
- Aligning manufacturing and accounting practices

Look for CoPs when you discover situations in which your organization faces competitive or regulatory pressures, major procurements or facilities planning, the need for infusion of new talent or technology know-how that might stimulate acquisitions or mergers, or the need for learning simple project management techniques. Groups of individuals from different departments often find their casual discussions and shared expertise make for the desire to move to an electronic or office meeting space on a regular basis to strategize or problem-solve. Managers from loosely linked but unrelated groups may encourage their subordinates to "get-together" to thrash out a problem that affects both.

No matter what the reason or origin, these CoPs are a fundamental asset to the organization and a core for critical knowledge that needs to be recognized, and factored into the audit. Document the existence of CoPs you uncover and discover in your audit. Identify team leaders and key contributors that you might want to interview. Categorize these teams and establish a ranking system to prioritize how they should be audited. Find out how they capture and track their teamwork.

As your discovery progresses, you will undoubtedly discover that some groups, which may have seemed important early in the project, are not significant factors in the larger context of the work of the organization; their knowledge, while valuable, may be less important than that of other more influential groups. It is a balancing task to make such judgments, but if the goal of your audit is to improve knowledge flow and provide valuable context for assembling and sharing knowledge, you must eliminate insignificant activities, as interesting as they may seem. As a case in point, the author usually uncovers one or two groups or individuals who have initiated Web sites, blogs, or wikis to expand on or plug holes in the organization's knowledge base. Their enthusiasm and energy around these activities always seems to disguise the fact that their work is not heavily used by others. It is tempting to treat these *loud* efforts as significant, but channeling the participants into new programs after the audit is probably a better use of their talents. You need to *focus on in-depth auditing of resources that have gained trust, respect, and a following.*

# What and How Is Project Information Captured?—Phase III

When you have established both formal and informal "maps" of how your organization is structured, you will have a set of guideposts to programs and projects for which knowledge and knowledge flow are crucial. In addition to this compendium of knowledge repositories, you should also seek out planning documents, strategic reports, and third-party reports that may have resulted from work performed for the organization under contract. These will contribute to your understanding of both current work and directions for future projects. Chart major and minor projects on a timeline that shows:

- Active engagements
- Scheduled programs
- Contemplated work

Include notations about current or likely contributors, and any information you have gathered about key players and content repositories (data files, databases, or collaboration applications) where information is being routinely contributed for each project.

As you engaged your subjects in Phase I you were probably assembling a lot of impressions about the processes and technologies currently in play for capturing knowledge, sharing ideas, and finding human and content resources. Using your timeline of current and planned organization programs, coupled with these insights, lay out a final round of interviews and meetings to flesh out how knowledge flows within the organization.

Among the more detailed information that you will seek is:

- Where is knowledge sharing happening, in what groups, for what purpose, and what is the process?
- What specific collaboration activities are being employed and who are the collaborators? What are their outputs?
- How information about projects and programs is recorded, organized, and retrieved needs to be documented in process charts that reflect what the content is, its scope, the technologies used, and factors of accessibility.

- Finally, you need to uncover gaps in knowledge resources, where important individual contributors, teams, or groups seem to have no culture of sharing, collaborating, or documenting events that can, will, or have affected the business.

This chapter on audits has mentioned technology only in passing, but by this phase, the technology infrastructure and software applications in use throughout the organization need to be documented as well. In the best of all cases, you will have a starting point in a document or series of documents from your information technology group. Network architecture schematics are often available, and applications software licenses in use and by whom are usually inventoried and audited on a regular basis. Organizations with a history of controlling these technology assets centrally will have better records than organizations that allow groups and divisions free reign in selection and application of technology. A complete knowledge audit will include a state-of-the-technology-landscape map that links hardware and software to content repositories and points of access to content.

As you are making a final pass to gather information about content, it is appropriate and wise to validate what you have learned about the technological landscape and try to discover any technology assets not documented elsewhere. Above all, you want to learn what "best practices," user-friendly, and heavily adopted technologies are benefiting the organization even in isolated cases, and where there are deficiencies and bottlenecks in the transfer and flow of knowledge. Some of the answers you get may be more people or process related, while other successes or problem areas may relate directly to technologies. Expect to discover chronic problems in technology infrastructures. Both hardware and software components contribute to significant "siloing" of knowledge resources because the parts simply do not work in an integrated fashion. Look for barriers to effective retrieval, since this is where many technologies break down by not delivering to meet user expectations.

How you gather Phase III information will be quite different than during the first phase when you were building relationships, gathering impressions, and establishing a foundation for documenting the status of knowledge conditions. Throughout Phase II you will have returned to some of the first subjects and expanded your network of contributors to individuals or even groups the first subjects recommended. If you have worked the network effectively and established a good communication mechanism with all those you have engaged, you are probably receiving periodic contributions via e-mail, by phone, or in person as people remember or run across other evidence they believe will be helpful. The more of this that has occurred, the more complete your audit will be. Keep track of this material and use it as further anecdotal supporting evidence for tracking down details to flesh out the scope of your descriptions. Assemble focus groups, host "brown-bag" lunches to discuss a process you are trying to understand, or follow up with a more detailed survey approach; these can all be employed. Sharing some of the anecdotal material may help explain to subjects why you need more data.

## Reporting and Communicating Phase III Results

The quality of the analytical work you do after gathering Phase III information depends heavily on several factors:

- Your record keeping and the consistency of how records were maintained throughout the process
- The evenness of the scope across the organization
- The reputation and trustworthiness of your sources
- The methods for information gathering and explanation of their validity
- The completeness of data
- Your honest treatment of data, including assessments of problems and successes
- Acknowledgement of individuals who helped with contributions to the study

Nothing makes for a more credible report than work that is organized, well documented, and from trustworthy sources. It is also true that the clarity of your mission and how it shows through in the final product will be enhanced significantly if the problems that are documented are accompanied by suggested remedies.

As you assemble your material, begin to organize it, and think about presentation, there are several steps to the analytical process you should consider:

- Explore personally as many content and collaboration repositories as you have uncovered and develop an inventory of what you find. The inventory should note topical scope, types of material, contributors, amount of content, age of material, frequency of contributions, and accessibility requirements (for future security considerations).
- Think about how to contextually relate people and content; this means creating logical frameworks to bring CoP members into alignment with content they need to further their business objectives.

- Rank successful and problematic content management and retrieval efforts that you have uncovered.
- Begin framing recommendations and for every recommendation work on business justifications. Make risk assessment part of your justification to give an honest view of what the organization has to gain by moving on each recommendation, or to lose by not acting.

## The Report Components

The largest part of your report will be data in whatever form you capture the results of your interviews and research, and your analytical output. The latter may be primarily in the form of graphics but it is important to have a narrative tying the pieces together. All of this material belongs in Appendices but it is helpful to provide links to these parts from appropriate places in the narrative of the report.

A suggested outline for a report follows. The author recommends also developing a cover letter, even if the report is distributed via e-mail, which conveys the professional weight of the project. A distribution list that reflects dissemination at the highest level of the organization helps to show the strategic intent of the audit. Others reading it will take the contents more seriously if they believe that top management is a participant. That said, the writing and tone must reflect the fact that it is intended to influence leadership to action; it should be straightforward and formal, getting to the point quickly:

- **Cover page** containing a title, names of author(s) and supporting auditors, time period of execution, and for whom it is being written.
- **Table of Contents,** hyperlinked if the report will be issued electronically.
- **Preface** describing the intent of the audit and its scope (e.g., which parts of the organization or the entire organization) with acknowledgment of sponsors and special assistance.
- **Introduction** giving a more detailed description of methods, scope, dates of performance for each phase, and study contributions. This may also describe for readers how to use the report.
- **Executive Summary** is really the heart of what you want organization leaders to see and act upon. It should briefly include a statement of work, generalized description of the outcomes, specific recommendations, and business risk factors. In electronic versions the executive summary should link to specific sections of the Detailed Findings and Appendices.

- **Detailed Findings** are the long narrative of the report with recommendations that detail justifications.
- **Appendices** include data collected, diagrams and charts derived from analysis, and a list of participants with their professional roles relating to the study.

# Summary: Concepts for Consideration and Why This Stuff Is Hard

Knowledge auditing is not a science and outcomes are often unpredictable, especially in organizations with very loose or fluid structures. A realistic outcome is to identify opportunities for improving knowledge flow, sharing, and exchanges with little investment in technology while leveraging existing frameworks in the organization. These opportunities can become obvious as the audit moves along, and if they do, you may ask for input from others you interview about the potential for adoption and success.

Still, a thorough vetting of knowledge in the organization and how people have self-organized into communities of practice will reveal also the *complexities*, and probably conflicting agendas, of groups. Expect to find a great deal of complexity among people, how they operate, modes of communicating, and practices for managing information. Other factors that will become apparent are business and personality disruptors, the actual amount of information, and how technology contributes to the speed of transfer of information content in huge unvetted quantity, which outstrips humans' ability to absorb and adopt or reject it. Placing a value on resources quickly is an art that requires a lot of practice, as is skill in knowing what and when to reject. Few of us can perform these processes with the speed of content accumulation. Finally, a great complicating factor that can often be as fortuitous as it is disruptive is serendipity. In fact, building models of contextual relevance in our knowledge systems should have a goal of increasing serendipity because that fosters innovation.

Factor in the *asynchronous* and *asymmetrical* nature of organizational activity feeds, and you find another layer of complexity. The heavy usage of e-mail and collaborative spaces like Sharepoint contribute to volumes of overlapping actions and commentary, and an egalitarian environment for contributions by anyone at any level of the organization. It is common behavior to open these forums with little governance in the spirit of increasing communication and sharing opportunities.

The result is lack of context, leading to difficulty in navigating the threads, determining the timelines of the contributions, and following the actual outcomes of overlapping inputs.

Another complexity factor is the numbers and types of *orthogonal processes*, activities and the types of knowledge facets represented by them. Auditors need to build logical frameworks for the relevance of work in one part of the organization to another, as a means of juggling all the knowledge flows that are perpendicular to each other, related but scaling on different axes.

So, complexity makes the auditing job hard; asynchronous, asymmetrical, and orthogonal flows of knowledge creation and transfer processes require the audit leader to maintain a clear mental model of how the results of discovery fit together. The resulting data, once carefully analyzed and presented, become the building blocks for a contextual framework that links people to knowledge resources.

## BIBLIOGRAPHY OF RELATED ARTICLES

Because Dr. Srikantaiah's bibliography, with revisions from Paul Burden, is so comprehensive, though published in 2000, it is a great place to begin for readings on audits. The ideas and methods reflected are just as relevant today. The other two citations come from the author and a reaction to her previous ideas on the subject.

Knowledge Mapping/Information Audit. (2000). In *Knowledge Management, The Bibliography*, revised and expanded version by Paul R. Burden, prepared under the editorial supervision of Prof. T. Kanti Srikantaiah, Ph.D., Director, Center for Knowledge Management, Dominican University, 2000. [Citations from mid-1990s through 2000.] domin.dom.edu/faculty/SRIKANT/lis88001/kmbib.html# InformationAudit

Moulton, Lynda W. (2005). KM as a framework for managing knowledge assets. *The Gilbane Report*, *12*:9. Available at gilbane.com/artpdf/GR12.9.pdf

Vinson, Jack. (2005). *Reactions from Jack Vinson to "KM as a Framework for Managing Knowledge Assets."* Chicago: Knowledge Jolt. Available at blog.jackvinson.com/archives/2005/05/05/km_as_a_framework_for_managing_knowledge_assets.html

# CHAPTER 7

# PKM: A Bottom-Up Approach to Knowledge Management

Dave Pollard

Meeting of Minds, Consulting Services

In North America at least, knowledge management (KM) budgets are under constant siege, KM leaders' salaries and department headcounts have been cut back, the Knowledge Director role has been relegated to a subordinate back-office role, and many CEOs are searching for ways to outsource the function entirely. In other words, most executives either do not see KM as strategic to their organizations, or have lost faith that investment in KM offers an appropriate return on investment (ROI).

It's time for the knowledge "champions" of the world to get together and get our *act* together. As much as the idea of increasing the sharing and effective use of information and ideas is appealing to just about everyone, KM has not delivered on this promise. I believe time is running out.

The story of KM so far has been, for the most part, a failure—failure to articulate, to imagine, and to implement. We allowed the bold vision of knowledge-sharing to be diminished and appropriated by those who saw it as merely an exercise in automating the acquisition, storage, and dissemination of documents. Many information technology (IT) departments saw it as another facet of technology—as competition for resources and as little more than an extension of the document management and Web site management functions they were already responsible for. Many training departments saw it as the "content" side of training, and wondered why it didn't report to them. Most executives saw it as a means to speed up and reduce the cost of the back office, the same way the assembly line had reduced manufacturing times and costs. And the creative people who often had the Knowledge Director thrust upon them conceived of KM as a means for increasing organizational innovation, customer satisfaction, and employee retention.

Now, a dozen years after the debut of KM, there has been little significant change in the efficiency, effectiveness, or value of information processes or content in most organizations. Many companies that jumped early onto the KM bandwagon have all but abandoned it, while many organizations that waited are now repeating the mistakes of the pioneers. Despite this, interest in KM remains substantial, and this is because, while its promise has not really been realized, its potential is still enormous. And CEOs of many organizations, having studied the lessons of Enron, 9/11, Katrina, and the flu, have a nagging feeling that no matter how great the cost of investing in KM may be, the cost of not knowing is even greater (Figure 7.1).

What most organizations essentially did with KM was automate existing information processes. They took the paper "stuff" in manuals and memoranda and newspapers and converted it into digital form. That made it easier and (sometimes) cheaper to maintain, but did not increase its value, which was, if you were to ask most of the people on the front line, pretty marginal anyway. Organizations provided staff with access to the Internet, but most of those who were inclined to

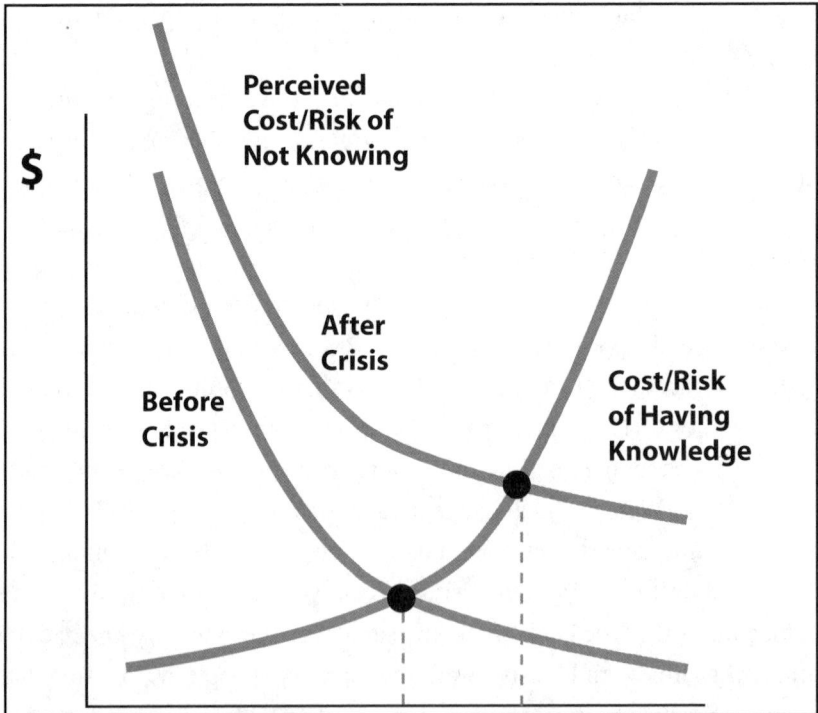

Figure 7.1  Cost of not knowing

use it already had it at home and were using it there, without the restrictions imposed by the company—so that, too, was of marginal benefit. In some cases, employees are *still* forced to shuttle critical information between their work and home PCs. Most organizations, too, refused to abandon the top-down centralized information model that was already in place, merely institutionalizing it with firewalls; access restrictions; monster centrally managed one-size-fits-all databases and Web sites; and over-engineered, over-managed collaboration and community-of-practice tools.

Essentially, neither managers nor early KM practitioners "got it": *KM is all about enabling people to obtain relevant, context-rich information, and connection with appropriate experts easily, when they need it, so that they can be more effective doing their unique jobs.*

As a result, the critical business information flows, shown in Figure 7.1, are essentially unchanged from what they were a decade ago. There have been some minor changes in the technologies used for these flows, but for the most part these have not been significant in improving front-line effectiveness of workers, and in some cases have actually made work more difficult. Management continues to rely on well-entrenched IS to promulgate instructions and policy decisions and to extract, often annoyingly and disruptively, information from the front lines that it needs to make business decisions. To traditional managers, information is still all about telling employees what to do and making sure they do it.

Customers, outside the corporate firewalls and disinclined to participate in technology initiatives designed for the suppliers' needs rather than theirs (as most e-newsletters, e-rooms, and extranets are), continue to interact, information-wise, with suppliers the same way they always have—receive (and usually turf) the marketing mail, put in their orders, and rely on their "relationship manager" to decipher the former and process the latter effectively. Business as usual, largely unaffected by KM.

Things happen the way they do in organizations for a reason. When people are unable to get the information they need within the system, they will find workarounds to get it in other ways. This is nothing new, and it is commendable—it shows people care about the quality and effectiveness of their work. The #1 means of getting and sharing information is, was, and probably always will be *conversations*. Pick up the phone, walk down the hall, use instant messaging (IM) (if your company allows it), use Skype (if your company allows it), or, as a last resort, send an e-mail to the people who might know what you need to know.

It would make sense that KM would *facilitate* conversations, but if anything it has tried to *obsolesce* them—substituting context-poor databases that purportedly have the information you used to get from talking with people, more efficiently. Not surprisingly, this has rarely worked.

What we in KM need to do is go back to the original premise and promise of KM and start again—*but this time from the bottom up*:

- Develop processes and programs, and buy or build tools that measurably *improve the effectiveness of front-line workers* in the performance of their unique and increasingly specialized jobs
- Refocus from top-down centralized content acquisition and collection to *peer-to-peer content-sharing*
- Develop processes and programs, and buy or build tools that measurably *improve sense-making: the value and meaning of content in context*
- Refocus from top-down community-of-practice management to enabling *peer-to-peer expertise-finding and connectivity*

This bottom-up approach to KM directed at the needs of individual employees and their peer-to-peer interactions has come to be called Personal Knowledge Management (PKM). It offers tremendous possibilities and could finally realize the original promise and expectations of KM, but it can't be done within the budget that most organizations set aside for KM. It requires recognition from management that the four sets of activities bulleted previously *will*, if properly implemented, yield huge improvements in the quality and effectiveness of the organization's people's work—repaying the investment many times over. The quote in Figure 7.2 is what one executive told me when I suggested his company make such an investment. It shows that, in many companies, labor costs are still seen as a necessary evil to be minimized, and an additional investment in people, or knowledge for them, is out of the question.

Fortunately, management of most organizations has more sense than that. The breakeven point for an investment of two hours of personal coaching for each employee in an organization is, after all, a mere 0.1 percent improvement in that employee's work effectiveness. And, while some executives may be impatient and disenchanted with the return on their KM investment to date, they still appreciate Drucker's argument that improving front-line worker productivity is "the greatest

"If our front-line employees need 'productivity improvement' training, maybe the answer is just to fire them and hire some who don't."

## Figure 7.2  Personal knowledge management

challenge of the 21st century"—that the answer isn't to do as much with less investment, but to do much more with more.

The diagram in Figure 7.3 shows what's *possible*—how valuable information flows *could* be enabled and facilitated by PKM. Step by step, here is what we would need to do to realize this potential:

**Revamp and upgrade the role of Information Professionals from content managers to personal work effectiveness enablers.** Most knowledge workers have figured out how to get the content they need to do their jobs well, without any help from KM. Centralized content management initiatives offer little or no incremental value to them. What they need is hands-on help *using the information and technology at their disposal more effectively in the context of doing their own unique jobs*. This does not lend itself, in most organizations, to either classroom or computer-based training; it needs to be face-to-face, anthropological: The information professional (IP) needs to observe how workers use technology and information now, and then advise them how to do so more effectively. And at the

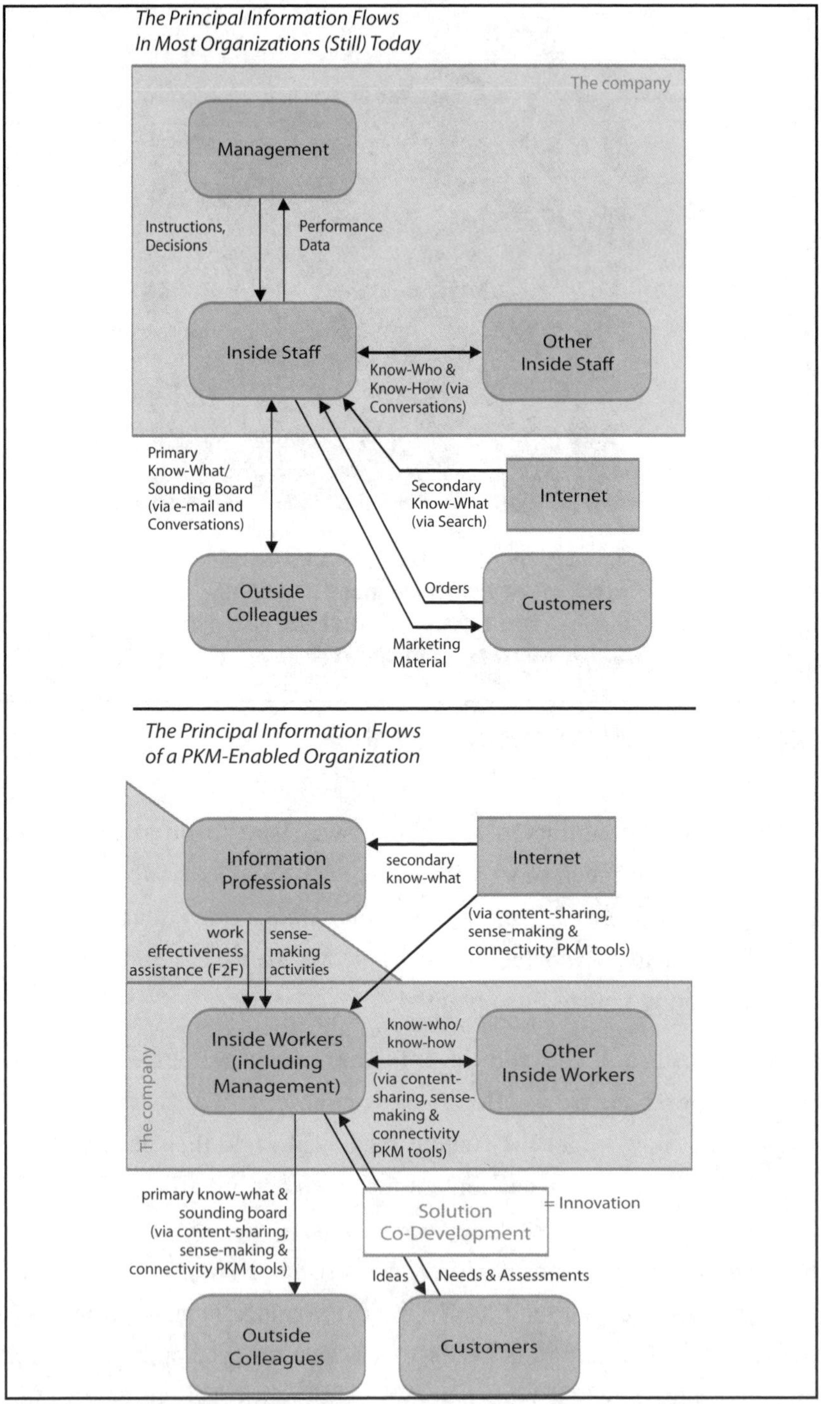

Figure 7.3  PKM enabled organization

same time, the IP needs to help workers *organize their personal content* so that they can manage it effectively and find (again) what they need when they need it. We need to get IPs away from their collections and help-desks and out into the field helping workers one-on-one. This is the essence of PKM.

**Reintermediate Information Professionals to filter and add sense, meaning, and value to information content.** One of the initial goals of KM was disintermediation—getting rid of the layers between front-line people and useful information. The problem is that most front-line people are now overwhelmed with the volume of information coming at them, and find most of what is available on the Internet too raw for their needs: They need help *making meaning and sense of this information*. IPs, as reintermediaries, can fill this need in two ways: They can massage raw information using visualizations, maps, tableaux, systems thinking charts, single frames, decision trees, and other techniques, and they can add insight by synthesizing, analyzing, organizing, and providing context for this information so that, in the hands of the knowledge worker, it is easily understandable, compelling, and ready to apply.

**Develop simple, automated mechanisms to facilitate peer-to-peer content-sharing with others inside and outside the organization.** These mechanisms include:

- Customizable, easy-to-use, context-rich *personal workspaces* (similar to Weblogs, but with additional functionality, security, and flexibility, while still being easy to learn and use) where all personal information that is shareable with others can reside
- Automatic *peer-to-peer publishing and subscription* mechanisms that allow employees' shareable content to be accessed by others, and high-value content from the Internet, and from other employees and outside colleagues, to flow automatically to the employee's desktop
- Automatic *knowledge harvesting* mechanisms that pull employees' shareable content into a central searchable archive copy, to obviate the need for submitting knowledge to central repositories

**Develop mechanisms to enhance meaning and context of information content so that it makes more sense and has more value to users.** These mechanisms include:

- Templates, e-mail lists, lists of experts and other aids for identifying and asking the right people for the right information on a quick-turnaround basis, in a single, easy-to-use *just-in-time canvassing* application
- Templates and models for creating high-context *stories and narratives*
- Templates, models, and self-study modules for creating *visualizations*, maps, single frames, and other compelling and meaningful representations of information
- Templates, models, and self-study modules for creating systems thinking charts, structured thinking documents, analytical reports, and other *insightful distillations and interpretations* of information
- Templates, models, and self-study modules for creating mindmaps, open space events, and other support mechanisms that *enhance the effectiveness of, and document, conversations*
- Templates, models, and self-study modules for *improving observation, listening, and attention* skills (e.g., cultural anthropology tools)
- Tools and mechanisms for *surveying employees, customers, and the informed public* and otherwise tapping the "Wisdom of Crowds" (including "prediction markets" and decision support applications)

**Develop mechanisms to enable peer-to-peer expertise finding and connectivity.** These mechanisms include:

- Simple, one-click *virtual presence* applications for connecting person-to-person with people (individually and in groups), with full audio (including ability to record), video, whiteboard (see what others in a conference are looking at and doing), and application sharing capabilities
- Simple, intuitive *collaborative workspaces and worktools* (enhanced, simplified versions of wikis, BaseCamp, etc.)
- Well-designed, automated *people-finding applications* and directories
- Simple *presence-detecting and peer-to-peer introduction applications* (enhanced, simplified versions of Dodgeball, etc.)

Table 7.1 contrasts the traditional, top-down, just-in-case content-and-collection KM approach with the bottom-up, peer-to-peer, just-in-time, reintermediated, context-connection-and-sensemaking PKM approach.

Executives preoccupied with risk and cost minimization will continue to wait on the sidelines for pioneers to show them that the risks and costs of such programs are far outweighed by the benefits of: better productivity; more engaged,

## Table 7.1  PKM Approach

| KM Program Objective | Traditional KM Approach | PKM Approach |
|---|---|---|
| Knowledge 'User Training' | Enterprise Application Training (classroom, CBT and newsletters distributed top-down) | Personal Productivity Improvement (PPI) Personal Content Management (PCM) |
| Content Sharing* | Top-down Collection in Central Repositories Formal Submission Process | Personal Shared Workspaces P2P Publishing & Subscription Automatic Content Harvesting |
| Sense-Making & Context Enhancement | (Not Addressed) | Just-in-Time Canvassing Stories & Narratives Visualizations Insight Analyses Conversation Support Observation Support Surveying, Predicting & Decision-Making |
| Connectivity* | Community of Practice Management Network Mapping | Virtual Presence Collaborative Workspaces/Tools People-Finders P2P Presence Detecting and Introduction |
| Role of Information Professionals | Repository Management Web Site Management | Personal Work Effectiveness (PPI + PCM) Sense-Making & Context Enhancement |

*Content sharing and connectivity tools are collectively known as "social networking" applications.

informed, and insightful employees; better connectivity; more context-rich knowledge sharing; and improved collaboration among employees and outside experts (as shown in Figure 7.4).

I first got interested in the idea of bottom-up PKM focused on the unique needs of each front-line employee in 2003, my last year as Global Director of Knowledge Innovation for a major professional services firm. I'd been asked to investigate a leveling-off of use of the firm's award-winning centralized knowledge resources, and decided to do the research through personal interviews with *non-users*, rather than the usual user surveys. We did about 100 interviews, and tried to get at the root causes of the problems and concerns they cited. So, for example, while many interviewees said they couldn't find what they were looking for, we tried to discover why this was: Was the tool too complex? Was the training inadequate? Was there too much content to wade through? Did they just not know where to look? Was the content badly indexed? Was it in the wrong format for convenient (re-)use? Or perhaps what they sought didn't exist at all. Or worse, they weren't motivated to make the effort to look for it.

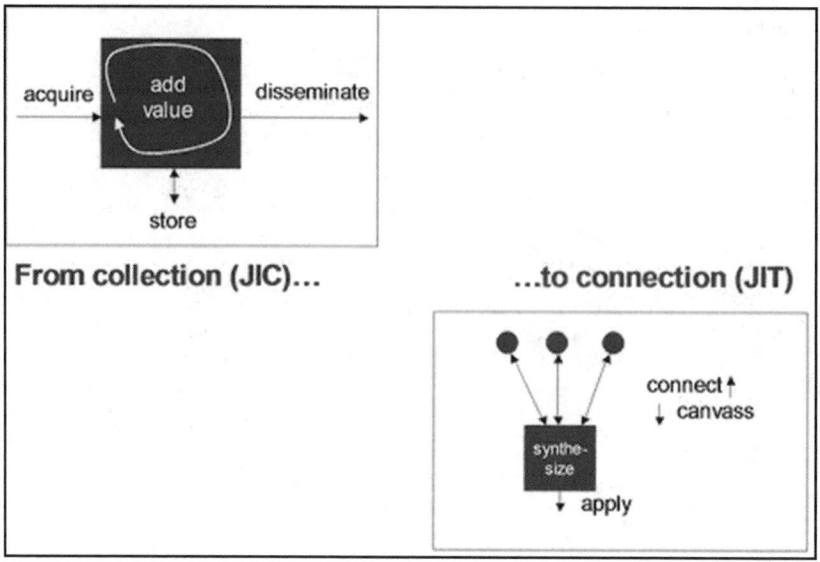

**Figure 7.4  PKM approach**

In describing this work, I've used three of the interviews that were especially illuminating. One of these was a corporate finance practitioner who confessed he'd completely stopped reading newspapers because general knowledge was unnecessary for his work, and used his PC only for e-mail and business valuation spreadsheets. A second was an audit manager who said she couldn't afford the intrafirm charge for research work and simply had no time to do such research herself, so she did without; she also confessed that she'd never been taught how to find stuff on her own PC and could never find what she needed on her own hard drive. A third was a tax partner who delegated all knowledge work to subordinates or assistants, even printing out and routing his e-mails. When I asked him about IM, he said he "handled it the same way." Ouch!

My conclusion from the interviews was that most of the firm's front-line people didn't use the knowledge resources because they didn't know how. I had been reading about a KM process that entailed one-on-one coaching of front-line people to use knowledge and technology effectively, and named this (for internal selling purposes, and with a tip of the hat to Drucker) Personal Productivity Improvement (PPI). When I proposed PPI as the solution to ineffective knowledge use, however, my boss said he was doubtful that, if they weren't willing to take the time to attend the firm's courses or computer-based training on the use of knowledge resources, employees were just as unlikely to make time for PPI. He sent me back to find out *why* practitioners didn't know how to use the resources effectively.

When I went to conduct the second round of interviews, it became clear that some of the interviewees had given me the answers they thought I wanted to hear because they *didn't know* the real answers. They were also blunter and more forthcoming when I went back to suggest that perhaps their ignorance of use of the firm's knowledge resources was partly *their fault*. This time, the corporate finance practitioner told me he was paid for his specialized technical knowledge, not for his understanding of business issues. He described the powerful, integrated newsfeeds and personalizable news profiles, the painstakingly populated databases, and the collaborative spaces we provided as "nice to have, not need to have." He was, he said, "unmotivated, so far" to learn more about what we had made available.

The audit manager pulled out an independent consultant's report that listed in the criteria clients used to select a professional services firm. In order, they were (1) strong pre-existing relationship with someone on the team, (2) fit and likability of the pursuit team, (3) senior face time spent with client key decision makers during the pursuit process, (4) technical competency and experience of the pursuit team, (5) understanding of the client's processes and organization, and (6) understanding of the client's business and industry. There is just no time, she told me, for stuff that clients don't think is very important. If she had more time, she said, she would be spending it out at clients building relationships, not at her PC looking for knowledge. (I later interviewed some clients who somewhat sheepishly corroborated the findings in this report, and said this audit manager was wise in setting her priorities.)

And the tax partner grabbed me as I passed near his office, whisked me inside, and told me how delighted he was that, after I'd mentioned it, he'd got his assistant to show him how to use IM. "If a client calls me on the phone with a question, sometimes I can IM a staff member and get confirmation of the answer while the client is still online, so I save research time and the client is very impressed," he told me. "It's stuff like this IM that really makes you guys valuable, not those giant repositories you build." If that weren't distressing enough, he confided that he was concerned that some of those giant repositories were accessible to everyone in the firm, and could we please restrict access to these to tax practitioners only? He patted me on the back. I sighed.

So my conclusion this time around was that the centralized content we spent so much time and money maintaining was simply not very useful to most practitioners.

The practitioners I talked to about PPI said they would love to receive PPI coaching, provided it was focused on the content on their own desktops and hard drives, and not the stuff in the central repositories.

Subsequently I met with a number of the firm's competitors and KM leaders of several other organizations that have experienced some frustration with the performance of their KM programs, and almost all of them expressed substantial interest in (and sympathy for) these findings and this approach.

From these interviews and subsequent discussions with leading KM gurus, notably the U.K.'s David Gurteen, emerged the concept of PKM. Some of the PKM elements are starting to be used, at least in part and in pilots, in quite a few organizations.

Here's a primer on how some of these elements can be introduced in your organization:

**Personal Productivity Improvement** *(leading practice: Ernst & Young, KPMG)*

1. Pre-interview each employee in the organization to understand their job, what knowledge and technology they use, and how they use it.
2. Pre-assemble a file of possible "leave-behinds"—cheat sheets, step-by-step instructions, FAQs, bookmark lists, and so on that the employee is likely to find useful, based on your previous PPI sessions with others with similar jobs or learning styles.
3. If you don't already have a personal content management program (see later), get this set up for the employee first.
4. Schedule about an hour face-to-face with the employee. The first half-hour should be spent observing and asking questions of the employee to identify significant productivity problems. The second half-hour should be spent *showing* the employee more effective ways of doing their work, stepping them through the leave-behinds, answering questions, and getting feedback from the employee on the value they feel they have received from the session.
5. Compile a list of observations and systemic problems that PPI cannot resolve, and present them to senior management for them to address.

**Personal Content Management**

1. Work with each individual employee to help them organize and index their My Documents and e-mail folders in a way that makes sense for them. A standard firm-wide taxonomy is rarely appropriate and with

current technology it is no longer necessary. Each person's files should be set up the way they would set up their personal filing cabinet if the documents were all hard-copy. Rather than by subject-matter, the most effective organization scheme is often "taskonomic" rather than taxonomic—indexed by how or when it will be (re-)used.

2. Deploy Google Desktop or some other fast, simple, powerful desktop search tool.
3. Use RSS feeds to simplify publishing and subscribing to others' content, and show employees how to use them and how to integrate this content into their personal taxonomy.
4. If you have canvassing and/or harvesting programs (see later), show employees how to use them and how to integrate this content into their personal taxonomy.
5. Develop and disseminate (with simple one-page instructions or FAQs) routines and practices for effectively capturing, filing, and finding relevant knowledge in the context of what it is to be used for.

**Personal Shared Workspaces, Publishing, and Subscription**

1. Educate the project team.
2. Identify the pilot group: There are three constituencies in organizations who will more readily see the benefits of using personal shared workspaces and who are therefore natural pilot groups: (a) subject matter experts who are inundated with requests for information and advice, who could benefit from having their electronic filing cabinet accessible to and browsable by others in the organization, (b) those in the company who are already publishing newsletters and similar regular bulletins, and (c) those who are coordinating community of practice networks.
3. Develop a starting personal "taskonomy" and starting personal content archive for each pilot group member.
4. Select and adapt a commercial Weblogging tool and/or develop your own personal shared workspace tool.
5. Get the IT subteam to convert personal content archives to HTML and bulk publish them, create a personal table of contents (TOC) for each group member, and develop a password protection scheme.

6. Offer everyone in the firm a brief seminar on personal shared workspace publishing and subscribing. Let interest in using these tools spread virally.
7. Talk up personal shared workspaces outside the organization.
8. Set up a personal shared workspace help/monitoring group.

**Automatic Content Harvesting** *(leading practice: Hill & Knowlton)*

1. Create separate public and private My Documents and e-mail folders on each employee's hard drive.
2. Whenever users save or store a document or message, prompt them to decide whether the document should be stored in the public (shareable) or private folder.
3. Establish an automated mechanism like RSS to regularly harvest the public folder information, to a central mirror site that other users can browse, and/or in response to just-in-time canvassing searches (see later), peer-to-peer.
4. Encourage people in the organization who maintain the most valuable context-rich content (e.g., subject matter experts, network coordinators, and newsletter editors) to use personal shared workspaces (discussed earlier) to post and archive their content as part of their public folder.

**Just-in-Time Canvassing, and People-Finders** *(leading practice: Lend Lease Corporation)*

1. Use social network analysis (mapping or interviewing) to identify the *de facto* networks of expertise and trust in the organization.
2. Use these to identify network coordinators, the "people to go to first," on key subject matter areas for your organization.
3. Have these coordinators create, maintain, and publish Canvassing Lists (e-mail groups) with e-mail, IM, phone, and other contact information for the people in these subject matter networks, so that anyone in the firm who wants to canvass people in a network can do so with one click. These lists should include experts outside as well as inside the organization.
4. Create Canvassing Templates, forms that people can fill in quickly and simply to describe what expertise they're looking for, and then send them to one or more Canvassing Lists.
5. Devise a simple one-page instruction sheet/FAQ on how to effectively use the Canvassing Lists and Templates, which communication media can use

in different circumstances to contact them, and how to deal with tele-phone tag, non-responses, and other situations when canvassing response is inadequate. It should also deal with appropriate etiquette and protocols to ensure the canvassing process isn't abused.

6. If you also have an Auto-Harvesting program (discussed earlier), consider putting experts' Weblogs and other context-rich resources in the Canvassing List to use as a surrogate for people who are unable or unwill-ing to respond to canvassing requests personally.

For many organizations, the traditional approach to KM is no longer a viable option. I believe PKM offers a sensible alternative, one that draws on some of the success stories in social networking and some pioneering programs of some of the world's leading knowledge-enabled organizations. It also resonates with the ways in which we have always shared what we know most effectively: through conver-sations; stories; just-in-time inquiries through those we know and trust; learning by watching others; and copying others on documents, messages, and learnings we believe they would find valuable.

This is a *complex system* approach to KM: It respects that things happen in organizations the way they do for a reason, and that people will find workarounds whenever processes, including knowledge processes, work suboptimally. Rather than trying to impose new processes and infrastructure on people, PKM attempts to support and reflect the ways we intuitively learn and share what we do. It adapts technology to people's behavior, rather than forcing behavior to adapt to new technology.

Still, what is missing are more pioneers. Cost reduction, outsourcing, and risk management are the strategic issues of the day in the corner offices of most organ-izations, and improving employees' work effectiveness and the quality of their work are not as high on the priority list. The onus is on us as KM champions to create new, compelling value propositions for KM (and specifically PKM), to pro-duce business models that measure what's important and come up with astonish-ing ROIs for investment in PKM activities, to stress the "cost of not knowing" without scare-mongering, and to continue to do small-scale experiments and share the results of our experiments with each other. That's the only way to get the attention of senior executives, and get them to start investing again.

And this time, once we do get that attention and investment, we'd better learn from past mistakes and do the job right.

# Part II

---

# Knowledge Management Strategy

# Knowledge Management Strategy
## Foreword

Chapter 9, by Boiko, is a very pragmatic and down-to-earth prescriptive on how to derive your knowledge management (KM) strategy. He starts from a very simple proposition: You need to develop strategy statements of the sort "By delivering <information> to <audience> we will be better able to <goal> because <justification>." It sounds simple, and in its fundamentals it is, but Boiko richly develops how that simple notion can be elaborated and developed into a persuasive and successful strategy. It is well worth reading not only by anyone planning to develop KM systems, but by anyone in the field, as KM strategies must be continually developed, justified, and re-justified.

The other three chapters all relate to the relationship between an organization's business strategy and the knowledge strategy or KM strategy that derives from it and supports it. An obvious "should do" for any KM manager or KM professional is to step back and ask, "What is my organization's business strategy, where is my company in its life cycle, and how does my KM strategy relate to and support that? How could the fit be better?" The remaining three chapters all facilitate the asking and the answering of those questions.

Kasten (Chapter 8) presents the results of a study of organizations' knowledge strategies. From the study, he develops a typology of knowledge strategies: Where does your organization's knowledge strategy fit? He observes that an organization's knowledge strategy is typically an emergent phenomenon from its business strategy, not an explicitly derived strategy.

McGrath (Chapter 10) reviews the classical organization and business literature on industry evolution, life cycle parameters, organization theory, and the resource-based view of the firm, and relates it to business KM strategy and particularly to the knowledge conversion mechanisms used at different stages of different organizational evolutions. That obviously leads to the question, "In attempting to support our business strategy, are we addressing the appropriate knowledge conversion mechanisms?"

Simard (Chapter 11) takes the track of thinking about how a modern networked organization should be organized, and from that develops the concept of a "framework" for such organizations. From that descends both a content value chain and a knowledge services value chain, and an accompanying knowledge services framework. This provides another construct against which to check your KM strategy: Where does it fit in? What might you be doing that you aren't doing?

Also, check the Strategy for KM theme in the Roadmap.

# CHAPTER 8

# Knowledge Strategy: The Linkage Between Business Strategy and Knowledge Management

Joseph Kasten
Dowling College

The recognition of knowledge as an asset of the firm has a strong history in the business literature. McNeilly (2002) notes that knowledge of the competitor, knowledge of the customer, and knowledge of the market are all assets that the firm must manage and nurture as they would any other asset. However, knowledge is not like other assets such as raw materials, money, or real estate. Knowledge assets have a level of importance that exceeds that of many other assets. Knowledge exists within a group of assets sometimes referred to as strategic assets. Strategic assets can be defined as those assets controlled by the organization that play a primary role in the achievement of its strategic goals.

We can view knowledge as the set of "assets that can be developed and used to create business value" (Skyrme & Amidon, 1997, p. 180). Beckett, Wainwright, and Bance (2000) go further when they assert that competitive advantage comes from a firm's ability to exploit knowledge. The exploitation of knowledge leads to increased innovation, more and better products and services, and increased abilities to react to changes in the marketplace. However, knowledge does not suffer from the same shortcomings as other assets such as capital or plant and equipment. Because of its characteristics, knowledge, if properly protected, cannot be bought or copied by the competition. It does not expire as patents do, but it must be kept up to date. Also, unlike most other assets, to share knowledge within the organization makes it grow rather than depleting it. Knowledge grows when it is synthesized with other knowledge, thereby making it more valuable when it is spread in a manner that supports the firm's goals.

Organizations often respond to the need to harness and apply knowledge by turning to knowledge management. Knowledge management, like knowledge itself, suffers from a plethora of definitions, each with a specific view of the phenomenon. A well-accepted working definition of knowledge management is a systematic process for creating, acquiring, disseminating, leveraging, and using knowledge to retain competitive advantage and to achieve organizational goals (Nicolas, 2004). A close reading of this very broad definition reveals that it is referring to a set of operational rather than strategic level processes. We have defined a wide range of tools, techniques, and plans that are directed at supporting the organization's strategic goals, but the implication is that the goals are defined external to the knowledge management system. The knowledge management system requires an externally defined strategic direction (Wenger, 2004). However, it is unlikely that an organization's overall business plan will include enough detail to provide sufficient guidance to the knowledge management system's designers. The link that aligns the business strategy and the knowledge management system is the knowledge strategy (Kim, Yu, & Lee, 2003; Maier & Remus, 2003).

The concept of knowledge strategy is a rather new one. Business or corporate strategy has a long history in the literature. Sub-strategies such as human resources strategy and technology strategy have both received growing attention as well. However, only recently (within the last 10 to 15 years) has a stream of research emerged that concentrates on the strategic use of, and planning for, knowledge. Within this stream of research, a range of definitions has emerged for knowledge strategy. For the purposes of this discussion, we can define knowledge strategy as the set of guidelines and beliefs that shape an organization's identification, acquisition, development, management, application, and ultimately the dispersal of organizational knowledge.

Knowledge strategy has a number of characteristics that are important to understand. First, it is directly influenced by the organization's business strategy. In a study in which the knowledge strategies of organizations from various industries were analyzed, Kasten (2006) found a strong relationship between the fundamental strategies followed by the organizations and their strategic treatment of knowledge. This relationship is discussed further in a subsequent section.

The second important characteristic of knowledge strategy is that it rarely exists as an explicit strategic plan. Rather, it is typically of an implicit or, to follow Mintzberg and Waters (1985), emergent nature. By labeling a strategy as emergent, it signifies that there is no formal explication of the particular strategy, but its effects are seen in the operations of the organization. Moreover, if the strategic decisions made by the organization are analyzed in a longitudinal manner, the strategic guidelines will be apparent and can be identified and analyzed just as any explicit strategic plan.

In the study just mentioned, Kasten (2006) used interview and case study data to identify and classify the emergent knowledge strategies of the organizations under study, which resulted in a typology of knowledge strategies. The study involved the analysis of knowledge strategy in the healthcare, banking, financial services, accounting, and insurance industries, as well as a county government. A representative organization from each industry group (two hospitals in the case of the healthcare industry) was analyzed using interviews of top executives. These interviews provided insight into the role played by organizational knowledge in the strategic planning process as well as the methods by which the knowledge assets of the organization are brought to bear on its strategic goals. In addition, these data shed light on the manner in which organizational knowledge needs are developed based upon strategic direction.

Two organizations, a hospital and the financial services firm, were selected for case studies. The case studies involved interviews of additional members of the management team, spread throughout the organization and occupying lower levels of the organizational structure. These case studies provided a perspective on the strategic planning process that created a richer understanding of the role played by knowledge. None of the organizations in the study had developed an explicit knowledge strategy, but by observing the decisions made by upper and middle management regarding the identification, acquisition, development, management, and application of organizational knowledge, Kasten (2006) was able to infer the characteristics of each organization's emergent knowledge strategy. Once identified, these emergent knowledge strategies were analyzed and categorized.

## A KNOWLEDGE STRATEGY TYPOLOGY

During the analysis of the interview and case study data, Kasten (2006) found that a number of dimensions emerged along which the organizations in the study defined their knowledge strategies. Each of these dimensions represents some variable or factor that helps to both categorize the organization's actions with regard to knowledge and allow the prediction and analysis of future knowledge-based operations. There are many of these dimensions hidden within the data, but for the sake of clarity and usefulness, we will consider three that appear to have a great deal of influence upon the success organizations have with their knowledge strategy. These dimensions are labeled as orientation, milieu, and scope.

Before describing these three dimensions, their general character should be discussed in some detail. Each of these dimensions is described by using their endpoints, or extreme values, as the focus. This should not be taken to mean that their possible values are binary in nature. Quite the opposite is true. Each dimension represents a continuum with an infinite number of locations. In fact, none of the organizations in this study occupy the endpoint of any of the dimensions, though their character is located sufficiently close to one of the endpoints as to make them useable as exemplars of the type of organization described.

In addition to the existence of an infinite number of values along each dimension, an organization or components of an organization might also rest in multiple places along that continuum simultaneously. The difference in knowledge strategy between management teams, departments, and individuals manifests itself by the organization's occupation of multiple points on the dimension in question. As the organization fashions a more coherent, articulated knowledge strategy, the number of locations occupied on each dimension will be reduced.

The **orientation** of the knowledge strategy refers to the degree to which an organization is proactive or reactive in its gathering and development of knowledge. Proactive organizations seek to gather and develop knowledge that will help them deal with anticipated changes in their competitive position or chosen marketplace. Examples of proactive knowledge acquisition include the application of knowledge to the analysis of customer data in order to spot changes in demand patterns or the research activities that lead to new product or service introduction. Organizations on this side of the continuum constantly try to use or develop knowledge as a means of creating a competitive advantage for themselves, or in some cases for their clients. Examples of organizations taking a proactive approach to knowledge strategy in this study are the healthcare institutions and the software firm. The hospitals, and especially the healthcare system to which one of them belongs, are constantly trying to locate new and better processes, both clinical- and business-related, that will allow them to offer preeminent care to their patients within the cost constraints of the industry. The software firm's approach to the development of knowledge extends beyond the software industry into the industries of its clients. This extended knowledge allows them to anticipate the changes in those industries and develop software to enable its clients to take advantage of those changes.

Organizations taking a reactive approach to knowledge acquisition and development will prefer to acquire knowledge that helps them cope with the changes around them. Rather than expend resources developing new knowledge in the hope of being able to use it profitably, they will acquire knowledge once they are certain it is necessary and useful. Firms that begin training employees to deal with new regulations only after their announcement are following a reactive knowledge strategy. Firms in this study that appear to be more reactive to knowledge creation are the bank and the accounting firm. The bank and accounting firm are both closely tied to the regulatory machine of the federal government, and as such, they must react to changes in the regulatory structure with new training programs and knowledge repositories for their employees. For these organizations, the acquisition of knowledge is not a path toward competitive advantage but rather a necessary process to ensure survival.

The **milieu** of an organization's knowledge strategy refers to its predisposition to embed knowledge in its people or in its technology. Another way of looking at this dimension is whether the organization stresses tacit or explicit knowledge forms (Koenig, 2004). Tacit knowledge is normally held by the organization's people while explicit knowledge is usually found in either documentation or other embodiments such as software. The reason for stressing the use of technology in this dimension is that all firms in the study used some form of information technology, such as an intranet, to store their explicit organizational knowledge.

Organizations in this study that tend to emphasize the development of the tacit knowledge of their employees include the healthcare institutions, the insurance firm, and the accounting firm. Both healthcare organizations stressed the importance of tacit knowledge for two primary reasons. First, "book knowledge," as one Chief Operating Officer (COO) put it, is not as useful as that knowledge acquired over years of practical experience, especially when dealing with non-standard situations, which is something very common in a hospital. Second, time is often a major consideration in healthcare, and knowledge must be available immediately. There is often no time to look things up in a reference source. The accounting firm stresses tacit knowledge for reasons similar to the healthcare providers, though lives are not at stake. Rather, the well-educated employee is better able to serve customers, much of which is done on the customer's site, making reference material much harder to come by. The appearance of an auditing staff with a strong knowledge of the processes and regulations creates a sense of confidence for the client. The insurance firm uses the tacit knowledge of its employees as an adjunct to the organizational knowledge embedded in the algorithms they use to predict healthcare costs for potential and current client firms. Much of the data collected and analyzed as insurers try to predict their exposure for the upcoming year lends itself to quantitative analysis. However, that analysis must be tempered and adjusted for implicit data, and that requires tacit knowledge borne of many years of experience in this field. In each of these cases, the tacit knowledge of their employees represents the organization's core competency, and the organization depends upon it for their competitive advantage.

Organizations in the study that depend more on their technology to store knowledge include the software firm and the financial services firm. Both of these organizations depend heavily upon intranets, knowledge management systems, and software algorithms to leverage their organizational knowledge. The software firm makes use of its knowledge management system to ensure that all employees have instant access to knowledge regarding its client's business environment and any other knowledge they might need to create new software. The financial services firm depends on computer-based models and algorithms to predict market moves and signal trading preferences for equities and other financial instruments. Each of these organizations depends heavily on information technology to implement its organizational knowledge, but the reader is reminded of the continuous nature of these dimensions. Stockbrokers develop a great deal of tacit knowledge regarding the market over the course of a career and the software developers each have a deep appreciation of their client's needs as they work to develop software for them. Every organization depends on tacit knowledge to operate; no organization envisions a group of automaton employees who only follow explicitly presented rules and procedures. However, the emphasis in these organizations, as reflected by the data gathered in the study, is the embedding of organizational knowledge into the technological, rather than biological, storage devices.

Knowledge **scope** is the last dimension in this typology. It refers to the breadth of topics in which the organization seeks to acquire knowledge. Organizations with a broad scope of knowledge acquisition seek knowledge that goes beyond the realm of their immediate activities. It might include basic research in fields that are complementary to those of the organization in the hopes of finding a synergy. It might also include knowledge acquisition in areas that are not of immediate concern but that might become adjacent lines of business in the future. The underlying commonality of a broad knowledge focus is the future, rather than immediate, benefits of the knowledge. Another reason to maintain a broad knowledge focus is that the nature of the organization does not lend itself to narrow fields of endeavor, but instead requires that a broad knowledge focus be maintained in order to support a wide range of activities.

Each of the organizations in the study follows a much more focused knowledge strategy. Each one focuses on only that knowledge required to either maintain their service level, such as the bank or the accounting firm, or increase their service level, as in the case of the healthcare institutions. For each organization, the span of the focus differs with the breadth of its activities. For example, the financial services firm performs knowledge acquisition on the various activities of its clients and the markets in which they trade. This includes foreign as well as domestic markets, and a very wide range of financial instruments. This is admittedly a very wide area in which to acquire knowledge, but it is still focused only on their current lines of business. Likewise, the focus of the healthcare institution is strictly on health-related matters and the administrative support they require, but it is still focused in that it does not include any knowledge structure they do not deal with directly. The only broad knowledge acquisition knowledge strategy in the study was the county government. This approach to knowledge acquisition is driven by its wide-ranging areas of responsibility to its constituents.

The model representing the typology of knowledge strategies is a $2 \times 2 \times 2$ matrix in which one dimension is the knowledge orientation, the second is the knowledge milieu, and the third is the knowledge scope. There are other dimensions along which we could classify knowledge strategies, but these three in particular capture the essential elements of the knowledge strategies observed in this study. With only the endpoints of each dimension shown, the model is comprised of eight cells, as shown in Figure 8.1. The typology is summarized in Table 8.1.

# RELATIONSHIP OF KNOWLEDGE STRATEGY WITH BUSINESS STRATEGY

The business strategy of each of the organizations in the study was categorized according to the well-known Generic Strategies Model developed by Michael Porter. In addition, they were also assigned to a cell on the Knowledge Strategy typology based upon the characteristics of their knowledge strategy. Once all of the organizations had a place in both models, it was clear that there is indeed a

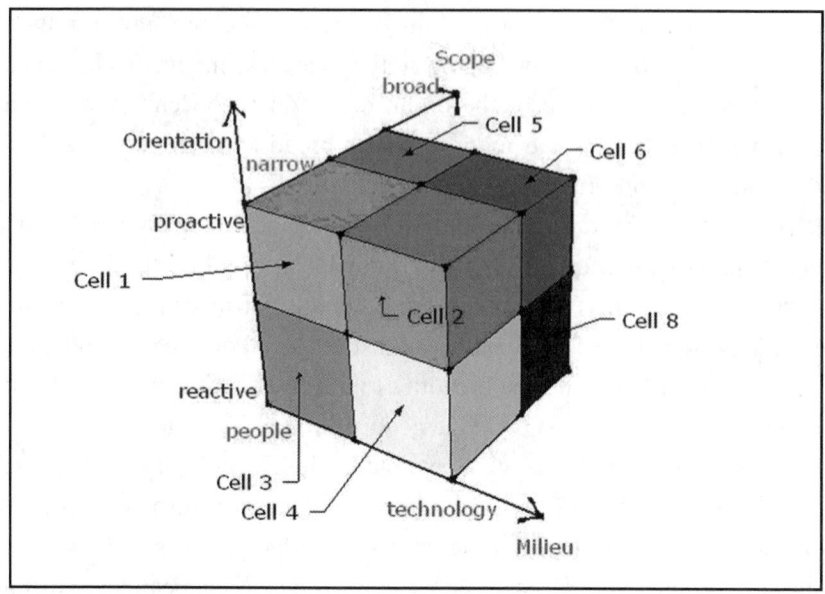

## Figure 8.1  Model of knowledge strategy typology

relationship between the business strategy followed and the manner in which knowledge is addressed. The mapping from Porter's (1985) Generic Strategies Model to the knowledge strategy typology model (Figure 8.1) is summarized in Table 8.2. Organizations occupying the cost leader position in the Generic Strategies model tend to position themselves in either Cell #1 (proactive orientation, people milieu, narrow scope) or Cell #4 (reactive orientation, technology milieu, narrow scope). Organizations battling an unstable competitive environment tend to follow a people-oriented, proactive knowledge strategy. This approach allows them to embed their knowledge in their people, which enables faster reaction time and better service while not having to invest in expensive technology that must be constantly updated. Their proactive orientation allows them to maintain their technical edge but not have to waste money chasing knowledge that is not appropriate or will not improve their operating ability. These are the firms in Cell #1. Those in a more stable environment allow the organizational knowledge to reside in the technology because updates are much less frequent and costly. They find it appropriate to allow other organizations to take the development risks surrounding the creation of new knowledge and knowledge instruments, hence their location in Cell #4.

## Table 8.1  Summary of knowledge strategy typologies

|             | Cell 1    | Cell 2    | Cell 3   | Cell 4   | Cell 5    | Cell 6    | Cell 7   | Cell 8   |
|-------------|-----------|-----------|----------|----------|-----------|-----------|----------|----------|
| **Milieu**      | people    | tech      | people   | tech     | people    | tech      | people   | tech     |
| **Orientation** | proactive | proactive | reactive | reactive | proactive | proactive | reactive | reactive |
| **Scope**       | narrow    | narrow    | narrow   | narrow   | broad     | broad     | broad    | broad    |

## Table 8.2  Mapping between Porter's generic strategies and KS typology

| Generic Strategy | Knowledge Strategy Cell |
|------------------|--------------------------|
| Cost Leader | Cell #1 (proactive, people, narrow) |
|  | Cell #4 (reactive, technology, narrow) |
| Product Leader | Cell #2 (proactive, technology, narrow) |
|  | Cell #3 (reactive, people, narrow) |

Those firms using their product or service to differentiate themselves (Product Leader) tend to map to either Cell #2 (proactive orientation, technology milieu, narrow scope) or Cell #3 (reactive orientation, people milieu, narrow scope). Again, those organizations operating within an unstable environment use their proactive orientation to combat the rapid changes in knowledge required to operate effectively but allow their technology to carry most of the knowledge burden due to its complexity and the requirement that it be available throughout the firm, and they occupy Cell #2 of the matrix. Those within a more stable environment depend on their people to apply their knowledge as a means of differentiating themselves and rely on the stability of their industry to adopt a more reactive stance toward knowledge development and acquisition, putting their knowledge strategy in Cell #3.

# CONCLUSION

An organization's business strategy should form the foundation for the development of its sub-strategies, such as its technology, human resources, and knowledge strategies. Likewise, an organization's knowledge strategy should form the basis for the creation of tools and processes that support the use of knowledge to pursue its strategic goals. In the case of knowledge management tools, the methods of gathering, managing, and applying knowledge should be aligned with the organization's business strategy, and this alignment can be achieved by using the characteristics of its knowledge strategy as design aids as the functionality of the system is developed. By doing so, we can encourage the development of KM tools that support the use of knowledge best suited to the organization, its people, and its mission.

# References

Beckett, Alan J., Wainwright, Charles E. R., & Bance, David. (2000). Knowledge management: Strategy or software? *Management Decision*, *38*(9): 601.

Kasten, Joseph. (2006). *Knowledge strategy drivers: An exploratory study*. Unpublished doctoral dissertation. Long Island University.

Kim, Young-Gul, Yu, Sung-Ho, & Lee, Jang-Hwan. (2003). Knowledge strategy planning: Methodology and case. *Expert Systems with Applications*, *24*: 295–307.

Koenig, Michael E. D. (2004). Knowledge management strategy: Codification versus personalization (a false dichotomy). In Michael E. D. Koenig & T. Kanti Srikantaiah (Eds.), *Knowledge management: Lessons learned*. Medford, NJ: Information Today.

Maier, Ronald, & Remus, Ulrich. (2003). Implementing process-oriented knowledge management strategies. *Journal of Knowledge Management*, *7*(4): 62–74.

McNeilly, Mark. (2002). Gathering information for strategic decisions, routinely. *Strategy & Leadership*, *30*(5): 29–34.

Mintzberg, H., & Waters, J. (1985). Of strategies, deliberate and emergent. *Strategic Management Journal*, *6*: 257–272.

Nicolas, Rolland. (2004). Knowledge management impacts on decision making process. *Journal of Knowledge Management*, *8*(1): 20–31.

Porter, Michael E. (1985). *Competitive advantage: Creating and sustaining superior performance*. New York: Free Press.

Skyrme, David, & Amidon, Debra M. (1997). *Creating the knowledge-based business*. London: Business Intelligence, Ltd.

Wenger, Etienne. (2004). Knowledge management as a doughnut: Shaping your knowledge strategy through communities of practice. *Ivey Business Journal*, January/February 1–8.

# CHAPTER 9

# You Want Systems But You Need Strategy

Bob Boiko

Metatorial Services Inc.

*To do knowledge, content, document, or any other kind of management well, you must be able and willing to form simple propositions about what information should do for your organization. You must also be willing to reiterate your propositions over and over again. At some point, every conversation needs to come back to one of your propositions about what information could be doing for the organization.*

Strategy is dead center of the universe for an information leader. A clear, simple sense of what information could be doing for your organization is the most important tool in your belt. The Chief Information Officer (CIO) of a healthcare institution might believe that an educated (read information-consuming) customer base will be healthier. A retailer might believe that if customers knew about their great deals they would surely buy more. The CIO of a world aid organization might contend that if potential donors only knew, they would surely give, and if leaders only knew, they would surely change policy. Whatever the sector, whatever the focus, the leader must have a firm idea of what value information brings.

Even from simple propositions like these, all the details of information management practice can grow like the roots and branches of a tree. The proposition spreads roots to tap into more and more of the information implied by the proposition. It grows branches to deliver information to more and more of the people implied by the proposition. The healthcare proposition, for example, needs roots into more and more sources of good information on healthy living. It needs to branch out to more and more customers whose health is in jeopardy. Like a tree, at every point in its life the information management system is self-supporting; the roots are always sufficient to support and feed the branches. Information should not be collected if it will not be delivered. The branches provide the energy to grow the whole system; the gains from the information your system already provides should justify continued investment into the further growth of the system.

If you want to make information really work in your organization, you must be able and willing to make simple, intuitively obvious propositions about information value, and you must be willing to reiterate your propositions over and over again. At some point, every conversation needs to come back to one of your simple propositions.

"So how does this system you are proposing make our customers healthier?" the healthcare CIO might ask.

An overall information strategy results from an interlocking set of these simple propositions backed by carefully staged plans that operationalize the propositions. To begin, merely answer this question: What information do we have to deliver to which types of people to most significantly impact the goals of our organization?

If you can manage to come up with a good answer to this question, you will have all you need to lead both your team and executive teams. If you can prove that the impact on goals is profound, then you have all you need to lead your organization's board as well. As your team proposes and executes projects, you can use your answers to this question to assure that they do the right thing. As your executive team proposes and executes enterprise strategy, you can use your answers to advise and lead them. Better still, based on your strategy, you can go beyond simply supporting the plans of others and begin to directly address goals and drive the organization forward.

As obvious as this concept of strategy seems to me, it continually astounds me how few organizational, departmental, or even project managers begin from this premise. Instead, they begin way downstream at the point where strategy should already have been firmly established. For example, here is the sort of discussion I have had far too many times with potential clients:

**Me**: What can I help with?

**Them**: Help us choose a system.

**Me**: I can do that. Do you have a good set of requirements for the system?

**Them**: We have talked to users and have a pretty long list. We also want to see what the systems can do before formalizing our requirements.

**Me**: Hmm … What sort of executive support do you have?

**Them**: He's the one who told us to build the system.

**Me**: Did he say why you needed to build this system.

**Them**: I think it has come up over and over again at his meetings and he finally needs to do something about it.

**Me**: Hmmm … So how does this system fit into your organizational strategy?

**Them**: I'm not sure what you mean.

**Me**: Well, what goals is it helping you meet.

**Them**: Oh, why are we doing it? Well, customers have been complaining that they can't find information. Plus, the old system is a mess, it is too hard to use so people don't contribute. Mostly, we just have too much information. We are drowning in it. We figure we can save some money and make our lives a lot easier with a new system.

**Me**: Hmm … How about audiences? I mean users. Who are the people who most need to get information from your system?

**Them**: It could be anyone really. We have all sorts of people who need information.

**Me**: Hmm … What kinds of information do you think they need?

**Them**: Oh, all sorts. It's all over the place, really. That's why we need a system.

**Me**: Hmm … Okay, how will you deliver all the information to all the people?

**Them**: It will be a Web site.

**Me**: Of course.

**Them**: Actually, if you could just tell us what system to buy, we could skip a big selection process and get right on to implementation.

So, what is going on here? First, as best I can, let me climb into the head of the client. She is being hit from all angles: too much information, contributors unwilling to contribute, unhappy audiences, and a boss who wants something done. She knows there are products out there that say they fix all that, but she is wary. She knows that some products are better than others. They are expensive and she wants to make the right choice. It's as simple as that.

Now let's look at the conversation from my perspective. The client is jumping into the middle of the process. Selecting a system is about half way between concept and system roll out. Before selection comes planning, after selection comes implementation. So, the first part of the process is done, or she prefers not to do it, or she doesn't know it needs to be done. I walk through the strategy questions that define the first phase of the project: Goals, audiences, and information. The client does not seem to have established any of these three to the extent needed to either decide if the project should be done or what project success should be based on. But then why should she have figured these things out? Her boss already told her the solution. There is no strategy to inform projects or systems. All anyone sees is the enormity of the information and their inability to manage it. I throw in the question about delivery on the off chance that "a Web site" will not be the immediate answer, but that she might have some further ideas about how to get information to people.

There is no one to blame here; at least not unless the project fails (which it probably will). But if there were a way to apportion blame, much of it would go to the boss. The boss has issued a directive without a solid idea of why. There is no wider strategy to which the project responds, or if there is, it has not been shared with my client. In the rush to build something, the groundwork needed to know what success is has been overlooked.

So, what is success and what does delivering information have to do with it? Success is different for every organization. For some, it means more profit, for others, social change. Government organizations want to pass and execute laws and educational institutions want students to come and learn. In any organization, there are scores of implicit and explicit goals that define and drive them. Anything that helps the organization advance toward its goals is valuable, and worth pursuing. Inasmuch as information can advance your organization toward its goals, it is valuable and worth pursuing. Given that everyone gets the preceding idea and all agree that that information is valuable, it's surprising how hard it is for most people to say exactly what that value is.

Clearly, you can calculate the cost of an item of information to your organization if you have bothered to keep track of its creation or acquisition process. The item took a certain amount of handling time, which can be equated to cost. It may have required the purchase of software and hardware, so a portion of this capital expenditure can be assigned to the cost of the information. It may have required training and other support costs, all of which can be apportioned to the pieces of information you create. So, theoretically, the cost of information can be calculated, but probably you are not organized enough to do so. Think about that. Any manufacturing organization that took such a casual attitude toward its product would soon be out of business. It is a fair measure of how young the information age is that we pay so little attention to the very asset upon which our economy is supposedly based.

Whether or not we are also in the information age, we are clearly in the industrial age. We take it for granted that we have to know the cost of production for our material goods. More importantly, we have no problem assessing the value of those same goods. Subtract the cost from the value and you know immediately if the good is worth producing. You perform valuation on material goods all the time. When you walk into a grocery store, you enter armed with a vast knowledge of what food "should" cost. You can compare two food items and decide if they are the same or different. Having determined that they are the same, you can decide if one is worth more than the other. Then you can look at the two prices and decide which to buy.

When we are confronted with two pieces of information, the situation is quite different. Except in limited situations, we have no knowledge that allows us to assess the value of each item (and we often don't even know what an item is!). We do not have enough knowledge to decide what to buy. Worse still, in most situations, we expect not to have to pay at all for information. What kind of information age is it when we think that most information is not worth paying for? How can we ever start doing information management based on value if we have no idea of the value of information? We have to find some way to measure information value.

Simply stated, an item (or, more generally, a type) of information is more valuable if it gets you further or faster toward your goals. A good strategy gives you the data to make this calculation. A type that serves more important goals and audiences is more valuable than one that serves fewer goals and audiences.

The units of value in this system are not necessarily dollars, so they can't always be directly subtracted from costs. Still, a strategy can provide a practical and flexible way to assign value and drive business justifications for the projects that you do.

Maybe someday we will be able to say that one article, report, or service description is worth three dollars while another is only worth two, but for today, I think we have to be satisfied with less specific measures. In particular, we will have to be satisfied with a relative value. You are asking too much right now if you try to put a dollar value on an item of information. You are not asking too much if you instead ask if one type of information is more valuable or less valuable than another. If you follow the methodology I propose for coming to a strategy, you will have all you need not only to consistently use information to serve your organization, but also to begin to look at information in the same terms your peers have been looking at other assets (money and hardware for example).

# MAKE STRATEGY STATEMENTS

Strategy Statements link the three most important information management elements. I created the idea of Strategy Statements to try and boil information management down to simple memorable statements of the form:

By delivering <information> to <audience> we will be better able to <goal> because <justification>

Each Strategy Statement describes one inarguably good thing you can do with your information. This Strategy Statement is no more than a restatement of the question that I base all strategy on: What information do we have to deliver to which types of people to significantly impact the goals of our organization? The crucial differences are:

- In the Strategy Statement there are slots for named goals, audiences, and information. You have to be specific.
- A short justification is required. Simply stating that there is a relationship between delivering information and meeting goals is not as good as proving it.
- There can be any number of these Strategy Statements. There can also be sub-Strategy Statements that further refine and extend the more general statements.

With a little work, these simple statements can form the basis of a comprehensive information strategy. Forming a short, sharp statement about what to do is a great way to get clarity for yourself. Armed with a crisp statement, you can begin to win over others. As you explore the terrain of statements that are undeniably true, they begin to connect. The same ideas come up again and again. As you go even further, the simple statements begin to form a comprehensive landscape and you are on your way to an information strategy.

Strategy Statements are a powerful tool. With one Strategy Statement, you can design a convincing business case for a project. With a comprehensive set of Strategy Statements that spans your most important goals and audiences, you have a basis for a full information strategy. If a proposal can't be related to a Strategy Statement then either you need a new Strategy Statement or the proposal is not justified.

You can build a strategy from an interconnected set of Strategy Statements that cover all the most important goals of your organization. They state, as specifically as possible, how information delivered to people can help you meet your goals. This method is deceptively simple. You just list a set of goals, decide what people are needed to meet those goals, and then decide what information will encourage them to help you meet your goal. The first difficulty comes in naming and organizing all the goals, audiences, and information types. The real difficulty comes in making a simple justification that intuitively links audiences and information to a goal. The final hurdle is getting those around you to behave in accordance with what your formulation states.

In an ideal world, you would have the entire organization participating in the creation of Strategy Statements. In the real world, you may have to begin alone. I hope you can at least recruit some of your more enlightened staff to help you. When you get comfortable with the process, you might also begin to draw in some of your peers. The nice thing about the Strategy Statements is that they can be done on the back of a napkin by someone who knows nothing about information management.

As a general process, you might follow these broad steps:

1. **Play first**. Before getting serious, be sure to just try out the process on a lot of napkins and whiteboards.
2. **Make a high-level pass**. Before working through to a complete analysis, work at a global level. Choose big, easy to understand goals, well known audiences, and clearly important information (for example, "By delivering compliance documentation to regulators we can keep our CEO out of jail").
3. **Revise iteratively**. Make multiple passes through the analysis, each time deepening it one level and interrelating your statements.

When you finally get down to the lowest level of details, the result should be an efficient system of highly interconnected Strategy Statements. At each iteration, pit your own ideas and analysis against the best wisdom of key people in your organization and think hard about how to synthesize the two.

# A Sample Strategy Statement

In Table 9.1, I have listed a part of the Strategy Statement analysis that Allied Financial Systems (AFS) might have done.

### Table 9.1  Audience information

| Goal | Audience | Information |
|------|----------|-------------|
| Establish more relationships | Customers | Industry backgrounders |
| Establish more relationships | Customers | Layman product descriptions |
| Establish more relationships | Customers | Staff profiles |
| Establish more relationships | Customers | Competition smack-downs |
| Establish more relationships | Customers | Questions and answers |

The Strategy Statements you might derive from this analysis are as follows:

- By delivering Industry Backgrounders to Customers we will establish more relationships. The backgrounders will help the customer sort out what they want from us, focus their questions, and establish our credibility.
- By delivering Layman Product Descriptions to Customers we will establish more relationships. The descriptions will help the customer sort out what they want from us, focus their questions, and establish our credibility.
- By delivering Staff Profiles to Customers we will establish more relationships. The profiles will help them get comfortable with their sales person and choose an analyst with whom they can bond.
- By delivering Competition Smack-Downs to Customers we will establish more relationships. The smack-downs will help customers decide in favor of us over the competition.
- By delivering Questions and Answers to Customers we will establish more relationships. They will help move customers past their confused state and onto the ability to commit.

Establishing more customer relationships is something that AFS wants to accomplish. This goal happens to be part of a wider goal of national expansion. You can imagine that there are other sub-goals that also support this larger goal. Also, there may be other larger goals that the goal of more customer relationships supports as well (raising revenue, for example). At any rate, the information leader has decided to focus on this goal because he suspects that information can help AFS reach it.

Customers are obviously critical to getting AFS to this goal. The customers have to want to establish the relationships or they will not happen. So how do you get potential customers to want to start a relationship? According to the Strategy Statement, if customers feel "safe, comfortable, and well served from the first interaction," they will begin more relationships. That is not the only way to get customers to engage, but it is clearly one way. Very importantly, the logic here is simple: If customers feel comfortable, they will engage. If the leader finds other ways to get customers to engage, he can form other Strategy Statements. Similarly, if different kinds of customers have different triggers for engaging, then the leader can break this broad audience category into smaller ones, all with their own Strategy Statements.

The kinds of information listed should all contribute to making customers feel safer, more comfortable, and well served. If they do contribute, then these types of information will also contribute to the larger goal of forming more relationships. When you break information into types and give each type a memorable name, an interesting thing happens. Rather than thinking about information as a continuous undifferentiated mass (like when you say "we need to supply customers with comforting information"), the names force you to think very specifically about information. It turns information into different kinds of objects that you can imagine creating, storing, and delivering. Naming types is the first big step to making information manageable.

For each row in Table 9.1, one Strategy Statement is listed. Here, too, the logic should be simple.

By delivering Staff Profiles to Customers we will establish more relationships. The profiles will help them get comfortable with their sales person and choose an analyst with whom they can bond.

The argument should sound straightforward and reasonable on its face. Others in the organization may agree or disagree with it, but they cannot fail to understand it. In the usual course of events, there should be lots of debate about the efficacy of this Strategy Statement. People can argue with the logic, or they can argue that there are information types that would better meet the goal. Those are arguments you want to have. By putting forward a Strategy Statement with a simple and immediately graspable logic, you have provided just the right forum for debate. Whatever Strategy Statement emerges from the debate will also have to be just as understandable and reasonable. Spend less time assuring that your first Strategy Statements are right and more time assuring that they frame the coming debate in a productive way.

In the end, the Strategy Statements you turn into strategy should be true and important. Their logic should be unassailable and their impact on the goal should be significant. You should be able to take the information types specified in the Strategy Statements and begin to build the process and technology for delivering them to the audience. You should be able to quantify the types. What is a Staff Profile composed of? How many will we need to create? How often do they change?

The Strategy Statement also takes you to the heart of the rhetoric of information as well as its type. Rhetoric is persuasion. Making customers feel more comfortable is an act of persuasion. The content of a Staff Profile, not simply the delivery of it, is what will persuade. So in addition to the easy questions about "who" and "how much," you need to start asking the much harder questions about the arguments, credibility, context, narrative, and style. Even something as seemingly data-like as a staff profile is essentially a persuasive communication.

Of course, information management can't do everything. No matter how persuasive the information you deliver is, customers may remain uncomfortable for reasons beyond your control. If the attitude of the sales person, the press AFS has received, comments from the competition, or a thousand other factors make the customer fearful, then all the persuasive information you deliver will be regarded as so much propaganda. You can't control these outside factors, but you can consider them. Ask "what outside factors might render our information less valuable?" If you think that there is a fair chance of those outside factors intervening, then maybe you should choose another type of information that is more immune to these factors.

One small goal matched with one audience yielded five Strategy Statements. Clearly, there are a lot of Strategy Statements needed to fully elaborate your strategy. Once again, information management shows itself to be a lot of work. You can cut this work down drastically by making sure to surface a small set of audiences and information types that impact the largest set of goals. Do a good job on your Strategy Statements to create the tools to contain the explosion of information in the rest of your organization.

# A Simple Strategy Statement Exercise

You can make the process of generating and linking Strategy Statements as official as you want. You can assign project management, canvass widely for input, and have stakeholder "smack-down" sessions where you work together through to the final product. Regardless of how official or casual your process is, however, actually generating Strategy Statements can be fairly simple. In this section I'll walk you though that process. You can use it to do Strategy Statements yourself or do them jointly with a small group. You can also show the process to a wide range of people, let them all use it, and then collect, collate, and review the results.

## Find Goals

To begin, simply list the top three goals of your organization, along with a justification for why this goal is important enough to make your list, in Table 9.2.

### Table 9.2  Goal and justification table

|    | Goal | Justification |
|----|------|---------------|
| 1. |      |               |
| 2. |      |               |
| 3. |      |               |

Before you go on, pause for a moment. Do you fully understand and embrace these goals? If you don't really understand them, now is a good time to get with the executive program and find out all you can about these drivers. If you don't support one or more of these goals, maybe you should choose others to work on that you do support. And, of course, the big question to ask yourself is:

Do you really think that information can get you closer to any of these goals?

If information can get you closer, how much closer? Remember that whatever you do will probably cost a lot of money, so the impact you make on a goal had better be significant. If you don't know whether information can impact these goals, keep going. By the end of this exercise, you should at least be able to come up with something to start with.

## Relate Goals to Audiences

From the three goals you came up with, choose one to continue on with. Use the one that you feel can be best advanced by delivering information to particular people. You may not think of your customers, members, employees, constituents, or users as audiences, but don't worry about that right now. Look back at your top goal and decide on three types of people that are most pivotal to your organization meeting this goal. List these in Table 9.3.

### Table 9.3  Audience and justification table

|   | Audience | Justification |
|---|----------|---------------|
| 1. |  |  |
| 2. |  |  |
| 3. |  |  |

As with the goals, give each audience a good name and a justification that states how they support your goal. Try to put yourself in their shoes and decide what actions or thoughts on their part will get you closer to your goal. This last column is important. Think hard and be sure you understand this relationship. For the purposes of this exercise, these people are means to your ends (but not outside this exercise please). In the next step, you will decide what information to give them based on how you think they can help you reach your goal. For now, think about what you want them to think, believe, or do to help you reach your goal.

At this point in the exercise you have decided upon the people who are most pivotal to the success of your organization. These may not be the ones you ultimately end up serving information to, but they are definitely the ones you want to serve if possible. Now, take a hard look. Can you move these people with information? If not, go on to other audiences or maybe even other goals. Are there so few of them that you are better off giving them a call rather than building them a system? If so, go on to other audiences. If you are still lost, and have no idea if or how information can move these people to think or do what you need them to, you have one more section to figure it out. But first go back to what you want them to do or think. What does that have to do with information? On the other hand, I'm hoping that some light bulbs are beginning to appear over your head. I'm hoping that you are already seeing some obvious connections between goals and audiences that are mediated by information.

## Relate Goals and Audiences to Information

Up until now in the exercise, you could have been doing a marketing exercise. But you are not doing marketing, you are doing information. To finish the exercise, take the number one audience for the number one goal and decide on three types of information you can deliver to them in order to help (persuade, provide incentives, etc.) them help you meet your goal. List these in Table 9.4.

### Table 9.4 Information and justification table

|    | Information | Justification |
|----|-------------|---------------|
| 1. |             |               |
| 2. |             |               |
| 3. |             |               |

As always, be careful to choose a good name. This name may be a bit harder than the others if you are not used to naming information types. Try to avoid saying "Information about …" Give it a try and be prepared to work your names over a few times before they are ready to be used in conversation.

The justification here should follow naturally from the justification you created for how the audience impacts your goal. For example, suppose the goal is a national expansion, and single women are key because you expect them to be the first adopters of your services. Figure out what information will help them be those first adopters and why the information type you chose particularly will do that.

Try to come up with justifications that are so obvious that no one in your organization could possibly disagree. If you can't create such a simple justification, reconsider this information type or even the audience or goal that led you to it. The value of this exercise lies precisely in the simplicity of your logic. If you can't find at least one goal and audience that is incontrovertibly served by information, how will you ever justify an entire strategy?

## The Finished Strategy Statements

You should now have all you need to make three pithy, powerful statements about what your information management systems should do in the form:

> By delivering <information> to <audience> we will be better able to <goal> because <reason>

Review your completed strategy statements and ask yourself if they hang together. Are you convinced that if you could somehow deliver these sorts of information to these sorts of people your organization would necessarily move a significant distance forward toward the goal? What further support for this argument would you need to make the case unassailable? The way I designed the exercise, whatever you come out with should be important enough to do, but stop and consider. If it came to pass that these people got your information and did what you wanted, how big of a deal would it be for your organization?

Next ask yourself how understandable the statement is. Would someone get it at a first hearing? Is the vocabulary unfamiliar? Do you need to have some background knowledge before you could fathom the relationships you have made? Try saying the Strategy Statement to a few people and see how they respond. Work with the language to increase the lucidity and impact of the statement.

Finally, ask yourself how doable this Strategy Statement is. Can you clearly envision collecting this sort of information and getting it in a usable form to the audiences? If your Strategy Statement makes it past all these barriers, it is ready to be used as is, or interrelated with other Strategy Statements to form a complete strategy.

In this exercise, you have crafted three strategy statements for one goal and one audience. With all three goals and all three audiences times three information types, you could have as many as 27 Strategy Statements at your fingertips. I think you can see both the great potential of this method as well as the challenge of keeping it under control. Of course, many of the Strategy Statements you come up with will not pan out. Other Strategy Statements, however, will present themselves as you think of new goals, audiences, and information types. But for now, you should be happy to have at least three rock solid, understandable, sound, and doable strategy statements.

I'm hoping that by doing this short exercise, you have gotten a good taste for what it means to lead information. The Strategy Statements you arrived at are a clear expression of three important things your organization should do with information. Anyone who comes to you with a reasonable proposal for how to turn this strategy statement into a working system should be welcomed. Anyone who comes to you with a different project proposal should be prepared to back it up with reasoning at least this strong. When your boss asks you what you are doing and why you belong at the strategic level of the enterprise, you can trot out these and other statements that show first, that you know how to think strategically, and second, that you have specific and important ideas of how to make information central to the success of your organization.

## FLESH-OUT YOUR STRATEGY STATEMENTS

As mentioned earlier, in an ideal world, you would have the entire organization participating in the creation of Strategy Statements. In the real world, you may have to begin alone. I hope you can at least recruit some of your more enlightened staff to help you. When you get comfortable with the process, you might also begin to draw in some of your peers. The nice thing about the Strategy Statements is that they can be done on the back of a napkin by someone who knows nothing about information management.

Again, to review, as a general process, you might follow these broad steps:

1. **Play first**. Before getting serious, be sure to just try out the process on a lot of napkins and whiteboards.
2. **Make a high-level pass**. Before working through to a complete analysis, work at a global level. Choose big, easy to understand goals, well known audiences, and clearly important information (for example, "By delivering compliance documentation to regulators we can keep our CEO out of jail").
3. **Revise iteratively**. Make multiple passes through the analysis, each time deepening it one level and interrelating your statements.

When you finally get down to the lowest level of details, the result should be an efficient system of highly interconnected Strategy Statements. At each iteration, pit your own ideas and analysis against the best wisdom of key people in your organization and think hard about how to synthesize the two.

A simple way to position yourself between enterprise strategy on one side and projects on the other is to own the organization's information problems. Projects lead to systems that solve those problems. To be acceptable, a project has to address one or more identified problems.

If you have done significant work on a strategy then you know the range of problems that you are here to solve. In my strategy, that range includes goals, audiences, and information types. These three factors form a sort of three-dimensional space of the problems that are in need of solution, as Figure 9.1 shows.

Goals, audiences, and information form a three-dimensional space into which your projects ought to fall.

You can imagine your goals listed on the vertical axis with the most important ones higher up. Similarly your audiences and information can be listed on the other two axes with more important ones further to the right and further into the page respectively. One goal, audience, and information type (what I call a Strategy Statement) is one point in this space. Projects cover some number of Strategy Statements and so are bigger than single points. Eventually, you would like to cover the entire space. Existing systems cover some of the space. New projects must lead to systems that cover the rest of the space. Systems that overlap in the information dimension need to integrate somehow so they can share the information. Systems that share audiences need to be unified in their audience

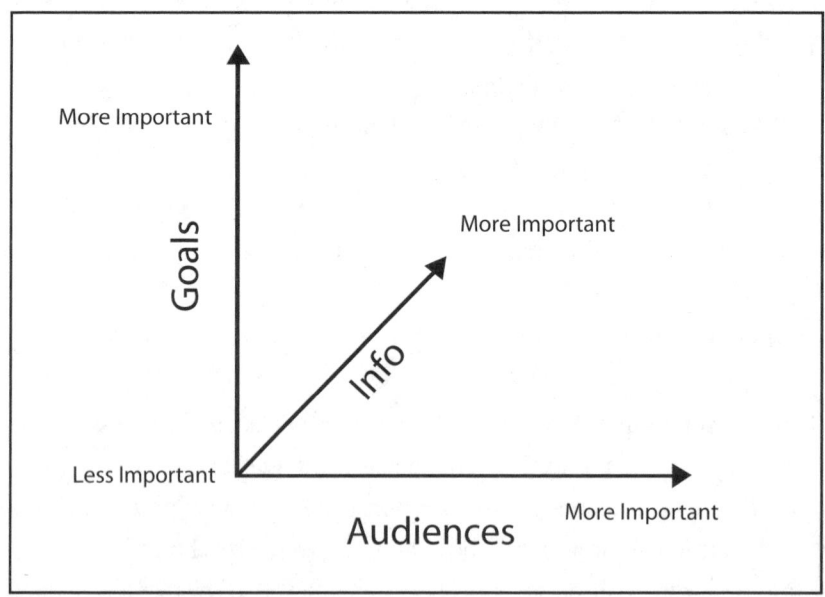

Figure 9.1  Problem space

approach. Systems that share both information and audiences may very well be redundant.

A high-value system covers a lot of the high-value space, as Figure 9.2 shows.

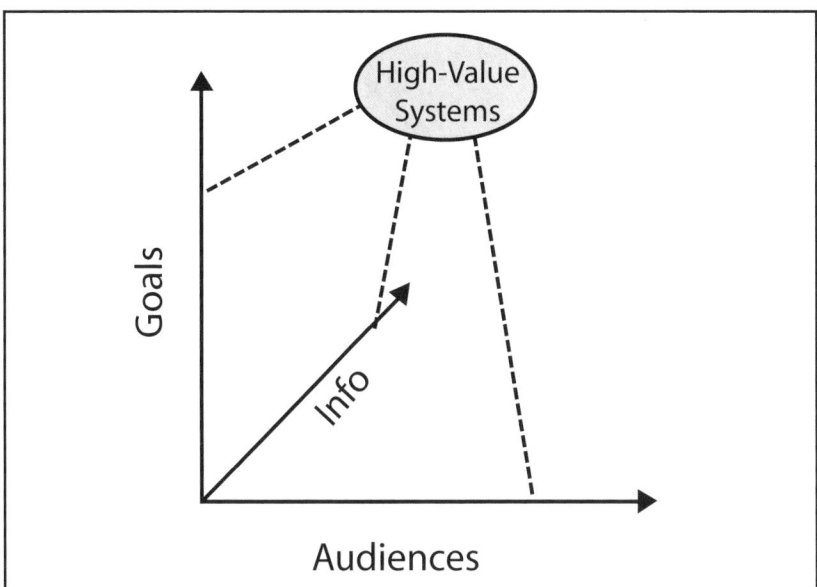

**Figure 9.2 Problem space, high value**

High value systems serve high priority goals, audiences, and information.

The system delivers high-value information to important people in order to meet key goals. All systems do not have to occupy this space to be worth doing, but the closer they come to this area, the more resources they should command. Systems with lower value are still worth doing as long as they cover some of the space, as shown in Figure 9.3.

Low value systems serve low priority goals, audiences, and information.

Systems that are not worth doing don't cover any of the space.

This way of looking at systems helps you decide what sorts of projects most need to be accomplished and how much of your resources they should command. For example, maybe you have large blank areas of the problem space with no project proposals pending and other parts that are crowded with proposals. What can you do to encourage projects in the blank areas?

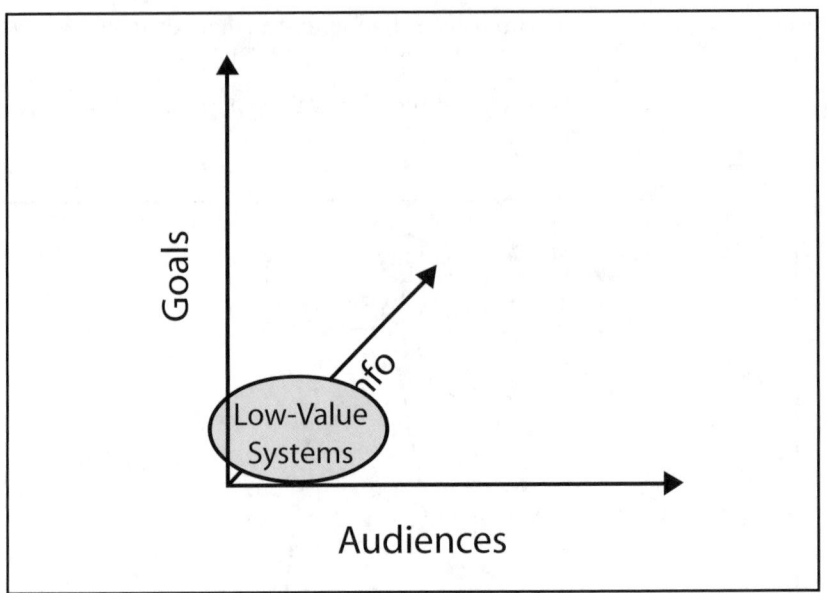

**Figure 9.3 Problem space, low value**

Or maybe you have one project that seems to be covering all the space (external Web sites are often a good example). Is there a way to break this unwieldy project into smaller ones, each with a more contained problem? Or maybe you have a predominance of projects in the low value range and need to increase their impact on goals. If you chart your projects in this way all sorts of possibilities will present themselves.

## Play First

Go through the Strategy Statement exercise quickly a few times. Form only one Strategy Statement. It does not have to be the most important goal or audience, it just has to make sense and be clearly worth doing. Jot on napkins and envelopes to show that you are just playing. Don't get committed to the answers you come up with at these early stages.

Then, do a lot of brainstorming. Try getting out a lot of Strategy Statements without worrying too much about how to relate them all or how important each one is. See how far across the goals and audiences you can make it.

Revise your understanding of goals, audiences, and information. After working through Strategy Statements for a while, you should come to know just how much or little you really know about the goals, audiences, and information of your organization. After you have a good set of Strategy Statements on the table, but before you begin to solidify them, take a break. Go back and look hard at the three players in their own terms. Work up an outline of goals and validate it with your peers. Form an outline of audiences and compare it with what your marketing, public relations, or corporate communications groups think. Find out what types of information your various editorial groups manage now. As you do this work, you will be refining your understanding and finding the people who get what you are talking about. You will need both.

Go out then, and find some of these people. Engage them in a general conversation about the relation of information to goals. Try getting them to do a back-of-the-envelope Strategy Statement of their own. I recommend that you do not show them your Strategy Statements. Whether you like it or not, the act of showing and discussing your Strategy Statements so soon in your process will cause you to commit emotionally to them more than is wise at the moment. More than anything, you want to identify collaborators and make friends. You want to open a career-long conversation with them about information management.

## Make a High-Level Pass

Try to construct a small handful of clearly important global Strategy Statements that talk in broad terms. Concentrate on the goals as you do this. You should have a good outline of organizational goals at this point, so you should be pretty confident that you know what the most important ones are and how they divide into sub-goals. At the end of this exercise you should have no more than a few Strategy Statements for each goal. Don't kill yourself trying to come up with a Strategy Statement for tough goals. A goal without a Strategy Statement indicates that you believe that information management can do nothing significant at this time to advance the goal. Choose broad audience and information categories without worrying too much about how vague and undefined they might be.

Next, begin to drill down the goal outline you created. Starting with the sub-goal that is most important or most supports the parent goal, create a Strategy Statement. The audiences and information you choose for these sub-Strategy Statements should be related to those you chose for the parent Strategy Statement, but should also come from the analysis you did on audiences and information. Don't be afraid to rename and rearrange your information types and audiences to get this all to fit together. What is most important is that it does fit together, not that you stick to what you came up with first. Drill down by goal priority until you either get exhausted or start to feel that you are making up audiences and information types that no one else knows about.

Take naming seriously. Take your time coming up with names and don't be afraid to change them as you go along. The names you choose need to be short, memorable, immediately understandable, and maybe just a bit controversial (to give them relevance and interest). For example, the goal "Win Big at the National Level" is better than the goal "Expand market share per marketing projections across the continental U.S."

Finally, go back again to the organization. At this point you should have a collection of quite a few loosely interrelated Strategy Statements. I can't say how many without seeing your goal hierarchy, but more than a few dozen at any rate. They should share audiences and information types to some extent, but you will work on that more later. It is time now to go back to the organization and validate your work. Find the people who know about the goals, audiences, and information types you have come up with and talk to them. Don't try to convince them that your Strategy Statements are "right." Rather, have your Strategy Statements in the back of your mind as you ask them about the relationships between people, information, and getting to goals. Be most sensitive to the language they use. More often than not you should adopt their terms and throw away your own. If they seem lost for a name, offer but don't impose yours. You are not there to convince them but to engage them in your world and get them to contribute. With this attitude, I guarantee that the next time you come to them they will be happy to work more with you. When you are done, you should have had a number of great conversations, collected a great many ideas, and significantly changed your way of looking at your Strategy Statements.

## Revise and Interrelate the Strategy Statements

With a lot of background information from your discussions with people in the know and a lot of your own good thinking in the form of a set of preliminary Strategy Statements, you are finally ready to get down to business. You might begin by revising the words of your Strategy Statements to meet the words your organization uses. On one hand, you want to be sure that your Strategy Statements are immediately understandable and convincing. Use their words to make sure this is the case. On the other hand, you probably know things now that others do not. You have likely come up with just the right name for an information type that may or may not exist. You may have split audiences in a new way that makes great sense. Your challenge is to choose words that teach others what you know while also reinforcing what those others already know.

So task #1 is to find the right language in which to state your Strategy Statements. Intertwined with this language edit, you must also combine and solidly interrelate the Strategy Statements themselves. The key here is to find the minimum number of information types and audiences that will span all your Strategy Statements. Look for audiences that could easily be combined because they share all the same information types. Look for information types that are essentially the same or are unnecessary (the information type "Document" is a great example of a type that can be portioned out to other types). Lump and split audiences and information types to create a more streamlined system.

It is likely that you have little ability to change the goals of the organization (although you may very well have some good ideas at this point). You likely have somewhat more ability to modify the way your organization looks at audiences. Your biggest competitor for defining audiences will be the marketing folks (in whatever department they live in your organization). If you have worked with them already then you should know what the trouble areas are. However, they will deal almost exclusively with external audiences. Your audiences will span internal, partner, and external audiences. So listen to marketing but understand that your needs are broader than theirs.

You may have the most ability to influence information types. For one thing, few people will oppose your choices. For another thing, your Strategy Statements are themselves strong arguments for why a certain type of information needs to be produced.

Do the work to make a consistent system, but don't go too far. The set of Strategy Statements you create will continue to be mashed around for all eternity. Stop when you are basically satisfied and leave plenty of room (and emotional openness) for others to put their stamp on your work. Also, don't fall into the trap that your professional staff finds themselves in. Don't get so enamored by the "beauty" of the Strategy Statement system that you lose track of the very practical reason you are creating this system. The information architect must ask herself "is this tag necessary." Even though it makes her architecture more complete and takes more uses into account, if people can't or won't populate the tag later, it does not belong. You must ask yourself "is this Strategy Statement necessary."

Even though it may complete the system or fill a perfect niche, if you can't use it to drive projects, it does not belong.

When you are done with this phase, you will have the smallest set of Strategy Statements that cover the largest number of the most important goals. You will have immersed yourself deeply in the strategic use of information and you will have all you need to articulate a very strong information strategy.

If you want, you can go back around the loop again, revising and validating your approach, but you don't have to. You will inevitably be forced back around the loop many times on many Strategy Statements as you try to get them to drive real decisions.

## Go Top-Down and Bottom-Up

To be sure your strategy is right, you need to drive it from both directions. The Strategy Statements and information audit methods I describe have a basic top-down skeleton onto which substance can be added from the bottom-up. The top-down skeleton works from goals of the organization to the information (and later the information systems) that you need. The bottom-up substance you can add to this skeleton includes:

- **Input from stakeholders:** People at every level of the organization can tell you about goals, audiences, and information. The advice you get from the audience-facing staff is often the best you will receive.
- **Review of systems:** Systems now in place might be serving an important information type to important people. What do these systems tell you about the wider strategy you should pursue?
- **Competitive analysis:** What sorts of information and audiences are other organizations working with? If you spend some time looking at your peers or competitors, you add validation and depth to your strategy analysis.

If your strategy is to succeed, it will need to integrate the ideas you derive logically from goals with the ideas that bubble up from the large base of people and other organizations you will come in contact with. If your organization is ready, you can take the next step and drive the strategy process out of your team and into the rest of the organization. Just like budgets percolate up and down through the organization, matching local needs to global realities, your information strategy can do the same. Unfortunately, few organizations are really ready to do strategy on this scale. Until then, you can make sure that your team gets input from above and below as it builds a viable strategy.

# Turn Your Statements into Strategy

You have created strong taxonomies of the most important goals, audiences, and information types. Each has been named and defined so that anyone can understand and hopefully remember what it is. You related goals, audiences, and information types to themselves in outlines. Your goals outline, for example, shows how main or high-level goals are divided and subdivided.

Now it's time to establish the relationships between all these three entities to form a full set of Strategy Statements. Your overall goal is to find the smallest set of audiences and information types that span the widest set of goals. In addition to simply stating that a particular goal can be served by delivering information to an audience, you will have to support the statement with a strong convincing argument.

That's a lot. In fact it is all you need to create a comprehensive strategy for how to get information to work for your organization. The Strategy Statements themselves are also great touchstones for projects and proposals. Each endeavor you pursue has to impact one or more of the Strategy Statements or, by the very definition of the Strategy Statements, it is not worth doing. However, it is not the end, but the beginning of your strategy. The statements provide the motivation for information management but say nothing about how to implement it.

## What Your Strategy Must Accomplish

Still, the strategy you make the Strategy Statements into has to do a few more things. In particular, it has to:

- **Definitively define**: The strategy needs first and foremost to frame the organizational debate over information and its management. By definitively defining audiences and information (and to some extent goals as well) the strategy sets the agenda for any future debate over who gets what information and why. Of course, the strategy can only do this if it is understood and accepted.
- **Prioritize**: The strategy has to state which goals are best served by information. In so doing, it also states which audiences and information are most important. Important information and audiences should receive more attention than less important ones. I'll leave it to you to decide exactly how quantitative you want to be in setting these priorities. But one

way or another, you have to be able to assign relative importance, and thus value for the audiences and information you serve.

- **Communicate out**: The strategy must present a strong and clear approach to the organization at large. It has to clearly say what the IT group will be doing and why. It should clearly reference and relate to the strategies of other departments. If the goals in your analysis are the same as those in other groups' analyses, this should be easy to establish. What might be a bit more difficult to establish is how your methods of meeting these goals will mesh with the methods other groups will use.
- **Establish the terms of engagement**: Your strategy sets the terms upon which you want to interact with other units in the organization. If the other unit wants to engage on an issue that is covered in the strategy, they should have a willing ear in your group.
- **Communicate in**: The strategy must present a strong and clear set of guiding principles for your group. It should be able to serve as an arbiter for discussions about information management projects and be the "Rule of Law" that people appeal to in arguing for or against a proposition. In addition, it should serve as the basis for building business cases and establishing the value of an approach or project.
- **Found further work**: The strategy is simply a statement of what you want to have happen. If it is based on Strategy Statements, it should be able to suggest and stand behind all your further ideas for how to make all this good stuff actually happen.

## Present Your Statements

Depending on your audience, your strategy should take different forms. For an executive audience, it needs to be concise and high level; for peer groups, it needs to be detailed for goals, audiences, and information they are concerned with and high level for everything else. For your team, it needs to be detailed across the board.

The most detailed presentation of the strategy is, of course, the long list of Strategy Statements. If you add priorities to this list, you will have a great reference for your team and the groups you work with. If you add goal, audience, and information type outlines and definitions, your group will have all it needs. Your group can cite the proper terms and arguments in discussions with each other and establish the relative merits of different proposals. If you deliver this large and highly interconnected information base in a way that's easy to navigate and re-use, you will do a lot to make it *the* standard resource for project specification and justification.

The less detailed view of the Strategy Statements, of course, requires a bit more work. Here are a few approaches you might take:

- **Combine outlines**: The style I illustrate shows one way to concisely relate goals and audiences. It is compact enough to show a lot of goals and audiences but detailed enough that you can directly read it. It gets a bit unwieldy if you try to add information to it as well, but it can be done. In fact, you can merge any of your outlines at any level. For example, you might find it useful to create an audience/information outline where information types appear under the audiences and sub-audiences you have defined. Or, you can create an information/goals outline where goals appear under the various information types you have concocted.

- **Summarize branches**: You might try listing only the top branches of your goals, audiences, and information outlines. This is not always so easy because the high-level goals often do not map to high-level audiences and information. You might also try creating Strategy Statements at the high levels of the goals outline and summarizing the lower branches.

- **Graphics**: Flowcharts, mind-maps, and other charts that show the connections between goals, audiences, and information can really help communicate. A large wall chart that shows the complete sets of all interrelated entities is a great way to see the whole context all at once (it is also a great way to impress everyone with how complete and organized you are).

- **Scenarios and use cases:** A scenario is a story that charts a typical audience member's use of your information. Use cases are a more technical and formalized approach to the same idea. Both methods walk a person from a state of information need to a state of information satisfaction. What you would add to the story in your strategy is the steps after information satisfaction where the audience member goes on to do what you want them to, and the final step where your organization clicks one notch closer to its goal. Unconvincing arguments that can successfully hide in the Strategy Statement often stand out like bad actors in a scenario.

- **Personas**: Personas are composites of an audience profile that humanizes the profile, makes it more memorable, and knits it into a coherent person.

In the strategy, your personas can "flesh-out" your audience distinctions and more importantly present a convincing argument for why this sort of person can reasonably be expected to behave in the way you have said they would.

Using these methods, and others I'm sure you can think of, you can render the base of information you have collected into a variety of understandable and compelling forms for your team, your partners, and your peers. If all of this is starting to look like the beginning of an information system all its own, you are on the right track. Your strategy is less a particular publication than a system that collects information about strategy from various authors, stores and organizes it in some repository, and then publishes it out through a number of different channels into a number of different publications for a number of different audiences.

## Present Context

The Strategy Statements you create are the heart of your strategy. But you will need to draw some conclusions and general implications from the Strategy Statements to put flesh around that heart. Here are some types of context-giving implications you might want to consider:

- **Create principles**: You can elevate certain key Strategy Statements to principles. For example, noticing that customer fear and confusion comes up over and over again in the Strategy Statements, you might create the principle that "customer-facing information must use only layman's terms." You can also elevate justifications. For example, you might notice that building credibility is a key justification that comes up again and again, leading to the principle that customer-facing information must be reviewed for credibility arguments before it is made public.
- **What are the organizational implications**? What sorts of organizational changes are implied by your Strategy Statements? Should one group's capacity to create information be increased? Should other groups be merged? Should your own group change staffing, or its position in the organization chart? Be careful not to go too far advocating change before you are sure that the arguments your Strategy Statements make for them are accepted.
- **What are the systems and technology implications**? You can hold back the technology questions only so long. People will want to know what all this strategy has to do with software and hardware. They will want to

know the implications for their favorite systems or venders and they will want to know how it affects their job. By the time the strategy hits the organization, you will have to be able to at least address these concerns.

- **What are the information implications**? Before the strategy, the organization produced whatever information it produced with little methodical connection to its value. After the strategy you know exactly what information you should be producing and what sorts you have little reason to produce. How will you affect this transition? Believe me, it won't be easy.

You will not know the full implications of your new organizational strategy until you begin to put together the details of your departmental strategy and tactics. So I would advise being calculatedly vague about specific implications. Focus instead, on the large-scale and general changes that your analysis entails.

# Putting Strategy to Action

A fleshed out and well-presented strategy can drive the rest of the information management you do. In this section, I'd like to briefly describe some of the issues you might want to consider as you roll your strategy out to your organization.

If you have not engaged a range of influential people in the process of forming the strategy, you will now regret it. You will need the support of these people to make the strategy stick. If you don't have them on your side, you will now need to explain your process to them and get them to look seriously at your results. You may prefer to get tacit acceptance from them rather than a lot of proposed changes, but the proposed changes are better. They signal that the influential people have really engaged with your strategy and will (hopefully) make it a better strategy.

In addition to the allies you want to win among the influencers in your organization, you should have a set of natural allies at your disposal. As you developed the strategy, you will have talked to any number of people at all levels of the organization who understood and supported what you were doing. Also, you should be able to figure out which people will gain a lot from the implementation of your strategy. For example, if it turns out that delivering product support information to a wider audience is very important, the product support group might contain some strong allies of your strategy.

First, you need to establish who you need to support you, and then you need to get them to do so. You might also take into account anyone who is likely to oppose or (more likely) ignore you. Then, you will be ready to plan how to include them in the roll-out of your strategy.

Roll-out includes these concerns:

- **How much hoopla**? Should you launch your strategy with a big bang or let it simply become a fait accompli? Even if you have a lot of support, you might consider staying a little "low-key" if this is your first run at a strategy or if previous strategies have failed. On the other hand, if you are ready for an information management takeover maybe a big splash is just the launch you need.

- **How do you get the strategy understood**? If you have done a good job on your Strategy Statements, they will sell themselves. However, they will only sell themselves if you can get people to pay attention long enough to consider them. How will you raise the issue of an information strategy, and get people to understand that it is worth their attention? Given their attention, what will you do to hold it long enough for your ideas to sink in?

- **How do you get the strategy ensconced**? The strategy you put in place is just the beginning of an ongoing process of review, update, and use of the strategy. How will you institutionalize the strategy process so that it becomes a natural part of the life of your organization?

- **How do you push out ownership**? The next time you go through the strategy process, how will it be less your job than it was the first time? Who should take a more active role and how will you get them to commit now, when the energy around the current strategy is at its maximum?

- **What are the project sweet spots**? With luck, there are at least a few places where the information management planets have aligned to create a great opportunity. Find the groups that are ready and willing to produce the information types that some audiences really need to push a goal. Find a simple way to package and deliver some of those types for delivery through an existing channel and publication. See if you can't put together a quick turn-around project to snatch this low hanging fruit early in the strategy roll-out process.

- **How will you transition**? You were doing information management in some way before the strategy. After the strategy this way is likely to change. How will you stage this transition? How will you begin to divert resources to new and existing projects that deserve them? How will you put the sacred cows out to pasture? How will you retool your own team and the teams they work with to meet the new strategy?

Finally and most importantly, a strategy is just the beginning of the story for your group. You will need to plan now for how to turn your organization-level strategy into a department-level strategy and then how to turn the department strategy into tactics for making information management real.

# CHAPTER 10

# Knowledge Management in Strategic Context

Robert N. McGrath

University of Maryland University College

## INTRODUCTION

Strategy is an abused term; Knowledge Managers should understand strategy in proper theoretical context in order to practice it. This chapter views Knowledge Management in the context of organizational strategy and structure in business settings.

Driven by economic, market, technological, and other forces that are well understood, industries and organizations tend to evolve from stages of early dynamism to later stages of sclerosis. Aside from managing the day-to-day aspects of a "chaotic" climate, it is imperative for strategic managers to understand the larger, long-term evolutionary patterns of their environments. They must understand where the industry is heading so that they can position the firm for the future.

An important part of strategic positioning is to understand that as environments evolve, so must organizational structure. It is romantic to consider that strategic managers should "take hold" of a situation and shape the environment to their wishes, but this chapter assumes the more typical opposite. Managers must first ensure that their organizations are structured appropriately for the present environment, then are flexible enough to not only adapt to change, but also to proactively morph so that organizational change occurs in synch with environmental change.

Since organizational structure has such a dramatic impact on the nature and flow of information, the implications for Knowledge Management are straightforward. Environmental evolution, organizational evolution, and knowledge management evolution at the organizational level should be contemporaneous.

Drawing upon Strategic Management and Organization Theory, this chapter details the theory of industry evolution and organizational evolution, integrates the two, and draws implications for knowledge managers. The three patterns of evolution will evolve together one way or the other. It is better to participate knowingly and proactively.

## Industry Evolution

Industries evolve (Grant, 2005; Utterback, 1996). At least, industries change in ways that are not chaotic, in the sense that major forces tend to act and interact in predictable ways at strategic levels of analysis. Not all industries evolve in the same way—very far from it. Theoretically, each industry can, and perhaps does, evolve uniquely. This discussion will center on the prevailing model of industry evolution that forms an important basis of Strategic Management theory and practice.

In our model of the industry life cycle, industries pass through four stages of evolution: introduction, growth, maturity, and decline. There is no necessary length of time for any of these stages, nor the overall industry life cycle. Some industries are more than 100 years old; others come and go in much shorter periods of time. The salient point is that the discussion is addressing the life cycle of an entire industry, and not any single product. This point is important because the well-known product life cycle is characterized by the same four phases. Here we are talking about entire industry life cycles. The term "product" as used here is an all-encompassing term, referring to all products in a product category that circumscribes an industry.

Of course, this begs a clear understanding of what an industry is. An industry can be defined in any of several ways, each suitable to a specific purpose. For present purposes, an industry will be defined as a "group of firms producing products that are close substitutes for each other" (Porter, 1980, p. 5). While no specific industry will be chosen as an example, the model that will be discussed best fits industries that become capital intense and experience economies of scale.

## Life Cycle Parameters

The reason that the Industry Life Cycle is divided into four phases is because, as a rule, each phase is different according to certain parameters. This section

## Table 10.1   Industry life cycle characteristics (Grant, 2005)

|  | Introduction | Growth | Maturity | Decline |
|---|---|---|---|---|
| **Key Success Factor** | Product innovation, brand image | Process innovation, new product development | Efficiencies, scale economies, capacity utilization | Low overheads, commitment |
| **Demand** | Early adopters, price insensitive, technophile | Mass market emerges | Mass market, repeat business; sophisticated, price sensitive | Obsolescence |
| **Technology** | Disparate versions, rapid innovation | Standards, dominant design | Well-diffused, small improvements | Little innovation |
| **Products** | Frequent changes, relatively low quality | Rationalization around standards, quality improves | Commodities, difficult to differentiate | Commodities, difficult to differentiate |
| **Production** | Short runs, high skill content and level | Mass production, supply chains develop | Overcapacity, deskilling, long runs; price competition | Chronic overcapacity |
| **Competition** | Few | New entrants | Shakeouts | Price wars, exit |

briefly discusses how the life cycle evolves in accordance with each parameter, as summarized by Grant (2005) and shown in Table 10.1.

*Market Demand.* In the introduction phase of the industry life cycle, demand is usually driven by "early adopters." This segment tends to be price-insensitive, willing to pay a premium price for products. Importantly, they tend to have an urgent need for a new technology, or a strong desire. Often early adopters are government/military customers, intra-industry customers (B2B), or technophiles (a.k.a. "geeks"). All serving as experimental ground, expansion from this segment to the more price-sensitive mass market denotes transition to the growth phase—growth is often exponential once this breakthrough occurs. As the mass market saturates, the industry matures, a period when consumers are very sophisticated about the product and its producers. Very suddenly in evolutionary terms, growth flattens, leaving the competition scrambling, mostly for repeat business. Product obsolescence marks the decline phase.

*Technology.* In the introduction phase, technology is relatively new and crude; indeed, an industry may be inaugurated by a technological innovation, or "breakthrough." Innovation is not only rapid, but widely disparate; competing technologies may be incompatible with each other. A "winner take all" scenario can especially hold back the mass market, as this type of consumer can be techno-phobic and unwilling to invest in a potentially losing and incompatible design. Eventually a technology standard or "dominant design" emerges around which the remaining players compete, allowing the emergence of the mass market (growth) and refocusing innovation on process improvements. By maturity the technology is well-diffused, and proprietary improvements are difficult. In decline innovation is almost gone.

*Products*. When introduced, products are relatively crude and full of "bugs." There are many efforts to experiment with the right consumer formula. Together with these phenomena, rationalization around standard designs begets rapid industry growth and quality makes great strides. During maturity products tend toward commoditization, meaning that they are difficult to differentiate. Seemingly, every major product innovation that can be tried has been tried. Most failed, commercially speaking. The product is important but unexciting. Competition is based more on price than high performance, which has become an expectation. This intensifies during decline.

*Production*. When introduced, production may be by the unit or in small batches/runs. Labor content is high and highly skilled. Again, in concert with these phenomena, growth is enabled by a transition to mass production/customization. Because so many competitors are racing for market share, chronic overcapacity may occur. Overall industry overcapacity ruins unit cost structures, greatly stressing the competition. Long production runs, deskilling of labor, and obsession with cost denotes maturity. Few players survive even for the decline stage.

*Competition*. As one would expect, there are few competitors when the first products are introduced. Emergence of the mass market lures new entrants, often too many in the sense that not all can survive. Characteristics of maturity cause a series of "shakeouts" and chronic price wars, continuing through the decline phase.

*Key Success Factors*. While all of these factors are highly interrelated and, indeed, recursive in effect, a few key success factors can be identified—those few imperatives that must be the focus of strategy in order to gain or hold an advantage.

In the introduction phase, product innovation is paramount. As corollary, company and brand image must be established in the minds of early adopters—it is always perception in the minds of consumers that is really being sold.

As growth happens and product innovation dwindles to rationalization around the technology standard or dominant design, process innovation and supply chain rationalization become paramount. About as important, however, is the speed of product innovation because once market share is captured, it is fairly easy to defend. Conversely, being first to market with a poor-quality product can be disastrous to brand and company image. This is a time when the mass-market still needs some convincing.

Once convinced, mature consumers demand high quality at low prices, so during this phase, cost efficiencies become paramount through capital and scale intensity, capacity utilization, and low costs of resources.

Decline can be managed by keeping overhead low, careful market niche selection, and sending signals that one intends to stick it out. Those without nerve, leave.

Readers will recognize that as complex as these dynamics can become, the model is still oversimplified. For example, it ignores complications such as regulatory restrictions, world affairs, social and cultural change, macroeconomics, unforeseen shocks, to some degree globalization, and so forth. Also, as opposed to a biological model of evolution or life cycle, not all industries are destined to go into decline and disappear. Many industries rejuvenate, and we understand how managerial action can make that happen. On that note, let us not take the notion of evolution too literally. There is one enormous difference between a biological theory of evolution and the model of industry evolution. In the biological model, each individual creature is essentially doomed to a fate determined by its genetic makeup. In the industry model, where organizations are the creatures in an essentially economic environment, organizations can change their essential natures and adapt. We turn to Organization Theory.

# Organization Theory

There is no single, unifying theory of Strategic Management (Mintzberg, 1994). The field has always been an eclectic amalgam of theories taken from fields such as Industrial-Organization Economics (the previous discussion, for example), Marketing, Organizational Behavior, and Finance, and is adopting ideas from fields such as Chaos Theory. Another important contributor is Organization Theory. In this field, there are models of organization life cycles. Naturally, and borrowing a key idea from Systems Theory, no theory or organization or organization life cycle can

## Table 10.2 Organization life cycle characteristics (Daft, 2005)

|  | Nonbureaucratic | Prebureaucratic | Bureaucratic | Very Bureaucratic |
|---|---|---|---|---|
| **Goal** | Survival | Growth | Stability | Reputation |
| **Structure** | Informal | Some procedures | Division of labor | Small company thinking |
| **Management Style** | Entrepreneurial | Direction-giving | Delegation, control | Team approach |
| **Products** | Single product | Variations | Product line | Multiple lines |
| **Innovation** | Owner-manager | Employees plus managers | Separate group | Institutionalized R&D |

be meaningful without considering the environment at large (Scott, 1992). We will see how industry life cycles and organizational life cycles relate.

There are several models of organizational life cycles, and most are similar to that shown in Table 10.2. Viewed in isolation from the environment at large, it implies an evolution that is driven by increasing organizational size. The view here, however, is that the phases of the organizational life cycle may be seen as adaptations to environmental change. The four phases of the organizational life cycle correlate well with the four phases of the industry life cycle, with an important exception: The organizational life cycle does not presume decline—quite the opposite. It presumes a fourth phase where the downside of bureaucracy is addressed through management techniques that attempt a return to many of the benefits of small-company characteristics and attempt to capture the best of both organizational types. It is probably true that such techniques are partly accountable for the rejuvenation of many industries, an ironic reshaping of the environment by those that live in it.

In the introduction phase of the industry life cycle, everything is new and untested, and the future is uncertain except perhaps in the broad strokes painted earlier. Organizations, too, are new and therefore small, often being created by an entrepreneur who is himself/herself the creative genius. Organizations are properly unstructured, informal, and staff is highly dependent on the boss. Visionary leadership and cultural buy-in are keys to simple survival in this treacherous stage.

As the growth phase ensues, imperatives change. Radical product ideas become unnecessary and perhaps counterproductive as product innovation must focus on emerging standards. Processes and time-to-market become more important. As the organization increases in size, some codification of procedures becomes necessary, and management becomes less "entrepreneurial" and more "professional."

At the same time, innovation processes become less dependent on the founder-genius and more diffused at the loci of product line variation.

The transition to industry maturity is a critical time. Rapid growth of the industry has lured many entrants, and existing players have expanded capacity to overly optimistic levels. The resulting industry overcapacity means that some firms will have disastrous unit-cost structures unless they are prepared for the flattening of market demand. Commoditization of the product makes premium pricing very difficult, and in fact competition becomes mainly about price. Cost is king and overall efficiencies and economies drive the organization to the classical model of bureaucracy. Division of labor is clean. Controls are everywhere, especially where it concerns the quality of the product line, which has broadened and may even be "full." By this time innovation may be disassociated from production, being the province of dedicated groups who themselves are not immune from the efficiency imperative.

For several decades, many management scholars and many more practicing managers have not resigned themselves to industry or organizational decline, and have sought ways to reconcile efficiency imperatives with the quest for organizational renewal and industry rejuvenation. This discussion will not address the huge amount that has been written on this subject. But concluding a look at our model, Table 10.2 indicates that team approaches are part of a successful formula. Even in an organization that is diversified in terms of product line, teams (by any of several names and purposes) are a way to re-instill small-company thinking and culture.

Again, it should not be presumed that industry and organizational life cycles coincide. Obviously, hundreds of organizations ordinarily come and go throughout the duration of an entire industry's existence. Many firms never get beyond the entrepreneurial stage. Conversely, a new entrant in any phase of the life cycle is likely to be entrepreneurial. Some organizations are able to grow despite lack of growth industry-wide. A phase of an industry life cycle may be so long that many organizational innovations are tried with varying levels of success. The salient point is that organizational structure should take into account not only current environmental characteristics, but future ones as they evolve. Strategic managers are accountable for being prescient in this regard, to the extent possible.

But strategic managers don't really manage environments. They manage resources.

# Resource-Based View of the Firm

Strategic Management is the quest for sustainable competitive advantage; this term is badly misused in practice. It is one thing to have an advantage in business; it is another to have an advantage that can be defended for strategically meaningful periods of time—usually years.

There are several theoretical frameworks that scholars have developed to understand sustainable competitive advantage. The positioning school reigned during the 1980s, positing that it is imperative for managers to understand their competitive environments and develop an organization that is well-suited to the present and prepared for the future. This is an implication of the earlier discussion about industry evolution.

However, the positioning school fell short of offering a full explanation. One obvious shortcoming was that it treated organizations as "black boxes," in the sense of not thoroughly extending theory to intra-organizational factors. During the 1990s, the Resource-Based View (RBV) of the firm advanced to theoretical prominence, though it is still under theoretical development. As such, there are still slight terminological inconsistencies within the body of RBV scholars. Just one set of terms and definitions will be offered here for the sake of illustration (Barney, 1997) and simplified by the author.

RBV notes that organizations are bundles of resources and competencies. Resources can be either tangible or intangible, and research regularly discovers the particular importance of intangible resources (Hamel & Prahalad, 1990.) A competency resides at a fairly low level of organizational analysis, is human-based, and is something an organization does well. If the competency lies at the heart of the organization's value-creating proposition, it is a core competency. A distinctive competency is one that is done better than the competition. Hopefully core competencies and distinctive competencies are the same, but one can imagine that this is not always the case. Resources and competencies together comprise broad, organization-wide capabilities, the theoretical loci of true sustainable competitive advantage.

But in order for sustainable competitive advantage to occur, capabilities need certain attributes (Barney, 1997). First and at the most basic level, they need to be valuable—enabling the firm to respond to threats and take advantage of opportunities. Second, they need to be rare—not widely held by other competitors. These two attributes are fairly obvious, and minimally necessary even for competitive parity.

Third, they need to be difficult to imitate—more precisely, costly to imitate. For example, imitation might be blocked because of unique historical circumstances. An advantage may be traceable to a path-dependent organizational history that cannot be copied, at least not quickly enough to really matter. Or, imitation may be too costly because of causal ambiguity. The intangibility of some resources plus the tacitness of some competencies may be very difficult for the competition to fully understand, let alone imitate. Similarly, imitation may be too costly because of social complexity, say, because of a deep organizational culture. Finally, a direct inference is that the firm must be properly organized in order to take advantage of its capabilities.

Though RBV is not evolutionary, it is clear that sustainable competitive advantage is difficult to build overnight. Deep and complex organizational culture, intangible resources such as reputation, causally ambiguous and historically rooted competencies, and so forth may take many years to develop and institutionalize. Therefore, while no theoretical integration can be attempted here, it can be suggested that managing an organization from the RBV should take into consideration environmental change. Capabilities that deliver value are rare, difficult to imitate, and properly organized, and should evolve with the nature of the market or prevailing technology, especially as knowledge diffusion (i.e., erosion of competitive advantage) is practically inseparable from evolutionary processes. In fact, knowledge diffusion is a key evolutionary force.

We are left with a key theme of sustainable competitive advantage. From the RBV of the firm, advantage based on intangible resources such as tacit knowledge is generally more defensible than advantage based on tangible resources and codifiable knowledge, which clearly diffuse as industries and organizations evolve (Tidd, Bessant, & Pavitt, 2001). This presents a challenge to Knowledge Managers.

## Knowledge Management

Given the objective of this chapter, a relevant definition of Knowledge Management is "a process for helping an organization continuously build its capabilities to maintain and improve organizational performance" (Kotnour, 1999, pp. 3–27). Let us maintain the strategic view and assume that organizational performance means gaining and sustaining competitive advantage. In this context, the concept of Knowledge Management Strategy becomes much more intriguing. Surely, Knowledge Management Strategy must support overall Business Strategy, and Knowledge Management might be seen as a special case of the RBV (Grant, 1996). "From the viewpoint of organizational knowledge creation, the essence of strategy lies in developing the organizational capability to acquire, create, accumulate and exploit knowledge. The most critical element of corporate strategy is to conceptualize a vision about what kind of knowledge should be developed and to operationalize it into a management system for implementation" (Nonaka & Takeuchi, 1995, p. 74).

Return to the Key Success Factors that were suggested for each of the phases of the industry life cycle—basically and in order: (a) radical product technology innovation, (b) process innovation and new product development around emerging standards, (c) production efficiency and cost management, and (d) either managed decline or organizational renewal. Since these are organizational activities, let us assume that these are also capabilities that can be the basis of competitive advantage. In a dynamic sense, a capability that may be the basis of advantage for one firm at one point in industry evolution (e.g., superb product technology innovation in the introduction phase) may find it is no longer a basis in a later phase (e.g., product technology innovation during maturity when cost is king).

The message is simple. In order for advantage to be sustained and to the extent that industries evolve, it is likely that strategically critical capabilities must change from one type to another, not just be continuously improved. This is especially true in scenarios where knowledge is easily codified and diffused throughout organizations because such knowledge is relatively easy to observe and imitate by other firms.

Applying these definitions of Knowledge Management and Knowledge Management Strategy now implies the need for great care. It is being argued that Strategic Managers and Knowledge Managers must develop joint strategies not only for building capabilities, but simultaneously preparing for evolutionary change. The implied linearity of "creation, assimilation, dissemination, and application of organizational knowledge" needs to take into careful account the type of knowledge assumed and its importance to competitive advantage at any point in time. Codifiable knowledge is a relatively weak basis for competitive advantage, so the basis of competitive advantage often evolves as knowledge diffusion happens industry-wide.

## Table 10.3  Knowledge conversion mechanisms (Nonaka & Takeuchi, 1995)

| From | To | Mechanism |
|---|---|---|
| Tacit | Tacit | Socialization |
| Tacit | Explicit | Externalization |
| Explicit | Tacit | Internalization |
| Explicit | Explicit | Combination |

Nonaka and Takeuchi (1995) proposed a knowledge conversion matrix that has been modified as Table 10.3. It acknowledges four different ways that two different types of knowledge may be converted, one into the other (explicit knowledge is essentially the same as what has been termed codified knowledge). Nonaka proposed a dynamic model of organizational learning where all four conversion mechanisms are used to co-develop ever-increasing organizational and individual learning, but it can also be adapted to illustrate the strategic context where resources, core/distinctive competencies, and capabilities change from one type to another, as discussed.

Table 10.4 combines the essential points made in other figures, and extends it to consider Nonaka and Takeuchi's matrix. It offers one very simple version of how Knowledge Management might co-evolve with an industry and organization. In the introduction phase, when technologies, markets, and products are new and organizations are entrepreneurial, it may be best to manage product technology knowledge with the goal of keeping tacit knowledge tacit, but diffusing it intra-organizationally through socialization processes common to natural ways of communicating in such an environment. The key is shared experiences that develop mental models and technical skills through observation, imitation, and practice. Common examples include apprenticeships and on-the-job training (Nonaka & Takeuchi, 1995).

As the industry and organization near transition to the growth phase, product technology is, practically by definition, diffusing to the growing number of competitors, and in fact becoming standardized. That being the case, the new critical capability becomes process innovation and new product development, meaning that tacit to explicit management of product technology knowledge, through externalization techniques, can be used to begin to institutionalize that knowledge

## Table 10.4 Integrated cycles

|  | Introduction | Growth | Maturity | Beyond |
|---|---|---|---|---|
| **Key Success Factor/ Capability** | Product technology innovation, brand image | Process innovation, new product development | Efficiencies, scale economies, capacity utilization | Decline or rejuvenation |
| **Goal** | Survival | Growth | Stability | Reputation |
| **Structure** | Informal | Some procedures | Division of labor | Small company thinking |
| **Conversion of Product Technology Innovation Capability** | Tacit to tacit | Tacit to explicit | Explicit to explicit | Explicit to tacit |
| **Conversion Mechanism** | Socialization | Externalization | Combination | Internalization |

without losing competitive advantage. It is more important to manage the tacitness of the emerging basis of advantage, to keep it difficult and costly to imitate through the growth phase. Triggered by dialogue or collective reflection, externalization techniques include the use of metaphors, analogies, concepts, hypotheses, and models that help promote reflection and interaction.

As the industry and organization transition to maturity, the strategic argument about product technology asserts that there are no big secrets left, so explicit to explicit mechanisms (combinations) may be used to fully exploit their inherent economies without losing any advantage in product technology because that is now long gone. Even process innovation, key to advantage in the growth phase, is becoming well-diffused and can be made more-or-less safely explicit. The new basis of advantage is cost management, triggered by networking new knowledge and existing knowledge intra-organizationally. Examples of combination techniques include documentation, meetings, conversations, electronic communications, and databases, then reconfiguration through sorting, adding, combining, and categorizing (Nonaka & Takeuchi, 1995).

Finally, in the fourth phase of evolution, explicit to tacit knowledge management (internalization) is loosely offered as a means of organization survival or renewal, as this phase may be characterized by anything from widespread decline to total rejuvenation. Learning by doing triggers internalization; techniques include documentation into manuals and oral stories, where people experience the experiences of others. The idea is to trigger a new spiral of knowledge creation (Nonaka & Takeuchi, 1995).

Certainly, not all industries evolve in the way discussed in this chapter. The model is most relevant to capital intense industries, and many information-age industries do not evolve this way because of the economics of information technologies that are beyond this discussion (Grant, 2005). But we do not have a model of information-age industry evolution that is nearly as well-specified as the classical model. It does not matter for the purposes of this chapter. The point is that industries do change in ways that are not truly chaotic or random from a macro point of view. To the extent that industries do change in foreseeable ways, strategic managers should exercise all available foresight. The basis of sustainable competitive advantage may change predictably, shifting the relative importance of resources, competencies, and capabilities. The relative tacitness vs. explicitness of knowledge can therefore be seen as the basis of Knowledge Management Strategy first and foremost.

## Conclusion

Words like strategy and strategic management are often overused and misapplied, as are terms like sustainable competitive advantage, distinctive competence, and capability. These terms have important theoretical and practical meanings that provide a context for business decisions at other levels of analysis and within constituent business functions. This chapter has suggested how Knowledge Management might better be guided by this context when properly framed. A conclusion drawn from a simple explication of basic Strategic Management theory suggests that if the organizational locus of sustainable competitive advantage changes with environmental change, the focus as well as the nature of a Knowledge Management Strategy may need to shift as well.

## References

Barney, Jay B. (1997). *Gaining and sustaining competitive advantage*. Reading, MA: Addison-Wesley.

Daft, Richard L. (2004). *Organization theory and design*. 8th ed. Mason, OH: Thompson Southwestern.

Grant, Robert M. (1996). Toward a knowledge-based theory of the firm. *Strategic Management Journal, 17*: 109–122.

Grant, Robert M. (2005). *Contemporary strategy analysis*. 5th ed. Malden, MA: Blackwell.

Hamel, Gary, & Prahalad, C. K. (1990). *Competing for the future*. Boston: Harvard Business School Press.

Kotnour, Timothy G. (1999). Knowledge management. In Richard C. Dorf (Ed.), *The technology management handbook* (pp. 3-27–3-31). Boca Raton, FL: CRC Press.

Mintzberg, Henry. (1994). *The rise and fall of strategic planning*. New York: Free Press.

Nonaka, Ikujiro, & Takeuchi, Hirotaka. (1995). *The knowledge-creating company: How Japanese companies create the dynamics of innovation*. New York: Oxford University Press.

Porter, Michael E. (1980). *Competitive strategy*. New York: Free Press.

Scott, W. Richard. (1992). *Organizations: Rational, natural, and open systems*. Englewood Cliffs, NJ: Prentice-Hall.

Tidd, Joe, Bessant, John, & Pavitt, Keith. (2001). *Managing innovation: Integrating technological, market and organizational change*. 2nd ed. Chichester, U.K.: Wiley.

Utterback, James M. (1996). *Mastering the dynamics of innovation*. Boston: Harvard Business School Press.

# CHAPTER 11

# Knowledge Services: The "Why" of Knowledge Management

Albert J. Simard

Natural Resources Canada

## INTRODUCTION

*The traditional hierarchical designs that served the industrial era are not flexible enough to harness the full intellectual capability of an organization. Much less constrained, fluid, networked organizational forms are needed for effective modern decision-making.*

–Debra M. Amidon (1997)

It is generally recognized that science creates new knowledge that increases the standard of living in developed societies. The same can be said for innovation that uses knowledge to develop products that satisfy the wants and needs of consumers. At a grand scale of scientific and technological progress, it can be said that knowledge flows from its source to society. At a scale of knowledge organizations, however, the reality is that some knowledge flows: somehow, somewhere, sometime.

In a knowledge organization, people use systems and processes to generate, manage, and use knowledge to support organizational goals, learning, and adaptation. From this definition, we see that knowledge management (KM) provides a link between generating knowledge and using it and that this is done within the context of achieving organizational goals. Goals specify what a private- or public-sector organization wants to accomplish in relation to its business or mandate, respectively. This chapter is about the business of a knowledge organization—

transferring knowledge-based products and services to clients or citizens through knowledge markets.

Since the invention of writing, information and knowledge have been the lifeblood of organizations. Bartlett (1999) notes that: "Organizations aren't just structure. Structure is just the skeleton. Organizations also have a physiology—the flow of information and knowledge is their life blood—and a psychology, representing people's values and how they think and act." Similarly, Evans and Wurster (1999) point out that: "Fundamentally, information and the mechanisms for delivering it are the glue that holds together the structure of businesses." Buckman (2004) takes the argument even further: "Ever since the first human clan enjoyed the warmth of the first tame fire, it's been true that knowledge shared is knowledge multiplied. The more a group knows of what its members know, the better it can perform in the world." In essence, if the internal flow of information stops, an organization cannot function very well.

From a broader perspective, organizations are systems that exist within the context of their socioeconomic environment. Lynch and Kordis (1988) state: "Open, or living, systems are always exchanging matter or energy with the outside environment." Similarly, Amidon (1997) notes that: "No enterprise is an island—especially in the knowledge economy. … The flow of knowledge must transcend traditional organizational boundaries." Finally, McGee and Prusak (1993) point out that: "In an information economy, organizations compete on the basis of their ability to acquire, manipulate, interpret, and use information effectively. Organizations that master this information competition will be the big winners in the future, while those organizations that don't will be quickly overtaken by their rivals." It is apparent that in both business and government, the consequence of not providing something that markets or society want or need is that the environment will not provide the resources, in the form of profits or a budget that the organization needs to sustain itself.

From these arguments, it is evident that knowledge organizations must do two things well to remain relevant and sustainable: run the organization efficiently and provide knowledge-based products and services to their clients. As with yin and yang, neither is complete nor sufficient without the other. Without satisfied clients, an organization cannot sustain itself, and without an organization, there is no way to provide services that satisfy clients. Yet, in an era of specialization, those who use knowledge to serve clients and those who use other knowledge to run organizations tend not to fully appreciate the importance of nor understand the other side of this inseparable duality. Unless we bridge the gap between knowledge management and an organization's business, KM will remain a "factor of production"—a function that is poorly understood by business leaders, with costs to be minimized. How much better for KM to be viewed as a "strategic investment" in the business—something that should be proportional to the return on that investment.

This chapter presents a framework for managing organizational content (data, information, and knowledge) that addresses and integrates both organizational management and client service. The framework is based on a knowledge-services system model developed by Natural Resources Canada (Simard, Broome, Drury, Haddon, O'Neil, & Pasho, 2006). Although the model is based on government science-based organizations, it should be applicable to a broad range of knowledge organizations in both the public and private sectors.

As noted by Davenport and Prusak (1998), "Although simple answers to complex problems are intuitively appealing due to their apparent clarity, knowing more usually leads to better decisions than knowing less." One finds many seemingly elegant models in the management literature, claiming only five or seven steps to nirvana. Only by drilling down into the details of such models, however, can we be certain of the correctness of their logic and the completeness of their systems. With the service framework described here, the service system upon which it is based ultimately includes enough detail to accurately represent real-world complexity.

The chapter begins by discussing the need for an organizational framework for managing content. It then describes four framework dimensions. This is followed by overviews of how content flows in organizations and through the knowledge services system, from a value-chain perspective. The paper discusses the advantages of a knowledge services approach for managing organizational content, and concludes by outlining an approach to implementation.

# Management Frameworks

*Networks will not replace or supplement hierarchies; rather, the two will be encompassed within a broader conception that embraces both.*
–Stanley M. Davis (1977)

This section explains what a framework is, why an organization needs one, and describes some key attributes of the service framework.

## Definitions

As an emerging concept, I define key terms at the outset to establish a common understanding of the subject as discussed here:

- **Knowledge organization:** An organization in which people use technology and processes to generate, manage, share, use, and transfer knowledge to support organizational goals, learning, and adaptation.
- **Knowledge services:** Programs that produce or provide content-based outputs with embedded value, intended to be used or transferred to meet user wants or needs.
- **Output:** Collective term for content, products, services, or solutions that have been produced and transferred by an organization to satisfy external user wants or needs.
- **Framework:** Structural outline of the essential components of an organization, system, or processes, and the relationships among them.

From these definitions, we see that a knowledge organization produces, uses, and transfers knowledge; knowledge services are the programs through which this is done; output is what is produced, used, and transferred; and a framework is how it all fits together.

## Purpose

A framework is positioned roughly in the middle of a hierarchy of organizational processes that range from why an organization exists to daily work activities. The business processes are: business case, vision, charter, governance, policies, strategy, *framework*, plans, programs, projects, and services. A framework lists everything needed to implement an organizational strategy and describes relationships among the elements. A framework provides an outline for planning how programs, projects, and activities will be undertaken.

The position of a framework in this hierarchy is pivotal. Starting from the top leads to a results-based or demand-driven approach to managing an organization. That is, what business are we in and how do we conduct that business? Starting from the bottom leads to a capacity or supply driven approach. That is, what do we do well and how can we market what we do? Using a cooking analogy, a top-down approach involves deciding what to cook (intended result), finding a recipe that lists the ingredients (the framework), and buying the ingredients (capacity-building). By shopping first, an infinite variety of meals can be prepared. A bottom-up approach involves searching through recipes (the framework) to find a list of ingredients that corresponds to what is available in the pantry (supply) and following the instructions for cooking that meal (plan). One can vary the meal, but the choices are limited by what is available. Returning to our organization, regardless of the management approach, a framework is both central and pivotal.

Frameworks serve a number of organizational roles:

- A framework provides structure in a complex environment. By revealing hidden patterns and functional relationships, a framework helps in understanding complex processes—a necessary precursor to measurement and management.
- A framework shows what the picture looks like. Like a blueprint or architectural drawing, seeing the intended end result, and how individual pieces relate to that result and to each other, helps to organize the many pieces of the management puzzle.
- A framework provides a basis for planning and action. Structure and organization provide a sound basis for selecting an approach, prioritizing work, and planning activities.

## Framework Attributes

Desirable attributes of a service-based framework are:

- **Independence:** The framework should be independent of content, issues, or organization; it should be applicable to any knowledge services.
- **Level:** The framework should be based on a single department or enterprise; mandates, authorities, and resources are tied to legally constituted organizations.
- **Scalability:** The framework should be scalable upward to multiple departments or businesses and downward to specific domains or business lines.
- **Primary driver:** The primary driver should be the departmental mandate or business charter because an organization must first exist and have the means to produce outputs.
- **Secondary driver:** The framework should also respond to user needs for organizational outputs to reflect a demand-driven approach to services.

- **Process:** The framework should be based on use rather than delivery of services to actively lead to outcomes and benefits, rather than passively lead to receipt of outputs.

# FRAMEWORK DIMENSIONS

*To compare and classify the immense variety of shapes, structures, and phenomena around us we cannot take all their features into account, but have to select a few significant ones. Thus we construct an intellectual map of reality in which things are reduced to their general outlines.*

–Fritjof Capra (1975)

A service framework has four dimensions: scale, infrastructure, content, and outputs (Figure 11.1). They are discussed in order of increasing relative importance for our purposes. Each framework dimension is part of all subsequent dimensions. Thus, scale is part of infrastructure, both are part of content, and all three are necessary to manage outputs.

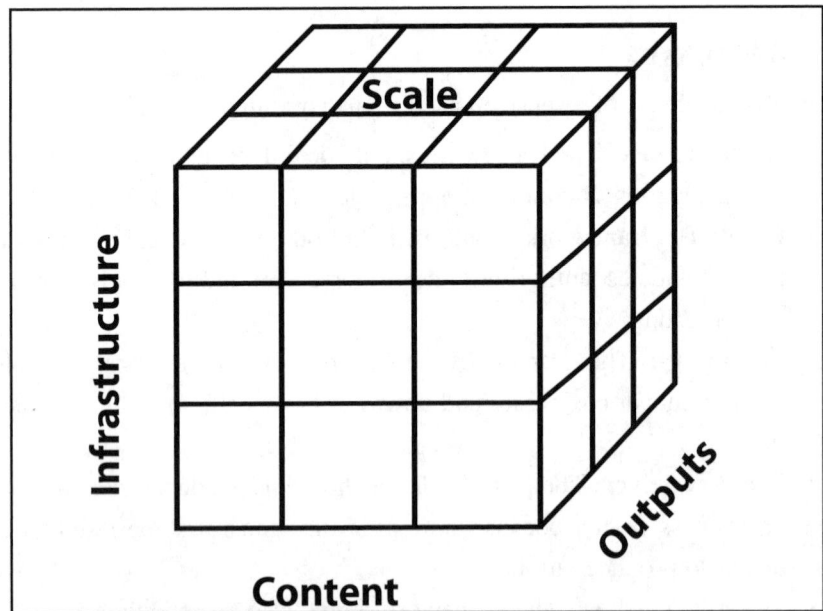

Figure 11.1 Framework dimensions

The four dimensions are defined here and discussed in the remainder of this section:

- **Scale** is the spatial, temporal, process, and organizational magnitude, span, or level of outputs and their intended use.
- **Infrastructure** is the underlying foundation of human resources, organizational management, work processes, and technology that enables an organization to generate, manage, use, and transfer outputs.
- **Content** is the message or signal, with embedded value that is carried by objects, data, information, knowledge, or wisdom. Content is the basic building block or raw material of a knowledge organization.
- **Outputs** are content, products, services, or solutions with embedded value, derived from, dependent on, or in support of content. Simard, et al. (2006) provides a detailed list of definitions and descriptions of outputs for Natural Resources Canada.

## Scale

Scale is ubiquitous. It is everywhere and it affects everything. Yet, scale is often poorly understood, relegated to background status, or omitted entirely in most systems, models, or frameworks. Scale is important as a framework dimension because it is essential that the scale of outputs be similar to that of their intended use. It is also important that the scale of multiple outputs be similar to enable their integration for combined uses. Finally, scale considerations include techniques to integrate outputs and uses across scale boundaries or to differentiate between adjacent scales.

Lack of compatibility between the scale of outputs and uses has a number of consequences. Too much detail wastes time, resources, and effort for both producing and using outputs. Too little detail may conceal processes that are essential to obtaining useful results—a key limitation of simplistic models of "knowledge cycles." Although a transition between adjacent scales may be possible, it is only one way. While integration is generally feasible, differentiation into component parts is often impossible.

If outputs differ by more than one scale class from the intended use, they are unlikely to be usable (Simard, 1992). National-scale outputs are poorly suited to local applications, and vice-versa. Annual averages are of little value when up-to-date statistics or the weather is needed. Global climate-change models tell us little about regional impacts.

There are four aspects of scale: space, time, process, and organization:

- **Space** is the spatial context of outputs and intended uses. It has attributes such as: place (coordinates, place names, relative locations), relative size, magnitude, or extent. Spatial classes are: point, spot, site, area, zone, region, continent, and global.
- **Time** is the temporal context of outputs and intended uses. It has attributes such as when (clock, date, event), duration, interval, and flow (delay, past, present, and future). Temporal classes are: instant, immediate, brief, current, short-term, mid-term, seasonal, and long-term.
- **Process** is the context of the complexity and magnitude of outputs and intended uses. Complexity can be classified as: static, dynamic, flow-through, feedback, learning, reasoning, and goal changing. Magnitude classes are: micro, mechanical, sensory, meso, synoptic, macro, and global.
- **Organization** is the context of the hierarchical and management level of outputs and uses. Although organization is a subset of process, it is identified separately because of its importance to the subject at hand. Hierarchy classes are: society, government, department, sector, branches, programs, projects, and tasks. Management classes are: business case, vision, charter, governance, framework, policies, strategy, and plans.

Although scale is an essential framework dimension, it is more attribute than driver. Thus, although scale is a part of all subsequent dimensions, it is not a candidate for the primary dimension of a framework for a knowledge organization. The next section moves up the framework hierarchy to organizational infrastructure.

## Infrastructure

Infrastructure includes everything needed to manage an organization. That is, infrastructure connects and enables people in an organization, using technology and work processes, to produce content and provide services. It follows, therefore, that a management infrastructure includes four components: people, the organization, technology, and work processes (Figure 11.2). These four exist for the purpose of generating and using content and for providing content-based services.

All components are equally necessary to success. Downplay any one and organizational productivity suffers:

- **People** are persons and groups who perform information and knowledge work. Information and knowledge are human constructs. People create,

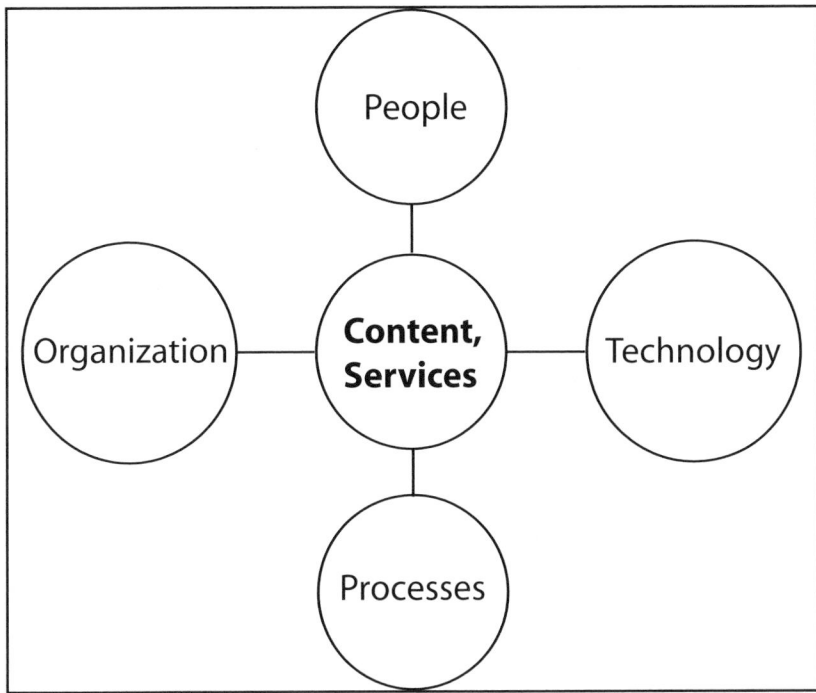

Figure 11.2 Management infrastructure

manage, and use content to accomplish organizational goals. Managing people involves human resource activities, such as staffing, pay, motivation, and evaluation. In knowledge organizations, it also involves expertise, sharing, learning, and adaptation.

- **Organization** is a legally constituted governance, administrative, and functional structure that fulfills its mandate by transforming authority, responsibility, and resources into programs that produce outputs and provide services. Without an organizational structure, nothing else follows.
- **Technology** is the means of production in a knowledge organization. It is impossible to succeed in the information society or the knowledge economy without information and communication technology. Information technology includes: computers, applications, systems, communications, and networks.
- **Process** is the development, implementation, and operation of methods to acquire, organize, preserve, and provide access to content to enable its use or transfer. Process is the way in which information and knowledge work are done.

We will drill one level down into process. As pointed out by Galliers (1987), "Information is both elusive and illusive; [*it is*] difficult to define ... and deceptively easy to underestimate." One difficulty in developing this framework is the lack of a generally accepted vocabulary to aggregate all processes or types of content under a common term or to distinguish between overlapping but different processes or types of content. For example, *Webster's* (Mish, 1991) has nine different definitions for information and 10 for knowledge, some of which are in terms of each other (not to mention data), so that either can mean almost anything. Further, authors frequently interchange terminology, which adds to the confusion. Each type of content and its related processes are defined individually here. Examples are for Natural Resources Canada:

- **Collections** are groups of objects or artifacts that facilitate and support the generation of content. Curators acquire, organize, preserve, and provide access to collections. Collections include: rocks, minerals, fossils, wood samples, insects, plant materials, or diseased tissue.
- **Libraries** are collections of intellectual property. Librarians acquire, organize, preserve, and provide access to their holdings. Intellectual property (IP) includes: books, publications, reports, documents, maps, photographs, images, artwork, and audio or video recordings. Note that libraries may not own IP rights to the material that they hold.
- **Data** are recorded, ordered symbols or signals that carry information and patterns. Data managers acquire, organize, preserve, and provide access to data and data-based products. Data are organized into elements, files, data sets, databases, and statistics (data in context).
- **Information** is meaning and context, arising from processing, interpreting, or translating data to extract an underlying message or pattern. Information managers acquire, organize, preserve, and provide access to information and information-based outputs. Information includes: documents, reports, images, maps, brochures, presentations, or multi-media recordings.
- **Records** are content that is specifically related to organizational management. Records managers acquire, organize, preserve, and provide access to organizational records. Records include data (e.g., finance, personnel, operations), information (decisions, meeting minutes, proposals, reports), and knowledge (e.g., experience, policies, guidelines, contacts).
- **Knowledge** is understanding arising from integration, analysis, or synthesis of data or information to reveal cause and effect relationships that

facilitate the explanation and prediction of natural or social phenomena. Knowledge managers acquire, organize, preserve, and provide access to knowledge and knowledge-based outputs. There are many types of knowledge, including: factual, experience, skill, tacit (mental), and explicit (codified or documented).

It is apparent that each type of content involves similar processes (acquire, organize, preserve, and provide access). This partially explains why there is so much confusion among them. Yet, each process involves specialists who use different management practices and vocabulary. Libraries and collections generally manage physical objects. To use information, one "only" needs to find it, access it, and "read" it. To use data, one must also know its format, codes, and the software that was used to prepare it, as well as be able to extract and manipulate subsets of it. A key aspect of using knowledge is an ability to find and interact with an expert. Records are not simply a subset of information, but include organizational data and knowledge as well.

The four components of an organization's infrastructure all exist to enable or support the management of an organization's content and outputs. It is the similarity of goals rather than functions that unites the processes and requires their coordination. In the final analysis, however, although, managing organizational infrastructure is necessary, it emphasizes "how" an organization does work, rather than "what" work it does or "why" it does it. The bottom line is that clients are not interested in how work is done; rather they are interested in what outputs are produced—the subject of the next section.

## Content

As indicated in the previous section, content includes much more than information. Although some classify data, knowledge, and records as subsets of information, or vice-versa, we have seen that they are generated, managed, and used differently. Therefore, the term content management is preferable to information, knowledge, or records management. Content is essential to managing an organization, and generating it is the first stage of providing services. This section describes content from three perspectives—value chains, flow, and context.

### Value Chains

Content can be described from a value-chain perspective. Value chains are well understood in the private sector as production or distribution channels. They describe a sequence of steps in which inputs are transformed into increasingly refined and higher-value outputs that are eventually sold to consumers. For example, a tree is cut into logs, which are transported to a mill, where they are sawn into rough lumber, which is milled into finished lumber, which is transported to a distributor and then to a retailer, where it is sold to a consumer. Each step in the chain adds value through production or distribution, some of which can be extracted as profit.

A content value chain is the flow of content through a sequence of stages in which its form is changed and its value or utility to users is increased at each stage. From a domain perspective (e.g., subjects, topics, issues, markets), objects are measured to yield data (a signal that is carried); data are interpreted to yield information (meaning in context); information is synthesized to yield knowledge (understanding how things work); and finally wisdom (experience and judgment) leads to the correct application of knowledge (Figure 11.3). Note, however, that value and utility must be viewed in the context of use. For example, a manager who needs knowledge to solve a problem consults an expert rather than collecting data to study the problem. In contrast, information has less value to a scientist because it cannot be disaggregated into its source data that are needed to create new scientific knowledge.

From an organizational perspective, data (e.g., finance, personnel, operations) are transformed into records (e.g., decisions, minutes, reports), which in turn become know-how (e.g., processes, procedures, practices), and, ultimately, experience (e.g., policies, rules, guides). Thus, content value chains apply equally to providing services and to running an organization. Methods are similar for both value chains, even though their drivers differ substantially (Table 11.1).

In general, as content moves "downstream" along the value chain, its value and utility increases. Moving downstream involves knowledge work and associated costs, which reflect increased value of the content produced at each stage (assuming that the inputs and transformation processes are acceptably correct). Thus, the further

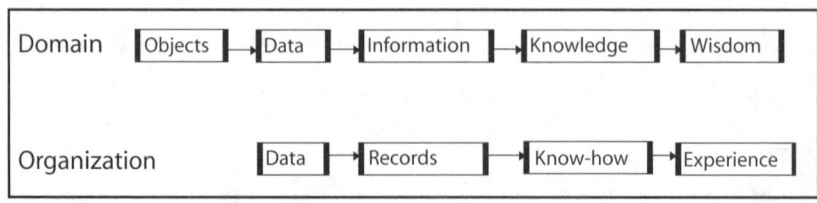

Figure 11.3  Content value chains

**Table 11.1  Comparison of content value-chain drivers for organizations and domain outputs**

| Driver | Organization | Domain Outputs |
|---|---|---|
| Purpose | Run the organization | Fulfill mandate, make a profit |
| Infrastructure | Laws, regulations, policies | Market forces, domain standards |
| Level | Plans, management strategy | Business case, content strategy |
| Focus | Internal needs, efficiency | External needs, effectiveness |
| Evaluation | Audit | Market feedback |

"upstream" one has to move to solve a problem, the greater the cost. Science is an exception to the linear flow portrayed in Figure 11.3, in that scientific knowledge arises from analyzing data and the knowledge is then transformed into information, in the form of publications and reports.

### Flow

The flow of content integrates everything that an organization does. As shown in Figure 11.4, content flows from the executive to the operational level and vice versa. This flow normally takes place through a vertically oriented infrastructure of people in programs (e.g., science, statistics, policy), supported by technology, doing work. Further, two types of content flow through this network—domain-related and organizational records. Finally, content also presumably flows across the organization, as individual programs or production processes add value through different kinds of knowledge work.

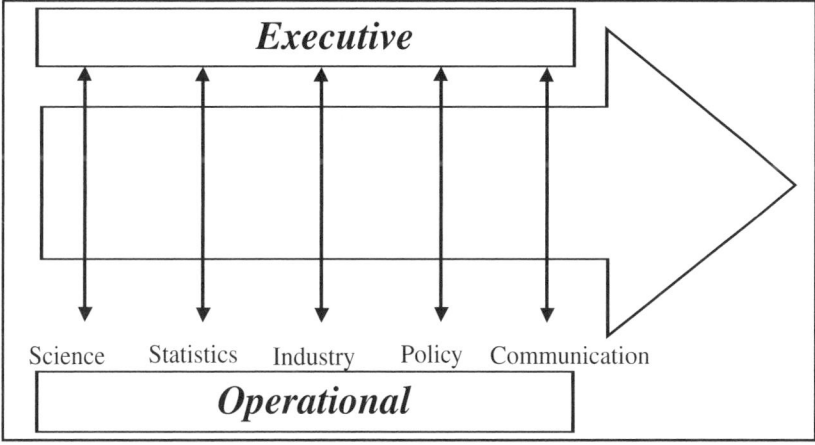

**Figure 11.4  Flow of content in an organization**

## Context

Managing the flow of content is not as simple as it might, at first, appear. There are many considerations that affect government departments and/or businesses. These can be grouped into three categories: rights, strategy, and management:

- **Rights:** Many information "rights" are encoded in law. Citizens have a right to privacy with respect to personal information. Departments have a legal obligation to safeguard information relating to security, while businesses do so for competitive reasons. Citizens have a right to access government information not excluded by the previous rights and obligations. Finally, government policies require that certain standards be followed for all information (e.g., bilingual content, common look and feel, universal accessibility). These rights constrain what can be done and mandate what must be done with information. Further, specific rights may conflict with each other, as in individual privacy versus national security, or when access is limited because the cost of meeting required standards is prohibitive.

- **Strategy:** Delivery strategy relates to an organization's natural or chosen position along a spectrum of content richness. At the rich end of the spectrum, communication involves relatively complex messages transmitted to small, knowledgeable audiences. Science and technology organizations emphasize richness. At the reach end of the spectrum, communication involves relatively simple messages transmitted to large, general audiences. The government as a whole and mass marketing emphasize reach. As will be shown in the section "Knowledge Services," content needs and service delivery methods at the two ends of the richness spectrum are not compatible with each other.

- **Management:** There are many criteria and indicators of how well an organization manages its content. A few are included here. Does an organization have a formal content management infrastructure? How efficient are the content management practices? Is there adequate technological capacity to manage organizational content? What is the quality of the content? How effective are the content management practices? Not surprisingly, content managers often have considerable difficulty in setting priorities.

Ultimately, the purpose of content management is to enable an organization to produce outputs and provide services of interest to clients, customers, and citizens.

Traditionally, organizations have tended to manage each form of content independently, within domains or markets. But this is not enough; it emphasizes what an organization does in vertical program silos or business lines. Outputs and the services that they support are the reason why a knowledge organization exists; they are what clients, customers, and citizens see and want. Therefore, basing a management framework on outputs and services is preferable as such an approach directly relates to an organization's business. This is the subject of the next section.

## Outputs

An organization produces four types of outputs: content, products, services, or solutions. Each is defined and described here. Common to each type of output is the idea that it contains embedded value and that it is intended to be used by or transferred from an organization to satisfy user wants or needs. The definitions are limited to those outputs derived from information or knowledge work rather than those produced from physical materials. Other types of service defined by the Government of Canada (2005) include transactions, intervention, and interaction. Because knowledge is often at the root of most government programs, the framework provides for knowledge being used as an input to other types of service:

- **Content** is embedded value, in the form of the message or signal contained within all elements of the content value chain that are held or owned and intended to be transformed, used by, or transferred from an organization to satisfy user wants or needs. There are five types of content: objects, data, information, knowledge, or wisdom.
- **Products** are tangible, storable commodities, or merchandise wholly or partly derived from and dependant on, or in support of, content, with embedded value, intended to be used by or transferred from an organization to satisfy user wants or needs. Products produced by Natural Resources Canada are: databases, scientific articles, technical reports, promotional material, geospatial products, statistical products, standards, policies, regulations, systems, and devices.
- **Services** are intangible, non-storable work, functions, or processes, wholly or partly derived from, dependent on, or in support of content, with embedded value and intended to be used by or transferred from an organization to satisfy user wants or needs. Services provided by Natural Resources Canada are: answers, advice, teaching, facilitation, support, and laboratory.

- **Solutions** result from the successful use of content, products, or services to embed or extract value by accomplishing organizational objectives, and intended to be transferred from an organization to satisfy external user wants or needs. Solutions transferred from Natural Resources Canada are: direction, operations, plans, positions, integration, and results.

We can define a knowledge-services value chain as the flow of knowledge services through a knowledge services system in which value is embedded, advanced, or extracted by the organization, sectors, and society (Figure 11.5). The knowledge services value chain includes nine stages: generate, transform, manage, use internally, transfer, add value, use professionally, use personally, and evaluate. As with the content value chain, downstream services generally have higher embedded value than upstream services.

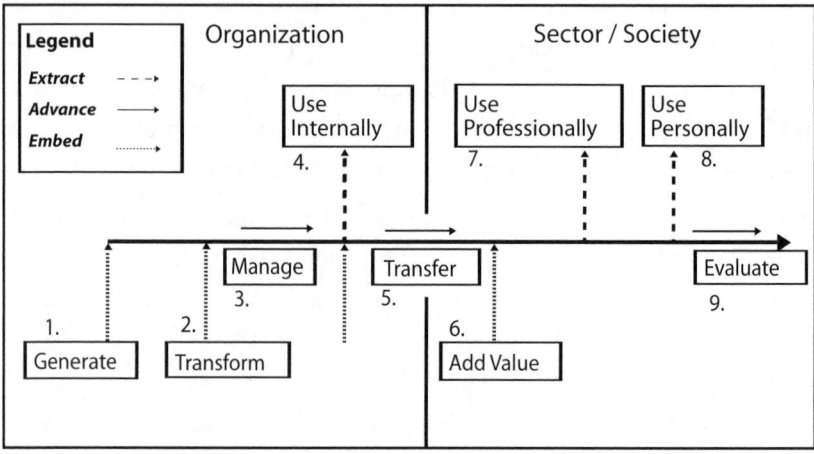

## Figure 11.5  Knowledge services value chain

The purpose of each stage of the knowledge services value chain is as follows:

1. **Generate:** *Content* with intrinsic value and potential utility must be generated as the first stage of the knowledge services value chain.
2. **Transform:** Content may be transformed into *products* and *services* to increase its utility or value to users.
3. **Manage:** Existing knowledge services must be preserved and their flow enabled to permit their internal use or external transfer.
4. **Use Internally:** Knowledge services may be used internally to produce *solutions* that accomplish organizational objectives.

5. ***Transfer***: Organizational *outputs* must be transferred, through transactions and interactions, to intermediaries, clients, citizens, or customers to enable external use.

6. ***Add Value:*** Intermediaries may increase the availability, utility, or value of knowledge services.

7. ***Use Professionally****:* Knowledge services may used by clients with sector-related knowledge to benefit an identifiable sector.

8. ***Use Personally****:* Knowledge services may be used by citizens or customers to realize personal benefits.

9. ***Evaluate****:* The system should be evaluated to improve its performance in supplying or fulfilling demands of knowledge markets.

Three stages (1, 3, and 5) are mandatory; all *must* function for subsequent stages of the knowledge-services value chain to function. This is good news for knowledge management (stage 3). One or more (but not all) of the other six stages *may* be bypassed without stopping the value chain. However, at least one value-extraction stage (4, 7, or 8) must function for the value chain to have useful meaning.

Information and knowledge markets have been variously described as enabling, supporting, or facilitating the sharing, exchange, or mobilization of information and knowledge among individuals or groups who have it and those who need it (Davenport & Prusak, 1998; Simard, 2005; Stewart, 1997). This approach focuses on facilitating transactions and interactions through which content is transferred from providers to users (Figure 11.5, stage 5). This approach generally assumes that content is, somehow, available for transfer and that it is wanted or needed for some purpose—a passive delivery approach. Provider-user models are applicable in situations with autonomous providers and users. That is, in markets with little or no control or influence over the production and availability of content and little or no interest in how or why it is used.

A provider-user model is inadequate in situations where a provider not only controls the production and distribution of knowledge, but is also mandated to promote and facilitate outcomes and benefits for citizens, as are government agencies. In such cases, providers and users are not simply facing each other with connecting infrastructure between them. Rather, providers and users interact at multiple points along the knowledge-services value chain. The value chain shown in Figure 11.5 allows managers to evaluate the complete sequence of transformation processes from the original generation of content to its eventual use—a proactive outcome approach.

A value-chain approach to knowledge services demonstrates a number of key principles:

- Knowledge services are much richer and more complex than simply transferring knowledge from providers to users.
- A knowledge value chain comprises nine stages in which value is embedded, advanced, or extracted at each stage.
- Distinguishing between internal and external use resolves the confusion arising from providers also being users.
- Distinguishing between professional and personal use resolves the confusion arising from knowledge services intended for clients and those intended for citizens and customers.

# KNOWLEDGE SERVICES

*Every work, both of nature and of art, is a system; and as every particular thing, both natural and artificial, is for some use or purpose out of and beyond itself, one may add to what has been already brought into the idea of a system, its conduciveness to this one or more ends.*

–Joseph Butler (1692–1752)

A "knowledge services system" provides the underlying infrastructure and processes that support the knowledge services value chain and, ultimately, knowledge markets. Yet, a knowledge services system does not actually exist as an identifiable entity in the real world. It is an artificial construct that combines many components and flows across organizations, sectors, and the society they serve. Although driven by organizational mandates, it has no place in the organization chart and no line item in the budget. That it has not been previously identified as an entity partially explains why no one has previously described what it does. Yet, to understand, measure, and manage knowledge services, we must bring together in one place all of the many processes that collectively transform organizational outputs into benefits for citizens and customers. We have to be able to "heat water at one end and see steam coming out at the other."

## Knowledge Services System

We begin by bending the knowledge services value chain so that it closes on itself, forming a circular value chain (Figure 11.6). We then use a framework of

*Who* is *Working* on *What* and *Why* to define three types of components and a purpose for each stage. The purpose of each stage has been described in the "Outputs" section:

- **Who:** Persons, groups, or organizations who do knowledge work.
- **Work:** Processes, activities, or actions that embed value into, advance value, or extract value from knowledge services.
- **What:** Inputs to and outputs from each stage of the knowledge services value chain.

Figure 11.6 shows 34 components of the nine stages of the knowledge services system as a cyclic flow. The cycle begins with an organizational mandate to generate content, and it ends with recommendations to the organization about the effectiveness of and need for services. The first five stages are internal to the organization while the four remaining stages are external to the organization. A "/" indicates more than one component within one "box." Stages marked with (*) are necessary for the system to function because everything must flow through them, while others may be bypassed without stopping the system. Each stage performs one of three functions: embedding value, advancing value, or extracting value.

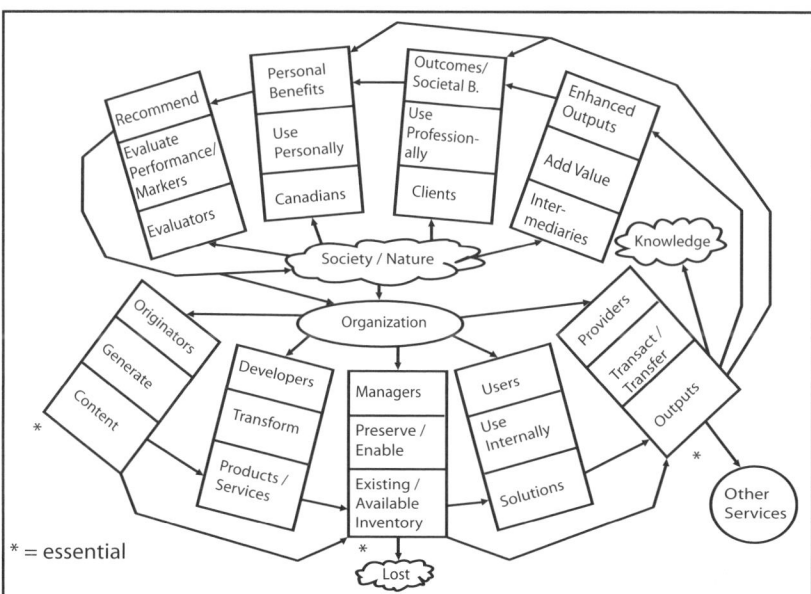

Figure 11.6  **Knowledge services system**

The knowledge services system also includes parameters that interact with multiple stages of the knowledge services value chain and that notably affect the overall system (Simard et al., 2006). Parameters can be thought of as generic processes that lie in a layer above the system and that interact with it at many points. The knowledge services system includes nine parameters: channel, quality, utility, scale, intellectual property, ownership, source, criteria, and indicators.

## Content Richness

The knowledge services system (Figure 11.6) shows that a knowledge organization may distribute outputs and provide services to any or all of six destinations (individuals are split into two groups—customers and all residents). These destinations can be thought of as regions of a content richness spectrum. Like colors in the electromagnetic spectrum, we can name regions of the content richness spectrum, even though we cannot precisely define boundaries between them: unique, complex, technical, specialized, simplified, and mandatory (Table 11.2). As with a blue-green color, sub-regions can also be identified. For example, university professors need both concepts and management practices while high-school teachers do not need professional knowledge, but they require more than a casual acquaintance.

Table 11.2 lists seven attributes associated with each region of the richness spectrum: system destination, audience size, market segmentation, architecture, difficulty of understanding, level of interaction, and use, along with examples of output or service. Each type of output is generally intended for one region of this spectrum. The terms used in each box are not categorical; rather, they are intended to show a progression from one end of the richness spectrum to the other.

## Table 11.2  Selected regions on the content richness spectrum

| Rich | | | | Reach | | |
|---|---|---|---|---|---|---|
| Region | Unique | Complex | Technical | Specialized | Simplified | Mandatory |
| Destination | Other services | Knowledge | Intermediaries | Practitioners | Customers | All residents |
| Audience | One | Few | Few | Some | Many | All |
| Market | Customized | Specialized | Tailored | Sector | Categories | Mass |
| Architecture | None | Formats | Specifications | Domain | Standards | Common |
| Difficulty | Complex | Conceptual | Complicated | Professional | Popular | Fool-proof |
| Interaction | Intervene | Support | Promote | Explain | Advertise | Provide |
| Use | Particular | Research | Enhancement | Management | Interests | Instance |
| Example | Question & answer | Scientific articles | Product specifications | Consultation & advice | Self-help guides | Forms & instructions |

The spectrum can be divided into three zones: rich, middle, and reach (Figure 11.7). Two opposing processes take place across the richness spectrum: distribution and interaction. At the rich end of the spectrum, distribution of a few copies requires only minimal effort while interaction in the form of conversations is critical to knowledge transfer. Conversely, at the reach end, distribution to millions of customers or residents requires substantial effort while significant personal interaction is infeasible. In Table 11.2, audience, market, and architecture are distribution processes while difficulty and interaction are interaction processes.

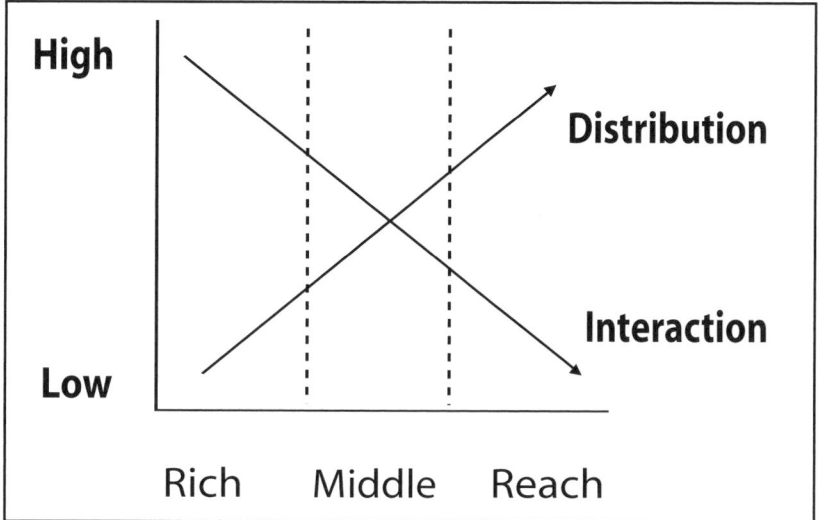

Figure 11.7  Content richness spectrum

The most appropriate channels and methods for transferring information and knowledge or delivering services at the ends of the spectrum are generally self-evident. For example, conversations or scientific publications are generally used for rich content, while the World Wide Web and mail are typically used for reach. As a corollary, the methods of either end are generally inappropriate and ineffective at the other end. Selecting appropriate transfer processes is more difficult in the middle region of the spectrum, which combines some aspects of both rich and reach communication. Delivery of any particular service is not limited to any particular channel. Many services are delivered through multiple channels, as appropriate.

This framework does not preclude someone with a personal interest (e.g., someone who is sensitive to pollution) from acquiring professional or richer levels of understanding. The essential point is that in producing content, an organization may assume a level of understanding appropriate to the richness region. Similarly, because all citizens or customers *may* access and use content in their areas of interest, content needs to be popularized and disseminated, but it does not have to be provided at the same level of simplicity and accessibility as content that all residents *must* access and use.

The flow to other services is closest to the "rich" end of the spectrum because it tends to be *unique*. It is often intended for one or two persons, is specifically tailored to a particular end use, and is often transferred through dialogue involving questions and answers. Next, *complex* content flows to the pool of knowledge. It is generally conceptual in form and is transferred to scientists conducting research in related areas through scientific articles.

In the middle region, *technical* outputs are destined for a few intermediaries who add value in a variety of ways (e.g., customize, innovate, simplify, analyze) and move the enhanced content toward the reach end of the spectrum. Continuing, *specialized* content is transferred to a broader group of practitioners through advice and recommended management practices to achieve sector outcomes.

Approaching the "reach" end of the spectrum, many citizens or customers use *simplified* outputs, such as self-help guides to realize benefits in areas of personal interest. The reach end of the spectrum is the domain of government agencies that are *mandated* to interact with all residents, regardless of their interests. A key strategic decision for any organization is the positioning and distribution of its mix of outputs and services along the content richness spectrum.

## Business Context

> *Senior executives must begin to explicitly articulate and define the role information will play in the design and execution of their company's competitive strategy, or they will risk being at a serious disadvantage to the hands of information-enabled rivals.*
> —James McGee and Lawrence Prusak (1993)

The knowledge services framework has a number of business advantages over functional records, knowledge, or even content management approaches:

- It helps identify important questions. Describing the components and interactions reveals key strategic patterns and relationships that underlie management issues.

- It emphasizes horizontal flow rather than management processes. This fosters and promotes enterprise-wide integration across organizational silos.
- It supports an organization's business. Content management should be more successful by using a value proposition that is meaningful to senior managers.
- It promotes sector or market outcomes. Focusing on user needs rather than organizational efficiency supports an evolution to results-based management.

The advantages can be grouped into four categories: the business model, service strategy, management role, and attributes. Each is discussed in this section.

## Business Model

Sinclair (2006) states that "KM is probably the single best hope for successfully moving the monolith of government towards a new and improved business model, one that can better respond to the information age demands of an on-line and computer-savvy generation." The Government of Canada (GoC) service transformation vision represents nothing less than a new business model for government. Although knowledge management is relegated to a functional specialty in the service framework the concept is equally applicable here.

Leonard notes that: "Companies, like individuals, compete on the basis of their ability to create and utilize knowledge; therefore, managing knowledge is as important as managing the finances. In other words, firms are knowledge, as well as financial, institutions." Stewart (1997) extends the argument with: "Knowledge assets, like money or equipment, exist and are worth cultivating only in the context of a strategy. You cannot manage intellectual assets unless you know what you are going to do with them."

The service-based framework is positioned in the center of a hierarchy of business processes (Figure 11.8). Although direction flows from the business model through the content strategy to the framework, the framework should also influence the strategy and, in turn, the organization's business model. For example, if an organization is currently using a traditional vertically oriented, domain-specific, and functional business model, recommendations about its limited suitability to the information society and knowledge economy might be appropriate before starting to implement a service-based framework. Alternatively, implementation will be

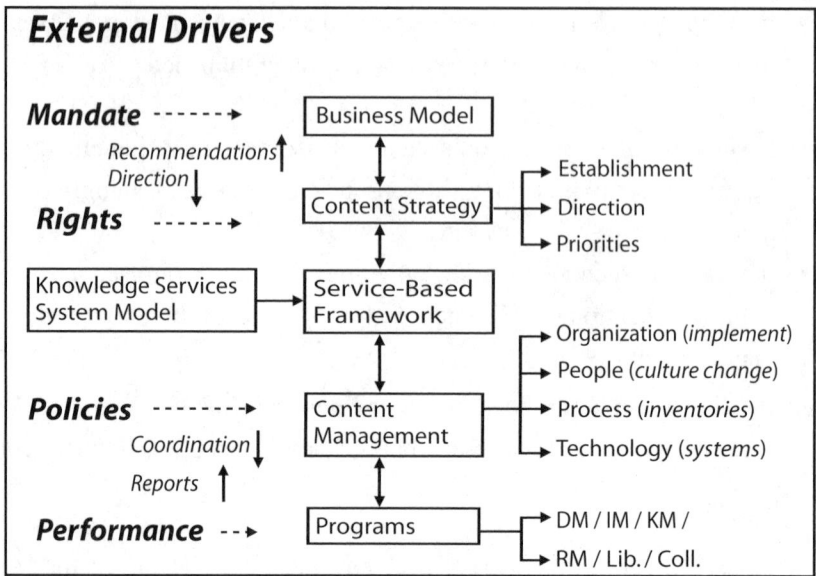

**Figure 11.8  Knowledge services business framework**

limited to adapting the service framework to the existing business model, to the extent possible.

It is important to understand how the framework fits into the hierarchy of business processes. There are four content drivers: mandate, rights, policies, and performance. These impact business processes, the business model, content strategy, management plans, and programs, respectively (Table 11.3).

From a content perspective, external drivers impact a department or business at four different levels. At the top, the mandate defines the business, but there is considerable flexibility in interpreting how that mandate will be fulfilled. Rights affect the content strategy, policies affect content management, and performance

**Table 11.3  Hierarchy of external drivers and business processes**

| External Drivers | Business Processes |
|---|---|
| The **Mandate** defines the business. | The **Business model** interprets the mandate. |
| **Rights** impact on the content strategy, which cannot exceed the legal limits of what must and must not be done. | The **Content strategy** supports the business model by linking content management to business outputs. |
| **Policies** impact on content management, which must implement institutional rules and procedures. | **Content management** supports the content strategy by linking program outputs to the content strategy. |
| **Performance** standards impact on programs, which must meet specified requirements. | **Programs** support content management by implementing and operating content-specific technology and processes. |

standards affect programs. It should be evident that this structure is fraught with opportunities for inconsistency and sub-optimal decisions. If, for example, rights, policies, or standards require content management practices that are not consistent with the business model and not budgeted at an appropriate level, the former will be difficult to implement. Clearly, the functional needs of managing an organization's content cannot be considered in isolation.

## Service Strategy

McGee and Prusak (1993) discuss the importance of an information strategy that establishes the use of information as a strategic resource to help the organization attain its goals. This should not be confused with a typical information management strategy that establishes how information will be managed. The former presents a business case whereas the latter is limited to functionality. Most information management strategies begin with motherhood statements that information is important and then move directly to how it will be managed. Rarely do they show why it is important, even critical, to the business in ways that are convincing to senior managers. Until content management (in its broadest sense) is seen as an investment in organizational success and relevance, it will be just another function whose costs should be minimized.

A content strategy is a high-level direction and approach for using content as a strategic resource to support an organization's business. A content strategy can be framed as a hierarchical set of issues that need to be addressed: organizational role in knowledge markets, market approach, intended audiences, richness spectrum, and finally, a management framework:

- **Organizational role:** What is the appropriate organizational role in external (sector, national, and international) information and knowledge markets? Once it is understood that external markets exist and function with or without the organization, the question of appropriate organizational roles becomes self-evident. There are risks associated with non-participation as well as benefits of participation. Three types of market roles need to be considered: content (provider, user, intermediary), participant (owner, partner, manager, developer, member), and support (champion, facilitator, funding, infrastructure). Each of these terms are defined and described in Simard, et al. (2006). Clearly, most organizations will have multiple roles in external knowledge markets. The key point is that they should be explicitly identified, selected, and managed so as to support the organization's business.

- **Market approach:** What is the desired organizational balance between supply- and demand-driven approaches to knowledge markets? All organizations operate somewhere between the end points of supply and demand. Further, unless an organization produces only one output or service, they will likely be distributed at both ends of this range. Supply versus demand has significant ramifications. Although promoted by the government's service transformation vision, a demand-driven approach requires shifting current organizational capacity and implementing processes to continuously adapt that capacity to shifting market demand. These may require substantial organizational transformation.

- **Intended audiences:** What is the intended distribution of outputs among internal, professional, and personal users, as well as the pool of knowledge, other services, and intermediaries? This addresses a key question of who are the clients for organizational outputs. This question relates directly to an organization's mandate, business, and strategy. Does the business emphasize producing outputs, industry support, making a profit, sector outcomes, or benefits for citizens? As with supply and demand, most organizations will distribute its outputs among various categories and sub-categories of audiences.

- **Richness spectrum:** What is the most effective position of organizational outputs along the content richness spectrum? This relates to the nature of the outputs and services that must be provided to facilitate usability by different categories of users. The spectrum also affects the appropriateness of various types of system architecture, distribution channels, and transfer processes. The key point is that the closer to the reach end of the spectrum an organization wants to position itself, the more that outputs will have to be adapted to user wants and needs.

- **Management framework:** What is the most appropriate framework for managing organizational content? Although this chapter demonstrates the advantages of a service-based framework, that choice must be made by decision makers at various levels in the organization. The answer to that question provides the starting point for developing a content management strategy and the segue to implementation and performance measurement.

## Management Role

The capacity of content management to help an organization achieve its goals is governed by the level of investment in the process. How broad should the role of content management be in an organization? Some specialists maintain that it is everywhere—from the inception of an idea through the termination of work, and even beyond. And they are right. Others argue that it is focused in certain critical areas—that of enabling an organization to do work (Figure 11.6, stage 3). And they are also right. These seemingly contradictory views are both partially correct because much like the blind men and the elephant, each view represents only part of the whole.

Data, information, and knowledge are the lifeblood of any organization. Programs, projects, and processes cannot interact and work collectively to achieve a common purpose unless they exchange content among themselves. Thus, it is correct to say that content management is (or should be) everywhere, supporting the work of the organization.

However, an organization consists of people working in groups. People and groups have beliefs and values, perceptions and opinions, behavior and dynamics. They also take pride in their work and their role in the organization. Unlike technology, which can be centrally controlled (to the frequent annoyance of those who use it), information and knowledge cannot be conscripted; they must be volunteered. If content management portrays itself as the center of the organizational universe, it will dissipate its energy in territorial battles rather than in serving the organization.

Consider functionality. Content management does not generate content, except for what is needed to demonstrate its performance, as with other programs. Similarly, it does not transform content into products and services; program subject-matter experts do that. It also does not use content to carry out the business of the organization; that is the mandate of other programs. Functionally speaking, content management is mandated to perform the critical work of enabling the rest of the organization to achieve their mandates. Although this is no small purpose, it is a support and not a business function.

If programs perceive content management as "invading their space," or a "tax" that reduces their budgets, they are likely to resist with every bureaucratic device available to them, resulting in much motion but little movement. Conversely, if content management is perceived as supporting, facilitating, and promoting programs, they are more likely to support changes that are necessary to move the enterprise forward. The service framework clearly distinguishes between organizational programs that generate, transform, and use content to provide services and the functional need to manage content so that it can be used for the good of the enterprise.

## Service Framework Attributes

The knowledge services framework has a number of attributes that enhance its functionality. The systems model on which the framework is based is intended to work operationally; it is not a simplified overview that conceals more than it reveals about managing organizational services. All necessary components and connectors are included, although assembly will be required. Although the framework does not describe what to do or how to do it, it lists everything that an organization should consider in managing its content from a service perspective:

- It is independent of content or issues. It should be applicable to a broad range of knowledge organizations and programs.
- It is based on a sound logic model. There should be no "fatal flaws" or parts that don't work to be discovered after implementation begins.
- It addresses real-world complexity. This avoids the problem of solving a problem based on its symptoms only to have another problem arise elsewhere.
- It is complete. It includes everything that an organization should consider in managing its infrastructure, content, and services as a whole.
- It is detailed. The sub-components are sufficiently detailed to permit bureaucratic identification and classification of all relevant organizational activities.
- It supports performance measurement. Criteria and indicators can be developed for evaluating any of the interactions and flows portrayed in the knowledge services system.

## CONCLUSION

The knowledge-service framework presented here goes beyond information and content management to provide a direct link to an organization's business. A service-based business case for knowledge management should be stronger and more successful than one based on functional necessity. Further, the framework focuses on external clients, customers, and citizens—the ultimate reason why departments and businesses exist. Finally, the framework promotes a shift from supply-driven information and knowledge markets to demand-driven markets. Organizations that use a service framework will decreasingly ask: "Can you use what we have?" and increasingly ask "What do you need from us?"

# References

Amidon, Debra M. (1997). *Innovation strategy for the knowledge economy.* Boston: Butterworth-Heinman.

Bartlett, Christopher A. (1999). The knowledge-based organization. In Dan Holtshouse and Rudy Ruggles (Eds.), *The knowledge advantage* (p. 119). Dover, NH: Capstone.

Buckman, Robert H. (2004). *Building a knowledge-driven organization.* New York: McGraw Hill.

Capra, Fritjof. (1975). *The tao of physics.* Berkeley, CA: Shambhala Publications.

Davenport, Thomas, & Prusak, Laurence. (1998). *Working knowledge.* Boston: Harvard Business School Press.

Davis, Stanley M. (1977). *Future perfect.* Reading, MA: Addison-Wesley.

Evans, Philip B., & Wurster, Thomas S. (1999). *Blown to bits: How the new economics of information transforms strategy.* Boston: Harvard Business School Publishing.

Galliers, Robert. (Ed.). (1987). *Information analysis.* Reading, MA: Addison-Wesley.

Holmes, Douglas. (2001). *E-Gov: E-business strategies for government.* London: Nicholas Brealey Publishing.

Kaplan, Robert S., & Norton, David P. (2004). *Strategy maps: Converting intangible assets into tangible outcomes.* Boston: Harvard Business School Press.

Leonard, Dorothy. (1995). *Wellsprings of knowledge.* Boston: Harvard Business School Press.

Lynch, Dudley, & Kordis, Paul L. (1988). *Strategy of the dolphin.* New York: William Morrow and Company.

McGee, James, & Prusak, Laurence. (1993). *Managing information strategically.* New York: John Wiley & Sons.

Mish, Frederick C. (Ed.). (1991). *Webster's ninth new collegiate dictionary.* Springfield, MA: Merriam Webster.

Nonaka, Ikujiro. (1998). The knowledge creating company. In *Harvard Business Review on Knowledge Management* (p. 21). Boston: Harvard Business School Press.

Simard, Albert J. (1992). Fire severity, changing scales, and how things hang together. *International Journal of Wildland Fire, 1*(1): 23–34.

Simard, Albert J. (2000). *Managing knowledge at the Canadian Forest Service.* Ottawa: Natural Resources Canada, Canadian Forest Service.

Simard, Albert J. (2005). Global disaster information network. In *UN World Conference on Disaster Reduction.* Kobe, Japan, Jan. 18–22.

Simard, Albert, Broome, John, Drury, Malcolm, Haddon, Brian, O'Neil, Bob, and Pasho, Dave. (2006). *Understanding knowledge services at Natural Resources Canada.* NRCan, Knowledge Services Secretariat.

Sinclair, Niall. (2006). *Stealth KM: Winning knowledge management strategies for the public sector.* Burlington, MA: Butterworth-Heinemann.

Stewart, Thomas A. (1997). *Intellectual capital: The new wealth of organizations.* New York: McGraw-Hill.

# Part III

# Knowledge Management Techniques and Technology

# Knowledge Management Techniques and Technology

## FOREWORD

This section contains two chapters by Bedford (Chapters 12 and 14) that constitute an excellent primer on information description as well as search and retrieval techniques, taxonomies, ontologies, metadata, and query processing in Chapter 12; and metadata, concept extraction, clustering, and summarization and text extraction in Chapter 14, with discussions of the capabilities and limitations of each.

Chapter 13 by Hawamdeh and Refai is a review and discussion of what will be an increasingly important topic in knowledge management (KM): the use of video material. Video will be important because of its increasing use to capture the knowledge of a rapidly retiring workforce, and because the workplace will be making increased use of videoconferencing and video enhanced person-to-person connection, both of which will be grist for KM systems. Video can also convey context in a fashion that text cannot. In that role, too, we can expect more use of video in KM. The chapter gives examples of video use, particularly Project Exodus of the U.S. Department of Defense. It also discusses techniques and technology, including specific hardware.

Rao's chapter (Chapter 15) is a very informative chapter on KM practices among companies in the infotech sector. First, it analyzes the practices at some 17 companies. Then, it analyzes commonalities and patterns among those companies using a technique, the "8 Cs" audit, which provides a very useful strategic checklist in its own right. The "8 Cs" are:

1. Connectivity
2. Content
3. Community
4. Culture

5. Capacity

6. Cooperation

7. Commerce

8. Capital

Whether or not the reader has an interest specifically in KM in the infotech sector, the editors advise every reader to check out the "8 Cs" checklist.

# CHAPTER 12

# How to Build a Smart Search System Using Taxonomies and Ontologies

Denise A. D. Bedford
World Bank

## BUILDING SMARTER SEARCH SYSTEMS

Users' expectations for intelligent search systems are increasing. Users expect to search for any information they need regardless of where it exists, whenever they need it, wherever they are when they need it, and in a language they can understand. Users expect search systems to find their spelling mistakes and fix them, to understand what they mean by their search terms and interpret them when they search, to make suggestions for other related concepts, to tell them something meaningful about the search results, and to be able to sort and manipulate search results.

Making search systems smarter is well within our capacity. Search systems are not black boxes, which are beyond the average person's understanding. There is no magic algorithm that makes a search system smart. The simple truth is that the more we expect a search system to do and the more intelligent we expect it to be, the more sophisticated the search architecture we need and the more human intelligence we have to build into it. Taxonomies and ontologies are valuable tools for building the intelligence into search.

Let's start with a vision of a smarter search system (Figure 12.1), and consider how taxonomies and ontologies make search smarter (Figure 12.2). Next, we will consider where taxonomies live in a search system, and how they work.

## VISION OF A SMARTER SEARCH SYSTEM

How is this vision of a search system smarter than most others? It is smarter because it uses taxonomies in order to:

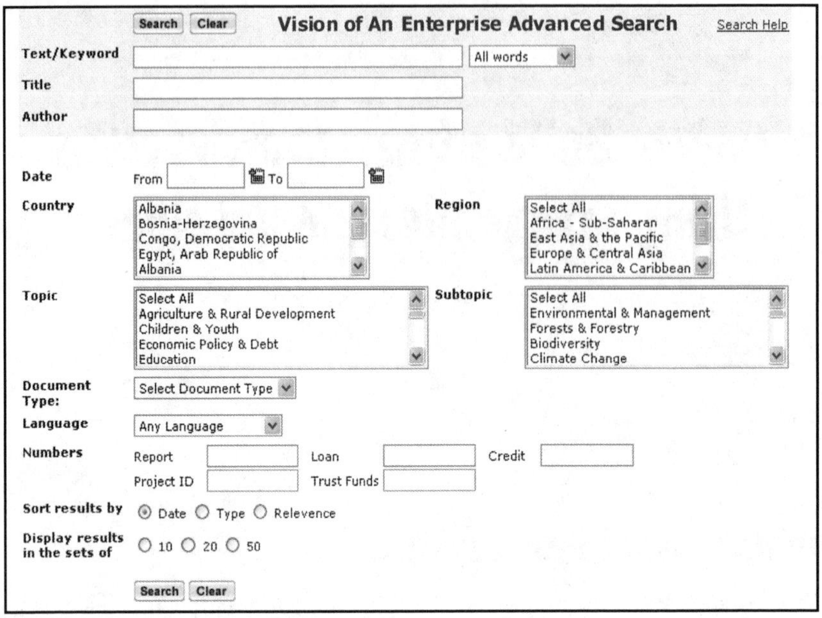

**Figure 12.1  Vision of a smart search interface**

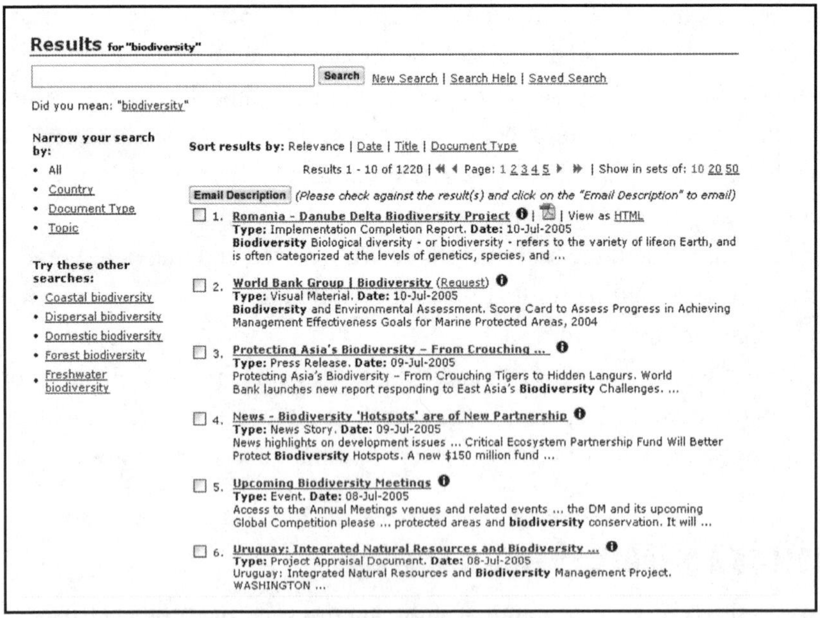

**Figure 12.2  Vision of smart search results presentation**

- Allow users to specify the parameters of a search across many systems (*faceted taxonomy*)
- Determine the variations in country names over time (*ring taxonomy*)
- Detect and fix spelling mistakes (*ring taxonomy*)
- Detect and search for synonyms (*ring taxonomy*)
- Suggest other related searches (*network taxonomy*)
- Contextualize search results by topic (*hierarchical taxonomy*), by country (*ring taxonomy*), by region (*hierarchical taxonomy*), by date (*flat taxonomy*), and by content type (*flat taxonomy*)
- Determine different forms of an author's name (*ring taxonomy*)
- Allow the searcher to narrow the search (*faceted taxonomy*)
- Allow the searcher to sort results (*faceted taxonomy*)
- Present predictable and sufficient information about a result to let the searcher better judge relevancy (*faceted taxonomy*)
- Recommend other items that are similar to the results a user selects (*network taxonomy*)
- Infer relationships among objects such as people working in an area or products that pertain to processes (*network taxonomy*)

These features may seem simple and intuitive. However, they are only possible through the use of taxonomies, and a search system architecture that supports taxonomies.

# Kinds of Taxonomies and How They Work

There are five different kinds of taxonomies, including: (1) faceted taxonomies; (2) flat taxonomies; (3) ring taxonomies; (4) hierarchical taxonomies; and (5) network taxonomies. Let's take one more look at the vision of a smart search engine—this time with taxonomies in mind (Figures 12.3 and 12.4). What kinds of taxonomies are supporting search?

In order to design taxonomies into search system architectures, we need to have a basic understanding of taxonomy structures and behaviors.

## Facet Taxonomies

Faceted taxonomies are represented as "star" structures (Figure 12.5). Each node in the star describes an aspect or parameter of the center node. The center node can represent any type of object, for example: a Web site, a book, a person,

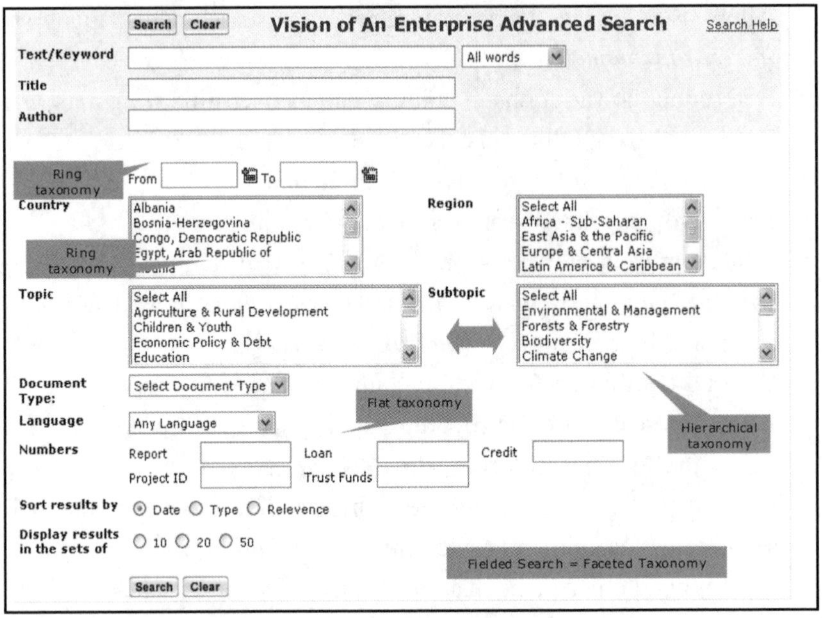

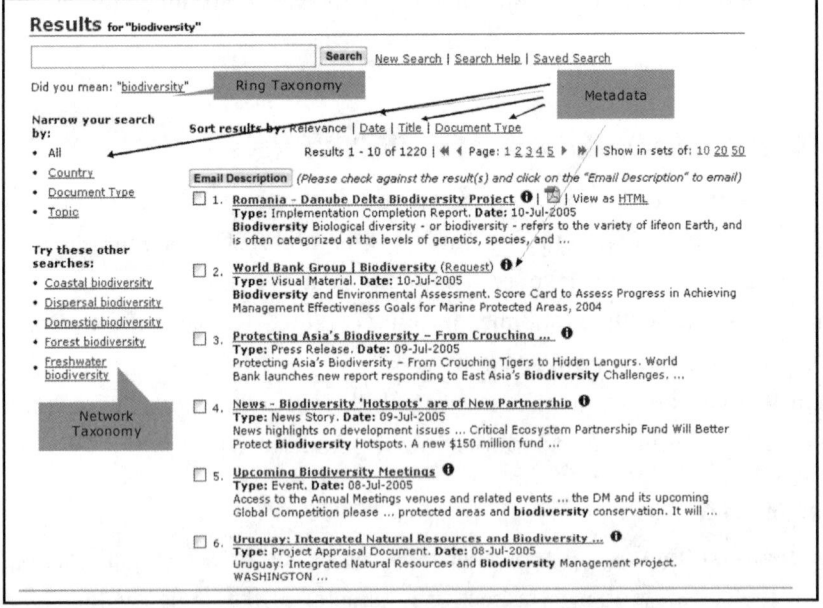

**Figure 12.3 Use of taxonomies in smart search interface**

**Figure 12.4 Use of taxonomies in smart search results presentation**

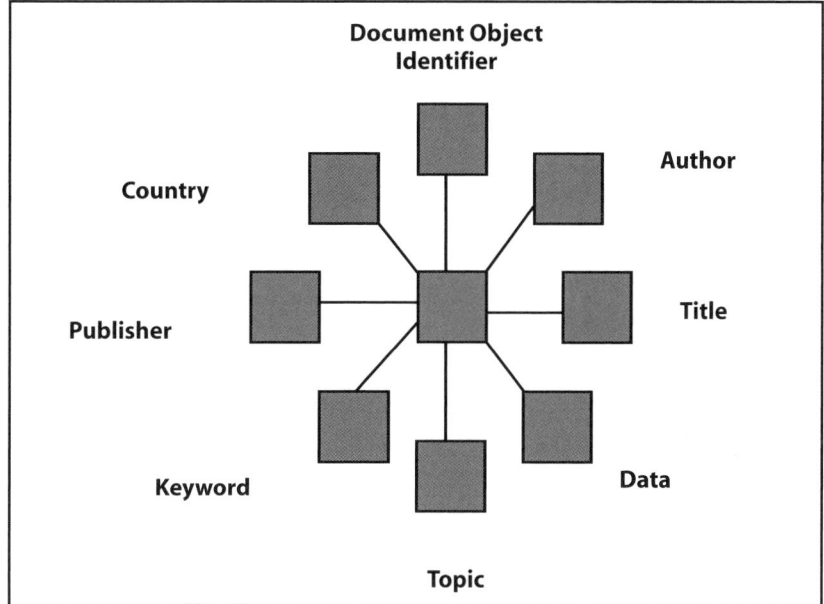

## Figure 12.5  Faceted taxonomy data structure

a report, a company, or a country. Faceted taxonomies are the structures we use to represent metadata about information objects.

Search systems use faceted taxonomies to support parametric search, and to narrow and sort search results. Each facet in the taxonomy represents a searchable parameter. Search indexes can be constructed for individual parameters, or a single index can be parameterized for metadata attributes (i.e., all values in the index can be associated with a parameter or facet). Where metadata is used for full text searching, the faceted taxonomy is discarded.

Faceted taxonomies support the following search features:

- Ability to search by a parameter or field
- Metadata displayed in search results
- Ability to narrow the search by a field or parameter
- Ability to sort the results

## Flat Taxonomy Structure

Flat taxonomies are represented as simple list structures (Figure 12.6). Each node in the list represents a value. The values in the list have no inherent relationship to

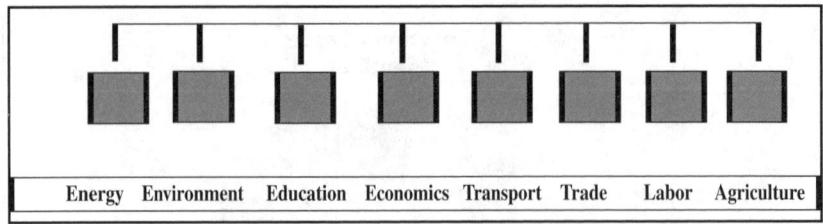

**Figure 12.6   Flat taxonomy data structure**

each other beyond the fact that they represent the same kind of entity or object. A list of states, of content types, of services or products—all are examples of flat taxonomies.

Search systems use flat taxonomies to present simple selection options to users. They improve search by ensuring that the user is always using the search term the search system expects. Flat taxonomies are helpful when users don't know what values are supported or included in the "universe," or may not know how to describe the values.

In the previous search example, flat taxonomies support the following features:

- Selection of document types
- Selection of languages

## Ring Taxonomies

Ring taxonomies (Figure 12.7) are represented as logically circular data structures. Any node in the circle is equivalent to the other nodes.

Search systems use ring taxonomies to discover synonyms, and include them in an expanded search. The searcher may select any of the nodes and gain access to all the other synonymous values. Ring taxonomies are important for handling all kinds of synonyms, including: lexical variants, variant spellings, misspellings, abbreviations, acronyms, initialisms, and cross-language synonyms.

Ring taxonomies can be used to handle misspellings. The misspelling might be in the search index or in the search terms. Misspellings are common in search logs—one only needs to see how many different ways a searcher might spell the country name Afghanistan (Afganastan, Afhghanistan, …) to understand the value of a ring taxonomy.

Ring taxonomies also support concept searching, rather than simple word searching. A simple word search for "biodiversity" will not find results where

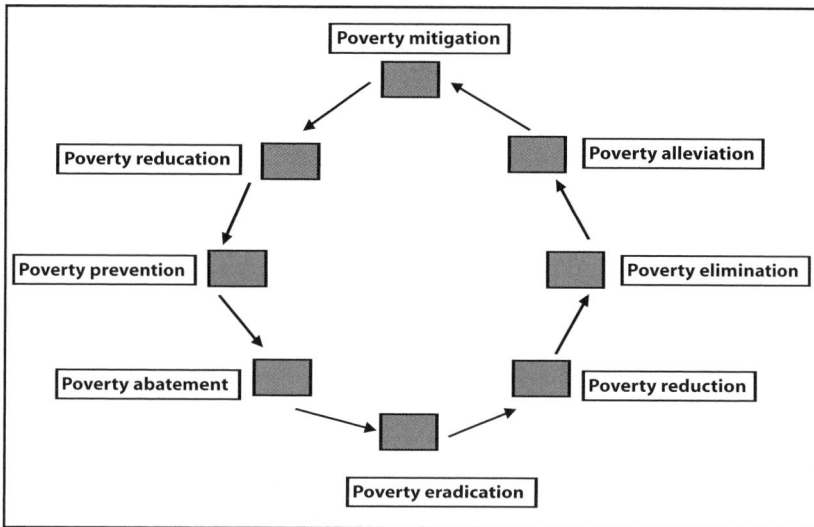

Figure 12.7  Ring taxonomy data structure

"biological diversity," "species diversity," and "species diversification" are used. A simple full-text, "word-based" search will miss 50 to 60 percent of the relevant results.

Ring taxonomies also support variant spellings and cross language synonyms. For example, a full-text or metadata search for "labor organizations" will not find results for the variant spelling "labour organizations." If the searcher intends to find only American results, ring taxonomies are not important. If the searcher does not differentiate by country, though, the word-based search results will miss important results.

A search system leveraging ring taxonomies will search not only UNESCO but also United Nations Economic Social and Cultural Organization (including other language versions of this). Where the two terms are used in the same document, a full-text or metadata search that rates relevancy by simple frequency of occurrence will lower relevancy because it is rating on only one rather than both forms.

In the previous search example, ring taxonomies support the following:

- Harmonizing variant forms of author names
- Variant forms (historical and current) of country names
- Correcting spelling mistakes

## Hierarchical Taxonomies

Hierarchical taxonomies are represented as tree data structures (Figure 12.8). The tree structure consists of nodes and links. The link between nodes has meaning. The link is a parent-child relationship. Moving upward in the structure broadens the concept searched; moving down in the structure narrows the concept searched.

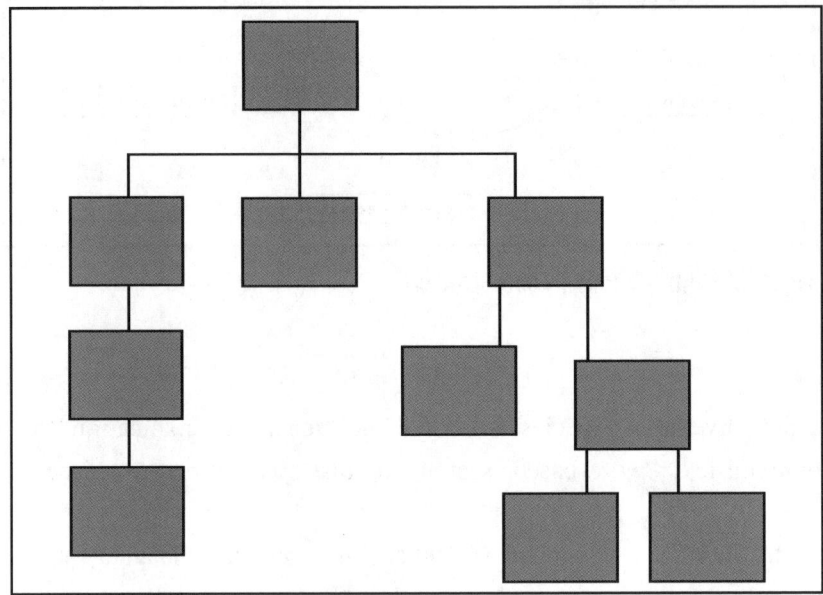

**Figure 12.8  Hierarchical taxonomy data structure**

Search systems use hierarchical taxonomies to partition the searchable resources into sets. Hierarchical taxonomies help to improve the relevancy of search results by providing a more focused collection of information within which to search. They also make it possible for users to narrow or partition search results. Hierarchical taxonomies are the basic structures used for browsing. They also make it possible for users to switch between searching and browsing, and browsing and searching.

## Network Taxonomies

Network taxonomies are represented as plex data structures (Figure 12.9). Each node in the taxonomy can have more than one parent. Any node in the plex structure can be linked to any other node. In plex structures, both the links and the

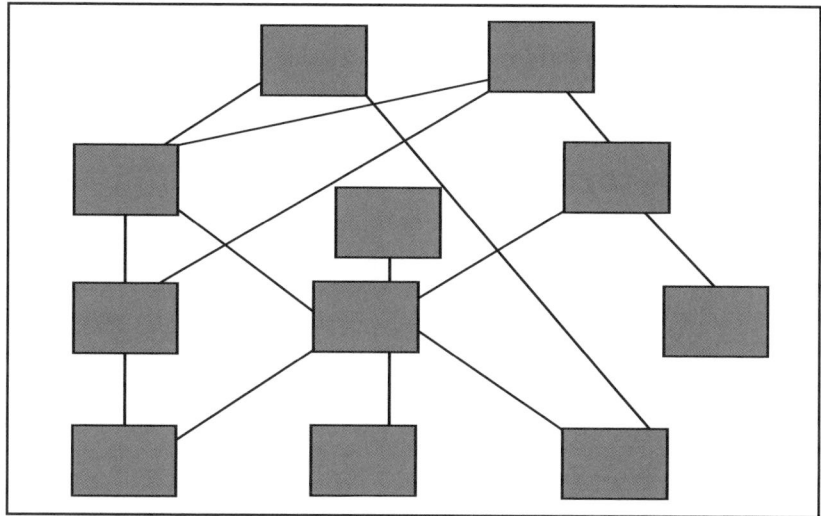

**Figure 12.9 Network taxonomy data structure**

nodes have values. The meaning of the links helps us to move from a traditional network taxonomy (thesaurus) to a semantic network (ontology).

The meaning of the links can help a search system to infer other concepts based on the search terms. The following are examples of types of relationships that might be used for inference or query expansion:

- Causes and effects
- Processes and products
- Products and properties

Search systems use network taxonomies to identify related terms for searching. In the search example here, network taxonomies support the following:

- Index terms and keywords
- Other search recommendations

## ONTOLOGIES

It is the shift in focus from the node (concept) in a taxonomy to the link (meaning) that moves us from taxonomies to ontologies. By using taxonomies in search, we are using a component of an ontology. To use a full ontology in search, though, we need one more component—an inference engine (Figure

12.10). This component leverages the search system components, but goes a little further. Integrating an ontology or a network taxonomy into search—outside of an inference engine—has the potential to dramatically increase the results set without improving relevancy. This does not make search smarter. Rather, it generates information overload.

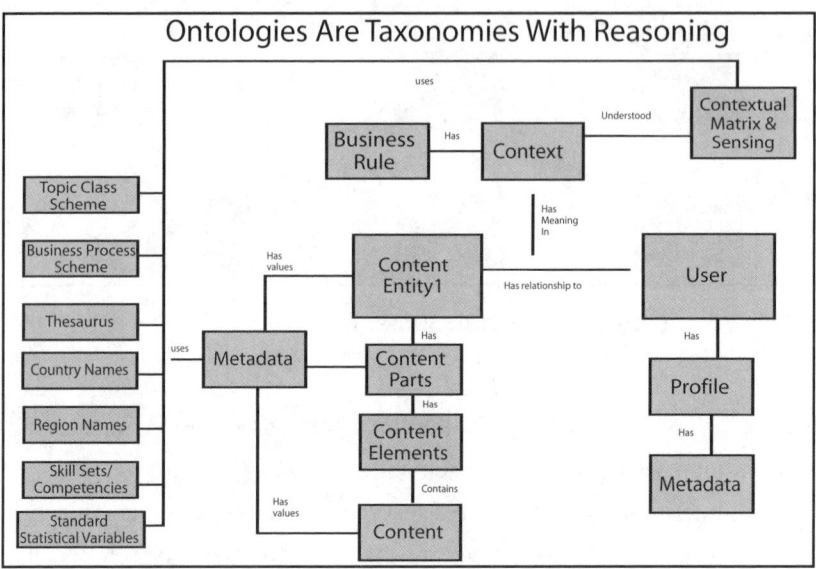

## Figure 12.10   High-level ontology reference model

From an ontology we might be able to learn who is working in a domain, who performs a kind of process, what products result from a process, or who works with whom. Ontologies support inferencing across attributes and across entities. Ontologies can support discovery, answer questions, and make recommendations for other results or entities like the one the searcher identifies.

## TAXONOMIES IN SEARCH SYSTEM ARCHITECTURES

We found taxonomies at work in our vision of a smarter search system (Figures 12.3 and 12.4). This vision, though, was only at the search interface level—the query screen and the search results screen. In order to understand how taxonomies *truly* support search, we need to look a little deeper into search system architecture.

Search systems are basically systems—they have inputs, processes, and outputs. Figure 12.11 illustrates the basic architecture of a search system. The output side of search is what most of us see every day, but this is only about 10 percent of what makes up a search system. Most search systems are not WYSIWYG (what you see is what you get). The inputs to a search system determine what you are searching against and how you can search for it. The processes of a search system determine how your search query is processed or transformed and what rules the system uses to match your query against the search system's index.

Taxonomies have a role to play in every component of the model. Let's consider where they fit and how we can configure search to use them.

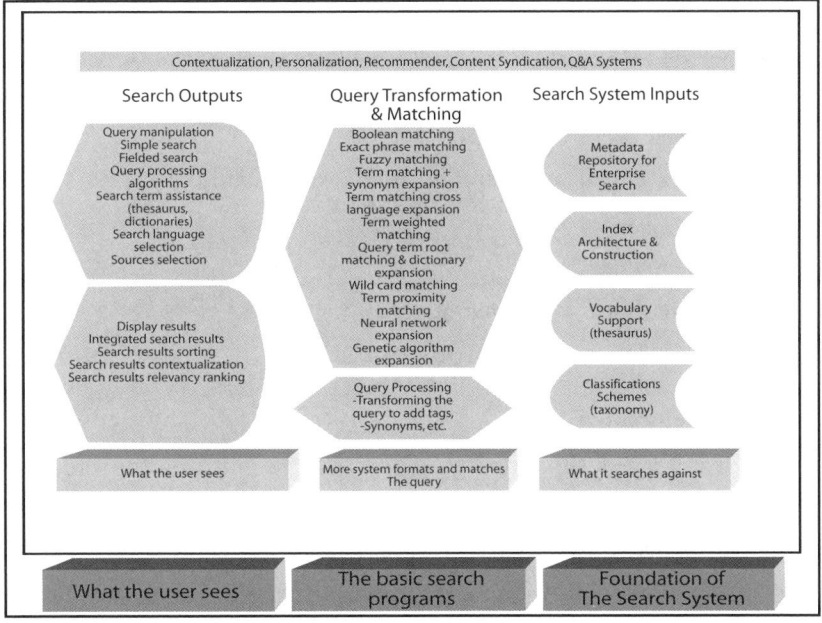

Figure 12.11 Search system architecture

# Search System Inputs

Search system inputs may include: (a) metadata surrogates for searchable information; (b) indexes; (c) vocabulary support tools; and (d) classification schemes. Inputs use all five types of taxonomies.

## Metadata and Index Architectures

Let's start with a discussion of metadata. Metadata is data about data. Metadata provides a surrogate record for information. Metadata is represented as a faceted taxonomy. Examples of metadata include: (a) title, (b) creation date, (c) topic, (d) country, and (e) language.

Metadata and index architecture are closely related in search architecture. The type of index architecture you can build depends on what kind of information you have available to put in the index. If you have metadata, then you can build parametric indexes. If you only have full text, you will probably build a full-text index.

Indexes are structures that make it easier for people or search systems to find the information they're looking for. An index is the only required input for a search system—bare bones full-text search systems still have an index. If you didn't have an index behind a Web search engine, how long do you think it would take to get a set of results? Decades? Centuries?

There are four kinds of index architectures we can build:

- Full-text index
- Parametric index
- Parametric index with integrated full-text
- Full-text index with integrated metadata

### Index Architecture Type 1: Full-Text

Full-text searching is supported by a single large index or concordance. In a full-text index (Figure 12.12), every word in every information object is an entry point. There is no way to contextualize or parameterize each word beyond its position in the information object. No sense-making is possible in full text because all context is removed from the word in the index. Searching a full-text index for news stories about Kenya will retrieve any information where the word, Kenya, is mentioned. The stories may not be about Kenya, though. There is no way to specify Kenya as a country focus in a full-text index.

There are advantages and disadvantages to full text. The advantages include:

- Indexes are dynamic.
- Every word in every reference is an access point.

The disadvantages include:

- Generates very large results sets

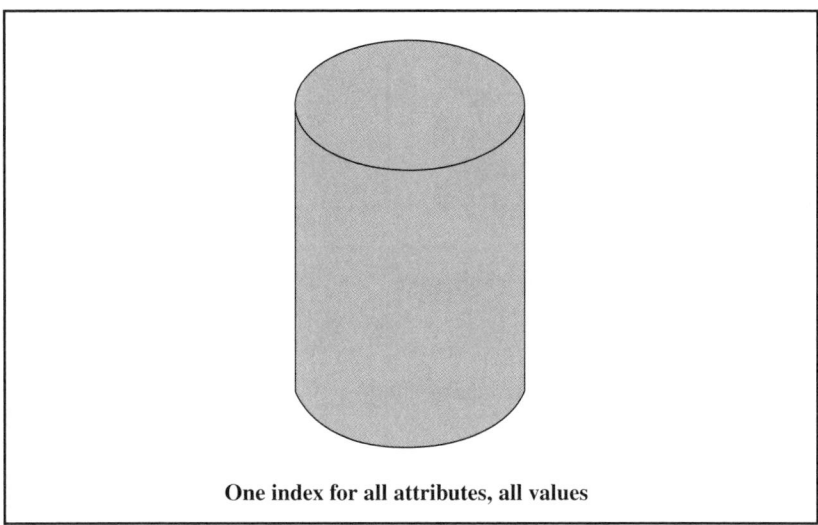

**One index for all attributes, all values**

## Figure 12.12   Full-text search index

- Generates zero result sets when you didn't search using the author's words
- Does not resolve ambiguity (contagion: financial or disease?)
- Results in false coordination (car polish vs. polish car)
- Does not compensate for current and outdated forms (polio or infantile paralysis)
- Does not support contextualization
- Does not support sorting of results
- Does not support narrowing or refining a search

There are no taxonomies inherent to full-text indexes. Clustering technologies that make use of network taxonomies may be used to mitigate some of the disadvantages of full-text search. Clustering is a way of identifying common sets of concepts in full-text documents and organizing the documents according to the sets. However, the user does not have any control over the clusters that are generated. In addition, the clusters are typically of only a small subset of the total results (i.e., the top 200 results). Without any foundation for applying taxonomies, it is a challenge to add intelligence to full-text search.

### Index Architecture Type 2: Parametric

Parametric index architectures (Figure 12.13) build an index for each searchable field or parameter. Parametric architectures can support searching by: author,

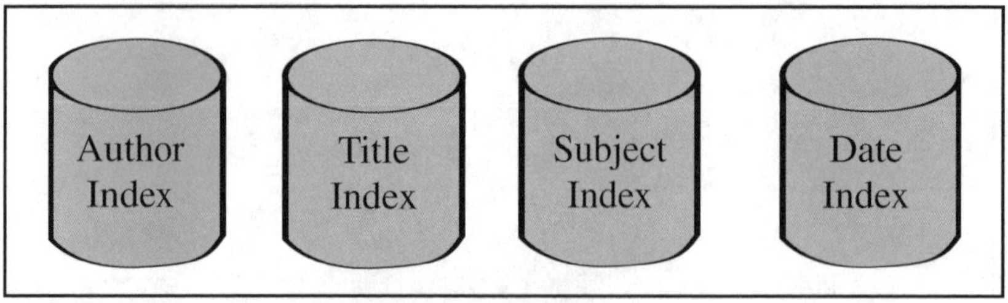

**Figure 12.13 Parametric index architecture**

title, topic, document type, format, or language. Parametric index architectures are built on metadata (faceted taxonomy). Like full-text search, parametric search presents advantages and disadvantages.

The advantages of parametric search include:

- Allows us to build indexes on individual parameters and across attributes, such as: (a) author, (b) title, (c) date, (d) topic, (e) country, (f) format, (g) language
- Supports sorting and prioritization of results
- Supports harmonizing parameters across information systems
- Supports the discovery of synonyms and other concepts, but does not include them in the search
- Supports optimization of index structures and values depending on the values and kinds of taxonomies (country index, topic index, etc.)

There are disadvantages of parametric searching, including:

- Because it relies on metadata, where metadata does not exist or is of insufficient quantity or quality, it cannot support a parametric search:
  - Full-text index architecture is chosen, and the metadata is added to the index word by word, removing the context from the metadata
  - Parametric index architecture is chosen, and the full text is indexed as a single attribute, typically as a keyword or subject attribute

A hybrid approach to indexing is also possible. There are two ways to create a hybrid index architecture: (a) integrating full-text into a parametric index, or (b) integrating metadata into a full-text index.

### Index Architecture Type 3: Integrating Full-Text into Parametric Index

This hybrid index architecture leverages the parametric index architecture. In this approach, the full text has to be transformed into and represented as metadata. We are trying to apply some context to the full text by fitting it into a single facet in a taxonomy (Figure 12.14).

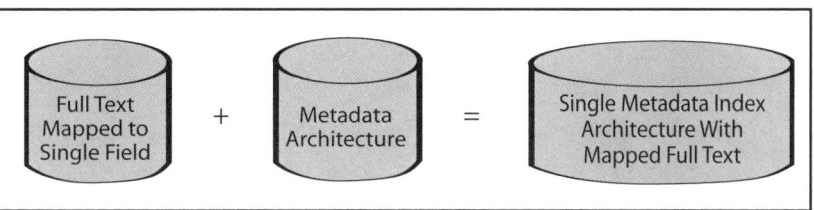

**Figure 12.14  Full-text integrated into parametric index**

The solution is to select an attribute to which you will map your full-text words—typically to keywords or subjects. The result, though, is that the full text overwhelms the keywords or indexing terms in metadata. The result of this type of mix is that you get all of the fuzziness of full-text mixed with the well-disciplined keywords:

- Balance is very difficult to achieve in this hybrid architecture—very high risk that users will be unable to find what they're looking for if it isn't in the top 10 results
- The fuzziness overwhelms the well-disciplined data—pushes it down further in the results sets
- If you have rich keywords which are concentrated, though, the keywords can overwhelm the full-text

### Index Architecture Type 4: Metadata Integrated into Full-Text Index

This hybrid index architecture uses the single, full-text index architecture as a base. All metadata is reduced to single words. All metadata is tokenized and added to the full-text index as individual words (Figure 12.15). All context is lost but you have a single index against which to search. Generally, the metadata is overwhelmed by the sheer weight of the full-text content. The investment put into creating the metadata is lost in the full-text index. In this case, we have engineered the faceted taxonomy out of search. In effect, this strategy results in "dumbing down" the search.

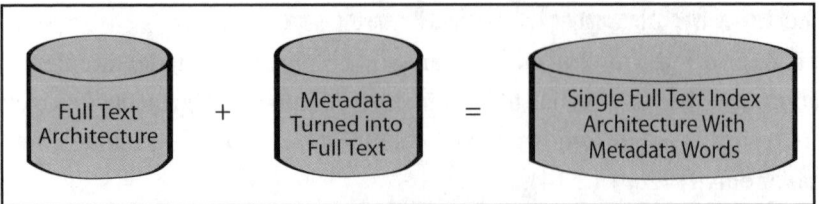

**Figure 12.15   Metadata integrated into full-text index**

## Vocabulary Tools

The vocabulary component supports: (a) simple picklists; (b) synonyms, misspellings, abbreviations, and language variants; (c) cross-language variants; and d) related terms.

### Picklists

Picklists are represented as flat taxonomies. Flat taxonomies can improve the performance of search by ensuring that the best value is selected by the user. For example, a list of languages from which to select ensures that the user is aware of all the languages available and selects the value that will have the most effective search result (i.e., will match the index entries most effectively).

### Synonyms

Synonyms are represented as ring taxonomies. When ring taxonomies are present in search system architectures, synonyms can be detected and added to a search. When synonyms are included in the search, relevancy ratings and recall performance improve.

Synonyms can include:

- Variant forms of names—personal, corporate, country
- Proper and misspelled forms of terms (Alignment, alignement; Millenium, millennium; Afganastan, Afhghanistan)
- True synonyms (biodiversity, biological diversity, diversity of species, species diversity)
- Cross-language equivalent terms
- Abbreviations and fully spelled-out terms

### Related Concepts

Related concepts are derived from a thesaurus (network taxonomy). When a thesaurus is available in search, the search system can recommend other terms to search for related information. Related concepts should never be automatically expanded in the query as are synonyms. Rather, the decision to search for a related concept should always be a user decision.

## Classification Schemes

When classification schemes are part of the search architecture, searchers can select classes or sets of information within with to search. Classification schemes are represented as hierarchies of controlled values. The values are linked to information through tags or metadata values.

Classification schemes allow us to predefine the classes for users and to let them select the class from a list at the point of query. Searching within a class allows users to search for the concept "contagion" in a subset of "financial" versus "health" information. Classification schemes also improve precision of searching by holding back information that does not pertain to the context.

# SEARCH SYSTEM PROCESSES

Search system processes include Query Processing Algorithms and Query Matching Algorithms. To the average searcher, these two appear to be one and the same. However, they are distinct processes.

## Query Processing Algorithms

Query Processing Algorithms (QPAs) determine what is done to the search terms before they are matched against the index. QPAs determine whether each word in the query is "tokenized" (i.e., treated as a single entity—"girls" and "education") or whether words are treated as a concept string ("girls education"). QPAs determine whether Boolean operators are inserted into the query, and if so, where and which operators.

QPAs also consult the vocabulary tools to determine if synonyms exist for any of the search terms. If synonyms exist, they are added to the query and used to calculate relevancy of results.

One day in the not too distant future, QPAs will parse the search terms, make a best guess as to whether the searcher means a country when they search "Afghanistan" and a person when they search "Bill Clinton," and contextualize the query for the user. In this example the QPAs are applying a faceted taxonomy to the query before attempting to match it against a parametric index.

Stemming and dictionary expansion is another form of QPA. This strategy does not use taxonomies, though. Stemming can either: (a) use simple pattern matching of root words to root words in the index, or (b) look up root words in an embedded dictionary and expand the query using grammatical forms. The first approach is more common. Neither of these approaches uses a taxonomy. Both of these approaches can lead to decreases in relevancy. The fact that expansion words have the same root does not mean that they are synonymous.

## Query Matching Algorithms

Query Matching Algorithms (QMAs) determine how the search terms will be matched against the index, what constitutes a match, and which matches are the most relevant. If we have a parametric index architecture, we can tailor the QMAs to improve relevancy and to suit the context (Figure 12.16).

If we have implemented vocabulary tools for some of the fields, we can further improve the relevancy ratings by calculating all synonyms detected.

# SEARCH SYSTEM OUTPUTS

It should be clear at this point in the discussion that the search system outputs—what we see in the interface—are largely determined by the features we have engineered into the inputs and processes. Even though the interface (outputs)

| Author | Exact phrase matching = authority control expansion | Relevancy = 100% or 0% |
|---|---|---|
| Title | Default to ALL WORDS (AND operator) with EXACT PHRASE matching (no expansion or stemming) | Relevancy = 100% or 0% |
| Country | Default to EXACT PHRASE matching + authority control expansion | Relevancy = 100% or 0% |
| Topic | Default to EXACT PHRASE matching + authority control expansion | Relevancy = 100% or 0% |
| Keywords | Default to EXACT PHRASE matching + synonym expansion | Relevancy is calculated by degrees depending on the number of occurences and the fields in which they occur (title, keyword, abstract) |
| Format | Default to EXACT PHRASE matching | Relevancy = 100% or 0% |

Figure 12.16  Query matching algorithms by parameters

is the aspect of search that receives the greatest attention, it is the part of the system with the least amount of control.

If all you have to work with is full text indexes and a limited set of QPAs, there isn't much you can do to make search smarter at the interface level. You cannot sort, you cannot narrow your search, you may not be able to control the results displays, and you are limited to a simple word search.

# CONCLUSION

There is no magic bullet that will make search systems smarter. In order to be smart, search systems need to think and act like smart people. Adding intelligence to search systems requires a deliberate and systematic effort. Just as people become smarter by organizing and analyzing knowledge, search systems can add intelligence through the use of taxonomies. Not all search systems have architectures that can support taxonomies. Not all organizations have formalized taxonomies to work with. Where either of these components is lacking, there will be constraints to improving search.

# CHAPTER 13

# Video Management and the Transfer of Knowledge through Audiovisual Material

Suliman Hawamdeh and Hazem Refai
University of Oklahoma

## INTRODUCTION

The strategic role of knowledge in today's economies combined with the advances in information and communication technologies have sparked interest in knowledge management and knowledge processes such as knowledge creation, acquisition, discovery, retention, organization, sharing, and transfer. The increased interest in knowledge management can be attributed to several factors, but one of the key drivers of knowledge management nowadays is the aging workforce in many of the developed countries and the realization by private as well as public organizations of the need to retain their valuable knowledge (DeLong, 2004; Ernst & Young, 2006; Federal Interagency Forum on Aging-Related Statistics, 2000). However, most of that valuable knowledge is in the minds of people, and it is not possible to capture it in a form that can be documented or stored in computerized databases. Our ability to understand what can be captured and what cannot be captured in electronic records is a key to knowledge retention and transfer.

The complexity associated with human knowledge has puzzled philosophers and scientists for thousands of years (Spender, 1998; Stark, 1958). This is why the term knowledge has been defined in different ways and from different perspectives. Our ability to break the knowledge concept into smaller components could be the key to effective knowledge management. However, this could prove to be illusive and time-consuming. A number of knowledge taxonomies were identified and discussed in the literature (Aguayo, 2004; Blacker, 1995; Boist, 1998; Lundvall & Johnson, 1994; Machlup, 1980; Mokyr, 2002; Wiig, 1999; Zack,

1999). Some of these include knowledge embodied in action in the form of skills and cognitive abilities, encoded knowledge or information, procedural knowledge or organizational routines and ritual, practical knowledge, relational knowledge, casual knowledge, social knowledge, spiritual knowledge, substantive knowledge, and scientific knowledge.

Nonaka and Takeuchi (1995) identified types of knowledge, namely explicit knowledge and tacit knowledge. The first type is explicit knowledge or information. This type of knowledge is normally expressed in words and numbers, documented, and can be stored in databases as electronic records. The second type of knowledge is tacit knowledge, which includes subjective insights, skills, and competencies (Nonaka & Takeuchi, 1995). Al-Hawamdeh and Hussein (2001) discussed four different types of knowledge in an attempt to facilitate knowledge retention and transfer: know-what, know-why, know-how, and know-who. The "know-what" refers to facts; "know-why" refers to scientific knowledge about the principles and laws of nature; "know-how" refers to skill(s) or the capability to do something; and "know-who" involves knowing "who knows what and who knows how to do what" and requires special relationships to access experts and their knowledge. "Know-who" is most critical when managers and organizations have to respond to changes (Bawany, 1999). Though "know-what" and "know-why" can be obtained from explicit sources such as books and references, "know-how" and "know-who" are more difficult to codify, as a high degree of personal tacit knowledge is usually involved.

The other type of non-quantifiable knowledge is knowledge about social situations and social practices (Brown & Duguid, 2000; Linde, 2001; Snowden, 1999; Spender, 2003). This type of knowledge is best conveyed to others by telling stories, or narrative. Social knowledge can be broken down into knowledge of individuals and that of groups. Each person in the group, in order to fit into the group, must find a way to incorporate the accepted stories of the group into his or her own story and to incorporate his story into the group narrative. Although Linde found that narrative is a very important aspect of transferring tacit knowledge, she points out that, because telling stories is a social process, capturing them for future use is complicated. Stories are often tailored to the listener and thus are made relevant by the teller. Video may work well if the storyteller is skilled, but transcribing and managing large collections of video manually can be inefficient and expensive. Voice and frame recognition can enhance knowledge retention and transfer using narrative through video (Ricci, 1994).

# AUDIOVISUAL INTERACTION AND KNOWLEDGE TRANSFER

Recognizing the complexity associated with managing tacit knowledge, it becomes clear to researchers as well as practitioners that the best way to retain knowledge within the organization is to transfer it from one person to another through interaction and socialization (McDermott & O'Dell, 2001; Monero, 2001; Nonaka & Konno, 1998). Many terms have come to be used for knowledge transfer, among them, knowledge sharing, dissemination, exchange, and distribution. Knowledge transfer typically transcends geographical distance and time. It may be unidirectional (or largely so) or bi-directional. It may be vertical (between superior and subordinate) or horizontal knowledge sharing. Knowledge transfer can take place when people get together and interact. It can happen in on-the-job training, through discussion and dialogues in formal and informal events, and by being engaged in e-learning and watching television. Narrative and storytelling can be effective in preserving organizational memory, and can be used to convey values, create role models, reveal how things work around the organization, and communicate complex ideas (Snowden, 1999; Stewart, 1998).

Video and audio technology has unique properties that allow individuals as well as organizations to capture and record events and moments in time (Fish, Kraut, Root, & Rice, 1993). If a picture tells more than a thousand words, then a video is worth much, much more. Video enables us to simulate our co-presence through direct synchronous mode or indirect asynchronous mode. Face-to-face (technology mediated) knowledge sharing can take place in videoconferencing, listservs, groupware, newsgroups, virtual team rooms, e-mail, voicemail, and so on. Coincidence of location is not required, but the coincidence of time may be required (e.g., videoconferencing), or may not be required (e.g., e-mail). The key difference between this mode and the document is the ability to customize the knowledge shared in a real-time or near real-time fashion. A technological infrastructure is required to facilitate the mode of knowledge sharing. Innovative applications have been developed to enable audiovisual interaction in the form of collaborative virtual workspace, simulation, and video conferencing applications.

Polycom is one of the leading companies in providing video conferencing solutions. In a recent article published on the company Web site, it talked about how doctors and researchers at Johns Hopkins are using video conferencing to consult and share knowledge and best practices (www.polycom.com/company_info/1,, 3699,FF.html). According to Alexander Nason, senior manager of telehealth for

Johns Hopkins Medicine International, "Videoconferencing is helping us reach people more efficiently than was previously possible." Johns Hopkins is using videoconferencing to share knowledge through its educational program, the JHI GlobalAccess Lecture Series. The series provides physicians around the world with the latest medical updates and education from doctors, clinicians, and researchers at Johns Hopkins. It includes more than 200 topics in more than 30 medical specialties, from cardiac surgery to endoscopy. Each 60-minute program features 45 minutes of lecture and 15 minutes for an interactive question-and-answer session. Nason added that people in other countries can access Johns Hopkins lectures more frequently because the price tag is not cost prohibitive, and physicians at Johns Hopkins are considerably more accessible thanks to video conferencing. It's a lot easier to commit to teaching a one-hour class over video than it is to travel two days to teach that one-hour class.

Video conferencing is used frequently for conventional distance learning applications in universities and educational institutions. It enables visual contact as well as collaborative classroom experience for students on different campuses and between different sites. Besides the visual interaction, videoconferencing can improve retention and appeal to a variety of learning styles by including diverse media such as video or audio clips, graphics, animations, and computer applications. It also enables connections with experts at different sites, bringing a richer content to the classroom. It also provides access to special-needs students, giving them the opportunity to connect and interact with the classroom (Reed & Woodruff, 1995; Woodruff & Mosby, 1996). Besides classroom experience, videoconferencing is increasingly used for meetings and bringing people together from different locations. It provides information exchange and problem solving without the normal burden of travel.

Heath and Luff (1991) postulate that interactions via video cause asymmetries in the interaction. When people interact face-to-face, nonverbal communication is just as important to the interaction as the spoken word. For example, speakers rely heavily on the visual and vocal conduct of the recipient to achieve co-participation. Fish et al. (1993) found mixed results when testing their system in a real-world environment. The system was a computer-based audio and video communications system intended to mimic face-to face, informal communication. Each user had his or her own network terminal that was capable of four types of interactions: cruise, which opened an audio/visual channel with a specific target or list of targets; glances, short, video-only connections to a target; autocruises, where the system itself called random targets (intended to mimic spontaneous conversation like that generated when people meet in the halls); and waylay, where the caller keeps an open link to an absent target, watching for the target's return (much like "camp on" when calling a busy telephone number). Although users of the Cruiser system used it almost as often as they used the telephone, and for similar purposes (setting up face-to-face meetings), users did not find the system useful for complicated interactions. The autocruise feature, which was supposed to facilitate information communication, was found to be much too intrusive. It seems that even though the Cruiser system provided face-to-face-like interactions, it did not allow the subtle social cues found in actual fact-to-face interactions that allow people to govern informal conversation.

Chakraborty and Victor (2004) looked at the effectiveness of compressed video used to present extensive information literacy training simultaneously to on-site students and distance learners. The facilities for the off-site students were not equal to those of the on-site students—off-site students did not have computers with which they could follow along, as did the on-site class; off-site students did not have the opportunity to stop by the reference desk for further consultation. (These students were repeatedly encouraged to contact the instructor, but most did not.) The authors saw this discrepancy between facilities as a major obstacle to the success of the off-site students. But because they did not examine a situation where the facilities were identical, it is hard to say with certainty whether the lack of facilities or some other character unique to off-site students (such as limited experience with library research or some factor related to being distant from the library) was the source of their inferior performance. However, the authors concluded that, while not as effective as face-to-face interactions, if the instructor makes the extra effort to include the distance learners, videoconferencing could be a viable alternative to face-to-face interactions. In a very different use of video to bridge the gap between distant peoples, Gibson (2003) tells of an Intermediate Technology Development Group (ITDG) project that taught women in Kenya, Zimbabwe, and Peru how to produce videos of the "challenges and aspiration of the women" (p. 14). Operating under the theory that women rarely have a voice in discussions about poverty, even though poverty predominately affects women, the members of ITDG wanted to give women a way to tell their policy leaders what they needed. The videos were shown to government ministers, housing directors, donors, and nongovernmental organizations (NGOs) and were broadcast on national television. The result was that these women made contact with policy makers and other groups.

Research into the use of electronic media versus face-to-face communication often shows a contradiction: the medium used often lessens the richness of the communication, but this loss of richness does not lessen the positive results. Kock (2005) argues that it is true there is a loss of richness in the communication, such as nonverbal communication, touch, and so on, and an increase in cognitive effort when using technology, which is a result of the unnaturalness of the communication medium. In other words, relying on the media naturalness principle, Kock argues that humans, having evolved their forms of communication in the richest medium possible (face-to-face), human physiology predisposes them to lose meaning when communication is not face-to-face. In spite of this, Kock argues that the compensatory adaptation principle accounts for the apparent contradiction when people collaborating via electronic media often have results as good as or better than people who collaborate face-to-face. This principle, based on the evolutionary principle that people adapt to new situations when necessary, states that when people are faced with a loss of richness in their communication, they compensate (or overcompensate) to make up that difference by increasing the cognitive energy needed to make the communication work.

## THE ROLE OF TECHNOLOGY IN KNOWLEDGE TRANSFER

Technology plays an important role in the acquiring, interpreting, and disseminating of knowledge. Where knowledge is primarily tacit, technology supports the personal interaction required for its sharing and creation. A coordinated exchange and management of explicit and tacit knowledge will thus lead to the creation and sharing of knowledge (Nonaka & Konno, 1998; Smith, 2000). Managing explicit or documented knowledge is not new. Libraries and information centers are the best examples of efforts through history to manage documented knowledge. Recently, researchers have started to take into account the value of tacit knowledge and the need to develop a framework that integrates the tacit knowledge components. Recognizing that capturing and managing tacit knowledge is a complex task, knowledge management necessitates the process of rethinking information management. There is a need to create a knowledge management environment that encourages people to share knowledge. There is a need for the development of a framework in which tacit knowledge can be identified and tapped when the needs arise. This requires the development of a new generation of information systems that facilitate and encourage knowledge sharing and collaboration. The transformation process from tacit to explicit knowledge and vice versa can only happen when people are part of the process.

Technology enables individuals to coordinate the logistics of face-to-face meetings. It can also be used to catalog the experience and expertise of organizational members, making knowledge sharing possible. Computer-mediated communication such as e-mail or computer-conferences can help to maintain continuity and connection between conversations, especially for those in different locations. One of the key technologies that is driving knowledge management is collaborative technology, such as groupware, intranets, videoconferencing, and document management. Collaboration tools enable a company's professionals to work together virtually regardless of the geographical location. Web technology allows organizations to build Web and knowledge portals that can handle substantial amounts of information and make it accessible to users on a 24/7 basis.

The objective of knowledge management (KM) is to make appropriate knowledge available from knowledge providers to receivers when and where needed. The providers could be individuals or other forms of sources of knowledge such as stored knowledge. Although the traditional modes of sharing knowledge such as face-to-face meetings, conferences, printed reports, and books continue to be useful, today's environment requires knowledge to be accessible as and when needed. That is where Information Technology (IT) can be leveraged to establish effective and efficient tools to enable all the facets of knowledge management, from capturing knowledge, to sharing it, and then applying it.

Knowledge management tools are technologies, broadly defined, that enhance and enable knowledge generation, codification, and transfer (Ruggles, 1997). Typically, they are designed to ease the burden of work and to allow resources to be applied efficiently to the tasks for which they are most suited. Importantly, not all knowledge management tools are computer-based, as paper and pen can certainly be utilized to generate, codify, and transfer knowledge.

Document management systems, groupware, and intranets are a few of the types of applications that can be used to support an organizational knowledge database. Though they do not contain knowledge per se, they provide pointers to it. For example, Yellow Pages, an online directory of expertise, is structured by skill and discipline. Novartis created the "Blue Pages," which contain details of "external experts with whom they collaborate" (Skyrme, 1999). Other approaches include "embedding backup resource material" to access organizational memory, such as is used in CIGNA, and a workflow software that "blends computer held knowledge with human knowledge." CIGNA's "click here for help" screen icon triggers an e-mail for a computer-generated phone call to a human expert, while the workflow software applies rules to differentiate transactions that are straight-forward, and therefore can be handled automatically by computer, from those that require human intervention (Skyrme, 1999). Firestone (2001) defines a knowledge management system (KMS) as an adaptive system with agents that continuously produces, maintains, and enhances the system's knowledge base. A system produces knowledge by gathering information and compares concepts in describing or evaluating its experiences, with its goals, objectives, and expecta-tions. A system maintains knowledge by evaluating its knowledge base against new information.

## ORGANIZING AND MANAGING AUDIOVISUAL MATERIAL

For many organizations, the thought of organizing the vast growing digital resources manually is horrifying. The cost of employing staff to manually build tax-onomies and manually classify information is prohibiting and discouraging organi-zations from embarking on large knowledge organization projects, especially if these projects involve audiovisual material. The current automated statistical-based keyword indexing methods are limited in many ways and lack the semantic capa-bilities needed when dealing with audiovisual information. Many vendors are offering semi-automated solutions to indexing and organizing digital information. They are encouraging their customers to use taxonomies and information archi-tectures in order to combine content and context.

Among the software companies that provide semi-automated taxonomies and content management include Factiva (factiva.com). Factiva has developed a soft-ware solution called Factiva Synaptica Knowledge Management System (KMS) for building and maintaining taxonomies and thesauri. It allows users to create vocabulary files, design metadata elements, configure rules to govern taxonomy behaviors and customize display formats, and perform data import and export functions. Inxight (inxight.com), a spin-off of the famed Xerox Palo Alto Research Center (PARC), is another taxonomy builder and content management vendor. Inxight's product offerings include its LinguistX natural language pro-cessing platform as well as the Hyperbolic Tree software and Summarizer Plus.

Recently, Inxight Software launched an extended service for Google. The application allows Google Search Appliance and Google Desktop users to find relevant documents faster and locate hidden information in document sets and individual documents. The extended service is powered by Inxight's ThingFinder extraction technology, which automatically clusters search results on-the-fly and enables users to filter their results sets by certain categories such as people, companies, places, concepts, and other information contained within the retrieved documents. GrapeVine Technologies (grapevinetechnology.com), with GrapeVine for (Lotus) Notes and GrapeVine for Compass, provides rules-based document discovery and classification, as well as collaboration components, in addition to its set of vertical taxonomy templates. Autonomy (autonomy.com), Plumtree (plumtree.com), and Hummingbird (humming bird.com) also have applicable product offerings as well as significant product developments in the pipeline.

It is important to note that most of these products deal with textual and digitized information and do not support an automated indexing and retrieval of video and audio information. When it comes to video and audio information, there are limited numbers of solutions available. This is because most of the systems available do not provide an automated or even semi-automated method for extracting and indexing video and audio data. Manual indexing of video and audio information is very expensive and time-consuming. With the recent advances in audio and video recognition, it is now possible to build automatic storyboarding software that will produce shot-by-shot storyboards in real time during video capture (Aigrain, Zhang, & Petkovic, 1996). Audio recognition can be used to assist in identifying phrases or concept that can be used to index a specific frame in the video. Some approaches to speech recognition include word spotting (Jones, et al., 1996), speaker recognition (Kazman & Kominek, 1997), and sub-word or phones recognition (Schäuble, 1997). Word spotting is used in mail retrieval by using predefined sets of words.

Several models, techniques, and technologies for video integration in various operations have been developed or are being developed around the world. Some of those techniques include structured and unstructured video data modeling approaches (He, et al., 1999; Tonomura, 1991) and stratification (Davenport, Aguierre-Smith, & Pincever, 1991). In the structured modeling approach, the video is divided into atomic shots, representing the set of basic concepts. The stratification approach, on the other hand, divides the video sequence into overlapping chunks, each chunk representing only a single event that can be easily described. To facilitate retrieval, all useful semantic objects and their attributes appearing in the video shots (or chunks) must be indexed. Because of the time-dependent nature of video data, these semantic units need to be indexed with respect to time as well. As existing image analysis techniques are not sufficient to identify the necessary semantic units, current approaches (Davenport, Aguirre-Smith, & Pincever, 1991; Tonomura, 1991) use text to describe manually the necessary semantic units and their contextual information. The use of keywords or free text, however, suffers from the problem that the descriptions are likely to be incomplete and subjective. Additional techniques are needed to tackle this problem. The process of segmenting video sequences into shots and describing the semantic contents of the resulting video shots using text is known as "logging" in the video industry. The video shots logged are then stored for subsequent retrieval.

# Project Exodus

Project Exodus addresses the critical loss of knowledge through the retirement of senior staff that is expected to occur throughout the Department of Defense (DoD) during the next decade. As part of the project, a prototype is being developed at the University of Oklahoma in collaboration with the Army Defense Ammunition Center (DAC) at McAlester to automate the processes of transcribing video-based interviews and enabling indexing and retrieval of video clips associated with those interviews.

The manual process of video transcription is slow and expensive, and does not allow for the effective capture of valuable knowledge in a timely manner. The transcribed text is used to publish the video on the Internet and make it searchable using free-text search. The indexing process is simple and only a small part of the video that corresponds to certain concept(s) is segmented and placed on the Web. However, given the fact that this is a manual process, only small parts of the interviews are published and made searchable online. Figure 13.1 shows the existing process of video capture and retrieval.

There is a need to automate the process as much as possible to enable more effective and efficient ways of harvesting knowledge from key personnel who will be retiring or leaving. The proposed approach is illustrated in Figure 13.2. Audio and/or video is captured in an interview setting and recorded in either analog or digital format. After converting from analog to digital, if necessary, the quality for both speech and text recognition must be determined. Speech recognition software converts speech to text for indexing and publishing transcripts on the Web.

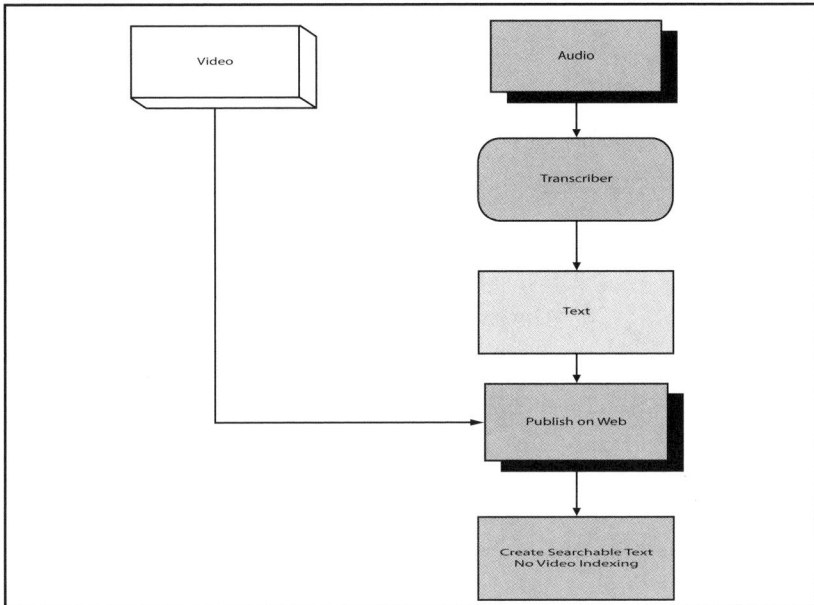

## Figure 13.1  Manual process of video management

The speech recognition module captures text associated with the recorded interviews. Keyword indexing on text associated with the recordings is the best approach for retrieving particular segments. Identifying significant keywords or concepts and linking them to segments within the recordings enables users to navigate and browse the recordings.

Caption recognition is only needed when certain frames in the video contain contextual information that could be useful in indexing the video content. In this case optical character recognition software can be used to capture the text and link it to those specific frames within the video. Keyword indexing enables users to search any format (text, audio, and video) and locate occurrences of certain keywords therein. However, keyword indexing will likely retrieve too many hits that would overwhelm the user and hinder navigating or browsing. A thesaurus would reduce the number of hits and enhance navigating or browsing the content. Creating a controlled vocabulary identifies keywords or phrases that are important to the user and associates those keywords or phrases with significant or key frames in context. These frames form the basis for frame indexing and thumbnail browsing capabilities.

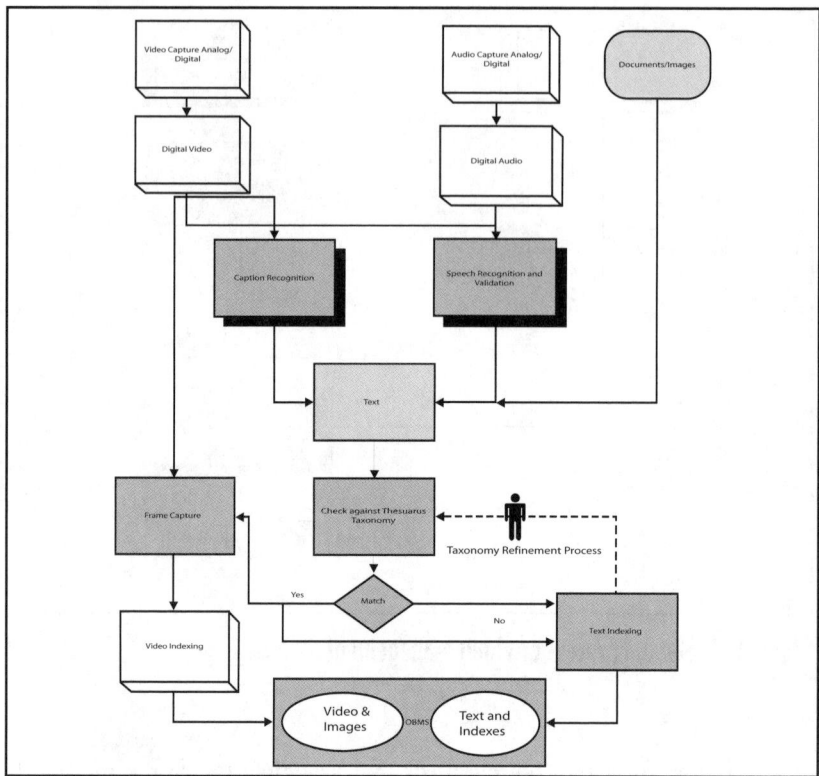

**Figure 13.2 Automated process of video management**

Identifying key frames for indexing is illustrated in Figure 13.2. Once the keywords are extracted from the content, we determine whether these keywords match a pre-defined controlled vocabulary or thesaurus. If there is a match, the frame that corresponds to that keyword is then captured and indexed using the specified keyword, phrase, or subject heading defined in the thesaurus. If the keyword does not match any of the pre-defined keywords or subject headings, the keyword is indexed using free text indexing but without any association to any key frames within the video. The keyword is added to the taxonomy. The user will still retrieve the video shot but without the specific location of that keyword. This normally happens with keywords that are common and occur too often within the associated text.

Free-text indexing combined with relevance feedback capabilities allow key frames to be clustered in such a way as to facilitate navigation and browsing of segments. Each key frame identifies the start of the retrieved segment. For example, in a one-hour recording, there may be 30 to 40 segments, each of which may be one to two minutes in duration. In other words, 30 to 40 key frames will have been identified for that recording. With 30 to 40 key frames, the user can easily navigate through the key frames and play the recording at any position within those segments.

# Summary

Video and audiovisual materials are considered the most effective medium for capturing tacit knowledge in the absence of real-world interaction and networking. Besides the entertainment dimension of video, it becomes a medium for capturing important moments in time and documenting events that most of the time it is very difficult to describe using text. Because of its expressive power, video is also a suitable medium to demonstrate complex and dynamic concepts that cannot be easily explained or demonstrated using text or other media. Combining the advantages of video and the power of today's computers and video capture devices, it is possible to deploy this technology in unconventional situations such as realistic battle zone experience or simulated dangerous environments. Applications that can benefit from integrating video, sound, and text can be used for a variety of applications such as computer-based training and simulation, medical systems, visual databases, virtual reality, point-of-sale systems, and more importantly, harvesting valuable knowledge.

The automation of the process of distilling and codifying transcripts within the Exodus Project context reduces the labor cost and speeds up the availability of key knowledge for training and decision making purposes. Automatically capturing the text associated with the video and at the same time augmenting it with taxonomy assist in eliminating the large number of false hits, which normally happen as a result of keyword indexing. The taxonomy will assist in reducing the noise associated with keyword indexing and enable users to locate key frames in the interviews and associated video for exact retrieval. Users can also navigate within the interviews and the associated videos reducing the time it normally takes to locate the relevant information and get to the desired video segments.

# References

Aguayo, Rafael. (2004). *The metaknowledge advantage: The key to success in the new economy.* New York: Free Press.

Aigrain, Philippe, Zhang, HongJiang, & Petkovic, Dragutin. (1996). Content-based representation and retrieval of visual media: State of the art review. *Multimedia Tools and Applications*, *3*: 179–202.

Al-Hawamdeh, Suliman, & Hussein, Hanna. (2001). Knowledge and Library Information Portal (KLIP). *Singapore Journal of Library and Information Management*, *30*: 54–62.

Bawany, Sattar. (1999). Managing in the knowledge-based economy: Creating and sustaining the organisation's competitive advantage through knowledge management. *Today's Manager*, October–November: 53–56.

Blacker, Frank. (1995). Knowledge work and organizations: An overview and interpretation. *Organization Studies*, *16*(6): 1021–1046.

Boist, Max H. (1998). *Knowledge assets: Securing competitive advantage in the information economy*. Oxford: Oxford University Press.

Brown, John Seely, & Duguid, Paul. (2000). *The social life of information*. Boston: Harvard Business School Press.

Chakraborty, Mou, and Victor, Shelley. (2004). Do's and don'ts of simultaneous instructions to on-campus and distance students via videoconferencing. *Journal of Library Administration*, *41*(1/2): 97–112.

Davenport, Glorianna, Aguierre-Smith, Thomas G., and Pincever, Natalio. (1991). Cinematic primitives for multimedia: Toward a more profound intersection of cinematic knowledge and computer science representation. *IEEE Computer Graphics and Applications*, *11*(4): 67–74.

DeLong, David W. (2004). *Lost knowledge: Confronting the threat of an aging workforce*. New York: Oxford University Press.

Ernst & Young. (2006). The aging of the U.S. workforce: Employers' challenges and responses. Available at www.ey.com/global/download.nsf/US/Arnone_Aging_US_Workforce/$file/AgingUSWorkforceEmployerChallenges.pdf

Federal Interagency Forum on Aging-Related Statistics. (2000). *Older Americans 2000: Key indicators of well-being*. New York: The Forum.

Firestone, Joseph M. (1998). Knowledge management metrics development: A technical approach (June 25, 1998). Executive Information Systems White Paper. Available at www.dkms.com/white_papers.htm.

Firestone, Joseph M. (2001). DKMS brief no. eight: Enterprise information portals and enterprise knowledge portals. Available at www.dkms.com/papers/ekpandeip.pdf

Fish, Robert S., Kraut, Robert E., Root, Robert W., & Rice, Ronald E. (1993). Video as a technology for informal communication. *Communications of the ACM*, *36*(1): 48–61.

Gibson, Sandra. (2003). ITDG's approaches to knowledge sharing. *African Research and Documentation*, 93.

He, L., Sanocki, E., Gupta, A., & Grudin, J. (1999). Auto-summarization of audio-video presentations. In *Proceedings of the ACM Multimedia, 99* (pp. 489–498), October 1999, Orlando, Florida.

Heath, Christian, and Luff, Paul. (1991). Collaborative activity and technological design: Task coordination in London Underground control rooms. *Proceedings of European Conference on Computer-Supported Cooperative Work, 91* (pp. 65–80). Dordrecht, The Netherlands: Kluwer Academic Publishers.

Jones, G. J. F., et. al. (1996). Robust talker-independent audio document retrieval. *Proceedings of the International Conference on Acoustics, Speech, and Signal Processing, Atlanta, GA.* Washington, DC: IEEE Computer Society.

Kazman, Rick, and Kominek, John. (1997). Supporting the retrieval process in multimedia information systems. *Proceedings of the 30th Annual Hawaii International Conference on Systems Sciences.* Wailea, Hawaii, January 1997.

Kock, Ned. (2005). Media richness or media naturalness? The evolution of our biological communication apparatus and its influence on our behavior toward e-communication tools. *IEEE Transactions on Professional Communication, 48*(2): 117–130.

Linde, Charlotte. (2001). Narrative and social tacit knowledge. *Journal of Knowledge Management, 5*(2): 160–170.

Lundvall, B. A., & Johnson, B. (1994). The learning economy. *Journal of Industrial Studies, 1*(2): 23–42.

Machlup, Fritz. (1980). *Knowledge: Its creation, distribution and economic significance.* Princeton, NJ: Princeton University Press.

McDermott, Richard, & O'Dell, Carla. (2001). Overcoming barriers to sharing knowledge. *Journal of Knowledge Management, 5*(1): 76–85.

Mokyr, Joel. (2002). *The gifts of Athena: Historical origin of the knowledge economy.* Princeton, NJ: Princeton University Press.

Monero, Alfredo. (2001). Enhancing knowledge exchange through communities of practice at the Inter American Development Bank. *Aslib Proceedings, 53*: 296–308.

Nonaka, Ikujiro, & Konno, Noboru. (1998). The concept of "ba": Building a foundation for knowledge creation. In James W. Cortada & John A. Woods (Eds.), *The knowledge management yearbook 1999-2000* (pp. 37–51). Boston: Butterworth Heinemann.

Nonaka, Ikujiro, & Takeuchi, Hirotaka. (1995). *The knowledge creating company: How Japanese companies create the dynamics of innovation.* New York: Oxford University Press.

Reed, Jodi, & Woodruff, Merry. (1995). Using compressed video for distance learning. Available at www.kn.pacbell.com/wired/vidconf/Using.html

Ricci, Katrina E. (1994). The use of computer based videogames in knowledge acquisition and retention. *Journal of Interactive Instruction and Development, 7*(1): 17–22.

Ruggles, Rudy. (1997). *Knowledge tools: Using technology to manage knowledge better.* Working Paper, Ernst & Young Center for Business Innovation.

Schäuble, Peter. (1997). *Multimedia information retrieval: Content-based information retrieval from large text and audio databases.* Norwell, MA: Kluwer Academic Publishers.

Skyrme, David J. (1999). *Knowledge networking: Creating the collaborative enterprise.* Oxford: Butterworth-Heinemann.

Smith, David E. (Ed.). (2000). *Knowledge, groupware and the Internet.* Boston: Butterworth-Heinemann.

Snowden, David. (1999). Storytelling: An old skill in a new context. *Business Information Review, 16*(1): 30–37.

Spender, J. C. (1998). Foreword. In Max H. Boisot (Ed.), *Knowledge assets: Securing competitive advantage in the information economy* (pp. vii–x). Oxford: Oxford University Press.

Spender, J. C. (2003). Exploring uncertainty and emotion in the knowledge based theory of the firm. *Information Technology & People, 16*(3): 266–288.

Stark, Werner. (1958). *The sociology of knowledge: An essay in aid of a deeper understanding of the history of ideas*. London: Routledge and K. Paul.

Stewart, T. (1998). The cunning plots of leadership. *Fortune,* 138(5):165–166.

Tonomura, Yoshinobu. (1991). Video handling based on structured information for hypermedia systems. *International conference on multimedia information systems, 91* (333–344). Singapore: McGraw-Hill.

Wiig, Karl M. (1999). Introducing knowledge management into the enterprise. In Jay Liebowitz (Ed.), *Knowledge management handbook* (pp. 3.1–3.41). Boca Raton: CRC Press.

Woodruff, Merry, & Mosby, Jennifer. (1996). A brief description of videoconferencing. Videoconferencing in the classroom and library. Available at www.kn.pacbell.com/wired/vidconf/description.html#what

Zack, Michael H. (1999). Developing a knowledge strategy. *California Management Review, 41*(3): 125–145.

# CHAPTER 14

# Knowledge Discovery, Metadata, and Semantic Interoperability

Denise A. D. Bedford

World Bank

## DIMENSIONS OF KNOWLEDGE AND KNOWLEDGE DISCOVERY

Knowledge discovery is multidimensional because knowledge is multidimensional. There are three dimensions of knowledge discovery:

- **Content dimensions:** The aspects or dimensions of knowledge itself
- **User dimensions:** Who is looking for knowledge
- **Use dimensions:** Why they're looking for knowledge

Knowledge discovery tools are designed to leverage the dimensions of knowledge. Typical knowledge discovery tools include:

- Faceted search
- Clustering engines
- Recommender engines
- People profiles and directories of expertise
- Business architectures and rules
- Business intelligence systems
- Social networking and tagging
- Inferencing engines

To support knowledge discovery, these tools need rich metadata. These tools do not work effectively on linear, full-text representations of knowledge. One of the greatest challenges to effective knowledge discovery, therefore, is the lack of metadata to run these knowledge tools. Metadatas enable the three dimensions of knowledge discovery. In order to support knowledge discovery, we need three kinds of metadata: metadata about knowledge content, the user, and the use/context.

Metadata about knowledge *content* includes: (a) authoritativeness (who created the content, their provenance, relationship to other people and institutions, publishing or authorizing institutions); (b) temporal context (when it was created); (c) conceptual focus (topics, keywords); (d) geographic context; (e) type of content (data, publications, learning events, communications, people, services); and (f) relationship to other content (citations, derivations, links).

Metadata about the *user* includes: (a) who the user is (identifying metadata); (b) what the user knows (area of expertise, credentials, level of knowledge, languages; (c) what the user does (roles, responsibilities, experience); (d) geographical focus (where the user is, cultural comfort, and assumptions); and (e) who the user knows (people in the user's knowledge domain, people with similar profiles).

Metadata about *use* includes: (a) task at hand (business functions, stage of work, business rules); and (b) type of content suited to task.

## Metadata Challenges—Availability and Interoperability

We know the value of metadata and we have knowledge discovery tools. Why are we still using single-dimension knowledge discovery tools? The reason is that there are many challenges associated with metadata.

There are availability problems associated with all three kinds of metadata. *Content* metadata is:

- Often available only for high profile and high value content because creating metadata is expensive and time-consuming
- Not available to describe users (user profiles)
- Not available to describe the context (business architectures)
- Often not available in the language of the content
- Sparse where it does exist, and is not sufficiently rich to support deep conceptual indexing and contextualization
- Not sufficiently rich to describe the multiple dimensions of discovery

*User* metadata is:

- Scattered across systems
- Created for different reasons, in varied syntax and forms
- Rarely descriptive of the interests and knowledge of the person or community in depth or according to an accepted classification scheme

- Rarely able to capture the level of knowledge of a person or community

*Use* metadata is:

- Frequently unavailable due to the predominance of context-insensitive applications (Web applications)

There are interoperability problems associated with all three kinds of metadata. Metadata is not usable because it is:

- Subjective and constrained to the perspective of the creator
- Created to suit different schemes and different business rules
- Not suited to the way users and systems think about the knowledge referenced
- Not to be interpreted or understood outside of the source application where it was created

All of these challenges could be met if we had unlimited human resources and unlimited time. Unfortunately, we will never have enough people or enough time to generate the metadata we need to support knowledge discovery. We describe a solution to meet the metadata challenges, specifically: (1) automated generation of metadata, and (2) designing an interoperable metadata architecture.

# Challenge 1: Availability of Metadata

Semantic technologies help us to solve the metadata availability challenge. Semantic technologies that meet the challenge have two essential components: a *decomposition component* and a *composition component*. Semantic *decomposition* involves breaking down the semantic components of knowledge to make it understandable at a machine level. Semantic composition involves teaching the technologies to behave like a human being solving metadata challenges.

## Semantic Decomposition

Semantic decomposition mimics a human being's most primitive attempt at processing knowledge. Semantic decomposition makes use of natural language processing techniques. Semantic technologies leverage a language's grammatical rules and extensive language dictionaries to "part of speech" tag knowledge. Figure 14.1 illustrates how a sentence is tagged as "part of speech" to identify nouns, verbs, and verb phrases. Reference sources such as names of political figures, groups, or institutions are checked to provide canonical forms and increase our understanding. At this level, the system recognizes the language, sentences, and grammatical forms.

This step, however small, gives us a basis for teaching the system how to look for the kind of metadata values we're interested in extracting or inferring. Once we have decomposed knowledge, we can overlay it with the metadata rules.

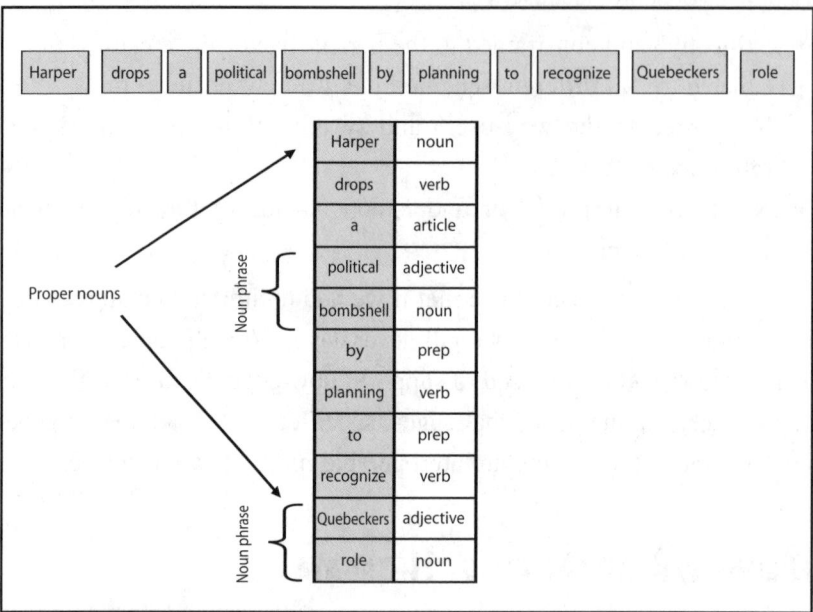

**Figure 14.1  Example of semantic analysis for knowledge decomposition**

This step, and a semantic engine, is critical to successful programmatic generation of metadata. While there are many products available on the market today that are labeled as natural language processing, not all have a semantic foundation. Some tools have a statistical foundation and apply the metadata rules directly without semantic decomposition. This type of tool treats parts of speech as data objects, applying statistical analysis methods directly to words as if they were patterns or numbers. This approach tells us which words appear together in patterns, but they do not give us a foundation for semantic composition or for applying metadata rules. These types of tools might tell us that "artisanal" and "water" frequently co-occur in reports about water resources management. But, we already know that "artisanal water" is a concept. While these kinds of natural language

processing tools have value in knowledge discovery, they do not support semantic decomposition.

## Semantic Composition

The second part of the process is semantic composition. By semantic composition, we do not mean machine level composition of knowledge. Rather, we refer
to the ability of machines to interpret and apply rules for generating metadata. The
critical success factors in automated metadata generation are:

- The accuracy of the rules
- The suitability of the rules to the metadata task
- The ability of a technology to represent and implement the rules

The process of machine generation of metadata should resemble the process
that a person follows to create metadata. People use different processes to create
different kinds of metadata. The rules a person follows to determine who is the
author of a report are different than the rules a person follows to infer a classification to the same report.

We need a set of natural language processing technologies, not a single tool, to
generate metadata. One size, one tool, does not fit all metadata challenges.

# MATCHING SEMANTIC TECHNOLOGIES TO THE METADATA CHALLENGE

In order to solve the metadata challenge, we need a set of *natural language processing* (NLP) technologies, including:

- Concept extraction technologies (rule-based and grammar-based)
- Rule-based categorization technologies
- Summarization technologies
- Clustering

Each technology can be used to generate a different kind of metadata (Table
14.1).

Let's look at each of these natural language processing technologies to understand what they do and how we can use them to greatest advantage. The illustra-
tions provided here are taken from the Teragram tool set. Teragram is a
commercially available tool set, but there are other technologies on the market
today that also provide these natural language capabilities.

## Table 14.1 Metadata and semantic technologies

| Metadata for: | Semantic Technology |
|---|---|
| Authors | Rule-based concept extraction |
| Titles | Grammar-based concept extraction |
| Important numbers (ISSN, ISBN, procurement #) | Rule-based concept extraction |
| Topics or subjects | Rule-based categorization |
| Index terms or keywords | Rule-based concept extraction |
| Country focus | Rule-based categorization |
| Business focus | Rule-based categorization |
| Summary | Text extraction/summarization |

## Rule-Based Concept Extraction

Rule-based concept or entity extraction is a simple pattern recognition technique that looks for and extracts named entities. Any kind of entity can be defined as long as you can describe the rules for identifying the entity in a way the machine can understand. Pattern matching compares the rules or list of entity names to what it finds in the decomposed content. Regular expressions also can be used to match sets of strings that follow a pattern but contain some variation. Figures 14.2, 14.3, and 14.4 illustrate the use of rule-based categorization to extract ISBN and ISSN numbers, and the names of organizations.

Figure 14.2 illustrates how pattern-matching rules can be overlaid onto semantically decomposed text to identify and extract ISBNs. Any standard number

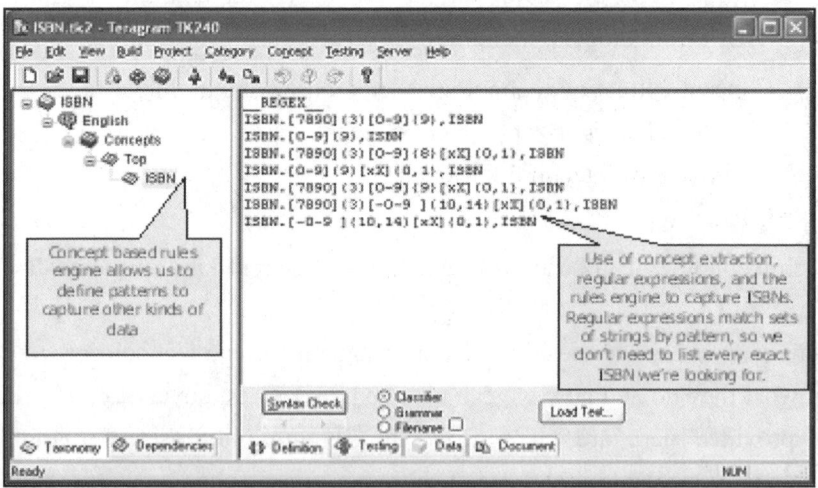

## Figure 14.2 ISBN extraction using regular expressions

```
<?xml version="1.0" encoding="UTF-8" ?>
- <TERAGRAM_XML>
  - <RESPONSE>
    - <ENVIRONMENT>
        <SOURCE name="W:/Teragram Tests/eLibrary Training Sets/Labor and Income/bank.pdf" type="file" />
      </ENVIRONMENT>
    - <CONCEPT name="ISBN">
        <CONCEPT_ITEM name="ISBN" info="ISBN">ISBN 0-8213-2164-1</CONCEPT_ITEM>
      </CONCEPT>
    </RESPONSE>
  </TERAGRAM_XML>
```

## Figure 14.3   Numbers extracted

whose patterns can be specified as a regular expression rule can be extracted, including ISSNs, classification numbers from cataloging in publication, project numbers, procurement numbers, or bid numbers.

Figure 14.4 illustrates how an authority control list of variant forms can be used as a rule set to identify organizations referenced in text. In this case, the rules engine identifies the variant form as the lead-in or entry term, and the preferred form as the output form (as shown in Figure 14.5).

Rule-based concept extraction also can be used to generate additional metadata for knowledge content (authorizing institution, publisher), and metadata that describe the context or use. In the examples here, we can reliably define the rules.

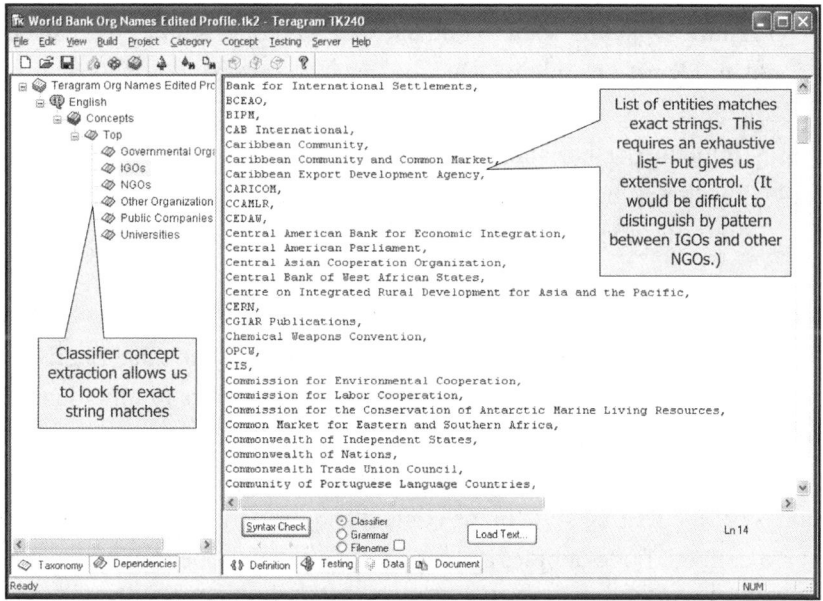

## Figure 14.4   Using rule-based concept extraction to discover organizations

```
- <CONCEPT name="ORG_NAME_EDITED">
    <CONCEPT_ITEM info="na" name="IGOs">IMF</CONCEPT_ITEM>
    <CONCEPT_ITEM info="na" name="IGOs">OECD</CONCEPT_ITEM>
    <CONCEPT_ITEM info="na" name="IGOs">G8</CONCEPT_ITEM>
    <CONCEPT_ITEM info="na" name="IGOs">Bank for International Settlements</CONCEPT_ITEM>
    <CONCEPT_ITEM info="na" name="IGOs">World Bank</CONCEPT_ITEM>
    <CONCEPT_ITEM info="Bank of America Corporation|BAC|NYSE" name="Public Companies">Bank of
      America</CONCEPT_ITEM>
    <CONCEPT_ITEM info="na" name="NGOs">IEA</CONCEPT_ITEM>
    <CONCEPT_ITEM info="na" name="NGOs">ESF</CONCEPT_ITEM>
    <CONCEPT_ITEM info="na" name="NGOs">World Congress of rhe Internatiopal Economic Association</CONCEPT_ITEM>
    <CONCEPT_ITEM info="na" name="NGOs">ATM</CONCEPT_ITEM>
    <CONCEPT_ITEM info="na" name="NGOs">IEA World Congress</CONCEPT_ITEM>
    <CONCEPT_ITEM info="na" name="NGOs">Hungary</CONCEPT_ITEM>
    <CONCEPT_ITEM info="na" name="NGOs">Economic and Social Research Institute</CONCEPT_ITEM>
    <CONCEPT_ITEM info="na" name="NGOs">International Economic Association</CONCEPT_ITEM>
```

**Figure 14.5   Organizations extracted**

The greater the difficulty in specifying the rules, though, the less reliable the extracted metadata.

Generating metadata that describes users and use is a greater challenge. The challenge of building metadata for users is that users are dynamic, multi-dimensional, and require a body of knowledge about the user. Collecting the body of knowledge about the user is a significant challenge.

## Grammatical Concept Extraction

Grammatical concept extraction uses the underlying grammar rules built into the semantic engine. In this case, composition involves defining grammars to describe the entities that you want to find and extract. For example, you can define proper nouns to identify people's names or sentence fragments to discover titles. In this example there is no explicit authoritative list or rule set. Rather, this technology uses implicit parsers and part-of-speech taggers to identify the entities. Figure 14.6 illustrates how grammars can be used to define names of people. Figure 14.7 illustrates the names that were extracted from a document using these grammars.

This technology works only as well as the underlying dictionary and grammars. In order to do metadata generation in languages other than English, you need to have a semantic engine that understands the grammars of other languages and has a well-developed dictionary.

Grammar-based concept extraction sometimes generates "noise" depending on the goodness of the writing style in the content and the way the grammatical components are defined. For example, a person recognizes a proper noun by a combination of case-sensitivity, knowledge of the entity described, and its context in a sentence. If the pattern defined for a proper noun is defined too simplistically on

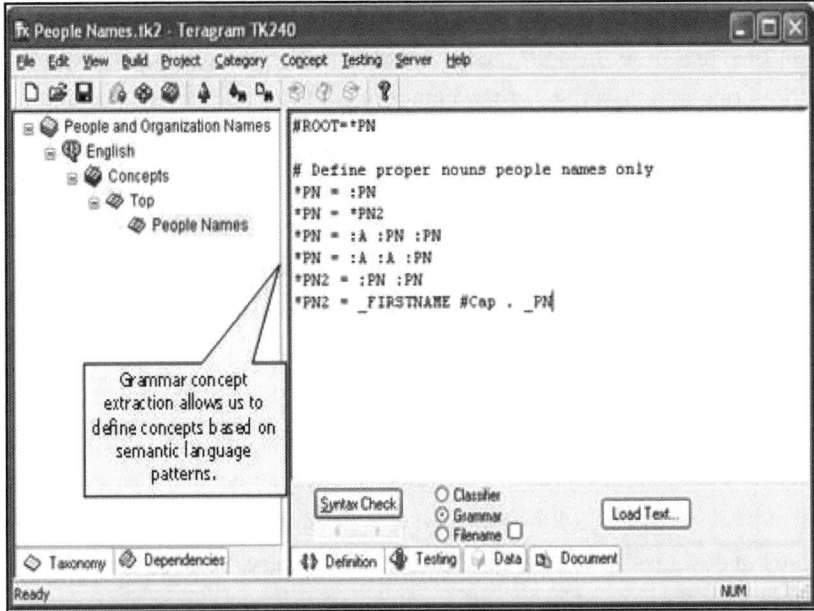

**Figure 14.6  Discovery of people names using grammar-based concept extraction**

```
</Source><Profile_Name> PEO P LE_O RG</Profile_Name>

<keywords>Abdul Salam Syed, Aruna Roy, Arundhati Roy, Arvind Kesarival, Bharat Dogra, Kwazulu Natal,
Madhu Bhadurt, </keywords><keyword_count>7</keyword_count>

</Proper_Noun_Concept>
```

**Figure 14.7  People names generated**

format alone, the system might extract a string of uppercase text that is not a proper noun. In order to think like a person, the system has to have access to as much knowledge as a person.

## Rule-Based Categorization

Categorization is the process of grouping things based on characteristics. Categorization technologies classify documents into groups or collections of resources. An object is assigned to a category or schema class because it is like the other resources in some way. Rule-based categorization assigns knowledge to a predefined set of categories.

Rule-based categorization is an "inferencing" task, whether it is performed by a person or a machine. In both cases, the human and the machine have to understand the scope and coverage of the category in order to categorize accurately.

In order to categorize to a predefined scheme, we first build the scheme. Figure 14.8 illustrates how a rule-based categorization profile is constructed. In the left panel of the screen is the classification scheme. The right panel of the screen contains the domain vocabulary that defines each class in the scheme. The scheme needs to have as much knowledge about a category as a human in order to categorize as well as a human. It is not sufficient to use a few keywords to describe a category.

Humans bring a wealth of tacit knowledge about subject domains to the categorization task. The challenge of categorization is to make this tacit knowledge explicit in the form of a profile. Figure 14.9 illustrates the recommended classifications for a document by a semantic tool. Most of the categorization technologies on the market today are not designed to work with a domain vocabulary. Most of the categorization technologies are actually clustering tools (statistical concept clustering).

Figure 14.9 illustrates the topics that are inferred for a single document using the topic categorization profile described in Figure 14.8. The topics are generated

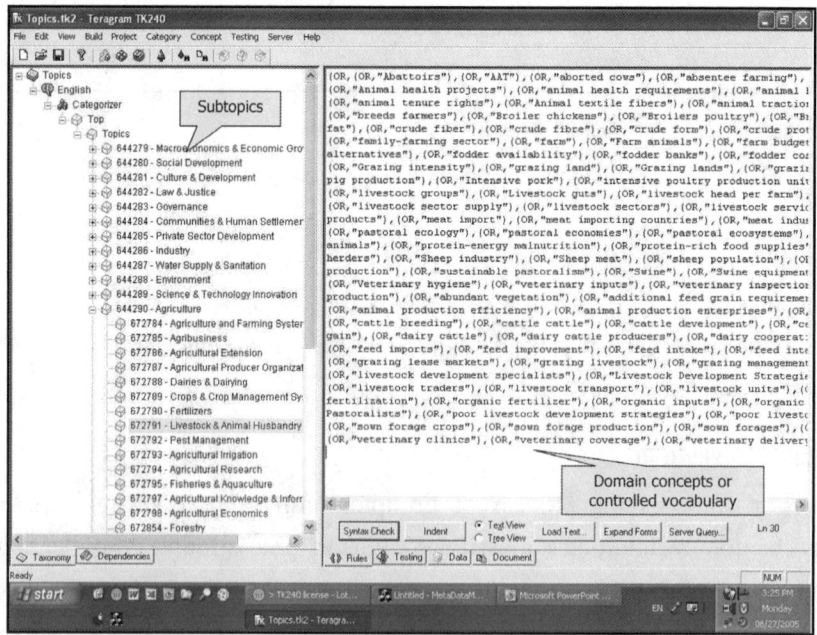

**Figure 14.8  Topic categorization using rule-based categorization**

```
    </ENVIRONMENT>
    <LANGUAGE codepage="CP1252" name="ENGLISH" />
  - <CATEGORY name="Topics">
      <CATEGORY_ITEM mdk="672884" name="Banks and Banking Reform" relevant="1092.0" />
      <CATEGORY_ITEM mdk="672893" name="Financial Intermediation" relevant="729.0" />
      <CATEGORY_ITEM mdk="672888" name="Financial Crisis Management and Restructuring" relevant="568.0" />
      <CATEGORY_ITEM mdk="672634" name="Economic Theory and Research" relevant="567.0" />
      <CATEGORY_ITEM mdk="672885" name="Insurance and Risk Mitigation" relevant="465.0" />
      <CATEGORY_ITEM mdk="672856" name="Public Sector Economics & Finance" relevant="456.0" />
      <CATEGORY_ITEM mdk="672685" name="Settlement of Investment Disputes" relevant="436.0" />
      <CATEGORY_ITEM mdk="672897" name="Non-Bank Financial Institutions" relevant="392.0" />
      <CATEGORY_ITEM mdk="672642" name="Investment and Investment Climate" relevant="387.0" />
      <CATEGORY_ITEM mdk="672635" name="Fiscal and Monetary Policy" relevant="385.0" />
    </CATEGORY>
```

# Figure 14.9   Topics inferred

in an xml format, which is easy for information systems to ingest. Each topic inferred has a relevancy ranking, which indicates the strength of the inference. The relevancy rating is specific to the document or information object. The rating indicates the incidence of occurrence of the domain vocabulary in the document. The categorization method resembles the implicit categorization process followed by a cataloger or subject analyst.

A combination of concept extraction and categorization technologies is the best fit for generating indexing terms or keywords. Concept extraction alone is not sufficient to support high quality machine-assisted indexing. The combination, though, mimics how a person indexes:

- Determine the general focus of the document (implicit categorization)
- Identify key concepts that are substantively treated in the document (implicit concept extraction)

When used in combination, these two technologies generate rich and quality controlled indexing terms. If the quality controlled domain vocabulary (thesauri) is integrated into the natural language processing technologies, the indexing terms generated will be, by definition, also quality controlled. Figure 14.10 provides a selection of the 279 rich concepts generated for the document described in Figure 14.11. Notable is the fact that the indexing terms are not single words, but actual multi-word concepts.

The productivity improvements resulting from the categorization and concept extraction methodologies are numerous and significant. The most noteworthy, though, is the ability to substitute rich conceptual indexing for full-text searching.

Rule-based categorization can be used to generate additional metadata about knowledge (e.g., geographical context, business context), about the user (area of expertise, level of knowledge), and about the context (business role).

```
- <KEYWORD count="279">
    <KEYWORD_LIST>accountability, Accounting, accounting principles, accounting rules, agriculture, annual financial
    statements, asset valuation, auction, auctions, audited financial statements, auditing, auditors, balance sheets,
    bank accounts, bank deposits, bank failure, bank failures, bank loans, bank management, bank supervision,
    banking law, banking laws, banking regulation, banking sector, banking services, banking supervision, banking
    system, bankruptcy, banks, borrowing, Capital Adequacy, Capital requirements, capitalization, CAR, cash
    management, central bank, central banking, civil service, clearinghouse, collateral, collateralization, commercial
    banks, competitiveness, compulsory insurance, connected lending, consolidated supervision, consolidation,
    consumers, contingency planning, contract enforcement, contractual savings, corporate governance, corporate
    sector, cost recovery, CPSS, credit boom, Credit exposures, credit facility, credit institutions, credit risk, credit
    risks, Credit Unions, currency assets, current accounts, debt restructuring, deficits, demand deposits,
    denominated loans, Deposit Insurance, deposit insurance coverage, depositors, deposits, development policies,
    disclosure, distressed banks, diversification, domestic borrowing, earning assets, Earnings, economic growth,
    economies of scale, effective governance, electricity, euro, excess liquidity, exchange policy, exchange rate,
    exchange rate depreciation, exchange rate risk, exchange rates, export growth, external debt, external
    financing, factoring, financial accounting, financial information, financial institutions, financial intermediaries,
    Financial Intermediation, financial management, Financial Markets, financial products, Financial Reporting,
    Financial Reporting Standards, financial risk, Financial Sector, financial services, Financial Stability, Financial
    systems, fiscal consolidation, fiscal costs, foreign assets, foreign banks, foreign currency, foreign currency
    deposits, foreign exchange, foreign exchange market, foreign exchange operations, foreign exchange policy,
    foreign exchange rates, foreign exchange risk, foreign nationals, foreign ownership, GDP, government debt,
    government securities, Gross Domestic Product, guidelines, housing, IAIS, income statements, inflation, inflation
    rate, institutional investors, insurance companies, Insurance Industry, insurance law, insurance products,
    insurance regulations, Insurance Supervision, Insurance Supervisors, insured deposits, insurers, integrity,
    interbank markets, interbank payment systems, Interest margin, interest rate, interest rates, International
    Accounting Standards, International Association of Insurance Supervisors, international credit rating agencies,
    international financial institutions, international firms, International monetary Fund, international reserves, joint
    ventures, laws, Legal Framework, legal protection, legal provisions, legislation, LEK, liberalization, life insurance,
    life insurance companies, liquid assets, liquidity management, liquidity ratio, litigation, loan agreements, loan
    classification, macroeconomic performance, market forces, maturities, migration, monetary policies, monetary
    policy, monetary policy operations, Money laundering, money market, mortgage loans, mutual funds, non-bank,
    Nonperforming loans, Open market operations, operational risk, operational risks, organizational structure,
    Payment Systems, payments systems, Pensions, per capita income, policyholders, political interference,
```

## Figure 14.10  Example of rich conceptual indexing

## Clustering

Clustering is the use of statistical and data mining techniques to partition data into sets. The partitioning is based on statistical co-occurrence of words, and their proximity to or distance from each other. Words that have frequent occurrences and occur in close proximity to one another are assigned to the same cluster. Clusters are defined by co-occurring terms. Clustering tools are resource intensive to run. Statistical generation of clusters from 50 knowledge objects can require several hours of processing time and consume a significant amount of server resources.

Clustering applications should be carefully and thoughtfully selected. Clustering is an effective method for defining relationships among a predefined set of concepts (i.e., defining a semantic network of concepts in a single domain). Some clustering engines will generate clusters of a predefined set of concepts.

Figure 14.11 illustrates the clusters of concepts that were found in a set of 100 documents. In this case, the clustering was guided by the extensive wildlife resources controlled vocabulary. The wildlife resources vocabulary was fed into the clustering engine and the clustering rules were set to discover associations anywhere within the same document. Clustering rules can be constrained to within a specified number of words, sentences, or paragraphs.

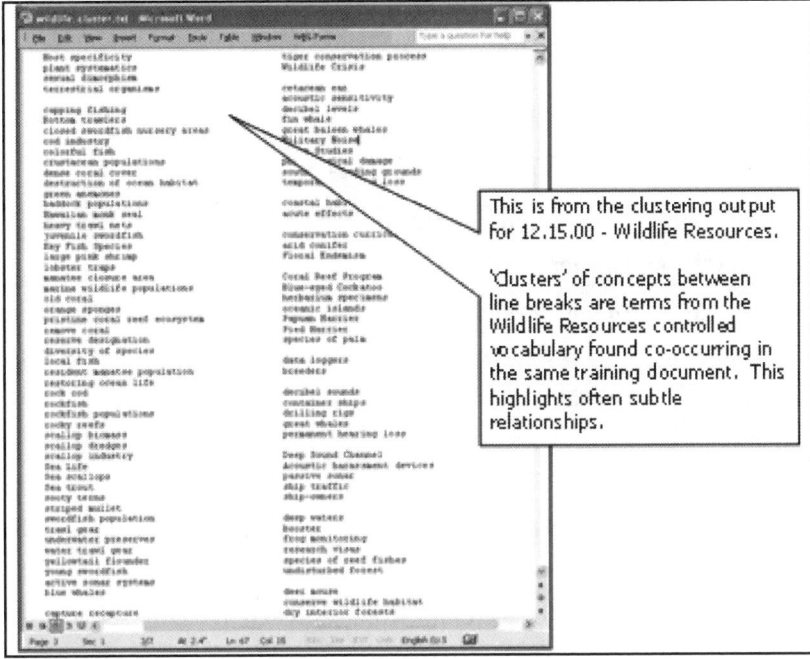

The clusters described in the image are from the clustering output for 12.15.00 - Wildlife Resources.

'Clusters' of concepts between line breaks are terms from the Wildlife Resources controlled vocabulary found co-occurring in the same training document. This highlights often subtle relationships.

## Figure 14.11  Clustering predefined concepts

The clusters described in Figure 14.11 suggest that there are relationships among the following concepts:

> Capping fishing, bottom trawlers, closed swordfish nursery areas, cod industry, colorful fish, crustacean populations, dense coral cover, destruction of ocean habitat, green anemones, haddock populations, Hawaiian monk seals, heavy trawl nets, juvenile swordfish, key fish species, large pink shrimp, lobster traps, manatee closure areas, marine wildlife populations, old coral, orange sponges, pristine coral reef ecosystems, reserve designations, diversity of species, local fish, resident manatee populations, restoring ocean life, rock cod, rockfish, rocky reefs, scallop biomass, scallop dredges, scallop industry, …

The clustered concepts provide a basis for investigating the relationships and building semantic links among these and other related concepts. This technology can be used to enable thesaurus construction and semantic networks.

Clustering can be used to discover other kinds of affiliations (information, people, institutions) based on metadata similarities.

# Summarization and Text Extraction

Summarization is rule-driven pattern matching and sentence extraction. It is important to distinguish summarization technologies from information extraction technologies. Many of the products on the market extract sentence fragments around a predefined keyword or concept. These technologies do not substitute for human generated abstracts, but they are sufficient to give the user a sense of the knowledge object.

Rules and conditions can be defined to resemble how a human abstractor analyzes knowledge for abstracting (Figure 14.12). Sentence extraction rules and conditions allow us to define: (a) the number of sentences to extract; (b) the concepts to use to select sentences for extraction; (c) where the concepts might occur in the sentence; and (d) which sentences to exclude. Rule sets can be defined for different kinds of knowledge.

The most effective summarization technologies combine text extraction technologies with explicit extraction rules and conditions. The most effective technologies can recognize and extract full sentences. Not all summarization tools work with rules and conditions, though. Many are "readers." The reader method uses clustering and weighting to promote sentence fragments. Simple extractors use internal format representation and word and sentence weighting to select sentences.

In summary, automated metadata generation is possible with the right tools and a realistic modeling of human metadata generation processes. We can meet the first metadata challenge.

# Semantic Technologies in Other Languages

We have used English examples in this chapter. Each of these technologies, though, works in other languages, on content that is written in other languages. The semantic foundations are suited to the language. To do rule-based concept extraction in German, we need to use German grammars. To do rule-based categorization, the concepts fueling categorization need to be in German.

| Code | Where would appear in the sentence | It is likely to be included | Syntax |
|---|---|---|---|
| 5 | anywhere in the sentence | It is likely not to be included | copyright/2004,5 |
| 9 | anywhere in the sentence | Definitely not included | for/example,9 |
| 7 | anywhere in the sentence | Definitely to be included | got/the/top/grade,7 |
| 10 | anywhere in the sentence | It is likely to be included | pull/off/that/coup,10 |
| 2 | anywhere in the sentence, followed by the second | It is likely to be included | evidence,2:collected |
| 1 | beginning of the sentence | It is likely to be included | we/report,1 |
| 6 | beginning of the sentence | Definitely to be included | reporting/on,6 |
| 8 | beginning of the sentence | Definitely not included | copyright/reserved,8 |
| 3 | beginning of the sentence; only if the preceding sentence qualifies | It is likely to be included | however,3 |
| 4 | beginning of the sentence; only if the preceding sentence qualifies | Definitely to be included | the/former,4 |

Figure 14.12  Sample summarization rules and conditions

# CHALLENGE 2: INTEROPERABILITY OF METADATA

The second metadata challenge is semantic interoperability. It is difficult to support knowledge discovery when metadata cannot be used across systems, or understood outside of the context in which it was created. The traditional approach to semantic interoperability involves integrating, mapping, and reconciling metadata from different contexts. This works to a limited degree, but is expensive, unsustainable, and unscalable. This approach requires the maintenance of reference mappings, continuous monitoring of metadata in all contexts, consultation, and devising solutions. This is a "feeding the beast" approach.

A second option leverages the automated metadata generation strategy across systems to generate semantically interoperable metadata when knowledge is created. This strategy allows us to get ahead of the semantic interoperability challenge and actually manage it, rather than perpetually chasing it.

Figure 14.13 illustrates enterprise-level profiles for each of the core metadata attributes. Each profile is built once, and used many times. Each profile is built to generate metadata according to established quality standards, and is built by the information quality team.

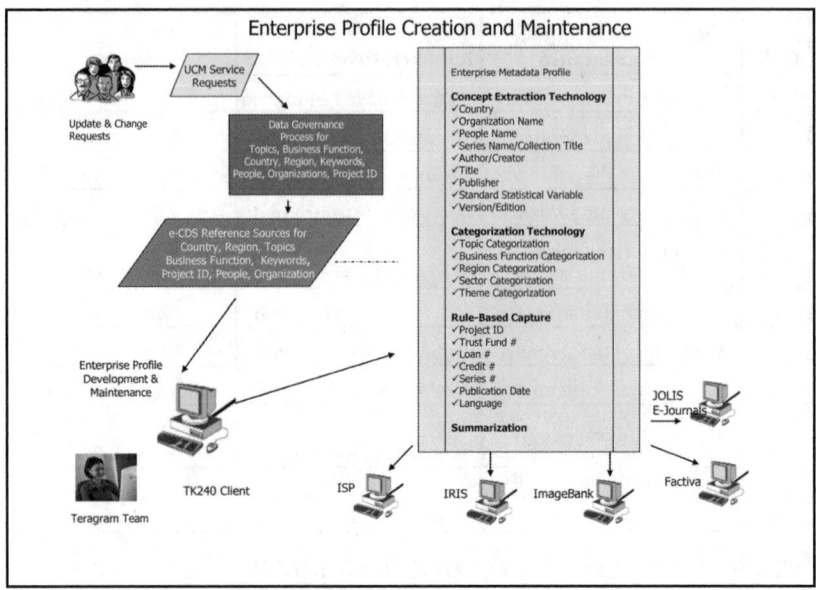

**Figure 14.13 Semantic architecture**

By institutionalizing the metadata profiles described earlier in the chapter, the metadata generated across systems by definition are semantically interoperable. Institutionalizing the profiles means defining an institutional profile for each metadata attribute, and allowing different systems to generate the metadata they need when they need it. It means having an open metadata architecture designed around the semantic technologies. It means shifting the efforts of cataloguers from cataloguing to building metadata profiles and maintaining reference sources (as shown in Figure 14.14).

In this architecture, metadata profiles are designed to support individual metadata attributes. All metadata outputs are xml-formatted for easy consumption by information systems. Each information system generates semantically interoperable metadata when needed.

## SUMMARY

The productivity improvements resulting from a programmatic metadata strategy are significant. The improvements are both direct and indirect. Direct improvements include:

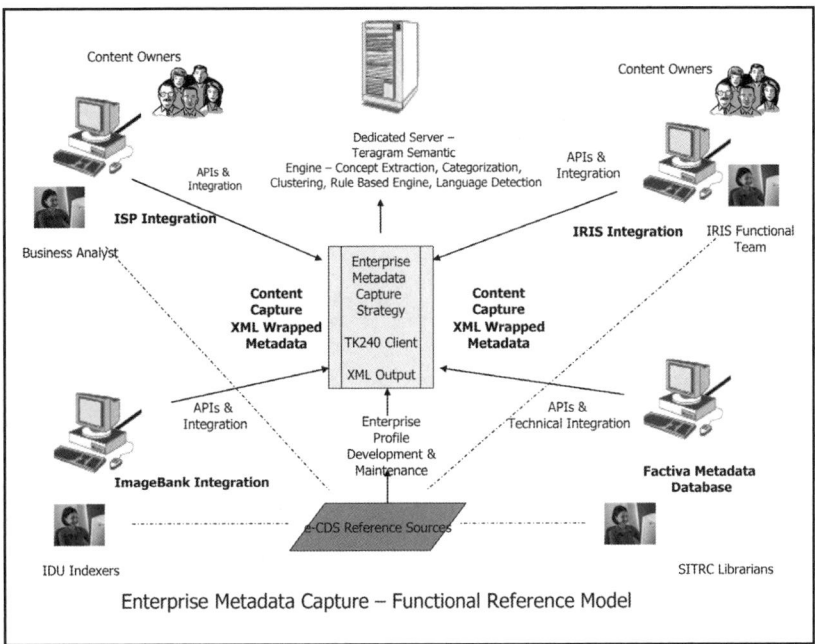

Enterprise Metadata Capture – Functional Reference Model

# Figure 14.14 High-level view of semantic technologies in open metadata architecture

- Reduction in per unit processing cataloging times (where human review is part of the process) from 20 minutes to under 1 minute
- Throughput of PDF formatted documents in batch processing (without human review) of anywhere from 1,800 to 3,000 per hour
- Increase in metadata quality for all attributes
- Increase in richness (quantity) of metadata for individual attributes
- Increased availability of metadata attributes for all kinds of content
- Automatically harmonized metadata values generated for content across diverse information systems

Our conclusions are that we can meet the metadata availability and interoperability challenges using semantic technologies wisely and building our human intelligence about metadata into the technologies.

# CHAPTER 15

# Knowledge Management: Best Practices in the InfoTech Sector

Madanmohan Rao

Asian Media Information and Communication Centre

## INTRODUCTION

This chapter surveys knowledge management (KM) practices in the infotech sector. As an industry vertical, information technology (IT) companies tend to dominate global KM rankings such as the MAKE (Most Admired Knowledge Enterprise) Awards. KM heads of more than a dozen IT companies contributed full-length narratives of their KM experience, summarized in a separate book. This chapter extracts key learnings as captured along the author's "8 Cs" framework for KM: connectivity, content, community, culture, capacity, cooperation, commerce, and capital.

KM can be defined as a systematic discipline and set of approaches to enable information and knowledge to grow, flow, and create value in an organization; this involves people, information, workflows, best practices, alliances, and communities of practice.

KM concepts, theories, and practices seem to have matured over the past decade and spawned a whole industry of vendors, consultancies, thinktanks, task-forces, consortia, magazines, journals, books, Webzines, events, benchmarks, and awards.

This paper reviews recent literature on KM trends and methodologies, provides a framework for analysis of KM practices, surveys KM practices in IT companies, contextualizes these findings with respect to the KM framework, and identifies areas for future research.

# The Road Thus Far: A Decade of Learning and Knowledge Literature

Drivers for KM today include increased workforce mobility, growing complexity in business environments, the need for lifelong learning, willingness by companies to invest in KM, the need to reduce loss of intellectual assets from employee turnover, the need to avoid reinventing the wheel, faster pace of innovation, the need to operate at a global level, increasing shift from tactical to strategic adoption of KM practices, and the steady absorption of Internet and wireless technology.

Gamble and Blackwell (2001) explain that KM is more organic and humanistic as compared to the various business strategy paradigms of the last few decades—but also caution that KM need not be a guarantee of success or survival, though it can certainly improve the odds. There is also the possibility that without proper planning, users may merely become "information rich but knowledge poor."

KM is now being acknowledged not just as a source of wealth but as a mechanism to maintain market position, avoid failure, and beat the competition (Bahra, 2001); Hatten and Rosenthal (2001) also tie KM to competitiveness via concepts like "experimental knowledge gained" and "strategic stretch."

Dixon (2000) identifies five key categories of lesson sharing in large companies: serial transfer, near transfer, far transfer, strategic transfer, and expert transfer. They differ in terms of who the intended knowledge receiver is (same or different from the source), the nature of the task involved (frequency and routine), and the type of knowledge being transferred (tacit/explicit).

In sum, recent literature and study on KM reinforces the importance of knowledge strategy driven by a combination of technology, people, and process considerations, keeping in mind the complex nature of organizational behavior and the uncharted terrain of business and competition in the current global economy.

# The "8 Cs" of Successful Knowledge Management

Over years of consulting and writing, this author has evolved a framework for assessing and enabling success of 21st century KM practices, called the "8 Cs" framework (parameters that begin with the letter C): connectivity, content, community, culture, capacity, cooperation, commerce, and capital (Table 15.1). In other words, successful KM practices can be facilitated by adequate employee

## Table 15.1  KM framework: The "8 Cs" audit

| 1. Connectivity | What connectivity devices, bandwidths, interfaces, technologies, and tools do your knowledge workers have when they are in the office or on the road? |
|---|---|
| 2. Content | What knowledge assets are relevant to the context of your workflow, and what are your strategies for codification, classification, archival, retrieval, usage, and tracking? |
| 3. Community | What are the core communities of practice aligned with your business, and what organisational support do you have for identifying, nurturing, and harnessing them? |
| 4. Culture | Does your organization have a culture of learning where your employees thirst for knowledge, trust one another, and have visible support from their management? |
| 5. Capacity | What are your strategies for building knowledge-centric capacity in your employees, for instance via workshops, white papers, mentoring, and e-learning? |
| 6. Cooperation | Do your employees have a spirit of open cooperation, and does your organization cooperate on the KM front with business partners, industry consortia, and universities? |
| 7. Commerce | What commercial and other incentives do you use to promote your KM practice? How are you "pricing" the contribution, acceptance, and usage of knowledge assets? |
| 8. Capital | What percentage and amount of your revenues are invested in your KM practices, and how are you measuring their usage and benefits in monetary and qualitative terms? |

access to KM tools, user-friendly work-oriented content, communities of practice, a culture of knowledge, learning capacity, a spirit of cooperation, commercial and other incentives, and carefully measured capital investments and returns.

Each of these "8 Cs" is critical for success of a KM practice, and inadequate focus on even one of these parameters can cause the practice to flounder. Let us look at this framework in action in the analysis of KM practices around the world.

# KM in IT Companies: Practitioner Reports

KM typically manifests its impact in four key business processes: design of products/services, customer relationship management, employee management, and business analysis. It works particularly well in situations where timeliness, accuracy, and strategic relevance of information are key; typically, such organizations are in sectors like technology, global consulting, pharmaceuticals, research and development (R&D), and manufacturing (Honeycutt, 2000).

This chapter analyzes KM practices in the IT sector. For this study, numerous KM professionals in the IT sector around the world were approached in person, via e-mail, or on the phone to narrate the story of their KM practices based on parameters like evolutionary trends, infrastructure, knowledge assets, communities of practice, return on investment, cultural issues, capacity building, and incentive schemes (based on the "8 Cs" framework outlined in the previous section).

KM practitioners from more than 15 organizations agreed to contribute to this study. Let us now survey the salient features of KM practices in the profiled IT companies in alphabetical order.

## EDS

Over a dozen years, EDS has perfected a mix of top-down, bottom-up, and regional approaches for knowledge sharing across vertical and horizontal domains, now institutionalized via the Knowledge Management Office and line-of-business KM Champions. EDS has a vast architecture for knowledge sharing and innovation across its global force, which includes the Techlore technical knowledge repository, the EDS Fellows Program for top performers in the company, the innovation engine portal for employees to submit innovative ideas, the Idea2Reality program to make an idea succeed in the real world, the Innovation Centre Network to spur collaboration between Innovation Centres, and 114 communities of practice with more than 28,000 members. The annual EDS Innovation Forum brings together top innovative thinkers from across the globe, and awards are given to the patent of the year, innovator of the year, and community of the year. KM metrics are driven by the Intellectual Capital Balance Sheet, and collaborative research with a top U.S. business school. A mix of "leading, seeding, feeding, and breeding" has made KM successful at EDS.

## EMC

The evolution of the KM system and culture at storage solutions company EMC is a fascinating case study in the impact of rapid technological change, expanding market focus, and stiff competitive pressures on customer service methodologies and attitudes in an IT company. Evolving from a period when it was sufficient to answer customer calls without formally recording the nature of the transaction, EMC's advanced KM practice today has helped improve worldwide sharing of known solutions to technical questions and shorten learning curves of new hires. EMC's secure Web portal, Powerlink, facilitates collaboration between thousands of customer service agents who access more than 21,000 knowledge articles in the EMC Knowledgebase. Metrics that safeguard

Knowledgebase quality, top management support, training programs, and formal awards have ensured that KM culture is ultimately nurtured via peer pressure. Future enhancements include tapping into outside knowledge sources by letting partners and customers create solutions for the Knowledgebase.

## Fujitsu Consulting

Formal KM practices at Fujitsu Consulting (FC) actually got off to a bumpy start, with rampant database proliferation, inadequate budgetary support, multiple technical platforms, and cultural confusion. Things got back on track with awareness programs, top-level support, the Knowledge Access System (KAS) portal, a Results Chain model for realizing benefits, formation of a community called "The Knowledge Underground," and a global Knowledge Support Office (KSO), which works round the clock in different time zones. Today, KM at FC blends both a top-down strategic approach and a bottom-up operational approach. FC's KM practice has helped increase the quality and consistency of work and decrease the cost of proposals, and has delivered a measurable improvement in gross margin via tools like ProjectFinder. Upcoming trends to watch include the use of handheld wireless devices in the spread of KM at multiple "trigger points."

## Hughes Software Systems

A major player in mobile network solutions, Hughes Software Systems (HSS) spends about 14 percent of its revenue in technical R&D, for which KM is a key driver; KM also extends to customer relationships, e-learning, and procurement. In addition to an evolving and closely monitored KM architecture, HSS taps into external sources of knowledge such as industry consortia and collaborative research agreements with universities around the world. Top management support, quality certification groups, KM workshops, and a daylong knowledge-sharing event help foster a culture of knowledge sharing.

## i2

Though barely 15 years old, supply chain software leader i2 has moved quickly from informal collaboration mechanisms to formal knowledge codification strategies in areas ranging from software engineering to constraint theory. Its Knowledge Base and Project Workbench help product developers and marketers in India and the U.S. improve upon software quality for their products and supply chain performance for their customers. KM leaders are appointed from various regions, and their performance in KM implementation is included in their quarter-end appraisals. Knowledge-centric strategies have been successfully used to position the company's products for medium-sized companies instead of just Fortune 500 giants, by leveraging knowledge assets to develop scaled-down products, speed up implementation time, and educate customers via e-learning modules. The company identifies e-learning, cognition studies, and organizational learning as key productivity areas to watch out for in the future.

## IBM

IBM's research into KM from the early 1990s shows that effective KM requires components like corporate vision, process design, organizational roles, and metrics. In 1998, a formal corporate KM effort was launched. A corporate-wide award called Knowledge Advantage as well as individual business units' KM awards help incentivize usage of new KM programs. Systemic metrics ensure that KM practices help corporate business objectives like innovation, responsiveness, efficiency, and competency. IBM also uses an approach called the "HealthCheck" to determine the maturity of its CoPs. IBM conducts extensive research on KM in its own labs as well as client-focused consortiums such as the IBM Institute of Knowledge-Based Organizations. Future KM trends identified by IBM include tighter linkage of KM to human resource (HR) initiatives and Enterprise Content Management; the biggest hurdles are culture, scale, and infrastructure.

## i-flex

Financial software and services firm i-flex has launched a combination of enterprise-wide strategic KM initiatives as well as smaller individual initiatives of a more tactical nature. As is the case with other leading software firms, i-flex's KM initiative is heavily based on process automation, as per the Capability Maturity Model (CMM) framework developed by the Software Engineering Institute (SEI) at Carnegie-Mellon University. i-flex has unveiled a plethora of schemes and tools on its i-Share KM portal—like the QuBase repository of methodologies, the Promotr project tracking tool, Project Closure Documents (PCD), the i-CleaR corporate learning repository, QPati quiz program, i-Suggest process improvement suggestion scheme, K-Forum for employees to seek solutions on unresolved issues, business intelligence monitoring contextualized with respect to i-flex's positioning, and K-Webcast conferences with i-flex experts hosted on the intranet called i-Opener.

## Infosys Technologies

In addition to a culture of sharing, Infosys cleverly leverages its self-engineered KM technology platform to give its employees a hands-on view of KM in action and an opportunity to grow the intellectual asset base of the company. Infosys' KM initiative for domain areas like software engineering is built on the KM Maturity (KMM) model, and is promoted via the motto "Learn Once, Use Anywhere." A formal KM practice with a central KM group, KM steering committee, knowledge research group, and knowledge editors was launched in 1999, and the KM portal KnowledgeShop helps the company improve teamwork, refine software, re-use code, and meet growth expectations. A particularly useful incentivization scheme consists of Knowledge Currency Units (KCUs) whereby employees can award points to knowledge assets posted by their colleagues, and can also earn points when their own posted knowledge assets are utilized. More than 99 percent of respondents in a survey expressed the belief that KM is very essential for the company.

## MITRE

Founded in 1958, MITRE has been deploying asset-harnessing mechanisms like clusters of excellence for decades. Offline and online strategies for leveraging communities have included physical collaborative space design, the award-winning MITRE Information Infrastructure (MII), Technical Exchange Meetings (TEMs), and social network analysis to unearth pockets of expertise in real-time via the XpertNet. Top-level support comes from MITRE's Director of Knowledge Management, along with business unit KM champions. In 1996, MITRE created the Innovation Team (I-Team) and the KM CMM framework was adopted in 2002. An annual KM summit, research partnering with universities, publishing articles and books, the president's KM Achievement award, 10 Corporate KM Recognition awards, and an award for the best published paper have raised the profile of KM at MITRE. Interesting innovations include KM with partners via an extranet, and the Knowledge Partners initiative for retirees. Tangible benefits of KM have been realized in reduced operating costs and improved staff productivity.

## Novell

Novell offers a superb case study of the complexities, opportunities, and challenges that can arise on the KM front at a time of company mergers: in this case, with Cambridge Technology Partners and SilverStream. With proper CEO support and professional KM drive, the tremendous opportunities for synergies have been harnessed while also understanding and coping with the needs of new communities of practice that appear almost on a weekly basis. This calls for the KM function to be nimble, flexible, and proactive.

## Open Text

Open Text's Livelink platform for document management and collaboration is a market leader, and is used by thousands of global companies—including Open Text itself. The company's corporate intranet, OLLIE, hosts the global Knowledge Library and three key communities of practice: Competitive Intelligence Forum, Customer Dashboard, and Knowledge Centre. Open Text has also launched Livelink Wireless, which is being used by its knowledge workers on the road. Open Text launched an extranet in 1997 to improve collaboration with its Affinity Partners, participates in industry KM initiatives like APQC, and has a Knowledge Management Advisory Board (KMAB) consisting of representatives from about 20 of its top customers. Future areas of research and development include tools to improve learning and productivity during and after meetings. A key learning has been that KM solutions are always evolving, and there may be no "perfect" KM solution.

## Oracle

Though decentralized processes for harnessing intellectual capital were in place for more than a decade, Oracle's formal KM-centered programs kicked off in 1997. Its success relies on a network of change agents—including KM Leads, Domain Mentors, and Portal Managers. Web-based project libraries have helped consultants readily find reference material and decreased the number of technical assistance requests from customers. Of Oracle EMEA employees, 30 percent are members of the 80 communities of practice or "Professional Communities," and more than 70 percent of the members say that their communities add value to their performance. Technology is not just "another" enabler for KM but a "key" one; technology-assisted platforms like My.Oracle.Com, GlobalXchange, Knowledge Areas, and Community Areas help KM concepts to be put into action. Future steps include extending KM beyond the enterprise via the Oracle Technology Network and Oracle Partner Network.

# SAS

SAS, the world's largest privately held software company, is such a firm believer and supporter of social capital that it enjoys one of the lowest employee turnover rates in the IT industry. Its understanding and commitment to people-based knowledge sharing ranges from free M&Ms as an incentive for getting people into coffee rooms, to formally designated knowledge support officers who assist busy employees in creating, editing, and translating knowledge assets. SAS has a knowledge repository called ToolPool with loads of useful tips, tricks, and technical papers. An open culture, CEO support, human flexibility, responsiveness, internal marketing, commitment, and scalable technical infrastructure are important components of SAS's KM success.

## Sun Microsystems Philippines

Digital KM platforms can have a transformative power in environments where paper and face-to-face meetings constituted the bulk of knowledge transfer. Sun Microsystems Philippines (SunPhil), a joint venture between Sun Microsystems and erstwhile distributor Philippine Systems Products, was formed in 1999. Sun technology was used to launch the SunPhil Corporate Portal and its Knowledge Management System, with features like document rating, profiling and filtered search, and collaborative authoring. The time taken to prepare proposals and project documentation has been reduced tremendously, and innovative approaches are being explored to harness information mobilization and real-time expert contact via personal digital assistants (PDAs) and SMS (the Philippines, after all, is the world's SMS capital). SunPhil professionals are now partnering with clients, sharing their home-grown experience and expertise in the area of KM. SunPhil is even taking the KM message to the national level through its active support of the Knowledge Management Association of the Philippines (KMAP).

## Unisys

Unisys is deploying KM via a centrally led, but decentrally energized initiative. The KM objectives range from workforce transformation and capture of "proven practices" to developing organizational agility and enhancing stock valuation. A formal KM initiative was launched in August of 2000, with special focus on 11 critical success factors (like alignment with corporate strategy, holistic treatment, and institutional support via a KM Community Council). Architecturally, this is facilitated via the Knowledge.Net portal and Ask

Knowledge.Net expertise location management application. Fifteen communities of knowledge are operational, thanks to a Behavioral Change Method and capacity building exercises like the KM@Unisys_introductory e-learning course available through Unisys University. KM-specific questions regularly feature in employee surveys conducted every 18 months.

## Xerox

Xerox has a high profile in the KM community thanks to its pioneering work in innovative technologies, sponsorship of KM forums, and active participation in consortia such as APQC. There are 10 domains of KM at Xerox, applied to areas like customer service, sales and marketing, software engineering, and call center operations. Xerox launched its Knowledge Management initiative in 1996, and funded the first "Professorship in Knowledge" at the University of California, Berkeley. Xerox's Eureka practice for sales engineers is credited with solving over 350,000 problems annually with savings in excess of $15 million a year. Its Code Exchange initiative (CodeX) has now grown to more than 1,000 registered users and saves more than $3 million annually in software-license fees, servers, and other infrastructure costs. Some of the key learnings include the importance of seeding and supporting communities in a bottom-up fashion, the power of on-the-job learning, and the key role of a people-centered focus.

# KM in IT Companies: Analysis of Findings

Let us now contextualize these findings with the "8 Cs" framework as well as other observations about the nature and performance of IT companies, particularly on the KM front.

IT can be viewed through two lenses: as an industry, and as an instrument. As an instrument for computation, information management, and communication, IT has profoundly transformed consumer behavior, organizational structuring, and the nature of work, ushering in the Information Age. IT-enabled processes are becoming key instruments of KM strategies in the 21st century (with equal importance to culture as well, of course).

And the IT industry itself has been through tremendous turbulence over the past decades, particularly during the spectacular dot-com boom and bust amplified by a global economic downturn and increasing political uncertainties.

Through good times and bad, KM practices have been at the core of the more successful IT firms. "IT companies are leveraging KM to keep up with rapidly changing technology, complexity of implementing solutions, and customers' expectations," observes APQC's Cindy Hubert.

Global IT firms are successfully leveraging KM to capture best practices, improve project management, nurture innovation, enhance customer service, re-use software code, and expand across boundaries of technology generations and varying maturity levels of markets.

In fact, IT companies feature very prominently in the list of winners of awards like the annual MAKE Awards (Table 15.2), conducted by Teleos in association with The KNOW Network. IT companies account for the largest single industry sector in MAKE rankings over the years and across regions. Thus, the IT sector seems to be a good choice to analyze KM in a single industry vertical.

In the IT sector, software is often called the "quintessential knowledge industry," with software being an artifact that is purely a knowledge creation and that defies industrial-age economics thanks to a zero cost of duplication and near-zero cost of distribution in the Internet Age.

One of the advantages of applying IT-enabled KM processes to the development of software itself is that many KM-centric behaviors can be easily embedded in the workflow, directly into development activities themselves. With proper planning and execution, software companies with appropriate levels of quality certification (e.g., SEI-CMM) can leverage software-enabled KM strategies like few others can.

Some other characteristics of the software industry include the relatively high degree of autonomy of the workers, their independence in career planning, a higher proportion of tele-work or remote computing, high degrees of churn as

## Table 15.2  The MAKE Awards criteria: Knowledge performance dimensions

| |
|---|
| 1. Success in establishing an enterprise knowledge culture |
| 2. Management support for managing knowledge |
| 3. Ability to develop and deliver knowledge-based goods/services |
| 4. Success in maximizing the value of the enterprise's intellectual capital |
| 5. Effectiveness in creating an environment of knowledge sharing |
| 6. Success in establishing a culture of continuous learning |
| 7. Effectiveness of managing customer knowledge to increase loyalty/value |
| 8. Ability to manage knowledge to generate shareholder value |

employees quickly move to other pastures or hive off their own start-ups, and the requirement of co-location in customer premises for contracts involving outsourcing (which can raise problems in terms of connectivity to remote systems and even cultural mismatch). Each of these throws up interesting twists for HR managers and KM planners of IT companies.

In terms of the "8 Cs" framework, the individual narratives in the KM case studies seem to support the validity of the eight parameters as discussed next, thus opening the door for more exhaustive and comprehensive benchmarking studies.

## Connectivity

All featured companies have robust connectivity for employees to the intranet and thereby to standardized KM tools, knowledge repositories, and communities of practice. KM at Fujitsu Consulting got off to a bumpy start partly because of lack of standardization of connectivity and KM platform. Many companies have also identified wireless connectivity as the next level of knowledge mobilization to workers like sales staff. Open Text has launched Livelink Wireless, which is already being used by its sales staff on the road. Information mobilization and real-time expert contact via PDAs and SMS are high priorities at SunPhil (Filipino subscribers are the heaviest users of SMS worldwide).

## Content

The featured IT companies have all evolved sophisticated strategies to manage content. These include EDS's Techlore technical knowledge repository, EMC's Knowledgebase for tech support, Fujitsu Consulting's ProjectFinder, i2's Knowledge Base and Project Workbench, knowledge asset editors at Infosys, and i-flex's Project Closure Documents (PCD). SAS has formally designated knowledge support officers who assist busy employees in creating, editing, and translating knowledge assets. Improper planning at an earlier stage led to rampant database proliferation and knowledge clutter at Fujitsu Consulting, which was subsequently rectified. Digital content-management platforms have completely transformed the merged entity SunPhil, which had an archaic paper-based environment prior to merger.

## Community

All profiled IT companies have sophisticated top-down and bottom-up strategies for large numbers of communities of practice (CoP), such as EDS's 114 communities of practice, Fujitsu Consulting's "The Knowledge Underground," MITRE's

Technical Exchange Meetings (TEMs) and XpertNet, Oracle's "Professional Communities," and Open Text's Competitive Intelligence Forum and Customer Dashboard. IBM uses an approach called the "HealthCheck" to determine the maturity of its CoPs.

## Culture

A culture of knowledge-centricity and innovation right from the top levels of management was present in all featured companies. EDS has a Knowledge Management Office and an innovation engine portal for employees to submit innovative ideas. EMC aims to have KM culture ultimately nurtured via peer pressure. i2 preserves its start-up oriented culture of learning fast. IBM conducts extensive research on KM and formulates concepts like the Cognizant Enterprise Maturity Model. i-flex has the QPati quiz program and K-Webcast conferences with experts. Infosys uses mottos like "Learn Once, Use Anywhere." Oracle has a network of change agents. Novell has promoted a culture of synergy during its acquisition of companies like Cambridge Technology Partners and SilverStream. And MITRE aligns KM systems with three corporate values: "people in partnership," "excellence that counts," and "outcomes in the public interest." Quiver (acquired by Inktomi) had to deal with cultural obstacles like the "engineering versus the rest" attitude and "sell and forget" mindset; its merger with a larger company also required cultural adjustment to harness KM. Fujitsu Consulting went through a period of "cultural confusion" in the early days, which even led to a period of "dis-enlightenment" with KM until the program was put back on track. In a QAI survey of KM in 100 software companies, three out of 10 projects on knowledge management were found to fail because of insufficient support from a change management roll out plan.

## Capacity

Building capacity for knowledge-centric behaviors received strong support from all featured IT companies: For instance, EMC has formal training programs, Hughes Software Systems hosts KM workshops and a day-long knowledge-sharing event, and i-flex invests heavily in software process certification for its employees. QAI recommends the use of external consultants for capacity building in KM. Inktomi provides its knowledge workers with training on cost-performance activity, Unified Modeling techniques, statistical charting processes, and job rotation opportunities to understand knowledge impacts on performance measures and productivity gains.

## Cooperation

The more forward-looking IT companies promote a strong culture of internal cooperation between employees and business units, and external cooperation with industry consortia and universities. For instance, EDS conducts collaborative research with a top U.S. business school. HSS taps into external sources of knowledge such as industry consortia and collaborative research with universities. IBM conducts extensive research in client-focused consortiums such as the IBM Institute of Knowledge-based Organizations. MITRE's Knowledge Partners initiative includes contributions from highly qualified MITRE retirees. Open Text has a Knowledge Management Advisory Board with representatives from about 20 of its top customers. Oracle plans to extend KM beyond the enterprise via the Oracle Technology Network and Oracle Partner Network. And Xerox is active in sponsorship of KM forums and participation in consortia on learning, knowledge, and productivity such as APQC. In an inspiring move, SunPhil is even taking the KM message to the national level through its active support of the Knowledge Management Association of the Philippines (KMAP).

## Commerce

Many of the featured IT companies have a mix of commercial and non-commercial incentives to "price" and reward knowledge contributions. Infosys has devised Knowledge Currency Units (KCUs) whereby employees can award points to knowledge assets posted by their colleagues, and can also earn points when their own posted knowledge assets are utilized or ranked by their colleagues; these can be cashed in for gifts at a local e-tailer. MITRE has a $5,000 president's KM Achievement award (presented by the CEO), 10 Corporate KM Recognition awards of $1,000 each (presented by the CIO), and an award for the best paper that makes an external contribution to KM theory/practice. EDS has an EDS Fellows Program for top performers in the company and the annual EDS Innovation Forum for top innovative thinkers from across the globe; awards are given to the patent of the year, innovator of the year, and community of the year. IBM has a corporate-wide award called Knowledge Advantage and individual business units give their own KM awards.

## Capital

Substantial investments were made in the KM systems of the featured companies, and strict metrics adopted to assess RoI. Xerox's Eureka is credited with solving more than 350,000 problems annually that otherwise would have been recreated by other customer service engineers (CSEs) wasting both parts and labor as they try to find a solution—parts and labor savings are in excess of $15 million annually, with increased customer satisfaction and faster learning cycles for the CSEs. At EDS, KM metrics are driven by the Intellectual Capital Balance Sheet. EMC's KM practice today has helped improve worldwide sharing of solutions and shorten learning curves. Fujitsu Consulting has delivered a measurable improvement in gross margin via KM tools like ProjectFinder. i2 has used knowledge-centric strategies to position new products to new clients in less time. IBM uses systemic metrics to ensure that KM practices help corporate business objectives like innovation, responsiveness, efficiency, and competency. Infosys' KM portal KnowledgeShop helps the company improve teamwork, refine software, re-use code, and meet growth expectations. At MITRE, tangible benefits of KM have been realized in reduced operating costs, improved staff productivity, and cost avoidance.

In sum, paying close attention to all the parameters of the "8 Cs" framework has helped the profiled IT companies develop successful KM practices. The most successful IT companies also have KM practices that have been successively benchmarked as among the best in the world.

# FUTURE RESEARCH

The analysis of KM in the IT companies profiled in this chapter throws open a fascinating series of future research questions, at the level of the individual, the business unit, processes, technologies, organizations, sectors, vocations, and even nations and regions.

KM practices, like many other management paradigms and fads, go through successive phases before they mature. They tend to be sparked off by a technology trigger, reach a peak of inflated expectations, then hit a trough of disillusionment; a slope of enlightenment then emerges, followed by a plateau of productivity, according to the Gartner Group.

While those in the IT industry may be familiar with Gartner's "hype cycle" model, it is now being applied to KM as well. KM practices and technologies that have reached the "plateau of productivity" stage include document management and best practice programs. Auto-indexing and knowledge bases are in the "slope of enlightenment" phase, while content management and knowledge mapping are slowly emerging from the "trough of disillusionment."

Communities of practice, collaboration, expert location, and enterprise portals are at the "peak of expectations" phase, while recent technology triggers have sparked off personal KM systems, advanced e-learning, and inter-enterprise KM.

All this has serious implications for KM; let us look at just some of the questions that can arise. How will the emerging "third wave" of the Internet and intranet (mainframes, PCs, handhelds) affect work habits, organizational structures, and knowledge-enabled workflows? Whither personal knowledge management? What new analytics and discovery technologies can be used to mine content assets? What directions will KM standards take? Will KM benchmarks emerge that are geared uniquely toward a particular industry vertical or horizontal function? What are the key learnings from failed or floundering KM practices? How successful will the EU and Southeast Asia be in developing regional knowledge strategies? How can knowledge clusters and learning organizations be promoted in cities and countries around the world? And what's beyond intellectual capital—emotional capital, spiritual capital? What are some future directions of KM literature?

And finally, technology plays an intriguing role in KM practices of globalized organizations in the 21st century—digital interfaces, platforms, and tools can provide knowledge workers with direct and visible proof of KM in action, but can also be mistaken for a one-stop quick-fix solution for KM.

# REFERENCES

Bahra, Nicholas. (2001). *Competitive knowledge management*. New York: Palgrave.

Dixon, Nancy. (2000). *Common knowledge: How companies thrive by sharing what they know*. Boston: Harvard Business School Press.

Gamble, Paul, & Blackwell, John. (2001). *Knowledge management: A state of the art guide*. New York: Kogan Page Limited.

Hatten, Kenneth, & Rosenthal, Stephen. (2001). *Reaching for the knowledge edge*. New York: AMACOM.

Honeycutt, Jerry. (2000). *Knowledge management strategies*. Redmond, WA: Microsoft Press.

Rao, Madanmohan. (2003). *Leading with knowledge: Knowledge management practices in the global infotech sector*. New Delhi: Tata McGraw-Hill.

# Part IV

---

# Knowledge Sharing

# Knowledge Sharing
## Foreword

The chapter by Chait (Chapter 16) is first in this section for a reason: It contains three very important elements. First is his transformation of Bacon's "Knowledge is power" to "The sharing of knowledge is power." An obvious step, of course, particularly given that for a few years there was an audible murmur in the KM community that knowledge management was a rotten name and that the name ought to be knowledge sharing, as practiced in the World Bank.

More important, though, is Chait's extensive analysis of why people don't share knowledge. Particularly illuminating is his stress on the importance of person-to-person communications, particularly in the context of context. The reader interested in this topic should also consult the Roadmap under Collaboration and Collaboration Tools, and under Communities of Practice (CoPs).

Finally, very useful for the KM developer or the KM manager reviewing the success (or not) of their KM system is Chait's discussion of the influencing of behavior. He reviews the "Seven Methods of Influencing Behavior" tool and relates it directly to KM systems.

Marek (Chapter 17) discusses the role of a digital library in supporting KM and the learning organization. Her use of Cliff Lynch's definition of a digital library: "A customized set of information resources and services designed to support a specific kind of work by a specific community" can also serve as a definition of the explicit knowledge resources behind any KM system, and clearly makes the point about relevance of digital libraries to KM. The article is a good review of the issues involved in setting up the explicit knowledge resources behind a KM system. In particular, Marek emphasizes findability and the role of metadata. In addition, she points out two issues not often explicitly touched upon in the KM literature: the issue of localization versus interoperability and the issue of sustainability.

Chait points out that people are often reluctant to share their knowledge with an inquirer whose context is unknown. That occurs not so much because they want to get recognition and to get cited as it were, but because they want to understand the context to which their knowledge and their best practice might be transferred. They want to be able to judge how relevant or applicable their knowledge will be in that context. They want to be able to interact with the requester and discuss parallels, differences, the degree of transferability, and applicability. In short, they want to ensure that their knowledge or lesson learned is put to use appropriately. Chait brings this point out well, and brought it out well at his presentation at the KMWorld meeting in San Jose in November 2006, in a fashion that the co-editors had never before heard articulated so clearly.

Zhang and Ma (Chapter 18) analyze the role of corporate blogs in KM. They describe three different styles of blogs in terms of how they are produced, who is the originator, and their different styles in terms of content. While they report that at least among large corporations, four companies have adopted corporate blogs, they see substantial utility for blogs in facilitating the development of communities of practice. In addition, they report on two research studies, and make some comparison between and draw some conclusions about corporate blogs as a cross cultural context.

# CHAPTER 16

# Sharing Knowledge:
# Problems, Root Causes, and Solutions

Laurence P. Chait

Chait and Associates, Inc.

Sir Francis Bacon, back in the 16th century, was first credited as saying, "Knowledge is power." His declaration became part of our common vernacular, and it proved true for several centuries. But today, Bacon's wisdom has largely lost its luster. In the knowledge age, "knowledge" is not power; rather, the "*sharing* of knowledge" brings power.

The true value of knowledge can only be achieved and realized when knowledge is shared among people. It is through such sharing that improvements are made, new ideas are generated, and innovations occur.

Sharing knowledge can improve processes and speed staff assimilation. It can stop the all-too-common pattern of "reinventing the wheel." And it can reduce waste and improve productivity. Many positive outcomes result from sharing knowledge more effectively.

## BIRTH OF A KNOWLEDGE-SHARING INITIATIVE

As a vice president of a global consulting and contract research firm with more than 25 years of consulting experience, I saw this shift first hand. Because of competitive pressures in a changing business environment, our firm found sharing knowledge an increasingly important factor in its success—sharing across consulting practices, among offices, and around the world. Sharing knowledge more effectively would bring significant benefits for the firm. It would help us to sell more competitively, deliver services more profitably, and deliver higher valued services. It would help us to grow allowing us to assimilate staff faster and more effectively and by enriching and enhancing our products. Also, it would create value by helping us to develop and leverage proprietary technology and consulting products.

In response to the competitive pressures we faced, we embarked on several programs to unify the firm's far-flung operations. We introduced an international sales and support effort to meet the needs of its global clients. We undertook a strategic program to ensure that it showed a single face across the world. And we launched an initiative to ensure that the firm's global knowledge and expertise was effectively leveraged to the benefit of its clients, staff members, and the firm as a whole.

I was asked by the CEO to establish the firm's Knowledge Management (KM) function. Working with a handpicked team, I developed and won approval for the KM strategy, governance structure, operational plan, and budget from the Executive Committee and Board. I then led the effort to create the firm's "knowledge taxonomy," establishing the logic structure for key data about staff, clients, projects, products, tools, "learnings," and reusable methodologies.

With a core staff of eight KM specialists, I led the effort to define and deploy critical KM processes, and to appoint, train, and support 120 Knowledge Stewards to ensure on-going capture of reusable information company-wide. My team embedded KM into the firm's culture, creating physical/virtual "communities of practice," networks, intermediary roles, and events to share explicit and tacit knowledge.

The effort was launched in six months, with 10,000 initial "knowledge objects" providing information on clients and employees worldwide. We introduced leading-edge collaboration tools, including electronic bulletin boards, videoconferencing, mini-repositories, and shared document access. System usage was closely monitored and driven higher; in two years, it grew to 137,000 "pages viewed" per month. More important, the initiative was beginning to have the anticipated effects that senior management had projected for the firm's bottom line.

## Emergence of a Knowledge-Sharing Problem

Thus, much was done to foster increased sharing of knowledge and expertise. But after three years of increasing success, we were surprised and disappointed when we discovered that people were not contributing and sharing content as planned. The question was, "Why?" Everyone said the answer was obvious—our consultants were simply independent, self-absorbed experts. "Of course," people said, "experts do not share because to them, 'knowledge is power'"—by which they meant that our experts hoarded their personally gained knowledge as a sign of their position and rank.

That answer troubled me. After two decades in the firm, I knew from personal experience that consultants from across the organization shared their knowledge and expertise fully and freely when working on a specific client's assignment. There had to be something beyond "knowledge is power" at work.

I decided to dig deeper, to try to identify the root causes of the non-sharing behavior that had been observed. We conducted interviews of a sample of the firm's professionals at multiple levels and in different offices. We also executed a broad survey related to our KM initiative, with attitudes and behaviors on sharing as key components.

As I had suspected, the root cause of the lack of contribution to our knowledge repository and the general lack of sharing was definitely *not* protecting one's knowledge turf. Instead, we found three underlying reasons people were not sharing knowledge.

First, people craved civility. They wanted to be asked "please" before they gave up their knowledge, and they wanted to be told "thank you" after the transfer had taken place. The impersonal nature of our computer-based access to our knowledge repository eliminated peoples' ability to have these sorts of interactions.

The second reason was equally important—and even more significant. People who had expertise were genuinely and correctly concerned that their "knowledge," now captured out of context in a document of some sort, might be applied inappropriately by the new user. They feared that used in such a way, their knowledge might lead to the wrong conclusions—to the potential detriment of the client, themselves, and the firm.

What they wanted was the opportunity to have a brief conversation with the requester to learn the basics of the problem being addressed and why their knowledge was being sought. Then, they wanted the chance to provide caveats and advice to ensure that their knowledge would be properly applied.

Third, experts said that some knowledge simply could not be reduced to a few words on a page. Such knowledge was in the realm of wisdom and what Professor Dorothy Leonard (Leonard & Swap, 2005) of the Harvard Business School calls, "Deep Smarts." This type of knowledge can only be shared within a very well understood context, and it demands interaction between the requester and the expert for such sharing to take place.

I have come to see the need for interaction between requester and expert—be it the quick call or e-mail, or the more intensive discussion—to be present in most instances where experts in less scientific/engineering domains are asked to share their knowledge. Such experts are most willing to share their knowledge, but are seriously concerned that their knowledge be used safely and effectively.

# Problem Solved

So what did we do? The first thing we did was to acknowledge to our user community that we recognized there were valid reasons people might not be willing to simply pour all of their knowledge into our common pot (i.e., our repository). We noted that people wanted the courtesy of a "please" and "thank you." We also made it clear that some knowledge was best not shared openly—and, at times, could not be shared simply through words on a page. In such cases, context and discussion would be needed before knowledge could be safely and effectively used. Finally, we provided the solution to these issues.

It turns out that much of the solution was already in place. We already had the facility for a knowledge holder to add an abstract of his/her content—and to require that the requester call or send an e-mail to gain access to the actual knowledge. And we had made the calling/e-mailing relatively painless. Phone numbers were available in the companion staff directory. Sending e-mails was even easier. Where a knowledge-holder's name appeared, it was accompanied by an envelope icon; by clicking on the icon, the requester could send an e-mail referencing the desired content—from directly within the knowledge portal application.

We also modified our training programs to share these issues and solutions with staff members. Especially with more junior consultants, we stressed the importance of communicating directly with experts to ensure that those experts' knowledge would be used appropriately.

## Other Knowledge-Sharing Problems

*Sorry, no time.* Sometimes people don't share because they don't have the time. When people are under time pressure, they think they can solve a problem by themselves faster than they can if they ask others for help—especially if the others are not known to them, and sitting right next door. Such situations are one of several causes of the productivity blocker known as "reinventing the wheel."

One remedy for such situations is to make it easier to find answers—by proactively developing social networks among employees, or by providing easy-to-use equivalents to yellow pages so that staff can quickly find trusted sources of knowledge. A second solution is to make it clear that reinventing the wheel is not an accepted form of behavior. By rewarding sharing and penalizing reinvention, an organization can impact and change people's behaviors.

*Not as much fun.* At other times, some people would really *rather* reinvent the wheel than leverage someone else's knowledge and have a problem solved. Such people get strong feelings of accomplishment from analyzing problems and meeting new challenges by themselves. To them, such activities provide personal enjoyment and enhance self-worth.

The solution in this case is more challenging. Reinvention may have become a key element in job satisfaction, so simply penalizing it could have serious undesirable side effects. One way to address this issue is to institute a new requirement for sign-off on significant decisions that requires the requester to show he/she has contacted a fellow-employee somewhere else in the organization to get his/her inputs—not with a requirement to follow any advice given, but rather only to discuss and listen.

During these discussions, the requesters often learn things that can significantly improve their cases and the likelihood of management approval. If a person is faced with a good idea—or better yet, a proven solution—he/she will be hard pressed to ignore what's been heard and insist on starting from scratch.

*No way simply.* At times, people don't share knowledge because they don't have the means to share. They may not know who has the knowledge they need. Or, it may be that the organization has not kept such knowledge. And even if the knowledge is there—somewhere—there may be no effective way for a person to locate and access it.

In such situations, building social networks, developing yellow pages, creating repositories, and providing knowledge portals can all be elements of the solution.

*Not my job.* In organizations with a piecework or piecework-like model, where people are paid for the number of widgets they assemble or number of applications they process, there is a negative reward—a penalty—for taking the time out to share knowledge. Helping others can actually reduce their pay.

While promoting the value of knowledge sharing can't hurt, it probably won't go very far toward solving this type of problem. In these environments, the piecework model has to be opened up with other rewards to enable experts to share what they know without penalizing them for doing so. Lower quotas and/or higher piece rates can do this.

***Knowledge really is power.*** Regrettably, in some cases, the long-held belief that "knowledge is power" *can* be a driving force in the failure to share knowledge. It can result from several factors, the most important being where knowledge is the primary currency in getting and keeping a job. In such situations, people's value is measured largely by what they know, or what knowledge assets they have. In such organizations, the reward system, role models, and one's relative position in the organizational pecking order all strongly support the "knowledge is power" syndrome.

Such situations create a highly competitive work environment, one in which *not* openly and freely sharing knowledge is the unwritten rule. It takes some serious *quid pro quo* or strong outside pressure to break the rule and share.

***And many, many more.*** These half-dozen reasons for the failure to share knowledge simply scratch the surface. Two recent articles uncovered myriad barriers to the effective sharing of knowledge:

- Peter Yih-Tong Sun and John L. Scott (2005) conducted a Delphi study and identified 39 barriers, as well as multiple sources of barriers at the individual, team, and organizational levels.
- Andreas Riege (2005) reviewed current KM and related literature and identified 36 barriers, which he categorized as individual, organizational, and technological.

Based on my experience, the most frequent barriers include:

**Personal**
- No time to share
- Don't know whom to call
- Poor social networks connecting people
- Little faith that knowledge will be used appropriately
- Low levels of trust between individuals

**Organizational**
- Poor alignment of knowledge initiatives with corporate goals and objectives
- Ineffective communication of the value proposition for knowledge sharing
- Low ranking of knowledge initiatives among management's key programs
- Lack of shared values
- Work environment that stifles sharing

- Poor "any-to-any" communication channels or infrastructure
- Incentive system that inhibits knowledge sharing
- Highly competitive internal environment
- "Knowledge" as the primary currency for advancement

**Technological**
- Technology tools that fail to support and promote knowledge sharing
- Failure to build comfort in using technology tools

While all of these barriers certainly don't doom knowledge sharing, they can make it a very challenging endeavor. The following section will discuss ways to identify and mitigate the root causes of knowledge-sharing problems.

# FINDING ROOT CAUSES

To identify the reasons—and root causes—that knowledge is not being shared effectively requires observation, inquiry, and analysis. At times, the reasons for a lack of sharing are obvious and can be easily observed. A piecework environment is an example of a situation with an obvious reason for non-sharing, and in such an environment, the obvious reason for a lack of sharing *is* the root cause.

While reviewing the lists in articles such as those mentioned here can provide initial insights, it does not necessarily identify the root causes that must be solved. As we saw in the consulting-firm example, the immediate answer is not always the root cause of the failure to share knowledge effectively. The initial reason given there—that "knowledge is power"—was a *symptom*, or a possible explanation, but not the root cause.

In the consulting firm, the initial reason might just as well have been, "people don't have time to share." Had that been the case, we might have discovered that those people didn't have time because the organization pressured them to be billable at the expense of sharing knowledge. Or, we might have found that people didn't make the time to share knowledge because they perceived such sharing to be unappreciated and unrewarded.

Where there is a need to dig further, interviews and/or surveys can help to uncover root causes, as they did in the consulting example. The objective in such situations is to probe further, and identify the causal factors of observed behavior.

A key tool in identifying the root causes that knowledge is not shared is the word "why." With the "why technique," the investigator takes a page from the average five-year-old and repeatedly asks, "Why?" And whatever the response, the investigator asks "Why?" again and again …

Often, the investigator also uses a set of categories to prompt questions and structure responses. For example, in a knowledge-sharing situation, the categories might be "individual, organizational, and technological," or "reward system, role models, and official communications." The investigator might ask, "Are there any technology barriers to sharing knowledge?" or, "Is there anything in the reward system that impacts how you share knowledge?"

After a more coherent reason is identified, it is often necessary to revert back to the why technique. If the reason is, "People don't share because they can't find the knowledge they need," you could start asking why that knowledge isn't available. Is it because the extraction and codification of knowledge isn't valued? Is it that there is no system to manage or provide access to the knowledge that has been captured? Is it that people don't know that the knowledge exists? Or is it that people don't know how to access the knowledge?

The key is to continue to ask "Why?" until you are certain you have reached a root cause.

However, in analyzing very complex knowledge-sharing issues, basic interviews and surveys often do not go far enough or dig deep enough. In such situations, a more structured tool, such as the "Seven Methods" model discussed later, may be required.

## INTRODUCING A TOOL

The enlightened self-interest of the individual is a key factor in the analysis and mitigation of barriers to knowledge sharing. We all do what we perceive to be in our best interest, and that perception is a product of an individual's life experience and a set of organizational factors. While managers cannot change life experience, they do have the power to shape and mold the work environment to help ensure desired behaviors—in this case, knowledge sharing.

The "Seven Methods of Influencing Behavior" is a tool that can help identify barriers to knowledge sharing and develop initiatives to mitigate them. This tool was first described in "Intentional Revolutions" and further developed by Dr. Joan Lancourt and myself (Nevis, Lancourt, & Vassallo, 1996).

The model states that there are "Seven Methods" (Figure 16.1) that influence behavior:

- **Persuasive communication:** Messages from the organization and its managers that share what is happening, what should be done, and why
- **Participation:** Messages from co-involvement and community that enable the individual to take ownership of goals, objectives, and ideas
- **Role modeling:** Messages from others, especially role models who embody accepted forms of behavior
- **Expectancy:** Messages emanating from the *expected* behavior of others that influence the behavior of the individual
- **Organizational standards and requirements:** Messages from "rules," which, if followed, can make or break the status quo
- **Rewards and recognition:** Messages from incentive programs that impact individual action
- **Structural rearrangement:** Messages from organizational changes that redefine processes and relationships

In the everyday world, each of these "Seven Methods" is constantly broadcasting its message across the organization. Most often, these messages are sent independently of one another, with no coordination among or between them. When the messages are in harmony, they have a positive impact on the individual and what he/she perceives to be in his/her enlightened self-interest. But when the messages

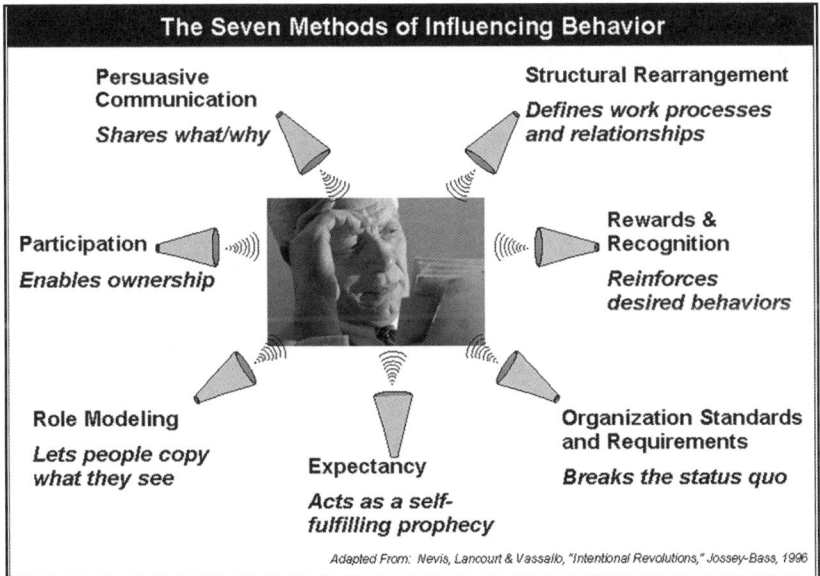

**Figure 16.1 Seven Methods model**

are dissonant, they can promote confusion and inconsistent actions among staff members, can ultimately block any initiative's progress, and even create chaos.

Imagine a situation in which a manager says one thing, but does another. How are those two conflicting messages interpreted by the individual? Which one is to be given precedence? Alternatively, what happens when a manager says to do something, but the incentive system penalizes that thing and rewards its opposite?

By understanding the messages and their impact, it is possible to identify the dissonance and plan multiple interventions over time. The messages can be relatively easily discerned by a combination of observation, interviews, and/or surveys. With this understanding, the messages can be modified and brought into alignment with whatever the change that management is trying to achieve—in our case, more effective knowledge sharing.

## Developing a Solution

Once root causes that block knowledge sharing are surfaced, the next challenge is to mitigate them. Here, the concept of the "Seven Methods" can play a central role.

Managers have a choice of several levers that they can push or pull in an attempt to modify employee behavior. But, as explained in the discussion of the "Seven Methods" tool, it is critical to ensure alignment of the messages employees receive from multiple sources.

An approach to ensure such alignment is to consider the "Seven Methods," asking:

- What messages is each method sending today?
- What messages need to be sent to mitigate the root causes that have been identified?
- What further adjustment in the messages is needed to ensure continued alignment?

In the consulting-firm example, the "Seven Methods" tool was used to help develop a set of initiatives to counter the lack of knowledge sharing:

- In "Communication," messages were broadcast to acknowledge the valid reasons knowledge was not being shared, to reiterate the importance of sharing, and to advise people on how their knowledge could be shared civilly and safely.

- In "Role Modeling," a concerted effort was undertaken to promote knowledge sharing by key managers and thought leaders—the role models in the organization.
- In "Structural Rearrangement," the processes for identifying and linking to experts were enhanced.
- In "Participation," multiple efforts were undertaken to involve staff members at all levels in programs and events related to the KM initiative and knowledge sharing.

A caveat: Pushing and pulling management levers can often have unanticipated and unintended negative side effects. Thus, after the newly aligned messages have been sent and had their initial effects, it is necessary to circle back and analyze whether management's actions have had the desired effect—or its opposite. Have behaviors begun to change, and has the level of knowledge sharing begun to improve? If the trajectories are not as desired, is it necessary to revisit and review the messages once more? In the most complex situations, it can take three or four iterations to "turn the battleship" and set knowledge sharing on a positive course.

## An Example of Clear Messaging

One of the organizations that has been on the forefront of successful knowledge sharing is British Petroleum (BP). Lord John Browne, CEO, has been a major force in transforming the organization from an also-ran to a world performance leader.

In the case of BP, consistent communication from the top has played a major role in the success of knowledge management and the business itself. In John Browne's own words: "Anyone in the organization who is not directly accountable for making a profit should be involved in creating and distributing knowledge that the company can use to make a profit" (Prokesch, 1997).

The consistency and clarity of Browne's communications sent clear messages down and across the organization. In addition, he was an active participant in knowledge activities, and thus established himself as a clear role model for his people. It appears now, in light of the report on BP's safety and maintenance failures, that Browne's internal messages were often at variance to the external projection of what was being communicated.

## Summary

Sharing knowledge has always played a role in an enterprise's success. But today, with global competitive pressures, a changing business environment, and a knowledge-centric economy, sharing knowledge has become a *critical* factor in that success.

Both research and empirical observation have pointed to myriad reasons that knowledge is not shared easily or effectively within organizations. The challenge for each organization is to uncover the root causes of the lack of knowledge sharing in its own environment, and to determine ways to mitigate those root causes.

For successful implementation of knowledge sharing, a tool such as the "Seven Methods of Influencing Behavior" can play a key role in both uncovering the root causes of the lack of knowledge sharing and removing them.

## References

Leonard, Dorothy, & Swap, Walter. (2005). *Deep smarts*. Boston: Harvard Business School Press.

Nevis, Edwin C., Lancourt, Joan, & Vassallo, Helen G. (1996). *Intentional revolutions*. San Francisco: Jossey-Bass.

Prokesch, Steven E. (1997). Unleashing the power of learning: An interview with British Petroleum's John Browne. *Harvard Business Review*, 75(5): 146–168.

Riege, Andreas. (2005). Three-dozen knowledge-sharing barriers managers must consider. *Journal of Knowledge Management*, 9(3): 18–35.

Sun, Peter Yih-Tong, & Scott, John L. (2005). An investigation of barriers to knowledge transfer. *Journal of Knowledge Management*, 9(2): 75–90.

# CHAPTER 17

# Digital Libraries and Librarians in the Learning Organization

Kate Marek

Dominican University

*Key question: How can digital libraries support and extend a learning organization?*

The rapid development of computer technologies, including information systems that store and share data across electronic networks, has provided a springboard for the field of knowledge management (KM) and its growth in the past two decades. The question "How do we know what we know?" demands conceptual answers, but to move from the theory of identifying and capturing knowledge content to the complex reality of making that content available on the other end—the usage end—requires information technology-based knowledge systems. Examples of those systems are software programs such as groupware, content management systems, and sophisticated electronic communication tools. This chapter will deviate from the discussion of these typical knowledge management information technology (IT) tools, and will instead investigate a newly developing arena in information storage and retrieval with significant KM potential: the digital library. A key question in this discussion is: How can digital libraries support and extend a learning organization?

## CREATING A LEARNING ORGANIZATION

An overview of the conceptual elements of the learning organization is a useful preparation for discussing information systems, products, and services that support the learning organization and, specifically for this chapter, the digital library.

Essentially, a learning organization is one that not only captures the knowledge and new ideas generated from its personnel and processes, but that also is able to implement behavior changes based on the captured content. This ability to make systemic changes based on noticing, and then capturing, knowledge and ideas requires first a culture open to change, and then various consistent action steps where that knowledge is incorporated into the organization's processes.

A key part of the learning organization is communicating ideas to the organization as a whole. Garvin (1998) defines the learning organization as one that is "skilled at creating, acquiring, and transferring knowledge, and at modifying its behavior to reflect new knowledge and insights" (p. 49). Argyris (1998) refers to the new "knowledge worker" as needing to combine skill mastery with the ability to work effectively in an organization full of other highly skilled people, forming relationships and working in teams, and to "critically reflect on and then change their own organizational practices" (p. 85). Argyris is also known for his emphasis on double-loop learning, where individuals and organizations can learn from mistakes, and extend knowledge based on a deeper level analysis of problems and events.

While a culture focused on organizational learning is the essential foundation of the learning organization, the implementation of this kind of knowledge management requires sophisticated tools. Contemporary capabilities of IT provide opportunities for identification, capture, and access of an organization's information assets. But how are information assets defined? Three concepts are important at the outset of this discussion: information, knowledge, and ultimately the *containers* of that information and knowledge, discussed here as "information products."

## INFORMATION PRODUCTS IN AN ORGANIZATION

Orna (2005) describes a cyclical process of transformation from information to knowledge, and knowledge into information. She defines information as "knowledge which has been put into the outside world and made visible and accessible through a series of transformations" (p. 11). A person's own individual knowledge, according to Orna, is developed due to his ability for "knowledge observation," recognizing information in the outside world that can be internalized and transformed into personal knowledge. "Information products" are intentionally developed to assist in that transformation; they may be developed at a variety of levels for a variety of purposes, such as for personal, organizational, or social use. The content of information products may be stored in a variety of formats, including print, audio, graphics, and moving images. These information products, then, can be stored in a variety of containers, both physical and digital. "Meta-containers" such as Web sites and intranets store additional information products.

Orna's description of the transformation process from knowledge to information and information to knowledge varies from the one-directional continuum ordinarily presented in information literature, which begins with data, moves to information, then knowledge, and finally wisdom. What her definition of the transformation cycle allows us to do is focus more specifically on the importance of the *information product* in the knowledge creation process; we raise the level of importance of the information product, highlighting it as an essential part of the knowledge creation process rather than as an auxiliary byproduct of an organization's "real" work.

This focus on the information product is critical in the discussion of knowledge management, as the effective development and use of an organization's information products, information artifacts, or information assets is essentially the backbone of a learning organization. Librarians, or information managers as they are sometimes identified in the corporate world, create digital libraries through selection, organization, storage, access, and management of specialized sets of information products. These digital libraries are an important component in the overall landscape of KM systems.

## DIGITAL LIBRARIES

A "library," broadly speaking, serves as the information center of an organization. Indeed, many organizations use names such as Information Center to describe the traditional collection of information and services found in today's corporate library. A traditional librarian's functions are to collect, organize, store, and make accessible a variety of information products relevant to the organization's needs. These needs may be diverse, ranging from material supporting research and development to material important to the organization's historical record.

The digital library (DL) is not a replacement for the physical library, but rather an extension of these services. What can digital libraries do for the learning organization that traditional libraries cannot do? To answer that question, we must first define the concept itself.

Witten and Bainbridge (2002) define a digital library as "a focused collection of digital objects, including text, video, and audio, along with methods for access and retrieval, and for selection, organization, and maintenance of the collection" (p. 6). This definition highlights various elements of the library, including the materials (information products as digital objects), users (issues of access and retrieval), and the librarian (activities of selection, organization, and mainte-nance). Lynch (2003) explains a digital library in a way that is most relevant to KM and the learning organization, calling it "a customized set of information resources and services designed to support a specific kind of work by a specific community" (p. 195). Implicit in the explanation of the digital library is the poten-tial for remote access through internal and external electronic networks. This combination of customization and access is what makes the digital library an exciting resource for KM.

# Building the Digital Library: Materials, User Perspectives, and Librarian Roles

## Information Products as Digital Objects: Materials in the Digital Library

The process of creating library collections is a cycle that begins with assessing the organization's information needs. First, "information" should be identified within the context of the organization's mission and business goals. An informa-tion audit may be needed to help identify the resources and information products currently in use, how those materials are used, the outcomes of their use, and the value added to the organization of the information resources' use (Evans, 2000). The overall library collection should not only respond to identified information needs but should also anticipate needs.

Subsets of the library collection may be developed to target a specialized project or information need. The digital collection makes perfect sense for these project-based efforts, as they offer the significant advantage of anytime/anywhere access by a select community of users.

Information products may be packaged in a variety of containers in a variety of forms: text, such as reports, policy statements, and articles; images, such as pho-tographs and architectural drawings; audio files, such as speeches and meeting transcripts; or video, such as records of events and instructional presentations. These information products may be born analog or born digital, and thus they may or may not require conversion before being included as digital objects (DOs) in a digital library collection. Conversion from analog to digital will add an administrative layer to the digital library project that should be incorporated into the project management plan; equipment selection, staff time, and data storage will need to be considered.

Another aspect of the digital library for KM is that the information products may originate from within the organization (internal information products), or they may be purchased or licensed from outside publishers or contractors (external information products). Internal information products in a digital library may be the documents traditionally found in KM content management systems, but selected specifically for a particular purpose in a customized collection. The internal documents may be supplemented with external products such as commercial databases and periodical indexes.

A digital collection, for example, could support the work of a law firm through access to internal information products (case-specific support materials) and external information products (case law and statutes, electronic news services, etc.). Additional items such as forms, contracts, and wills could be made available in a targeted collection to support work practices and projects (Borgman, 2003).

The digital library may be a first-rate collection of information products, but if it is not relevant to the organization's and the users' needs, it will not be used, and therefore will waste valuable institutional resources. "If we build it, they will come," while tempting in many regards, is an insufficient planning model. Digital libraries, according to Agre (2003) will be evaluated "in terms of the ways that they fit, or fail to fit, into the institutional world around them" (p. 219). Robust content framed by a specific project or information need creates a digital library with the highest potential of use within the organization.

Finally, items selected for the digital library should meet the criteria of authority and credibility; quality digital objects are selected not only for content but also for issues of organizational values. Van House (2003) encourages concern "with how people decide whether to trust others' work and to incorporate it into their own and how the DL supports or undermines these processes" (p. 279).

## User Perspectives

Literature from KM frequently emphasizes the importance of building systems based on how users actually work and what they need. For example, the importance of social practices in information system design is a consistent theme in the work of John Seely Brown and Paul Duguid (Brown, 1998; Brown & Duguid, 1996). A system designed not to predict work practices or create a designer-imagined interface, but rather to maximize existing usage patterns of the user population in question is the most desirable system.

That same theme is prominent in digital library literature, as evidenced in the work of Arms (2000), Borgman (2003), Lynch (2003), Morville (2005), and Nardi and O'Day (1999). Research consistently shows the importance of building information environments based on social rather than technical priorities. Agre (2003) states, "A digital library does not require its users to extract themselves from their ongoing patterns of activity. To the contrary, the library can conform itself to those patterns of activity in numerous ways" (pp. 222–223). An important first step in digital library planning and design is recognizing the organization's social networks and practices.

Nardi and O'Day (1999) discuss "information ecologies" that highlight the symbiotic relationship of the people, technology, practices, and values included in a digital library project. Their ecology metaphor stresses the interdependence of the various parts of the whole, thus making the user as important as the technology and the content. Marchionini, Plaisant, and Komlodi (2003) describe a human-centered design principle that links digital libraries to two clusters of constructs: people and their needs, characteristics, and contexts; and design, implementation, and evaluation.

Effective learning organizations are well positioned to create digital libraries with user-centered design. Quality KM systems will already reflect these design priorities, and the digital library collections should mirror the functionality of these systems. Strong partnerships should exist between the information technology staff of a learning organization and the librarians or information managers; these partnerships will guarantee an important consistency in the delivery and access of the institution's digital information products across all systems.

## Access and Retrieval

As mentioned earlier, an important benefit of the digital library is its anytime/anywhere accessibility via electronic communications. As more workers depend on ubiquitous access to communications technologies (sometimes called "ubicomp"), creating information services to meet those needs becomes essential. Issues of security, usability, and search are important considerations for those systems.

## Security

When security is a priority, access to digital libraries may require authorization or authentication (Arms, 2000). Various situations might require restricted access to the digital library, including the existence of proprietary internal information products as well as subscription-based external information products. In addition, protections may be necessary for reasons of data integrity: Who has access to adding or removing information products, and who is authorized to make changes to the documents themselves are examples of questions that must be answered.

Issues of intellectual property may also come into play, such as in the case of content donated with specific rights granted or restricted, or in the case of external information products that are protected by copyright. Materials accessed through the digital library are available for subsequent use, and the individual user is required to abide by protections associated with those works. Internal policies regarding issues such as intellectual property, copying, and use of protected materials should be clearly articulated and made visible within the digital library. The American Memory Project, maintained by the Library of Congress, does an excellent job of displaying rights and permissions with each digital object within the collection, and serves as a valuable illustration of this point (see memory.loc.gov).

Alternatively, the material may be created as an open access resource using the company's existing Web site as a direct portal. However the organization chooses to make the digital library accessible, rules regarding the use of the information products should be clear to the user. External controls such as authentication and authorization should be supplemented with internal policy statements outlining the organization's rules and restrictions surrounding internal and external information products. These information policies are a critical part of the organization's rulebook, and should not be overlooked.

## Usability, Design, and Findability

The primary consideration in terms of access, once issues of security have been determined, is ensuring effective navigation and searching within the digital library. These are issues of architecture, design (including the issue of aesthetics), and usability. Jakob Nielsen (2000) encourages Web designers to begin from the perspective of usability; his definitive work on usable Web interfaces stresses simplicity, consistency, and legibility. When building digital libraries, a consistent format is essential, as users will quickly lose patience with a system that must be relearned from page to page. As stressed earlier in this chapter, understanding users' work processes is also a necessary consideration at the design stage.

There are two dominant methods of analyzing Web page usability, and these are directly applicable to the discussion of digital library design. One standard involves the use of heuristics, or rules of thumb, which can be measured against a proposed or existing interface. Nielsen identifies 10 Usability Heuristics (www.useit.com/papers/heuristic/heuristic_list.html), which include "consistency and standards" as well as "aesthetic and minimalist design." A second method of usability analysis is through user testing, done most effectively by direct observation of a constituent who is asked to "think out loud" as he uses the digital library. These observations and resulting annotations serve as a framework for interface evaluation and revision, including general user reactions as well as any specific frustrations in navigation or search.

Morville's (2005) term "findability" is perfect for describing an essential part of the digital library user's experience: the ability to quickly and easily locate valuable resources within an electronic collection. It is a more complex concept, however, than one might initially think. Structuring findability, or "ambient," ubiquitous findability, must be thoughtful and deliberate, and must rely on established tools such as metadata but must also continue to improve through the design of additional tools. "Ambient findability is less about the computer than the complex interactions between humans and information" (p. 13). Once again, we hear the important message regarding social aspects of information products and their users.

## Aesthetics

While usability is the key factor in system design, aesthetics should not be ignored. Pink (2005) suggests that in our age of abundance, aesthetically pleasing design has emerged as a significant market factor and is ushering in an era of opportunities for "right brained" thinkers, those with "R-Directed sensibilities— beauty, spirituality, emotion" (p. 33). Morville (2005) agrees: "Design has emerged as one of the world's most powerful forces" (p. 103). But by emphasizing aesthetics, Morville and others are not necessarily advocating graphic-heavy interfaces or broad splashes of color. The combination of simplicity, elegant design, and usability creates the best interface; ultimately the designer tries to create a complete and positive *experience* for the user.

Morville describes a "rich, dynamic, interconnected blend of qualities that shape the user experience," including usefulness, accessibility, and "findability" (2005, p. 109). The resources must also be credible and valuable to the user, but this attention to structuring for findability is an essential consideration when creating collections of digital objects.

## Metadata

Computer-based tools can be identified which aid in search and discovery of information products within a collection, facilitating findability. Chief among those tools is metadata, or brief chunks of descriptive information presented within machine-readable formats, or schemes. Metadata is assigned to the underlying structure of a digital object, which then helps identify that object's subject, origin, and structure. Digital objects can be built with attention to enhanced access through the incorporation of descriptive, structural, and administrative tagging.

Descriptive metadata serves to aid in the location, identification, and analysis of the digital object as a resource. Administrative metadata is associated with the management of the digital object (including designations of date, person, or department responsible for the object) and rights management information. Structural metadata helps connect related digital objects, such as individual chapters of a book, pages within the chapter, or related audio and image files. Structural metadata provides a way to identify relationships between objects and is important for navigation of electronic resources (Caplan, 2003).

There are numerous metadata schemes, developed and used for specific kinds of digital objects or for specific types of collections. The Dublin Core metadata scheme is a general-purpose scheme consisting of 15 data elements for resource description. Other schemes include EAD (Encoded Archival Description) for archival collections, VRA (Visual Resources Association) Core for visual materials, and GILS (Government Information Locator Service) for government documents.

Selecting a metadata scheme is an important step in developing a digital library collection. Issues of interoperability with potential partners, projected longevity of the standard, and extent of resource description in each scheme are all important considerations when evaluating metadata scheme options. Institutions hoping to share digital collections must be especially concerned with issues of potential interoperability. However, private organizations are somewhat less confined by potential partnerships in digital library creation. Issues of metadata scheme selection can be more localized than those in regional consortiums, specific academic or scholarly communities, or specialized institutions such as museums. While general standards such as basic ISO conventions are necessary, system creation and design can be responsive to the organization and its existing KM systems, while also potentially influencing the evolution of those systems.

It is, however, worth adding a cautionary note when discussing metadata standards and system architecture. Consistent change is the norm, and any system architecture that is strictly proprietary is somewhat risky. Including standard metadata tagging can ensure greater longevity to your digital objects, even when the collection of objects may have outlived its function. Persistence over time is an important consideration.

## Search Features

Building a system that can be easily searched is a function of information storage and retrieval theory. This discussion of digital libraries assumes digital objects as content; in this case, search clues are embedded in the structure of that digital object. The previous discussion of metadata is closely linked to issues of digital object location and retrieval. In digital collections that will be organized as Web sites, linguistic clues and keywords can be built directly into the source code using both metadata and the basic HTML tag structure.

Ultimately, however, decisions will still need to be made regarding search term designation; selecting a controlled vocabulary such as the Library of Congress Subject Headings or the National Library of Medicine's Medical Subject Headings (MeSH) taxonomy is one option, while a loosely structured "natural language" keyword index structure may be preferred instead. Newly popular "folksonomies," or taxonomies created by the user group itself, can also be used. Whatever option is selected, terms will need to be assigned to each digital object and included in the metadata structure and/or the system design. File type is another consideration, as text documents, and image, audio, and video files will also be distinguishable via appropriate metadata tagging.

While the taxonomies are important, there are additional ways of searching the collection. Browsing materials by broad category, for example, may satisfy a particular kind of information search. Using the earlier example of a digital collection within a private law firm, a user might choose to search by specific case by name or by citation, for a particular judge, within a particular district, by date, or by plaintiff name. Ultimately the metadata scheme's fields should closely match the anticipated search fields.

## Additional Interface Considerations

Finally, interface design should consider the emerging popularity of alternate displays such as those in portable, wireless handheld devices, such as cell phones and pocket personal computing (PC) devices. More and more workers travel and depend on portable devices to access organizational resources. While it is out of the scope of this chapter to discuss the technical aspects of designing for small screens and for portable devices, this is an important area of consideration for contemporary digital library design.

## Sustainability and Stewardship

A final stage of digital library project planning is identification of methods for long-term collection management. Over time, technologies will evolve as will user needs and preferences. Attention must be paid to sustainability of the digital library collection and its digital objects; archival issues are also important.

Computing structures, including software, language structures, and hardware, continue to evolve rapidly. This environment of change is challenging for librarians working with digital information products when viewed from the perspective of archiving and stewardship. Arms (2000) states it well:

> There is no computer in the world that can run programs for some computers that were widespread only a short time ago. Some formats are fairly simple. ... Other formats are highly complex. It is hard to believe that anyone could ever decipher MPEG compression with a record of the underlying mathematics, or that anyone could understand a large computer program on the basis of its machine code. (pp. 259–260)

Thus digital archiving includes not only preservation of the digital objects (DOs) themselves, but also preservation of methods for understanding the DO's type, structure, and format (Arms, 2000). In order to circumvent the obvious problems this creates at an organizational level, data migration has become standard. Data is transferred to newer systems, preserving the content while leaving behind outdated formats. Even metadata structures evolve and must be continually assessed for potential revision. The reality is that, unlike print, digital objects truly do require constant attention throughout their life; lack of migration ultimately leads to their death.

For organizational archiving, digital library collections should be captured in snapshots on a regular schedule. An organizational archival plan will provide a framework for this process; digital libraries should not be forgotten as an important part of the organization's information assets and part of its historical record.

# CONCLUSION

In sum, a digital library must be useful, usable, aesthetically pleasing, credible, authoritative, timely, accessible, and easily searched. A digital library serves learning organizations by providing a cohesive set of information products to an identified "community of interest" (Brown & Duguid, 1996).

A digital library can help create a learning organization and meet its information needs through access to specialized collections of information products, built for user needs, and supported by librarians' services, such as selection, organization, methods of access, and sustainability. These digital libraries extend the physical library through their ability to be flexible, responsive to user information needs, and continually available to dispersed groups of users from remote locations. Digital libraries take their place among other KM information technology solutions, such as content management systems and collaborative workspaces, as an important part of an overall knowledge management environment.

# REFERENCES

Agre, Philip E. (2003). Information and institutional change: The case of digital libraries. In Ann Peterson Bishop, Nancy A. Van House, & Barbara P. Buttenfield (Eds.), *Digital library use: Social practice in design and evaluation*. Cambridge, MA: MIT Press.

Argyris, Chris. (1998). Teaching smart people how to learn. In *Harvard business review on knowledge management*. Cambridge, MA: Harvard Business School Press.

Arms, William Y. (2000). *Digital libraries*. Cambridge, MA: MIT Press.

Borgman, Christine L. (2003). Designing digital libraries for usability. In Ann Peterson Bishop, Nancy A. Van House, & Barbara P. Buttenfield (Eds.), *Digital library use: Social practice in design and evaluation*. Cambridge, MA: MIT Press.

Brown, John Seely. (1998). Research that reinvents the corporation. In *Harvard business review on knowledge management*. Cambridge, MA: Harvard Business School Press.

Brown, John Seely, & Duguid, Paul. (1996). The social life of documents. *First Monday*, (1)1. Accessible at www.firstmonday/org/issues/issue1/documents

Buchanan, George, Jones, Matt, & Marsden, Gary. [n.d.]. Exploring small screen digital library access with the greenstone digital library. Accessible at www.cs.waikato.ac.nz/~mattj/SmallScreenDLsFinal.pdf

Caplan, Priscilla. (2003). *Metadata fundamentals for all librarians.* Chicago: American Library Association.

Evans, G. Edward. (2000). *Developing library and information center collections.* Englewood, CO: Libraries Unlimited.

Garvin, David A. (1998). Building a learning organization. In *Harvard business review on knowledge management.* Cambridge, MA: Harvard Business School Press.

Lynch, Clifford. (2003). Colliding with the real world: Heresies and unexplored questions about audience, economics, and control of digital libraries. In Ann Peterson Bishop, Nancy A. Van House, & Barbara P. Buttenfield (Eds.), *Digital library use: Social practice in design and evaluation.* Cambridge, MA: MIT Press.

Marchionini, Gary, Plaisant, Catherine, & Komlodi, Anita. (2003). The people in digital libraries: Multifaceted approaches to assessing needs and impact. In Ann Peterson Bishop, Nancy A. Van House, & Barbara P. Buttenfield (Eds.), *Digital library use: Social practice in design and evaluation.* Cambridge, MA: MIT Press.

Morville, Peter. (2005). *Ambient findability.* Sebastopol, CA: O'Reilly Media.

Nardi, Bonnie A., & O'Day, Vicki L. (1999). *Information ecologies: Using technology with heart.* Cambridge, MA: MIT Press.

Nielsen, Jakob. (2000). *Designing web usability.* Indianapolis, IN: New Riders Publishing.

Nielsen, Jakob. (2005). Ten usability heuristics. Accessible at www.useit.com/papers/heuristic/heuristic_list.html

Orna, Elizabeth. (2005). *Making knowledge visible.* Burlington, VT: Gower Publishing Company.

Pink, Daniel H. (2005). *A whole new mind: Moving from the information age to the conceptual age.* New York: Riverhead Books.

Star, Susan Leigh, Bowker, Geoffrey C., & Neumann, Laura J. (2003). Transparency beyond the individual level of scale: Convergence between information artifacts and communities of practice. In Ann Peterson Bishop, Nancy A. Van House, & Barbara P. Buttenfield (Eds.), *Digital library use: Social practice in design and evaluation.* Cambridge, MA: MIT Press.

Van House, Nancy A. (2003). Digital libraries and collaborative knowledge construction. In Ann Peterson Bishop, Nancy A. Van House, & Barbara P. Buttenfield (Eds.), *Digital library use: Social practice in design and evaluation.* Cambridge, MA: MIT Press.

Witten, Ian A., & Bainbridge, David. (2002). *How to build a digital library.* San Francisco, CA: Morgan Kaufmann.

# CHAPTER 18

# Corporate Blogs and Communities of Practice

Qiping Zhang
Long Island University

Shanshan Ma
Drexel University

In this chapter, we will first review the literature on corporate blogs and communities of practice. We will then report on our two empirical studies on corporate blogs: one focusing on the usage of corporate blogs, and the other regarding cross-cultural comparison of corporate blogs. Finally we will discuss the three different perspectives on how corporate blogs cultivate a community of practice.

## INTRODUCTION TO CORPORATE BLOGS

Blogs were used for publishing online journals when they were first introduced. Personal bloggers use a blog for personal expression and communication. Nardi, Schiano, Gumbrecht, and Swartz (2004) discovered five major motivations for personal blogging: documenting one's life, providing commentary and opinions, expressing deeply felt emotions, articulating ideas through writing, and forming and maintaining community forums. Moreover, a blog has also been used as a knowledge management tool. While experts use their blogs to publish their thoughts and ideas on a particular topic, readers can interact and exchange knowledge with experts through their comments (Brady, 2005).

Other than personal use, blogs can be created and maintained by multiple authors within a workplace, a team, or a family as a computer-mediated communication tool. Wackå (2004) defined a corporate blog as "a blog published by or with the support of an organization to reach that organization's goals. In external communications the potential benefits include strengthened relationships with important target groups and the positioning of the publishing organization (or individuals within it) as industry experts. Internally blogs are generally referred to as tools for collaboration and knowledge management."

Early practitioners in corporate blogs include Microsoft, Sun Microsystems, SAP developers, Oracle, and Macromedia. Although it was predicted that corporate blogs would be commonplace for most marketers in the future, statistics from Socialtext show that only 5.8 percent of the top Fortune 500 companies have corporate blogs at the time of this writing.

The launch and maintenance of corporate blogs is mainly driven by business motives, which were identified by Cohen (2005) as: establishing expertise, creating alternative media, extending corporate communications, and building communities. At first, leading companies in certain fields used corporate blogs as a tool to provide professional opinions. A company can establish its reputation as an industry expert by offering domain knowledge. Second, a corporate blog can serve as an extra medium for announcing new products and services. Third, a corporate blog can serve as a channel for direct communication with customers. Blogs allow companies to act quickly in response to customers' feedback. More importantly, blogs are a two-way communication channel in that customers can leave comments and interact directly with the company. Fourth, a community composed of enthusiastic blog readers would be built up as a corporate blog develops. In addition to these four business reasons, a corporate blog is also used for more practical purposes such as optimizing the search engine ranking of a corporation. Given that current popular search engines like Google and Yahoo! usually give high credits to constantly updated and link-rich Web pages (e.g., a blog site), small businesses can use a corporate blog as a tool to increase its visibility among numerous search results. In general, most companies that launch a corporate blog find that the blog provides a means of enabling the corporation to connect with its customers in a personalized, immediate way (Levine, et. al., 2000).

# Community of Practice (CoP)

## Definition of CoP

Community of practice (CoP) is the concept described by Jean Lave and Etienne Wenger in 1991 in the context of collaborative learning. It is "a set of relations among persons, activity, and world, over time and in relation with other tangential and overlapping communities of practice." In other words, this involves a social process of collaborative learning among people who have a common interest in some subjects or problems. Since 1991 the "community of practice" has been the grounding concept in education, organizational learning, and many other kinds of settings. Explicit knowledge and tacit knowledge are learned by observing and interacting with other community members.

According to Wenger (1998), a community of practice consists of three basic elements: what it is about (its joint enterprise as understood and continually renegotiated by its members), how it functions (mutual engagement that binds members together into a social entity), and what capability it has produced (the shared repertoire of communal resources—routines, sensibilities, artifacts, vocabulary, styles, etc.—that members have developed over time). Members of a community come together for a reason. This reason is the "joint enterprise" that brings members to the community. After the community is formed, members inside the community function cooperatively to sustain the community. The learning and interest of its members are what keep a community of practice together. And finally, members of a community develop the shared repertoire of communal resources through their mutual engagement.

## Success of CoP: Identify Key Elements for CoP Elements or Framework

Hildreth (2004) summarized 12 successful characteristics of a community of practice: common ground, common purpose/motivation, legitimate peripheral participation (LPP), fluidity, evolution, relationship, community and identity, narration, dynamism and new knowledge creation, informal, unofficial/voluntary, and similar jobs.

Among these characteristics, *common ground* refers to the knowledge, beliefs, and suppositions shared by members of the community; *common purpose/motivation* is what gives the group an internal impetus to come together; *legitimate peripheral participation* (LPP) is the process by which a newcomer to the group gradually becomes an established member of the CoP; *fluidity/regeneration* refers to the arrival of newcomers and the eventual departure of old-timers; *evolution* refers to the process through which a community evolves; *narration* is the process of storytelling by which CoP members share knowledge; *informal* means that there is no hierarchy inside a CoP and there is no specific deliverable.

Characteristics such as common ground, common purpose/motivation, and similar jobs belong to the category of "what it is about" in Wenger's (1998) discussion. Characteristics like LPP, fluidity, relationships, community and identity, narration, informal, and unofficial/voluntary belong to the category of "how it functions as a community." Characteristics like evolution, dynamism, and new knowledge creation belong to the category of "what capabilities its practice has produced." Learning in the process of participation and reification is the key point in the concept of CoP. Mutual engagement, joint enterprise, and shared repertoire are the three key dimensions of practice as the property of a community (Wenger, 1998).

The concept of community of practice is easier to understand in physical settings: students who are enrolled in the same program and classmates who take the same class, employees who work in the same company or the same department, partners who collaborate on the same project, and people who live in the same neighborhood. We all hold multiple identities living in a society. We fulfill our identities by functioning in the different communities to which we belong. In virtual communities, however, some characteristics of CoP are not so apparent. For instance, a new member who just joined a discussion board may not know the most active IDs or the default talking style of this particular group. Such knowledge can only be obtained during the process of learning, since everyone holds a virtual identity in the community.

## Benefit and Impact of CoP

Fontaine and Millen's (2004) empirical study revealed three levels of CoP benefits: individual benefits, community benefits, and organization benefits. *Individual benefits* constitute the basic motivation for why people choose to participate in a community. In Fontaine and Millen's study, individual benefits cover issues like skills and know-how, personal productivity, job satisfaction, personal reputation, and sense of belonging. *Community benefits* consist of the overall productions in a community that are realized by connection, interaction, and collaboration among members, such as knowledge sharing, expertise and resources, collaboration, consensus and problem solving, community reputation and legitimacy, and trust between members. *Organization benefits* are tangible business outcomes such as operational efficiency, cost savings, level of service or sales, speed of service or product, and employee retention.

From another perspective, Wenger (2000) discussed the value of a CoP based on time efficiency: immediate value, long-term value, and professional value. *Immediate value* refers to the most straightforward benefits that a CoP brings, helping to deal with the current job. *Long-term value* helps a CoP to renew itself and build capabilities that assure the long-term viability of the enterprise. *Professional value* helps a CoP to develop professionally.

# Two Empirical Studies on Corporate Blogs

## Study 1: Content and Management Style of Corporate Blogs

It is a trend to start a corporate blog for a company, but it is not clear what is being done with them. What kind of content should be posted on a corporate blog? How should a corporate blog be managed? Because of their different motivations, the content and style of corporate blogs vary. In this study, we investigated the top ten popular corporate blogs at present and provide our findings on their contents, management styles, and posting volumes.

### Content Types of Corporate Blogs

Different researchers have very different opinions regarding content types of a blog. First, Blood (2002) identified three basic types of blogs: filters, personal journals, and notebooks. The content of *filters* is external to a blogger (world events, online happenings, etc.). The content of *personal journals* is internal (the blogger's thoughts and internal workings). *Notebooks* refer to long topic-focused essays. Later, Herring et al. (2004) replaced the category of notebook with *k-log*, intending to "functionally resemble hand-written project journals in which a researcher or a project group makes observations, records relevant references, and so forth about a particular knowledge domain." Second, Bar-Ilan (2004) listed three categories of blogs: *associative, personal and self-expressive*, and *topic oriented*. In her categorization, topic blogs refer to the blogs aimed at talking about topics related to a hobby or to the author's profession.

In the case of a corporate blog, Dugan (2004) identified three corporate blog models: *intranet blogs*, *event blogs*, and *product blogs*. Intranet blogs are the blogs maintained inside a company, and are not open to the public. In our study, we only collected public corporate blogs. Based on the observation of our data and the literature, we proposed three types of corporate blogs in terms of the content: event blog, product blog, and knowledge blog. *Event blogs* are announcements or the broadcast of current events of the company. *Product blogs* refer to the entries that introduce the company's new product or describe the new features of the product. *Knowledge blogs* refer to the entries that discuss the general topic in the field without a direct relationship with the company's products or services, such as industry information or relevant literature (Angeles, 2003).

## Management Style of Corporate Blogs

Management is less of a problem for a personal blog than for a corporate blog. While a personal blog is maintained by an individual, a corporate blog is usually supported by multiple individuals. Though a corporate blog empowers employees to talk freely with their colleagues and customers, in an open environment, certain topics like financial information can be very sensitive under such circumstances. Therefore the ability to monitor and control what is being published on a corporate blog is a major concern for companies. The problem is increasingly complicated when the company has a large number of employees. On the one hand, some companies set their corporate blogs as only open to employees. Such an intranet corporate blog serves as a group communication tool to help employees communicate with each other without any outsiders peeking. On the other hand, some companies control the content of a corporate blog by limiting the number of people who can publish blogs. In summary, companies have adopted different strategies to manage their corporate blogs depending on the companies' culture, the size of the company, industry domain, and other factors.

## Posting Volume and Updating Frequency

Some people believe that bloggers have to update their blogs on a certain level to attract readers and to keep their blogs alive. But it is not clear how often is often enough and how long each post should be. Louis (2005) did a length analysis of blog entries from five A-list blogs. The results showed that the top five bloggers actually created an average of 30 entries in one day, with each entry being less than 150 words. Liao (2006) suggested that blog posts should be human-hand sized long, given the fact that people won't be willing to read long articles. Although it sounds reasonable that shorter posts makes more frequent updating possible and more posts are better for generating readership with RSS, other issues like topic, comprehensive coverage, quality of post, and reader attention span (Rowse, 2006) also deserve consideration when bloggers decide on the proper posting volume and updating frequency. Corporate blogs aim at building a long-term relationship with customers and should pay particular attention to the posting volume and updating frequency, because this can affect the company image on a certain level. In this study, we are interested in looking into the overall patterns of posting volume and updating frequency among the top-ten most popular corporate blogs.

## Method

Sundar (2006) reported a list of the top ten corporate blogs based on the number of inbound links provided by Technorati. Nine out of the top 10 corporate blogs were chosen for our study (the one dropped from our data is an aggregation of personal employee blogs, rather than a normal corporate blog). These nine corporate blog sites were monitored for one month, from June 1 to June 31, 2006.

Table 18.1 lists basic information about the nine corporate blogs, among which there are three search engines (Google, Yahoo! Search, and Ask.com), one software manufacturer (Sunbelt Software), two online media learning companies (Otter Group and O'Reilly Radar), one automaker (GM FastLane), one online management consultancy firm (Tom Peters), and one small business (English Cut).

## Table 18.1   Basic information of nine corporate blogs in our study

| Company | URL of Blog Site | Industry |
| --- | --- | --- |
| Google | googleblog.blogspot.com | Search engine company |
| O'Reilly Radar | radar.oreilly.com | Online media learning company |
| Yahoo! Search | www.ysearchblog.com | Search engine |
| Tom Peters | www.tompeters.com | Online management consultancy |
| Ask.com | blog.ask.com | Search engine |
| GM FastLane | fastlane.gmblogs.com | Automaker |
| Sunbelt Software | sunbeltblog.blogspot.com | Software manufacture |
| English Cut | www.englishcut.com | Small business |
| Otter Group | www.ottergroup.com | Online media learning company |

A total number of 262 blog entries from the nine corporate blog sites were analyzed. For each blog entry, information about author, topic, and posting length were recorded. Content analysis was conducted to decide the content category of the blog entry.

For each corporate blog, basic information about every blog post during the whole month was recorded. Basic information includes posting date, authorship, number of internal links, number of comments, number of trackbacks (if applicable), number of pictures, number of audio and video components, and posting length.

## Findings

### Content Types of Corporate Blogs

In our study, three types of corporate blogs were identified based on their contents: event blog, product blog, and knowledge blog. Overall, among the 262 blog posts, there were 23 percent event blogs, 21 percent product blogs, and 56 percent knowledge blogs.

There are different patterns of distribution of the three types of blogs and blog entries among different industry domains. Figure 18.1 illustrates our findings with three search engine companies, in which 40–60 percent of their blog entries fall into product blogs. Figure 18.2 presents the results with three online companies. An average of 91 percent of their blog entries are knowledge entries, focusing on general topics in the field and discussion on current trends. The averages of their product entries and event entries are 4 percent and 5 percent respectively.

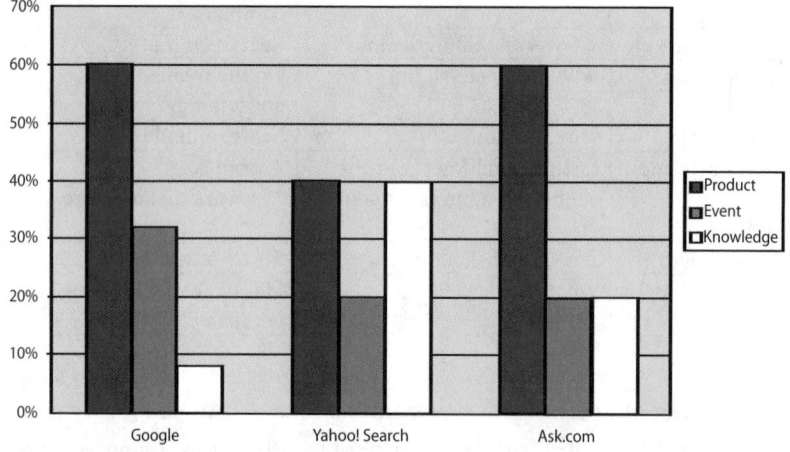

**Figure 18.1   Percentage of three types of blog entries among three search engine companies**

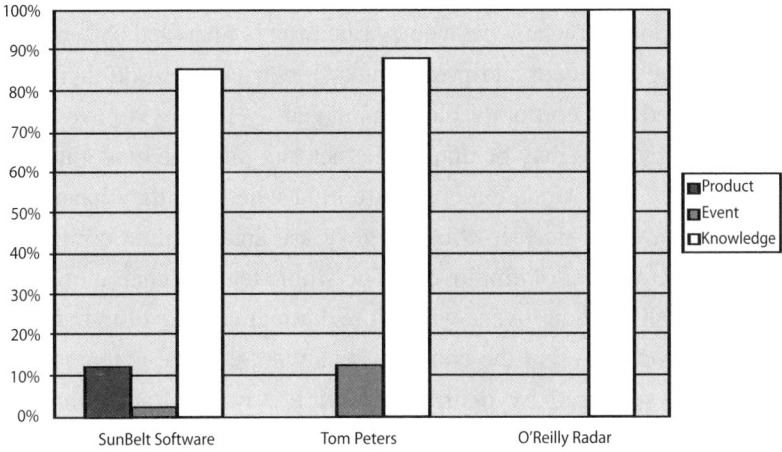

**Figure 18.2   Percentage of three types of blog entries among three online companies**

## Management Style

Three different types of corporate blogs are identified in terms of their management styles.

### Centralized Style

The centralized style means that a corporate blog is managed by one moderator, although multiple authors contribute contents. The moderator acts like an editor. Company employees send the moderator entries that they want to post. The moderator would then decide whether to post it. When a blog entry is posted, usually the author's name and position in the company are displayed. Companies with a large number of employees and multiple departments tend to adopt this style. For instance, Google's official blog (googleblog.blogspot.com) is managed with the centralized style. Individual employees send their articles to the moderator, and the moderator publishes their articles as blog entries. In the nine corporate blogs we studied, four of them are managed this way: Google, Yahoo!, Ask.com, and GM's FastLane blog. There are some advantages to this style. First, it's easy to control what content is published. The moderator's role guarantees that the content published is in line with the company's policy. Second, blogs can be published with a more consistent tone, so that they not only represent the single authors, but also the company as a whole.

### Distributed Style

The distributed style means that a corporate blog is managed by multiple moderators. They blog as a team and post their own entries based on their own preferences. We found that corporate blogs managed by this style have the highest updating frequency. This may be due to the fact that multiple moderators also act as active bloggers. They update a corporate blog whenever they have new items to share. Usually, companies in this category are small online companies who don't have a large number of employees. The whole team in charge of a corporate blog consists of all the employees within the company. They blog independently from each other yet represent the company as a whole. In the nine companies we studied, two are managed by distributed style: O'Reilly Radar and the Otter Group. O'Reilly Radar's blog is managed by five writers, who basically constitute the whole company.

### Mono Style

The mono style refers to a corporate blog that is written and managed by one single person. Usually it applies to small business companies. For example, English Cut, an English tailor company's corporate blog, is managed by the tailor himself. In the nine cases we studied, three of them are managed in mono style: Tom Peters, Sunbelt Software, and English Cut.

### Posting Volume and Updating Frequency

All corporate blogs demonstrated the relatively short length of blog entries. The overall average length of the blog entries is 300 words, with a minimum of 114 words and a maximum of 570 words. This result is in accordance with the findings from a previous study (Louis, 2005). The short blog entries will not cost readers too much time in reading them, and will therefore catch readers' attention to the blog site.

As for updating frequency of a corporate blog, our results showed varied ranges with the most frequently updated blog posting 2.83 entries a day (Sunbelt Software), and the least frequently updated blog only posting two entries a month (English Cut). Overall, the average updating frequency is one blog entry per day.

### Conclusion

We performed this study with nine popular corporate blogs. The results revealed three types of blogs in terms of contents: product blog, event blog, and knowledge blog. In addition, three management styles were also identified: centralized style, distributed style, and mono style. It was also found that corporate blogs have a relatively shorter blog entry and lower updating frequency. In addition, our study established a framework for analyzing corporate blog usage and contents. It will help practitioners understand how other corporations manage their blogs.

## Study 2: Cross-Cultural Comparison of Corporate Blogs

Cultures vary along a number of dimensions that may impact group processes and outcomes, such as *individualism vs. collectivism* (the extent to which people prioritize their personal benefit vs. that of the larger group; e.g., Hofstede, 1983; Triandis, 1995), *low vs. high context of communication*, (how much contextual information is required for communication; Hall, 1976), and *task vs. relationship orientation* (whether people focus on getting work done or on establishing rapport with their partners; e.g., Triandis, 1995). These and other cultural dimensions may interact with features of corporate blogs to create different effects on blog contents and management styles in different cultures.

We have little fundamental knowledge about what role culture plays in a corporate blog. In the context of a corporate blog, will people's blogging behavior be technology-specific or culture-specific? In other words, do bloggers from different countries while working for the same international corporation show similar (technology driven) behavior or different (cultural specific) behavior? There are reasons to believe that studies based solely on Western participants will not translate straightforwardly to the practices of other cultures.

### Cultural Effect or Technology Effect

In cross-cultural research there has been substantial debate about the definition of culture, as well as about the number, size, and significance of dimensions along which cultures vary (e.g., Hofstede, 1983; Oyserman, Coon, & Kemmelmeier, 2002; Schwartz, 1992; Triandis, 1995). For the purposes of this chapter, we define culture as *a set of norms, roles, and values emphasized by a culture and adopted, to greater or lesser degrees, by members of that culture through such processes as imitation and teaching.* We focus on two cultural dimensions—individualism/ collectivism and power distance—that affect processes central to collaborative work. These dimensions are not intended as an exhaustive description of how cultures differ, but rather as a way of focusing our investigation on those dimensions most likely to influence bloggers' behavior in a corporate blog.

*Individualism/collectivism.* Virtually all dimensional culture theories distinguish between individualistic cultures, those in which people tend to identify themselves as individuals and focus on their own personal gain, and collectivistic cultures, those in which people identify themselves as a member of a collective and focus on the betterment of that collective (e.g., Hofstede, 2001; Triandis, 1995). Nisbett (2003) describes a wide range of cognitive processes affected by membership in individualistic vs. collectivistic cultures, including reasoning styles and memory processes. Hofstede's (2001) analyses of survey responses from a global sample of IBM employees shows how individualism/collectivism is associated with preferences for business practices, child-raising, and many other aspects of culture.

*Power Distance.* This refers to the extent to which the less powerful members of organizations within a culture expect and accept that power is distributed unequally (Hofstede, 2001). In low power distance cultures, there is limited dependence of subordinates on superiors and a preference for consultation. However, in high power distance cultures, there is considerable dependence of subordinates on superiors, and subordinates are unlikely to approach or question their superiors directly.

In Study 2, we focus primarily on two cultures—the U.S. and the People's Republic of China (PRC)—for two reasons. First, the rising frequency of American–Chinese international teamwork makes an understanding of how the differences between these two cultures can shape team processes and outcomes especially pertinent. Second, American and Chinese cultures differ dramatically along the two cultural dimensions we have discussed. American culture is typically characterized as individualistic, low power distance whereas Chinese culture is characterized as collectivistic, high power distance (e.g., Hofstede, 2001; Nisbett, 2003; Triandis, 1995). By selecting cultures that are at opposite ends of these continua, we can most readily identify how cultural differences impact a corporate blog.

The official corporate blogs of Google—Google China and Google U.S.A.—were chosen for this study since they share the same corporate culture, but vary in national culture. The goal is to investigate blog usages within a working environment, particularly to see whether there are cultural differences in blogging behavior (frequency of updating, length of the blog, theme-topics, power structure of the bloggers, etc.).

Given the power distance in Chinese culture is higher than in the U.S., we predict:

*Hypothesis 1a: Chinese bloggers tend to be high level managers, while American bloggers are more equally distributed among regular employees and managers.*

Given that Chinese culture is more collectivistic and American culture is more individualistic, we predict:

*Hypothesis 1b: The content of Chinese blog entries places a focus on company/group news, while American blog entries focus on individual or individual group news.*

Our study is exploratory in nature given the fact that there are no such cross-cultural studies on corporate blogs based on our knowledge so far. An alternative hypothesis to cultural effect prediction is technology-driven prediction, that is, it is technology (a blog in this case) instead of national culture that determines bloggers' behavior.

*Hypothesis 2: Both Chinese and American bloggers show similar behavior patterns in terms of entry length, updating frequency, and management style.*

## Method

Google China (googlechinablog.com) and Google U.S.A. (googleblog.blogspot.com) were chosen for the study. Blog entries posted from April 1 to June 29, 2006, were collected from these two sites.

Three sets of measures were analyzed with the blog entries: bloggers' position title, types of blog contents, and updating frequency. For position titles, six categories of position titles were identified based on our collected data: guest blogger, regular engineer or researcher, moderator, product manager, senior manager, and product team. For types of blog contents, we used the same categories as were used in Study 1: event blog, product blog, and knowledge blog. For updating frequency, we used number of entries per day as we did in Study 1.

## Results

### Comparison of Position Titles of Bloggers

Table 18.2 shows the percentage of bloggers in each category of position titles for both Google U.S.A. and Google China. The Chi-square test showed significant cultural differences in terms of bloggers' position titles ($x^2(5) = 15.41$, $p < .01$). Contrary to our prediction, actually more managers and senior managers posted entries on the American site than on the Chinese site.

## Table 18.2  Percentage of position titles in two cultures

|                  | U.S.A.     | China      |
|------------------|------------|------------|
| Guest            | 0 percent  | 11 percent |
| Regular employee | 30 percent | 36 percent |
| Moderator        | 2 percent  | 23 percent |
| Manager          | 38 percent | 14 percent |
| Senior manager   | 19 percent | 2 percent  |
| Group            | 13 percent | 14 percent |

### Comparison of Types of Blog Contents

Figure 18.3 shows the percentage of three types of blog contents in Google U.S.A. and Google China corporate blogs. The Chi-square test showed significant cultural differences in terms of different types of blog contents ($x^2(2) = 27.29$, $p < .00$). Google U.S.A. has more product blog entries while Google China has more knowledge blog entries. Both corporate blogs have a similar amount of event blog entries.

### Comparison of Updating Frequency

Both Google U.S.A. (0.69 entry/day) and Google China (0.49 entry/day) showed similar updating frequency, that is, less than one entry per day.

## Discussion and Conclusion

On the surface, our results seem to support cultural-specific hypotheses as shown in the cultural differences in position titles and types of blog contents. However, an alternative explanation to such cultural differences might be due to factors irrelevant to cultures. For example, Google China has fewer product lines

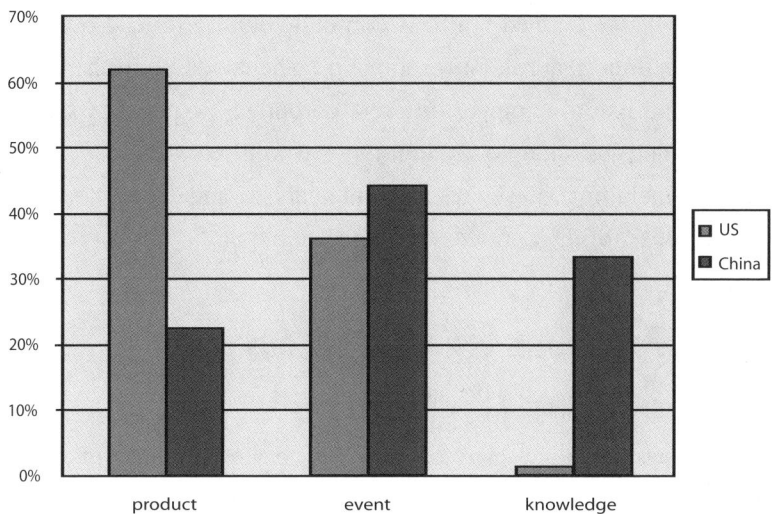

## Figure 18.3  Percentage of three types of blogs in two cultures

than Google U.S.A. even though they belong to the same company. Different markets, different products, and different engineering expertise may lead to different blog contents and blog behavior. Chinese Google bloggers tend to post fewer product blogs, but it may be simply because they don't have the same rich product lines as their peers in Google U.S.A. In terms of position titles, it turns out that Google has internal policies regarding who is allowed to blog. Such policy constraints prohibit us in some sense from observing "natural" cultural behavior. Therefore our observation of more manager bloggers in the U.S. does not necessarily reflect the cultural behavior.

When we combined the updating frequency result with the content result, it was clear to us that frequent updating seems very important for keeping corporate blogs live. It seems that when Google China had fewer products to post in their corporate blog, they supplemented it with knowledge blogs to keep up their updating frequency.

In summary, we concluded that our data tends to support the technology-driven prediction. That is, corporate blog behavior is mainly influenced by blog technology and company policy instead of national culture.

### Future Work

From our study, we learned that it is corporate culture instead of national culture that plays an important role in corporate blog behavior. To further test this prediction, we would like to compare different corporate blogs in the same domain, for example, Yahoo! vs. Google. In addition, we would like to adopt multidimensional methods including interviews, content analysis, and experiments to develop an in-depth analysis of the contents of corporate blogs.

# Cultivate CoP through Corporate Blogs

## Communication: Corporate Blogs–A New Way of CoP

Corporate blogs are a new way of establishing a community of practice. The learning process occurs informally during the interaction between company and customers, between bloggers and readers, and between the commentators themselves. Members of the community come together because of their common interest in the company and its products. The common ground they maintain is the basis upon which the community is formed. Some of them start reading corporate blogs because they want to know more about the product information of a particular company with a human voice from blogs rather than the official information from the Web site. Some others are the truly loyal customers who want to follow what's new in the company and use the blogs because corporate blogs are usually updated more frequently than Web sites. Some commentators are field experts who build up a close relationship with the particular company by providing valuable insight in comments.

New members join the community by first reading the blogs and comments from others. The degree of participation gradually grows as the new member becomes familiar with the community. There is no rigid membership in this community. Some constant visitors may subscribe to the RSS feed so that newly updated blogs would be sent directly to their e-mail inbox. Some may just visit the blog when they feel like it. Commenting is not obligatory. The corporate blog community can be very fluid, with most members visiting without leaving comments or commenting anonymously. The community of corporate blogs evolves during the process. New knowledge is created in the informal interaction among bloggers, readers, and commentators.

## Corporate Blogs and Other Technologies for Knowledge Management and Community of Practice

There are many tools developed to serve the function of knowledge management across organizations. Tools like bulletin boards, discussion forums, and chat rooms have been employed by companies to build up community and enhance communication with customers. Different tools have different functions and work most efficiently in the right context. Some tools are good for collaboration, some are good for discussion, some for publication, and still others for group editing.

Corporate blogs enable people to accumulate knowledge as well as share and manage it. But blogs are merely tools; knowledge is synthesized by communication between people who come to this community formed around corporate blogs. Blogs facilitate this by making people easier to find, and by providing immediate and direct communication channels once these contacts have been established. Bloggers do not merely publish information, but also use the blogosphere as a source of increasing their own knowledge and supporting or disproving their claims. Blogs could be utilized as an ideal tool for knowledge management. It has the following advantages: ease of use and capture, decentralized aggregation, distributed knowledge, a flexible data model, extensiblity, and inferencing capability (Cayzer, 2004).

## REFERENCES

Angeles, Michael. (April 15, 2003). K-logging: Supporting KM with Web logs. *Library Journal.* Available at www.libraryjournal.com/article/CA286642.html

Bar-Ilan, Judit. (2004). An outsider's view on "topic-oriented" blogging. *Proceedings of the 13th International World Wide Web conference*, New York: 28–34.

Blood, Rebecca. (2002). *The Weblog handbook: Practical advice on creating and maintaining your blog.* Cambridge MA: Perseus Publishing.

Brady, Mark. (2005). Blogging. *Personal participation in public knowledge-building on the Web.* Chimera Working Paper. Available at www.essex.ac.uk/chimera/content/pubs/wps/CWP-2005-02-Blogging-in-the-Knowledge-Society-MB.pdf

Cayzer, Steve. (2004). Semantic blogging and decentralized knowledge management. *Communications of the ACM, 47*: 47–52.

Cohen, Heidi. (2005). Corporate blogs, measure their value. Available at www.clickz.com/showPage.html?page=3517546

Dugan, Kevin. (2004). Emerging corporate blog models. Available at prblog.typepad.com/strategic_public_relation/2004/11/emerging_corpor.html

Fontaine, Michael A., & Millen, David R. (2004). Understanding the benefits and impact of communities of practice. In Paul M. Hildreth & Chris Kimble (Eds.), *Knowledge networks: Innovation through communities of practice.* Hershey, PA: Idea Group Pub.

Hall, Edward T. (1976). *Beyond culture.* New York: Doubleday Anchor Books.

Herring, Susan C., Scheidt, Lois Ann, Bonus, Sabrina, & Wright, Elijah. (2004). Bridging the gap: A genre analysis of Weblogs. *Proceedings of the 37th Hawaii International Conference on System Sciences* (*HICSS-37*).

Hildreth, Paul M. (2004). *Going virtual: Distributed communities of practice*. Hershey, PA: Idea Group Pub.

Hofstede, Geert. (1983). Dimensions of national cultures in fifty countries and three regions. In J. Deregowski, S. Dzuirawiec, & R. Annis (Eds.), *Explications in cross-cultural psychology*. Lisse, Switzerland: Swets & Zeitlinger.

Hofstede, Geert. (2001). *Culture's consequences: Comparing values, behaviors, institutions, and organizations across nations*. Thousand Oaks, CA: Sage.

Liao, Bill. (2006). Scoble on tips for joining the A-list. Available at www.stoweboyd.com/message/2006/02/scoble_on_tips_html

Levine, Rick, Locke, Christopher, Searls, Doc, & Weinberger, David. (2000). *The Cluetrain manifesto*. Cambridge, MA: Perseus Publishing.

Louis, Tristan. (2005). Secrets of the A-list bloggers: Lots of short entries. Available at tnl.net/blog/2005/05/24/secrets-of-the-a-list-bloggers-lots-of-short-entries

Nardi, Bonnie A., Schiano, Diane J., Gumbrecht, Michelle, & Swartz, Luke. (2004). Why we blog. *Communications of the ACM, 47*(12): 41–46.

Nisbett, Richard E. (2003). *The geography of thought: How Asians and Westerners think differently ... and why*. New York: The Free Press.

Oyserman, Daphna, Coon, Heather M., & Kemmelmeier, Markus. (2002). Rethinking individualism and collectivism: Evaluation of theoretical assumptions and meta-analyses. *Psychological Bulletin, 128*(1): 3–72.

Rowse, Darren. (2006). Post length—how long should a blog post be? Available at www.problogger.net/archives/2006/02/18/post-length-how-long-should-a-blog-post-be

Schwartz, Shalom H. (1992). Universals in the content and structure of values: Theoretical advances and empirical tests in 20 countries. In M. Zanna (Ed.), *Advances in Experimental Social Psychology, 25*. New York: Academic Press.

Sundar, Mario. (2006). Top 10 corporate blogs (Technorati ranked). Available at mariosundar.wordpress.com/2006/07/16/top-10-corporate-blogs-technorati-powered

Triandis, Harry C. (1995). *Individualism and collectivism*. Boulder, CO: Westview.

Wackå, Fredrik. (2004). Your guide to corporate blogging. Available at www.corporateblogging.info/2004/06/corporate-blog-short-definition.asp

Wenger, Etienne. (1998). Communities of practice. Learning as a social system, systems thinker. Available at www.co-i-l.com/coil/knowledge-garden/cop/ lss.shtml

Wenger, Etienne. (2000). Communities of practice: Stewarding knowledge. In Charles Despres & Daniele Chauvel (Eds.), *Knowledge horizons: The present and the promise of knowledge*. Boston: Butterworth-Heinemann.

# Part V

---

# Knowledge Management Measurement and Assessment

# Knowledge Management Measurement and Assessment

## FOREWORD

The inclusion in this book of a section on measurement and assessment can be seen as a metric of a certain maturity for knowledge management (KM). The domain of information and knowledge is notoriously difficult to quantify and metricize, and the metrics we have are far less compelling than we would like, but they are a start.

Chapter 20 by Chua and Chaudhry is the result of the compilation of the metrics used for KM measurement by a number of organizations. For each organization they present a table listing the measurements foci and the principal indicators used. Then they summarize, first by the "Dimensions of Measurement" (Outcomes, Technology, Culture, Human Development) and then by KM processes. Each table provides samples of key indicators both at the organizational level and at the economic (more or less national) level. The result of course is a very useful list of candidate metrics.

Fonseca and Fonseca (Chapter 19) contribute a fascinating account of the development of an Organization Knowledge Assessment (OKA) tool by the World Bank Institute. The tool is still under development, but it promises to be very useful in the KM world. Considerable detail is provided. Also, a number of tentative (based on pilot studies) conclusions are needed. One interesting conclusion is that the development of the tool seems to function as a very effective marketing tool for the development or further development of KM. This is particularly striking in that the typical response overall was to report lack of success with KM initiatives. In addition, they report some intriguing results comparing which knowledge areas tend to score high and which score low.

Also check the KM Measurement and Assessment theme in the Roadmap.

# CHAPTER 19

# Measuring Knowledge in Organizations: The Organizational Knowledge Assessment Tool

Ana Flavia Fonseca

University of Joao Pessoa

Arnoldo Fonseca

Consultant

## ABSTRACT

Rapid advancement of information and communications technologies has transformed the cost structures that have constrained knowledge creation, capture, and dissemination. As a result, knowledge has become indispensable for economic success, and the management of knowledge within organizations has become critical for sustaining success in the long term. In spite of this, work evaluating the nature of knowledge management (KM) within and across organizations has been fragmented, commonly the purview of one-off improvement projects within large corporations and institutions. To address this void, the World Bank Institute (WBI) is developing a didactic survey instrument that consolidates much of the salient, accumulated best practices of knowledge management. Much like its Knowledge Assessment Methodology (KAM), which measures country-level knowledge capacity, the Organizational Knowledge Assessment (OKA) tool can be use to provide relative indications of knowledge management capacity within organizations. Presently, OKA has been tested through multiple pilots, including a WBI-sponsored workshop with diverse organizations in Brazil. Although the evolution of OKA is ongoing, this chapter overviews the OKA tool and reviews some preliminary findings.

# INTRODUCTION

Knowledge is increasingly a critical basis for competitiveness and social well being. Rapid advancement of information and communications technologies has transformed the cost structures that constrained knowledge creation, capture, evaluation, storage, transformation, and dissemination. Unleashed, these knowledge activities have accelerated innovation and adoption cycles within almost every industry and facet of human life. Public- and private-sector organizations that have leveraged knowledge to create greater value added within their respective areas of business have been driving economic transformation.

Evaluation and improvement of knowledge activities within the organizational context is critical for continued economic and social gains, but systematized mechanisms for achieving this are sparse. Although customized, organization-specific evaluation projects can generally provide the richest results, few organizations have the resources to engage outside experts or devote internal resources for this task. The World Bank Institute's role in helping its client countries transition to a more knowledge-intensive economy has motivated it to develop a didactic instrument that helps organizations frame their strengths and deficits with respect to KM. Since organizations tend to be prime actors in motivating macro-level adoption of knowledge-promoting policies, investments, infrastructure, and behaviors, greater understanding of knowledge at the organizational level can yield a grassroots approach to knowledge-economy adoption that can complement top-down government policies.

The OKA tool provides a manner in which to collect and study key pieces of information about the management of knowledge within an organization. Although management of knowledge has become increasingly important, relatively few organizations effectively treat knowledge as a strategic tool or understand what levers to use to foster knowledge activities. The goal of the OKA tool is two-fold: to serve as a didactic tool that exposes organizations to critical facets of knowledge management and to provide a relative measure of knowledge management capacity within organizations. The latter can in the long term provide a benchmark, which can be utilized for motivating improvement within organizations.

# THE ORGANIZATIONAL KNOWLEDGE ASSESSMENT CONSTRUCT

KM is a management principle that aims to leverage the information, knowledge, experiences, and intuitions of the organization in order to generate value. Its relevance within organizations has been heightened as consensus has pointed to knowledge as a basis for sustainable competitive advantage. The challenge faced by organizations is that KM for the most part is "soft" and intangible; its artifacts are implicit and locked within the people, processes, and systems of an organization. People, processes, and systems are essential for the operationalization of action within all firms. In order to successfully apply KM across the firm, management must create conditions within each of these that promote and enable value creation from intellectual assets.

An assessment of an organization's knowledge environment should strive to quantify its capacity and capability in the leveraging information, knowledge, experience, and intuition through its people, processes, and systems in order to achieve its goals and generate value. Using this as a guiding rubric, the OKA was conceived as assessing firm capacity and capability in leveraging intellectual assets through the prism of people, processes, and systems. Use of the People-Process-System framework also makes the OKA more accessible and understandable to executives, leaders, and other persons not necessarily schooled in the field of KM.

Within each of the three arenas of the framework are specific dimensions that are used to measure KM within the firm. Each dimension emerged as a result of extensive literature research and extensive discussion with practitioners of KM. Each dimension included was identified as critical for accurate assessment of KM practices within an organization. Figure 19.1 illustrates the relationship between dimensions and the three-part framework. Table 19.1 contains more information about each dimension. In addition to the dimensions listed here, demographic information about an organization and its industry is also collected.

Prior research on KM by the authors served as a base from which to generate an initial list of possible dimensions. Literature review with specific focus on knowledge assessments, organizational knowledge, and KM was also undertaken to identify additional dimensions. Sources used in this research are inclusive of those cited at the end of this chapter. The dimensions were gradually refined, combined, or eliminated with the aid of other practitioners of KM and inputs from

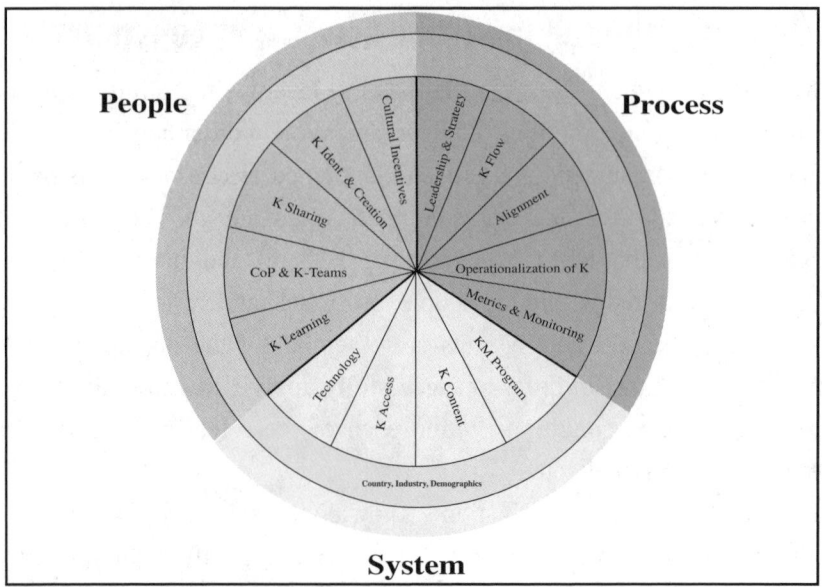

## Figure 19.1   OKA framework and dimensions

WBI. The dimensions remaining from this process represent the key areas of KM that are believed to adequately describe the nature of KM within an organization.

Dimensions were grouped into the framework based upon the area in which each had a disproportionate impact. For instance, Knowledge Sharing certainly has technological (Systems) and policy (Process) aspects, but for Knowledge Sharing to fundamentally make a difference and where it makes the biggest contribution to KM is in People.

## OPERATIONALIZATION OF THE OKA

It was recognized early in OKA's development that a knowledge assessment of organizations would require a qualitative approach to data gathering. Relatively few standard statistics exist for measuring organizational knowledge, and relatively few organizations have the wherewithal to collect such data. As a result, the OKA is operationalized through a survey that respondents answer either individually or within a workshop setting.

In order to guide the development of survey questions, specific measures were formulated for each dimension. Each measure represents an aspect or facet of its respective dimension that was deemed important and measurable. Table 19.2

## Table 19.1 Expanded description of OKA dimensions

| People | |
|---|---|
| *Culture and Incentives* | The implicit and explicit cultural attitudes, beliefs, and incentives that exist within the firm to shape, create, and support the use of intellectual assets (including knowledge) to reach firm goals. |
| *Knowledge Identification and Creation* | The capability of the firm and its stakeholders to identify and create knowledge (and other intellectual assets), especially those that contribute to the goals of the organization. |
| *Knowledge Sharing* | The capacity of the firm and its stakeholders to share intellectual assets in ways that enable the firm to reach its goals. |
| *Communities of Practice and Knowledge Teams* | The existence, nature and use of pools of people within the enterprise that can be effectively leveraged to solve problems and enable the organization to reach its goals. |
| *Knowledge and Learning* | The existence and capacity of the firm to build human capital through training and other structured or formally driven knowledge-building activities. |
| **Process** | |
| *Leadership and Strategy* | The adoption and execution of KM as a management principle by the leadership of an organization. |
| *Knowledge Flow* | The nature and capability of knowledge and other intellectual assets to flow within the enterprise. Includes capture, storage, dissemination, and some aspects of delivery. |
| *Operationalization of Knowledge* | The capacity of the organization to integrate and apply knowledge into its business and operational processes (including new product development, marketing, and others). This is essentially the feedback loops of knowledge into the core business processes and outputs of the firm. |
| *Alignment* | The degree to which the goals of the KM Program and outcomes try to fulfill or realize the objectives and goals of the organization. |
| *Metrics and Monitoring* | The capacity of the organization to measure itself with regard to management of intellectual assets and to monitor and identify best practices, external information, and learning that can improve the innards of the company and to generate value for the firm. |
| **Systems** | |
| *KM Technology Infrastructure* | The existence and capacity of the technological infrastructure that enables knowledge management and sharing best practices. |
| *Knowledge Access Infrastructure* | The capability and infrastructure existent enabling stakeholders to access and interact with the firm's intellectual assets (whether in its system or in other people). |
| *Content Management* | The types of content and information management tools that the organization produces or manages to execute KM. |
| *KM Environment Infrastructure* | The nature, design, and capacity of the KM program as constructed within the company, involving people, units, groups, etc. |

highlights some examples of metrics used for dimension within the People arena. Questions were developed that either directly or indirectly assessed each measure. Once questions were developed, they were rearranged and regrouped in a manner that afforded better logical flow of the questions from the user perspective. The final survey contains 183 questions.

## Table 19.2  Example of metrics for dimensions within People arena

| **Culture and Incentives** |
| --- |
| The degree to which organizational policies reward knowledge activities, including mechanisms like CoPs and teams |
| The degree to which the organization is tolerant of innovation-related risk and behavior |
| The degree to which the firm supports learning activities by employees |
| The receptiveness of the organization to employee-driven change |
| The degree of employee participation in improving the organization's performance |
| The degree to which the firm is receptive to external ideas |
| **Knowledge Identification and Creation** |
| The organization's receptiveness to new information as a basis for formulation of new knowledge |
| The organization's (and employee's) ability to create knowledge |
| The degree to which the organization promotes "cross-border" (cross-disciplinary, cross-unit, etc.) communication and information sharing |
| The degree to which the organization invests in and optimizes human capital through the acquisition and retention of employees who have a diverse of set of topical knowledge |
| The effort undertaken by the organization to find information important for its business and objectives |
| The nature/"how" of identification and clarification of KM opportunities |
| The measure of outcomes from knowledge identification and creation |
| The degree to which external pressures on the business require change and innovation |
| **Knowledge and Sharing** |
| The degree to which the firm has organizational structures that favor knowledge sharing |
| The degree to which knowledge sharing is widespread in the organization |
| The degree to which the organization supports information knowledge sharing activities |
| The degree to which the organization shares tacit knowledge |
| The degree to which the organization shares explicit knowledge |
| The degree to which the organization converts tacit to explicit |
| The degree to which the organization converts explicit to tacit |
| The degree and quality with which the organization shares knowledge with clients, partners, vendors |
| **Communities of Practice and Knowledge Teams** |
| The ability of the organization to support the creation of various knowledge pools and knowledge-sharing groups within the organization |
| The nature of communities of practice within the organization |
| The effectiveness of communities of practice |
| The capacity of the organization to dynamically coalesce teams that use knowledge to solve problems or support goals of the organization |
| **Knowledge and Learning** |
| The organization's attitude and approach to building human capital |
| The quality of the learning environment |
| The degree to which the firm has training aimed at behavioral change or improvement |
| The degree to which the organization has built knowledge processes into their business processes |
| The degree to which the organization uses or re-uses knowledge and know-how |
| The degree to which the organization transfers knowledge and know-how |
| The degree to which the organization incorporates external information into its learning activities |

The OKA survey is presently delivered to users through an online survey platform. This facilitates the data collection and manipulation process once users complete the survey. The ideal format through which to administer the OKA survey is through a workshop, where several persons from a single organization each take the survey and reconcile results. From pilots of the OKA, we have found that this experience leads to a richer learning experience for users and helps to better approximate an organization's true knowledge capacity. Owing to the needs for discussion and negotiation of answers between the various participants, the experience itself is reported to facilitate creation of common language and understanding among participants, which can be especially valuable if these participants represent disparate functions or parts of the organization. A common understanding is important for empowering action that leads to improvement within the organization. The other approach to OKA administration is to have it be filled out by an individual who responds on behalf of an organization. This approach is more straightforward and is a means for organizational evaluation, but it provides only limited learning and momentum for action.

## Scoring of OKA Results

Different types of organizations are likely to have relatively different KM requirements, which lead to different notions of how good their KM programs are relative to other organizations. A sample of the OKA online survey is shown in Figure 19.2. This is at the crux of the complexity of the scoring methodology employed by an instrument like OKA. To make the OKA scores comparable across organizations, two scoring methodologies were explored during the development of OKA: a weight-based scheme and a rules-engine-based scheme. Use of a rules engine or inference engine, while potentially more precise and accurate, was believed to be too complex to implement in the short term, so the weight-based approach was selected. The weight-based approach relies upon a multi-factor weighting process based upon demographic-related values. Scores of each dimension are tabulated and then transformed based upon weights, which are created from a combination of organizational demographics, such as firm size and industry. Figure 19.3 depicts this scoring approach.

Since the OKA is still collecting an initial set of data, implementation of the scoring methodology has not yet been undertaken at the time of this writing; scores are presently being collected "raw" and being aggregated without adjustment for each dimension. Driving the decision was a paucity of data collected as well as the possibility for survey changes, which could make results non-comparable for some organizations. Once more data has been collected to support at least anecdotally the use of some demographic variables as weights, the full-fledged weight-based approach will be warranted. The OKA tool will likely require one year's worth of use and data collection before it is truly stabilized and an appropriate set of scoring weights can be developed.

Although crude, this present scoring approach provides current respondents with some notion of relative strengths and weaknesses between dimensions of

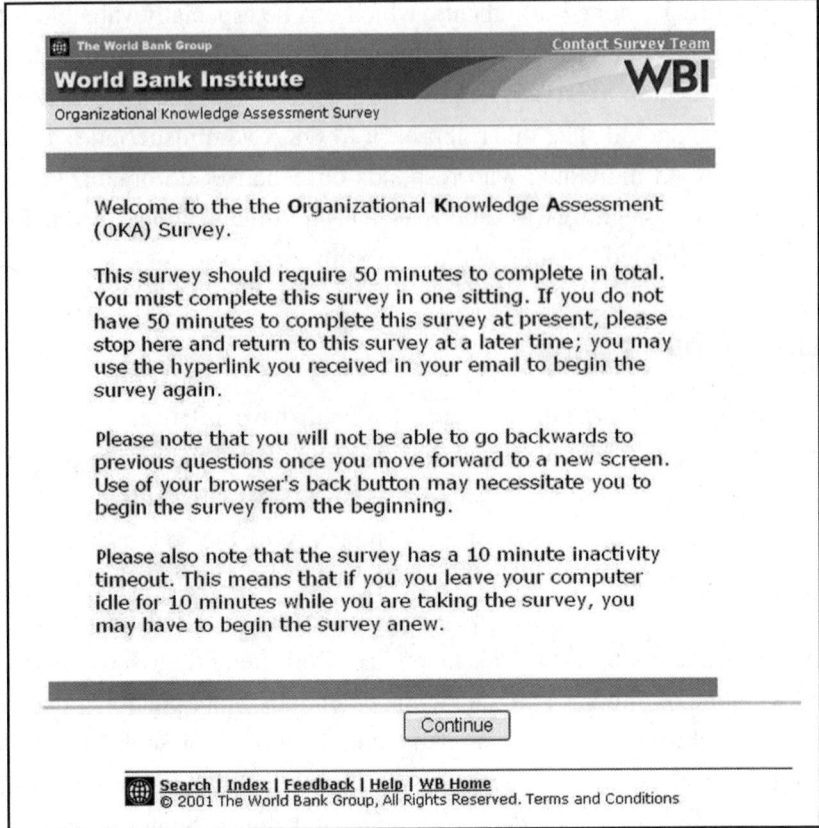

**Figure 19.2  First page of the OKA online survey**

their organization. Comparability between organizations that are significantly different are problematic, however, because the interpretation of questions is likely to be impacted by demographic factors, particularly organization industry and size. KM entails an entirely different meaning and level of sophistication between a small, domestic manufacturing company and a large, multinational service company; nevertheless, two respondents may answer questions similarly owing to their understanding of the meaning of the question vis-à-vis the context of their organization. Consequently, score comparability between these two companies could be very misleading.

Each answer choice of each survey question has been coded with a numerical value between 1 and 10 indicative of whether that answer choice indicates greater levels of KM capacity within the organization. A question's value is the sum of

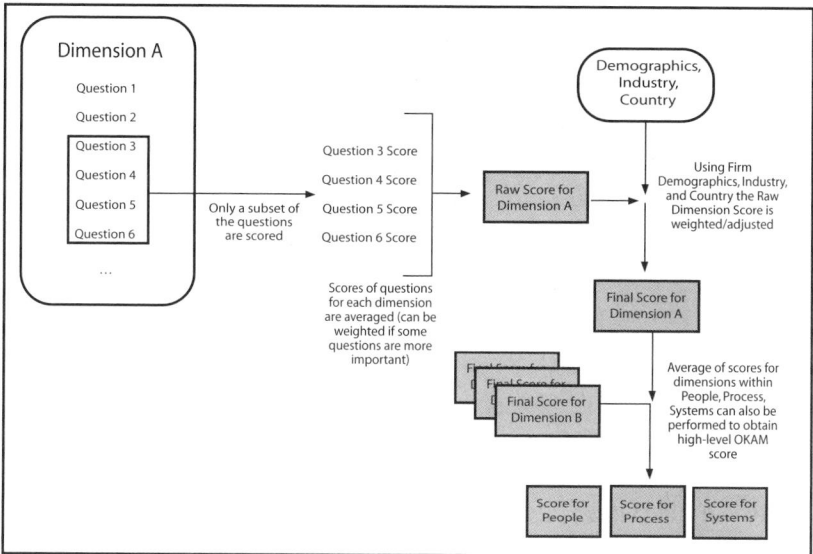

**Figure 19.3  Weight-based scoring approach**

the selection of answers that a respondent chooses. Scores of all questions within a dimension are aggregated to arrive at a final numerical value for the dimension.

The output of the OKA tool is a spider chart similar to WBI's Knowledge Assessment Methodology (KAM), which measures country-level knowledge capacity. An example chart for a real organization tested using the OKA is provided in Figure 19.4.

## PRELIMINARY OKA RESULTS

In order to operationalize and improve OKA, two sets of test pilots were undertaken involving 36 organizations. Organizations represented included several U.S. government agencies, Fortune 500 companies, and smaller private sector firms. Most of the organizations involved in the pilot were public sector related (government or non-governmental organizations). The exceptions were health-related firms that comprised a large percentage share of the sample. Owing to these demographics, the majority of organizations were large (more than 501 employees) and possessed relatively stable employee tenure (longevity with low turnover rates).

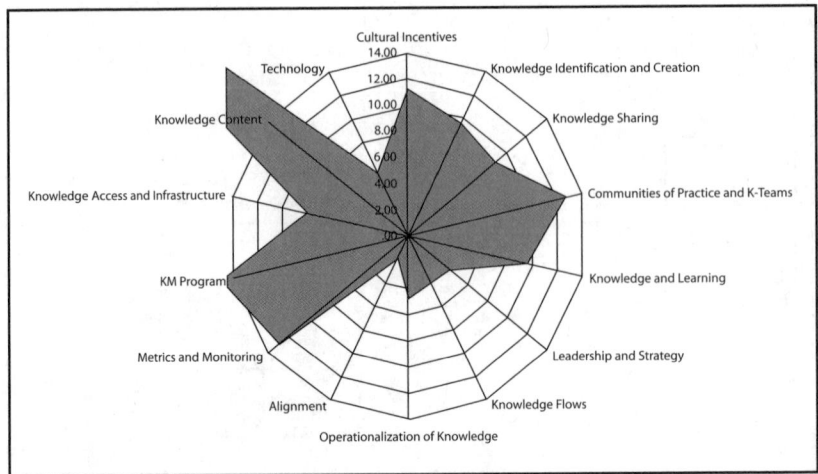

**Figure 19.4 OKA results for actual organization using OKA tool**

The education level across organizations was fairly distributed, with college education generally comprising between 5 percent and 75 percent of the workforce.

One set of test pilots was undertaken by two classes of part-time MBA students taking an online KM course at the University of Maryland University College (UMUC). Students used the OKA to evaluate their organization and provided feedback about their survey results vis-à-vis their expectations. Students were encouraged to contact colleagues within their organization to aid in the response of questions. Another set of pilots was conducted during WBI-sponsored workshops at two large Brazilian organizations, Serviço Federal de Processamento de Dados (SERPRO), a data processing firm for government agencies, and Companhia Hidroelétrica do São Francisco (CHESF), a major water utility. For these two organizations, a workshop approach was used where multiple representatives from different parts of each organization were involved. WBI and other workshop administrators from the Sociedade Brasileira de Gestao do Conhecimento (SBGC) helped to facilitate discussions and reconciliations of scores among the participants.

The pilots yielded several beneficial results for the development of the OKA instrument as well as for insight into KM practices within large organizations. With regard to the latter, owing to the changes that the survey has undergone during its development as well as the small samples employed, such data should only be interpreted as indicative rather than descriptive. Figure 19.5 presents the average

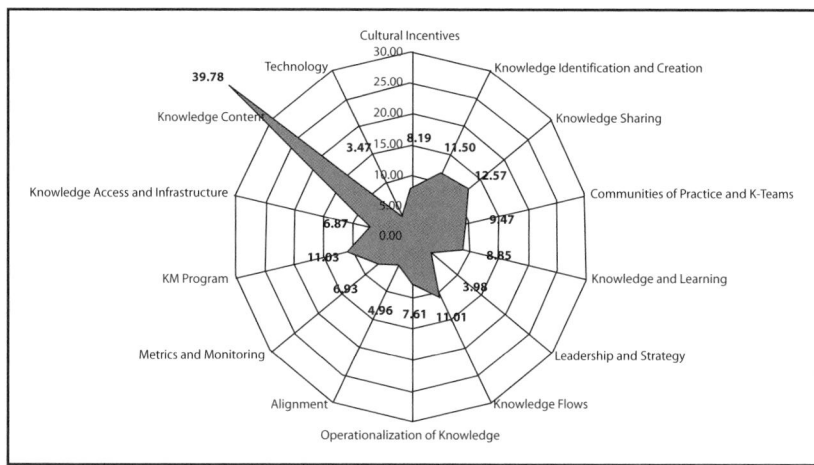

## Figure 19.5  Running average score for OKA after 36 organizations

score for each dimension across all 36 organizations (the "Knowledge Content" dimension is presently unbalanced in its scoring; the defect is presently being addressed). While at this point, there is no particular meaning that can be attached to a particular score level, it is interesting to note dimensions where organizations seem to be lacking relative to other dimensions.

## Observations Related to OKA

Both pilots generally yielded results that were consistent, lending credence to the results obtained, especially as related to conclusions deduced about the OKA instrument.

*Participants found OKA useful.* The majority of participants found OKA useful as a means to understand the full breadth and scope of KM. They also liked the OKA framework as a way to represent the KM landscape and found the graphical representation of the framework very useful for discussions with their managers. They seemed to realize that KM encompasses much more than what they thought before. Through the framework they said they could quickly comprehend all the factors that they needed to have within the organization in order to have a proper environment for KM.

*Participants were excited by the scope of KM.* The encompassing nature of the framework enabled many participants to realize that their organizations were already fostering competencies within a number of these dimensions. Often this was occurring under a different name than "knowledge management." Many participants came to conclude that an organization does not need to have a formal KM program to enjoy the benefits of having an environment that promotes and sustains knowledge activities.

***Participants wanted a more multi-factored scoring for OKA.*** The majority of participants suggested that questions needed to differentiate between organizations that had formal KM Programs and those that did not. At the root of this observation was their concern that different types of organizations would answer the same questions using different standards of judgment. As discussed, a multi-factored weight-based scoring approach will help to correct this in the future.

In addition to these observations, participants provided valuable feedback regarding individual questions, structure, and other aspects of the OKA survey, which have been incorporated into the tool.

# RESULTS ABOUT KNOWLEDGE MANAGEMENT PRACTICES

The pilot yielded interesting results about KM within organizations. Again, the small sample of organizations analyzed should prevent any firm conclusions from being drawn; rather, these results can be understood as possible indications and avenues for future hypothesis testing.

***Some dimensions consistently scored highly.*** The "Content Management," "Knowledge Identification and Creation," and "Culture and Incentives" dimensions generally scored highly across all organizations. This suggests that most organizations have at least commenced to address KM issues through improved document and content management systems and practices and are leveraging these systems/practices through deliberate knowledge-forming activities.

***Some dimensions were consistently problematic.*** Both "Operationalization of Knowledge Management" and "Leadership and Strategy" consistently yielded low scores across all organizations. Initially, it was believed that poorly worded questions within these dimensions were causing these results and further work was done to improve these questions. Operationalization of KM was also believed to be skewed by its relatively low number of questions, and more questions were added to match the average number of questions per dimension. Following improvements, these organizations still tended to score low in these dimensions, suggesting that these two dimensions represented areas where organizations seemed to have problems implementing. Other dimensions presenting some diffi-culty for some organizations included "Alignment," "Knowledge and Learning," and "KM Technology Infrastructure." It is interesting to note that the Process and Systems arenas are heavily represented in these problematic dimensions.

*Most organizations scored highly in the People arena.* The following dimen-sions scored relatively well most frequently across pilot organizations: "Cultural and Incentives," "Knowledge Identification and Creation," "Knowledge Sharing," "Communities of Practice and Knowledge Teams," "Metrics and Monitoring," and "Content Management." These dimensions are skewed to the People arena of the OKA framework. A possible explanation could be that survey takers are less familiar with the organization's systems and processes while another explanation is that questions in the other two arenas were not sufficiently clear or were too technical. Questions in both arenas were reviewed and edited. Another possible explanation for these results is that organizations are generally trying to foster KM practices within their organizational culture (or people) before making large alterations or investments in their processes or systems. A last possibility is that KM practices are emerging within organizations even without formal company investments or structures; this would tend to occur through People-oriented dimensions before those requiring formal organizational investment. Despite the real underlying reason, a safe conclusion seems to be that Process and System elements tend to lag People elements within organizations with respect to KM activities.

*Most organizations reported a lack of success in KM initiatives.* The majority of organizations reported a lack of clearly articulated KM strategy for their organ-ization. In fact, 57 percent of respondents felt that their organization's KM initia-tives have been "somewhat unsuccessful" or "very unsuccessful" in achieving observable results.

*Most organizations had informal KM Programs.* Most organizations did pos-sess several elements of an informal KM program. Almost as many organizations said they had communities of practice as said they did not. The majority did use teams to solve problems. Learning activities and sharing of tacit knowledge within the organization was generally achieved through training workshops and attending conferences. Knowledge sharing was generally achieved through e-mail, telephone, and unit meetings as well as video/audio conferencing. Most organizations reported using a high level of electronic communication to transact their daily work. These results demonstrate a fairly capable infrastructure for practicing KM despite the lack of formalized KM approach.

***Organizations actively collect best-practice knowledge.*** When asked about the types of knowledge collected by the organization, the top two categories predictably involved knowledge about procedures and business processes of the firm. The third-highest ranked knowledge type was best-practice knowledge.

# Future Developments

The OKA tool has already reportedly provided value to pilot participants, and as it evolves it promises to help enrich work in the KM field. As OKA is further tested, we anticipate possibly shortening the survey, once data is able to identify which questions seem to be most relevant and important for score discrimination. Using a large-enough data set will also enable development of data-driven weights for a more rigorous and meaningful scoring methodology to be implemented. Lastly, refinements in the methodology for delivery of the survey to users will also be better crafted. While a workshop format is ideal, practical constraints may lead to alternative approaches. The OKA data, in the long run, will not only provide a benchmark for organizations, but may also help tell the story of how most organizations evolve to a knowledge enterprise—in other words, which dimensions are emphasized at what points in time and with what resources. This promises to enable better and more effective guidance of organizations into the knowledge-intensive economy.

# Acknowledgments

Construction of the Organizational Knowledge Assessment tool was undertaken with appreciable support from the World Bank Institute. WBI provided valuable review, advice, and evaluation of the project, but at the same time provided sufficient flexibility to enable it to evolve on its own. Testing of the tool could not have been possible without the collaboration of MBA students from the University of Maryland University College and several Brazilian organizations, particularly Companhia Hidroelétrica do São Francisco and Serviço Federal de Processamento de Dados. These groups tested and helped improve the OKA tool.

# References

APQC. (2007). Measuring Knowledge Management. Available at www.APQC. com

Bassi, Laurie J., & Van Buren, Mark E. (2000). New measures for a new era. In Daryl Morey, Mark Maybury, & Bhavani Thuraisinghem (Eds.), *Knowledge management: Classic and contemporary works* (pp. 337–353). Boston: MIT Press.

Bontis, Nick. (2000). Managing organizational knowledge by diagnosing intellectual capital. In Daryl Morey, Mark Maybury, & Bhavani Thuraisinghem (Eds.), *Knowledge management: Classic and contemporary works* (pp. 375–402). Boston: MIT Press.

Delphi Group. (2007). Why do a knowledge audit? Available at www.destinationkm.com/articles/default.asp?ArticleID=633&keyWords=why++A

Denning, Stephen. (2007). Measuring knowledge management programs. Available at www.stevedenning.com/measurement_knowledge_management. html

Earl, Sarah, Carden, Fred, & Smutylo, Terry. (1971). *Outcome mapping: Building learning and reflection into development programs.* Ottawa: IDRC.

Hylton, Anne. (2007). A knowledge audit must be people-centered & people focused. Available at www.hyltonassociates.com

Hylton, Ann. (2007). The knowledge audit is first and foremost an audit. Available at www.hyltonassociates.com

Kaplan, Robert, & Norton, David P. (2000). Classic work: The balanced scorecard: Learning and growth perspective. In Daryl Morey, Mark Maybury, & Bhavani Thuraisinghem (Eds.), *Knowledge management: Classic and contemporary works* (pp. 317–336). Boston: MIT Press.

Lee, Lawrence Lock. (2000). Knowledge sharing metrics for large organizations. In Daryl Morey, Mark Maybury, & Bhavani Thuraisinghem (Eds.), *Knowledge management: Classic and contemporary works* (pp. 403–419). Boston: MIT Press.

Liebowitz, Jay, & Wright, Kathy. (1999). A look towards valuating human capital. In Jay Liebowitz (Ed.), *Knowledge management handbook* (pp. 5-1–5-13). Boca Raton, FL: CRC Press.

Liebowitz, Jay, Rubenstein-Montano, Bonnie, McCaw, Doug, Buchwalter, Judah, & Browing, Chuck. (2000). The knowledge audit. *Knowledge and Process Management*, January/March: 3.

Lopez, Kimberley. (2007). Measurement for knowledge management. Available at www.APQC.com

Moore, Carl R. (1999). Performances measurements for knowledge management. In Jay Liebowitz (Ed.), *Knowledge management handbook* (pp. 6-1–6-13). Boca Raton, FL: CRC Press.

National Electronic Library for Health. (2007). Conducting a knowledge audit. Available at www.nelh.nhs.uk/knowledge_management/km2/audit_toolkit.asp

Skyrme, David. (2002). Knowledge audit. Available at www.skyrme.com/services/kmaudit.htm

Sveiby, Karl-Erik. (2000). Measuring intangibles and intellectual capital. In Daryl Morey, Mark Maybury, & Bhavani Thuraisinghem (Eds.), *Knowledge management: Classic and contemporary works* (pp. 337–353), Boston: MIT Press.

Vestal, Wesley. (2002). Measuring knowledge management. Available at www.providers edge.com/docs/km_articles/Measuring_KM.pdf

# CHAPTER 20

# Knowledge Management Measurement: An Agenda for Organizations and Economies

Alton Y. K. Chua and Abdus Sattar Chaudhry

Nanyang Technological University

## INTRODUCTION

The notion of knowledge management (KM) has attracted immense attention especially in the past decade. This interest is largely fueled by the realization that knowledge is the source of competitive advantage for any organization or economy to thrive in the knowledge-based era. Efforts to implement KM have proliferated around the world as evidenced by the substantial increase in corporate spending on KM (Ithia, 2003). Correspondingly, the number of KM-related publications has also surged significantly from 1996 onward with little indication of decline even after nine years (Koenig, 2006).

Amid the euphoria is a gradual shift in focus toward the issue of measurement. When the dust of implementation settles, the quantifiable benefits KM brings and the manner in which KM is measured inevitably come under scrutiny. However, an attempt to measure knowledge itself is no simple undertaking. For one, knowledge possesses characteristics including subjectivity, transferability, embeddedness, self-reinforcement, spontaneity, and perishability, all of which are markedly different from those aspects commonly associated with tangible assets such as land and equipment (Kluge, Stein, & Licht, 2001). Nonetheless, KM measurement remains an important priority in knowledge-intensive environments. This is because measurement serves as the basis on which knowledge processes can be controlled, evaluated, and improved (Ahmed, Lim, & Zairi, 1999). Furthermore, measurement accentuates critical knowledge assets and allows increments in the value of knowledge assets to be calibrated. In the long run, measurement helps foster a performance-oriented culture (Kannan & Aulbur, 2004).

This chapter examines KM measurement from two ends of the spectrum, namely, the organizational level and the economic level. First, four organizations that had implemented KM initiatives are briefly introduced. The discussion centers on the set of performance indicators used by each organization to ascertain the impact of KM. Thereafter, the unit of analysis is extended to the economy. Various indicators to measure KM and its impact on economic clusters such as the Organisation for Economic Co-operation and Development (OECD) and Asia-Pacific Economic Cooperation (APEC) as well as individual nations such as the United States and Australia are surveyed. In conclusion, this chapter summarizes the common underlying themes in KM measurement between the organizational and economic levels.

# KM Measurement in Organizations

Organizations often use financial indicators to measure the impact of KM. Such an approach remains very appealing because financial figures are easily derivable. Furthermore, closely stitching KM to the bottom line offers an unambiguous view to KM's value proposition. However, these indicators make poor proxies to other equally important but intangible consequences of KM including brand name, goodwill, and intellectual capital. Some organizations have thus expanded the suite of indicators to include non-financial ones such as customer satisfaction and employee morale. Still, most of these measures are not precise enough to assess the impact of KM. Their underlying constructs continue to hold to a commodified and static view of knowledge.

As time passes, a slew of frameworks such as the Intangible Assets Monitor (Sveiby, 1997), Skandia Navigator (Edvinsson & Malone, 1997), and the Balance Scorecard (Kaplan & Norton, 2001) have been developed to capture the impact of KM more holistically. For example, the Intangible Assets Monitor can be used to track and value intangible assets while the Balanced Scorecard provides four different perspectives on which KM could exert an impact: financial, internal processes, learning and growth, and customer.

Several studies have been conducted to examine KM measurement within the organizations. In particular, Chaudhry and Dhansukhlal (2002) explored KM measurement in four organizations, namely, Fuji Xerox, Microsoft Corporation, Arthur Andersen, and Infosys Technologies. These organizations were selected on the basis of their successful KM efforts and well-documented KM measurement regimes. Data were drawn from an extensive review of their Web sites as well as interviews and e-mail communications with their local representatives. The findings revealed that KM in these organizations was guided by clearly articulated visions and invariably represented overt efforts to support business operations. The objectives of KM measurement and the level of sophistication of measurement indicators, however, varied among them.

Fuji Xerox developed "Eureka" as a platform to capture and disseminate tried-and-tested tips and insights culled from the day-to-day experience of its technical representatives. The purpose of measurement was to track the extent to which the Eureka system was relevant to the ground. For example, it was found that more than 150,000 problems were solved using Eureka. The measurement foci were in the areas of deployment, knowledge content, and productivity, as shown in Table 20.1.

## Table 20.1  Expanded description of OKA dimensions

| Measurement Foci | Sample Indicators |
|---|---|
| Deployment | • # of users connected<br>• % of users updating weekly |
| Knowledge content and quality | • # of solutions submitted<br>• Number days taken to validate solutions |
| Productivity | • # of customer problems solved<br>• % reduction in service hours<br>• % reduction in parts dollars<br>• Total $ saved in cost of service and support |

Being the first organization to conceptualize and implement the "Digital Nervous System," Microsoft sought to extract "actionable information" from the masses of data it already housed. The system enabled Microsoft to look at its strategic strengths, weaknesses, and goals for clues where KM could have a high impact on the organization. The KM measurement was focused on products and services design and development, customer and issue management, business planning, and employment management, as shown in Table 20.2.

Arthur Andersen launched its Global Best Practices, a repository of knowledge about world-class business practices that consultants could use as a reference point

## Table 20.2   Foci of KM measurement in Microsoft

| Measurement Foci | Sample Indicators |
|---|---|
| Product and services design & development | • Product success rate<br>• Cycle time<br>• Low design rework |
| Customer & issue management | • Customer satisfaction<br>• Needs captured in products<br>• Breadth of service coverage |
| Business planning | • Discovering trends<br>• Crisis response times<br>• Competitive awareness<br>• Acting on complete information |
| Employment management & development | • Education levels<br>• Training participation<br>• Skills alignments |

## Table 20.3   Foci of KM Measurement in Arthur Andersen

| Measurement Foci | Sample Indicators |
|---|---|
| Strategy | • Time saved in proposals and engagements |
| Process | • Number of contributions<br>• Contributors<br>• Organizing office<br>• People accessing documents<br>• Usefulness of documents |
| Culture | • People's reaction to KM |

to guide performance improvements for clients. The purpose of measurement was to justify the investments in the system. The emphases were on strategy, process, and culture as shown in Table 20.3.

With a "learn once, use anywhere" paradigm, Infosys Technologies brought together an organization-wide, integrated KM plan from pockets of disparate knowledge sharing initiatives. The purpose of KM measurement was to provide a

## Table 20.4   Foci of KM measurement in Infosys Technologies

| Measurement Foci | Sample Indicators |
|---|---|
| Customers (external structure) | • Growth/renewal (revenue and new customers)<br>• Efficiency (sales/customers)<br>• Stability (repeat business and sales to large customers) |
| Organization (internal structure) | • Growth/renewal (IT and R&D investments)<br>• Efficiency (proportion of staff and sale)<br>• Stability (average age of support staff) |
| People (competence) | • Growth/renewal (education index)<br>• Efficiency (value added per employee)<br>• Stability (average age of all employees |

value to the off-balance-sheet assets of the company and to show the financial and non-financial parameters that determined its long-term success. Customer, organization, and people were identified as the main measurement foci, as shown in Table 20.4.

Despite having different KM measurement systems, at least three common threads can be seen among them. First was the inclusion of customer-related elements. Fuji Xerox considered the number of customer problems solved; Microsoft tracked customer satisfaction, needs, and breadth of service coverage; Arthur Andersen was concerned about the turnaround time on proposals and engagement with customers; Infosys Technologies identified the customer as one of the main foci of measurement. The next common thread was the recognition of staff involvement and contributions. Fuji Xerox measured its deployment of KM by the connections from technicians; Arthur Andersen measured individual knowledge-sharing behavior and the usage of the corporate intranet; in Infosys Technologies, the competence of people was expressed and tracked in terms of educational level and value added per employee and average employee's age. Finally, there was an attempt in all four KM measurement systems to account for intangible outcomes. For instance, Fuji Xerox tried to quantify knowledge content and quality by indicators such as the number of solutions submitted and the number of days to validate the solutions. Similarly, Infosys Technologies used the percentage of revenue from image-enhancing customer, sales from the five largest customers over the total revenue, and value-added per software engineer to measure the intangible aspects of its KM efforts.

# KM Measurement in Economies

Not unlike organizations, economies around the world are also grappling with KM measurement, albeit at a macro level. There has been much interest in measuring the impact of knowledge on the economy through indicators such as the World Competitive Ranking, growth in gross domestic product, and income per capita. However, particularly after the Organisation for Economic Co-operation and Development (OECD) first coined the term "knowledge-based economy" (KBE) in 1996, the focus has been enlarged to consider the extent to which knowledge is created, disseminated, and exploited in an economy. Common definitions of the KBE include "an economy which is directly based on the production and use of knowledge and information" (Organisation for Economic Co-operation and Development, 1996) and "one in which the production, distribution, and use of knowledge is the main driver of growth, wealth creation, and employment across all industries" (Asia-Pacific Economic Cooperation, 2000). Requirements to build, maintain, and grow a KBE include an economic government that incentivizes the use of knowledge, the presence of an educated and skilled workforce, and a dynamic information and communication infrastructure, as well as a system of innovation comprising knowledge-intensive organizations such as research centers, universities, and think-tanks (Sigurdson, 2000). However, there is currently no internationally agreed-upon framework to measure the extent to which an economy is knowledge based.

The OECD economies use a scorecard, shown in Table 20.5, that specifies indicators related to five areas, namely, investment in intangibles, investment in ICT, investment in Science and Technology, internationalization of technology, and trends in international trade and foreign investment (Organisation for Economic Co-operation and Development, 2001). Through the scorecard, the growing role of knowledge in driving economic performance can be seen in some OECD countries. For example, there is greater international job mobility, especially among highly skilled workers. R&D expenditures particularly in the services and high-technology sectors have seen a steady increase.

Building on the OECD model, the APEC economies use a four-dimension framework that comprises business environment, ICT infrastructure, human

## Table 20.5  Foci of KBE measurement in OECD Economies

| Measurement Foci | Sample Indicators |
|---|---|
| Investment in intangibles | • R&D intensity in business sector <br> • # of R&D researchers |
| Investment in ICT | • % of GDP spent on ICT <br> • Price of assessing Internet |
| Investment in science and technology | • Size of venture capital market <br> • # of scientific publications/patents |
| Trends in international trade and foreign investment | • % of high-tech industries in total trade <br> • % of foreign direct investment in GDP |
| Internationalization of technology | • Share of foreign affiliates in R&D <br> • # of technological alliances, nationally and internationally |

resource development, and innovation system (Asia-Pacific Economic Cooperation, 2000) (shown in Table 20.6). The indicators represent a combination of "hard" or objective measures, such as service export as a percentage of the GDP, and "soft" or opinion measures, such as the ratings from the World Competitive Yearbook. A salient feature about the APEC framework is the inclusion of people development as an important priority of the KBE.

## Table 20.6  Foci of KBE measurement in APEC Economies

| Measurement Foci | Sample Indicators |
|---|---|
| Business environment | • % of service exports in GDP <br> • Rating on government, financial competition policy , and openness |
| ICT infrastructure | • Mobile phone subscription rate <br> • Index of business usage of ICT |
| Innovation system | • % of GDP spent on R&D <br> • # of US patents per million population |
| Human resource development | • Secondary school enrollments <br> • Human Development Index (HDI) |

## Table 20.7    Foci of KBE measurement in U.S.

| Measurement Foci | Sample Indicators |
|---|---|
| Knowledge jobs | • Employment of IT professionals<br>• Educational levels of the workforce |
| Globalization | • Export orientation of manufacturing<br>• Amount of foreign direct investment |
| Economic dynamism and competition | • Rate of economic "churn" (function of new business start-ups and existing business failures)<br>• Value of Initial Public Stock Offerings (IPO) by companies |
| Transformation to a digital economy | • # of ".com" domain names registered<br>• Internet and computers used by farmers |
| Technological innovation capacity | • # of jobs in tech-producing companies<br>• Venture Capital activity |

The U.S. uses the New Economic Index (Atkinson & Coduri, 1999), shown in Table 20.7, to benchmark its economic transformation in the KBE. The Index comprised five dimensions, namely, the quality of knowledge jobs, globalization, economic dynamism and competition, transformation into a digital economy, and technological innovation capacity. A closer examination of the indicators such as "Internet and computers use by farmers" and "number of .com domain names registered" reveals that some are now clearly out-dated.

In Australia, the effort to measure knowledge in the economy and society was championed by the Australian Bureau of Statistics (ABS). While the Australian rendition was drawn from the earlier OECD and APEC frameworks, it recognizes the reciprocal influences between the economy and the society. Hence, as shown in Table 20.8, the ABS framework comprises five dimensions, namely, innovation and entrepreneurship, human and social capital, the role of ICT, the economy, society and environment, and finally, economic and social impacts (Australian Bureau of Statistics, 2001).

It is clear that different economies hold different perspectives on the KBE. The foci of KBE measurements reflect their varying needs and priorities. For example, the OECD economies are concerned with the development of high-technology industries. Thus, several of their indicators are technology related. Likewise, given that research and development are seen as the key driver of innovation to the APEC economies, a high number of the research and development indicators have been specified. In Australia, the choice of indicators shows the nation's concern for the effects of knowledge on society as well. Common among all economies

## Table 20.8   Foci of KBE measurement in Australia

| Measurement Foci | Sample Indicators |
|---|---|
| Innovation & entrepreneurship | • Cross-border ownership of inventions<br>• # of business R&D by industry |
| Human & social capital | • Availability of tertiary courses<br>• Immigration and emigration of skilled adults |
| Role of ICT | • Household access to computers<br>• ICT sector share of total employment |
| The fundamentals—economy, society, and environment | • GDP trend per capita<br>• Income distribution |
| Economic & social impacts | • Growth in productivity<br>• Teleworking patterns among the workforce |

are the foci on the output of the industries, the use of information communication technology in businesses and by the populace, as well as the development of human resources.

## DISCUSSION

KM measurement appears to be a multi-faceted effort whether at the organizational or the economic levels. On the basis of the various organizations and economies presented earlier, a few overlapping dimensions of KM measurement are apparent. They include the outcomes for which KM was intended to achieve as well as KM-enablers such as technology, culture, and human development shown in Table 20.9.

An important but obscured dimension of KM measurement is the measurement of KM processes (Chaudhry, 2003). While the precise descriptions and demarcations among KM processes are debatable, they are commonly identified as knowledge creation, knowledge dissemination, and knowledge application. Knowledge creation refers to the addition of new knowledge to the existing stock of knowledge by developing it internally or acquiring it from external sources. Knowledge dissemination involves transmitting knowledge content or sometimes establishing a connection between the knower and the one seeking knowledge. Knowledge application is the process of capturing knowledge from an experience and packaging it into a form suitable for repeated use in future similar experiences. Sample indicators of how KM processes can be measured at the organizational and economic levels are proposed in Table 20.10.

These indicators were reviewed by experts in the Economic Development Board in Singapore and found appropriate for measuring the contribution of KM

### Table 20.9   Dimensions of KM measurement at the organizational and economic levels

| Dimensions of Measurement | Sample Indicators | |
|---|---|---|
| | Organizational Level | Economic Level |
| **Outcomes**: Business results or economic and societal outcomes | • Profit-and-loss figures <br> • Market share <br> • Financial savings | • GDP growth <br> • World competitiveness ranking <br> • Income per capita |
| **Technology**: The development of technology and the extent to which technology is accessed and used | • Investments in IT <br> • # of users connected | • % of GDP on ICT spending <br> • Household access to computers |
| **Culture**: Openness to embrace KM | • People's reaction to KM <br> • # of contributions made to a repository <br> • Online participation rates | • # of technological alliances, nationally and internationally <br> • Immigration and emigration of skilled adults |
| **Human Development**: The development of human resources | • Training participation <br> • Educational levels of the employees | • Availability of tertiary courses <br> • Educational levels of the workforce |

by different types of organizations toward the knowledge-based economy (Chaudhry & Fong, 2006; Chua, Chaudhry, & Fong, 2006).

# Conclusion

This chapter attempts to examine the foci of KM measurement both at the organizational and the economic levels. The KM measurement practices at Fuji Xerox, Microsoft Corporation, Arthur Andersen, and Infosys Technologies are examined. Common across all four organizations are the inclusion of customer-related elements, the recognition of staff's involvement and contribution, and the attempt to account for intangible outcomes. At the economic level, the rendition of KM measurement is the knowledge-based economy. Based on the review of the KBE measurement adopted by the OECD, APEC, U.S., and Australia, it can be observed that all economies focus on the output of their industries, the use of information communication technology in businesses and by the populace, as well as the development of human resources. The common themes that underlie KM measurement at both the organizational and economic

### Table 20.10 Measurement of KM processes at the organizational and economic levels

| KM Processes | Proposed Sample Indicators | |
|---|---|---|
| | Organizational Level | Economic Level |
| Knowledge Creation | • R&D expenditures<br>• Strategic partnerships with other organizations<br>• Provision of internal platforms for cross-fertilization of ideas | • % of GDP spent on R&D<br>• # of mergers and acquisitions activities<br>• # of national brands registered |
| Knowledge Dissemination | • Ease of access to knowledge and experts<br>• Level of trust among staff<br>• Openness to knowledge sharing | • Major newspapers circulation figures<br>• Extent of deregulations in ICT and the media |
| Knowledge Application | • Availability of past lessons learned<br>• Attitude toward adopting and adapting among units in the organization | • Number of start-ups<br>• Monetary value of Intellectual Property (IP) commercialized by industry |

levels are the outcomes for which KM was intended to achieve as well as KM-enablers such as technology, culture, and human development. An obscured dimension of KM measurement is in the measurement of the KM processes. Thus, a number of indicators to measure the processes of knowledge creation, knowledge dissemination, and knowledge applications for organizations as well as economies have been proposed.

KM is a complex venture whose wide-ranging impact, enabling mechanisms, and associated processes can only be comprehensively measured with myriad measurement indicators. This chapter is thus a modest attempt to provide a guide for KM practitioners and economists in their KM measurement efforts.

## REFERENCES

Ahmed, Pervaiz K., Lim, Kwang K., & Zairi, Mohamed. (1999). Measurement practice for knowledge management. *The Journal of Workplace Learning*, *11*(8): 304–311.

Asia-Pacific Economic Cooperation. (2000). *Towards knowledge based economies in APEC*. Singapore: APEC Secretariat.

Atkinson, Robert D., & Coduri, Rick. (1999). *The new economy index: Understanding America's economic transformation*. Washington, DC: Progressive Policy Institute.

Australian Bureau of Statistics (2001). Measuring the knowledge-based economy: A statistical framework for measuring knowledge in the Australia economy and society. Accessed December 20, 2004, from www.unescap.org/stat/cos12/wgse12/wgse12-06.asp

Chaudhry, Abdus Sattar. (2003). What difference does it make: Measuring returns of knowledge management. In Elayne Coakes (Ed.), *Knowledge management: Current issues and challenges* (pp. 52–65). Hershey, PA: IRM Press.

Chaudhry, Abdus Sattar, & Dhansukhlal, Jasna. (2002). Measuring the impact of knowledge management. IRMA 2002 International Conference. Seattle, Washington, May 19–22.

Chaudhry, Abdus Sattar, & Fong, Pin Fen. (2006). Validating the indicators for the knowledge based economy: A case study of economic development board of Singapore. 2006 Information Resources Management Association International Conference—Emerging Trends and Challenges in Information Technology Management. Washington, DC, May 21–24.

Chua, Alton, Chaudhry, Abdus Sattar, & Fong, Pin Fen. (2006). Pursuing the holy grail of knowledge-based economy assessment: The case of Singapore. Third International Conference on Knowledge Management. Greenwich, U.K., July 31–August 2.

Edvinsson, Leif, & Malone, Michael S. (1997). *Intellectual capital: Realizing your company's true value by finding its hidden brainpower*. New York: HarperBusiness.

Ithia, A. (2003). UK lawyers spend more on KM. *KM Review*, 5(6): 11.

Kannan, Gopika, & Aulbur, Wilfried G. (2004). Intellectual capital: Measurement effectiveness. *Journal of Intellectual Capital*, 5(3): 389–413.

Kaplan, Robert S., & Norton, David P. (2001). *The strategy-focused organization: How balance scorecard companies thrive in the new business environment*. Boston: Harvard Business School Press.

Kluge, Jurgen, Stein, Wolfram, & Licht, Thomas. (2001). *Knowledge unplugged: The McKinsey & Company global survey on knowledge management* (pp. 63–67). New York: Palgrave.

Koenig, Michael. (2006). Leadership roles for information professionals. In *Asia-Pacific Conference on Library & Information Education & Practice* (pp. 11–17). Singapore, April 3–6.

Organisation for Economic Co-operation and Development. (1996). *The knowledge-based economy science, technology and industry outlook*. Paris: OECD.

Organisation for Economic Co-operation and Development. (2001). *The new economy: Beyond the hype. Final report on the OECD growth project*. Paris: OECD.

Sigurdson, Jon. (2000). Singapore means to turn into a knowledge based economy. The Stockholm School of Economics.

Sveiby, Karl Erik. (1997). *The new organizational wealth: Managing and measuring knowledge-based assets*. San Francisco: Barrett-Kohler.

# Part VI

---

# Knowledge Management and Project Management

# Knowledge Management
# and Project Management
## FOREWORD

It is increasingly being recognized that project management and KM are very much linked, first by the fact that a major project management undertaking should be supported by a KM initiative, and second by the fact that a major KM initiative should be viewed as something requiring project management skills and techniques. The chapter by Shobha (Chapter 21) comes from the latter perspective. Shobha's chapter contains a very useful table, which for each of nine different knowledge areas of KM, presents challenges, knowledge capture techniques, and knowledge dissemination techniques. A major thread of the chapter is not just on KM for the project per se, but upon the utility of not treating each project as a "silo," and creating a broader structure in which lessons learned from one project can be background and management information for subsequent projects. Even within the same project, if at all long term, personnel turnover, particularly in the IT field where professionals are notorious for desiring new challenges and new assignments, means that the utility of KM as a tool for knowledge retention and preservation is a must.

Hutchinson and Anklam (Chapter 22), in describing the development of collaborative software projects, also succeed in describing very good project management techniques for applications in the domain of KM. They cover not just techniques, but metrics and critical success factors as well. This chapter could just as well have been placed in the "Knowledge Sharing" section, but that is what the Roadmap is for.

This overlap between KM and project management is also discussed in some detail in Chapter 3 by Srikantaiah.

# CHAPTER 21

# Knowledge Management in Software Projects

C. S. Shobha

Perot Systems

*A manager is responsible for the application and performance of knowledge.*

–Peter Drucker

## INTRODUCTION

World Bank, in its World Development Report of 1998–1999, describes knowledge as light, weightless, and intangible; it can easily travel the world and enlighten the levels of people everywhere. At the organizational level, knowledge management (KM) is attributed to organizational assets. These assets may include databases, documents, policies, and procedures, as well as previously untouched expertise in individual workers. KM is the systematic process of identifying, capturing, organizing, and disseminating/sharing explicit and tacit knowledge assets that add value within an organization. It is a product of the 1990s and is a hot topic in organizations, with many practitioners drawn from different disciplines such as business, engineering, education, epistemology, communication, and information management, among others. KM embraces those disciplines and treats knowledge as an entity dynamically embedded in networks, processes, repositories, and people. Billions of dollars are invested worldwide in KM.

In a project, knowledge is power—but only if it is readily accessible, organized, analyzed, and disseminated to meet the project needs. Knowledge in projects should focus on the proper access and delivery methods for explicit knowledge on the desktop and should also concentrate on tacit knowledge unknown and unavailable to most people involved in these projects.

## Project Management

Projects are part of organizations. Of late, organizations are focusing more on projects to meet their objectives. Internal environments that affect the organization are business plans, strategy, funding, staffing, processes, architecture, politics, and culture. Externally, the organizations are influenced by industry, market, economic, political, social, and technology environments.

When we deal with projects in organizations, project management is different than general management. All projects will have start and end dates, in addition to a detailed project plan, budget, schedule, human resources, and deliverables. Every project will be unique in nature and will have a temporary structure. General management differs in all these areas.

Project Management Institute (PMI) in its PMBOK Guide (2004) defines a project as a temporary endeavor to create a unique product, service, or result.

There are several phases to a project life cycle. According to the PMBOK Guide, projects can be divided into phases to provide better management control. Collectively, these phases become the project life cycle. Many organizations identify a specific set of life cycles for use in their projects. However, all project life cycles will connect the beginning of a project to its end. There is no single best way to define an ideal project life cycle. Some organizations have established policies that standardize all projects with a single life cycle, while others allow the project management to choose the most appropriate life cycle for the team's project. Project life cycles generally cover the following aspects:

- How technical work should be completed in each phase
- How deliverables should be generated in each phase
- How each deliverable is reviewed, verified, and validated; people involved in each phase; and a plan to control and approve each phase

Project life cycle descriptions can be very general or very detailed. Most project life cycles are generally sequential and are usually defined by some form of technical information transfer or technical component handoff. Cost and staffing levels are low at the start, peak during the intermediate phases, and drop rapidly as the project draws to an end. The first phase involves identification of a problem or need. The second phase involves the development of a proposed solution to the problem or need. The third phase is actually doing the project, utilizing resources and meeting the stated objectives. The fourth stage involves terminating the project. Although all projects go through all four phases of the project life cycle, they vary in duration and complexity.

The Guide also lists nine knowledge areas in project management:

- **Project Integration Management:** This area is concerned with how the resources are manipulated throughout the project. It includes processes and activities to identify, define, combine, and coordinate the various activities required. A contingency plan cost estimate will require the integration of planning in the project cost management, time management, and risk management processes.

- **Project Scope Management**: Describes the processes involved in determining that the project includes all the work required, and only the work required to complete the project successfully. It includes scope planning and scope definition.

- **Project Time Management**: Describes the processes concerning the timely completion of the project. It includes activity definition, activity sequencing, and activity resource estimating.

- **Project Cost Management**: Concerned with the process that ensures the project is completed within the approved budget. It also includes planning, estimating, budgeting, and controlling costs. While primarily concerned with the cost of resources, it should also consider the effect of project decisions through the project life cycle.

- **Project Quality Management**: Describes the processes involved in assuring that the project will satisfy the objectives for which it was undertaken. It includes quality planning and performing quality assurance. Processes may include planning to identify project roles, acquiring project team members through the life of a project, developing skills and competencies of project team members, and tracking performance.

- **Project HR Management:** Describes the processes concerned with HR related project management issues, including recruiting and assignment, motivation, and retention, and with a particular emphasis upon employee professional and managerial development.

- **Project Communications Management**: Describes the processes concerning timely and appropriate generation, collection, dissemination, storage, and ultimate disposition of project information. It includes communication planning, information distribution, and performance reporting.

- **Project Risk Management**: Describes the processes concerned with risk management of a project. It includes risk management planning, risk identification, qualitative risk analysis, and risk response planning.
- **Project Procurement Management**: Describes the processes that purchase or acquire products, services, or results as well as contract management processes. It also includes the plans for purchases, acquisitions, plan contracting, selecting sellers, requesting seller responses, and contract administration.

Although some projects do not contain all of the nine areas described, knowledge is generated in some areas of the project. In terms of KM, knowledge capture and knowledge dissemination become the two most important issues.

Knowledge is created and flows through all the nine areas of project management and in the all phases of the project life cycle. Project managers and staff constantly seek knowledge to address various problems: resources, deadlines, deliverables, goals/objectives, team composition, planning, communications, and conflicts.

Earlier, the emphasis for project management was on developing tools and techniques such as critical paths and earned value analysis. Later, the project management shifted to evaluation-based success criteria. It is the responsibility of the organizations' senior management to ensure that they create an environment in which projects can succeed. The advantage of managing knowledge in projects is that they can successfully deliver and remain competitive. Organizations need to learn to manage the knowledge that they acquire and accumulate from their previous projects more effectively so that other projects in the organization can benefit.

Knowledge can be embedded within an individual, a group, or an organization. Knowledge gained is learned from the failures or successes of projects, which is a vital aspect of long-term sustainability and the ability to compete in business environments. Unlike organizations, projects do not have organizational memory because projects are temporary in nature. Knowledge types in projects may include sector knowledge, technical knowledge, and organization knowledge. KM helps in all these areas and also aids staff in sharing the vision of the project.

## Criteria for Managing Knowledge in Projects

- **KM is about people.** It is directly linked to what people know, and how what they know supports business and organizational objectives. Although technology can support a KM effort, it shouldn't begin there.

- **Effective KM is orderly and goal-directed.** It is inextricably tied to the strategic objectives of the organization. It uses only the information that is the most meaningful, practical, and purposeful.
- **KM is ever changing.** There is no such thing as an incontrovertible law in KM. Knowledge is constantly tested, updated, and revised, and oftentimes knowledge that was applicable at one time may no longer be practicable. It is a fluid, ongoing process.
- **KM is value-added.** It draws upon pooled expertise, relationships, and alliances. Organizations can further the two-way exchange of ideas by bringing in experts from the field to advise or educate managers on recent trends and developments. Forums, councils, and boards can be instrumental in creating common ground and organizational cohesiveness.
- **KM is visionary.** This vision is expressed in strategic business terms rather than technical terms, and in a manner that generates enthusiasm, buy-in, and motivation for managers to work together toward reaching common goals.
- **KM is complementary.** It can be integrated with other organizational learning initiatives such as Total Quality Management (TQM). It is important for knowledge managers to show interim successes, along with progress made on more protracted efforts such as multiyear systems developments infrastructure or enterprise architecture projects.

## Benefits from KM in Projects

- **Strategic advantage:** Projects rely on knowledge to create a strategic advantage. With available knowledge widely dispersed and fragmented, project teams often waste valuable time and resources in "reinventing the wheel" or failing to access the highest quality knowledge and expertise that is available.
- **Retention**: Without effective mechanisms in place to capture the knowledge of experienced employees, project teams may be making costly mistakes or have to pay again for knowledge they once had on tap.
- **Sharing of best practices**: Projects could cut costs by taking the knowledge from their best performers and applying it in similar situations elsewhere.

- **Successful innovation**: Other companies applying KM methods have found that through knowledge networking they can create new products and services faster and better.

# Projects Demography

The project context, size, and scope play key roles in terms of the importance of KM. The projects can be very short term, with one set of deliverables, or they may consist of multiple projects done for the same customer, executed as program management. The project can be as short lived as three weeks, or may run as long as 10 years. Most of the long running projects will be maintenance projects.

The challenges presented by various kinds of projects differ greatly. As an example, software projects can be utilized to achieve the following objectives:

- Fresh development
- Maintenance of existing applications
- Enhancements to existing applications
- Migration of projects from one platform to another in terms of technology/databases
- Re-engineering existing applications
- Agile development, where project scope is not completely defined at the outset of a project, but continuously develops on an ongoing basis, capturing requirements in an agile mode, and delivering them in multiple short-term releases
- Deploying package solutions and working on customization around them
- Product development

With total outsourcing deals, the scope of the project would be extended into transitioning existing customer employees to its organization, and going through a total change of management in terms of culture, human resources, compensation, and people aspects.

What we see in service provider software companies is that all the knowledge from one project may not be relevant to other projects. There we get into segmentation of knowledge, which offers opportunities to look at apples versus apples, and not apples versus oranges. (Just as a Web development project in J2EE Technology can be compared to a similar project, but not to a mainframe project.) There are certain aspects in a project like project management that can be compared and some concepts that are relevant across all projects, irrespective of the technology or domain.

Today, an engineer who works on a project needs to have multiple competencies relevant to that specific project. In senior roles, the need for understanding is broad. It includes an understanding of organizations' internal process for inter-group co-ordination, such as how to acquire resources for a project, how to procure software, how to book meeting rooms, how to request training for team members, and so on.

The common knowledge needs in software projects will be in the following areas:

- Project context, scope, organization
- Understanding the customer's business, including their organization structure, people, and their way of working
- Technology used—languages, operating systems, databases, middle layers, architecture, etc.
- Tools being used in the projects—for project management, estimation, requirements capture, design, automated code generation, testing, configuration management, release, problem management, defects tracking, time sheet tracking, etc.
- Process, standards, guidelines used in the project—both from their own organization and customer specific
- Security policies, data protection acts, etc.
- Knowing who the experts are in specific areas—so that there is a "go to" person when the need arises

These needs would be addressed by acquiring people with the right competencies, or by supporting them with training programs. Another means of support would be to allow access to existing knowledge repositories of the organization through mentoring, in addition to continuous communication through meetings, KM sessions, and communities of practice, as well as a list of experts available for interactions during the projects.

# LIFECYCLE OF KM IN PROJECTS

The role of KM software projects can be viewed at these three stages:

- At project initiation
- During project execution
- At project shutdown

## At Project Initiation

The projects will have resources assigned at various phases of the project, and the resources would be required in multiple competencies, experience levels, roles, skills, and expertise. There are some implementation instances where projects have developed Project Induction programs as Kiosks, where more interaction, steps, and evaluation of the members are ongoing through this program. They will have information available in a structured manner for team members to go through, and do self-learning.

If an organization has a repository of earlier projects, there is also a great opportunity to look at any information gained through previous projects that is relevant and can be adopted in current projects. Some examples may be experience with tools, re-usable components, approach papers, coding standards, and GUI guidelines, in addition to current performance in terms of metrics goals like productivity, defect density, effort at the various life cycle stages, etc. CMMI framework recommends looking at defect prevention based on previous experience at the start of a project. In this case, the project team would look for prevention of certain defects in projects previously faced by looking at root causes and lessons learned. This can be made a mandatory step at the beginning of the project as part of a defect prevention process. The practical issue one faces here is that, unless there is organized information available and one can easily identify relevant best practices and have the necessary artifacts easily available, it becomes a challenge to get the right information from the maze of information available. Especially in a global delivery model, the ability to know where the right information is available can happen only with the right repositories, taxonomies, metadata tagging, and tools to search and access them seamlessly.

In many organizations there are different teams who work on putting up proposals for the engagement and actual execution of the project. Typically the proposal work would be done by the business development team and supported by domain and technical experts. Once the proposal is accepted and the actual project starts, there may be many discussion points, such as understanding context and objectives, as well as changes that happen in conjunction with customer teams at various levels that do not get recorded. This knowledge is very rarely captured, and usually only the finally accepted terms are updated in the proposal documents. When the project actually starts with an allocation of a project manager in delivery mode, many of the earlier discussion points, context, and assumptions are never passed on. This is one key point where tacit knowledge gets lost. One of the best practices in such a scenario is to organize project kick-off meetings with all stakeholders and the people who were involved in the proposal and solution preparation phase of the project to share the details of discussions, thoughts, and assumptions that went into this activity. Some of the details that would be useful are understanding why a particular architecture, technology, approach, solution, and business solution has been decided upon.

## During Project Execution

During project execution, it is essential to be in touch with all stakeholders in the project to get to know about changing business needs, changes to existing architecture, designs, tool deployments, test strategy, environment, etc. Today, we work in global delivery models where teams from different organizations, different geographical locations, and different time zones work on the same project. They all need to share the immense collective knowledge on life cycle phases, as they use common code, test cases, object models, architecture etc. We have seen projects where the same code is being accessed by multiple teams simultaneously. Project teams need to be aware of common components. In many situations, common components themselves go through changes and impact on other artifacts. Change management is so intense and critical in today's projects that it is similar to running continuously on a treadmill. By the time you have written and unit tested the code, you need to put it through a change management process and take it to system integration to absorb all the changes that have occurred in that short period.

The advanced configuration management principles and tools are used extensively to address all these needs. Projects will have central or distributed repositories and all the project artifacts are stored and maintained in a structured manner. Teams use well defined processes to check documents in and out from them and also have appropriate naming conventions, version management, amendment history, review, approval, and test steps to manage them. The project teams would conduct configuration audits to ensure that configuration practices are actually in place and backed up in addition to running disaster drills.

Specifically in programs with multiple projects for the same customer, there are many opportunities to share lessons learned across teams. The customer would also like to see collective knowledge and experience being reflected in such engagements. A team would have figured out the best way to use a defect tracking tool, or a better performance ability, or a design principle. The sharing of such practices offers an opportunity for the team to connect and subsequently improves the team's performance.

Adopting KM in project execution helps to eliminate unproductive repetitive tasks. If for every task there could be a best practice approach and available information about an expert in that domain, each task could achieve peak performance in the optimal time period.

The best practices in this area are to develop a tool/template that documents the project learnings on a continuous basis and is based on the PMBOK structure: e.g., all scope and risk management learnings are documented separately. This will enable further consolidation at an organizational level. At any given frequency it is possible to consolidate learnings from multiple projects being handled during that interval in the organization and a best practices book can be published within the organization.

## Maintenance Projects

The continued maintenance of projects in production needs more knowledge leverage by its nature. The applications and systems developed need to be maintained for the shelf life of the project. The defects and problems in such systems need to be addressed in defined Service Level Agreements (SLAs), so that end users have better service available to them. Most often these SLAs are very stringent to the extent that problems need to be dealt with within 4 to 48 hours, depending on criticality. What this means is that the project teams responsible for handling such prompt response times need to be on top of the application, technical, and business knowledge at all times. Only well structured, documented, and accessible information within a continuous exchange of knowledge combined with expert help can make these goals achievable.

In long-term maintenance projects, the retention of knowledge within the various teams becomes all the more critical. The challenge for software service providing companies is to retain people for a longer duration to continue working within the projects. Most often software engineers do not like to work on the same project on a long-term basis. They feel that by working on the same application they cannot keep up with the pace of technology growth. They would like to move out to other projects after a one- to two-year stint in the same project. But, the customer expects to retain these resources on a long-term basis for better delivery. The best practices applied in such situations have been to implement a rotation plan—a systematic way to induct new team members onto a project by putting them through an actual mentoring phase for three to six months, which will allow them to support the applications keeping up the agreed SLAs. In this step, a knowledge repository should be developed that can contain business process documents, help files, documenting solutions, frequently recurring problems, and a detailed log of major breakdowns, in addition to operational manuals, etc. These are also supported by tools, which help in the analysis and impact of change in one artifact against the rest.

## At Project Shutdown

The entire experience of the project can be captured at this stage. This process can be institutionalized to capture these experiences systematically into the system. The organization groups that manage process, tools, business, and KM may receive various triggers for further improvements going forward. The project performance metrics can be placed into an organization metrics repository, and can be further utilized for organizational baselines. The customer feedback at this stage is also a key input to understanding project performance. The best practices in these areas are to conduct knowledge sharing sessions with the fellow project management community on challenges faced, what worked, what did not work, and what could have been done better. Many times, in this type of session the real, honest, and detailed sharing will not be accomplished. These types of meetings are typically conducted at a high level and are usually limited to the few points the project manager can think of at that time, when they are in a hurry to close down the current project and move on to the next assignment. Unless a continuous log of learnings is kept alive during the project execution, this briefing has very limited use. Yet another good practice is to make key people in the project like the business analyst, architect, designer, test engineer, and developer share their experiences, not limiting this session to only the project manager. This session can be structured as a panel discussion with a third person moderating the discussion. Projects are like history, either one learns from the past or they are destined to repeat the mistakes of the past.

# Contribution of ISO 9001, CMM, CMMI Frameworks

Applying these Software Quality Management standards has greatly improved the maturity in the project management and software engineering arena. The best practices from these frameworks have enhanced the ability organizations have to manage basic information and core processes in a predictable and consistent manner. This type of maturity has enabled organizations to maintain a project history and enhanced communication and knowledge dissemination across the organization.

## Collaboration with the Customer

There is a trend and growing need of working more collaboratively with customers in software projects delivery. Customer organizations are also reaching maturity in terms of developing methodologies, frameworks, and processes conforming to ISO, CMM, and CMMI standards. In many cases, there has to be an agreement as to which process model is to be adopted for a specific project. Typically a fusion of processes will be adopted. There are examples where coding standards of companies are merged to form a common best practices set and there are also cases where established customer standards receive priority. In either case, orientation programs should be scheduled for the team on both methodologies where a process framework shall be discussed and agreed upon and can be documented as part of the project quality plan.

When handling multiple projects for the same customer, there is an expectation that the multiple project teams would work as a single team. Therefore the input the customer has given in the context of one project may be expected to be carried over to all the projects. This cannot be achieved unless integrated teams are established and processes are put in place to capture inputs and communicate them to the entire team. However, in many engagements the different projects work in a vacuum. Each project will have its own project organization and oftentimes they do not have a view of what is happening in other projects for the same customer.

There are many situations where customers do not have any standard process and they do not support defining any specific process. They may like to skip certain steps, for example, start coding directly instead of going through the requirements such as gathering, analysis, and design. This becomes an issue in terms of working out cost estimates and scheduling these types of engagements.

## Collaboration with Subcontractors

In this era where we need to look at projects with a "wing-to-wing" view, anyone who is part of the project cycle should have a link to the knowledge and collaborative viewpoint of the project execution; subcontractors are not exempt from this. They also contribute to the defined scope of the project and hence all the relevant information, best practices, standards, methods, processes, and tools need to be shared with them as well. The best practice in this area is to include them in all project-specific training and share the project knowledge artifacts in a collaborative manner in order to get them connected to experts.

## Infrastructure/Environment

The physical places—including desk spaces, meeting rooms, conference room, training facilities, informal coffee places, and access to library and conferencing facilitates—all play an important role in facilitating knowledge exchange in projects. Oftentimes increased knowledge exchange happens in an informal setting. The availability of collaborative tools, such as telephone connections, offers ease of communication and enhances knowledge sharing behaviors. The "K-café"—an informal coffee area available specifically for knowledge exchange—is a practice implemented in some organizations.

# Knowledge Capture/Dissemination on Nine Areas of Project Management

The challenges to knowledge capture and dissemination practices that have been observed in my experience have been consolidated in Table 21.1. This table

## Table 21.1  Nine knowledge areas in project management

| Knowledge Areas of Project Management | Challenges | Knowledge Capture | Knowledge Dissemination |
|---|---|---|---|
| Project Integration Management | Large volumes of knowledge captured, but not contextualized or shared.<br><br>*Teams work in silos.* In projects with multi-vendor scenario, integration with other vendors, managing dependencies, timelines, and standards is a challenge.<br><br>*What gets overlooked is the right information being available to the right person at the right time, even though information is readily available in some form.* | *Have a project kick-off with all parties involved in order to identify and establish integration points, dependencies, schedules, and underlying standards. Integration aspects from requirements to design and testing should be documented and shared. Specifically the information that gets overlooked is:*<br><br>Shared vision.<br>Contract terms.<br>External assumptions, constraints, dependencies.<br>Historical information about the project.<br><br>Capture/research on the associated topics that pose a challenge to the project scenario. | *Share aspects related to integration and changes that happen during the project life cycle on a continuous basis. This can be done by having all related information in a common repository accessible to all parties involved or by having a mechanism of sharing via e-mail with each party updating their individual repository. Have an owner for sharing all such knowledge.*<br><br>The shared vision is to be communicated on a continuous basis between all teams and validated at various points of reference as people keep moving in and out of the project at various points of time. |

# Table 21.1  (cont.)

| | | | |
|---|---|---|---|
| | | Focus on optimized process and automation for integration.<br><br>Get external experts to bring in new perspectives and advice on critical knowledge areas. | Use virtual collaboration tools/platforms for sharing project information.<br><br>Share with the customer any research information that is relevant to the project in a summarized form.<br><br>Connect knowledge seekers and providers. Facilitation is key to getting the team to work together.<br><br>Tools and technologies are areas where many best practices and problem solving help can be sought from experts outside the project teams and organization. |
| **Project Scope Management** | Getting in-depth knowledge on requirements from customers.<br><br>There is not enough time made available for the team to internalize the requirements in a complete and detailed sense.<br><br>Scope creep, scope changes, unambiguous requirements, understanding of requirements, sharing of requirements to all concerned, and understanding within project teams pose a challenge. | *Document in detail all the requirements, along with priority and clarity status. Capture as much information as is available from customer.*<br><br>*Elicit requirements from the right experts. If the customer organization has corporate yellow pages, refer that to identify experts beyond references stated by the customer.*<br><br>Audio/video capturing of customer interviews on project expectations and context would be good source for project teams at any point in time.<br><br>*In the contractual documents, keep the terms and controls for dealing with changes in scope as open as possible.* | *Study tours.*<br><br>Get all related stakeholders to a common meeting to finalize on the project's scope and have subsequent formal meetings to discuss scope change and understanding.<br><br>Demonstrating requirements capture through visualization/prototypes. |
| **Project Time Management** | Understand priorities and schedules. | Look at tasks that are likely to take more time either by intrinsic challenge or by experience level of the individual, and assign expertise/mentors to address time delays. | *Share slippages in advance with customer.*<br><br>Prioritize important tasks on a regular basis within team . |
| **Project Cost Management** | Understand cost implications in regard to changes to scope and schedule, and try to predict cost overruns.<br><br>*Incentive schemes for knowledge sharing and ideas for productivity gains.* | *System to keep the cost parameters updated and available to all concerned.*<br><br>Look for tools/ideas to improve productivity. | *Share cost details and resource utilization during project execution, specifically with integrated teams.* |
| **Project Quality Management** | Understand quality requirements from customer's perspective within project teams. | *At the beginning of the project, look into organization repository at various intervals to assess* | Coaching/mentoring by experts within project, and also by external experts if needed. Provide self study |

# Table 21.1 (cont.)

| | | *reusable knowledge and best practices in the context of the current project.* | materials. Use of intranet, project portals, project kiosks, e-learning. |
|---|---|---|---|
| | *Experiential, subjective, and intuitive knowledge-based decisions are not documented and shared with the rest of the team and are not available for future reference.* | Making a search tool available to access the project repository will facilitate better access to the information. | Look at benchmarking data from industries and compare with current project data and analyze. |
| | *Opportunities for innovation will be missed.* | Capture the quality framework that needs to be used in project context as part of the plan. | Any industry/customer specific standards or guidelines that need to have compliance need to be shared with entire team at the beginning of their task. |
| | *Role definition for taking and participating in knowledge capture and sharing not defined.* | Conduct a knowledge audit during project execution to see that the information and expertise are leveraged and to identify if any gaps exist. | Keep looking at and analyzing the project performance data on a regular basis with all key stakeholders. |
| | *No sophisticated systems to learn what worked and what did not work from previous similar project scenarios.* | Map business processes/technology areas with staff. Identify key experts who have not transferred their knowledge in terms of guidelines, checklists, etc. Succession planning and mentorship programs can also be evolved with this audit. | Participate in knowledge sharing sessions from other projects and Communities of Practice. |
| **Project HR Management** | Sharing tacit knowledge. Motivation to share and re-use. | *Reward and recognize knowledge sharing behaviors.* | Provide a culture and platforms that allow people to express their opinions. |
| | | Include knowledge sharing/mentoring as part of job descriptions. A specific role of knowledge champion/co-coordinator for a project is a best practice. This can be a part-time role for small projects and a full-time role for large projects. | Have an experts list that is being maintained, getting into the details of customer and project specific technology/domain specific expertise. This list should include their contact numbers, e-mail, experience level, and expertise details. Peer recognition of these experts is vital to the identification of experts. Capture expertise of people beyond their current roles. |
| | | Provide training for in-house experts on presentation and teaching skills. Also provide time and resources for these experts to develop content. | When people leave the project teams or organization, make sure their tacit knowledge is captured in some form or another including their impression about who are the experts and their social, informal networks in the context of project setting. |
| **Project Communications Management** | Communication within the team and between geographical locations. | *Capture important decisions in documents, voice, or video form.* | *An external communication expert available for coaching in the handling of e-mail, telephone, video, Webinar, fax, and written, oral, formal, or informal communication if the teams have deficiencies in these areas and understanding cultural issues involved.* |
| | Cultural barriers against saying "no" to the customer. Making sure to ask questions at the right time and confronting ideas from customers. | The communication points must be well structured so that users can have ready access whenever they are needed by the right set of people. | |

## Table 21.1  (cont.)

| | | | |
|---|---|---|---|
| | *Tacit knowledge exchanged synchronously in formal meetings and casual conversations between selected groups of people are not communicated to the rest of the team.*<br><br>*Feedback mechanisms will be missing in many stages.*<br><br>*There is no established communication between experts and team members who seek that expertise.*<br><br>*Updating customers in advance about any shortcomings, bottlenecks, and delays in the output.* | Provide a framework where team members can post questions on any topic related to the project, which anyone in the integrated project team can answer, and which can also be built into a FAQ (Frequently Asked Questions) database. Problem solving can happen collectively in this framework.<br><br>Have a feedback system on critical success areas of the project in terms of available knowledge, gaps, and access. | Make the key decisions and minutes of meetings available in a common area that is accessible to all relevant project team members.<br><br>Have newsletters specifically in large long-term multi-location projects.<br><br>Availability of information/knowledge repositories. Have an owner identified for specific areas of knowledge in order to keep it updated and current.<br><br>Manage effective meetings with a well-defined agenda, having all stakeholders involved, and tracking actions for closure during entire project execution will keep the project understanding at its desired levels. These meetings can be virtual, telecom, video, etc. |
| **Project Risk Management** | Better risk mitigation steps and ownership. | Maintain an organizational consolidated risk database that has a recording of what worked and what did not work in their project scenarios. | From organization risk database, look for inputs, what mitigation steps worked in similar situations in previous projects. |
| **Project Procurement Management** | Understanding of timelines and service quality in terms of the purchase of hardware, software, time line, etc. | *Have database of vendors, product features, and services provided from both the external market and internal experience perspective.* | *Look for previous experience in the current context in the database.*<br><br>*Sharing experience on products/services bought with the vendors, and establishing constant communication with them on quality, timelines, and service attributes.* |

offers a snapshot perspective of the role KM plays in nine knowledge areas for the successful execution of projects. The seamless integration of KM into project execution will mark the maturity of managing projects in today's context.

## FINAL NOTE

Organizations are becoming involved in more and more projects to meet their goals. KM, which is an invaluable tool in fostering the institutional memory in organizations, has recently found practical applications in projects in addition to becoming a fundamental necessity for the success of these projects.

Projects can be successfully completed without a holistic formal KM approach. But they cannot excel in its execution without adopting KM concepts in some way or the other. For achieving execution excellence, KM is a must. KM methods would enable the achievement of high productivity, improve quality, delight customers, and also boost up the project team. It is a win-win situation for all stakeholders.

# REFERENCES

Koulopoulos, Thomas M., & Frappaolo, Carl. (1999). *Smart things to know about knowledge management*. Oxford, U.K.: Capstone Publishing Limited.

Love, Peter, Fong, Patrick S. W., & Irani, Zahir. (2005). *Management of knowledge in project environments*. Oxford, U.K.: Elsevier/Butterworth-Heinemann.

Project Management Institute. (2004). *A guide to the project management body of knowledge. PMBOK guide*. 2004 edition. Atlanta: Project Management Institute.

# CHAPTER 22

# Running Successful Collaboration Software Pilots

Joe Hutchinson and Patti Anklam

Hutchinson Associates, Consulting Services

## INTRODUCTION

Knowledge management practitioners have known that knowledge management (KM) is as much (if not more) about people and work practices as it is about technology, but this much is also clear: The KM work required to establish a culture of collaboration and knowledge sharing must be accompanied by a stable, usable software infrastructure that provides enabling tools.

Collaboration software is software that is architected to provide productivity tools to a community (a project management community or a community of practice, for example) rather than to a single user. For example, when a project manager creates a spreadsheet on her PC, she needs to take extra steps to share that spreadsheet with her team members, in some cases every time she updates the spreadsheet. Collaboration software provides a "team space" that allows spreadsheets, documents, databases, calendars, presentations, and other productivity artifacts to be created and shared in this space as well as communications and awareness (or "presence") tools for working with team members.

Collaboration software has proliferated over the past two years, with technology enthusiasts talking at a high decibel level about Web 2.0 and Office 2.0, and similar topics. (Web 2.0 refers to a "next generation" of Internet-based services, such as social networking sites, blogs, wikis, communication tools, and folksonomies, that emphasize online collaboration and sharing among users.)

Also, there are commercial collaboration packages that are Web based, like WebOffice and BaseCamp. These tools are all productivity producers but don't scale to the level of enterprise-class collaboration software, such as Documentum eRoom or Microsoft SharePoint.

By "enterprise class," we mean collaboration software that is full function out of the box. For users, this software offers rich integrated functionality for databases, participant profiles, announcements, polling/voting, messaging, contacts, real-time communications, calendaring features, project management, discussion, file/document, and real-time meeting features in the context of a shared Web page, most commonly called a "virtual team space." Figure 22.1 shows a screen shot from an enterprise collaboration package that shows a virtual team space set up "out of the box" for program management.

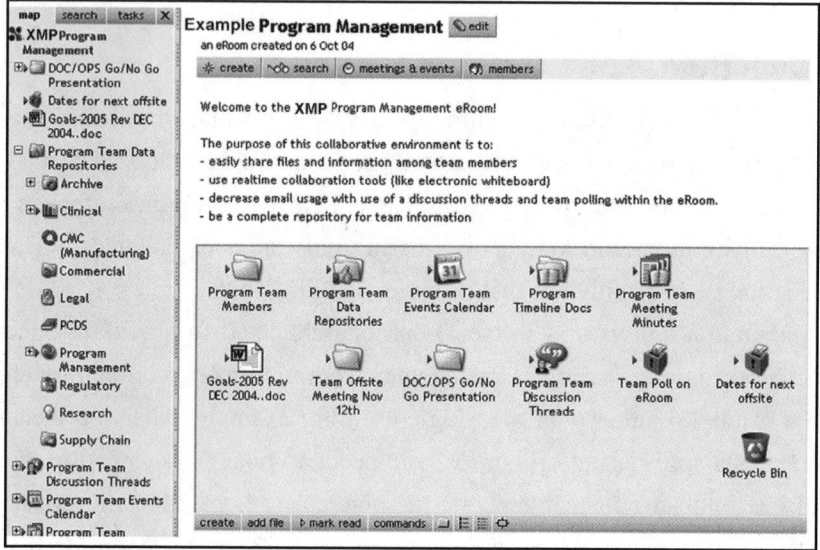

## Figure 22.1  A virtual team space

For administrators, this software comes with setup and configuration, user management, rights and permissions, and security features that let both team leaders and administrators measure and tune for effectiveness. This software is typically easily customizable by users with various levels of software sophistication.

The chapter covers the following topics:

- The business of collaboration: Why "believe" in collaboration as a part of a business strategy
- The network mind shift: Trends that allow for thinking about organizations as networks as well as hierarchies

- The nature of pilot activities: What does a pilot "look like," testing before investing
- Practical lessons for managing pilots
- Success factors

Our examples are taken from our experiences piloting collaboration software for two mid-sized corporations.

# The Business of Collaboration

Businesses see that collaboration is a significant boost to knowledge worker productivity. IBM, for example, made the broad underlying case for collaboration in a recently published study called Global CEO Survey 2006 in which they stated: "The upside of collaboration is underscored not only by qualitative CEO feedback, but also by the financial performance of companies with extensive collaboration capabilities. The Global CEO Study 2006 illuminates the degree to which strong collaborators enjoyed healthier revenue growth and average operating margin over their competition."

There are many reasons that companies are now moving to implement collaboration systems. Three examples of business forces are distribution and globalization of the workforce (mergers/acquisitions, outsourcing, off-shoring, etc.), more technology-savvy employees, and backlash against e-mail. In particular, companies have found that they need to leverage knowledge assets: promote ease of use and ease of reuse, reduce redundancy, rework, and the cost of not knowing, and generally find ways to preserve corporate memory. Likewise, many large companies find that they need tools that enable international teams to work efficiently toward common goals over distances.

The market for software that supports enterprise collaboration has grown between 15 percent and 18 percent per year over the last three years and is expected to continue—$681.7 million in 2005, a 16 percent increase over 2004, according to Gartner, Inc. By 2008, the market is expected to reach $1.1 billion. Products include:

- SharePoint
- Groove
- eRoom
- IBM Workspace
- Open Text LiveLink
- SiteScape

## The Technology Context for Collaboration: The Promise

When the first collaboration platforms arrived, the promises were twofold:

- For corporations, the promise was about managing knowledge assets—program and product deliverables—in a central location to:
  - Promote ease of use and ease of reuse
  - Reduce redundancy, rework, and the cost of not knowing
  - Preserve corporate memory
- For workers, the promise was to foster collaboration by providing a common environment for teams and ad hoc collaborators that would:
  - Ensure consistency of work practices and deliverables
  - Enable more cross-group idea generation and problem solving
  - Enhance social capital

When these technologies were introduced to the market, the vision was that they would enable geographically distributed teams to work together more efficiently, get products out faster, improve quality, and allow managers to get control of corporate content in increasingly dispersed organizations. The vision limped along over several years as early versions of the software presented performance and usability obstacles, but over the past two to three years the promise has come to fruition. Today, enterprise collaboration software enables personal productivity and knowledge management, small group productivity, large group productivity, and allows companies to manage and maintain control of corporate content in increasingly dispersed and more complicated organizations.

## Enterprise Collaboration Software Today

The "return on investment" or "time-to-value" question seems to be answered: According to Collaborative Technologies, more than 50 percent of the companies who adopt these technologies see the return on investment in less than seven months (Figure 22.2).

The areas that have seen improvement specifically and the collaboration software features that support these areas are shown in Table 22.1.

The user interfaces and the specifics of the features vary somewhat from platform to platform, but the significant factors in choice for an organization (particularly a large one) are:

- Existing IT infrastructure—Java or .NET, for example
- Requirements for integrating existing business applications—SAP, Oracle, Documentum, etc.
- Cost of ownership—including ease of use and cost to support

These are big issues, but information technology (IT) managers have usually considered them at some level before a decision is made to do a pilot. Whereas the infrastructure and business application compatibility issues are relatively easy to get a handle on (.NET, SAP, or others are usually already part of the corporate infrastructure), cost of ownership is not so easy to measure and is very frequently the reason to do a pilot. Ease of use and cost of support are functions of both "the human variable" and what you might think of as "the suitability variable."

## The Net Work Mind Shift: Getting From "Me" to "We"

The human variable refers to the fact that "one size" does not necessarily "fit all." Some tasks require lots of training, some not that much; some people learn more quickly, some more slowly; some people are technophobic, others enjoy using software tools; most people have tools that they don't want to give up (for example, e-mail), and the list goes on. People are used to their personal tools from office suite preferences through drawing programs and custom databases. The PC defines personal computing space; shifting users beyond that space requires real work and real motivation on the part of the worker to work within the context of a community.

The suitability variable comes into play in more project-specific terms, and answers questions like whether workers are geographically dispersed or all in the same geographic area and/or whether a given project lends itself to support by collaboration software. For example, project management and some research projects might lend themselves naturally to the use of collaboration tools whereas production line usages may not provide appropriate applications. For example, project managers have "net work" defined into their job descriptions; they are usually responsible for connecting and coordinating several functions, ensuring that those functions are in alignment and working closely, and on reporting on the state of their project.

Technology enables people who are already collaborating to do so more smoothly, but it can also connect people in a context (the virtual team space) that promotes collaboration. Powerful software functionality always faces the

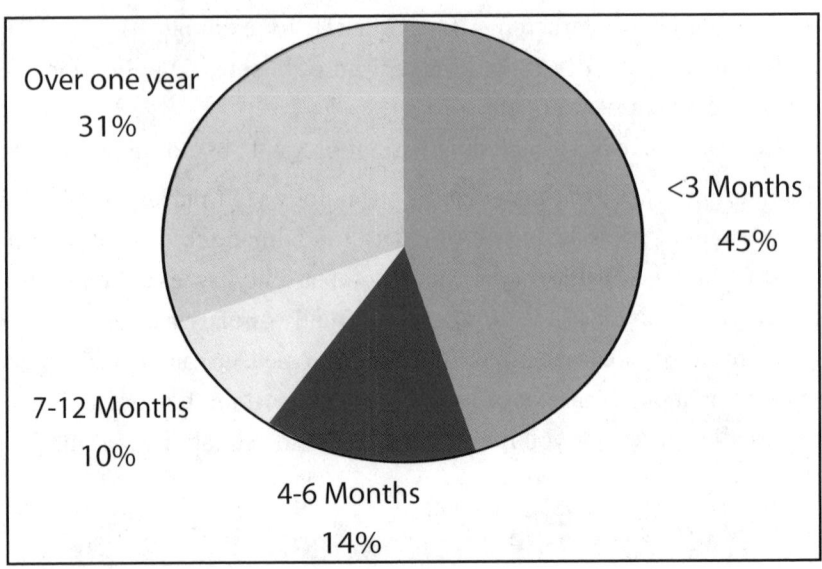

**Figure 22.2  Time to value for collaboration technologies**

**Table 22.1  Collaboration software features that promote productivity**

| Productivity Area | Software Features |
|---|---|
| Personal productivity and knowledge management | • Presence and messaging<br>• Subscription services<br>• File sharing<br>• Blogs |
| Small group productivity | • Calendars<br>• Task lists<br>• Wikis, discussions<br>• Polls<br>• Links<br>• Information management |
| Large group productivity | • Project management<br>• Workflow<br>• Document management<br>• Databases<br>• Integration with enterprise business applications<br>• People working on multiple projects<br>• Content in file shares, document management systems, individual e-mail folders uncategorized and not indexed by corporate search engines |

fundamental challenge of user adoption—you can bring the features to the people, but you can't make the people use them (at least not right away). How do you get from installation and rollout to adoption, leverage, and productivity? We believe that setting the appropriate social context, preparing teams to adopt the collaboration tools effectively and productively, is the key to the success of tools usage. This preparation is part of what we call "Net Work."

"Net Work" is about understanding and leveraging both the differences and the similarities in networks. One of the interesting questions about the acceptance and use of collaboration technologies is the relationship to the technology use and the connectivity of people. Do people who are already connected use the technologies to enhance the work and exchanges that they are already engaged in? Or will the technology enable more connections? Do three sets of people, when linked, become a collaborative workgroup? How important is it that this workgroup be open or closed?

Different networks take on different structures depending on their purpose and the type of value that they create. A very tight network, like that in the lower right of Figure 22.3, is a very focused team/project network. But it didn't get there by magic. Networks evolve like the ones shown in Figure 22.3.

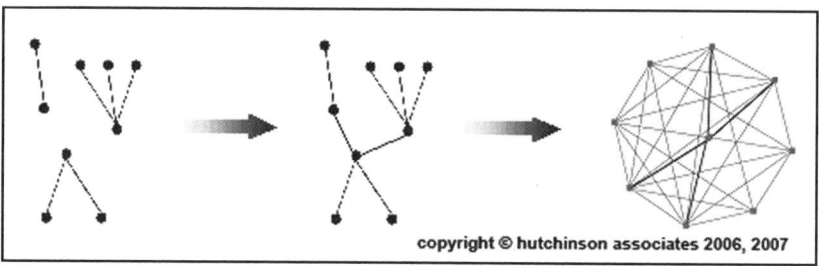

copyright © hutchinson associates 2006, 2007

## Figure 22.3  Network growth

On the left, imagine three "groups" with a common idea for innovation, then imagine that an intuitive engineer or marketer connects those three groups to focus their ideas and energies on a market, and then imagine that the corporation "discovers" them and puts them into a product cycle, which requires a densely knit team, the structure shown on the right.

## Visions, Teams, and Actual Work

Working with enterprise collaboration software requires that you satisfy top-down management expectations while enabling emergent teams and real work. In general, there are three categories of stakeholders you need to engage in order for a technology implementation to be successful:

- **Management stakeholders:** Define roles and responsibilities by establishing user communities and community leadership.
- **IT stakeholders:** Set policies and procedures and governance models.
- **User communities:** Clearly establish the purpose of the work per workspace, ensure that users have the appropriate tool set for the work, and integrate the workspace into existing work processes and productivity tools.

Commitment from management stakeholders at all levels is imperative. If the collaboration project is not supported by management, both management and workers responsible for participating in a collaborative environment may lack the motivation to make the project work.

Likewise, IT stakeholders need to fully commit to participation in the project. They hold the key to making the collaboration software easy to use within the context of the larger corporate technology environment.

Lastly, community leaders need to be engaged. Users' work context and processes need to be understood and the capability of individuals primarily involved in the pilot need to be assessed.

The substance of work happens within the dynamics of people and culture, the practices and processes people work with, and the overall systems (including technology systems) that support people in their work. The balance of this chapter emphasizes the non-technical factors that play the major role in influencing success in collaboration technology pilots.

Context is everything. In particular, when you implement collaboration software, you change the relationships among users. And, because you are changing the way that individuals do their work, you are changing the social relationship of individuals to the tools they use. "It takes time to collaborate," and when it comes to introducing software that changes the way people work, it takes time:

- To learn new tools (and unlearn old habits)
- To alter working relationships
- To adjust to working more openly and transparently

The result of a well-designed pilot is to accelerate the adoption of technology by decreasing these times—and effectively providing the organization with an enhanced ability to collaborate.

# The Nature of Pilots

Essentially, a pilot is a trial of software a corporation may want to invest in. The idea is to validate that a technology platform meets the needs of the stakeholder and user communities, identify potential hazards, set and test boundaries, and use the pilot experience to attract other users. But there is also the important element of discovery in the pilot: You are trying to find out how things "really work," and there will be insights and surprises along the way. Let insights from stakeholders help drive the planning and implementation process that follows the pilot.

It is useful to have a model to use to mine these insights as you go. We have used the model illustrated in Figure 22.4 to "wiggle through knotholes" in projects that didn't have obvious solutions.

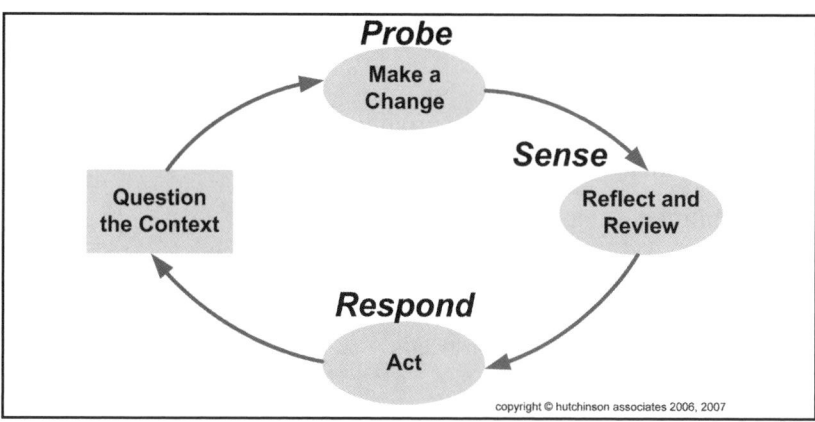

**Figure 22.4  Managing emergent learning from a pilot (Copyright© Hutchinson Associates 2006, 2007)**

When you manage a pilot, you must constantly be observing the environment; when a problem arises, you make a change you believe makes sense (probe), watch carefully the effects of the action (sense), and then respond based on whether the change fixed the problem. As you can see, this is a cycle you need to stay in because the collaboration environment is never standing still; it changes as the community or the corporation changes.

"Pilot," as we are using the word, refers to the exploration of a new method or tool. In nautical terms, a pilot boat is a smaller and more agile boat that assists large boats entering the harbor. It not only leads the way, but also tests the path to let captains know about changes in currents caused by weather, shifts in sandbars or other structures, or alterations to a channel. In general, the pilot boat marks a safe path for larger, more costly, more valuable vessels.

And just as buoys help the pilot (and other vessels) by marking the path, a well-planned pilot process lays out a path for successfully implementing collaboration systems. That's why, particularly in collaboration systems, pilots are useful—they help managers understand the underlying context in which the larger investment will be implemented.

Enterprise collaboration software often is very expensive and management has very real concerns about investment. Will the software really help the corporation and workers be more productive? What effects will the software have on policies and procedures, security, governance? How will this software enhance the infrastructure already in place: content management systems, intranets, portals? How much will it cost to support? And will the summary of answers to these questions be a net plus for the corporation?

A well-executed pilot program can provide answers to most of these questions. It can provide estimated requirements for:

- Capability development needs
  - Basic computer skills
  - Organizing information
- Work practice development needs
  - Process maturity
  - Team norms, practices, and commitments

Likewise, it can help uncover "underwater dangers" embedded in IT Infrastructure, incompatibilities in application development platform, intranet content management and Web platforms, and inconsistency in user interfaces.

Lastly, remember that as a pilot administrator, you need to develop a good deal of expertise in the product you are piloting, and there is the danger of coming to see the product as "the answer" rather than being a dispassionate observer, analyst, and documenter of the pilot process.

## MANAGING THE PILOT

There are a number of aspects of a pilot you need to think about in order to manage successfully. We've outlined some of the most important here.

## Focus: Narrow the Scope of the Pilot

To run a successful pilot, you and the client need to agree on what is being measured and on the questions the pilot needs to answer. So in the design phase, it is key is to assess the project both from the point of view of the business stakeholders and the user communities. Parallel investigation tracks ensure that the direction of the pilot emerges from both sets of viewpoints. Table 22.2 summarizes the tasks related to working with each group of stakeholders.

## Table 22.2  Tasks for working with pilot stakeholders

| Stakeholder | Tasks |
|---|---|
| Business | • Identify tasks within larger context of enterprise mission and IT architecture<br>• Interview IT stakeholders<br>• Interview business unit stakeholders<br>• Create framework documents for policies and procedures<br>• Review governance models, roles, and responsibilities |
| User communities | • Identify candidate projects and work practices for piloting<br>• Set up virtual team spaces for the pilot<br>• Provide individual training and coaching for pilot project leads to establish their spaces<br>• Orientation for whole team<br>• Ongoing support and measurement<br>• Rollout documentation and training |

Essentially, we are working "bottom-up and top-down" at the same time with the teams for whom the software is intended as well as the stakeholders whose concerns are with security, privacy, and costs.

## Map the Pilot Process

Mapping the pilot process in preparation for the pilot is always useful. Figure 22.5 shows one way to map the process and includes four basic activities: identifying potential pilot groups, qualifying those groups, coaching them through the startup phase of the pilot, and then managing the pilot learning cycle. Notice that each of these activities comprises several steps.

Feedback is key to this system. You always need to be listening to users and adapting the implementation based on their feedback. At the end of the pilot process, that feedback will have adapted and tuned the enterprise software to fit the needs of the larger corporate community. Notice that sometimes feedback leads to changes in the software implementation, but can also lead to process changes, insights and improvements, and new ways of thinking about how the software will be used.

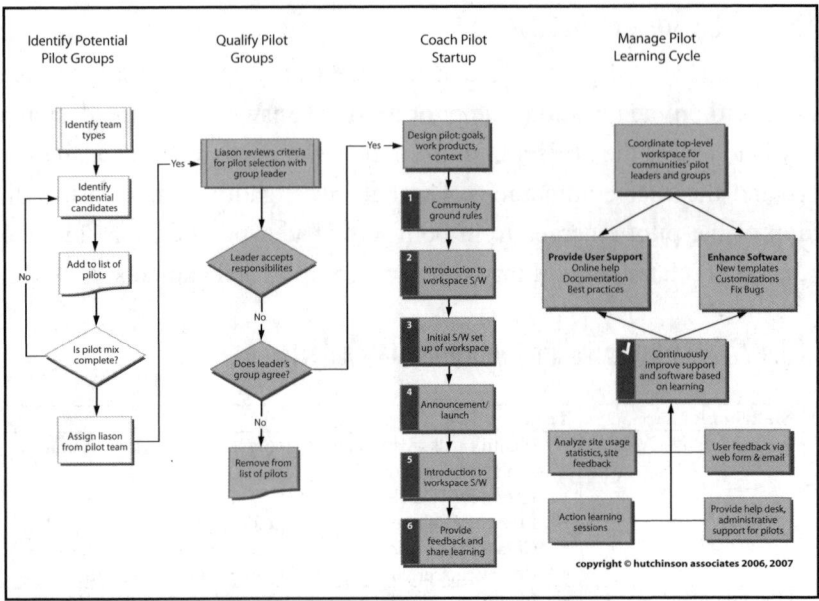

**Figure 22.5  Mapping the pilot process**

One of the big wins for one of our pilots was the establishment of "Learning Clinics." From the inception of the pilot process onward, these lunchtime brown-bag sessions were set up for users who had developed virtual team sites to share what they had done with others. At the same time, they could ask specific questions and get suggestions on recent problems. These sessions were valuable to the entire community, including those managing the pilot who were setting up the training courses and the policies and procedures.

## Create Communities in Context

Create communities in context and select pilot groups carefully. Figure 22.6 shows a typical IT-based portal infrastructure for a corporation.

Note that there are already places for communities of practice, project status, event announcements, and search-specific tools. When you are forming pilot communities/groups, make sure that the collaboration software complements existing infrastructure and that the collaboration space adds value beyond the existing portal tools.

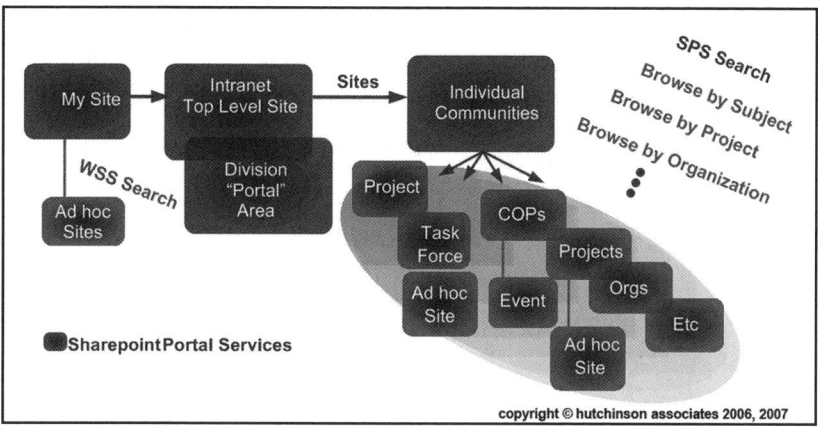

Figure 22.6   Information hierarchy of collaboration sites within an intranet

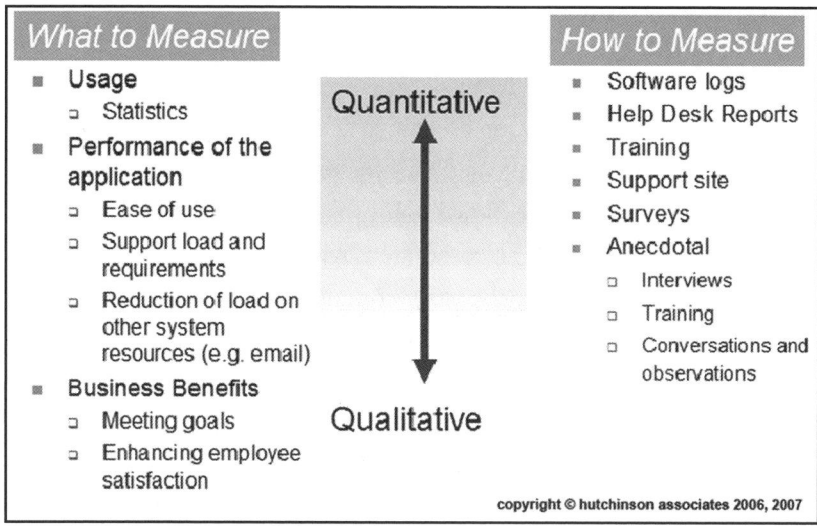

Figure 22.7   Setting metrics for pilots

## Establish Clear Metrics and Measures

Usually, pilots have hard deadlines and want to be "in a hurry." As we've already said, the collaboration software is a big investment, and it's important to put measurements in place that will tell your sponsor to what degree the software "works." Measurements vary depending on context and the sliding chart in Figure 22.7, which shows a range of measureables from qualitative to quantitative.

All enterprise collaboration software provides administrative statistics capabilities, though you may find that the environment requires more than the "out of the box" features. You might find that you need to customize to get at certain statistics based on how you set up the system. For example, if you want variations on how many new research communities might have been created, or how many visits there were to some subset of the executive communities, you might require custom software development. One of the findings from the pilot will be indicators of how much of this custom support you require.

Brainstorming sessions with technical administrators often surfaces very useful data. For example, collaboration software statistics will show that the use of the technology is increasing but may not show whether use of e-mail is declining at the same time, so you need to look for this kind of quantitative data outside of the collaboration software itself.

## Select an Appropriate Set of Pilot Groups

Seek diversity in determining representative teams. Limiting teams to technology-literate participants skews results and will make the results of the pilot less than accurate. Try to include a range of technology skills, a range of domain expertise, and corporate veterans as well as corporate novices.

We try to be sure that when the software goes into pilot, we have teams that represent an array of the community types that exist in the company. Each community type will need different features and a different approach to getting started, and will often require different levels of documentation, training, and support. The goal is to capture as much context as possible on how users work before you begin the pilot. Where you can, match real needs with software capabilities. For example, project managers use repositories for team data document review, publish announcements, and use calendars to manage meetings; researchers often use databases and spreadsheets. Use the native technical capabilities provided in the collaboration software to fit as closely as possible the needs of the users in a given community.

Qualify prospective pilots through dialog with team leaders. One of the principles for establishing an effective collaboration community is to designate a leader. Make sure at the beginning of the project that the leader understands the goals of the project, the general functionality of the software, and agrees with his/her specific responsibilities to the team and to the project.

## Table 22.3  Representative taxonomy of pilot community types

| Team Type | Business Area | Intended Usage |
|---|---|---|
| Program management | Marketing | Repository for team data, document review, publish announcements, calendar, manage meetings |
| Community of practice | Research | Data folders, reference links and folders, presentation folders, contact lists, databases, discussion threads |
| Task force | Strategy | Publish goals and progress, engage in discussions, Q&A, lists links to relevant research |
| Project team | Development | Team meeting agendas and schedules, file sharing, contact lists, databases, discussion threads |
| Executives | Communications | Meeting archives, file sharing, contact lists, customer reports, business performance dashboards |

Keep the introduction of tools in the context of the users. Table 22.3 shows an example based on one of the clients we worked with. We developed this taxonomy as part of the pilot team design process.

To get to comprehensive findings, you may also want to consider attributes of communities you select:

- **Knowledge-based or transaction-based:** Research communities will be knowledge-based and need tools that accommodate high levels of expertise and training. Project managers need transaction-based tools oriented around tasks and deliverables.
- **Open or closed:** A task force might be a closed community with very explicit boundaries designed to protect information until it is ready to be published. A community of practice might be open to all who want to have discussions about a given subject. Privileges you set up for such communities will make them easier to use and more attractive to users.

## Create Baseline Team Spaces

Most enterprise software packages come with template workspaces for "the typical cases." For example, in eRoom there are templates for product design, project management, governance, compliance, audit functions, and so forth. As the pilot administrator, you can use these templates as a base for customizing team spaces based on the specific requirements of the groups you have interviewed and

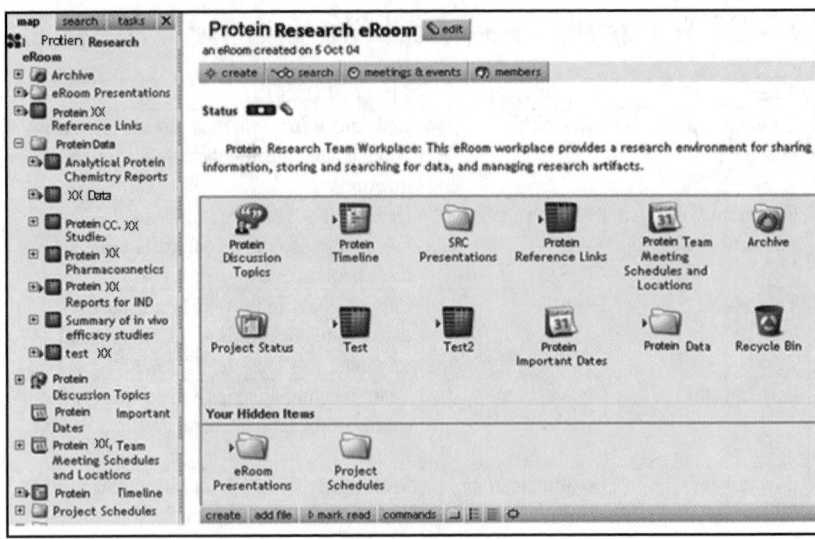

## Figure 22.8 Sample eRoom set up for a research team

who are going to be using the space. Figure 22.8 shows an example of an eRoom set up for a Research team.

This space includes shared folders for specialized protein test databases, discussions, calendar, polls, and other tools useful to a science research team. Note that you should include as many, but no more, features than will be used. Simplicity makes the space easier to use and less confusing to inexperienced or new users.

Collaboration software has come a long way toward ease of use, but that's still a relative term. What's easy to use for an employee of Microsoft is not easy to use by a program manager for a communications program in a pharmaceutical company or financial services company.

You may have heard the term "personal information and knowledge management" (PIKM). Tom Davenport, who has researched the topic, says, "Individuals need to recognize how much of their time and productivity is tied up in PIKM. Companies need to realize that their workers are wasting lots of time on this, and that better personal information and knowledge management means greater organizational success. Vendors need to do a better job on reliability, integration, and effective use. We all need more insights, role models, and instructors."

The key point that Davenport makes is that managers need to understand that it takes time to learn a new tool but that the investment in training and coaching pays off. The more you customize the training to the users' context, the more they will be able to see how it applies to them.

## Establish Roles and Responsibilities

Collaboration software implementation requires a spectrum of skills and roles across organizations. It also requires that users learn new skills, take on new tasks, or fill an entirely new job role in the organization. So it's easy to get confused about "who's on first" with respect to development responsibilities, governance, and ownership. Figure 22.9 shows one way to distinguish "who does what." It is a continuum and a good starting point for facilitating the conversation about what the work is and who is responsible for what tasks. It also is very good for making sure that you have identified all the resources you need.

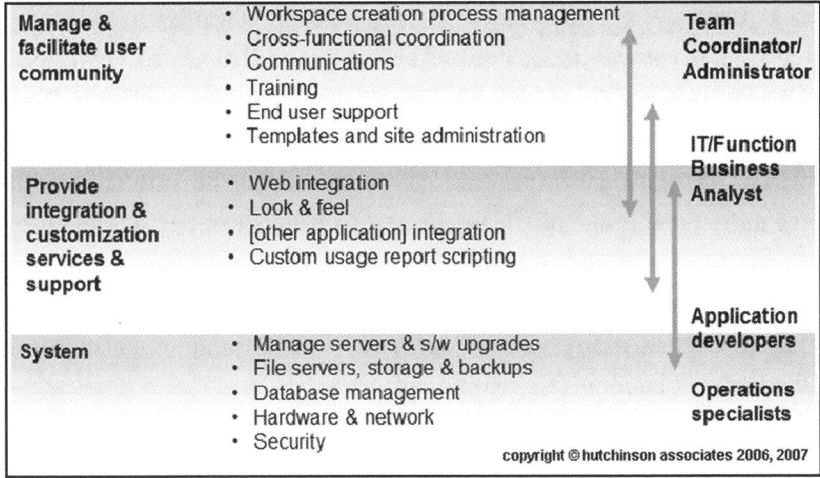

## Figure 22.9  Distinguishing roles and responsibilities

Usually the first roles involved in the implementation process come from IT organizations. For enterprise class systems, there are often several servers required to support the application, as well as architecture issues that need to be addressed before the pilot can be launched. Likewise, the IT organization is responsible for portals and other Web functionality across the corporation and they will want to ensure that the new team space application aligns with these existing infrastructure elements.

Once the architecture and infrastructure responsibilities are established, the pilot team leader must work with team leaders of the communities to ensure that they are well trained and understand their roles and the roles of their team members. For a large pilot, you may want to ensure that there are sufficient team coordinators/administrators to act as "coaches" or "liaisons" for the individual pilot communities.

Thereafter, team leaders are the first line of support. The pilot coordinator/administrator is the next line of support. It's important that the pilot team lead has as streamlined a working relationship as possible with the vendor supplying the team space software; the vendor is the last resort for support and training.

## Establish a Governance Model

Governance refers to the top-down issues in a company. Governance issues inevitably arise in collaboration environments so there needs to be a clear path to the people who can answer questions and make decisions about team spaces. Managers need to feel that they are being good stewards of the company's resources and employee time, but are also paying attention to legal needs and requirements of customer/client confidentiality, government regulations for retention of information and paperwork, and so on.

Typically, professionals from various domains want to influence policy for implementation and usage of shared spaces. Conflicts can begin at the user level when domains for various teams overlap or an influential contributor wants to use the tool in ways that overextend other corporate resources (like IT storage or firewall limits). Basically, any sort of conflict that exists in an organization will be reflected in the collaborative environment.

Establish the roles and rules for who can create virtual team spaces and delete spaces, and who has what levels of application privilege. Some corporations will want to tightly control creation of new spaces and archive and delete little-used spaces. Other corporations will delegate the control of these functions to the judgment of users. IT generally has a significant role to play, especially at the implementation time. IT is also affected by support costs for help desks and user groups, hardware infrastructure, and usually some portion of training.

Security is a major concern in most corporations, and the workspace managers need to work with IT and other management to make certain that team spaces have appropriate levels of security. Most enterprise class software has sophisticated functionality for defining private spaces versus public spaces and for setting up secure user privilege levels. Likewise, in implementations that go beyond corporate firewalls, there will be significant IT concerns to be negotiated.

## Be Prepared for the Results

Results using the same methods can vary widely depending on the scope of the pilot and the characteristics of the corporate communities participating in the pilot. The two pilots used as the basis for this chapter yielded very different results, each successful in its own dimension. The first pilot was conducted in an organization that was very computer literate, technically oriented, organizationally mature, and relatively homogeneous in terms of user profiles (mostly engineering background). It was, however, a very large project for a pilot and not without challenges. The results from the second pilot were less formal and centered around gathering information for making a purchase decision. For very low cost and a short timeframe, the sponsor was able to gather enough information to make important decisions that would affect the whole corporation.

### Pilot 1 Results

The goal of the first pilot (Fall 2003–Spring 2004) was to create about 30 communities by April 2004. Both the management and the user communities were already sold on the idea and the technology behind enterprise collaboration tools, so this pilot had some of the feel of a "beta test" for an implementation. As is almost always the case, when people hear about a new tool that helps in their work, they get curious and want to try it, so word about the collaboration tools spread virally and by July 2004, the number of communities topped 100. By April 2006, there were 897 communities, with 30 formed that April alone.

The groundwork on which this pilot was undertaken could not have been more ideal. Users in this pilot were almost all engineers and were, as mentioned earlier, technically oriented; they were often supported by equally PC-savvy group administrators. Management at this company "wanted this program to work." IT had done the homework and provided the required hardware and software infrastructure. The pilot project leader laid out the program and everyone was pleased with the results, as described previously.

### Pilot 2 Results

The second pilot was less of a beta test and more about gathering the data required to make a "go/no-go" decision about purchasing the collaboration product. It was based on a smaller sample group, which was comprised of people with varying levels of computer comfort, much more diverse user profiles (from scientists through non-technical administrators), and in a relatively younger and less technically oriented organization.

The sponsor especially wanted to understand the costs of support and the adoption rates of the software being urged on him by internal product champions from his scientist community and vendor sales. This pilot confirmed the intuitions of the sponsor that this product would not likely be easily and quickly adopted and that the costs and risks, at that point, were greater than he was comfortable with.

The goal of this pilot was to create six communities across three domains; three working communities actually emerged, despite intensive introduction, training, and one-on-one coaching and support. We found difficulties can occur in the following areas:

- **Capability needs:** We learned that it's important not to make assumptions about users' basic computer skills and information organization abilities. Working in virtual team spaces also requires a heightened attention to the needs of conversational dialog.
- **Work practice development:** Teams need to have a basic process maturity so they can understand the appropriateness of specific tools and features and be able to develop the necessary team norms, practices, and commitment processes.
- **IT infrastructure:** Collaboration software tools are most effective when they become integrated with other applications in the environment, hence there can be significant problems when the software is incompatible with the application integration platform. Attention must be paid to how the collaboration software fits into the existing intranet content management and Web platform—especially if there is inconsistency in the user interfaces.

None of these difficulties outweighs the potential hazard of misalignment between the stated needs of a user community and the constraints placed on implementation by the IT infrastructure.

## So What Did We Learn?

Over the course of these pilots, we made observations that could very likely apply in almost any pilot you conduct.

### Support Requirements Grow with User Sophistication and Tool Integration

Support ranges from Help Desk through one-to-one coaching and always needs to be available during the pilot. People need support for infrastructure issues like getting passwords and getting online through connecting collaboration software

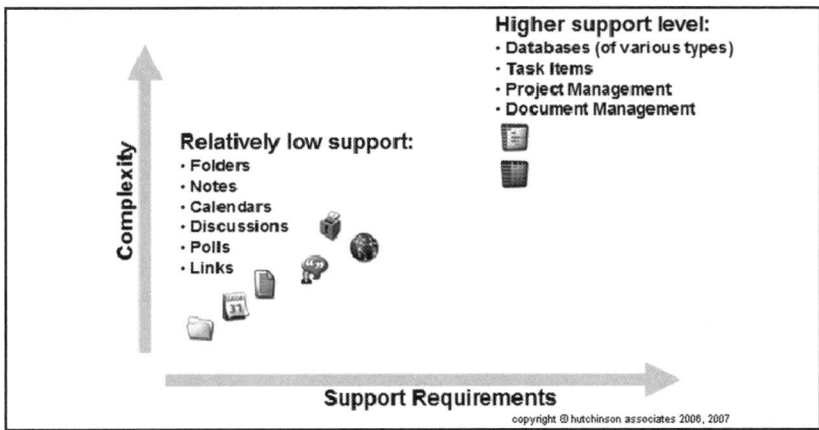

**Figure 22.10   Gauging support requirements based on use of software features**

to e-mail and other personal knowledge management tools. They need support for application functions like "Undoing," and in general learning new features to set up project work.

Figure 22.10 maps the features available in collaborative software with its support requirements.

Significantly, especially for IT decision makers, as the complexity of total usage increases support requirements increase also. At the beginning of the pilot when people are using simple tools like folders, notes, calendars, discussions, and so forth, all they need to learn are basics. However, when users wanted to learn how to use databases of various types, work with task items for project management, and use document management functions like check-in/check-out, support requirements increased. In fact, we found in both pilots that there would need to be a local expert who understood the collaboration software at a level that would allow for development of custom tools.

### Fast Feedback Is the Best Answer to the Productivity Question

In large well-planned knowledge management environments, many of the variables are known and can be readily measured. In the first pilot, the IT group agreed early on to collect and analyze statistics about the usage of the software. They collected information on the number of sites created, the type of site, the number of users, and so on.

More complex variables require that you "walk around" to directly gather user insights. For example, there can be anecdotal evidence like the following:

- Reduction in number of face-to-face meetings
- Reduction in travel time and other costs
- Ability to keep a global project going around the clock
- Decreased confusion about the "most current version" of a document
- Decrease in e-mail volume
- Increased confidence about being current with changes and updates
- Shift to openness in brainstorming and critiquing

In the second pilot, the IT manager sponsor for this project needed decision-making information on whether to buy the product, and there was neither the time nor the resources to set up formal measurement processes. Basically, we met with the manager face-to-face and worked weekly with him during the project. He wanted quick feedback: "What have we learned, what were the issues we were dealing with today." He wanted to get a feel for how the project was working and how/whether the product was being adopted and useful.

### Keep an Eye on the Big Picture and Changes in Context

Figure 22.11 gives another perspective on the relationship between complexity and support. It shows how collaboration software supports productivity not only at personal levels, but can also help an entire enterprise be more productive. In general, when the software is introduced, it is used in what we think of as the "personal productivity" level. Users readily identify with the idea of file shares, task lists, and e-mail as they appear in a collaboration space. During this stage, effective team leaders will use the collaboration space to drive team meetings and activities.

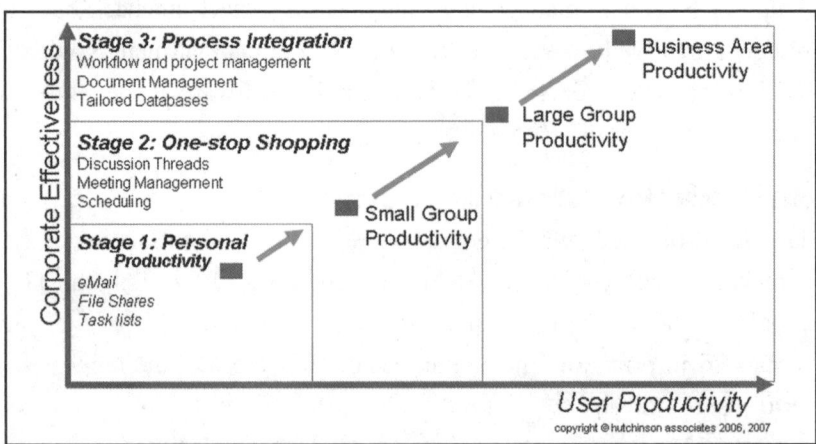

Figure 22.11  Long-term benefit of well-managed collaboration software systems

As users work with the tools and everyone on the team understands that the workspace is "the go-to place" for all team news, status, documents, work tasks, and so on, the group productivity goes up. There are fewer e-mails being missed, the project history is in one place, new people can get acclimated and up to speed sooner by reading through discussions, and so on. For any given project, team members recognize the team space as "one-stop shopping" for that project. These first two stages are really about applying technology to existing work practices.

At the enterprise productivity level, integration of the collaboration technology with corporate information systems and workflow actually changes work practices to improve corporate capability development and knowledge transfer at corporate levels. This macro shift may look different across different types of companies and may focus on different key applications:

- Pharmaceutical firms focus on document management.
- Consulting firms focus on the client engagement process.
- Production/manufacturing companies focus on project management.

For example, in a pharmaceutical environment where there are federal regulations for archiving information on drugs, the corporation can plan the path of a project database over time from its beginnings in the team room through to hardware tape archives. This means that that information becomes accessible across multiple functions in the corporation from its origin as a research document through usages in operational reports, in marketing, and in technical and customer support.

## CRITICAL SUCCESS FACTORS: LOOK AT THE SYSTEM

The identification of different community types is the basis for the design and getting the tools into the users' hands. From the overall systems perspective, you need to be aware of or put activities in place to make sure that, overall, the technology will fit systemically into the company's mission and purpose. Table 22.4 summarizes the critical success factors for successful deployment of the technology. Note that as a project, this is much less about the technology than it is about paying attention to what users need, what the business goal is, and then adapting the technology.

## SUMMARY: SUCCESSFUL PILOT MANEUVERS

We believe that although collaborative technology has evolved into highly productive team environments, the real barriers to collaboration are cultural. With that

## Table 22.4  Critical success factors

| Critical Success Factor | Key Activities |
| --- | --- |
| Technology and/or user acceptance criteria | • Pilot process design and implementation<br>• System architecture integration<br>• Work practices framework identifying policies, procedures, and guidelines required for consistent use of communications and collaboration tools across the enterprise |
| Business alignment | • Stakeholder interviews leading to chartered executive steering group<br>• Strategic plan for evolution of technology use that maps to corporate mission and challenges |
| User acceptance | • Contextual design of workspaces tailored to individual team type and work content<br>• Assessment of cultural and social factors that leverage adoption<br>• Support model for learning and problem-solving<br>• Group training |
| Organizational change management | • Identification of roles and responsibilities based on job and task definitions created by new technology<br>• Governance models for federated ownership of collaboration system<br>• Organizational network analysis |
| Work practices integration | • Coaching of pilot team leaders for collaborative development of new work practices<br>• Best practices approach to team learning and process improvement<br>• User-centered design and work practice modeling |

in mind, we approach working with collaboration pilots using an organizational model that applies to all knowledge management work. This model is based on elements of people, process, and technology, works both "bottom-up" and "top-down" to support the organization's mission. We focus on organizational infrastructure with clearly established roles and responsibilities for community and technology stewardship.

The pilot process relies on a structured but flexible rollout to carefully selected teams, matching real needs with software capabilities and pursuing an iterative development process based on continuous learning via user feedback and requests. Given a set of well-stated goals and metrics to meet the requirements of good business management and careful attention to connectivity, productivity, and satisfaction of employees through training and coaching in the context of their work, it's possible to accelerate the adoption cycle of this emerging class of technology and to enhance an organization's time to collaborate.

# Part VII

---

# Knowledge Preservation

# Knowledge Preservation
## Foreword

This section features two chapters that focus on the design and development of knowledge management (KM) systems designed very much with knowledge preservation in mind. In Chapter 23 by Rossion, the context is very high-tech, nuclear energy, specifically ONDRAF-NIRAS, the Belgian agency charged with the oversight of and research concerning radioactive waste and enriched fissile material. The subject of Srikantaiah and Rueger's chapter (Chapter 24) is at the other end of the spectrum—the World Bank's system for the capture, use, and preservation of indigenous knowledge for development. Both, of course, are designed with much more than preservation in mind—the ONDRAF-NIRAS system is also designed with content management and work group integration in mind, and the World Bank system very much with immediate application to development projects and programs in mind. Two points about the ONDRAF-NIRAS description will probably strike the reader. First, that it is designed to facilitate research projects that may well last more than 80 years, and second, the very useful metaphor of the Knowledge Management House both for the system design, and for the easy portrayal of the system to users.

Also check the Knowledge Preservation theme in the Roadmap.

# CHAPTER 23

# Transfer of Long-Term Knowledge and Expertise: A Case Study in the Nuclear Sector

Françoise Rossion
Ernst & Young Consultancy

## INTRODUCTION

This paper describes how a knowledge management (KM) system has been designed in order to safeguard contextual knowledge in the nuclear sector. It explores especially the Knowledge Management House, a metaphor that served as an entry card into the organization's discussions and planning process.

## START WITH THE KNOWLEDGE MANAGEMENT HOUSE

Applying the idea of narrative in KM is not new. A story helps people to understand "how it works," and it stimulates the imagination of the audience. In our case study, we have used an architectural metaphor to delineate the KM environment. The Knowledge Management House is a metaphor that tells a story about the configuration of the most important KM functions. Each room of the KM House expresses how people can have access to knowledge and what kind of knowledge is available in it (Figure 23.1).

### The Registration Room

The registration room is the place where you must enter when you visit the KM House. It is similar to the hall of a building: You can access it only if you have the pass to get in, otherwise the door is closed. The registration area reflects KM security and addresses issues like: Who is accountable for identifying and defining KM policy and rules? How do you ensure confidentiality, respect for copyright, and intellectual property rights?

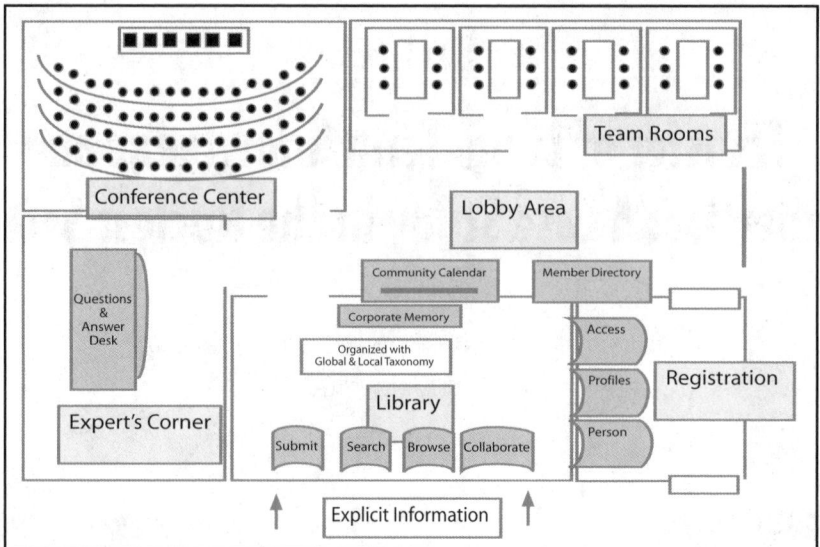

## Figure 23.1  The Knowledge Management House

## The Lobby Area

The lobby is a public and common space where people metaphorically stand to drink a cup of coffee, read some news, skim through corporate information, have a look at the company's current facts and figures, and retrieve the calendar of main events. In a KM context, the lobby illustrates the home page of the firm's intranet where corporate information is made available to the employees. It refers alike to the water coolers and coffee machines where people can informally connect and have a conversation.

## The Library

The library is the place to store tangible and explicit material such as books, periodicals, and journals. In the KM House, the library is a virtual space reflecting the corporate memory of the organization. It opens the door to structured and unstructured information such as manuals, description of procedures, company rules, internal project documents, administrative documentation, papers, articles, and so forth. Eventually, taxonomies support the research process, while quality guidelines and retention rules help point to the best and most reliable knowledge.

## The Expert's Corner

The expert's corner is an office where you can come in and ask questions of the recognized experts or scientists. It's a place with a great deal of focussed knowledge. So the KM expert's corner is a great place for accessing specialist and accurate knowledge. The expert's network is built on an internal process enabling one to identify and highlight employees' skills and know-how, and to facilitate the question and answer process.

## The Conference Centre

The conference centre is an open space where a speaker explains his experience to a large audience. In the KM space, the conference centre can be virtualized thanks to the e-learning applications and the Web conference tools: A teacher or a guru transfers knowledge to many listeners who can attend the event in real-time or in asynchronous mode.

## The Team Rooms

The team rooms are small spaces where employees meet to work together and address a project's difficulties, issues, and problems. The team rooms act as the community spaces in a virtual KM context: They focus on interactivity and connectivity and encourage collaborative teamwork; as such they are a great lever for innovation as they foster the exchange of ideas by bringing together people with similar objectives but potentially different perspectives.

Visitors to the KM House can visit the various rooms depending on their knowledge quest and needs. Some of the rooms have been thought of as mandatory, such as the registration room where you need to go for registering yourself as a member of the KM community, others are often considered optional, such as the expert's corner, even though this room is essential to access and expand the firm's expertise. All rooms are designed with open doors, enabling knowledge to flow from one space to another. By circulating knowledge, that knowledge can be transformed and, for example, be externalised in the library or socialized in the team rooms. In the KM House floor plan (Figure 23.1), the lower rooms store explicit forms of knowledge as they refer to current experts and to tangible information, while the upper rooms enable the transfer of tacit knowledge—knowledge that resides in people's minds. Those rooms are critical to capture ideas and experiences that cannot easily be articulated in other ways.

# FINDING THE PASTRY COOK'S EXPERTISE!

Have you ever made a pastry? Last week, I celebrated the birthday of my son and there were as many as 20 little but hungry boys invited to the party. I decided to prepare chocolate cake for the young public, but I must admit that I am a newbie to pastry making and I had no clue about cooking a chocolate cake. I first skimmed through my cooking books and found an attractive recipe, but the description of the cake's making was a little confusing to me. Exactly how much chocolate is required and which quality? Where to find the other ingredients such as the baking powder? What temperature is needed for cooking the cakes? I called a friend recognized for his cooking talents; he explained to me some tips and tricks and suggested looking at a pastry cooking video that he had at home. I took advantage of my visit to borrow a book, *Pastry Making for Dummies*. I felt more comfortable, but I still decided to test my skills by making a first cake, before the arrival of the invitees. The result was not so bad, but the cake was not thoroughly cooked. In an online chat, I learned that the doneness of the cake might be checked by inserting a small knife in the cake. When I repeated the experience, the new cake was a success!

In daily life, you can go on and on to find the information and expertise you need; generally, knowledge that is not too complex flows very readily from one location to another, and this flow tends to be more efficient if you pay for knowledge! This invites us to reflect on another reality of our environment: the atmosphere. When you visit a building, you may feel comfortable and warmly welcome, but you may also get feelings of trepidation and having absolutely nowhere to go because you feel uncomfortable and even rejected. If we come back to the KM House metaphor, there is a huge divide between the things that are visible and the things that are invisible and intangible: I refer to the values, the attitudes that are driving the atmosphere. In many organizations, there is often a disconnect between the KM talk and walking the walk! This means that you can't achieve a fluid flow of knowledge within the KM House if it is not sustained by enabling values such as spontaneity and integrity, recognition and team spirit, transparency, and openness. The architectural design of the KM spaces needs to match the desired collaborative atmosphere.

## TELL THE STORY TO MAKE KNOWLEDGE MANAGEMENT HAPPEN

Telling the KM House story can help greatly in compelling a common KM vision at Board level for driving corporate KM vision.

One of the first barriers in KM is a lack of understanding of the KM agenda and of the missing link between KM outcomes and organizational outcomes. A

KM strategy in its early stages needs alignment with business strategy, under-standing and commitment of management, and adoption by the staff.

With this purpose in mind, the complexity of KM can be explained in metaphorical and simple terms to management. You can visit rooms of the KM house and explain that each space features a range of KM processes, and those processes can be related to specific KM/business objectives. For example, the objective of developing the expertise regarding accountancy software so that the sales forces can provide demonstrations to customers needs to rely on a range of processes such as: identification of existing expertise (expert's corner), learning process (conference centre), exchange of tips and tricks regarding accountancy software (team rooms), and consultation of manuals (library).

Based on a sufficiently realistic picture of the KM environment, the dialogue with the managers can then be initiated by mapping ongoing knowledge-based projects onto the KM House and by interconnecting those projects when feasible. Generally this first phase resonates with the participants who then often imagine other projects that might support their business objectives.

All KM projects can be attached to one or more spaces in the house and then, if you can get that mapping process going, the KM House can be the *visualization instrument* of the firm's KM strategy and vision.

# APPLICATION CASE STUDY—THE RESEARCH DEPARTMENT AT ONDRAF-NIRAS

## Background and Context

Nuclear power, although controversial, produces approximately 17 percent of the world's electricity. There are more than 400 nuclear power plants throughout the world. Of those, about 100 are in the U.S. Many countries depend on nuclear power for their electricity supply, some more than others. For example, France is reputed to generate approximately 75 percent of its requirements from nuclear plants and the U.S. about 15 percent.

In this respect, the nuclear sector must ensure the security of the radioactive waste sites, protection of the environment, and the safety of the population, while it must develop and maintain the expertise acquired in building power stations. However, the long-term perspective that the nuclear industry must necessarily have—we routinely talk about decades and even longer—leads to huge issues in terms of knowledge sustainability and transfer. It is thus absolutely important that industries and governments involved in nuclear technology and research find appropriate answers to the safeguarding of nuclear knowledge and expertise over a long-term time horizon.[1] This scenario has been investigated by ONDRAF-NIRAS, a Belgian Agency operating in the area of radioactive waste.[2]

## ONDRAF-NIRAS

ONDRAF-NIRAS (French-Dutch acronym) is the Belgian Agency for Radioactive Waste and Enriched Fissile Material. It was created in 1980 by the Belgian government for ensuring that the general public is effectively protected from the potential hazards arising from radioactive waste. ONDRAF-NIRAS has to ensure, both in the short and in the long term, the safety of radioactive waste management. The protection of the environment and the security of populations are at the center of its preoccupations. It includes four basic missions, which are:

- To set up an inventory of the radioactive materials on Belgian territory and of the different radioactive waste producers
- To set up a safe management system for this radioactive waste
- To coordinate the decommissioning of nuclear facilities
- To manage enriched fissile materials

ONDRAF-NIRAS is structured in four main directorates (Figure 23.2): Disposal Directorate, Programming Directorate, Contracts and Finance Directorate, and Administration and Legal Affairs.

ONDRAF-NIRAS can perform the tasks mentioned previously either by making use of its own resources or by subcontracting to third parties operating under its responsibility and under its supervision.

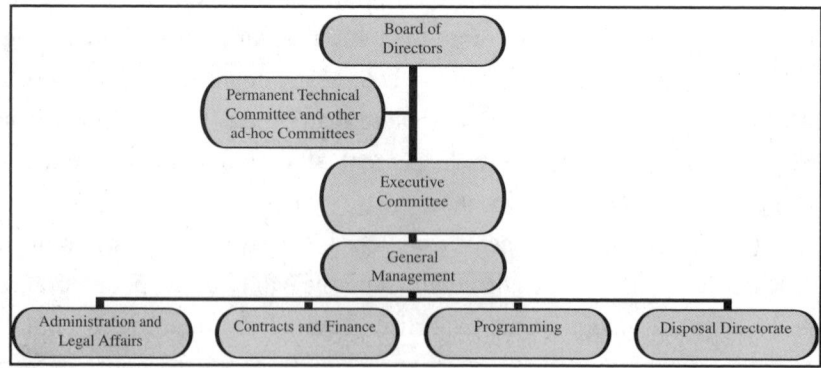

**Figure 23.2  Structure of ONDRAF-NIRAS**

## Why a Knowledge Management Approach at the Disposal Directorate?

The KM program has been initiated by the Disposal Directorate that is charged with undertaking studies and research projects. For conducting this research work, they need to collaborate with universities, research consultancies, research centres, engineering consultancies, and other specialized companies.

A research project at ONDRAF-NIRAS leverages a wide range of materials and involves both internal engineers and external researchers, the subcontractors. The KM reflection in the Directorate has been driven by the following observations:

- Research projects lead to huge sets of documents and often run over a period of more than 80 years, equivalent to three generations of engineers.
- Data consist of text fragments from larger units (including context, objectives, body of the report, figures, tables, original scientific data, etc.).
- Need for traceability and reproducibility of scientific results.
- Need for traceability of decisions that have been taken during the research projects.
- Need for peer reviews and audits at all levels of R&D results.
- The narrative aspects of the scientific work are important.
- A great deal of the research project is subcontracted.

## Envisioning Knowledge Management

Our KM journey in ONDRAF-NIRAS has started with the KM House. During a two-day session, ONDRAF-NIRAS research engineers reflected on what was the most crucial knowledge required for performing their job and ensuring the continuity and safeguarding of the contextual knowledge for future generations.

At the end of the session, they pointed out these key issues:

- The dissemination but yet disconnection of the different pieces of knowledge generated during a research project; that situation leads to a wide range of unstructured data and documents, often in paper format, stored in personal folders and categorized according to personal classification schemes.
- The absence of process for tracking the decisions and the reasoning of the experts along the project, and consequently no way to reproduce or justify the decisions that have been taken during the research process.

A powerful and common KM vision resulted from the brainstorming session: the need to move from fragmented research material—explicit knowledge—and experience—tacit knowledge—toward a collaborative research environment.

This fundamental shift had to be operated by implementing the following:

- Having a common and central store of project documents in order to replace individual classification schemes so that everyone can capture and access current and past documents
- Designing and applying consistent processes along the document life cycle so that the successive versions of the same report are tracked and secured
- Including the subcontractors in the documenting process so that their research knowledge and expertise is captured, safeguarded, and preserved for future engineers
- Tracking the reasoning of the researchers and documenting the decisions by conceptualising knowledge and documenting the decision process
- Automating the capture and tracking of the tangible documents and of the experts' arguments

## The E-Map Project

Sustaining the KM vision, the E-Map Project has been initiated by the Disposal Directorate and combines complementary strategies to preserve nuclear research knowledge.

The resulting KM system relies on Vignette Collaboration Server Technology, and it is based on a range of key principles.

### Modular Reporting

Traditional scientific reports are generally considered as a single entity by the researchers. Changing the ideas about scientific reporting has been part of the solution: the new statement is that the scientific report will be considered as a combination of knowledge entities, "the modules." Each module can evolve in an autonomous way, but yet be consolidated in a single document when it is required. For example, the subcontractors who intervene during the research project have access to the modules they must contribute to, whereas the internal researchers of ONDRAF-NIRAS have access to the whole report and can already draw some recommendations based on the findings of the subcontractors. Another benefit of the modular reporting is that it enables a non-sequential contribution to the report while respecting the security guidelines and authorizations of the company.

Metadata have been elaborated and serve as additional criteria that help users retrieve information needed. Figure 23.3 illustrates the modular reporting principle.

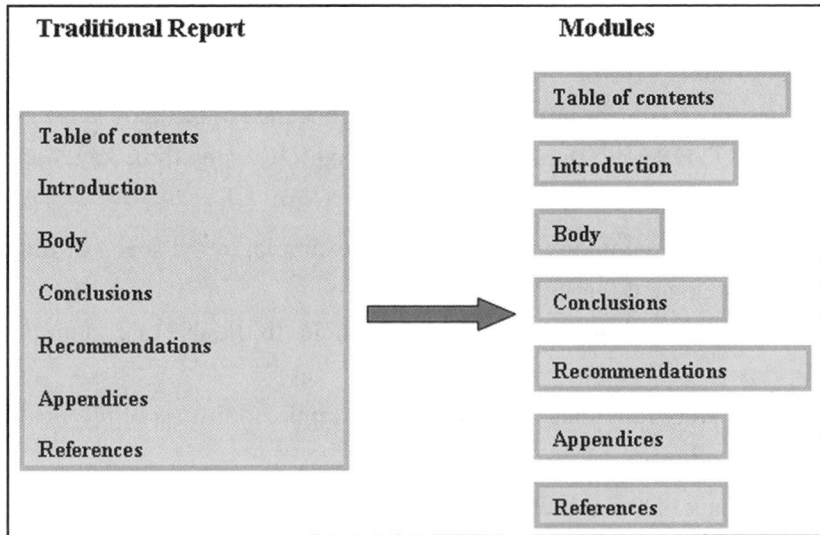

## Figure 23.3  Decomposition of a scientific report into modules

Given the focus on traceability, reproducibility, integration of scientific data, work, results, recommendations, and decisions, it is of the utmost importance that any user accessing the system has the opportunity to make queries of all sorts and on any selected part of the report and on metadata (headings, authors, keywords, etc.).

Typically, the system supports queries such as:

- List chronologically all the decisions relative to a keyword, a research study, or a group of research studies.
- What are the decisions that have led to that research study?
- What are the original data used in the research study XYZ?
- Draw all the conclusions from research studies done within a given time-frame within a certain research project space.
- Extract a specific table or figure from a research study.

### Argument-Based Case Building

The argument-based case building is the core of the KM solution designed at ONDRAF-NIRAS.

The rationale is the following: Over a decade, ONDRAF-NIRAS needs to present a major case that supports technical and environmental choices made by the research engineers. This can only be realized if the full tracking of the arguments justifying any decision or conclusion is captured. The argument-based system enables us to build consistency, traceability, and reproducibility of the scientific results and outcomes while keeping track of the *why* and *how* linked to one or more arguments.

How has this argument-based system been embedded in the knowledge system?

First, the ONDRAF-NIRAS arguments are built by using three key disciplines in the framework of their research studies:

- The phenomenology that relates, for example, to the speed of migration of an element through the clay
- The engineering that relates, for example, to the use of certain types of concrete
- The safety functions that relate, for example, to the use of physical inclusion, dilution

The elements of these three disciplines interact and lead to certain technical requirements and decisions (the so-called "arguments"). The resulting arguments of the interaction of the three disciplines need to be accessible. The capture of this information in the KM system is accomplished by using metadata. Those metadata support given choices and/or design instructions and are attached accordingly to the respective parts of the scientific report.

In the meantime, the knowledge acquired during the research study, including experts' advice, is linked alike to the report's module to which it refers (Figure 23.4). The resulting integration of the official scientific report, contextual information, metadata, and newly acquired knowledge during the life of the project leads to a document that enables ONDRAF-NIRAS to retrieve and justify at any time the recommendations and decisions taken during the research studies.

### Mapping and Visualizing for the Future Generations

A third focus of the KM system has been based on the need to visualize the research studies with their different entities of information on a time line, and to link the studies and reports that were the consequence of each other, for example, to demonstrate that such a recommendation or decision has led to a new research study.

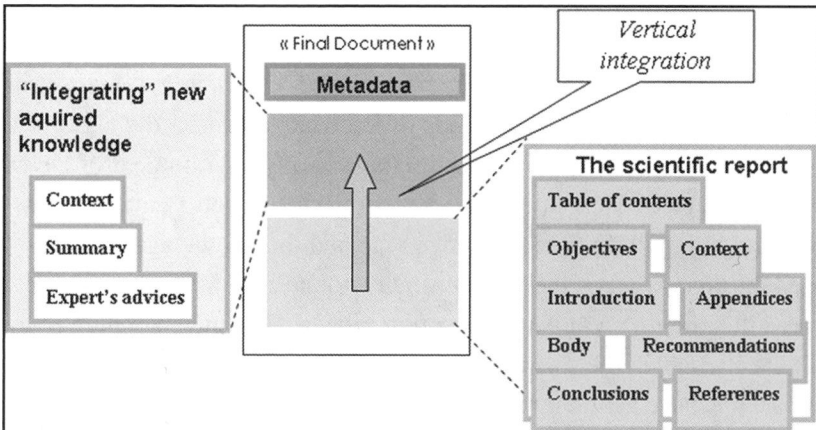

**Figure 23.4  Integration of newly acquired knowledge**

The visualization tool takes the form of a time line that maps any event of the study from the beginning of the study until the end. Each icon is a symbol of an event, for example, a hand refers to a range of recommendations and a smiley means that you can retrieve the advice of experts (Figure 23.5).

Conserving thus the main steps of the research study in a chronological way, the tool is fundamental for use by future generations, as it reflects, in a consistent map, the life cycle of the scientific projects.[3]

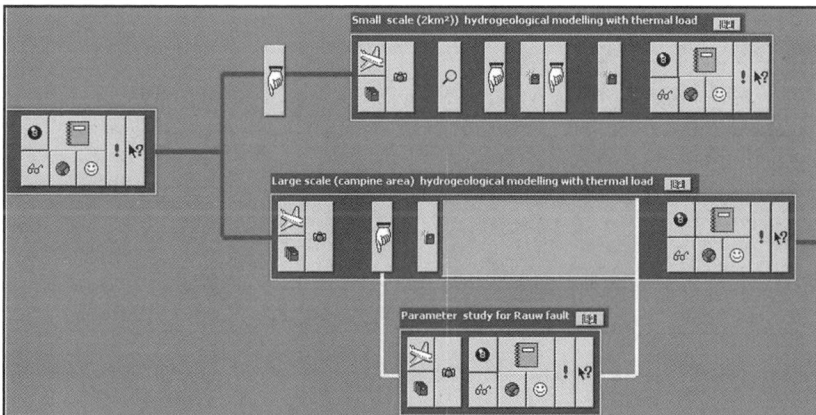

**Figure 23.5  Timeline of a research study**

## Conclusion

The KM House establishes the framework, the *visualization instrument*, that focuses attention on the different kinds of knowledge and on the ways to access it. The mapping of the KM House within the working environment of ONDRAF-NIRAS has enabled research engineers to project themselves into the KM environment and to highlight the knowledge map and the knowledge gap.

Based on this exercise, the Disposal Directorate has decided to design a KM system while initiating a modular reporting process. The main strength of the system is that it enables the users to visualize the story of a research study and to retrieve any decisive action impacting the life of the research study. Attaching narrative and contextual details to the formal scientific report is a crucial aspect of the solution and the necessary prerequisite for ensuring the understanding of the underlying arguments of the research studies. The concerted efforts made by the Disposal Directorate at ONDRAF-NIRAS have demonstrated that it is possible to design a KM system sustaining nuclear know-how in a narrative way and to preserve and manage nuclear knowledge thanks to an evolving perspective of the scientific report.

Here one must not lose sight of the fact that there has been a great emphasis on making knowledge available and sharing it. Intrinsic know-how—tacit knowledge—is rooted in the experience and expertise of individuals. This kind of system can be successful only if people belonging to the organisation support it.

## Endnotes

1. See *International Journal of Nuclear Knowledge Management (IJNKM)* (Inderscience Publishers, 2004).
2. www.ondraf.be/engels/5_niras_eng.html
3. The visualization interface is under development.

# CHAPTER 24

# An Alternative Knowledge System at the World Bank: A Case Study of the World Bank's Indigenous Knowledge for Development Program

Deepa Srikantaiah
University of Maryland

Claudia Rueger
World Bank

## ABSTRACT

Indigenous knowledge systems are of great economic importance globally and also in development practices. For example, in Southern Africa, the Commercial Products from the Wild (CPWild) project estimates the value of informal herbal remedies in the market to be between $75 million to $150 million per year. More than 1,000 indigenous crops and medicinal plants are traded in this informal market system, and more than 100,000 people are income earners in this industry. This one example, among others, illustrates that not only "mainstream" knowledge systems, but also alternative, local, or indigenous knowledge systems can be of great importance for the economy and for fighting poverty.

Alternative knowledge systems, however, are still marginalized in development practices. The marginalization of these knowledge systems leads to three important questions: (1) Why are alternative knowledge systems (indigenous, traditional, or local) still not acknowledged in development? (2) What are the challenges in using alternative knowledge systems in development practices? and (3) How can alternative knowledge community holders gain leverage of their knowledge systems to further their development? Using the Indigenous

Knowledge for Development Program at the World Bank as a case study, this chapter will address these questions and discuss the opportunities and challenges indigenous knowledge systems face in development practices.

> *In the Tanga region of Tanzania there is only one modern medical doctor for every 33,000 residents. There is, however, one traditional healer for every 343 residents and one traditional healer for every 146 rural residents.* (Scheinman, 2002, p. 51)

## INTRODUCTION

Tanzania is a microcosm of the developing countries who depend on World Bank funding for development projects in sectors such as education, health, and agriculture. The majority of rural areas in developing countries that rely on World Bank funding often do not have appropriate infrastructure and conditions to host modern medical resources, formal education systems, modern advances made in agriculture, and technology, such as information communication technologies (ICTs).

Due to cases such as that in Tanga, Tanzania, there has been an increasing interest in studying local resources and knowledge, particularly in pharmaceutical and medical techniques.[1] For example, in Southern Africa, the value of informal herbal remedies in the market is estimated to be between $75 million to $150 million per year. More than 1,000 indigenous crops and medicinal plants are actively traded in the informal market of this region and several hundred thousand people are income earners in this industry.[2]

This example demonstrates two important points: First, that not only "modern" scientific and technical know-how but also local, indigenous, or traditional practices can be of great economic importance, and second, since "modern"[3] resources and knowledge are not readily available and also not always appropriate to rural populations in developing[4] countries, local resources and knowledge may better compensate and, where appropriate, can be used to facilitate development practices.[5]

In development, scholars have also argued for years that development practices, especially in multilateral development organizations, should be reversed from the conventional "top-down" development practices to include community participatory methods and that development should be culturally sensitive to a community's traditions and knowledge.[6] This is the vision behind the Indigenous Knowledge for Development Program at the World Bank—a program that was created in 1998, three years after president Wolfensohn joined the Bank and declared the institution a "Knowledge Bank." The program supported a vision in which the poor participate as both users and contributors to knowledge in development practices at the World Bank.

This paper will examine the use of community and locally based knowledge systems in international development by studying the Indigenous Knowledge for Development Program (Indigenous Knowledge Program) at the World Bank as a case study. The paper is organized as follows: (1) Indigenous knowledge is defined according to International Development policies and practices; (2) the vision of the Knowledge Bank is described; (3) the vision, goals, and strategies of the Indigenous Knowledge Program are highlighted; (4) the function and operations of the Indigenous Knowledge Program are explored emphasizing the dissemination, exchange, and mainstreaming of indigenous knowledge to fit the vision and goals of the Knowledge Bank; (5) the opportunities and challenges of the Indigenous Knowledge Program are discussed; and (6) conclusions and future research are presented.

## WHAT IS INDIGENOUS KNOWLEDGE?

The word "indigenous" is problematized in literature. The difficulty in defining the term indigenous stems back to the disciplines from which the term originated. For example, Niezen (2003) writes that 20 years ago, the term indigenous was associated with physical science disciplines such as botany or environmental sciences.[7] He notes that the term gradually become equated with human identity and knowledge systems.

Associating the term indigenous with people, however, is also problematic. Who the indigenous are is political and generally left for individual governments to decide. For example, the Indian government does not discuss the indigenity of groups within India. They argue that their entire population is indigenous.[8] Many African countries also make a similar argument. Mexico, on the other hand, like many other Latin American countries, recognizes the indigenity of parts of its population and identifies 56 indigenous groups in that country.[9,10]

Indigenous knowledge,[11,12] in the sense the Indigenous Knowledge Program uses the term, can, in theory, break political and classification barriers because the knowledge is not limited to people or communities labeled as indigenous or other minority classifications. The program also refers to knowledge imported from other localities and which has been adapted by the community to its specific local and cultural conditions.[13] The Indigenous Knowledge Program follows this definition in its work program: Indigenous knowledge is "unique to every culture and society" and "embedded in practices institutions and relationships" and the "basis for local level decision making, agriculture, health, natural resource management."[14,15]

## VISION OF THE KNOWLEDGE BANK

The World Bank's World Development Report from 1998 to 1999 states that "knowledge is like light. Weightless and intangible, it can easily travel the world, enlightening the lives of people everywhere. Yet billions of people still live in the darkness of poverty—unnecessarily."[16]

Indeed, due to increasing globalization in the recent years, knowledge has become an important factor for development. It is steadily replacing labor and capital as production factors and is a major determinant for the success of social and economic development processes. Since 1998, from the start of Wolfensohn's presidency, the World Bank recognized the importance of knowledge and aimed to establish itself as a "Knowledge Bank." It aspired to become a knowledge broker for international development policy, and knowledge became seen as the "second currency." Wolfensohn, therefore, formalized the initiation of these knowledge activities through the field of "Knowledge Management."[17,18]

The formal establishment of Knowledge Management[19] at the World Bank allowed the organization to document and share the knowledge from its development projects and practices profitably to staff and clients (see Figure 24.1). It also enhanced its development projects by implementing knowledge activities in key areas of the World Bank. The Global Distance Learning Network (GDLN), for example, helps connect development clients from various regions and World Bank staff to engage in knowledge exchanges via videoconferencing.

In addition, the World Bank has documented knowledge of "best practices" from development projects and housed this knowledge in units such as the "Advisory Services."[20] These service centers create knowledge nuggets of "best practices" with the purpose of using this knowledge in future development projects. This knowledge can also be shared with clients.[21] The development of these

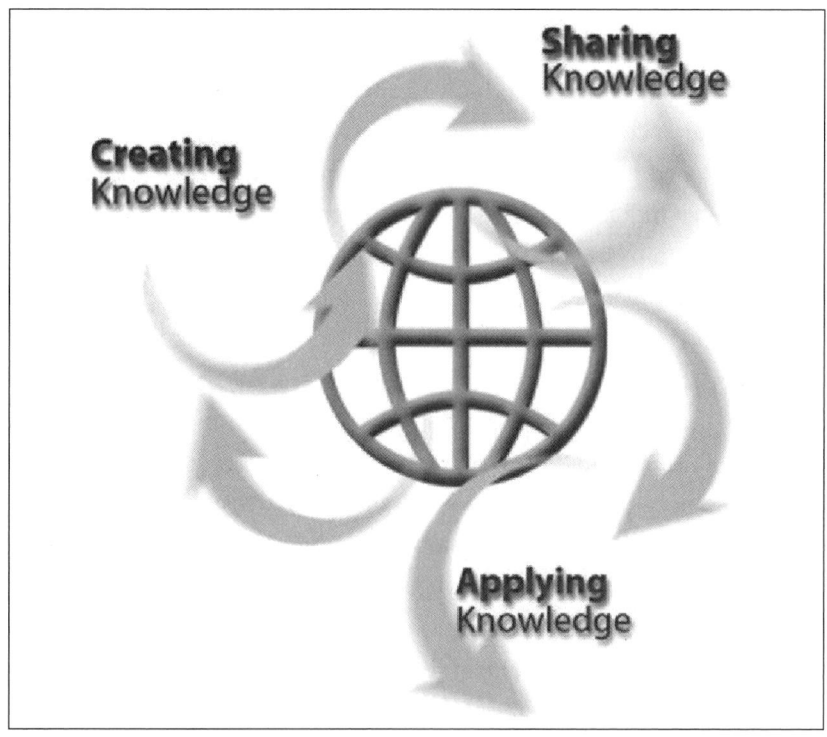

Figure 24.1   Major activities of the Knowledge Bank. (Source: B. Laporte (2002), "The Knowledge Bank in Action," Washington, DC: World Bank, p. 9.)

knowledge activities also allowed World Bank staff and clients to learn from the successes and failures of past projects, improve future development work, and meet the World Bank's main goal to alleviate poverty and increase economic growth.

In addition to capturing explicit knowledge,[22] the World Bank also worked at capturing the softer sides of knowledge or tacit knowledge.[23] The World Bank recognized that it is difficult to capture all dimensions of knowledge through conventional documenting systems or databases and, therefore, created programs, such as the Debriefings Program,[24] to make sure that World Bank staff's knowledge was properly captured and shared with others in the organization. Since much of indigenous knowledge is generally not codified and does not exist as explicit knowledge,[25] the Indigenous Knowledge Program, hence, worked with techniques developed in the area of tacit knowledge to capture all dimensions of indigenous knowledge from communities and introduce it in development projects at the World Bank.

## FORMATION OF THE IK PROGRAM

Within the framework of this new strategy, which made allowance for the increasing importance of knowledge, the World Bank's Indigenous Knowledge Program blossomed as a new and innovative initiative. In a document marking five years of the Indigenous Knowledge Program, Wolfensohn stated that the Bank should "not only … provide its own know-how gained through more than 50 years of development experience, but … equally learn from the practices of communities so as to leverage the best in global and local knowledge systems" (Woytek et al., 2004, p. vii).

Acting on the assumption that indigenous and community-based practices could contribute substantially toward achieving poverty reduction and improving livelihoods, the program was launched in an effort to foster and increase the use of indigenous knowledge in the development process. Figure 24.2 illustrates the program's philosophy.

The Indigenous Knowledge Program was started in 1998 after a Global Knowledge Conference was held in Toronto in June 1997. At the conference,

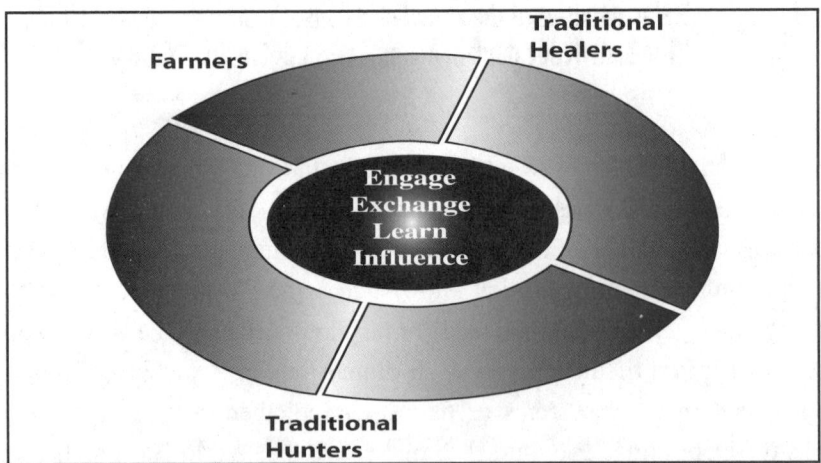

Figure 24.2   Engage, exchange, learn, influence: The philosophy of the Indigenous Knowledge Program. (Courtesy of the Indigenous Knowledge Program. See www.worldbank.org/afr/ik)

government leaders and civil society groups expressed concerns that the World Bank and other multi-lateral donors were not learning and developing development practices based on local communities' knowledge.

Also, around the same time, many World Bank client feedback surveys from African countries mentioned that country authorities and stakeholders wanted the World Bank staff to do a better job of working with and adapting local knowledge into development practices. Therefore, at the end of the Global Knowledge conference, the Vice President of the World Bank's Africa Region said the World Bank would "support a vision in which the poor would participate as both users and contributors to knowledge in development practices."[26]

The rationale of the Indigenous Knowledge Program was to introduce indigenous knowledge and practices in health, agriculture, and education, among other areas, into international development practices so that this knowledge is a part of global development discourses and development practices (Woytek et al., 2004, p. vii).

The program managers gave two main arguments for the integration of indigenous knowledge in development policies and practices at the World Bank: (1) Referencing the 1997–1998 World Development Report, which revealed that knowledge, not financial or material capital, is the key to sustainable development, the Indigenous Knowledge Program argued for building on local or indigenous knowledge, which was considered the basic source of any country's capital and thus resources for development; and (2) The Indigenous Knowledge Program addressed the "knowledge adaptation gap" (see Figure 24.3), which was evidenced by World Bank findings from client feedback surveys. The surveys had indicated that World Bank clients were highly satisfied with the World Bank staff's knowledge on international best practices, but dissatisfied with their effectiveness in adapting this knowledge to the respective country's and community's conditions. Therefore, the Indigenous Knowledge Program argued that a better understanding of the local conditions, including the knowledge basis of the local people, would help better adapt global technologies to the specific needs of local communities.[27]

Based on these assumptions, since 1998 the Indigenous Knowledge Program has been doing extensive work in capturing and documenting indigenous and community-based practices from all over the world, with a special focus on Africa.[28] During the creation of the program, different goals and strategies were developed wherewith to achieve the objective of fostering and implementing

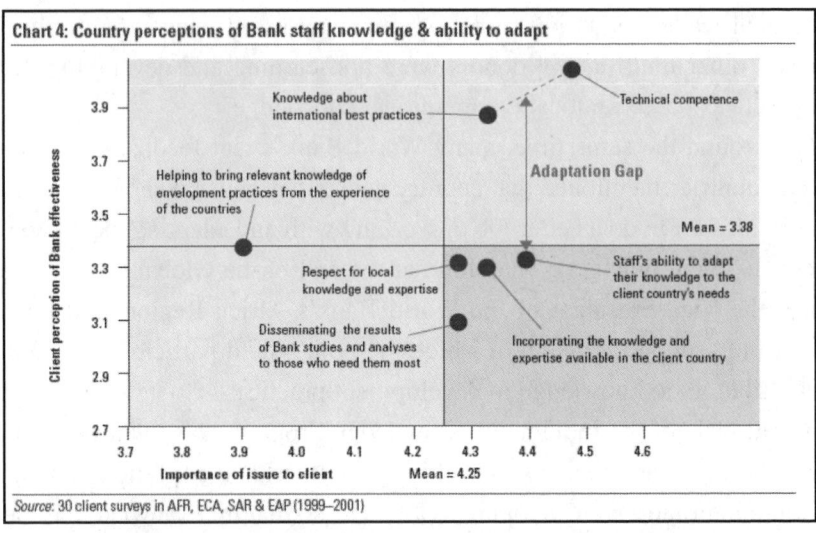

Figure 24.3  The knowledge adaptation gap. (Source: Capacity Enhancement
through Knowledge Transfer: A Behavioral Framework for Reflection,
Action & Results. See Gorjestani, 2005.)

indigenous knowledge in the development process in order to effectively reduce
poverty. These and the organizational creation and location of the program are
detailed in the next section.

# Function and Operations of the Indigenous Knowledge Program

## Organizational Location of the Program

The Program was first created as an initiative funded by a grant from the World
Bank's first Innovation Marketplace, which is a competitive forum that allows
people to informally present their antipoverty ideas to potential funding opportunities at the World Bank.[29] After surviving on a development marketplace grant
for a short period, the initiative was eventually integrated into a unit within the
Africa Region's vice presidency.[30] The vice presidential units are the main organizational units of the World Bank which address a continental region, a thematic
network or central function. As part of the structural renewal effort that began during the Wolfensohn presidency, the World Bank organizes most of its work along

two dimensions: thematic networks and regions. Thematic networks cut across the various regions and each of them covers several topics related to the different sectors of development.[31] Most of the networks operating globally, such as the Poverty Reduction and Economic Management (PREM) network, provide services in different development topics for World Bank staff and clients. However, unlike several programs addressing similar issues, such as the Indigenous Peoples Program or the Community Driven Development Program, the Indigenous Knowledge Program was not anchored at any globally operating network, but rather it was part of an operational department within the Sub-Saharan Africa region. Over the last eight years, in the "Knowledge and Learning" unit, however, the Indigenous Knowledge Program has done extensive work to pursue the goals of the program.

## Goals and Strategies

In order to track the outcomes of the Indigenous Knowledge Program, the "Framework for Action" established four pillars as the objectives for the Indigenous Knowledge Program: (1) Dissemination of knowledge and community-based practices that are relevant for the development process and reducing poverty; (2) facilitating learning and knowledge exchanges among communities; (3) applying (mainstreaming) of knowledge in national development policies and projects supported by the World Bank and other donors; and (4) building of partnerships in order to broker collaboration on knowledge issues between local practitioners, community-based organizations, governments, donors, the global scientific community, and other international organizations.

Different measures were undertaken over the last eight years to achieve these objectives (see Table 24.1). In order to *disseminate information* on indigenous knowledge in different areas, such as health, agriculture, natural resource management, education, conflict resolution, and others, a database on indigenous knowledge practices with approximately 300 entries was created on the Web site.[32] The database is a service to users from different countries and regions so that they can exchange indigenous or community-based solutions on development issues. Furthermore, in October 1998 the first "IK Note" titled *Indigenous Knowledge Systems in Sub-Saharan Africa: An Overview on indigenous knowledge systems in Africa* was published. The monthly publication reports on development issues and the effective application of indigenous knowledge. It publishes case studies from different development sectors written by development practitioners or scholars.[33]

## Table 24.1  Summary of the Indigenous Knowledge Program's goals and strategies

| Goal/Strategy | | Activities | | |
|---|---|---|---|---|
| Dissemination of indigenous practices | Database with 300 best practices | "IK Notes" | Indigenous knowledge Web site | |
| Facilitating learning and exchange of indigenous knowledge | Bank study tours | South-south study tours | Distance learning courses | |
| Applying and mainstreaming indigenous knowledge | Indigenous Knowledge Integration Fund | Advice to bank staff in integrating into bank-supported projects | Integrating into national policies | |
| Building partnerships on indigenous knowledge issues | Bank departments | NGOs, civil society groups | Global research institutes | |

The program's Web site aims at opening a gateway to development approaches that rely on indigenous knowledge systems. It is also supposed to raise awareness among the development community on the importance of indigenous knowledge and community-based practices and support the mainstreaming of these practices in World Bank's partner activities. Lastly, the program's Web site provides general background information on the debate about indigenous knowledge in academia and the development cooperation and publishes case studies, toolkits, and other instruments for the integration of community-based practices into development projects.

The objective of *mainstreaming the use of Indigenous Knowledge* in the development process is pursued through different measures. Besides hosting activities to raise awareness, such as presentations and workshops to demonstrate the relevance and effectiveness of locally based solutions, the program set up an Indigenous Knowledge Integration Fund for the amount of $250,000. The fund was allocated to task managers of World Bank-supported projects who planned to integrate indigenous knowledge in their work. In addition to receiving guidance from the Indigenous Knowledge Program staff, the fund provided the project teams with basic financial support for consultants, workshops, and the like to help them identify relevant knowledge and practices.

Following the creation of the implementation fund, different Bank operations in Africa and South East Asia planned to integrate indigenous knowledge-related activities in their operations work. The Agricultural Research and Training Project in Uganda, for example, built on indigenous practices in agriculture to make them part of the outreach program. The Africa Multi-Country AIDS Program plans to organize and train traditional healers on HIV/AIDS practices, while supporting the treatment of opportunistic infections using traditional medicine. After having been advised by the Indigenous Knowledge Program, several countries are exploring ways of incorporating indigenous knowledge into World Bank-supported projects. The means to support this process and the drive for results, however, remain limited due to relatively few financial resources and the lack of operational opportunities.

To several developing countries the program provided assistance in the formulation of national policies on indigenous knowledge. Following a multi-stakeholder workshop held in December 1999, Uganda, for example, formulated the Kampala Declaration on Indigenous Knowledge for Sustainable Development. This declaration eventually led to the integration of indigenous knowledge into the Uganda Poverty Eradication Action Plan (PEAP). The former president of Tanzania, Benjamin Mkapa, planned to draft a national action plan on indigenous knowledge, which was outlined in one of the program's publications (Woytek et al., 2004, p. 1). The Indigenous Knowledge Program has also worked with the government of Kerala in India to integrate indigenous knowledge into its five-year plan.

The program organized knowledge and learning exchange tours for World Bank staff working in the Africa region to visit successful development projects with indigenous knowledge components in South Asia. These exchanges allowed World Bank staff to learn of practices and encouraged them to integrate these indigenous knowledge systems and practices into World Bank operations in East Africa.

Similar cross regional tours called the "south to south" *learning* events were also organized in order to *facilitate knowledge exchanges* among communities between East Africa and South Asia. These exchanges aimed at enhancing local capacity to identify and apply indigenous knowledge and practices. The purpose of these tours was to allow South Asians to share their strategies of their indigenous knowledge activities with the East Africans, who could adapt similar strategies with their communities. For example, in 2004, local members of the Women's Development Initiative in Ethiopia and the Social Action Fund Projects in Malawi and Tanzania visited similar projects in South East Asia that had successfully used indigenous knowledge in their projects.[34, 35]

As follow up to the South-South tours, the program launched a series of distance learning courses. In 2005 and 2006, three learning events were organized, focusing on the role of indigenous knowledge in implementing the Millennium Development Goals (MDGs), combating HIV/AIDS, and managing natural resources.[36, 37] Facilitated by the Indigenous Knowledge Program staff, in each course participants exchanged information and practices on indigenous knowledge. Government representatives and traditional healers of six participating East African countries shared experiences and information on how traditional healing knowledge can be integrated into HIV/AIDS programs.

Lastly, the program conducted joint seminars with researchers, NGO representatives, and development practitioners from African countries to show how indigenous knowledge can be used to achieve the MDGs. Different toolkits, available on the program's Web site, were developed, such as documents, multimedia files, and case studies and examples on how to identify and integrate indigenous knowledge in development. These learning tools include literature, videos, interviews, and Web links that provide information and assist development practitioners to achieve the MDGs. Each toolkit presents successful approaches in achieving one of the MDGs based on practical country experiences. The toolkits also provide users a learning platform with timely access to lessons of experience on "what works" and "how to do it." The focus is on identifying the key success factors and providing users with practical guidelines on how to replicate and scale up successful practices.

On the strategic objective of building *partnerships*, the program worked with different NGOs, scientific institutions, and other donor organizations. A partnership with the Global Research Alliance, for example, has been established to help develop a collaborative process for the validation of traditional medicinal approaches and to promote innovation at the community level.

Over the eight years of its existence, the Indigenous Knowledge Program has done extensive work in different areas, as illustrated here.[38] However, despite these efforts and opportunities, the Indigenous Knowledge Program faced major challenges and limitations. We hypothesize that these challenges and limitations arose principally from the inconsistent use of different terms for "indigenous knowledge," the program's organizational location, and the predominant understanding of development and development cooperation at the World Bank.

## Discussion

We categorize the challenges faced by the Indigenous Knowledge Program into three major areas: (1) Appropriately defining and interpreting "indigenous knowledge" at the World Bank, (2) overcoming the organizational constraints of the institution in the location of the Program, and (3) validating the importance of indigenous knowledge in development.

As discussed in the first section, the Program defines indigenous knowledge loosely as local knowledge, tacit knowledge, or knowledge of a community, which spans beyond indigenous communities.[39] Researching the Indigenous Knowledge Program's Web site and publications, however, the terms "indigenous knowledge," "traditional knowledge," and "local knowledge" are inconsistently and interchangeably used. Although the rationale behind this may have been to facilitate the integration of indigenous knowledge into the World Bank's work program, this is actually very misleading.

The plurality of terms used to denominate the knowledge the program addresses—and the lack of a clear understanding of the term indigenous knowledge—leads to several problems and challenges. The program uses the term indigenous in a broader sense than the World Bank's Indigenous Peoples Program. The common understanding of indigenous in and outside the World Bank, however, is more related to indigenous peoples. Hence, an assumption can be made that World Bank staff and people outside the World Bank may think that the program addresses the knowledge of indigenous peoples, and perceive the program much more politically and less operation-oriented than it aims to be.[40] The fact that the program does not target indigenous peoples as its major focus group and attempts to avoid the political issues associated with the identification of indigenous peoples is actually confusing and misleading to staff regarding the aims of the program.[41] This is especially true in regard to the program's objective to mainstream the use of indigenous knowledge in World Bank operations. World Bank staff and clients may not relate their work to the Indigenous Knowledge Program's objectives if their work does not deal with indigenous peoples.

In Africa, this represents a major problem. The political debate about indigenous peoples in Africa is much less prominent than in Latin America and Asia. World Bank staff in the Africa region, therefore, may not see the applications of indigenous knowledge in their work.[42] This is especially important for the program because it is a demand-driven service and relies on the interest and awareness of project staff to integrate indigenous knowledge based on the Indigenous Knowledge Program staff's advice. Therefore, the use of the term "indigenous," which World Bank staff and stakeholders associate with indigenous peoples, should be endorsed by having the Indigenous Knowledge Program collaborate with the World Bank's Indigenous Peoples Program (which is currently not being done) or the term "indigenous" should be avoided. A different term, such as "local" or "context-specific" knowledge, may better clarify the program's technical focus on the application of relevant knowledge.

The term "context-specific knowledge"[43] may denominate more precisely the knowledge the program is addressing. It is difficult, however, to operationalize this term or use it in a global context. The knowledge a local organization or practitioner is working with is produced locally, in contrast to the knowledge produced by globally acting institutions, hence the local knowledge systems cannot claim to be globally applicable.

"Local knowledge," a term frequently used in place of indigenous knowledge, is actually a much broader term and refers to all knowledge systems that are shared in a local community of practice. A community of practice can refer to different kinds of groups and suggests that rural local communities, who are the target group of the Indigenous Knowledge Program, are one group of possible knowledge holders. If the Indigenous Knowledge Program uses the term local knowledge, the program would have to broaden its approach toward validating and integrating relevant knowledge systems of all participants in development. It would also have to concomitantly specify the holders of the knowledge it addresses. For example, the program staff would have to clearly acknowledge the "local knowledge of (rural) local communities." This approach is very close to the "Knowledge for Development" initiatives, where the importance is given to knowledge held by all development actors and how these knowledge systems can be used as a driving force in development. Using the term local knowledge then becomes close to general knowledge management approaches.

Between the terms local and context-specific knowledge, the term local knowledge seems to be the most appropriate way to address the knowledge the program is aiming to integrate in development. The Indigenous Knowledge Program should use the approach of local knowledge; however, it should lay major emphasis on the non-formalized knowledge of (rural) local communities and beneficiaries of development efforts. As demonstrated here, local, non-codified knowledge of communities can be of great importance for alleviating poverty and improving livelihoods. It is often not appropriately validated in development, however, because it is not formalized by conventional knowledge producing institutions and seems to be incompatible to the predominant understanding of development as a unilinear process to modernization.[44]

Besides the term "indigenous knowledge," the use of the acronym "IK" also leads to misperceptions of the program.[45] By using the acronym IK, indigenous knowledge is represented as a static technical toolkit and loses its dynamic character. Integrating indigenous or local knowledge in development activities, however, needs to go beyond incorporating techniques that are considered useful to achieve predefined goals. The concept of building on the knowledge of local people should be understood as an approach to development, not as a toolkit. However, using the acronym IK can contribute to a reduced perception of local people's knowledge. To make the development approach holistic, scientific knowledge and the knowledge systems of local people should be brought together to enhance the development dialogue. For the Indigenous Knowledge Program, this does not necessarily mean to question the (Western) concept of poverty alleviation through modernization and industrialization or even the concept of development. Integrating alternative knowledge systems into development practices means to approach development differently and as a process negotiated between development actors coming from different knowledge systems. As indicated on the program's Web site, the knowledge of local people is the basis for their decision making.[46] Referring to these knowledge systems in the form of a technical acronym should therefore be avoided in order not to reduce the contents of indigenous knowledge.

Second, besides defining indigenous knowledge and using appropriate terms to denominate the knowledge addressed by the program, it is also the organizational location, which represents a major challenge for the program. Although the location of the program has some advantages, there are also considerable disadvantages. Since the Indigenous Knowledge Program is in one of the Africa region's operational departments, the program's work can directly apply to World Bank operations in African countries. This means that efforts toward integrating indigenous knowledge can focus on specific projects in a region of similar socio-political conditions. However, the program should not be limited to the Africa region—particularly since indigenous knowledge is a global issue.[47] Building on the knowledge of local communities is an approach that should be embarked upon globally. Each region should have a separate Indigenous Knowledge Program that meets the specific needs of the region.

In order to set up such an initiative and to broadly integrate the use of indigenous knowledge in World Bank operations, however, the World Bank's approach to development and its understanding of valuable knowledge needs to change. If indigenous knowledge is to be mainstreamed in World Bank operations, staff and clients need to be aware of the importance and comprehension of indigenous knowledge. Therefore, it is equally important that the use of relevant indigenous knowledge and practices is integrated into key operations policies and procedures at the Bank. To do so, the program would need to be in a position that enables it to draft and establish new guidelines and policies. Being a part of the Quality and Knowledge Unit in the Africa region, which is basically in charge of improving and monitoring the compliance with existing World Bank policies through a monitoring and evaluation system and internal learning activities, the possibilities for the program in terms of introducing new policies, knowledge, and paradigms are limited.

On the other hand, the Indigenous Knowledge Program's relatively close connection to operations must not be underestimated. This connection offers the program the opportunity to work on specific activities of the World Bank instead of functioning in a parallel structure like many other minor innovative activities of the World Bank. Due to the lack of operational mandates and because of the predominant understanding of valuable knowledge at the World Bank, however, past activities were not sufficiently integrated in operations.[48]

Finally, indigenous knowledge systems need to be validated. In mainstream development, indigenous knowledge systems often take a back seat as solutions or approaches to development issues and are often referred to as a final alternative or not referred to at all. Although international development organizations, such as the World Health Organization, and leading research institutions, such as the National Institutes of Health, have created protocols to validate indigenous knowledge, practitioners at the World Bank and other multilateral organizations are hesitant to invest project funds in these knowledge systems. The following barriers need to be overcome in order to effectively and appropriately validate indigenous knowledge in development: overcoming the unilateral understanding of development, acknowledging and respecting indigenous knowledge, and scientifically validating indigenous knowledge to be on par with Western knowledge.

Unfortunately, due to dominant theories and practices, indigenous knowledge is not appropriately recognized as the social capital or valuable resources of the poor or local communities. "Modern" knowledge, generally thought of as knowledge codified by Western or American and European scientific institutions,[49] is more accepted to address development issues.[50] Although the development theory of modernization has been challenged by development scholars and its classical version is considered by development organizations as obsolete, current practices in development often still follow the basic principles of this theory, which suggest economic growth for development and exchanging "traditional" values for "modern" values.[51] In addition, simply put, what is not modern is considered traditional and obstructive to development.[52]

Following this theory, indigenous knowledge or the local knowledge in developing countries are sometimes simply labeled as traditional and a limiting factor and barrier to modernization and development.[53] Additionally, it is often implicit in development studies that indigenous knowledge systems are not scientifically valid and hence are not useful for development. Jegede (1999) and other authors[54] suggest that, due to this understanding of development, American/European knowledge has been dominant in development and has promoted the mission of Western education (including science)[55] in continents such as Africa.

Studying the African continent as a case study, Jegede (1999) notes that Western knowledge systems have dominated indigenous knowledge systems in science.[56] He points out that African indigenous knowledge systems follow different scientific methods or paradigms and interact closely with local community activities.[57] For example, in many African cultures, science is not compartmentalized, but is rather viewed holistically involving "worldview, communal organization, theory of knowledge, causality, religion, concept of time and space, kingship system, rituals, death, marriages, witchcraft, ancestor worship, storytelling and riddles, reincarnation, sorcery, spirits,"[58] among others.

Predominant science-based development theories, on the contrary, often suggest that the different environmental components be compartmentalized as separate activities. Following this dichotomized distinction between local indigenous and global scientific knowledge, indigenous knowledge often cannot be part of the knowledge stock relevant for development.[59] However, as seen in the activities of the Indigenous Knowledge Program, the approaches used by indigenous knowledge systems can in fact be extremely valuable in development processes.

## CONCLUSION

In conclusion, the Indigenous Knowledge Program is a great initiative embarked upon by the World Bank. However, the program faces major challenges mainly because the concept of indigenous knowledge follows a different development paradigm than that of the World Bank.

Unlike what many researchers suggest from a post-colonial perspective, integrating indigenous knowledge into the operations of the World Bank does not necessarily mean questioning the concept of development.[60] However, integrating indigenous knowledge should imply thinking of development as diverse and culturally bound. Local, non-formalized knowledge systems can be based on different "world views" such as environmental concepts, approaches to social justice, and gender relations. Building on such knowledge in development therefore implies recognizing the existence of different realities.[61]

Being one of the most powerful organizations in international development, the World Bank's mission and work, however, are based on the concept of modernization and economic growth as development—a concept that is based on modern scientific knowledge. Therefore, efforts to validate the importance of alternative knowledge systems have to be seen in this framework. The primary task of the Indigenous Knowledge for Development Program, hence, should be to help the institution expand its development paradigm without challenging theories of modernization. Building on the knowledge of local people and complementing this with global knowledge can help achieve desirable goals for all different participants in development: the reduction of poverty and improvement of livelihoods.

Therefore, in order for indigenous knowledge to be a central player in development at the World Bank, we believe the following needs to occur:

- There needs to be government support for indigenous knowledge. Local governments need to support their local research and development efforts in identifying and sustaining practices of indigenous knowledge.[62] In addition, they need to promote this knowledge when discussing funding of projects with the World Bank.

- Further support and funding should be given to research and development in scientific validation, quality assurance, and systematization of indigenous knowledge. This research will help governments to support their indigenous knowledge and also provide them the language and data in global and development dialogues. For example, the National Institutes of Health and the World Health Organization are working to validate these knowledge systems so that they are better accepted in mainstream healthcare.

- Development should be more decentralized. Indigenous knowledge refers to the knowledge in a country, not in the Washington, D.C. headquarters. Country World Bank offices should have greater autonomy and be able to integrate indigenous knowledge in the projects. This will probably yield better results and sustainability of projects at the World Bank and allow indigenous knowledge to play a central and key role in development.

Despite the challenges the Indigenous Knowledge Program encountered and the numerous changes that need to occur, at the level of the World Bank and in the countries, the program contributed to a major achievement at the World Bank and in international development. By identifying local solutions in international development, even though they were labeled as "indigenous knowledge," the program contributed to creating a new category of knowledge at the global level. It gave local people's knowledge a name and therewith allowed the knowledge to exist in international development.

At the moment, recognizing the diversity of knowledge and validating alternative concepts is of great importance. Recognizing the diversity of knowledge will also help the poor to be a part of the global development dialogue. Local knowledge is an important resource for new approaches, in addition to helping empower poor people and allowing them to participate in the global system; it is the values and perception of the present world view that cause the existing global problems. In the long term, these problems can hardly be solved within the current notions of development but need new convictions and new ways of thinking.

## ENDNOTES

1. A well known example is the Hoodia plant in South Africa. The pharmaceutical industry has shown increased interest in this plant, because it suppresses appetite and can be used to treat obesity.
2. See the Project Commercial Products from the Wild (CPWild): www.cpwild.co.za
3. All current knowledge can be considered modern; however, in this context modern knowledge is knowledge related to science dominated by industrialized countries. Modern knowledge can also be understood as knowledge imported into a region or knowledge that is not local to the region of study. See Evers (2003).
4. The World Bank categorizes countries based on GNP income per year. A Less Developed Country falls in their category of low-income to middle-income countries. These countries have a GNP of $765-$3,035 per year. See web.worldbank.org/WBSITE/EXTERNAL/EXTSITETOOLS/0,,contentMDK:202 64002~menuPK:534379~pagePK:98400~piPK:98424~theSitePK:95474,00.html#1
5. The World Health Organization (WHO) also reports that approximately 80 percent of Africans, such as rural communities in the country of Tanzania, rely on their traditional medicines as their primary health care. See www.who.org
6. See Warren (1992) and Chambers (1997) who advocate for the use of indigenous knowledge in development.
7. See Niezen (2003, p. 3).

8.    As discussed by Niezen (2003).

9.    See *Finance and Development*, December 2005, Vol. 42, No. 4.

10.   Although the World Bank recognizes that because indigenous peoples live in varied and changing contexts and that there may not be a universally accepted definition of indigenous peoples and also refers to groups as "indigenous ethnic minorities," "aboriginals," "hill tribes," "minority nationalities," "scheduled tribes," or "tribal groups," these classifications can also be politically influenced and determined by governments. See wbln0018.worldbank.org/Institutional/Manuals/OpManual.nsf/B52929624EB2A3538525672E00775F66/0F7D6F3F04DD70398525672C007D08ED?OpenDocument

11.   For consistency reasons, we use the term indigenous knowledge according to the Indigenous Knowledge Program's definition of the term, although we prefer the term "context-specific knowledge" or "local knowledge."

12.   In addition, it is important to note that knowledge and knowledge systems are used interchangeably, since the knowledge of individuals or communities usually refers to different content areas, which together can form a system. A knowledge system can be understood as the ensemble of individual knowledge parts.

13.   This is especially important regarding local innovations, which result very often from the interface of different knowledge systems. See Siebert (2004, p. 270).

14.   See Finding #70, November 2001.

15.   The Indigenous Knowledge Program uses the term Indigenous Knowledge as many academic researchers define local knowledge. The Program, however, was simply trying to highlight the knowledge of rural, poor, and marginalized communities in development.

16.   See World Bank (1999). Cited in *Knowledge for Development*. World Development Report 1998. Washington, DC, p. 1.

17.   A common definition of "Knowledge Management" is "the process of identifying, organizing, and managing knowledge resources. These include explicit knowledge (information), "know-how" (learning capacity), "know-how" (customer capacity), and tacit knowledge in the form of skills and competencies. See Al-Hawamdeh (2003).

18.   Knowledge Management, many World Bank staff have argued, was already an "underground movement" at the World Bank. For example, the Development Economics Group, one of the research units at the World Bank, has written reports from the early 1980s on the importance of documenting and incorporating knowledge in development practices. Academics and former World Bank staff, such as Mosely, Hararigan, and Toye (1991) and Denning (2001), note that these papers were not able to "rock the boat" of an organization dominated by economists. See discussion on this by King and McGarth (2001).

19.   The World Bank prefers to use the term "Knowledge Sharing" because it has come to the conclusion that knowledge should not be managed but shared.

20.   For example, the Human Development Network and Education Department's Education Advisory Service creates knowledge nuggets of best practices in Education operations projects and materials on numerous education topics. The knowledge service answers queries from World Bank staff and clients on topics in

education, designs and maintains the Education Web site, and performs other important activities to ensure effective knowledge transfer among Bank staff and clients. See web.worldbank.org/WBSITE/EXTERNAL/TOPICS/EXTEDUCATION/0,,contentMDK:20253087~menuPK:282440~pagePK:148956~piPK:216618~theSitePK:282386,00.html.

21. See King and McGarth (2001).

22. Knowledge already codified. See Davenport and Prusak (1998).

23. Knowledge that is not easily codified or documented. Oral histories can also be considered tacit knowledge. See Antweiler (1998).

24. The program conducts videotaped interviews with clients and staff on good practice and lessons learned in areas of regional strategic importance, either identified by interested World Bank staff or by Program staff to better document and exchange lessons of operational experience for improved development results. See www.worldbank.org/afr/debriefing. Davenport and Prusak (1998) agree with this and write that multimedia programs and other Internet programs help to capture the tacit dimension of knowledge.

25. For example, oral histories.

26. Gorjestani (2004) in Woytek, et al. (2004).

27. "… investing in the exchange of IK [Indigenous Knowledge] and its integration in development programs supported by the Bank and its development partners would help achieve the overriding development objective, the reduction of poverty. … We have learned that IK is a critical factor for sustainable development." Gorjestani (2004) in Woytek, et al. (2004).

28. The Program was located in the Africa region of the World Bank.

29. Created in 1998 and with an allocation of $3 million, the Innovation Marketplace was initially an internal World Bank program. In 2000, at that time called the "Global Development Marketplace," it was opened for external participants and received more than 1,000 proposals from within and outside the World Bank. See web.worldbank.org/WBSITE/EXTERNAL/OPPORTUNITIES/GRANTS/DEVMARKETPLACE/0,,contentMDK:20083068~menuPK:218640~pagePK:180691~piPK:174492~theSitePK:205098,00.html

30. Possibly because the managers of the initiative were working in this particular department.

31. Thematic networks host advisory services, data services, enhanced internet and the IT infrastructure, and aim at increasing staff learning through professional development and learning seminars. For example the ESSD Network answers internal Bank staff and external clients' questions on Environmental and Socially Sustainable Development (ESSD) related questions, publications, and related Web sites. The major networks of direct relevance for development operations are the Environmentally and Socially Sustainable Development Network, Human Development Network, Poverty Reduction and Economic Management Network, Private Sector Development Network, Infrastructure Network, Financial Services Network, and Operational Policies and Country Services Network.

32.    The Indigenous Knowledge Program's database documents to date 286 best prac-
       tices in using indigenous knowledge for development (see www4.worldbank.org/
       afr/ikdb/search.cfm). Database last checked on July 2006.

33.    For a recent survey of IK Notes readers see Rueger (2006). The publication is dis-
       tributed electronically and as paper copy and reaches about 15,000 readers. Since
       Internet access is still limited in developing countries, the majority of the hardcopy
       readers (about 7,000) live in developing countries, mainly Africa. See web.world
       bank.org/WBSITE/EXTERNAL/COUNTRIES/AFRICAEXT/EXTIND
       KNOWLEDGE/0,,contentMDK:20663953~menuPK:1693277~pagePK:64168445
       ~piPK:64168309~theSitePK:825547,00.html

34.    See South-South Learning Tours: web.worldbank.org/WBSITE/EXTERNAL/
       COUNTRIES/AFRICAEXT/EXTINDKNOWLEDGE/0,,contentMDK:20841231~
       menuPK:2287816~pagePK:64168445~piPK:64168309~theSitePK:825547,00.html

35.    See also Pidatala (2004, p. 75) on further descriptions of the South-South tours.

36.    See www.worldbank.org/afr/ik

37.    See also Prakash (2005, p. 84) on further descriptions of the Indigenous Knowledge
       Distance Learning Course.

38.    Major emphasis was put on indigenous or traditional knowledge in healthcare,
       especially the role of traditional medicine in treating HIV/AIDS opportunistic dis-
       eases. This may be due to the popularity HIV/AIDS has received in international
       development.

39.    www.worldbank.org/afr/ik

40.    Indigenous Peoples programs in and outside the World Bank address indigenous
       peoples as minorities and aim at supporting them in protecting their cultural, social,
       and political rights. See, for example, the World Bank's Indigenous Peoples
       Program Web site (web.worldbank.org/WBSITE/EXTERNAL/TOPICS/EXT
       SOCIALDEVELOPMENT/EXTINDPEOPLE/0,,menuPK:407808~pagePK:14901
       8~piPK:149093~theSitePK:407802,00.htm) or UNDP's Indigenous Peoples Program
       (www.undp.org/ cso/ip.html). Bilateral development organizations have similar work
       programs. See, for example, German GTZ: www2.gtz.de/indigenas/english

41.    This is explicitly visible when studying the program's Web site. The program
       addresses different aspects regarding the application of indigenous knowledge but
       rarely highlights the political issues surrounding the knowledge holders and the
       rights they may carry with them.

42.    Particularly in Latin America, the debate about political, cultural, and economic
       rights of indigenous peoples, generally considered to be the people living in the
       countries before colonization and also people that identify themselves as indige-
       nous, has been ongoing for several decades. In African countries, populations can-
       not easily be distinguished between descendents of former colonizers and those who
       have originally lived in the region before colonization. This is one reason for the fact
       that the political debate in this region has just recently started and is limited to dis-
       advantaged minorities such as the Pygmies in Central Africa.

43.    In theory, any knowledge system can be context specific when it is applied.

44.    For details on the production and construction of knowledge and reality by modern
       science institutions, see Lachenmann (1994).

45. The use of the acronym IK for Indigenous Knowledge is very common in research and development. See, for example, the "IK Pages" (www.ik-pages.net) or the "IK section" of the science and development network (www.scidev.net/dossiers/index.cfm?fuseaction=dossierfulltext&Dossier=7).

46. See web.worldbank.org/WBSITE/EXTERNAL/COUNTRIES/AFRICAEXT/EXTIND KNOWLEDGE/0,,contentMDK:20663799~menuPK:1692621~pagePK:64168445 ~piPK:64168309~theSitePK:825547,00.html

47. As seen in the Discussion section, the Program had activities addressing the knowledge exchange between African and South Asian communities. However, besides these efforts, the main focus lies on Africa, since the Program is anchored in the Bank's Africa region.

48. Limited financial means may also be an important reason for the Program's limited ability to mainstream the use of relevant indigenous knowledge.

49. As discussed by So (1990) and Lachenmann (1994).

50. After World War II and the end of British and French colonization in many countries, two countries dominated in the global arena: the United States and the former Soviet Union. During this time period, the United States became a world leader and other countries looked at it as "developed" and "successful economically." In addition, the United States led the reconstruction of Western Europe and worked hard to promote economic development and political stability in countries recently freed from colonization—which can also be thought of as "third world countries." Their involvement in these countries was important to them as they feared the spread of communism from the Soviet Union to these countries.

51. See So (1990, p. 36).

52. As discussed by Huntington (1976) in So (1990).

53. As discussed by Faschingeder (2001, p. 66).

54. See for example Lachenmann (1994).

55. See Jegede (1999, p. 124).

56. See Jegede (1999, p. 124).

57. This concept can also be thought of as the social capital of communities.

58. See Jegede (1999, p. 124).

59. See So (1990, p. 35).

60. For postcolonial perspectives on development see for example Escobar (1995) and Hobart (1993). See Briggs and Sharp (2004) for their critic directly about the World Bank's Indigenous Knowledge Program.

61. The topic of indigenous knowledge in development is often analyzed in the framework of theories on the construction of knowledge and reality. Many researchers understand integrating indigenous knowledge as recognizing the existence of different realities in development. See, for example, Chambers (1997).

62. For example, see details on the Sri Lankan Ministry of Medicine in Srikantaiah (2005b, p. 74).

# BIBLIOGRAPHY

Al-Hawamdeh, Suliman. (2003). *Knowledge management: Cultivating knowledge professionals.* Oxford: Chandos Publishing.

Antweiler, Christoph. (1998). Local knowledge and local knowing. An anthropological analysis of contested "cultural products" in the context of development. *Anthropos, 93*: 469–494.

Briggs, John, & Sharp, Joanne. (2004). Indigenous knowledges and development: A postcolonial caution. *Third World Quarterly, 25*(4): 661–676.

Chambers, Robert. (1997). *Whose reality counts? Putting the first last.* London: Intermediate Technology Publications.

Davenport, Thomas, & Prusak, Laurence. (1998). *Working knowledge.* Boston: Harvard Business School Press.

Dean, Bartholomew, & Levi, Jerome M. (2000). *At the risk of being heard: Identity, indigenous rights, and postcolonial states.* Ann Arbor, MI: University of Michigan Press.

Dei, George J. Sefa, Hall, Budd L., & Rosenberg, Dorothy Goldin. (Eds.). (2000). *Indigenous knowledge in global contexts: Multiple readings of our world.* Toronto: University of Toronto Press.

Easton, Peter. (1998). Senegalese Women Remake their Culture. In *Local pathways to global development* (IK Note # 3). Washington, DC: World Bank.

Escobar, Arturo. (1995): *Encountering development: The making and unmaking of the third world.* Princeton, NJ: Princeton University Press.

Evers, Hans-Dieter. (2003). *Local knowledge and the digital divide.* Unpublished working paper.

Faschingeder, Gerald. (2001). *Kultur und entwicklung: Zur relevanz soziokultureller faktoren in hundert jahren entwicklungstheorie.* Frankfurt a. M., Wien: Brandes und Apfel/Südwind.

Friere, Paulo. (1993.) *Pedagogy of the oppressed.* New York: Continuum Books.

Gorjestani, Nicolas. (2005). *Capacity enhancement through knowledge transfer: A behavior framework for reflection, action & results.* Washington, DC: World Bank.

Harragin, Simon. (2004). Relief and an understanding of local knowledge: The case of southern Sudan. In Vijayendra Rao & Michael Walton (Eds.), *Culture and public action.* Stanford, CA: Stanford University Press.

Hobart, Mark. (Ed.). (1993). *An anthropological critique of development: The growth of ignorance.* London, New York: Routledge.

Jegede, Olugbemiro. (1999). Science education in non-western cultures: Towards a theory of collateral learning. In Ladislaus Semali & Joe Kincheloe (Eds.), *What is indigenous knowledge?: Voices from the Academy* (pp. 119–142). New York: Falmer Press.

Lachenmann, Gudrun. (1994). Systeme des nichtwissens. In Ronald Hitzler, Anne Honer, & Christoph Maeder (Eds.), *Expertenwissen. Die institutionalisierte kompetenz zur konstruktion von wirklichkeit.* Münster, Germany: Westdeutscher Verlag.

Lachenmann, Gudrun. (2004). Researching local knowledge for development: Current issues. In Nikolaus Schareika & Thomas Bierschenk (Eds.), *Lokales wissen—sozialwissenschaftliche perspektiven.* Münster, Germany: LIT Verlag.

Laporte, B. (2002). The knowledge bank in action. PowerPoint Presentation. Washington, DC: World Bank.

McGrath, Simon, & King, Kenneth. (2004). *Knowledge for development? Comparing British, Japanese, Swedish and World Bank aid.* London: Zed Books.

Niezen, Ronald. (2003). *The origins of indigenism.* Berkeley and Los Angeles: University of California Press.

Prakash, S. (2005). *Indigenous knowledge-cross regional distance learning course— India, Sri Lanka, Uganda and Tanzania.* Washington, DC: Knowledge and Learning Division, Africa Region, World Bank.

Rueger, C. (2006). *IK Notes readers' survey. Final Results* (IK Notes, No. 97). Washington, DC: Knowledge and Learning Dvision, Africa Region, World Bank.

Sarangapani, Padma M. (2003). Indigenising curriculum: Questions posed by Baiga Vidya. *Comparative Education, 39*(2): 199–209.

Scheinman, David. (2002). Traditional medicine in Tanga today: The ancient and modern worlds meet. In *Local pathways to global development* (IK Notes, No. 51). Washington, DC: World Bank.

Semali, Ladislaus, & Kincheloe, Joe. (Eds.). (1999). *What is indigenous knowledge? Voices from the academy.* New York: Falmer Press.

Siebert, Ute. (2004). Welches wissen? Verständnisweisen von lokalem wissen in UNESCO programmen und Überlegungen zu einem sozialwissenschaftlichen konzept von lokalem wissen. In Nikolaus Schareika & Thomas Bierschenk (Eds.), *Lokales Wissen: Sozialwissen-schaftliche Perspektiven.* Münster, Germany: LIT Verlag.

So, Alvin. Y. (1990). *Social change and development: Modernization, dependency, and world-system theories.* Newbury Park, CA: Sage Publications.

Srikantaiah, Deepa. (2005a). *Education: Building on indigenous knowledge* (IK Notes, No. 87). Washington, DC: Knowledge and Learning Division, Africa Region, World Bank.

Srikantaiah, Deepa. (2005b). *Sri Lanka's ministry of indigenous systems of medicine. Indigenous knowledge note* (IK Notes, No. 83). Washington, DC: Knowledge and Learning Division, Africa Region, World Bank.

World Bank. (2006a). World Bank's indigenous knowledge for development results program. Available at www.worldbank.org/afr/ik

World Bank. (2006b). World Bank's indigenous peoples program. Available at web.world bank.org/WBSITE/EXTERNAL/TOPICS/EXTSOCIALDEVELOPMENT/EXTIND PEOPLE/0,,menuPK:407808~pagePK:149018~piPK:149093~theSitePK:407802,00.html

Woytek, Reinhard, Shroff-Mehta, Preeti, & Mohan, Prasad C. (Eds.). (2004). *Indigenous knowledge: Local pathways to global development.* Washington DC: World Bank.

# Part VIII

---

# Knowledge Management in Government

# Knowledge Management in Government

## FOREWORD

Chapter 25 by Davenport and Rasmussen is a fascinating analysis of a knowledge management (KM) failure, fascinating not only because it was a big messy failure, but because of the depth and the sophistication of the analysis. There is always much to learn from failure. Samuel Elliot Morrison, the late maritime historian, pointed out that in WWII the U.S. Navy had a great advantage over the Japanese Navy, because it lost the first battles. His point, of course, was that an organization is often forced to learn more, better, and faster from failure than from success. Davenport and Rasmussen analyze a major failure. It is clearly a failure of management to understand and appreciate context, but the analysis is undertaken at three levels:

- **Signification:** What did the various players understand it to mean to do knowledge work?
- **Domination:** Who controls the resources and assigns and prioritizes tasks?
- **Legitimation:** How is authority established?

These lenses, if you will, provide a technique with which to view and analyze almost any KM project, existent or proposed.

Droitsch's chapter (Chapter 26) is an equally fascinating look at KM implementation by the U.S. Government. It is largely a tale of misunderstanding and missed opportunities. The fault, Droitsch avers, lies to a great extent with the subordination of KM to a so-named Chief Information Officer (CIO), who is in fact required by the Clinger-Cohen Act (the Information Technology Reform Act of 1996) to be a Chief Technology Officer (CTO), as the name of the act suggests, not a CIO. He also sees the E-Government Act of 2002 as a major missed opportunity to correct the missed emphasis of Clinger-Cohen. Not all is bleak, however, in government undertakings. The Quicksilver e-government initiative of the

Office of Management and Budget (OMB) produced useful outcomes, though much less than what might have been accomplished if a KM perspective had been present. In addition, the author praises the Shareable Content Object Reference Model (SCORM) developed by the Advanced Distributed Learning initiative in the Department of Defense (but inexcusably ignored by the Department of Education). He also points favorably to the "Handle System" developed by the Defense Advanced Research Project Agency (DARPA), a digital object architecture for handling massive quantities of digital data, used by, among others, the Library of Congress and CrossRef (the article linking system development by the Publishers International Linking Association).

Also, check the KM in Government theme in the Roadmap.

# CHAPTER 25

# Knowledge Networking in a Public Service Agency: Contextual Challenges and Infrastructural Issues

Elisabeth Davenport
International Teledemocracy Centre

Louise Rasmussen
Napier University

## INTRODUCTION

This chapter presents a study of knowledge networking in a public sector agency (PuSA) in the U.K., where a number of knowledge management (KM) initiatives have been introduced since the inception of the U.K. "Modernising Government Programme" of 1999. PuSA is a quasi-governmental body that exists to stimulate commercial innovation and enterprise at national and regional levels. The study involves action research by an observant participant (Czarniawska, 2004), the second author, who worked for a number of years in PuSA. The case unravels some of the social and material consequences of an initiative to build a streamlined knowledge infrastructure. For seven years (1999–2006), senior management in PuSA based at HQ pursued an initiative to build a knowledge network—the Knowledge Working (KW) initiative—across the agency's 12 local subsidiary companies. Our study traces this initiative through a rich documentary archive of historical organisational material and personal research field notes. We focus particularly on a group of infrastructure intermediaries, or Knowledge Analysts (KAs), in PuSA. Like other accounts of public service networking (see, for example, Bowers, 1994), our study shows that the problems that arise in such projects are often unforeseen and intractable. The study raises a number of issues and challenges that confront managers of complex service infrastructures and the intermediaries who work with them.

## Knowledge Networking in PuSA: A Brief History

We start the story in April 1999 when PuSA approved a Knowledge Web project. The project was framed in terms of two main binary objectives: to address culture and behaviour and to improve processes with technology. One of 12 workstreams in this project was concerned with Knowledge Networking (KN) and with the recruitment of "Special-K People" (also known as "implants" and "analysts"), a cadre of intermediaries with specialist skills to manage a core knowledge system; provide professional support, advice, and training in managing knowledge; and, finally, monitor and maintain best practice in KM.

By July 2002, the Special-K People, or Knowledge Working Specialists as they became known, were recruited into a new KW team within the KM directorate at HQ. Structural tensions were present from the start. While the KW HQ team was responsible for developing and implementing tools and techniques for KW, the KAs were responsible for identifying and interpreting the knowledge needs of local staff in the distributed units. Utilising a participation framework called the "Knowledge Needs Route Map" (developed with the help of an external expert, an IBM consultant, between June and November 2003) and an associated KW toolkit, KAs were to recommend and implement appropriate KW tools and solutions, such as communities of practice (seen as a mechanism for harvesting tacit or implicit knowledge) and an intranet (the means to make tacit knowledge explicit).

In August 2003, 10 months after the KAs were first introduced, a Change Manager was brought in to provide strategic direction for the KA role. In an attempt to raise the status of the KA role and ensure that subsidiaries devoted more time to KW, he classified all the work the KAs did as "knowledge work," and this led to resource tensions. Toward the end of 2003 the KW team, KAs, their line managers, and other interested parties were taken through a two-day workshop and emerged as a trans-subsidiary Community of Practice, or CoP, a further structural complication. As a KW CoP, the KW team and KAs were to operate both vertically (between HQ and subsidiaries) and horizontally (across the different regional subsidiaries). The KW CoP members were geographically distributed and operated in a virtual manner using technologies such as the intranet, telephone, and discussion groups. However, the CoP was not a purely virtual entity, as some members were co-located; others met on occasion and all members met twice a year. The KAs' efforts in this initiative were only partially successful, as many of the local subsidiaries resisted to a greater or lesser extent HQ's efforts at integration.

In April 2005, a new CEO at HQ announced that the structure of the organisation would be reviewed. Details of this were not released until August 2006 and in December 2006, the KAs were disbanded—some left for other posts, and some were absorbed into other parts of the organisation.

## Managing Context or Building Infrastructure?

It would be easy to dismiss the story of knowledge networking in PuSA as another trite tale of an unsuccessful integration initiative that failed to address organisation-wide contextual issues of control and coordination. But this interpretation would not do justice to an initiative that was sustained for seven years and that delivered some of what was envisioned in some of the local units. It would also be easy to dismiss the story as another example of technological tunnel vision that failed to take account of context in the shape of the practices of local user groups. But this does not work as an explanation either—much of the remit of the KAs was concerned with cultural and behavioural transformation. In this chapter, we pursue a different line of explanation. The Knowledge Network was an attempt to build infrastructure, and there was a failure at many levels of management to understand how organisational infrastructure works. For managers in PuSA, infrastructure was a set of tools and services that would support trans-organisational knowledge work by providing common ground; the project was simply a matter of scoping and implementing, a minor workstream to be delivered by raw recruits. Managers failed to grasp the fundamental role of infrastructure as a site where organisational knowledge is produced, a site that is highly politicised and contentious. They thus failed to engage reflectively with the context of production of which they themselves were a part.

To explain how infrastructure works as a site of knowledge production, we draw on recent studies of knowledge management in project environments (Love, Fong, & Irani, 2005), and on emerging work on knowledge infrastructures in science. A recent series of studies by Newell and her colleagues of knowledge integration across units within organisations and within projects have focused on social capital formation. Newell and Huang (2005), for example, provide an account of failure to integrate in cross-functional projects, and Bresnen, Edelman, Newell, Scarborough, and Swan (2005) have recently published an account of a failed network project where lack of social cohesion was a major factor. In the case of PuSA, there is little evidence for the formation of proactive social capital, though a form of bonding in adversity is evident in many of the e-mails that were exchanged within the cadre of knowledge intermediaries. Lack of social capital does not explain, *per se*, the travails of the PuSA project, and we have pursued the issue of why there was little social capital formation, drawing on a study of conflict between two discourse communities in a public sector power utility by Carter and Scarborough (2001), one of several that constitute a research agenda based on the work of Foucault (e.g., 1977) in Information Systems research recently reviewed by Willcocks (2006). This alerted us to the effects of shifting regimes of power in distributed organisations where internal and external interest groups are involved in technological and managerial decision-making, and are thus implicated in the processes of knowledge production.

To date, the most comprehensive investigations of knowledge production in the context of very large infrastructures have been undertaken in the social studies of science domain as the research attention of different scientific communities converges on cyber-infrastructure and grid technologies. Very large knowledge infrastructures are the focus of an emerging field of study (Hine, 2006) where "memory practices" are seen not simply as sinks for output, but as drivers of science whose analysis allows us to understand how the world presents itself at a given point of observation, how things come to be as they are. Bowker (2005), in a recent monograph, describes memory practices in the sciences in terms of a rich set of infrastructures of differing reach and range. These emerge from complex chains of decision-making about who to involve and who to exclude, what to conserve and what to jettison, what to select and what to reject, and so on. Trajectories vary across domains and have considerable constitutive power. By making some materials available as points of reference and others not, such decisions shape what counts as knowledge in a given domain. Domains in science, the focus of Bowker's exposition, are discursive communities, and we suggest that his framing of infrastructures, memory practices, and the constitution of knowledge can be extended to a wider discussion of computer-mediated organisations.

# The Documentary Method

Bowker's text presents a number of methodological approaches to explore these issues. These include historical reconstruction/genealogy, discourse analysis, and ethnography. All of these involve longitudinal empirical work, and it is for this reason that research into memory practices relies heavily on the documentary method, the tracing of events across an archive of mixed sources.

As we noted earlier, the data that are used in the PuSA study consist of documentary, e-mail, and observational material gathered in the course of the researcher's work; interview data; and a range of generic documents (such as strategic plans, technology roadmaps, training checklists) from the wider organisational archive, each with its own distinctive discursive power. Three points of view are represented: those of a KA in two of the subsidiaries, and that of HQ. These have provided insight into decisions and negotiations that characterize complex infrastructure work. Analysis of documentation and observations has been ongoing; as Czarniawska (2004) points out, important events do not necessarily happen at the point of where an individual researcher observes, but at other times and in different places. In addition, she states that researchers cannot always determine that an event is significant when it takes place: Important events are sometimes "constructed" post hoc. We have used a time line, constructed post hoc, as a primary means of navigation through the assemblage of documents that constitutes the data archive for the study.

# Analysing the Knowledge Network at PuSA

In analysing the documentary archive, we have mixed two methods: discourse analysis and structurational analysis, an approach taken by Heracleous (2006; see Heracleous & Hendry, 2000). Historical analysis of knowledge management in PuSA reveals a number of different initiatives, or "versions," that emanate from the centre (HQ), that can be mapped on a time line and plotted in terms of key events or stimuli (seminars by influential consultants and gurus, for example, or shifts in personnel at senior management levels). The versions can be linked to competing KM discourses, championed by different senior agency officers at different times. These discourses problematize organisational knowledge in different ways, and the solutions that they entail provide different groups in the agency with an opportunity to bid for resources. The resource implications of a KM discourse may persuade bystanders to participate in a given initiative, as it is in their interest to do so;

where they have no interest, they will not take part. In the first phase of the study, we undertook a content analysis of key documents (strategy, planning, reporting) or texts that had traceable consequences for the knowledge intermediaries. A discourse analytic framework (Schultze & Leidner, 2002; and see Schultze & Stabell, 2004) was derived for the study that identified five main knowledge discourse elements from the documentary archive, and these were plotted against different discursive formations (Rasmussen, Davenport, & Horton, 2006). As high level units of analysis, they provided a starting point for unraveling the often complicated struggles that characterized KM implementation in PuSA, and a mechanism for scoping the Knowledge Network story in terms of three main discourse formations (value, psychology, object) each prioritizing different elements. To explore in detail the consequences of competing discourses in different phases in the knowledge network trajectory, we turned to structurational analysis.

In the analysis of PuSA, we were faced with an implementation that spanned a number of years, involved multiple management arrangements across distributed locations, computer applications and training techniques, and the appointment of specialist staff to facilitate adoption. The KAs who are the focus of the chapter were both producers of and produced by the knowledge network. Their formal duties and responsibilities (as described in project plans) refer to the former. But their power to produce was constrained because their duties and responsibilities fluctuated throughout their period of employment, as they were subjected to and were the subject of tensions on a number of fronts.

To accommodate these conditions, we followed a version of structurational analysis offered by Lyytinen and Ngwenyama (1992), who focus on computer support for cooperative work as their application area. Following Giddens (1984) they present social structures as instantiations of social actions over time intervals (compatible with our time frame in the PuSA study), virtual structures that are conceptualized in terms of the properties of social systems, namely rules and resources. Rules are generalizable procedures applied in the production/reproduction of social practices, and resources signify capacities to generate command over material and social objects. Stability and identity formation are important features of social ordering, and "ontological security" is an important theme of the paper; ability to monitor intentions and motivation is important here. Giddens provides a summary schema for structurational analysis. Three properties of social structure (signification, domination, and legitimation) are linked to three core capacities of social agents (communication, power, morality) by three modalities:

interpretive schemes (by means of which actors make sense of communicative actions), facilities or the ability to allocate material and human resources, and norms or sanctions. These are inextricably linked.

In the sections that follow we present the structures of signification, domination, and legitimation as they are manifested in PuSA. In the PuSA case, for example, a dominant discourse like "knowledge management adds value" can be anatomized in terms of signification (what does this mean to participants in the organization?), domination (who promotes this view and what resources can they command?) and legitimation (how does this discourse become naturalized in the organization?). Alternative discourses must compete and find their niche. In the text that follows, we offer a summary account of discourses and structuration in PuSA's Knowledge Network.

## Signification: What Does It Mean to Do Knowledge Work?

In the case of PuSA, we can observe a continuous struggle over signification. This was at its most basic in the terminology used for knowledge management activities. In a PuSA senior management paper written as far back as 1998, KM is mentioned as a mechanism for implementing the organization's strategy and its vision of becoming a knowledge organization. This remained the dominant discourse in spite of challenges from those implementing the Knowledge Network. At the time that the "KM as strategic asset management" terminology was adopted, knowledge of the economy and labor market helped PuSA formulate a strategy for economic development. For both in-house and outsourced knowledge services, PuSA operated a consultancy-based model whereby organisational staff or third parties imparted their knowledge to clients. PuSA states that it will "work with knowledge" to develop a strategy for economic development, understand and manage stakeholder relationships, and develop and deliver products and services to address market failure.

As we noted earlier, the original formulation of the Knowledge Web drew heavily on the "knowledge management adds value" discourse, a formation that appears to compete with other discourses throughout the project, a struggle that is reflected in continuously shifting nomenclature. The KAs were sometimes referred to as knowledge workers; under this rubric, their remit was presented as "working together more effectively by sharing knowledge with one another; it is about sharing views, ideas, insights, expertise and information, and having the tools, products, systems and processes in place which will allow us to use and manage that knowledge more effectively." But a year later, an alternative definition was offered by the Architecture Authority, a senior management group charged with designing a knowledge strategy for the overarching NT project: "Knowledge Working refers to the activities and behaviors required by [PuSA] to enable the creation, capture, sharing, storage, retrieval, analysis and application of knowledge. It embraces both the knowledge in the heads of individuals (tacit knowledge) and the knowledge held in documents and storage systems (explicit or codified knowledge)" (PuSA, 2004).

In a news item that appeared on the intranet in January 2003 introducing the KAs, they were described as "catalysts to bring about a change in culture within the network—a culture of Knowledge Working." Despite no agreed definition of KW, an internal job description described the KA as "the individual responsible for ensuring the effective management of Knowledge Working initiatives in their local [subsidiary]. They will work with senior management on the introduction of knowledge tools and new ways of working, ensuring that a knowledge sharing culture is embedded in the [subsidiary]."

While the KW HQ team was responsible for developing and implementing tools and techniques for KW, the KAs were responsible for identifying and interpreting the knowledge needs of staff and local support work. But there was little scope for KAs to assert a group identity, because the "needs framework" was developed in conjunction with an external expert, an IBM consultant. It was clear that the model first envisaged for KW was one whereby the KA acts in a consultancy capacity to identify business issues to address using KW tools and techniques. However, this was never made clear to the subsidiaries when the KA role was first proposed. The KAs were largely left to their own devices to communicate their role in their subsidiaries. Some KAs felt that it was difficult to communicate what they did because the term "knowledge working" was what the external world called "knowledge management." As the KW team was a team within the KM directorate and as such was associated with the KM activities of strategy, planning, research, and number crunching, the KAs could not recommend KM books or KM Web sites to other members of staff because they would associate KM with local usage at PuSA's HQ.

Confusion over definitions continued to June 2004 when the Change Manager and the KW Coordinator issued a report that was intended to encourage all of the regional subsidiaries to fall into line and subscribe to the KW initiative. While some KAs perceived a job-related task that was not common to all KAs to be KW teamwork, other KAs considered the same task to be an extension of their "other hats"—the other jobs they did. Around this time the Change Manager contended that there were different perceptions of KW depending on what the KAs thought their role was, what their boss perceived their role to be, and subsidiary circumstances. An attempt was made to define the role to subsidiary staff in terms of diagnosis, solutions, training, and support. The appointment of a new CEO led to further review, and in December 2006, the KA team was, as we noted earlier, disbanded.

## Domination: Whose Is the KA Resource?

In this section, we retrace the story to explore a further structural property of the knowledge network—domination. This account throws additional light on signification—the resources that knowledge work mobilized were tightly coupled to what knowledge work means. As we noted earlier, an organisational structure to accommodate KAs as both a central and local resource was implemented in May 2002. A human resource allocation model was proposed that specified the number of support and operational staff each subsidiary should have. Although PuSA wanted to increase the proportion of staff in "customer-facing" roles, the resource allocation model dictated that each subsidiary had to recruit a KA. These were to be included in a new team in each subsidiary. As the imposed (back-facing) KA support post represented a potential loss of an operational member of staff, the subsidiaries were reluctant to employ people whose role did not demonstrably add value in terms of their own local organizational objectives. Despite their concerns, the subsidiaries were required to adhere to the new staffing structure imposed by HQ and employ the KW specialists who were being recruited into a new KW team within the KM directorate in HQ. A number of local subsidiaries settled on a compromise, by allocating only a proportion of the activities of the new recruits to KW, thus reserving some resource for their own purposes.

In October 2002, before the KW PuSA team and the KA staff were all in post, the PuSA senior management team approved a conceptual Knowledge Architecture and Knowledge Working Strategy. The Knowledge Architecture and Knowledge Working Strategy were developed concurrently, in partnership between two PuSA HQ teams. The former was led by the PuSA KW team and the latter by the PuSA Architecture Authority. The strategy determined what needed to be done and the architecture determined how it should be done. The

Architecture Authority's role in assigning resources was to ensure that the ICT infrastructure and business processes of overall transformation project were "coordinated and mutually supporting" (PuSA, 2003a). Because the Architecture Authority was to disband following the implementation of the Network Transformation initiative, the KW team was assigned the ongoing role of changing and shaping the architecture in accordance with future organizational priorities. It was envisaged that the KW team would also be the "primary application vehicle" of the knowledge architecture (PuSA, 2003b). In addition, they were also tasked to lead on the development and delivery of the KW strategy (PuSA, 2003c). Not only were the KW team at HQ the strategists responsible for developing KW tools and techniques, but they were also tasked to support the KAs who would recommend KW solutions and apply them in PuSA.

The PuSA KW team at HQ recognised that KW concept was poorly defined and communicated and that there was considerable ambivalence about roles and line management. In August 2003, 10 months after the KAs were first introduced, a Change Manager was brought in to provide strategic direction for the KA role. Two senior managers (the Change Manager and the Coordinator) would form a bridge between the HQ KW team and each subsidiary KA. Coordination included setting up meetings, training events, and a spreadsheet to capture KA activities. A monthly meeting was scheduled to discuss work activities and share implementation experiences. KAs were to choose two projects and were prompted to consider a short description of the project, any network-wide implications or examples of best practice, use of KW tools to support the project, next stages, and support they might require to ensure completion.

The recruitment patterns of the knowledge intermediaries reflected tensions over definitions, which in turn reflected tensions over resource allocation. From the start, the posts were filled in a non-uniform way. In November 2002, seven KAs had been recruited, and the remaining five were recruited over the course of the following year. One joined in April 2003, two in July 2003, another in September 2003, and the last in January 2004. There was a mixture of full-time and part-time contractual and working arrangements across the different subsidiary agencies. In two cases, despite the role being communicated as being full-time, the KAs undertook other KM duties. In two subsidiaries, the individuals only found out that they were allocated the KA role when they received a group KA e-mail. They had to undertake KA duties in addition to their usual job functions. So in some cases, the KAs were undertaking the role on a part-time basis, while those that were full-time were given additional tasks that the subsidiary deemed important.

Regular monthly face-to-face meetings with individual KAs and each local "boss" were held, albeit separately. These meetings were an attempt to establish norms for managing KAs across the organization and to ensure that the KA workload was balanced, offer advice in implementing KW tools/techniques, gather KW good news stories, and identify areas where KA resources would need to be pooled. But KAs and local bosses never met as a cohort, and the Change Manager and Coordinator became the conduit for information on what each KA was doing. During meetings they recommended which KAs to speak to about undertaking a similar subsidiary activity. And if another KA or member of the KW team was required, for example, to facilitate a workshop, the two senior managers would act as liaison officers.

In early 2004, a spreadsheet was mandated for KAs to record their activity. This had four purposes. The first purpose was to provide an overview of what all KAs where doing to monitor length of time taken to implement KW solutions, plan future activities, and assess where KAs were being overloaded. It was also suggested that this would be helpful in discussions on priorities and workload with each local KA boss. All KA work had to be run through the Coordinator who would manage time and resources across the network. There was little or no dialogue with each KA's local boss regarding work that KW HQ team wished the KA to undertake, and it was left up to the KAs to clear work with their local boss and complete the worksheet. The spreadsheet was perceived by KAs as being just another mechanism to keep an eye on them. It was also anticipated that the spreadsheet would be replaced by an information technology (IT) system called Touchpaper. Eventually all KA work would be tracked online and the KW Team, KAs, KA line managers, and customers could monitor the stage a KA intervention was at. However, Touchpaper was never introduced.

In October 2004, it was decided to shift the monthly meetings, an important locus of central control, to a bi-monthly schedule. This was partly due to the fact that meetings were taking up too much time. The KA meeting in December was cancelled and no meetings took place until June 2005. A KW survey around this time suggested that HQ's "command and control" policy was not working. It was thought that the KW Director had asked the Change Manager and Coordinator to discontinue managing and coordinating the KAs. In January 2005 the PuSA KW Director announced that the role of the Change Manager and Coordinator had changed; they would both assume responsibility for managing and delivering the "tacit" agenda only, a major shift in focus by HQ. In August 2005, the KAs reinstated the KA meetings, but on a quarterly basis. They would now assume responsibility themselves for chairing the meeting and setting the agenda. While the Coordinator continued to attend some meetings, the Change Manager did not. Control of the resource had drifted yet again.

The KAs questioned the KW network structure on many occasions. More often than not, HQ developed network policies and procedures with little input from the subsidiaries, the operations arm of the business. Many of the local problems faced involved an issue with an HQ directive that couldn't be solved locally but at HQ level. As such, KAs found it difficult to intervene at a local level. Some KAs questioned whether local issues would be better addressed at a CoP level. This, it was felt, would be a better forum for KW interventions. But, some subsidiaries did not consider CoPs to be a local priority, and the KAs were not perceived to be delivering locally if they focused on an HQ initiative.

A survey in 2004 to elicit views of a proposed new KW structure highlighted a number of issues arising from this structural arrangement. It was felt that time spent on HQ and subsidiary priorities were deemed unimportant by opposing parties. In addition, the KAs were unable to focus on the job full-time and were pressured to focus exclusively on subsidiary priorities. To address these concerns, the HQ KW Director recommended that the subsidiaries continue to line manage KAs "whilst exploring increased commitment of KA time to KW activities (across business units where useful)" (KW Survey Recommendations, 2005). Subsidiary management was asked to agree to local and network priorities, gain consensus on the KA role, identify expected benefits, and agree on what amount of time should be devoted to KA activity (ibid). But, the recommendations fell short of asking the subsidiaries to work with each other and the KW team to concur on priorities, benefits, and resources. Instead, the KAs were later asked to submit subsidiary priorities to the PuSA KW team.

As we noted earlier, in April 2005 the new CEO confirmed at a staff away day that the structure of the organisation would be reviewed. This involved a great deal of consultation with staff, partners, and stakeholders. The restructuring announcement was delayed until August 2006. The KM directorate would now be named "strategy" and the KW team would disband. Two KW teams called "organisational learning" and "information management" would now form part of a new directorate that would encompass other support functions in the business such as human resources (HR) and ICT. The subsuming of KM discourses under those of traditional line management suggests that PuSA's engagement with knowledge networking had proved too complex to manage, and that the Knowledge Network and Knowledge Working initiatives had failed to achieve legitimacy, hence the retrenchment to an earlier discursive regime, that of traditional lines of business.

## LEGITIMATION: HOW IS AUTHORITY ESTABLISHED?

In this section, we go over the ground a third time, to explore legitimation, corporate morality, and norms and sanctions. To understand these in the context of PuSA, we focus on perceived authority, performance measurement, and training issues. Legitimation issues are tightly coupled with signification and domination: The KAs did not know how to define their role and did not always know whose resource they were. Managers, attempting to secure the KA resource, enacted multiple and conflicting initiatives. Though the KAs were hired at Senior Executive level, there was little indication of the organizational norms with which they were meant to comply. Three of the KAs were not on the same salary grading although they were expected to undertake the same role. Like most of the KAs, they had little experience of KW (or KM). Out of the KA and KW team, when recruited, only two of the KAs had any formal KM education. This would be addressed through a training programme and the production of guidance notes on what the KA tools were and how to implement them.

Because of the fluid nature of the KA job, it was virtually impossible for KAs to identify a forward schedule of work, and hence, articulate the potential benefit the organization might derive from their interventions. Consequently, it was very difficult to attribute any direct value to KW. As we noted earlier, in August 2003, 10 months after the KAs were first introduced, a Change Manager was brought in to provide strategic direction for the KA role. In September 2003, expert groups were set up to provide KAs with the skills they needed to deliver KW. Each expert group was led by a member of the KW team, and monthly training ranged from reviewing how an intranet search was conducted at a meeting to shadowing at a community development workshop. More formal training included attending in-house core skills courses such as facilitation, presentation, and influencing skills. Other training included consultant-delivered workshops in consultancy skills and business analysis. In addition, portions of the monthly KA meetings were devoted to development. This included inviting people from different areas of the business to talk about their work and how they thought KW could help.

As we noted earlier, the version of knowledge working promoted in the 2003 Architecture Authority document included a generic vision of all PuSA employees as knowledge workers capable of "positive knowledge exchanges" (or relationships) with texts and people (PuSA, 2003b). The former refers to the contribution to, and re-use of material in, the "knowledge base." The latter refers to the building and maintaining of relationships with internal and external people in their capacity as individuals or members of groups or networks. This was important as PuSA wanted to manage its relationships to improve customer satisfaction to convince stakeholders, partners, and customers of the economic value the organization provided. This should have boosted the legitimacy of KAs, as they would instill the requisite knowledge capabilities such as skills, technology, tools, processes, behaviours, and attitudes to enable these relationships. By improving these knowledge capabilities, it was thought that knowledge workers would constitute an effective knowledge-based network that would "contribute directly to business results" (PuSA, 2003b). Staff were encouraged to think of themselves as a PuSA community rather than separate autonomous organizations. They were asked to engage in this community by sharing and absorbing knowledge. Although it was the individual knowledge worker's responsibility to improve their knowledge capabilities, the onus would lie on the KW team and KAs to facilitate this. To be seen as reinforcing an organizational norm would strengthen the KAs' position.

At a meeting in March 2004, the KAs were told their stakeholders were not happy with their progress. To improve their performance, they would receive intensive training for the first six months and were then expected to deliver locally. However, by this stage most of the KAs had not yet had the opportunity to practice or shadow on many of the tools, and several expressed concern that they were to act as experts on the basis of minimal training. Most of the KAs were not happy to hear that they were not considered to be "delivering" and not operating at a senior executive level. The Change Manager also issued a mild threat: If the KAs did not perform well, they could be downgraded to an executive level. The published notes for the meeting included a senior executive level job profile to remind the KAs of the level they were expected to operate on.

# Discussion and Conclusions

The analysis says more about instability than stability. The properties of the network (or system) that are the focal points of structuration in our study are volatile, shifting outcomes of a continuous dialectic movement between managers and groups. The cadre of KAs who were charged with the delivery of a knowledge network were thus unable to consolidate identity, resources, or authority that were specific to the group. From the start, identity was compromised by a portmanteau job description that allowed local managers to select attributes to construct idiosyncratic versions of the KA role that produced variations across geographical regions. The KA role, as the analysis shows, also varied over time. In two regional subsidiaries, individual KAs achieved a productive *modus operandi* by working purely at local level according to specific agreements with local line managers, but such individual accommodations could only compromise further the cohesion of the group.

The line managers in charge of KAs implicitly followed a (conventional) "project management" script. Identity from this perspective meant "being identified with" externally defined sets of tasks and technologies—tending the intranet, for example, or delivering pre-defined training. KAs found this construction of their roles to be demeaning as they were cast as *attachés*, or at best lieutenants—leadership was not within the scope of their responsibilities and power was exercised persistently elsewhere. The creation of the CoP provides an example—this was implemented as yet another vehicle for knowledge sharing (perceived as a technical genre) rather than a means to forge social cohesion and reinforce identity among KAs. The initiative to transform KAs into "experts" was yet another example—an expert was construed as "someone who has undergone training," not a knowledgeable authority informed by cumulative experience and reflection.

Our analysis also says more about ontological insecurity than security. Lyytinen and Ngwenyama (1992) describe the former as the ability to reflect on intentions and motivation. In the case of the KAs, we can see a great deal of reflection on their predicament, and their uncertainty about the intentions and motivation of others—the line managers and senior managers who issued directives and initiated tasks. These directives produced a patchwork of contractual conditions, reporting arrangements, task portfolios, and expertises. This resulted in a form of negative *esprit de corps*—a sardonic sharing of commiseration, an adaptive strategy that may be compared with the "ironic appropriation" described by Poole and De Sanctis (1990).

PuSA is not, however, a unique organization. The world of fractured authority, dispersed legitimacy, and volatile signification is typical of organizations that operate within large networked infrastructures—the mode that characterises current societal institutions (Giddens, 1990). The certainties of stand-alone systems development and project management do not obtain in this environment, nor do traditional notions of center and periphery, when authority and legitimacy are "leased" to outside experts. Volatility and uncertainty are detrimental at the local project level, the perspective of the KAs, and the primary vantage point of the field researcher in our study. But they are less so at a larger level of systemic organization—the vantage point of senior management throughout the period of the study: These were triggered by management exposure to the ideas of consultants in seminars and in the prevailing academic and commercial literature. Thrift (2005) in a recent anatomy of "knowing capitalism" describes a nexus of industrialists, academics, and consultants—the "cultural circuit of capital." The knowledge network is a typical product of this context, inspired by the discourse of the day, and enacted by instant "experts" who can be reabsorbed and redeployed in the next wave of transformation. The impetus that drives activity in such environments is not delivery, but vision.

Vann and Bowker (2006) provide an alternative description of this phenomenon: In a recent study of NSF agendas for e-science, they delineate the issues and challenges that face what they call "technology-bearing labor," one practice among several that constitute infrastructure, or the "production of IT for epistemic practice" (in this case, scientific knowledge). Commenting on the blurring of production, consumption, and design, they highlight the challenges posed by conflicts of "knowledge production practices" and identify the different interest groups that are involved. These include what Vann and Bowker call "communities of promise" (p. 73). In the context of our study, public sector agencies, these comprise the managers, vendors, and consultants who produce the "prospective texts" (pp. 90–91) that drive large-scale infrastructure initiatives. Vann and Bowker suggest that "Consumers' interest in a technology is organized through their relations of use with the technology, but technology-bearing labour's interest in the technology is organized by the investments of others in their effort to produce it" (p. 85). By focusing primarily on providing a platform for consumers, the Knowledge

Network managers at PuSA did not take account of the interests of their "technology-bearing labor"—the Knowledge Analysts.

Many of the contributions to Hine's (2006) monograph (where Vann and Bowker's chapter appears) are concerned with the challenges of aligning the different interest groups who constitute the very large infrastructures of e-science. As we suggest here, methods and insights from this domain can be applied to other sectors, where more comprehensive accounts of networked knowledge are needed, specifically accounts of the work of what may be called "infrastructure intermediaries" whose focus is the context of production.

*Author's note:* The fieldwork has been undertaken under conditions of confidentiality. The names of the organization and of some of the roles have been changed.

# REFERENCES

Bowers, John. (1994). The work to make the network work: Studying CSCW in action. In *Proceedings of the ACM Conference on Computer Supported Cooperative Work* (pp. 287–298). New York: ACM Press.

Bowker, Geoffrey. (2005). *Memory practices in the sciences.* Cambridge, MA: MIT Press.

Bresnen, Mike, Edelman, Linda, Newell, Sue, Scarborough, Harry, & Swan, Jacky. (2005). A community perspective on managing knowledge environments. In Peter Love, Patrick S. W. Fong, & Zahir Irani (Eds.), *Management of knowledge in project environments* (pp. 81–102). Oxford: Butterworth-Heinemann.

Carter, Chris, & Scarborough, Harry. (2001). Regimes of knowledge, stories of power: A treatise on knowledge management. *Creativity and Innovation Management, 10*(3): 210 ff.

Czarniawska, Barbara. (2004). On time, space and action nets. *Organization, 11*(6): 773–791.

Foucault, Michel. (1977). *Discipline and punish: The birth of the prison.* New York: Vintage Books.

Giddens, Anthony. (1984). *The constitution of society: Outline of a theory of structuration.* Cambridge, U.K.: Polity Press.

Giddens, Anthony. (1990). *The consequences of modernity.* Cambridge, U.K.: Polity Press.

Heracleous, Loizos. (2006). A tale of three discourses: The dominant, the strategic and the marginalized. *Journal of Management Studies, 43*(5): 1059–1087.

Heracleous, Loizos, & Hendry, John. (2000). Discourse and the study of organization: Toward a structurational perspective. *Human Relations, 53*(10): 1251–1286.

Hine, Christine. (2006). *New infrastructures for knowledge production: Understanding e-science.* Hershey, PA: Information Science Publishing.

Love, Peter, Fong, Patrick S. W., & Irani, Zahir. (2005). *Management of knowledge in project environments.* Oxford, U.K.: Butterworth-Heinemann.

Lyytinen, Kalle J., & Ngwenyama, Ojelanki K. (1992). What does computer support for cooperative work mean? A structurational analysis of computer supported cooperative work. *Accounting, Management and Information Technologies*, *2*(1): 19–38.

Newell, Sue, & Huang, Jimmy. (2005). Knowledge integration processes and dynamics within the context of cross-functional projects. In Peter Love, Patrick S. W. Fong, & Zahir Irani (Eds.), *Management of knowledge in project environments* (pp. 19–40). Oxford, U.K.: Butterworth-Heinemann.

Poole, Marshall Scott, & De Sanctis, Geraldine. (1990). Understanding the use of group decision support systems: The theory of adaptive structuration. In Janet Fulk & Charles Steinfield (Eds.), *Organizations and communication technology* (pp. 173–193). Newbury Park, CA: Sage.

PuSA. (1999). NT foundation workshop presentation. Internal document.

PuSA. (2003a). How KM is applied at PuSA. Internal document.

PuSA. (2003b). Knowledge architecture. Internal document.

PuSA. (2003c). KW strategy. Internal document.

PuSA. (2004). What is KW? Internal document.

PuSA. (2005). KW survey recommendations. Internal document.

Rasmussen, Louise, Davenport, Elisabeth, & and Horton, Keith. (2006). Initiating (e-)participation through a knowledge working network. In Reima Suomi, Regis Cabral, J. Felix Hampe, Eija Koskivaara, and Jonna Järveläinen (Eds.), *Project e-society: Building bricks. 6th IFIP International Conference on e-commerce, e-business and e-government* (I3E 2006) (pp. 96–108), October 11–13, 2006, Turku, Finland. New York: Springer.

Schultze, U., & Leidner, D. (2002). Studying KM in information systems research: Discourses and theoretical assumptions. *MIS Quarterly*, *20*(3): 213–242.

Schultze, U., & Stabell, C. (2004). Knowing what you don't know? Discourses and contradictions in KM research. *Journal of Management Studies*, *41*(4): 449–573.

Suchman, Lucy. (1996). Supporting articulation work. In Rob Kling (Ed.), *Computerization and controversy: Value conflicts and social choices* (pp. 407–423). San Diego, CA: Academic Press.

Star, Susan Leigh, & Ruhleder, Karen. (1996). Steps towards an ecology of infrastructure: Design and access for large information spaces. *Information Systems Research*, *7*(1): 111–134.

Thrift, Nigel. (2005). *Knowing capitalism*. Oxford: Oxford University Press.

Vann, Katie, & Bowker, Geoffrey. (2006). Interest in production: On the configuration of technology-bearing Labor's for epistemic IT. In Christine Hine (Ed.), *New infrastructures for knowledge production: Understanding e-science* (pp. 71–97). Hershey, PA: Information Science Publishing,

Willcocks, Leslie P. (2006). Michel Foucault in the social study of ICTs: Critique and reappraisal. Department of Information Systems Working Paper Series, 138. London: London School of Economics and Political Science.

# CHAPTER 26

# Knowledge Management in the Federal Sector: A Review and Critique

Roland G. Droitsch

KM21 Associates

## INTRODUCTION

The recent growth in the field of knowledge management (KM) in both the federal and private sectors had its roots in the explosion of information made possible by the advent of the Internet.[1] During the early 1990s, the increased availability of the personal computer, coupled with advances in telecommunications, provided the framework for "file sharing," first among research institutions and followed by other public and private organizations. These efforts provided the building blocks of the World Wide Web, which led to the massive explosion of information sharing via the Internet in the latter half of the decade. It was during this period that most federal departments and agencies established Web sites. The period had an element of the "Wild West" to it, in that mounting such Web sites tended to be unstructured efforts. Agencies within a federal department mounted their own Web sites, often independent of any unified structure or guidance from senior departmental management. While departments typically had an official "home page," there often were no defined relationships between a department's home page and the many individual sites that were springing up among its agencies. Frequently, the departmental page listed these agency sites as links on the home page, but many departments still failed to have an overall design or a set of centralized standards that agencies had to follow.[2]

This problem of a free-for-all approach to mounting Internet sites was compounded by the unstructured procurement of hardware and software. Agencies within a department were using various servers with differing Internet software, browsers, and security protocols. Some servers were operated by the agency itself mounting a site, others piggybacked on servers in sister agencies, while still others outsourced their systems to Internet vendors. There was simply no unified approach to dealing with this new and dramatically growing technology. If there was a central computer "authority" in a department, it typically was the old established office that had the authority to operate that department's mainframe systems. But, with the advent of the widespread use of the personal computer (PC) and microprocessor, any unified overall information technology (IT) governance had vanished.

The private sector in many ways was experiencing a similar situation. It too had its traditional mainframe computer operations under the control of a defined organizational structure. It too was facing an explosion in the use of PCs and microprocessors, generally operating without any defined management structure. This desktop computing revolution typically was not the purview of a company's mainframe computer department. Most companies' computer staff had seen the growth of PCs as extensions of the typewriter and desk calculator, primarily used as word processors and spreadsheet tools. But with the advent of the Internet, the situation changed dramatically. Private sector companies, like the federal government, faced a rapidly growing investment in IT infrastructure led by the dramatic increase in personal computers and the growing use of the Internet. As with the federal sector, different units of a company were purchasing systems that were increasingly expensive and incompatible, and that posed security concerns for upper management. These concerns ultimately led to the establishment of the new senior level management official, a Chief Information Officer or CIO, whose mandate was to bring order into this new and otherwise disorganized world. His or her job was to bring under one umbrella a company's policies and practices with respect to all computer operations, including the investment in and use of personal computers and microprocessors. Ensuring hardware and software compatibility, eliminating redundant systems, establishing improved security systems, and providing for the professional development of the IT staffs became the primary functions of these CIOs. Companies generally standardized their word processing to one software application (i.e. Word or Word Perfect). The type and configuration of PCs were also typically standardized, with the IBM models being largely preferred to Macs in the corporate world. Unlike federal agencies, companies typically mounted a single corporate Web site, often developed by a contractor, focused on that company's business operations. Freelancing in the mounting of Web sites, as happened so often in the federal sector, was generally prohibited or discouraged.

The federal sector, facing many of the same problems as the private sector, began to follow the private sector's approach to addressing the situation. The growth in the use of personal computers operating outside of any organizing structure, their rising costs, and the lack of compatibility of these investments led to debate in Congress as to how best to address these problems. Drawing on the experience of the private sector, Congress in 1996 passed the Information Technology Management Reform Act. Better known as the Clinger-Cohen Act, this Act required the Office of Management and Budget (OMB) to establish an IT capital planning process throughout the federal government. Under guidance from OMB, all federal agencies were required to develop performance-based systems for the acquisition and management of their information technology investments. Specifically, the Clinger-Cohen Act required agencies to plan major investments, develop and use standards, develop enterprise architectures, address security concerns, and provide for professional staff development.[3] Again, drawing on private sector experience, one of the most critical aspects of the Act was to establish CIOs in each of the federal departments and major agencies. These CIOs were high-level positions, which were required to report directly to the secretary of a department or the head of an agency.

In reviewing the original purposes of the Act, it is clear that getting ahold of the spiraling costs of IT expenditures was foremost on the minds of its authors. The Act specifically required agencies to obtain a 5 percent reduction in IT expenditures in each of the coming five years starting in 1996. In addition, agencies were also required to achieve a 5 percent increase in efficiency in each of those five years. It is important to note that the duties outlined for the CIO did not in any way explicitly deal with issues related to the management of *information content* in the operation of these systems. Information content, it was assumed, would be the domain of the operating or program agencies using these new information technology tools.

## AN EMERGING DIVERGENCE

For a while it appeared that both the private and federal sectors were following similar paths with respect to channeling new and evolving information technologies. Both had come to the conclusion that some structure was needed to ensure that IT investments were undertaken within a defined "enterprise architecture." However, with respect to dealing with content-related issues, the two sectors began to diverge in certain ways. This became most evident with respect to how these two sectors handled the establishment of their Web sites and the information that was mounted on them. The federal sector agencies typically saw their Web sites as a new "add on" that departments and agencies had to mount as a matter of course. Generally, such federal sites were run by the IT staffs that relied on various program agencies for content to mount. As familiarity of the tool grew within a department, senior management typically might have directed the agency's Web staff to mount certain documents and information about new programmatic initiatives. What emerged was a group of IT Web staff who had the responsibility for maintaining the department's Web site. They were not integrated into program operations and were not seen as essential drivers in improving agency operations or performance. This separation built a wall between the program staffs and the operators of an agency's Web presence and limited the potential uses and benefits of the Web to a program's operations. Unless some informal relationships bridged the gap between agency programs and their Web operations, the potential power and benefits of this new Internet tool was lost.

The private sector, on the other hand, had begun to see the potential of Web sites and the Internet as a business-enhancing tool relatively quickly. It could be used to promote awareness about the company and its services. The Web's use as a means of making sales directly with customers began to be recognized. Fueled by such profit-maximizing behavior, and drawing upon the new and rapidly growing KM field, companies focused on Web *content*. They sought to use a growing set of tools such as intranets, content management systems, data mining, and e-learning systems. These and other uses emerging from new business applications, consulting practices, and academic research led the private sector to focus increasingly on content issues as opposed to only on hardware and software. Rather than simply looking for information to mount, the private sector began to ask what information they should upload to the Web site and how they could better use the information obtained from customers using this new tool.

The greatly expanded use of the Web and other content-oriented tools by the private sector led it to explore better ways to manage these operations. With corporate CIOs heavily focused on the fundamental hardware and software questions of compatibility, interoperability, and security, recognition grew in the private sector of the need for someone other than the CIO to focus primarily on content related issues.[4] Out of these deliberations came the introduction of a Chief Knowledge Management Officer (CKO) into private sector management structures. By 2000, approximately 20 percent of the Fortune 500 companies had established such positions and more than 70 percent of these companies had mounted knowledge programs.[5]

In the federal government, a number of important factors were at work during the latter half of the 1990s to place KM on a very different trajectory. First, and probably most significant, was the need to *implement* the Clinger-Cohen Act, which included many new complex requirements.[6] Federal agencies had to establish new offices, and hire CIOs and identify appropriate staffs. Unlike a private corporation, establishing such a new unit, identifying leadership, and recruiting staff was a major undertaking. Making the exercise more complex was the broad scope of the CIO's new authority, one that required the transfer of IT staff and resources from operating agencies and centralizing them under the CIO. Agencies, which up until that point had exercised control over much of their own IT operations, were not happy with the decision to centralize such authority, and in many cases did not willingly do so. Added to this was the host of new requirements under the Clinger-Cohen Act, which mandated that agencies submit spending proposals to this central CIO authority, which in turn was required to submit them to OMB for approval. Ultimately, undoubtedly as an unintended consequence, implementation of the Act involved the hiring of an army of consultants needed to fill out the reams of newly mandated documentation. The cost of hiring such consultants placed a substantial fiscal burden on top of the earlier noted Clinger-Cohen requirement to make annual budget cuts of 5 percent in their IT investments. Together, they cut deeply into the funds available to purchase needed IT equipment and services.

While struggling to implement the Clinger-Cohen requirements, another event loomed on the horizon that further shaped the nature of the federal CIO structure and the direction of federal IT management. The event was the potential impact of the coming millennium turnover to the year 2000, more commonly known as Y2K. There was widespread concern that the internal clocks of computers could only count to the year 1999, whereby the change to 2000 might lead to widespread system crashes. Fears were raised as to the federal government's ability to deal with the Y2K issue. This issue was at that time one of indeterminate scope and magnitude. OMB, acting through the newly established CIO Council, put forth a major effort whereby each federal agency had to inventory their IT systems and grade them as to their mission importance. Mission critical systems had to undergo a careful review to assure OMB that they could transition to the year

2000 without operational problems arising from any internal programming. Again, the energy and resources devoted to these efforts were substantial. And once again, there was heavy use of contracting staffs, the costs of which cut significantly into agency IT budgets. The Y2K exercise, on top of the basic implementation of Clinger-Cohen, resulted in the further concentration of power into the new CIO organizations. Agency IT staffs chafed under this constant transfer of authority and resources, but could do little in the face of the unfunded, legally mandated or OMB requirements. With the focus of these centralizing operations aimed primarily on hardware and software usage, content-related issues continued to take a backseat in the CIO's operational priorities.

The transition to Y2K went much more smoothly than expected, leading to some speculation that many of the efforts undertaken were unnecessary. However, no sooner had federal agencies been given some breathing space when the country was struck by the 9/11 catastrophe. Federal agencies reeled at the impact, uncertain as to how to address the then unknown problems that might emerge from such terrorist activities. What clearly emerged from the event, however, was the need for the federal IT community to significantly focus on tightening IT security. Once again, the role of the CIO was thrust into the fore to address this issue under the guidance of OMB.

# Early Knowledge Management Efforts in the Federal Sector

Although the establishment and growing power of CIOs was the predominant feature of federal sector IT management, there was growing interest among some federal agencies on the topic of KM. Just as the private sector and academia had provided leadership in establishing CIOs, they had taken the lead in this new and emerging field of KM. A number of individuals throughout the government were interested in adopting these new KM techniques in their departments or agencies. The problem they encountered, however, was that KM activities or investments fell squarely under the control of the CIO per the Clinger-Cohen Act. The combination of the increasingly widespread use of KM in the private sector and pressure from early adopters within agencies, though, led the CIO Council in March 2000 to establish the Knowledge Management Working Group (KMWG). The KMWG operated under the sponsorship of the CIO Council's Enterprise, Interoperability and Emerging Technologies Committee. The Working Group was to consist of several special interest groups (SIGs) including training, best practices, CKO competencies, and communities of practice. Membership, however, was to be constituted of a subset of CIO Council Members or others designated by the Council. Thus, first and foremost, the KMWG was a creature of the CIO Council and entirely beholden to it. This was a sharp departure from the private sector model, which was in the process of establishing CKOs working *with* but *independent of* a company's CIO.

Private CKOs typically had their own mandates and operating authority, and generally possessed different skill sets than the more traditionally IT-oriented CIOs. KM in the private sector emerged from a conglomeration of their staffs working with IT products, consultants, academics, and especially from their Web site itself. KM, thus, was transplanted into company operations as a tool set to address specific problems related to a business's operations.[7] The domain of KM involved such areas as organizational learning, building knowledge within an organization, and capturing value from knowledge assets, among others. These topics were significantly different from the traditional activities and training of a CIO, whether in the private or public sectors. The unfortunate circumstance of subordinating KM activities under the CIO in the federal sector was that the innovations that were emerging from the private and academic sectors were not being adopted by the federal sector. With a few exceptions, the CIO Council saw the KMWG simply as another operational task that was somehow related to its primary IT operations. In short, KM was not recognized as a separate (but related) domain that focused primarily on maximizing knowledge within an organization and applying it in a manner that would accomplish greater organizational efficiency.

With the establishment of the federal KMWG, the members, nevertheless, sought to establish a presence. A Web site was mounted that included links to some of the major areas of inquiry that the group planned to explore, including Communities of Practice, Education, Learning and Development, Taxonomies, Semantic Interoperability, Knowledge Retention, and KM Technology Community. Operational aids were put into place, such as a reference center, a calendar of events, and a listing of past events.[8] A number of federal departments developed KM programs as part of this early wave of enthusiasm. The Department of the Navy probably had the most articulated effort.[9] Significant efforts to build a structure of KM tools could also be found at the U.S. Department of Labor. This included an integrated department-wide Web design, a call center, expert systems, and a powerful e-learning authoring tool.[10] These efforts, however, were undertaken by "change agents" in the background who were able to convince upper management to devote resources to such KM initiatives. They did not emanate from guidance issued by OMB or the KMWG. Not having an official or statutory mandate, these agency efforts tended to fall by the wayside as these proponents of KM departed and other priorities forced themselves onto center stage.

A recent review of KM initiatives undertaken at the Department of Education is illustrative of the current state of KM in federal departments.[11] While the review lists a number of activities, such as the establishment of its ConnectED Intranet site and developing a "What Works Clearinghouse," the memorandum notes that, "The Department has not, however, created an inventory of employee skills or otherwise developed tools specifically designed to help share knowledge or document 'how things work' in the Department."[12] The memorandum essentially lists a series of activities that have KM aspects (such as e-learning, communities of practice, and document management systems), which are self-standing and not integrated into any organizational KM strategy. In sum, the review pointed to a collection of KM-related efforts that have little structure and certainly are not part of any systematic agency plan.

The KMWG itself, despite its charter from the CIO Council, also never gained any traction. Without a mandate, the KMWG essentially devolved into an informal group that came together from time to time to discuss issues related to KM. This limited interaction did not permit the group to move much beyond the discussion phase to bring proposed KM initiatives into operation. Viewing the official federal government KM site at the time this chapter was written, one finds that the last update to the Community of Practice page was made in March 2004. The site dealing with "References" was last updated on April 11, 2002. There is almost no information supplied under the Education, Learning and Development, Taxonomies, and the KM Technical Community sites. Opening the Semantic Interoperability site diverts you to an entry on this topic in Wikipedia.

# E-Government: A Federal Sector Substitute for KM?

The question may appropriately be asked if the federal government was involved in any broad-based KM efforts. The answer to this question is probably a highly qualified "yes." In July 2001, under the direction of OMB, the federal government launched its "Quicksilver" initiative, Citizen Centered E-Government. The initiative was "to enable citizens to expect the same level of IT quality from their government that the private sector provides its customers."[13] The initiative acknowledged that the private sector had *outstripped* the federal government in organizing and providing IT services to its customers. What it did not acknowledge was the route taken by the private sector.

As discussed earlier, the private sector grasped the Web because it was useful in marketing and selling products and services and it became a strategic tool for branding. To that end, it had employed a far wider spectrum of personnel and talent in identifying and building *customer-oriented* systems. As noted earlier, the more forward-looking private sector companies had identified the need to establish the position of a CKO who took the lead in implementing such customer-based initiatives. These CKOs and their staffs possessed different skill sets than the CIOs with their traditional IT-oriented staffs. The questions as to how best to serve customers required having good information on their wants and needs, questions ready-made for content-oriented KM practitioners.

In contrast, the federal government approached its Quicksilver initiative in a completely different manner. OMB led the effort and approached the task by establishing an interagency task force. The task force conducted interviews and sought advice from outside parties as to which projects should be undertaken. Of the initial 269 projects identified, 24 were eventually chosen.[14] OMB arbitrarily selected agencies to lead these projects often based more on political considerations than on an agency's specific knowledge and experience in the area. For example, the extensive IRS e-learning project that was well underway in terms of development was not utilized as a framework for e-learning. Rather, the Quicksilver e-learning project was initially given to the Department of Transportation![15] The projects were identified as belonging to four classifications: government to individual citizens, government to businesses, government to government, and lastly those that sought to improve internal efficiency and effectiveness.[16] Rather than identifying end-users and then working with personnel who possessed expertise in how best to organize and deliver the information, OMB appeared to see the initiative primarily as a cost saving, IT-efficiency initiative. The focus was on developing single systems that eliminated "redundancies" and organizing government-wide approaches to delivering e-government services that would produce cost savings.

The Quicksilver projects could be categorized into three distinct groups. First, a number of the projects simply consolidated an activity performed by many agencies into a single e-government-wide approach with the idea of garnering significant efficiencies through standardization and economies of scale. Among these projects, all involving Web-based solutions, were a unified federal payroll system (e-payroll), a government-wide travel system (e-travel), and a system of maintaining vital records such as births, deaths, and so forth (e-vital).[17] It would be difficult to classify such projects as experiments in KM since they presented no unique KM issues. Ultimately, it would also be very hard to show any net savings or efficiencies from such project or agency consolidations due to legacy and incompatible systems, infrastructures, software, and databases. If anything, there was a loss of knowledge in these consolidations as agency-specific information was lost in the process.

A second set of projects coordinated the co-location of information and provided such information to citizens, businesses, or government agencies. Again, these projects involved Web-based solutions that included providing information for businesses on how to comply with regulations (One-Stop Business Compliance Information), information to citizens about government benefits to which they were entitled (GovBenefits/Eligibility Assistance Online), development of a system of information regarding the availability of federal grants (e-Grants), and information regarding recreational activities (Recreation One-Stop). These projects involved a modest amount of structuring and ordering, along with building a tool set to assist the customer in obtaining the information sought. As such, they could be regarded as having some elements of KM utilized in their development, because some understanding of the interests of the intended customers was required in organizing the information.

Finally, there were several projects that could be said to involve a moderate amount of KM-related design and implementation. These included building an overall portal for obtaining information on federal government information, the FirstGov initiative. Also under this category was a government-wide e-learning portal, through which all government-training programs were to be run (GoLearn). Somewhat more complex was the construction of a portal providing information on ongoing federal rule-makings (Online Rulemaking Management). This portal also allowed citizens and institutions to respond to proposed rulemaking with their comments. These comments would need to be housed in an official "docket" requiring that a number of important legal considerations be followed.

The implementation of the Quicksilver projects offered the federal government an excellent opportunity to apply advanced KM techniques. Rather than simply compiling existing agency information, for example, overall knowledge frameworks might have been developed that would actively organize information through the use of ontologies or metadata. The information could then be verified; missing information could be identified and organized so as to deliver it to various customer groups in ways meaningful to them. Such systems, thus, would *build knowledge* rather than merely *distribute information*. For example, building the e-Training portal could have provided the framework for establishing federal agencies as learning organizations rather than merely providing a tool for delivering ad hoc course offerings. While not dismissing the efforts that were undertaken under the Quicksilver projects, the opportunity for building robust knowledge delivery systems and establishing knowledge organizations was missed. Nowhere is this aspect more clearly demonstrated than in OMB's recent efforts to measure the success of the Quicksilver projects. To this end, OMB asked agencies to focus on three areas: customer satisfaction, adoption, and participation.[18] Approached from a KM perspective, OMB might have asked agencies to query, "Was the information accurate with outdated information removed?" "Was the information complete, and, if not, what efforts were underway to provide such missing information?" "Was the information organized in ways useful for various customer groups?"

The missed opportunity by the Executive Branch to integrate KM into federal e-government implementation was mirrored by the Congress. It was during OMB's launch of its Quicksilver initiative that the E-Government Act was introduced in both the House and Senate. This Act could have established a more balanced approach to federal e-government activities by mandating a role for KM along with traditional CIO requirements. Unfortunately, as enacted, the unfunded E-Government Act missed an important opportunity to introduce appropriate KM requirements into federal government IT operations. It failed to understand that e-government was ultimately an area that dealt with the *content side* of IT and organizing such information in ways to build knowledge. Instead, it saw e-government as merely an extension of the role of traditional CIO-related activities.

The Act not only sought to codify the activities launched under Quicksilver, but identified a host of new requirements, including the establishment of the Office of Electronic Government, and statutorily establishing the CIO Council. The proposed Act directed the OMB Administrator of the Office of Electronic Government to (1) provide overall leadership and direction to the executive branch on e-government, (2) promote innovative uses of IT by agencies, (3) oversee the distribution of funds from and assure the appropriate administration of an e-government fund, (4) promote e-government and the efficient use of information technologies by agencies, and (5) assist the CIO Council in establishing policies to set the framework for government IT standards.[19] The E-Government Act gave OMB and the CIO Council even more sweeping powers with respect to every aspect of federal government IT activities. Through its Title II, "The Federal Management and Promotion of Electronic Government," the Act lists numerous requirements that federal agencies were to undertake to provide information to the public, virtually codifying and expanding the Quicksilver projects. The Act was signed into law in December 2002. The document is replete with references to interoperability, interconnectivity, and integrated Internet-based systems. It calls for developing "standards" for categorizing and indexing government information and "standards" for agency Web sites. The Act underscores that these requirements were to be accomplished through the direction and control of CIOs, not through the application of KM-based activities.[20]

The failure of the E-Government Act to incorporate a role for KM was a significant missed opportunity that also has had lasting implications on federal IT operations. The Quicksilver projects simply were OMB driven projects using agency CIOs to provide the basic management structure. OMB chose agencies to lead specific projects, defined time lines, and identified potential resources. The CIOs used traditional IT management techniques like wrapping each project into its enterprise architecture requirements, building a business case model, calculating the return on investment, and so forth. While the Quicksilver project's overall goal was to improve the way in which the federal government provides information and services to citizens, businesses, and other governments, OMB clearly saw the projects as a way to improve *efficiency* and provide *cost savings*. Many agencies were forced to give back "savings" claimed from earlier year's estimates that never materialized, resulting in terrible cutbacks that curtailed basic IT services to business units. Even when savings did result, agencies were rarely allowed to plow savings back into future projects that would continue to benefit the agencies. Successful projects were thus never rewarded. Kim Nelson, the former CIO of the Environmental Protection Agency noted that OMB "places the heavy emphasis on cost savings to the point where you are setting up expectations that every e-government initiative will save money. That is not always the case. One more important component is better serving the citizens."[21]

The Quicksilver projects became embedded in the President's Management Agenda (PMA) with the stated purpose of improving the effectiveness of federal

IT systems; however, cost savings remained foremost in OMB's PMA planning.[22] The failure to integrate KM into the Quicksilver initiatives set the course for federal e-government activities. The dominant feature of any IT project was to ensure that it fit into an overall Enterprise Architecture that was defined and structured by OMB and agency CIOs. This left little or no room for developing information architectures as might be defined by KM practitioners. Indeed, under the current dominance of the CIO structure and control, it is harder and harder to find clear KM initiatives that support agency programs and activities. Like the official KMWG site, KM activities in the federal sector appears have withered on the vine.

## SOME SURPRISING FEDERAL KM INITIATIVES

Although KM is not an established practice in most agencies of the federal government, a paradox exists in that some federal agencies are providing leadership and funding to a number of important KM initiatives. For example, the Department of Defense (DoD) is continuing to provide leadership in its Advanced Distributed Learning (ADL) initiative, an effort that dates back to the Clinton presidency.[23] In October 2006, the ADL released the latest version of its Shareable Content Object Reference Model (SCORM), a collection of standards for the development of e-learning content and software. The SCORM specification is divided into several subject matter areas—the Content Aggregation Model, the Sequencing and Navigation Model, and the Run-Time Environment Model—which are rapidly becoming worldwide accepted standards for the construction and delivery of e-learning.[24]

While working on improved versions of the SCORM, the ADL Co-Laboratory is working on a number of other important KM activities. For example, the ADL has developed a number of Intelligent Tutoring Systems (ITS), which "seek to mimic the methods and dialogue of natural human tutors, to generate instructional interactions in real time and on demand—as required by individual students."[25] ITS functionality include everything that a human teacher might do, such as select appropriate material, set up exercises, monitor student activity, and provide feedback to students.

The ADL Co-Lab has also done extensive work on digital repositories. Specifically, it is developing a Content Object Repository Discovery and Registration Architecture (CORDRA). As a near-term goal, it is building a registry for the DoD, which will include all the services at DoD under a single ADL Registry.[26]

The central Co-Laboratory, which is responsible for developing the SCORM standard, has spawned a network of sister Co-Labs both in the U.S. and abroad, including Canada, Great Britain, and Australia. In February 2007 an agreement was signed with South Korea making it the fourth country to establish an ADL Co-Lab.[27] Agreements have also been signed with Japan, Taipei, and a consortium of 13 Latin American countries. The U.S. DoD issued its instruction, 1322.26, which now mandates all DoD agencies to require SCORM conformance for all new training contracts. What is surprising in the face of this growing worldwide acceptance of this powerful KM tool is that most federal agencies have all but ignored it. The Department of Labor, one of the original partners of the original Co-Lab, has dropped out altogether despite its important role in workforce development and training. Likewise, the Department of Education appears to have no interest in adopting or promoting the SCORM specification despite its stated interest in promoting e-learning technologies.

Another major KM tool that was initiated under the federal government's leadership is the "Handle System." The system is essentially a digital object architecture that provides a means of managing vast quantities of digital information in a network environment. Sponsorship for the initiative was provided by the Defense Advanced Research Projects Agency (DARPA), working through the Corporation for National Initiatives. A digital "object" can include all types of information including documents, movies, sound recording, etc. The objects, however, carry unique identifiers and other metadata providing information about the digital object. The Handle System, thus, allows for the organization of databases within thousands of networks, allowing one to search and uniquely identify specific objects. The System provides users with an extremely powerful tool to seek information and knowledge objects around the world from a vast array of sources. And, as new objects are developed and entered into the system, the knowledge base of the Handle System will expand.

Early adopters of the Handle System included the Library of Congress, the Defense Technical Information Center, and, most recently, the CrossRef service offered by the newly formed Publishers International Linking Association. The Handle System has evolved within the digital library and electronic publishing communities as part of the move from paper-centric to digital-centric systems. However, the System has potential applications beyond the digital library area and can be used in any dynamic network environment as part of the overall process for managing digital objects.[28]

The ADL initiative and the Handle System are two examples of important KM research and development activities under federal sector sponsorship. While others can be identified, it is important to stress that they are not in the mainstream of how the federal sector is addressing and using KM to achieve its organizational goals. In nearly all federal departments, information technology initiatives are defined and controlled by agency CIOs with the larger initiatives requiring the approval of OMB. Few KM initiatives appear to be allowed through a CIO's IT-oriented gate keeping process.

# CONCLUSION

An examination of the Quicksilver projects shows that some KM practices have been utilized in their development by the federal sector. But an overall comparison of the federal sector with the private sector and academia would find that the application of KM practices in the federal sector is very weak. The outstanding characteristic of the federal sector is the presence of a strong structure of CIOs, whose statutory authority is derived directly from the Clinger-Cohen and E-Government Acts. This structure is further reinforced by the institutional role and mandatory guidance issued by OMB, such as through the PMA. Since the initial efforts to promote KM in the federal sector were placed under the umbrella of the CIO Council, KM has not been able to develop the strong institutional practices found in the private sector. Federal CIOs' staffs are populated by personnel with expertise in traditional IT skills focusing on hardware and software competencies. They are comfortable dealing with those issues that gave rise to CIOs in the first place, namely, to ensure that hardware and software systems were compatible, interoperable, operating efficiently, and not duplicative. They are concerned about the *efficiency and structure of files and databases* rather than what *content* is in them and whether such content is complete and organized for effective use by those that need the information. By contrast, the private sector led the introduction of CIOs into their organizations but also followed by incorporating KM personnel into their IT activities. The KM personnel have brought broad ranges of skills to their organizations including content management, expertise in building knowledge repositories, library science, implementing organizational learning, and so on.[29]

Driven by a series of events regarding the recent and urgent concerns with respect to security, CIOs in the federal sector have unprecedented power in the area of IT, including the application of and the investment in KM. Armed with the mandates and encouragement of OMB, agency CIOs have established vast paperwork requirements for all existing and new IT investments. Using an Enterprise Architecture approach for all such investments, a program office must produce reams of justification in order to demonstrate that any new investment fits tightly into the overall IT architecture. While it is difficult not to argue that an enterprise or federal agency should have compatible IT systems, the problem that emerges for KM is that it, too, is seen as being within the domain of the CIO. KM "architecture" is not easily defined by traditional criteria used in traditional enterprise architectures for IT hardware and software decisions. Further, it is especially problematic when the CIOs' IT-trained staffs are reviewing projects and have little or no understanding of KM practices or issues. If this understanding abounded within the CIO structure, one would find a rapid embracing of technologies such as the Handle System and the ADL initiative. To be sure, some KM practices are seeping into federal sector usage as advances in academia and the private sector make new systems available through commercial sales. However, such purchases are carefully scrutinized by the federal CIO structure, and frequently rejected as not fitting into the agency's enterprise architecture.

Operationally, it is still some of the successors of the E-Government or Quicksilver projects that come closest to defining KM activities in the federal sector. Although their focus is still on consolidation and garnering efficiencies, projects such as the FirstGov government-wide information portal (soon to be renamed as USA.gov) have had to come to grips with such issues as how to organize information on their Web sites and how to structure efficient search routines. It is within these projects where content-related issues must be addressed and where elements of KM have necessarily been applied. A much better solution would be to free KM from the CIO structure. As the private sector and the academic literature have found, IT and KM can live apart in harmony, but achieve organizational goals better when pursued together. Given that the structure of CIO activities is now deeply rooted in statutory foundations, and barring any new legislation addressing KM in the federal sector, any fundamental changes must come from the CIOs themselves. A first step would be the recognition of the importance of adopting KM practices in their departments and agencies.

# ENDNOTES

1.  The roots of KM itself date back much earlier to work done in various fields, for example, Artificial Intelligence and Rational Database Management Systems for explicit knowledge, Human Resources Management for tacit knowledge, and TQM for social knowledge.

2.  The author was responsible for mounting the Department of Labor's home page and working with the various agencies within the Department to mount their sub-sites. In querying other departments at that time, he found that no department had utilized a framework to structure or organize the information on its Web site. The closest "structured" approach came from those departments that had hired a contractor to mount a site that reflected activities in all its agencies, the Department of Housing and Urban Development being one such example.

3.  See Wikipedia entry for Information Technology Reform Act.

4.  Evidence for this growing interest in KM can be found in Michael E. D. Koenig, "KM: The Forest for All the Trees," *KM World* (April, 2006, pp. 1, 30). In the article, Dr. Koenig describes the growth of papers published on KM and their steep increase beginning in 1996. One needs only to survey the wide variety of articles in sources such as *KM World* to see how wide-ranging and fertile this new discipline has become.

5.  Barquin, R. C. (2000, May). *Knowledge Management in the Public Sector*, 1(12). Copyright 2000 by Management Concepts, Inc. See also discussion of The Emergence of KM in the Corporate Sector, Roland G. Droitsch, "Knowledge Management at the U.S. Department of Labor: A Case Study of Implementing Knowledge Management," in M. Koenig and T. Srikantaiah (Eds.), (2004), *Knowledge Management Lessons Learned* (pp. 333–334). Medford, NJ: Information Today, Inc.

6.  A number of federal departments and agencies had established CIO positions prior to Clinger-Cohen, but few had given these positions the prominence and the sweeping authority that Clinger-Cohen provided.

7.  See Leonard J. Ponzi, "Knowledge Management: Birth of a Discipline," in M. Koenig and T Srikantaiah (Eds.), (2004), *Knowledge Management Lessons Learned*. Medford, NJ: Information Today, Inc.

8.  The Education, Learning and Development SIG, for example, did a considerable amount of work on competency modeling, which included developing matrices that mapped training courses and competencies.

9.  See Alex Bennet, "Alive with the Fire of Shared Understanding: Implementing Knowledge Management in the Department of the Navy," in M. Koenig and T. Srikantaiah (Eds.), (2004), *Knowledge Management Lessons Learned* (pp. 279–292). Medford, NJ: Information Today, Inc.

10. See Roland G. Droitsch, "Knowledge Management at the U.S. Department of Labor: A Case Study of Implementing Knowledge Management," in M. Koenig and T. Srikantaiah (Eds.), (2004), *Knowledge Management Lessons Learned* (pp. 331–335). Medford, NJ: Information Today, Inc.

11. U.S. Department of Education, Office of the Inspector General, Memorandum from Cathy H. Lewis, Assistant Inspector General to Philip Maestri, Director, Management Improvement Team, "Review of the Department's Knowledge Management Initiatives and Best Practices from Other Federal Agencies (ED/OIG113E0022)," January 12, 2005.

12. Ibid., p. 2.

13. Daniels, Jr. Mitchell, "Citizen-Centered E-Government: Developing the Action Plan," (2002), www.whitehouse.gov.omb/memorandum/m01-28.html

14. An additional area was added later, the Department of Health and Human Services' project on Health Informatics, bringing the initial round to 25. Later, other projects were added as part of the President's Management Agenda.

15. Efforts by the Department of Transportation to completely centralize federal e-learning utilizing a single portal failed and OPM, which had campaigned strongly to be given the lead role, was subsequently given the lead. Rather than continue to seek a centralization of e-learning, OPM ran a competition to certify a limited number of vendors from which federal agencies were required to chose. Apparently, no consideration was ever given to the Department of Defense with its widely regarded Advanced Distributed Learning initiative.

16. See GAO, *Report to the Committee on Governmental Affairs*, "Electronic Government: Selection and Implementation of the Office of Management and Budget's 24 Initiatives," GAO-03-229 (November, 2002).

17. The author recognizes that KM involves a far broader spectrum of activities than those revolving around the Web and does not wish to give the impression of an equivalency between KM and the Web. However, federal KM-related activities focused almost entirely around Web-related projects as evidenced by the Quicksilver initiative.

18. Jason Miller, (2007), "OMB, Agencies Establish Consistent Ways to Gage Citizen Impact," *Government Computing News*, January 8.

19. See Library of Congress, *Thomas*, House Reports 107–787, "Summary of HR 2458 as passed 11/15/2002."

20. See Government Printing Office, *Public Law No. 197-347* (December 2002).

21. See Rob Thormeyer and Jason Miller, "The Test of E-gov: Efficiency and Effectiveness," *Government Computer News*, April 21, 2006.

22. See Office of Management and Budget, "Implementing the President's Management Agenda of E-Government," April, 2003. www.thefdp.org/EGov_Strategy_2003.pdf

23. For a discussion on ADL, see Roland G. Droitsch, "Knowledge Management at the U.S. Department of Labor: A Case Study of Implementing Knowledge Management," in M. Koenig and T. Srikantaiah (Eds.), (2004), *Knowledge Management Lessons Learned* (pp. 344–347). Medford, NJ: Information Today, Inc.

24. See www.adlnet.gov/news/articles/380.cfm for a discussion of the SCORM standard and the Advanced Distributed Learning initiative.

25. See www.adlnet.gov/technologies/Tutoring/index.cfm for a discussion and additional information.

26. See www.adlnet.gov/technologies/CORDRA/indes/cfm and also www.adlnet.gov/technologies/Repositories/index.cfm for further discussions on these topics.

27.    ADLNET.gov Newsletter, February 2007.

28.    For a good overview, see Laurence Lannom, "Handle System Overview," paper delivered at the 66th International Federation of Library Associations and Institutions, Jerusalem, Israel (August, 2000).

29.    See Dr. Jay Liebowitz, (2000), *Building Organizational Intelligence: A Knowledge Management Primer*, CRC Press. This book provides insights into the rich diversity of skills and activities that emerged at a relatively early stage of organizations implementing KM practices. It also underscores how different KM activities are relative to traditional IT skills and practices.

# About the Contributors

## Patti Anklam

Patti Anklam is a consultant with Hutchinson Associates, providing expertise in collaboration practices, social network analysis, and KM systems strategy and architecture. She is a recognized leader in the field of organizational network analysis for knowledge management, and is a frequent speaker and writer on the topic. Before becoming an independent consultant, Anklam held key positions at Nortel Networks, where she was Director of Knowledge, Digital Equipment Corporation, and then Compaq Computer Corporation (now HP).

## Denise A. D. Bedford

Denise Bedford is a Senior Information Officer at the World Bank Group in Washington, D.C. Since 1997, her duties at the World Bank have included management of the World Bank Group's Thesaurus; development of the Bank's core metadata strategy and the various taxonomies that support Bank metadata; functional lead of the enterprise search project; member of the Knowledge and Learning Environment working group; project manager for the implementation of the Teragram concept extraction, categorization, and summarization technologies and automated metadata capture; and project manager for the development of the World Bank Catalog in support of the Bank's Policy on Information Disclosure. Her work also has included collaboration with UNESCO Water Portal and UNAIDS on metadata, thesaurus, and taxonomy issues. Her current interests include multilingual information architectures, semantic analysis technologies, computational linguistics, and knowledge economics.

Dr. Bedford is an associate of the faculty of Georgetown University and the University of Tennessee, and former adjunct faculty of Catholic University of America. She received a Ph.D. from University of California, Berkeley, in Information Sciences, an M.A. from University of Michigan in Russian History, an M.S. in Library Science from Western Michigan University, and a triple major B.A. from the University of Michigan in Russian Language, German Language, and Russian/East European History. Her experience prior to joining the World Bank Group includes: University of California Systemwide Administration, Stanford University, Intel Corporation, NASA, University of Michigan, University of Maryland, and University of Southern California. She is a past member of the Board of Trustees of the Dublin Core Metadata Initiative, a current member of the Networked Digital Library of Theses and Dissertations Board of Directors, a Senior Fellow at the Montague Institute, member of the Board of the Federal CIO Council's Knowledge Management Working Group, an expert speaker for the U.S. Department of State, and a participant in the Ontolog community of practice. She is a current member of ASIS&T, SLA, ACM, SCIP, and AAAI.

## Bob Boiko

Bob Boiko, founder and president of Metatorial Services Inc., is a faculty member of the University of Washington Information School. Recognized worldwide as a leader in the field of content management, he has almost 20 years of experience designing and building Web, hypertext, and multimedia systems and tools for some of the world's top technology corporations (including Microsoft, Motorola, and Boeing). Boiko has sat on many advisory boards and is the recipient of many awards including the 2005 *EContent* 100 Award for leadership in the content management industry.

Boiko is author of *Content Management Bible* (Wiley 2005), widely recognized as the definitive work on the subject. He also wrote *Laughing at the CIO: A Parable and Prescription for IT Leadership* (Information Today 2007) and the ebooks Leading Information Strategy and Leading Information Departments, which extends his reach to organizational executives. He is internationally acclaimed for his lectures and workshops. In 2004, Boiko sparked the creation of CM Professionals, the first and foremost content management organization. Metatorial Services is a micro consultancy, specializing in content and information management strategy and design. With a range of commercial, governmental, and nonprofit clients of every size, Metatorial Services has worked on just about every aspect of information management.

Boiko's academic interests include metadata, business analysis, information initiative planning, information architecture, information system design, and public access to information. He has undergraduate degrees in physics and oceanography and a graduate degree in human communication.

## Laurence P. Chait

Larry Chait, Managing Director of Chait and Associates, Inc., enables senior managers and their teams to leverage their internal knowledge to achieve and sustain high performance. He brings 40 years of experience in knowledge management, business process improvement, and change management. He also supports clients as an insightful executive and team coach.

As a 23-year veteran of Arthur D. Little, Inc., Chait was VP and Chief Knowledge Officer, responsible for the launch of ADL's formal KM function—establishing KM processes, inducting 120 Knowledge Stewards, and embedding KM into the culture. Chait is also President of the Boston KM Forum, a Community of Practice for people involved in KM that sponsors 28 learning events a year. He has authored three books and 20 articles, lectured in seven post-graduate programs, and spoken at 40 conferences. He received his A.B. in Economics from Cornell University and his M.B.A. from the Harvard University Graduate School of Business Administration.

## Abdus Sattar Chaudhry

Abdus Sattar Chaudhry is Head of the Division of Information Studies (DIS) at the School of Communication and Information at Nanyang Technological University (NTU) of Singapore. DIS conducts graduate programs in three areas: information studies, information systems, and knowledge management. Before joining NTU in 1996, Dr. Chaudhry held teaching and professional positions in the U.S., Saudi Arabia, Pakistan, and Malaysia. He holds a master's degree from University of Hawaii and a Ph.D. from University of Illinois at Urbana-Champaign. His areas of teaching include information organization and knowledge management. His current research focuses on application of taxonomies and metadata for knowledge management. He can be reached by e-mail at aschaudhry@ntu.edu.sg.

## Alton Y. K. Chua

Alton Y. K. Chua is Assistant Professor at Nanyang Technological University (NTU), Wee Kim Wee School of Communication and Information. He teaches in the MSc (Knowledge Management) and MSc (Information Systems) programs. His research interests lie primarily in knowledge management and communities of practice. He has authored numerous papers in publications such as the *Journal of the American Society of Information Science and Technology* and the *Journal of Information Science*. In 2005 when he was Assistant Professor and Academic Program Content Manager at Universitas 21 Global, an online graduate business school, he won the Inaugural Faculty Research Award. In 2006, he was the recipient of the Highly Commendable Award for a paper entitled "The Mismanagement of Knowledge Management," awarded by Emerald Literati Network. Chua holds a bachelor's degree in computer science, a second bachelor's degree in arts, a master's degree in education, and doctorate in business administration.

## Elisabeth Davenport

Dr. Elisabeth Davenport is Professor of Information Management at the School of Computing, Napier University, Edinburgh, Scotland, where she is a member of the Social Informatics Research Group and an Associate of the International Teledemocracy Centre. She has been a Visiting Scholar in the School of Library and Information Science for more than a decade, and has been an invited speaker at a number of North American and European universities. She has published widely and taught in a number of countries in the areas of Knowledge Management, Information Management, and qualitative research methods. Her current research focuses in knowledge infrastructures in public sector agencies. She can be contacted at e.davenport@napier.ac.uk

## Roland G. Droitsch

Dr. Roland G. Droitsch is President of KM21 Associates, a consulting firm that specializes in knowledge management, strategic planning, and effectively integrating appropriate technology-based workplace productivity tools into an organization's operations.

Prior to establishing KM21 Associates, Dr. Droitsch was the Deputy Assistant Secretary for Policy at the U.S. Department of Labor and served in that position since 1987. Dr. Droitsch also was the Department of Labor's first Chief Economist and the Director of the Office of Macroeconomics and Economic Policy Review.

While at the Department of Labor, Dr. Droitsch led a series of efforts to bring important technologies to the Department. In the mid 1990s, he led the effort to mount the Department's Internet site. He then led the effort to mount a system of "expert systems" that provided employers and employees with compliance assistance information tailored to their specific situations. This initiative was followed by establishing a department-wide call center, the first for any federal department. And finally, he was the department's lead in working with the Department of Defense on its Advanced Distributed Learning Initiative. The latter has been responsible for establishing a standard for distributed computer based learning that is rapidly becoming recognized as an international standard.

Dr. Droitsch holds a B.A. from Columbia College in New York, an M.A. from the Maxfield School at Syracuse University, and a Ph.D. in Economics from Georgetown University.

## Ana Flavia Fonseca

Ana Flavia Fonseca is currently a Senior Technical Adviser to the University of Joao Pessoa–UNIPE, Brazil. Dr. Fonseca teaches Knowledge Management at the UMUC and also provides consulting services in Information and Knowledge Management. Before retirement, Dr. Fonseca was the Chief Information Architect and Information Services Manager for the World Bank in Washington, DC.

## Arnoldo Fonseca

Arnoldo Fonseca is a consultant in organizational management and corporate finance. He works with both for-profit and nonprofit organiations.

## Suliman Hawamdeh

Dr. Suliman Hawamdeh is a Professor and Program Coordinator of the Master of Science in Knowledge Management at the School of Library and Information Studies at the University of Oklahoma. He was the founding director of the first Master of Science in Knowledge Management program in Asia at Nanyang Technological University in Singapore. He was the founding president of the Information and Knowledge Management Society (iKMS). Dr. Hawamdeh was the managing director of ITC Information Technology Consultants, developing and supporting a line of products that included document management, drawing management, electronic commerce, and digital library. He is the author and editor of several books on information and knowledge management. He is the Editor in Chief of the *Journal of Information and Knowledge Management* (*JIKM*) as well as the editor of a book series on innovation and knowledge management published by World Scientific.

## Joseph Hutchinson

Joseph Hutchinson is a professional consultant focused on bridging communications gaps between end users, sales, and service organizations using systems analysis and information architecture skills. Hutchinson has more than 25 years of experience in marketing and technical communications, including design, management, writing, and training for sales and technical services professionals in technology markets. As a principle of Hutchinson Associates, Hutchinson's focus is enabling corporations to build, measure, and accelerate performance of collaborative work environments.

## Joseph Kasten

Joseph Kasten is an Assistant Professor of Computer Information Systems at Dowling College in Oakdale, New York. He earned his Ph.D. in Information Studies from Long Island University. His current research interests center on the alignment of organizational knowledge with business strategy. Prior to joining academia, Kasten was a Senior Engineer for the Northrop-Grumman Corporation, where he helped develop aircraft such as the F-14D and Boeing 777, as well as the International Space Station.

## Michael E. D. Koenig

Dr. Michael E. D. Koenig's background is primarily in information and knowledge management in the corporate area. His academic background is in information science and business. Prior to his appointment as Dean of the Palmer School, previous positions held by Dr. Koenig include head of information services for Pfizer Pharmaceuticals, Vice President at Tradenet, and Dean of the Graduate School of Library and Information Science at Dominican University.

Dr. Koenig is past president of the International Society for Informetrics and Scientometrics. His research interests include informetrics, database structuring, and the impact of information and information technology on society, in particular, the effect of library and information services and systems upon organizational productivity. In 2005, he received the Jason Farradane Award, which recognizes outstanding work in the information field.

## Shanshan Ma

Shanshan Ma is a Ph.D. student in the College of Information Science and Technology at Drexel University. She is interested in social issues in digital environment, including computer-mediated communication, computer-supported collaborative work, and personal and group information management using information technologies.

## Kavi Mahesh

Kavi Mahesh is a Technology Manager and Consultant with the Knowledge Management group, Infosys Technologies Ltd. He is also the Hewlett Packard Chair Professor of Computer Science at PES Institute of Technology, Bangalore, and the founder and CEO of EasySoftech, a company that develops specialized tools for information management. He has authored more than 30 papers and book chapters, and holds an MTech from IIT-Bombay and an M.S. and a Ph.D. in Computer Science from Georgia Institute of Technology.

## Kate Marek

Kate Marek is an Associate Professor at the Graduate School of Library and Information Science at Dominican University. She comes to graduate education from a long and diverse career in library practice, which began formally in 1980 with her MLIS from Dominican University. Before receiving her Ph.D. from Emporia State University, Marek worked in a private law library, an academic library, and a public middle school media center. In addition, she spent five years as a library consultant with an emphasis on technology development in public libraries. Marek's interests and expertise focus on technology development in information services, including digital libraries, Internet applications, and information policy.

## Robert N. McGrath

Dr. Bob McGrath is an Associate Professor and Project Management Program Director at University of Maryland University College. He began his career by graduating with honors from the U.S. Air Force Academy. He then served five years in the U.S. Air Force as an Aircraft and Munitions Maintenance Officer. Thereafter he worked for Texas Instruments' Defense Suppression Division as a logistics analyst, General Electric Aircraft Engines as a service engineer, and the Lockheed Aeronautical Systems Company as a material manager. Dr. McGrath also holds a Master of Arts degree in Public Administration from the University of Northern Colorado, a Master of Business Administration degree from Xavier University (Ohio), and a Ph.D. in Strategic Management and Technology Management from Louisiana State University in Baton Rouge. He teaches a variety of courses that apply both his professional experience and educational background, and has published more than 75 papers on related subjects.

## Lynda W. Moulton

Lynda Moulton is the principal of LWM Technology Services, a management consulting practice dedicated to leveraging organizations' knowledge. In 1980, she founded Comstow Information Services, which developed BiblioTech software products, forerunner of today's content management systems. In 1999, she sold BiblioTech to Inmagic, Inc.

Greenwood Press published her book *Data Bases for Special Libraries: A Strategic Guide to Information Management* in 1993. In addition to consulting on content and search technologies, taxonomy development, and text database design, Moulton is an active leader in the Boston KM Forum and a contributor to the publications and programs of The Gilbane Group. She is a past leader in the divisions and chapters of the SLA, where she co-authored the original document *Competencies for Special Librarians of the 21st Century.*

## Dave Pollard

Dave Pollard is director of his consultancy practice, Meeting of Minds, and he is the creator and architect of the blog How to Save the World. His extensive KM background includes more than a decade as chief knowledge officer for Ernst & Young Canada, where he designed the Idea eXchange Innovation Management System.

## Madanmohan Rao

Madanmohan Rao, a consultant and author from Bangalore, is research advisor at the Asian Media Information and Communication Centre (AMIC). He is the editor of three book series: *The Asia Pacific Internet Handbook*, *The Knowledge Management Chronicles*, and *AfricaDotEdu*. He is editor-at-large of *DestinationKM*, world music editor for *Rave* magazine, and contributor to the Poynter Institute blog on new media trends.

Rao is on the nominating committee of ICANN (International Corporation for Assigned Names and Numbers), which designs and manages the infrastructure of the global Internet, and was on the board of directors of CPSR (Computer Professionals for Social Responsibility). He is on the board of editors of the journal *Electronic Markets* and the *Journal of Community Informatics*, and was on the board of the journal *Convergence*. Rao was also on the international editorial board of the recently published book, *Transforming e-Knowledge.*

Rao was formerly the communications director at the United Nations Inter Press Service bureau in New York, and vice president at IndiaWorld Communications in Bombay. He graduated from the Indian Institute of Technology at Bombay and the University of Massachusetts at Amherst with an M.S. in computer science and a Ph.D. in communications.

Rao is a frequent speaker on the international conference circuit, and has given talks and lectures in more than 50 countries around the world. He has worked with online services in the U.S., Brazil, and India. His articles have appeared in *DestinationKM*, *Economic Times*, *Electronic Markets* magazine, *Economic and Political Weekly*, and the *Bangkok Post*. Rao is on the board of directors/advisors of numerous content and wireless services firms in Asia. He also participates in consultations at UNESCO, IDRC, and the Friedrich Ebert Stiftung (FES) foundation.

## Louise Rasmussen

Louise Rasmussen is a doctoral student in the Social Informatics Research Group in the School of Computing, Napier University, Edinburgh, Scotland. She has an MSc in e-Business from the Business School in Robert Gordon's University, Aberdeen, sign from Scotland, and has worked for a number of years in the public sector agency that is the focus of her doctoral work. Her posts there include e-Business Project Executive and Knowledge Analyst. She can be contacted at l.rasmussen@napier.ac.uk.

## Hazem Refai

Dr. Hazem Refai is an Assistant Professor in the School of Electrical & Computer Engineering-Telecommunication Program, University of Oklahoma–Tulsa. He is leading the effort in developing wireless communication and network graduate courses, laboratories, and research. He is the founder and director of the WECAD Center at OU-Tulsa. The Center offers industries technical expertise in solving electromagnetic compliance and design issues. His research activities are focused on several areas, including optical wireless communication, vehicle-to-vehicle communication, auto-collision avoidance system, technology insertion, and knowledge management.

## Françoise Rossion

Françoise Rossion was raised in Belgium and did a postgraduate degree in Information Sciences at Free University of Brussels. Her first position was as an information expert at the European Commission and then at Eurocontrol. In 1997, she was hired by PriceWaterhouseCoopers, where she established the Business Knowledge Center while liaising with the Global Knowledge Management team. In 2000, she joined Ernst & Young Consultancy and gained international knowledge management experience by working for great companies such as Totalfina and Delhaize Group. Since 2002, she has worked for HP Consulting and Integration Business Unit. Her current focus is on developing and delivering HP's services in knowledge and collaboration management. She speaks at international conferences and teaches at Belgium universities and at the Belgium Administration Training Institute.

## Claudia Rueger

Claudia Rueger has an M.A. in Political Science from the department of Political Sciences, Anthropology, and Romanic Studies from the University of Bonn in Germany. She specialized in development politics and development sociology. Internationally she has worked with several development organizations, including the German Association for Technical Cooperation (GTZ). She has also done extensive fieldwork and research in Chile. Rueger worked as a consultant with the Indigenous Knowledge for Development Program at the World Bank, where she developed evaluation frameworks and tools to assess the program. She has published an IK Note titled *IK Notes Survey Results*, in which she assessed whether the IK Notes publication series made a difference in readers' development work. Currently she is working as a consultant in the World Bank's Africa Region and her work focuses on Knowledge Management issues in the region. She also works with the Global Development Learning Network (GDLN), where she is integrating local knowledge and community perspectives into World Bank supported projects.

## C. S. Shobha

C. S. Shobha is the director of Quality and Operational Excellence for Perot Systems. She is an experienced professional in the area of Application Software – Analysis, Design, Development, Implementation, Project Management, Account Management with more than 19 years in IT, and 8 years specifically in Quality Management. Her domain areas include Banking, Portfolio Management, and Custodial System. Major strengths are knowledge on Software Engineering, Project Management, and Quality Management Models: ISO 9001, SEI CMM,

SEI CMMI, BS 7799, BS 15000, analytical skills, strategic quality management, leadership, and time management. During the last 10 months she has been driving Knowledge Management Initiative and Project Management Competency programs as part of Consulting and Application Solutions of Perot Systems. Additional strong points include planning, organizing, team building, people management, flexibility, and communication.

## Albert J. Simard

Dr. Albert J. Simard is the Director of Knowledge Strategies for Natural Resources Canada. As a research scientist for the Canadian Forest Service, he emphasized computer approaches to fire research. As a Project Leader for the U.S. Forest Service, he studied large, complex problems, such as measuring fire severity and El Nino and fire. From 1985–1997 he led the development of two national information systems to monitor and predict forest-fire activity. As Director of KM, he designed and developed a KM program for the Canadian Forest Service. He is currently developing KM strategies for Natural Resources Canada, including the knowledge services framework described in this book. He also developed strategic plans for two global information networks related to disaster management and forestry.

## Deepa Srikantaiah

Deepa Srikantaiah is pursuing her Ph.D. in International Education Policy (College of Education) at the University of Maryland, College Park. She received a B.S. in Microbiology and an M.A. in International Education Policy from the University of Maryland. She has published papers in conference proceedings, such as the *Journal of Materials Education* and the *International Journal of the Humanities,* and has presented at a number of conferences and venues, including the Comparative and International Education Society, The Materials Research Society, The International Humanities Conference at Cambridge University, England, and at the Indian Institute of Management, Bangalore.

She has experience working as a project coordinator and assessment coordinator for a number of science and engineering education programs, including the NSF-funded Graduate Fellows in the K–12 Classroom project (GK-12 Program) in Maryland, and has developed and coordinated teacher professional development programs and conferences at the University of Maryland. From 2001 to 2002, she was a Faculty Teaching Assistant in the Chemistry Department and won the Albertus Magnus Award for Best Teaching Assistant for General Chemistry. She has also worked as a student researcher at the National Cancer Institute and National Dental Institute in Bethesda, Maryland. Internationally, she has worked with the World Bank's Indigenous Knowledge for Development Program and the Human Development Network and Education Department at the Washington D.C. headquarters. At the World Bank, she helped develop and design a distance learning course, coordinated learning events, published two IK Notes, and provided research and analytical support for projects in education. Currently she is a graduate assistant in the College of Education's K–16 Development Center where she is working on partnership activities between the University and K–12 school systems. She is also a research assistant for the General Electric Funded Teachers Integrating Mathematics and Engineering (TIME) project, which is a joint project, between the College of Education and College of Engineering, to enhance Science, Technology, Engineering, and Mathematics (STEM) education in the state of Maryland.

## Taverekere (Kanti) Srikantaiah

Kanti Srikantaiah, Director and Professor, Center for Knowledge Management at Dominican University, joined the Dominican faculty in 1997. He teaches graduate courses in knowledge management and related courses in the Graduate School of Library and Information Science (GSLIS) and also cross disciplined courses with the Brennen School of Business (BSB) at Dominican University. Before joining Dominican, Srikantaiah had a distinguished career at the World Bank, where he headed varied and important assignments in the areas of information management at headquarters in Washington D.C. (and also at the World Bank's field offices in Africa and Asia). Prior to joining the World Bank, Srikantaiah worked on building a strong and advanced academic background in sciences, as well as in social sciences. Srikantaiah received his B.S. (Chemistry) from University of Mysore; M.S. (Geology) from the Karnatak University; M.S.I.S. from the University of Southern California; M.P.A. from the University of Southern California; and Ph.D. from the University of Southern California. He also worked at the Library of Congress as an area specialist and taught at the California State University as an Associate Professor. He has also taught for many years as an adjunct faculty at the Catholic University of America in Washington D.C, Syracuse University, University of Maryland, and at the University of Maryland University College (UMUC). His area of specialization includes systems analysis, content management, organization of knowledge, management of information repositories, environmental scanning, information audit, project management, and knowledge management. Among others, his research output covers several research studies and project reports at the World Bank and articles and presentations at IFLA and similar international organizations. He was invited to conduct KM workshops in Singapore and India in 2004. He was also a visiting professor at the Indian Institute of Management, Bangalore (IIMB) during June–August 2006. He was the chief editor of *Knowledge Management for the Information Professional*, published by Information Today Inc., as part of the ASIS&T Monograph Series. He was the co-editor for *Knowledge Management Lessons Learned: What Works and What Doesn't*, also published by Information Today Inc., as part of the ASIS&T Monograph Series. He has also published two other prominent books, one on systems analysis and the other on quantitative research methods.

## J. K. Suresh

J. K. Suresh is the Principal Knowledge Manager and Head of the Knowledge Management Group at Infosys Technologies Ltd. He has several publications in aerospace engineering, application performance testing, software engineering methodologies for Web-based systems, and knowledge management. He obtained his B.Tech and M.S. (Engineering) from the Indian Institutes of Technology at Kanpur and Madras respectively, and his Ph.D. from the Indian Institute of Science, Bangalore, India.

## Qiping Zhang

She is an Assistant Professor in College of Information and Computer Science at Long Island University. She is interested in facilitating productive collaborations of individuals who are geographically and culturally distributed. Her work encompasses not only just communication technologies, but also cultural issues that arise in inter-cultural, distributed collaborations. She has presented papers for conferences of ACM, ICKM, ALISE, International Congress of Psychology, and published papers at journals like *JIKM*. Dr. Zhang holds a Ph.D. and M.S. in information science from University of Michigan and M.S. and B.A. in cognitive psychology from Peking University.

# Index

## A

aboutness, 61
activity feeds, advantages/disadvantages, 92–93
ADL Co-Lab, 475, 476
Advanced Distributed Learning (ADL) initiative, 475–476, 480
advanced e-learning, phase of development reached, 272
Africa, indigenous knowledge/people, 416, 423–425, 433, 436
Africa Multi-Country AIDS Program, 424–425
agile development, 362
Agricultural Research and Training Project (Uganda), 424
Aguilar, Francis, 31
alignment, assessment, 329, 330, 337
alternative knowledge, 415–418. *See also* indigenous knowledge
America. *See* U.S.
American Memory Project, 295
Amidon, Debra M., 169
analysts, 446–447, 450–453, 454, 457–458, 459–460
APEC economies, knowledge management measurement in, 347–349
Arthur Andersen, 343–344, 345
Ask.com blog, 309, 311
Ask Knowledge.Net tool, 265–266
assessment. *See also* Organizational Knowledge Assessment tool
    benefits, 341
    challenges, 326, 341
    current status, 323
    dimensions, 329, 330, 336–337
    in economies, 346–351
    financial indicators, 342
    frameworks, 342
    methodology, 325, 328, 333
    in organizations, 342–346, 349–351
    performance, 64, 66, 70–75
associative blogs, 307
asymmetricity, 80
audio recognition, 231
audiovisual interaction, knowledge transfer via, 224–228, 235, 337, 418
audiovisual material, 227, 230–235
audits, financial, 33
audits, information, 33, 292
audits, knowledge. *See* knowledge audits
Australia, knowledge management measurement in, 348–349
authority, 460
auto-indexing, phase of development reached, 272
automatic content harvesting, 101, 103, 107, 108, 109
Autonomy content management tools, 231
awards, 257, 260, 262–263, 267, 270

## B

background axioms, 54
Bacon, Sir Francis on knowledge, 277
balance card, 69
Balanced Scorecard, 342
Belgian Agency for Radioactive Waste and Enriched Fissile Material, 401, 408–412, 414
best practice programs, phase of development reached, 272
best practices, 10, 338, 361, 366–367, 436
blogs, corporate
    benefits, 303–304, 319
    content types, 307–308

blogs, corporate (*cont.*)
  CoPs, establishing, 318
  cultural factors study, 313–318
  defined, 303
  example, 309, 311–312, 314–317
  history, 304
  as knowledge sharing tools, 107, 109
  management, 308, 311–312
  posting volume, 308, 312, 317
  search engine credit, 304
  studies on, 307–313
  types, 310–311
blogs, personal, 303, 307, 308
Blue Pages, 229
British Petroleum (BP), 287
Browne, Lord John, 287
*Building Organizational Intelligence: A Knowledge Management Primer* (Liebowitz), 481
bulletin boards, 319
Burden, Paul R., 93
business, knowledge management interrelationship, 171
business model, 191, 192
Business Process Reengineering, 5, 7
business strategy, relationship with knowledge strategy, 122–123
Butler, Joseph, 186
"by the Internet out of intellectual capital", 9, 10, 17

**C**

canvassing, just-in-time, 102, 103, 108
canvassing applications, 107–109
capability, organizational, 164, 167
Capability Maturity Model (CMM) framework, 69, 262
capacity assessment (8 Cs), 258, 259, 269–270
capacity-driven organizational approach, 172–173

capital assessment (8 Cs), 258, 259, 271
Capra, Fritjof, 174
caption recognition, 233
Caterpillar Inc., 13, 15
centralized blog style, 311
centralized content management, 25
centralized knowledge resources research, 103–106
change management, 365
chat rooms, 319
Chief Information Officer (CIO) role, 464–465, 467–469, 471, 474, 477–479
Chief Knowledge Management Officer (CKO) role, 466–467, 469, 471
Chief Knowledge Officer (CKO) Summit on taxonomies, 11
Chinese culture, 314, 315
CI (competitive intelligence), 21, 27–29
CIGNA, 229–230
CIO (Chief Information Officer) role, 464–465, 467–469, 471, 474, 477–479
CIO Council, 467, 468–469, 473, 474, 477
Citizen Centered E-Government, 443–444, 470–473, 474–475, 478
CKM (customer knowledge management), 67
CKO (Chief Knowledge Management Officer) role, 466–467, 469, 471
CKO Summit on taxonomies, 11
classification in search systems, 219
classification systems, 54–55
Clinger-Cohen Act, 443, 465, 467–468, 477, 479
closed research communities, 389
clustering, natural language processing, 215, 243, 248, 250–252
CMM (Capability Maturity Model) framework, 69, 262
CMS (content management system), 24–27

CMSS (content management systems strategy), 25
Code Exchange initiative (CodeX), 266
codifiable knowledge. *See* explicit knowledge
collaboration
  benefits, 377, 379
  with customers, 368
  organizational, 20
  phase of development reached, 272
  spaces/tools for, 92–93, 102, 103
  with subcontractors, 368–369
  user needs assessment, 24
collaboration software
  acceptance, fostering, 381–382
  barriers, 379, 381, 382, 397–398
  benefits, 229, 377, 396–397
  costs, 379
  described, 375
  ease of use, 390–391
  governance, 392
  history, 375, 378
  infrastructure, 391, 394
  market, 377
  productivity features, 380
  products, 377
  selection criteria, 378, 379
  success criteria, 397, 398
  suitability, 379
  time-to-value, 378, 380
  types, 375–376
collaboration software pilots
  described, 383–384
  difficulties, 394
  feedback, 395–396
  goals, 382, 383, 384
  groups, 386, 388–389
  metrics, 387–388
  participant roles, 391–392
  planning, 385–386
  sample, 383, 393–396
  support, 394–395

  team spaces, 389–390
collections, 178, 179, 292–293, 294, 338
combination mechanism of knowledge conversion, 165, 166
commerce assessment (8 Cs), 258, 259, 270
common purpose/motivation (CoP characteristic), 305–306
communication messages, 286
communications management, project, 359, 371–372
communities of practice (CoPs)
  assessment, 329, 330, 337
  benefits, 82, 306–307
  blogs, corporate, 318
  characteristics, 305–306
  described, 81, 304–305
  identifying, 87
  knowledge audits, 86–87
  knowledge loss, 13–15
  Knowledge working initiative, 446–447
  occurrence, 337
  phase of development reached, 272
  pilot teams, 389–390
  PKM approach, 103
  PuSA, 459
  retirees in, 13–15
  World Bank, 12
community (CoP characteristic), 305–306
community assessment (8 Cs), 258, 259, 268–269
compensatory adaptation principle, 228
competencies, organizational, 162–163, 167
competition, 20, 158
competitive advantage, 162–163, 164
competitive analysis, 146
competitive intelligence (CI), 21, 27–29
"Competitive Intelligence—An Overview" (Miller), 28
Competitive Intelligence Forum, 269
complexity, 80

complex regions, knowledge services system, 188–190
concept extraction, natural language processing, 243
conference centre (Knowledge Management House), 405
configuration management, 365
connectivity assessment (8 Cs), 103, 258, 259, 268
content
    delivery strategy, 182
    digital, conversion to, 26
    flow, 181–182
    harvesting, 101, 103, 107, 108, 109
    role in information market, 193–194
    sharing, 103
    types, 178–179
    volume, 25
content assessment (8 Cs), 258, 259, 268
Content Consumers, 23
Content Contributors, 23
content dimension (knowledge services framework), 174–175, 179–183
content management
    activities, 23–24
    assessment, 182–183
    described, 23, 57
    goals, 24, 195
    history, 23
    importance, 195
    information in, 24
    infrastructure, 25
    issues, 26
    organizational role, 192–193, 195–196
    phase of development reached, 272
    prioritizing, 182
    process, 26
    role in knowledge management, 21
    software, 26–27
    systems studies, 25
    term, 11, 179
    trends, 27
    types, 25
content management system (CMS), 24–27
content management systems strategy (CMSS), 25
Content Managers, 23
content maps, 24–25
content metadata, 240
Content Object Repository Discovery and Registration Architecture (CORDRA), 475–476, 480
content outputs (knowledge services framework), 174–175, 179, 183–186
content richness spectrum, 188–190, 194
content strategy, 191, 192, 193–194
content value chains, 180–181
context
    data attributes, 57, 59, 60, 63
    descriptors, 54
    enhancement, 103
    importance, 54–55
    information attributes, 58, 59–60, 61–62, 63
    knowledge attributes, 56, 58–61, 62, 64, 67–68
    matching, 53, 56
    representations, 55–56, 57–63, 67–68
    signatures, 55
    strategy statements, 150–151
    of use, 180
context-specific knowledge, 428, 436
controlled vocabulary, 298
conversation, 97–98, 103
cooperation assessment (8 Cs), 258, 259, 270
CoPs (communities of practice). See communities of practice
copyright, 295
CORDRA (Content Object Repository Discovery and Registration Architecture), 475–476, 480
core competencies, 162
corporate blogs. See blogs, corporate

Corporate Knowledge Management Recognition awards, 263
Corporation for National Initiatives knowledge management programs, 476
costs
    collaboration software, 379
    content, 180–181
    content management, 26
    information, 128–130
    knowledge-services, 184
    project management, 359, 370
CRM (customer relationship management), 67
CrossRef article linking system, 444
Cruiser system, 227
cultural anthropology tools, 102
culture
    assessment, 329, 330, 337
    blogs, influence on, 313–318
    Chinese, 314, 315
    defined, 313
    knowledge-sharing, 20
    organizational, 26
    U.S., 314, 315
culture assessment (8 Cs), 258, 259, 269
curators, 178
Customer Dashboard, 269
customer knowledge management (CKM), 67
customer relationship management (CRM), 67
customers, collaboration with, 67, 368

D

DARPA (Defense Advanced Research Project Agency), 444, 476
data
    described, 19, 56–57, 61, 178
    transformation, 291
    use, 179
data dump interviews, 14

data managers, 178
data mining, 250
Davenport, Tom, 390
Davis, Stanley M., 171
Debriefings Program (World Bank), 419, 435
decision making diffusion, 70
decision support applications, 102
Decision Support Systems (DSS), 15
Deep Smarts, 279
Defense Advanced Research Project Agency (DARPA), knowledge management programs, 444, 476
delivery strategy, content, 182
demand-driven market approach, 194
demand-driven organizational approach, 172–173
Department of Defense (DoD), knowledge management programs, 444, 475–476, 480
Department of Education, knowledge management programs, 444, 470, 476
Department of Health and Human Services, knowledge management programs, 480
Department of Labor, knowledge management programs, 469, 476
Department of Labor, Web sites, 479
Department of the Navy, knowledge management programs, 469
Department of Transportation, knowledge management programs, 480
descriptors, context, 54
Development Economics Group (World Bank), 434
dictionary expansion, 220
diffusion, decision making, 70
diffusion, knowledge, 163, 164, 349, 351
digital information, 20, 26
digital libraries
    accessibility, 294–295
    aesthetics, 296–297

digital libraries (*cont.*)
  archival, 300
  characteristics, 291–292, 294–295
  collections, creating, 292–293, 294
  defined, 275, 292
  Handle System, 444, 476–477
  intellectual property, 295
  interfaces, 299
  maintenance, 299
  metadata, 297–298, 299
  physical libraries, extensions of, 300
  search features, 298–299
  security, 295
  technological considerations, 293, 299
  usability, 295–296
  usage patterns, 294
Digital Nervous System, 343
directories, 102
direct transfer of knowledge, 53–54
discussion forums, 319
disintermediation, 101
Disposal Directorate, 401, 408–412, 414
distance learning, 226, 227, 425–426, 436.
  *See also* e-learning
distillations, information, 102
distinctive competencies, 162, 167
distributed content management, 25
distributed knowledge infusion, 70
Distributed Learning (ADL) initiative,
  475–476, 480
distributed style blog, 312
documentary method, 449
document management, phase of development reached, 272
DoD (Department of Defense), knowledge
  management programs, 444,
  475–476, 480
domain-related content, flow, 181
double-loop learning, 290
DSS (Decision Support Systems), 15
Dublin Core attributes, 58, 60
Dublin Core metadata scheme, 297
dynamism (CoP characteristic), 305–306

**E**

EAD (Encoded Archival Description), 297
early adopters, 157
economic conditions, 19, 20–21, 35–36,
  357
EDS, 260, 268, 269, 270, 271
EDS Fellows Program, 260, 270
EDS Innovation Forum, 260, 270
Education, Learning and Development
  SIG (KMWG), 479
E-Government Act (2002), 443, 473–474,
  477, 478
e-Grants, federal, 472
8 Cs framework, 258–259, 268–271
e-learning, 471, 472, 475, 480
electronic format, content conversion to,
  26
electronic information, 20
electronic publishing, 476
e-mail, advantages/disadvantages, 92–93
E-Map Project, 410–413
EMC, 260–261, 268, 269, 271
EMC Knowledgebase, 260–261
employees, 64, 66, 359, 366, 371
Encoded Archival Description (EAD), 297
English Cut blog, 309, 312
Enterprise Application Training, 103
enterprise-class collaboration software,
  376
enterprise portals, phase of development
  reached, 272
enterprise resource planning (ERP), 64,
  66, 67
entity extraction, 243, 244–246, 247–250
Environmental and Socially Sustainable
  Development (ESSD) Network, 435
environmental infrastructure, assessment,
  329, 330
environmental scanning, 21, 31–32
e-payroll systems, federal, 472
eRoom, 390

ERP (enterprise resource planning), 64,
    66, 67
ESSD (Environmental and Socially
    Sustainable Development) Network,
    435
e-training portal, 473
e-travel systems, federal, 472
Eureka (Xerox), 271, 343
event blogs, 307–308, 310
e-vital systems, federal, 472
evolution characteristic of CoPs, 305–306
executive teams, pilot, 389
Exodus Project, 235
expectancy, 285
expertise directory example, 61–63
expert knowledge transfer, 258
expert location, 272
expert's corner (Knowledge Management
    House), 404–405
explicit knowledge
    categories, 21
    conversion, 164–167, 228–229, 248
    described, 21–22, 24, 224
    holders, 119–120
external drivers, 192
external environments, 358
externalization mechanism of knowledge
    conversion, 165
extranets, 13

**F**

face-to-face knowledge sharing, 225, 227,
    228
face-to-face meeting technology, 229
facet taxonomies, 205, 207, 219
Factiva, 230
Factiva Synaptica Knowledge
    Management System, 230
fads, management, 5, 44–45
failure, learning from, 443

far knowledge transfer, 258
FC (Fujitsu Consulting), 261, 268, 269,
    271
federal government
    American Memory Project, 295
    effects on information flow, 182
    e-government, 443–444, 470–473,
        474–476, 478
    information content management,
        467–469
    information content responsibilities,
        465–466
    infrastructure, 465
    Internet/Web sites, 463–464, 465, 466,
        479, 480
    knowledge management programs,
        468–476, 477–478
    security, 468, 478
"The Federal Management and Promotion
    of Electronic Government"
    (E-Government Act), 474
filter blogs, 307
financial audits, 33
findability, 296
FirstGov government-wide information
    portal, 472, 478
flat taxonomies, 207–208, 218
fluidity/regeneration (CoP characteristic),
    305–306
folksonomies, 298
formal organization structures, 80–81
Formal Submission, 103
Fujitsu Consulting (FC), 261, 268, 269,
    271
Fuji Xerox, 343, 345
full-text index architecture, 214–215, 217
full-text search, 214–215

**G**

Gartner Group, 13, 271–272
GDLN (Global Distance Learning
    Network), 418

Generic Strategies Model, 122–123
GILS (Government Information Locator Service), 297
gist, 61
GlobalAccess Lecture Series (Johns Hopkins International), 226
Global Best Practices repository (Arthur Andersen), 343–344
Global CEO Survey 2006 (IBM), 377
Global Development Marketplace, 435
Global Distance Learning Network (GDLN), 418
Global Knowledge Conference (Toronto, 1997), 420–421
Global Research Alliance, Indigenous Knowledge for Development Program, 426
GM FastLane blog, 309, 311
GoC (Government of Canada), 183–184, 191
GoLearn e-learning portal, 472
Google blog, 309, 311, 314, 315, 316–317
GovBenefits/Eligibility Assistance Online, 472
Government Information Locator Service (GILS), 297
Government of Canada (GoC), 183–184, 191
grammatical concept extraction, 246–247
GrapeVine Technologies tools, 231

**H**

Handle System, 444, 476–477
hard copy information, 20
hardware barriers to knowledge transfer, 89
harvesting applications, 101, 103, 107, 108, 109
healthcare, indigenous knowledge for, 416, 425, 430, 433, 435–436

HealthCheck, 262, 269
Health Informatics, 480
herbal remedies market, 415, 416
hierarchical taxonomies, 210
hierarchy, organization, 176
high value systems, 141
HIV/AIDS, traditional medicine for, 435–436
Hoodia plant, 433
Horton, Woody (Forest W.), 49
Hughes Software Systems (HSS), 261, 269, 270
Human Development Network and Education Department's Education Advisory Service, 434–435
Human Relations Stage, 9, 10–11, 18
human resources (HR) functions, 66. *See also* employees
Hummingbird content management tools, 231
hybrid index architecture, 217–218
Hylton, Ann, 34
hype cycle, 271–272
Hyperbolic Tree software, 230

**I**

i2, 268, 269, 271
IBM, 262, 269, 270, 271
IBM Institute of Knowledge-Based Organizations, 262, 270
i-CleaR corporate learning repository, 262
Idea2Reality program, 260
identity characteristic of CoPs, 305–306
i-flex, 262, 268, 269
"if only Texas Instruments knew what Texas Instruments knew", 12
"if you build it they will come is a fallacy" stage, 9, 10–11, 18
"if you build it they will come" philosophy, 18

IK (indigenous knowledge) acronym, 428–429, 437
IK Notes, 424, 436
implants, 446–447, 450–453, 454, 457–458, 459–460
implicit concept extraction, 248
incentives dimension, assessment, 329, 330, 337
index architectures, search system, 214–218
indexing audiovisual material, 231–232, 233–235
India, Indigenous Knowledge for Development Program, 425
indigenous knowledge
  characteristics, 417–418
  economic importance, 415
  IK acronym, 428–429, 437
  medical, 416, 425, 430, 433, 435–436
  term, 427–428, 434
  validation/acceptance, 415–416, 430–431, 432, 435
  World Bank incorporation, 431–433
Indigenous Knowledge for Development Program (World Bank)
  accomplishments, 433
  best practices for use of indigenous knowledge, 436
  challenges, 426–431
  goals, 417, 419, 420–424, 434
  history, 417, 420–421, 422–423
  limitations, 437
  operations, 422–423
  strategies, 423–426
  strengths, 430
  terminology, 418, 427–429
Indigenous Knowledge Integration Fund, 424
*Indigenous Knowledge Systems in Sub-Saharan Africa: An Overview on indigenous knowledge systems in*

*Africa* (World Bank), 423
Indigenous Peoples Program, 427, 436
indigenous term, 417, 418, 427, 434
indirect knowledge transfer, 54
individualism/collectivism, cultural philosophy, 313–314
industries
  defined, 156
  life cycle, 156–159, 160–161, 164, 165–167
  market demand, 157
inference engines, 211–212
informal characteristic of CoPs, 305–306
informal organizational structure, 81–82
information. *See also* explicit knowledge
  categorizing, 133
  described, 19, 57, 61, 178, 290
  filtering/organizing, 101–102
  flows, 97–98, 100
  interpretations, 102
  sources, 28
  technology compared, 195
  transformation, 291
  types, naming, 133, 144
  value, 128–130
information audits, 33, 292
information management, 134–135, 193
information managers, 178
information market, 193–194, 363
information products, 290–291, 292–293
Information Professionals, PKM strategies, 99, 101–103, 109
information projects, 139–142
information strategy, 125–128, 130, 147–150, 151–153. *See also* strategy statements
information technology (IT), 9, 10, 355
Information Technology Reform Act (1996), 443, 465, 467–468, 477, 479
Infosys Technologies, 263, 268–271, 344–346

infrastructure
  assessment, 329, 330
  collaboration software, 391, 394
  components, 176–177, 195
  content management, 25
  environmental, 329, 330
  federal government, 463–464, 465
  knowledge access, 329, 330
  knowledge production, 460–461
  management, 176–179
  private sector, 464
  PuSA, 455
  science, 448, 460
  as site of knowledge production, 447
  software projects, 369
  study results, 337–338
  technology, 89, 177, 329, 330, 337
infrastructure dimension (knowledge serv-
    ices framework), 174–175
Inktomi, 269–270
innovation and knowledge sharing, 362
Innovation Centre Network, 260
Innovation Marketplace (World Bank),
    422, 435
Innovation Team (I-Team), 263
insight analyses, 103
Intangible Assets Monitor, 342
intellectual capital, 9, 10
Intellectual Capital Balance Sheet, 260,
    271
intellectual property, 295
Intelligent Tutoring Systems (ITS), 475
intended audiences, content output, 194
interaction services, 183
interactive knowledge ecosystems, 71–72
inter-enterprise knowledge management,
    phase of development reached, 272
Intermediate Technology Development
    Group (ITDG) project, 227
internal environments, 358
internalization mechanism of knowledge
    conversion, 165, 166

international investment, 35
Internet
  federal government sites, 463–464,
      465, 466, 479, 480
  information on, 20, 26
  knowledge management, influence on,
      9, 10
  limitations, 96–97
  private sector influence, 464
interpretations, information, 102
intervention services, 183
intranet blogs, 307–308
intranets, 10, 13
Inxight, 230–231
i-Opener, 262
IRS e-learning project, 471
i-Share KM portal, 262
i-Suggest process improvement suggestion
    scheme, 262
IT (information technology), 9, 10, 355
IT companies
  analysis example, 266–271
  examples, 260–266
  knowledge management in, 259
  research, future, 271–272
ITDG (Intermediate Technology
    Development Group) project, 227
I-Team (Innovation Team), 263
ITS (Intelligent Tutoring Systems), 475
"it's no good if they can't find it" stage,
    18

J

Johns Hopkins Medicine International,
    videoconferencing at, 225–226
journal blogs, 307
justifications in strategy statements, 150
just-in-time canvassing, 102, 103, 108

# K

KAM (Knowledge Assessment
    Methodology), 325, 328, 333
Kampala Declaration on Indigenous
    Knowledge for Sustainable
    Development, 425
KAS (Knowledge Access System) portal,
    261
KAs (Knowledge Analysts), 446–447,
    450–453, 454, 457–458, 459–460
k-attributes, 56, 58–61, 62, 64, 67–68
KBE (knowledge-based economy), 347
K-café, 369
KCUs (Knowledge Currency Units), 263,
    270
key success factors, industry evolution,
    158
K-Forum tool, 262
KIR (Knowledge Integrated Resources)
    group, 82
k-log blogs, 307
KM (knowledge management). *See* knowl-
    edge management
KM Achievement award, 263
KMAP (Knowledge Management
    Association of the Philippines), 265,
    270
KM Champions, 260
KMS (knowledge management systems),
    230
KMWG (Knowledge Management
    Working Group), 468–469, 470
knowing capitalism context, 460
knowledge
    characteristics, 19, 178–179, 357, 434
    collection, 338
    construction, 432, 437
    creation, 329, 330, 349, 351
    diffusion, 163, 164, 349, 351
    discovery, 239
    harvesting, 101, 103, 107, 108, 109

importance, 52, 53, 195
    individual, 290
    location, organizational, 52–53
    loss, 13–15
    management efforts, 228–230
    metrics, 68
    patterns, 21
    retention, 366
    sources, locating, 52
    technical, 360
    technology compared, 195
    transformation, 291
    types, 21–23, 224
knowledge access infrastructure, assess-
    ment, 329, 330
Knowledge Access System (KAS) portal,
    261
knowledge adaptation gap, 421, 422
Knowledge Advantage award, 262, 270
Knowledge Analysts (KAs), 446–447,
    450–453, 454, 457–458, 459–460
knowledge application, described, 349,
    351
Knowledge Assessment Methodology
    (KAM), 325, 328, 333
knowledge assets, 115
knowledge audits
    analysis, 90–91
    challenges, 92–93
    communities of practice, 86–87
    described, 33–35
    history, 49
    leaders, 79–80
    maps, 84–85, 89, 102
    organizational structure, 81
    overlapping, 79
    process phase I, 82–85
    process phase II, 85–88
    process phase III, 88–91
    reporting, 90–92
    resources, 93
    review/re-run, 79

knowledge audits (*cont.*)
    role in knowledge management, 21
    significance, identifying, 87
    software applications, 89
    technology infrastructure, 89
    timeline, 88
Knowledge Bank, 418, 419
Knowledge Base, 261, 268
knowledge-based economy (KBE), 347
knowledge-based research communities,
    389
Knowledgebase for tech support, 268
knowledge bases, phase of development
    reached, 272
knowledge blogs, 310
knowledge conversion mechanisms, 165
Knowledge Currency Units (KCUs), 263,
    270
Knowledge Desktop, 82
knowledge embodiments, 59
knowledge flows, 169, 329, 330
"Knowledge for Development" initiatives,
    428
knowledge identification, assessment, 329,
    330, 337
Knowledge Integrated Resources (KIR)
    group, 82
knowledge is power attitude, 278–279,
    282, 283, 357
knowledge management (KM)
    benefits, 223, 258
    challenges, 95–97, 327
    continuum, 19–20
    contributing factors, 20–21
    defined, 12, 45, 116, 163–164, 257,
        357, 434
    development stages, 9, 10–12, 17–18,
        34
    early implementations, 96–97
    effects, 326
    fads compared, 43, 44–45, 258
    focus, 19, 80

    functions enhanced by, 64, 259
    goals, 97, 229
    growth, 5, 7, 8, 36, 341
    history, 10, 17–19, 75, 257, 271–272,
        463, 479
    limitations, 258
    online resources, 40–41
    strategies, 164
    tools, 229–230
    trends, 12–16, 18, 36, 63–64
    uses, 52, 169
Knowledge Management Advisory Board
    (Open Text), 270
Knowledge Management Association of
    the Philippines (KMAP), 265, 270
Knowledge Management House, 403–405,
    414
Knowledge Management Office, 260
Knowledge Management Strategy, 164,
    167
knowledge management systems (KMS),
    230
Knowledge Management Working Group
    (KMWG), 468–469, 470
knowledge managers, 179
knowledge mapping, phase of develop-
    ment reached, 272
*Knowledge Mapping/Information Audit*
    (Srikantaiah/Burden), 93
knowledge maps, 34
knowledge model, 64–66
knowledge needs, 52, 53
"Knowledge Needs Route map" (PuSA),
    446
Knowledge.Net portal, 265
Knowledge Network, 446, 447, 448
knowledge organizations, 169–171, 172
Knowledge Partners initiative (MITRE),
    270
knowledge portals, 229
Knowledge Resource Planning (KRP), 49,
    67

knowledge services framework
  attributes, 173–174, 196
  benefits, 196–197
  business advantages, 190–191
  content dimension, 174–175, 179–183
  defined, 172
  infrastructure dimension, 174–175
  outputs dimension, 174–175, 179,
       183–186
  scale dimension, 174, 175–176, 179
  uses, 172–173
knowledge services system, 186, 187,
       188–190. *See also* knowledge-serv-
       ices value chain
knowledge-services value chain, 184–186
knowledge sharing. *See also* audiovisual
       interaction, knowledge transfer via
  advantages, 277–278
  assessment, 329, 330, 337
  barriers, 89, 280–282
  behavioral challenges, 278–283
  characteristics, 225
  dimensions, 328
  direct, 53–54
  example, 277–278, 287
  history, 463
  innovation, 263
  mechanisms, 54, 258
  organizational structure and, 67
  problems, identifying/resolving,
       283–287
  techniques, 280, 337
  technology role, 228–230
  term, 434
KnowledgeShop portal, 263, 271
knowledge strategy, 116–121, 122–123
knowledge supply management (KSM),
       67
Knowledge Support Office (KSO), 261
knowledge systems, 415–416, 434
knowledge teams, assessment, 329, 330,
       337

knowledge transfer. *See* knowledge
       sharing
"The Knowledge Underground" commu-
       nity, 261, 268–269
knowledge user training, 103
Knowledge Web Project, 446–447,
       451–457
Knowledge Working (KW) initiative,
       445–447
Knowledge Working Specialists, 446–447,
       450–453, 454, 457–458, 459–460
KRP (Knowledge Resource Planning), 49,
       67
KSM (knowledge supply management),
       67
KSO (Knowledge Support Office), 261
KW (Knowledge Working) initiative,
       445–447
K-Webcast conferences, 269

# L

large organizations, knowledge manage-
       ment in, 334–338
Latin America, indigenous peoples, 436
leadership, assessment, 329, 330, 336–337
learning. *See also* e-learning
  activities for, 337
  assessment, 329, 330, 337
  distance, 226, 227, 425–426, 436
  double-loop, 290
  from failure, 443
*The Learning Organization* (Senge), 18
learning organizations, 10–11, 290
legal issues, 26, 182, 295
legitimate peripheral participation (LPP),
       CoP characteristic, 305–306
legitimation property, 457, 460
Leonard, Dorothy, 279
lessons learned, 10, 338, 361, 366–367,
       436

librarians, 11–12, 178, 291

libraries, 178, 179. *See also* digital libraries

library (Knowledge Management House), 403

Liebowitz, Dr. Jay, 481

LinguistX natural language processing platform, 230

Livelink platform, 264

lobby (Knowledge Management House), 403

local knowledge term, 427, 428

logging video information, 232

low value systems, 141, 142

LPP (legitimate peripheral participation), CoP characteristic, 305–306

# M

MAKE (Most Admired Knowledge Enterprise) Awards, 257, 267

management framework, content, 194

Management Information Systems (MIS), 15

Management Network Mapping, 103

management organization classes, 176

management styles, influence on organizations, 20–21

management teams, program pilot, 389

mandate content drivers, 192

mandatory regions, knowledge services system, 188–190

maps, knowledge, 84–85, 89, 102

market research, competitive intelligence compared, 28

market role in information market, 193–194

McGee, James, 190

MDGs (Millennium Development Goals), 425, 426

measurement. *See* assessment

media naturalness principle, 228

medical knowledge, indigenous, 416, 425, 430, 433, 435–436

Medical Subject Headings (MESH), 11–12

memory practices, research on, 448–449

meta-containers, 291

metadata
availability tools, 241–243
components, 57–61
creating, 243
in digital libraries, 297–298, 299
extracting, 243–247
limitations, 241
in ONDRAF-NIRAS, 411, 412
programmatic strategies, benefits, 254–255
representations, 60–61
in search systems, 207, 214, 216, 217, 239–241
semantic interoperability, 253–254
types, 54, 240–241

metrics, 68, 329, 330, 337, 387–388

Microsoft, 343, 344, 345

middle zone of content richness spectrum, 189–190

milieu, knowledge strategy, 119–120, 121, 122

Millennium Development Goals (MDGs), 425, 426

millennium turnover, 467–468

Miller, Stephen H., 28

mindmaps, 102

MIS (Management Information Systems), 15

MITRE, 263, 268–269, 270, 271

MITRE Information Infrastructure (MII), 263

Mkapa, Benjamin, 425

"Modernising Government Programme" (U.K.), 445

modern knowledge, 430–431, 432, 433, 436

monitoring, assessment, 329, 330, 337

mono style blog, 312

Morrison, Samuel Elliot on failure, 443

Most Admired Knowledge Enterprise (MAKE) Awards, 257, 267

# N

naming information types, 133, 144

narration (CoP characteristic), 305–306

narratives, 102–103, 224, 225, 406–407. *See also* Knowledge Management House

Nason, Alexander, 225–226

National Institutes of Health (NIH), 430, 432

natural language processing (NLP)
  clustering, 215, 243, 248, 250–252
  concept extraction, 243, 246–247, 248
  keyword index, 298
  LinguistX platform, 230
  non-English, 246, 252
  rule-based categorization, 243, 244–246, 247–250
  summarization, 243, 252, 253
  text extraction, 252
  tools, 242–243

Natural Resources Canada knowledge-services system model, 171, 183–184

near knowledge transfer, 258

needs analysis, 24, 26, 52, 53, 363

Nelson, Kim, 474

Net Work, 379, 381

networks, 103, 108, 171, 381, 435

network taxonomies, 210–211, 212, 218–219

New Economic Index, 348

new knowledge creation (CoP characteristic), 305–306

NIH (National Institutes of Health), 430, 432

9/11 catastrophe, effect on federal agencies, 468

NLP. *See* natural language processing

notebook blogs, 307

Novartis, 229

Novell, 263–264, 269

nuclear power industry, 407–408. *See also* ONDRAF-NIRAS

# O

observation support, 103

OECD (Organisation for Economic Co-operation and Development), 346, 347, 348–349

Office of Electronic Government, 473–474

Office of Management and Budget (OMB), 443–444, 465, 474. *See also* Quicksilver e-government initiative

OKA. *See* Organizational Knowledge Assessment tool

ONDRAF-NIRAS, 401, 408–412, 414

One-Stop Business Compliance Information, 472

online information, 20, 26

Online Rulemaking Management, 472

ontologies, 54, 211–212

open research communities, 389

open space events, 102

Open Text, 264, 268, 269, 270

operationalization of knowledge management, assessment, 329, 330, 336–337

OPM, 480

optical character recognition, 233

Oracle, 264, 269, 270

Oracle Partner Network, 270

Oracle Technology Network, 270

oral histories, 435

O'Reilly Radar blog, 309, 312

Organisation for Economic Co-operation and Development (OECD), 346, 347, 348–349
Organizational Culture, 9, 10–11, 18
Organizational Knowledge Assessment (OKA) tool
  characteristics, 327
  data gathering, 328–331, 332
  development, 325
  dimensions of measurement, 327–330
  framework, graphical representation, 335
  future developments, 331, 338
  goals, 326, 327, 338
  information collected, 327
  People-Process System framework, 327, 328
  pilot testing, 333–335
  scoring, 331–335, 336
  study results, 336–338
organizational performance production and knowledge transmission, 68–70
organization aspect of scale, 176
organization infrastructure component, 177
organization knowledge, project, 360
organizations. *See also* knowledge services framework
  assessment in, 342–346, 349–351
  assets, knowledge, 357
  content flow, 67, 181
  economic conditions, influence on, 20–21
  evolution, 155
  forces to watch, 31
  goals, 169–171
  information, importance in, 170
  knowledge, 169–171, 172
  large, knowledge management in, 334–338
  learning, 10–11, 290
  life cycles, 160–161, 165–167
  management styles, influence on, 20–21

  market approach, 194
  standards/requirements, 285
  structure, 67, 80–82, 155, 170
  success factors, 80
organization theory, 159–161
orientation, knowledge strategy, 118–119, 121, 122
orthogonal processes, 93
orthogonity, 80
Otter Group blog, 309, 312
outputs
  audience for, 194
  defined, 172
  knowledge services framework, 174–175, 179, 183–186
  knowledge services system, 188–190
  product, 183
  search systems, 220–221
  service, 183
  solutions, 184
outsourcing, 64, 66, 67, 362

**P**

parametric index architectures, 215–216, 217
participant role in information market, 193–194
participation messages, 285, 287
passive delivery of knowledge services, 185
pastry cook metaphor, 405–406
pattern matching, 244–245
PCD (Project Closure Documents), 262, 268
PCM (Personal Content Management), 103, 106–107
PEAP (Poverty Eradication Action Plan), Uganda, 425
peer-to-peer content sharing, 101, 102
peer-to-peer introduction applications, 102

peer-to-peer presence detecting/introduction, 103

peer-to-peer publishing and subscription, 101, 103

People elements, 327, 328

people-finding applications, 102, 103, 108–109

people infrastructure component, 176–177, 195

People-Process System framework, 327, 328

performance assessment, 64, 66, 70–75

performance content drivers, 192–193

performance management, 70–71

performance production and knowledge transmission, 68–70

personal blogs, 303, 307, 308

Personal Content Management (PCM), 103, 106–107

personal content management programs, 106

personal information and knowledge management (PIKM), 390

Personal Knowledge Management (PKM), 49, 98–103, 106–109

personal knowledge management systems, phase of development reached, 272

Personal Productivity Improvement (PPI), 103, 104, 106

personal shared workspaces, 103, 107–108

personal work effectiveness, 103

personal workspaces, 101

personas, 149–150

personnel, 64, 66, 359, 366, 371

persuasion, 134, 285

phones recognition, 231

picklists in search systems, 218

piecework model, knowledge sharing in, 281–282, 283

PIKM (personal information and knowledge management), 390

pilot teams, CoP, 389–390

PKM (Personal Knowledge Management), 49, 98–103, 106–109

Plumtree content management tools, 231

PMA (President's Management Agenda), 474–475, 480

PMI (Project Management Institute), 29

policies content drivers, 192–193

Polycom, 225

Porter, Michael, 122

positioning philosophy, Strategic Management, 162

poverty, videos on, 227

Poverty Eradication Action Plan, Uganda (PEAP), 425

power distance cultural philosophy, 314

Powerlink Web portal, 260

PPI (Personal Productivity Improvement), 103, 104, 106

prediction markets, 102

presence-detecting applications, 102

President's Management Agenda (PMA), 474–475, 480

principles in strategy statements, 150

private sector knowledge management, 466–467, 469, 471, 477

proactive outcome approach of knowledge services, 185

process aspect of scale, 176

Process elements, 327, 328

processes
    described, 349, 351
    orthogonal, 93
    search systems, 219–220

process infrastructure component, 177

product blogs, 307–308, 310

production, industry evolution, 158

productivity training, 98–99, 101

product outputs, 183

Professional Communities, 269

program management teams, pilot, 389

Project Closure Documents (PCD), 262, 268

project cost management, 359, 370
Project Exodus, 232–235
ProjectFinder tool, 261, 268, 271
project management
    communications, 359, 371–372
    evolution, 360
    human resources, 359, 371
    integration, 359, 369–370
    knowledge areas, 359–360, 369–372
    knowledge management, 21, 29, 355
    procurement, 360, 372
    quality, 359, 370–371
    resources, 29
    risk, 360, 372
    scope, 359, 370
    time, 359, 370
Project Management Institute (PMI), 29
projects
    characteristics, 358
    components, 29
    defined, 29
    knowledge in, 357, 360
    knowledge management, 360–362
    life cycle, 358–359
project teams, pilot, 389
Project Workbench, 261, 268
Promotr project tracking tool, 262
provider-user models of knowledge serv-
        ices, 185
Prusak, Larry, 80, 190
public information, 28
Publishers International Linking
        Association, 444
publishing, 101, 103, 107–108, 476
PuSA (public sector agency). *See also*
        Knowledge Web project
    conclusions, 460–461
    described, 445
    discourse, 451–453, 458
    history, 457–458
    infrastructure, 455
    Knowledge Architecture, 453–454

Knowledge Network failure, 446, 447,
        448
Knowledge Working initiative, 445–447
Knowledge Working Strategy, 453–454
    reorganizations, 456–457
PuSA study
    analysis, 459–460
    challenges, 450
    domination, 453–457
    legitimation, 457–458
    methodology, 449–451
    signification, 451–453

**Q**

QMAs (Query Matching Algorithms),
        search system, 220
QPAs (Query Processing Algorithms),
        search system, 219–220
QPati quiz program, 262, 269
Quality Circles, 5, 6
quality controlled domain vocabulary, 249
QuBase repository, 262
Query Matching Algorithms (QMAs),
        search system, 220
Query Processing Algorithms (QPAs),
        search system, 219–220
Quicksilver e-government initiative
        (OMB), 443–444, 470–473,
        474–475, 478
Quiver, 269

**R**

RBV (Resource-Based View), 162–163,
        164
reach content delivery strategy, 182
reach zone of content richness spectrum,
        189–190
reader method summarization tools, 252
realignment, structural, 285, 287

recognition, 285. *See also* awards

records, 178

records managers, 178

Recreation One-Stop, 472

recruitment, employee, 64, 66

registration room (Knowledge Management House), 403

regular expressions, 244

regulation, organizational, 20

reintermediaries, 101

reinventing the wheel, 280–281, 361

related concepts in search systems, 218–219

relationship (CoP characteristic), 305–306

reorganizations, goals of organizational, 80

Repository Management, 103

research communities, types, 389

Resource-Based View (RBV), 162–163, 164

results-based organizational approach, 172–173

Results Chain model, 261

retention, employee, 366

retention, knowledge, 361

retirees, in communities of practice, 13–15

rewards, 285. *See also* awards

rhetoric, 134, 285

rich content delivery strategy, 182

richness spectrum, 188–190, 194

rich zone of content richness spectrum, 189–190

rights, information, 182

rights content drivers, 192–193

ring taxonomies, 208–209, 218

role modeling, 285, 287

RSS feeds, 107

rule-based categorization, natural language processing, 243, 244–246, 247–250

## S

SAS, 265, 268

scale, 174, 175–176, 179

scenarios, 149

schemas, representations, 60–61

scientific knowledge

  described, 433

  flow, 181

  indigenous knowledge, acceptance/validation, 430–431

  production, 436, 448, 460–461

SCIP (Society for Competitive Intelligence Professionals), 27

SCM (supply chain management), 64, 66

scope, knowledge strategy, 120–121, 122

SCORM (Shareable Content Object Reference Model), 444, 475, 476, 480

search systems. *See also* ontologies; taxonomies

  architecture, 213

  blogs, rating, 304

  classification, 219

  for content management, 107

  described, 213

  goals, 203–205

  improving, 221

  inputs, 213–219

  outputs, 220–221

  processes, 219–220

  user expectations, 203

SECI (socialization, externalization, creation, and internalization), 21

sector knowledge, 360

security, 295, 468, 478

self-expressive blogs, 307

semantic composition, 241, 243

semantic decomposition, 241–243

sense-making, 103

serendipity, 92

serial knowledge transfer, 258

service-based framework, role in business processes, 191–192

Service Level Agreements (SLAs), 366
service outputs, 183
service provider software projects, 362
Seven methods model, 284–287
Shareable Content Object Reference
    Model (SCORM), 444, 475, 476,
    480
signatures, context, 55
signification property at PuSA, 451–453,
    460
simplified regions, knowledge services
    system, 188–190
SLAs (Service Level Agreements), 366
SMS, 265
Social Action Fund Projects
    (Malawi/Tanzania), 425
social capital, 224, 447–448
socialization, externalization, creation, and
    internalization (SECI), 21
socialization mechanism of knowledge
    conversion, 165
social network analysis, 108
social networking applications, 103
social structure, 450
Society for Competitive Intelligence
    Professionals (SCIP), 27
software applications
    canvassing, 107–109
    content management, 26–27
    decision support, 102
    harvesting, 101, 103, 107, 108, 109
    knowledge audits, 89
    knowledge transfer, barriers to, 89
    peer-to-peer introduction, 102
    people-finding, 102, 103, 108–109
    presence-detecting, 102
    social networking, 103
    virtual presence, 102, 103
software industry, characteristics, 267–268
software projects. See also projects
    customer collaboration, 368
    demographics, 362–363

execution, 365–366
infrastructure, 369
initiation, 364–365
knowledge management requirement,
    373
knowledge needs, 363
life cycles, 363–367
maintenance, 366–367
outsourcing, 362
resources, 364–365
shutdown, 367
staffing, 366–367
subcontractor collaboration, 368–369
support role in information market, 363
tools, 69, 365–366
solutions outputs, 184
"south to south" learning events, 425
Soviet Union, post-World War II domi-
    nance, 437
space aspect of scale, 176
speaker recognition, 231
specialized regions, knowledge services
    system, 188–190
Special-K People, 446–447, 450–453,
    454, 457–458, 459–460
speech recognition, 231, 232–233
Srikantaiah, Prof. T. Kanti, 93
statistical clustering techniques, 248, 250
stemming, 220
stories, 102–103, 224, 225, 406–407. See
    also Knowledge Management House
strategic assets, 115
strategic knowledge transfer, 258
Strategic Management, 159, 162–163, 167
strategic positioning, 155
strategy, assessment, 329, 330, 336–337
strategy statements. See also information
    strategy
    analysis example, 132–135
    context, 150–151
    creating, 131–132, 135–139, 142–144
    described, 130

enhancing, 148–150
goals, 130, 134
interrelating, 144–146, 147
revising, 144–146
three-dimensional views, 140–142
uses, 130–131, 134–135, 138–139, 147
stratification modeling of audiovisual
    information, 231
structural realignment, 285, 287
structurational analysis, 450
structured modeling of audiovisual infor-
    mation, 231
Structuring Content and Assigning
    Descriptors, 10, 11–12
subcontractors, collaboration with,
    368–369
subscription, 107–108
sub-word recognition, 231
success, organizational, 128
summarization, natural language process-
    ing, 243, 252, 253
Summarizer Plus content management
    tools, 230
Sunbelt Software blog, 309, 312
Sun Microsystems Philippines (SunPhil),
    265, 268, 270
supply chain management (SCM), 64, 66
supply-driven market approach, 194
supply-driven organizational approach,
    172–173
support role in information market,
    193–194
survey, OKA, 328–331, 332
surveying, 102, 103
sustainable competitive advantage, 167
sweet spots, project, 152
SWOT analysis, 31
synchronicity, 80
synonyms in search systems, 218
System elements, 327, 328
systems, reviewing current, 146
systems study, content management, 25
Systems Theory, 159–160

# T

tacit knowledge
    categories, 22
    conversion, 165–166, 228–229, 248
    described, 21, 22–23, 24, 224
    history, 11
    holders, 119–120
Tanzania, indigenous knowledge and med-
    ical care, 416, 425, 433
task force, pilot teams, 389
taxonomies. *See also* strategy statements
    full-text index architecture, 215
    librarian role, 11–12
    organization-wide, 106–107
    pilot community, 389
    in search systems, 207–211, 212–213,
        298
    term, 11
    types, 205, 207–211, 223–224
team rooms (Knowledge Management
    House), 405
teams, organizational, 161, 337
team spaces, pilot, 389–390
Techlore technical knowledge repository,
    260, 268
Technical Exchange Meetings (TEMs),
    263, 268–269
technical knowledge, 360
technical regions, knowledge services sys-
    tem, 188–190
technology
    evolution, 157–158, 299
    information/knowledge compared, 195
    infrastructure component, 177
    knowledge management, influence on,
        272
    role in knowledge transfer, 228–230
    trends, 20
technology-bearing labor, 460–461
technology infrastructure, assessment,
    329, 330, 337

TEMs (Technical Exchange Meetings), 263, 268–269

Teragram tool set, 243

text extraction, natural language processing, 252

thematic networks, 435

thesauri, 210–211, 212, 218–219, 249

ThingFinder extraction technology, 231

time aspect of scale, 176

Title II, 474

Tom Peters blog, 309, 312

ToolPool, 265

topic oriented blogs, 307

Total Quality Management (TQM), 5, 6

traditional knowledge term, 427

training, 26, 66

transaction-based research communities, 389

transactions services, 183

transformation cycle, 291

tutoring systems, 480

## U

Uganda, projects/programs in, 424, 425

Uganda Poverty Eradication Action Plan (PEAP), 425

unique regions, knowledge services system, 188–190

Unisys, 265–266

unofficial/voluntary (CoP characteristic), 305–306

U.S.
   culture, 314, 315
   economic history, post World War II, 437
   economy, knowledge management measurement in, 348, 349

usability, 295–296

USA.gov, 472, 478

use cases, 149

use metadata, 240, 241

user metadata, 240–241

user needs assessment, 24

user profiles, content management, 26

## V

value chains, 179–181, 184–186

value information, 128–130

value realization, 68

value transformation production, knowledge transmission and, 68–70

videoconferencing, 224–228, 235, 337, 418

video data modeling, 231

video information, 227, 230–235

video interaction, 224–228, 235, 337, 418

virtual presence applications, 102, 103

virtual team space, 376

visualizations, 102, 103

Visual Resources Association (VRA) Core, 297

vocabulary tools, search system, 218–219

voluntary/unofficial (CoP characteristic), 305–306

## W

WBI. *See* World Bank Institute

Web 2.0 services, 375

Web-based collaboration software, 375–376

Weblogs. *See* blogs, corporate; blogs, personal

Web Site Management, 103

Web sites, 296, 466. *See also* Internet

Web technology, 229

WHO (World Health Organization), 430, 432, 433

why technique, 283–284

Wiener, Dr. Harvey, 81–82

wisdom, 19–20, 279, 291

Wisdom of Crowds, 102

Wolfensohn, James, 417, 418, 420

women, videos on poverty by, 227

Women's Development Initiative
(Ethiopia), 425

word spotting, 231

World Bank Institute (WBI). *See also*
Indigenous Knowledge for
Development Program;
Organizational Knowledge
Assessment tool

audiovisual interaction, knowledge
transfer via, 418

changes needed, 432–433

communities of practice, 12

Debriefings Program, 419, 435

Development Economics Group, 434

economic categorization, 433

history, 418, 434

indigenous knowledge, incorporating,
431–433

knowledge management program, 12

organization, 422–423

service centers, 418–419

World Development Report (1997-1998),
421

World Health Organization (WHO), 430,
432, 433

World Wide Web (WWW), 25, 463. *See
also* Internet

## X

Xerox, 266, 270, 271

XpertNet, 263, 269

## Y

Y2K issue, 467–468

Yahoo! Search blog, 309, 311

Yellow Pages, 229

# More Titles of Interest from Information Today, Inc.

## Knowledge Management Lessons Learned
### *What Works and What Doesn't*

*Edited by Michael E. D. Koenig and T. Kanti Srikantaiah*

A follow-up to Srikantaiah and Koenig's ground-breaking *Knowledge Management for the Information Professional*, this new book surveys recent applications and innovations in KM. More than 30 experts describe KM in practice, revealing what has been learned, what works, and what doesn't. Includes projects undertaken by organizations at the forefront of KM, and coverage of KM strategy and implementation, cost analysis, education and training, content management, communities of practice, competitive intelligence, and much more.

624 pp/hardbound/ISBN 978-1-57387-181-5
ASIST Members $35.60 • Nonmembers $44.50

## ARIST 42
## Annual Review of Information Science and Technology

*Edited by Blaise Cronin*

*ARIST,* published annually since 1966, is a landmark publication within the information science community. It surveys the landscape of information science and technology, providing an analytical, authoritative, and accessible overview of recent trends and significant developments. The range of topics varies considerably, reflecting the dynamism of the discipline and the diversity of theoretical and applied perspectives. While *ARIST* continues to cover key topics associated with "classical" information science (e.g., bibliometrics, information retrieval), editor Blaise Cronin is selectively expanding its footprint in an effort to connect information science more tightly with cognate academic and professional communities.

712 pp/hardbound/ISBN 978-1-57387-308-6
ASIST Members $99.95 • Nonmembers $124.95

## Computerization Movements and Technology Diffusion
### From Mainframes to Ubiquitous Computing

*Edited by Margaret S. Elliott and Kenneth L. Kraemer*

"Computerization movement" (CM), as first articulated by Rob Kling, refers to a special kind of social and technological movement that promotes the adoption of computing within organizations and society. Here, editors Margaret S. Elliott and Kenneth L. Kraemer and more than two dozen noted scholars trace the successes and failures of CMs from the mainframe and PC eras to the current Internet era and the emerging era of ubiquitous computing. Through theoretical analyses, systematic empirical studies, field-based studies, and case studies of specific technologies, CMs are shown to be driven by Utopian visions of technology that become part of the "ether" within society, creating a general bias in favor of computing adoption. The empirical studies presented here show the need for designers, users, and the media to be aware that CM rhetoric can propose grand visions that never become part of promising new technologies.

**608 pp/hardbound/ISBN 978-1-57387-311-6**
**ASIST Members $47.60 • Nonmembers $59.50**

## Knowledge Management for the Information Professional

*Edited by T. Kanti Srikantaiah and Michael E. D. Koenig*

With contributions from 26 leading KM practitioners, academicians, and information professionals, this book bridges the gap between two distinct perspectives, equipping information professionals with the tools they need to make a broader and more effective contribution in developing KM systems and creating knowledge management culture within their organizations.

**608 pp/hardbound/ISBN 978-1-57387-079-5**
**ASIST Members $35.60 • Nonmembers $44.50**

---

*To order or for a complete catalog, contact:*
### Information Today, Inc.
143 Old Marlton Pike, Medford, NJ 08055 • 609/654-6266
email: custserv@infotoday.com • Web site: www.infotoday.com